THE ENCYCLOPEDIA OF

MAGIC AND MAGICIANS

THE ENCYCLOPEDIA OF

MAGIC AND MAGICIANS

T. A. WATERS

Facts On File Publications
New York, New York • Oxford, England

THE ENCYCLOPEDIA OF MAGIC AND MAGICIANS

Library of Congress Cataloging-in-Publication Data

Waters, T. A.
    The encyclopedia of magic and magicians.

    Bibliography: p.
    1. Magic—Dictionaries.   2. Magicians—Biography—
Dictionaries.   2. Magicians—Biography—Dictionaries.
I. Title.
GV1542.5.W37   1987   793.8'0321   87-13464
    ISBN 0-8160-1349-7 (hc)
    ISBN 0-8160-1981-9 (pbk)
        88025280-41
Printed in the United States of America

10 9 8 7 6 5 4 3 2 1

CONTENTS

To the memory of my father

THURSTON A. WATERS

who inspired in me a love of magic and writing
this book is affectionately dedicated.

Dai Vernon; photo taken by Hal Phyfe in the 1930's.

INTRODUCTION

This is not the first attempt to create an encyclopedia of magic. In 1911 Ellis Stanyon, the editor of the British magazine *Magic*, attempted nothing less than a complete description of every known magical effect and technique. His dictionary was published in installments in the pages of *Magic*; some years later, when the magazine ceased publication, the entries had only reached the letter *c*—a testament both to Stanyon's thoroughness and the hopeless nature of his task.

It should be noted that Stanyon's efforts began over three-quarters of a century ago, when the literature of magic was a small fraction of its present size. Indeed, it has been said that more books have been written on the techniques of magic than on all other phases of show business put together. This may be overstating the case, but probably not by much.

In 1950 Henry Hay published his *Cyclopedia of Magic*—an alphabetically-arranged anthology of articles and notes, the bulk of which had been culled from early classic works on the subject. In 1954 John McArdle published his *Dictionary Of Magitain*, an interesting and idiosyncratic glossary of magical terms. In the 1960's an excellent glossary of conjuring definitions by S. H. Sharpe was published serially in the *Magic Circular*. In 1979 Geoffrey Lamb's *Illustrated Magic Dictionary* was published. None of these authors dared to suggest that their works were complete and comprehensive, and I can do no less than follow their excellent example.

My purpose in writing this book has been to provide a Technical Encyclopedia and Who's Who. To deal with these two aspects in turn:

The purpose of the Technical Encyclopedia is to provide a basic description of most known effects and routines and, where feasible, briefly describe the technique involved. I have also tried to provide comprehensive bibliographic references to guide the reader to further information.

The Who's Who is meant to give an overview of performers and creators of magic past and present. In this connection, I must note that within this text inclusion or exclusion should in no way be interpreted as an assessment of a performer or creator's worth. It is inevitable that some noteworthy persons will have been omitted.

In attempting to make this book as complete and correct as possible, I have enlisted the aid of five acknowledged experts in the field—Ricky Jay, Max Maven, Billy McComb, Jim Steinmeyer, and John Thompson—all of whom you will find described in these pages. These gentlemen have been kind enough to take time out from their busy schedules to go over the bulk of the manuscript and offer their suggestions and corrections. Their help is very much appreciated—and in justice to them I must point out that I have not in some cases agreed with them, and therefore all that follows is my responsibility and mine alone.

As should be evident from the foregoing, I do not pretend to omniscience in this field, and do not claim any sort of final authority. I have tried to make this book as complete and accurate as possible, within the limits set by the nature of the work. Any corrections or further information concerning the entries herein, *if accompanied by documentary evidence where relevant*, will be very much appreciated.

One final note: it is common in discussions of magic and—I am sorry to say—in much magical journalism, to state that "No one ever invents anything." It is as true in magic as in any other technical field that most creations are built on or inspired by the work of others;

this does not, however, make the act of creation any less real. Many who make these kinds of statements do so, I suspect, so that they need not consider a magical invention to be the real and private property of its creator—and therefore can take it for their own uses. My admittedly personal view is that it is only a brief step from not caring *who created* an effect or routine to not caring *how you obtain it*, and that this kind of thinking results in the hackneyed performances of copyists and plagiarists who at one time came very close to destroying magic as a theatrical art.

I have, therefore, made an effort to give credit where it is due; in a number of cases I have specified originators and creators other than those commonly associated with a given effect or technique. In nearly all cases my crediting has been based on documentary evidence, and in all cases on the best judgment I have been able to make given the available information. If I have erred in some respects, I am willing to be proven wrong—*proof* being the operative word.

Magic is one of the theater's most technically complex arts; if this book is able to render it a bit less complex, it will have succeeded in its purpose.

Special thanks to William W. Larsen Jr. for permission to reprint several photographs from the files of *Genii*; and to Ricky Jay for access to photographs and printed matter in the Mulholland Library.

Special thanks also to Robert Parrish and Jay Marshall for their valuable suggestions.

In the entries that follow many books are suggested for further reading. The great majority of these books are available only through magic shops and magic publishers and booksellers, and are thus not listed in *Books In Print* or similar sources.

Note: The text of this book is arranged alphabetically and is self-indexed through cross references. A word or phrase set entirely in capital letters within the text of an entry denotes a cross reference.

ABANAZAR

Evil magician in traditional British Christmas pantomime *Aladdin*; the role has been performed by many of Britain's top magicians, notably CLAUDE CHANDLER and EDWARD VICTOR.

ABBOT, ANTHONY

Nom-de-plume used by FULTON OURSLER.

ABBOTT, DAVID P. (1863-1934)

Author and inventor best known for his *Behind The Scenes With The Mediums*; written in 1907, this book is still one of the very best accounts of the techniques and methods used in fraudulent mediumship.

Abbott was also a master of more conventional areas of deception, and many of the greats of magic—KELLAR, THURSTON, HORACE GOLDIN, and THEO BAMBERG among others—visited his Omaha, Nebraska, "Mystery House" to be baffled and to learn. The FLOATING BALL routine made world-famous by Bamberg was devised and taught to him by Abbott.

The TALKING TEAKETTLE, invented by Abbott, could be shown empty, yet when the spout was held to a spectator's ear it would answer a question of which the spectator had been thinking; this was performed well before the advent of radio.

The SPIRIT PAINTINGS was Abbott's duplication of a trick performed as a genuine phenomenon by a pair of mediums known as the Bangs Sisters. Having devised an excellent stage presentation for the effect, Abbott revealed the method to a Dr. Wilmar, who promptly sold it as his own to SELBIT and Kellar, who featured it in their performances. Still performed today, it is a mysterious and beautiful effect; the slow appearance of a thought-of image on the examined canvas is truly eerie.

Abbott wrote a second full-length book, describing not only the "seances" given in his home but many magical feats which had astounded top professional performers; he died before it could be published, and for a long time the manuscript could not be found.

It was discovered by Walter Graham and published as *David P. Abbott's Book Of Mysteries* in 1977.

ABBOTT, PERCY (1886-1960)

Born in Australia, he toured the world for many years with a FULL-EVENING SHOW, traveling to the Orient, Russia, England and the United States. Settling in Colon, Michigan, he became a U.S. citizen and, with HARRY BLACKSTONE SR., founded the Abbott Magic & Novelty Co., first known as The Blackstone Magic Co. (the partnership lasted for only a short time). Today the firm is one of the largest APPARATUS and book companies, selling both to dealers and direct through its huge mail-order catalog. A family-oriented convention, Abbott's Get-Together, is held yearly in Colon.

Abbott was also the founder of TOPS Magazine.

A.B.C. FLY

An effect created by DAVID DEVANT in which a large model of a fly (the winged insect) crawled from a box the performer held to an easel on which was a display board bearing the alphabet. At the performer's command, the fly would move about to spell out words requested by the audience.

There were many variations in method, but the one

most often employed by Devant used a magnet within the board that attracted a steel disk on the fly's stomach; the magnet was controlled with threads by hidden assistants under the stage.

A later version of this effect was called ISIS.

ABRA (Magazine)

Technically titled ABRACADABRA, but known simply as *Abra*; begun in February 1946 by GOODLIFFE (C. Goodliffe Neale), this magazine is (as it proudly proclaims on each issue's cover) "The World's ONLY Magical Weekly." Magic magazines have a very high mortality rate, which makes the forty-year on-time record of *Abra* even more astonishing.

For many years FABIAN (E. Ray Griffiths) was Associate Editor; on his death, Donald Bevan was appointed to this position. With Goodliffe's passing Bevan became Editor, as he is today.

Published in England, *Abra* carries some strictly local news (such as magical society reports), but most of it is of general interest, from the dealer ads and the thought-provoking (and often controversial) editorials to the truly incredible amount of good magic appearing here over the years.

Abra has recently been acquired by the firm of L. DAVENPORT & Co.; what effect—if any—this will have on the direction of the magazine remains to be seen.

ABRACADABRA

Used (now rarely) by stage magicians as a "magic word", and as slang by the public to refer to magic in general, this was originally used in a cabalistic charm, its syllables forming a kind of acronym for the Hebrew letters symbolizing the Holy Trinity.

ACADEMY OF MAGICAL ARTS

The nonprofit organization which operates the MAGIC CASTLE as its clubhouse; it was the inspiration of WILLIAM W. LARSEN. It is run by a board of directors, of which WILLIAM W. LARSEN JR. is President for life. DAI VERNON is a member Emeritus as was the late Cary Grant; other members are voted in by election.

The Academy holds an awards banquet annually; Fellowship and Magician Of The Year awards are determined by the Board, as are any Award Of Merit citations. Other awards are for performances and lectures at the MAGIC CASTLE and are decided on by the entire regular membership.

There are two classes of membership in the Academy: regular, for magicians who must audition and be interviewed to determine their abilities, and associate, for friends and aficionados of magic. There is also a Junior Magicians Society for magicians under the age of 21.

ACE

The playing card with only a single center PIP; also, the side of a DIE with only one spot; from the Latin *as*, a unit.

While in numerical value the Ace is equivalent to a *One*, in most card games it is considered the highest valued card. If, therefore, the performer has to ascertain the identity of a card when one possibility is the Ace and the other is a Two, Three or Four this can be done by stating "You are thinking of a *low-value* card." Any hesitation on the spectator's part will indicate the *Ace*, since the spectator doesn't know if you are referring to numerical or gaming value (*see* PUMPING).

ACE ASSEMBLY

Synonymous with the FOUR ACES; also, effects in which the four Aces, placed in different parts of the deck, come together at one location. Some card specialists prefer to use this phrase only in the first sense given, to avoid confusion.

ACETABULARII

Magicians who specialized in performing the CUPS AND BALLS effect in early Rome. The Acetabularii are mentioned in writings by Seneca and Athenaeus.

The name is derived from the Latin term for "vinegar cup."

ACETONE

A volatile liquid used to remove rubber-based adhesives such as SPIRIT GUM or rubber cement. It is also sometimes used to dilute inks used on MARKED DECKS (*see* JUICE), or to remove ink or printing from a playing card.

ACQUITMENT

A SLEIGHT used to show the hand apparently empty while it actually contains an object. While this can be accomplished with one hand (*see* BACK PALM), it is usually done by means of a CHANGEOVER PASS. Unless done by an expert manipulator in the course of a logical movement, such sleights are unconvincing and are often disparagingly described as HAND-WASHING.

ACROBATIC CARD

An ordinary-appearing but ingeniously faked card, believed to have been invented by Joe Fenichel, which can be added to an ordinary deck; placed on the table or on the deck, the card will visibly flip over to reveal its face, powered by a sheet of rubber attached to a half-card flap.

Several uses for this card are described in *Acrobatic Cards* by ED MARLO.

ACROBATIC MATCHBOX

A popular CLOSE-UP effect in which a matchbox placed on the performer's hand goes through various gyrations, usually concluded with the drawer mysteriously sliding open. The effect is the invention of G. W. HUNTER.

ACT

A Performer's complete ROUTINE; "Act" usually denotes a performance of less than thirty minutes, often as part of a longer SHOW.

Act also denotes a specific routine within a FULL-EVENING SHOW (e.g., the SPIRIT CABINET act or the LEVITATION act.

ACT DROP

Another name for the FRONT CURTAIN (curtain nearest the front of the stage and/or footlights).

ADAIR, IAN (b. 1943)

Born in Britain, he at one time specialized in DOVE MAGIC but now works primarily as a children's entertainer. Adair is the author of over seventy books on magic and allied arts, including his monumental five-volume *Encyclopedia of Dove Magic*; many of his books are published by the SUPREME MAGIC CO., with which he is associated.

Adair also writes a regular column for MAGIGRAM, and contributes items to other magazines, including one-man Parades to the LINKING RING.

ADAMS, GRAHAM (1893-1974)

British magician noted for his entertaining card magic in which he specialized. Though not a full-time professional performer, he was a popular after-dinner entertainer in and around his home city of Manchester.

His approach to card magic was described in a series of articles which appeared in PETER WARLOCK's *Pentagram* magazine.

ADAMS, S.S. (1869-?)

Born Soren Adams in Denmark; he emigrated to the U.S. as a child. Adams founded a novelty and joke manufacturing company which became one of the largest of its kind. Among the items manufactured were several small pocket tricks, and in many cases it was an Adams-manufactured EFFECT that drew its buyer into a lifelong interest in magic.

An interesting profile of Adams is contained in *It Takes All Kinds* by Maurice Zolotow.

ADD-A-NUMBER

Originally a title name for a specific brand of mechanical writing pad which will produce, vanish or change writing of the magician or a spectator, this term is now applied generically to the many varieties of such devices.

The first marketed pad was designed by H. W. Brehaut; variants on the basic design have been published by Geoff Ogram and GEORGE BLAKE.

This device is often referred to as ADDANO.

ADDITION SLATE

A mechanical slate with a hinged central flap which may cover the upper or lower half of the slate, in much the same way as a FLAP CARD; invented by JOSEPH DUNNINGER, the slate will produce, vanish or exchange writing. The name comes from its use in a feat of MENTAL MAGIC in which the performer apparently predicts the total of a randomly given group of numbers. (*See* SIXTEEN-DIGIT TEST.)

Later versions of the **addition slate** created by AL BAKER and Harry Dobrin allowed the flap to be locked in position so that it could be safely handled by spectators. Slates not being as common as they once were, the effects once accomplished by this slate are now usually done with the ADD-A-NUMBER device.

ADD-ON

A technique first developed by DAI VERNON in which a number of INDIFFERENT CARDS are added to a PACKET—as is often required in (for example) FOUR-ACE effects.

The original Vernon move used a break held above a few cards at the back of the face-up deck. The deck was spread and the Aces were jogged upward; the deck was then squared with the Aces left projecting. The right hand took the deck above the break, and the left hand moved forward with the extra cards, adding them to the Aces as these were pulled from the deck. A very similar technique was used in Vernon's later

B.D.V. move, which appeared in the PHOENIX and later in BRUCE ELLIOTT's *The Best In Magic*.

There have been many techniques developed for accomplishing the add-on procedure, by FRED BRAUE and several others; in most of these procedures the packet is held from above as for the BIDDLE MOVE, and cards are added from above a BREAK in the deck held in the left hand.

In modern usage, the add-on term usually refers to these latter techniques; to differentiate them, a move of the Vernon type given above is called a strip-out addition.

AD LIB

Spontaneous, unscripted remarks or actions; also, to make such remarks or actions.

Though many performers have a ready wit and can take advantage of unique situations, they rarely trust to luck and fate; most have a large repertoire of performance material which can be applied to various circumstances.

ADRIAN, MONS. (?-?)

Performer (his name is variously spelled "Adrien" and "Adrean") who worked throughout the eastern U.S. and in Britain in the early part of the 19th century; in addition to magic, he performed PLATE SPINNING.

ADVANCE MAN

Person (male or female) who travels to a venue to inspect the performance area, arrange advertising, and take care of other business particulars prior to the performer's arrival.

ADY, THOMAS (?-?)

Writer of *A Candle In The Dark*, a book published in 1655 which contained a section on performance magic. Some of the information therein was similar to and likely taken from REGINALD SCOT's *The Discovery of Witchcraft*, but there was also new material.

AERIAL FISHING

An EFFECT in which the performer uses a fishing pole to cast a baited line over the heads of the audience; a fish appears visibly on the end of the line and then is removed and dropped into a fishbowl where it swims about.

Quite possibly Oriental in origin, this effect has been a popular one with magicians for many years; it was featured by (among others) CHUNG LING SOO

seventy-five years ago, by JOHN BOOTH and CECIL LYLE in the 1930's, and currently by ALAN SHAXON.

AERIAL SUSPENSION
See SUSPENSIONS.

AERIAL TREASURY
See MISER'S DREAM.

AFGHAN BANDS

Endless loops of cloth or paper which, being torn along their lengths, do not separate into single bands as should happen; instead, one attempt will find two bands linked together—another will produce a large band twice the size of the original loop—a third try will produce an equally large loop with an overhand knot in it.

This popular effect is over a century old; the above name, by which it is now known, was given by PROFESSOR HOFFMANN. It was first performed with paper bands; later routines use CARL BREMA's idea of cloth bands, which can be ripped rather than cut. Its operation is dependent on loops constructed as variations of Moebius strips. It is discussed and explained not only in magic books but also in works on recreational mathematics and topology.

A.F.T.R.A.

American Federation of Television and Radio Artists, the labor organization to which all performers making professional appearances on broadcast media must belong.

AGA
See LEVITATIONS.

AGOSTON, CHEVALIER (1821-1876)

German performer who toured Europe with a ghost show. Later he outfitted a boat as a floating theater and gave shows in cities along the Rhine, but this was not successful. He attempted to recoup his losses by performing in Switzerland, but returned finally to Berlin where he reportedly died of starvation.

A.G.V.A.

American Guild of Variety Artists, a labor organization for various kinds of performers. It is not as influential as it once was; many of its functions having been taken over by A.F.T.R.A.

A.I.M.C.

An advanced level of membership in Britain's MAGIC CIRCLE; the initials stand for Associate of the Inner Magic Circle.

AIRBORNE GLASS

A glass which floats in the air while the performer pours liquid into it from a bottle.

Many noted performers have featured this effect, from HARRY BLACKSTONE SR. to LANCE BURTON.

AIR CHECK

An audiotape or videotape recording of a radio or television performance. It may be studied by the performer to eliminate flaws in presentation.

A collection of segments featuring the performer may be edited into a sequence on a single tape which may then be used for audition purposes.

ALAN, ALAN

Born Alan Rabinowitz in Britain; professional performer specializing in sensational ESCAPES. A specialty is release from straitjacket or chain while hanging upside-down from a burning rope (*see* CHAIN ESCAPES; STRAITJACKET). He is also noted for his handling of classic CLOSE-UP MAGIC.

In addition to performing, Alan is a well-known London magic dealer.

ALAN, DON (b. ?)

A closeup performer who, after study at the CHAVEZ COLLEGE OF MAGIC, began his career at the "magic bar" of MATT SCHULIEN; his subsequent career has included not only appearances on many television talk/variety shows, but also his own series called *Don Alan's Magic Ranch*.

His relaxed and enjoyable approach to his work was highly influential on performers coming into magic in the 1960's; it is well described in the two books he has written on the subject of closeup magic: *Close Up Time* and *Pretty Sneaky.*

ALARM CLOCK PRODUCTION

Used in conjunction with a PRODUCTION device, this consists of a set of alarm clock SHELLs which nest together and which—produced one at a time—have the appearance of real alarm clocks. This appearance is enhanced by a special tray which not only holds the clock shells in an upright position, but also contains several ringing devices to create the illusion of the alarms being set off.

ALBENICE, JOHN (1913-1957)

Nightclub performer who toured North and South America; author of *Reel Magic*, a book of EFFECTS accomplished with the aid of a REEL.

ALBINI, HERBERT (1860-1922)

Born Abraham Laski in Poland, he began his performing career in Britain and then moved to the U.S. Albini was particularly noted for his routine for the EGG BAG, and also for his custom of beginning each of his card tricks by opening a new deck of cards; by the end of the performance the stage was littered with discarded decks.

ALEXANDER, C.A. (1880-1954)

Born Claude Alexander Conlin, he achieved fame as *Alexander, The Man Who Knows*. While the major feature of his act (which made him quite wealthy) was the answering of questions thought of by members of the audience, the first part of his show was conventional magic. The act was presented in a quasi-Oriental setting with lavish costuming for himself and several female assistants.

He wrote *The Life And Mysteries Of The Celebrated Dr. Q*, which, published in 1921, described several of his magic and mental feats.

ALL BACKS

A card EFFECT in which the faces of the cards are replaced by backs, so that the cards appear to have two backs and no faces. Some routines have involved the use of faked or prepared cards, but there are many in the literature which use only SLEIGHT-OF-HAND technique. An excellent version is that of DAI VERNON (who is believed to have invented the basic effect), and can be found in the *Dai Vernon Book Of Magic.*

There are several PACKET versions of the effect; one of the more popular ones is **Hofzinser All Backs**, by HARRY RISER, which appeared in the magazine *Epilogue.*

ALLEN, KEN (b. ?)

Performer, dealer and manufacturer; among the many popular items he has created are JUMPING GEMS and CHINATOWN QUARTER.

ALLEN, STAN (b. ?)

Performer who specializes in comedy magic, and is noted for his popular routine with a large puppet rabbit named Stewart; he performs in varied venues, most often on cruise ships and in INDUSTRIAL SHOWS (which he also creates).

He is the editor/publisher of *Inside Magic*, a monthly newsletter of news and information begun in January 1985.

ALLERTON, BERT (1889-1958)

Born Bert A. Gustafson, his fame arrived in middle age after a career as a businessman. Allerton became a star of CLOSE-UP MAGIC in nightclubs, and worked for many years in Chicago's Pump Room with great financial and artistic success. One of Allerton's features was the VANISHING BIRD CAGE, not usually considered a close-up effect.

Allerton's work is described in *The Close Up Magician*, written by ROBERT PARRISH.

ALMA, WILL (b. 1904)

Born into show business in Australia, Alma has had a long career in all phases of magic—as performer, inventor, collector, and dealer. He is a member of the Inner MAGIC CIRCLE (with Gold Star). His *Alma Con-*

Stan Allen and friend Stewart

juring Collection is now in the State Library at Victoria, Australia.

AL-'N-NATE BOX

A variant of the OKITO BOX, this box has a sizable hole in its bottom and is used in conjunction with a prepared coin incorporating the principle of MASKING. Fully described in J. B. BOBO's *Modern Coin Magic,* it is named for AL BAKER and NATE LEIPZIG.

ALPHABET CARDS

Cards bearing letters of the alphabet; these are used in venues where playing cards may be objectionable and quite often in effects of MENTAL MAGIC.

While such decks are available from magic dealers, some performers (particularly those doing mental magic) prefer to use Lexicon or Bali cards from the respective games, feeling that these decks appear more innocent than a specially printed deck.

ALTAR LIGHT, SACRED

A parlor/platform EFFECT invented by U.F. GRANT, using two candles separated by an upright sheet of glass; several puzzling effects take place in the ROUTINE. The flame of one candle, for example, apparently penetrates the solid bottom of a water-filled glass.

The routine is based on a clever application of the principles employed in PEPPER'S GHOST.

ALTERNATIVE DISCLOSURE

A principle most often used with two or more items, in which the performer makes it appear that an action occurs in accordance with a choice made by the spectator.

As an example, a ring and a coin might be borrowed, secretly taken from their supposed location, and loaded respectively into a DOVE PAN (tied with a ribbon to a bouquet) and a NEST OF BOXES. The performer asks for one of the objects to be named, and then carries out the revelation in accordance with the choice—the implication being that the same would have been done with either object. Presentation and staging helps to carry this idea through.

Sometimes confused with OPTIONAL DISCLOSURE.

AMAC, BILL (1890-1961)

Born Robert William Macfarland, he was a British magician who made his reputation with his FIND THE

LADY illusion, first in the U.S. and then in his native land. Though he began his career with varied small magic, in later years he presented FIND THE LADY by itself as a specialty act.

He also invented, among many other items, the popular pocket effect known as the EDUCATED PENCIL.

AMATEUR MAGICIAN

One who performs magic for the love of the art, without charging a fee; also, someone who does not make a living as a professional performer.

Often the word *amateur* is used as a pejorative, but in fact many amateur magicians have been highly skilled performers, while some full-time professionals are mediocre at best.

AMBIDEXTROUS

Capable of using both hands with equal facility. Most SLEIGHT-OF-HAND magicians are ambidextrous of necessity, though they may favor one hand for the more difficult manipulations.

AMBITIOUS CARD, THE

A classic card EFFECT in which a chosen card, repeatedly placed in the center of the deck, mysteriously rises to the top. In many ROUTINEs the card is signed by the spectator to eliminate the obvious possibility of duplicate cards.

Nearly every major card magician has a special way of performing this effect; the most widely used routines are those of DAI VERNON, published in the book *Stars Of Magic*, and HARRY LORAYNE, which will be found in his *Close-Up Card Magic*. A work devoted entirely to this effect is DARYL's *Ambitions Card Omnibus*, written by STEPHEN MINCH.

AMBUSH

A variant of the COLLECTORS in which the collector cards have a back design and/or color differing from the rest of the deck; it is the creation of ED MARLO.

AMEDEO (1890-1974)

Born Amedeo Vacca in Italy, he emigrated to the U.S. as a youth and was a professional magician by the age of 20. For the last three years of HOUDINI's career, Amedeo acted as his advance man; after Houdini's death, Amedeo returned to performing, working both in the U.S. and Europe.

His work is described in *Amedeo's Continental Magic* by FRANK GARCIA and George Schindler.

Amedeo (*The Mulholland Library of Conjuring & the Allied Arts, Los Angeles, California*)

AMERICAN MUSEUM OF MAGIC

Opened in 1978 in Marshall, Michigan, it was created by ROBERT LUND. In addition to APPARATUS, the museum features posters, books, and voluminous files of information on every conceivable subject relevant to magic.

AMMAR, MICHAEL (b. 1956)

Specialist in close-up magic; he has appeared on many television shows, including *The Tonight Show* and *Merv Griffin*, and in a number of other venues.

He is a co-editor of the *Magical Arts Journal*; his books include *Encore II, Encore III, Success In Magic*, and *The Topit Book*.

Ammar is a first place winner of the close-up competition at FISM; he has also twice received the Best Close-Up Magician award from the ACADEMY OF MAGICAL ARTS.

AMWELL, LORD (1876-1966)

British amateur, born Frederick Montague, who is noted as the inventor of the BLUFF PASS and the HANDKERCHIEF FORCE. His work is described in his book *Westminster Wizardry* and in many contributions to ABRA Magazine.

ANDERSON, GENE (b. 1941)

A chemist by profession, Anderson is noted for his trophy-winning act of newspaper magic, consisting almost entirely of effects of his own devising. Of these, undoubtedly the best known is his commercially-marketed version of the TORN AND RESTORED newspaper (probably inspired by an earlier version created by AL KORAN), which has been featured by DOUG HENNING through his entire career.

This effect is described (along with many others) in Anderson's book *Newspaper Magic*.

Anderson is also noted for his lecture (and book) titled *The Part-Time Pro*; dealing with the semi-professional performer, it stresses that—even when performing is not a person's only source of income—standards must still be maintained at a high professional level.

ANDERSON, HARRY (b. 1952)

Harry Anderson began his career doing STREET MAGIC; he also performed at the Ashland (Oregon) Shakespeare Festival, where he featured the BULLET CATCH. Long known as a comedy magician, his shows now blend broad comedy with poetic and mysterious presentations. He is, of course, also known for his lead role as Judge Harry Stone in the highly successful television series *Night Court*.

In his stage shows Anderson has often worked with wife LESLIE ANDERSON as partner. In addition to comedy routines, they have performed a TWO-PERSON MENTAL ACT; some of their techniques are revealed in their book *Eight Brass Monkeys*.

Other books by Harry Anderson include *The Shadow And Other Card Mysteries* and *The Final Couvert Seance*.

ANDERSON, JOHN HENRY (1814-1874)

Known best as the "Wizard of the North," a title he claimed had been bequeathed to him by Sir Walter Scott, Anderson was a showman-magician in the grand manner. With the possible exception of HOUDINI, he was the greatest exponent of publicity and promotion in the history of magic.

Anderson is generally credited with moving magic from the parlor and fairground into the theatre. He toured energetically through Great Britain, the United States, Europe, Canada, Russia and many other places.

Particularly notable in his show was his performance of the BULLET CATCH.

ANDERSON, LESLIE (b. 1952)

A specialist in MENTAL MAGIC, Leslie Anderson most often performs in a TWO-PERSON MENTAL ACT or an ESCAPE routine with husband HARRY ANDERSON. She is co-author with him of *Eight Brass Monkeys* (a book which describes some of the techniques used in the act).

ANDERSON, LOUISE (?-?)

Daughter of JOHN HENRY ANDERSON, she performed with him one of the earliest TWO-PERSON MENTAL ACT routines during the middle years of the 19th century. Louise was billed as the "Second-Sighted Sybil" and "Retro-Reminiscent Mnemosyne," and while securely blindfolded would describe articles handed to her father by members of the audience.

ANDREWS, VAL (b. 1926)

A prolific magical journalist and author, Andrews has, in addition to contributions to many magazines, written dozens of books. His works include *The Big Show*, *Card And Coin Magic Of Bobby Bernard*, *Circus Magic*, *Floorshow Fun And Phantasy*, *A Gift From The Gods*, *Goodnight Mr. Dante*, *Impromptu Show*, *Triumphs And Tragedies Of Horace Goldin*, *Val's Varieties*, *Whirlwind Of Wizardry*, and many more.

ANDRUS, JERRY (b. ?)

Most famous for his creation of the LINKING PINS, Andrus has also developed a number of other EFFECTs. In addition to magic, he has produced some startling three-dimensional optical ILLUSIONS and perceptual effects.

Andrus has a unique approach to magic, both in PLOT and method, and his effects are noticeably different from the usual run. An interesting aspect of his magic is that Andrus never says anything in his presentations that is not true, preferring to deceive the spectators by visual means alone.

ANDRUZZI, TONY (b. 1925)

Born Tom Palmer, he has worked in many phases of show business. As Palmer, he was noted for an award-winning comedy act which he debuted in the late 1960s. Many elements from this act have been used by various performers, and Palmer wrote a book describing the complete routine.

He devised a number of illusions, including his popular SATAN'S SEAT (a version of which was

Tony Andruzzi as Tom Palmer

featured in DOUG HENNING's Broadway show *Merlin*); this and other effects were described in his book *Modern Illusions*. Other books include *Cagey Doves*, *The Tie Pitch*, and *The Famous Flea Act*.

In the 1970s he adopted the family name of Andruzzi and began to specialize in BIZARRE MAGIC, often using the stage name Masklyn Ye Mage. In addition to writing several books on the subject (*The Negromicon Of Masklyn ye Mage*, *Daemon's Diary*, and *Grimoire Of The Mages*) he became editor of the *New Invocation*, a magazine devoted to bizarre and unusual magic.

In addition, he has created the **Invocational**, a yearly convention for those interested in the kind of magic described in the magazine.

ANGEL

A slang term to designate the individual who provides the financial backing for a show or act.

ANGELICO, SAM (b. ?)

Born in Australia, Angelico's SILENT ACT features him as an odd, humorous and intriguing character. He has performed throughout Europe, and has also appeared in Britain and the U.S.

He is a recipient of the Comedy Magic First Prize award at F.I.S.M.

ANGLE-PROOF

Term used to describe an EFFECT which can be performed with spectators on all sides without revealing its methodology. This is not a major consideration for the illusionist working on a PROSCENIUM-arch stage; for the nightclub performer, however—who often will work with an audience on three sides and the orchestra directly behind—it is of major importance; for the close-up performer working in informal circumstances it is essential.

A classic example of an angle-proof effect is the LINKING RINGS. CARD-FAN PRODUCTIONS, on the other hand, can only be effectively performed with the audience directly in front of the performer (*see* BACK PALM).

ANIMAL MAGIC

Magicians have always used animals and birds in their performances; in recent years this area has become much more popular, in great part due to the success of SIEGFRIED AND ROY (who feature such work). Indeed, many magicians have come to believe that lions and tigers are essential ingredients for any act hoping to play venues such as Las Vegas or Atlantic City. In the words of comedy magician MIKE CAVENEY:

"Use a cat, go to Vegas—it's the law."

This perception on the part of many magicians is not at all true; while exotic animals may add momentary interest, their presence alone will not sell an act. Many top acts such as JEFF McBRIDE and THE PENDRAGONS work these venues regularly without using animals.

Aside from their questionable necessity in an act, and the difficulty of keeping them healthy and happy in the unpredictable conditions of trouping, animals present another problem for a performer. Audiences are very sensitive to anything they may perceive as mistreatment of animals—whether or not this may actually be the case—and one slip or stumble of an animal, one loose birdfeather falling to the ground in the course of an effect, can kill the entire act stone dead.

The reverse of this picture is that when an animal seems to enjoy performing and has an obvious

Siegfried and Roy with their white tiger Zenza Sitarra and her three cubs.

affectionate rapport with the performer, it can add a great deal to an act—enough, sometimes, to make all the problems seem worthwhile.

It should be noted that there will always be a certain percentage of the audience who do not believe animals should be used in stage entertainment under any circumstances—either on the grounds of suspected cruelty, or simply because they do not consider such magic to be sophisticated entertainment. Performers should be aware of the possibility of such perceptions.

ANIMAL MAGNETISM

An obsolete term for the phenomenon of hypnosis; now sometimes used by magicians as a presentational concept for effects in which objects (pencils, cards, etc.) cling to the performer's fingertips.

See MAGNETIZED CARDS; DUAL CONTROL.

ANIMATED SELF-LIGHTING CIGARETTE

An amazing parlor effect created by JOHN KENNEDY in which a cigarette rises to the performer's lips from a pack held in the hand; the pack then changes to a box of matches.

The matchbox drawer opens—a match floats out, pushes the drawer closed, and then strikes itself on the side of the box; it then floats up to the cigarette, which it lights.

Interestingly, the EFFECT (now commercially marketed by Kennedy) uses no threads to create the floating effects. Not surprisingly, it was a major factor in building Kennedy's reputation as an innovative inventor.

ANNALS OF CONJURING

A history of stage magic and its performers by SIDNEY W. CLARKE, first published serially in THE MAGIC

WAND (1924-1928) and most recently in book form (photo-offset from the original magazine publication) by *Magico Magazine* in 1983.

While it tends to focus on European magicians, particularly those who performed in Great Britain, within those limits it is an invaluable reference work and essential background reading.

ANNEMANN, THEODORE (1907-1942)

Though now primarily known for his creation of EFFECTs in the MENTALISM field, Annemann began his career as a magician and maintained an active interest in it throughout his life. In his magazine—THE JINX—were published many of his magical effects as well as those of his contemporaries.

Annemann's most famous feat was, in fact, in the area of magic; this was his test-conditions presentation of the famous—and deadly—BULLET CATCH. He planned to present this effect, along with others, at a special FULL-EVENING SHOW in January of l942; however, two weeks before the show-date, Annemann was found dead—a suicide.

To learn of his general magic, a file of THE JINX is required; much of his card magic is available in *Annemann's Card Magic*, a book created from two earlier collections of effects from his magazine.

Many top magicians were persuaded by Annemann to contribute their best effects to THE JINX; just as valuable are his editorial columns, which he titled "Editrivia." Annemann was a keen observer of the magic world, and much of what he had to say is as valid today as when he wrote it.

ANTI-GRAVICO

A LIQUID EFFECT in which water poured into a cola bottle does not run out when the bottle is inverted, even though toothpicks, matches, and a pencil are inserted in the bottle's mouth to prove it is open. The effect, invented by Bob Andre, depends upon a commercially-available GIMMICK which employs subtle principles of surface tension to achieve its effect.

See HYDROSTATIC GLASS.

ANTI-GRAVITY GLASSES

Japanese in origin, and believed to have been invented by TENKAI; an EFFECT in which two glasses are placed mouth down on a book which has been wrapped in a handkerchief. The book is then inverted but the glasses mysteriously cling to it; if silks have been placed in the glasses these may be withdrawn without affecting the situation.

A version of this effect, using a cigarette case, a dollar bill and two "zombie" glasses, was featured by JACK GWYNNE; his routine is described in *Jack Gwynne* by David Charvet.

A number of variations of the basic effect have been developed over the years. In one version a folded newspaper replaced the book, and both paper and glasses were spun on the performer's magic wand. The most elaborate version to date uses a sheet of clear plastic and *three* glasses; it was commercially marketed by L. Davenport & Co. A ROUTINE for this version is LEWIS GANSON's **A Clear Case of Antigravity**, described in *The Lewis Ganson Book*.

ANVERDI, TONY (b. ?)

Born in Holland; baker by profession. Anverdi is noted for his many LIQUID EFFECTs using hydraulic and other principles, and latterly for his many electronically operated effects, which are currently commercially marketed, among them a miniature TALKING SKULL, a version of the SEVEN KEYS TO BALDPATE effect, and a JUMBO DECK designed for the RISING CARDS.

ANY CARD CALLED FOR

See CARDS FROM THE POCKETS.

APPARATUS

Any object, seen by the audience, which has been specially prepared to bring about a magical effect. The term is not dependent on size; a BILL TUBE and a LION'S BRIDE ILLUSION are both apparatus effects. This term is not classified by audience perception; while a matchbox may not *appear* to be magician's apparatus, if it has been secretly altered and prepared for the purposes of an effect, it is so regarded.

APPEARING CANE

Invented by RUSS WALSH, this cane is so constructed as to be compressible into a very small package; when pressure is released, it instantly springs out to full size. It also may be used as a silk-to-cane effect, the silk handkerchief being drawn into the cane as it expands.

Originally made of spring steel, it is now available in a plastic model (*see* VANISHING CANE).

APPORT

An object mysteriously brought into a locked SEANCE room or other location from elsewhere, by a MEDIUM or other person professing supernormal or supernatural abilities; the object may be anything from a small "spirit gift" or bouquet to a previously "lost" object to (in one well-known case) another medium.

To simulate this phenomenon by conjuring technique is elementary; it is, however, still demonstrated by many mediums and such others as URI GELLER and the East Indian Sai Baba.

APRON

That part of the stage beyond the footlights and/or nearest the audience; also, a central playing area which extends outward from the stage proper into the auditorium.

See THRUST STAGE; RUNWAY; RUNDOWN.

ARABIAN BEADS

Having been cut loose from their cord, a number of beads are magically re-strung, usually in a glass or in the performer's mouth. Often (erroneously) called the CARMO BEADS, after a popular version of the EFFECT; this version, invented by JOHN ALBENICE, does not use the same principle. (A similar version was published in THE MAGIC WAND by Charles Ramsey.)

See NEEDLE TRICK; RAZOR BLADE SWALLOWING.

ARCANE

Hidden; mysterious. Often used in reference to information requiring a secret key or special knowledge to understand.

Also, name of magazine begun in 1980 and published by JEFF BUSBY. Not a "house organ" in the usual sense (it carries no advertising), it was available only as a premium to purchasers of Busby's merchandise until its eleventh issue, when it became available by subscription. Subscriptions are by number of issues, since the publishing schedule is somewhat arbitrary.

It is noted for its high quality of production and thorough descriptions of routines and effects.

ARCANE was also the title of a French magic publication.

ARISTOCRAT

Brand of playing cards manufactured by the U.S. Playing Card Company; much favored for card magic, due to the finish, pliability, and aesthetically pleasing back design.

ARM BOX

A stage EFFECT, invented by U.F. GRANT, in which a spectator's arm is placed in a chimney-like wooden tube; upper and lower parts of the arm can be seen through openings at the front, but when a central door is opened, that section of the arm is not visible. A rear door is opened and the magician thrusts his own hand through the central section to show that part of the arm has vanished; the central doors being closed, the spectator removes his arm—none the worse for wear.

The effect is achieved by an application of the mirror principle. It can be used both on its own and as a logical preliminary to a presentation of the GIRL WITHOUT A MIDDLE. The APPARATUS was originally marketed under the name *Amputation*(!).

ARM DROP

With cards, a FLOURISH best described as a one-handed WATERFALL; the cards are allowed to drop in ribbon fashion from the hand, which then recaptures them in a scooping action. This is not an easy flourish to accomplish, and the student is advised to become proficient in the ARM SPREAD before attempting it.

ARM SPREAD

A type of FLOURISH in which a deck of cards is placed in a RIBBON-SPREAD on the arm; the arm is then dropped, and the cards fall into the hand. Alternatively, the spread may be given a toss and caught in a scooping fashion by the other hand; this is considerably easier, but still requires a good deal of practice.

After spreading the cards on the arm, some performers like to execute the TURNOVER SPREAD before catching the cards.

ARMSTRONG, GEORGE (?-?)

Noted British performer who was also for some years editor of the British periodicals *Magic Wand* and *The Wizard*, and the operator of Magic Wand Publishing Co.; he also contributed items to a number of magazines. His books include *George Armstrong's Premonition, Challenge Instant Hypnotism And Mass Hypnotism* and others.

ARRANGEMENT

In card magic, the particular order of cards in a STACK.

ARROWSMITH, GEORGE (1887-1978)

British clergyman and noted amateur magician; a founder of Cambridge University's magical society, later to become *The Pentacle Club*. He was a member of the Inner MAGIC CIRCLE.

He contributed to a number of magazines, including PENTAGRAM and THE MAGIC CIRCULAR, and also wrote a number of books: *Assorted Mysteries, Exceptional Concepts, Magical Mentalia, Magical Originalia* and *Arrowsmith's Mystery Box*.

ARTHUR

Illusionist's parlance (now rarely used) for a stage TRAP (possibly from the word *aperture*); depending on size, a trap might be called Big Arthur or Little Arthur.

ARTISTE

Term formerly used to indicate a performer/entertainer; now, in English-speaking countries, only used in an ironic sense.

ARTIST'S DREAM

An illusion invented by DAVID DEVANT early in his career, in which a painting of a woman seems to come to life—she steps from the painting and observes the "sleeping" performer. At the conclusion of the playlet the living woman vanishes back into the painting.

This illusion was the first presented by Devant in his debut at EGYPTIAN HALL. It was probably inspired by an earlier presentation of the same title which used the METEMPSYCHOSIS principle. This title has also been applied to the PRODUCTION of various items from a paper-covered frame, after they have been sketched on the paper.

ASCANIO Y NAVAZ, ARTURO DE (b. ?)

Born in Spain; magistrate by profession. He is noted for his analytical approach to card magic, and is best known for his invention of the ASCANIO SPREAD.

His books include *On The Psychology Of Palming, About The Handling Of Double Cards*, and *The All Backs Routine*. He is also the author of a book on the COLOR-CHANGING KNIFE, the English-language version of which (translated by Jose de la Torre) is *Ascanio's World Of Knives*.

ASCANIO SPREAD

A SLEIGHT invented by ARTURO DE ASCANIO in which a small group of cards (usually no more than six) are displayed by spreading them between the hands with apparent freedom; two or three cards, however, are kept in perfect alignment and thus appear as a single card. Thus the five-or-six card packet seems to contain only four cards.

A variant, in which four cards are shown as three, is known as a *Partial Ascanio*.

Interestingly, the sleight as usually performed is itself a variant on Ascanio's original handling, in which the cards were held by the sides; in standard usage the cards are held from above at the ends, the position being somewhat similar to that taken for a BIDDLE MOVE.

Earlier work on this kind of display maneuver was done by Dutch performer Eddy Taytelbaum. Techniques and applications of this sleight are described in *The Ascanio Spread* by JON RACHERBAUMER.

ASH TRICK

An EFFECT in which a bit of cigarette ash vanishes from the performer's hand and appears in the spectator's palm. This very effective feat, described in many basic books on magic, depends almost entirely on MISDIRECTION and HANDLING.

An excellent presentation for this effect will be found in EUGENE BURGER's *Intimate Power*.

See also SUGAR CUBE TRICK, which relies on a similar handling.

ASRAH

Invented by SERVAIS LEROY, an illusion in which a woman covered with a cloth is levitated and then vanishes in mid-air. *See* LEVITATION.

ASSEMBLY

Any effect in which a separated set of objects are made to come together in one location. Examples include the ACE ASSEMBLY, CHINK-A-CHINK, and MATRIX effects.

ASSISTANT

Person who is on stage as a helper to the performer, either as subject in an illusion or bringing on or taking off apparatus. Early FULL-EVENING SHOWs might carry twenty or more assistants, but few shows currently use anything close to this number.

The present trend is away from the "assistant" as such, and toward the act featuring two performers as partners—as, for example, JOHN and PAM THOMPSON, and THE PENDRAGONS.

The term *assistant* should not be confused with CONFEDERATE.

ASSISTANT'S REVENGE

A stage ILLUSION invented by ROBERT HARBIN in which the magician is secured by several straps to an upright frame by an assistant who then pulls a circular curtain around the frame. As this action is completed, however, the magician is seen holding the curtain; when the magician pulls the curtain back the assistant is revealed to be strapped into the frame. Correctly performed, the exchange is almost instantaneous.

This illusion, which bears a presentational relationship to METAMORPHOSIS, was first presented on British television's DAVID NIXON show. The version used there differed from many later models in that instead of straps it used modified automobile seat belts, which allowed for a very rapid presentation—an idea of the CONSULTANT to the show, BILLY MCCOMB.

ASTLEY, PHILIP (1742-1814)

British performer who built a large amphitheater in London where he presented various spectacles (he also built the London Palladium). He is regarded by many historians as the father of the modern circus. Among his many feats of magic was a presentation of the BULLET CATCH; Astley's claim to have invented this effect is exceedingly unlikely, though he may have developed a particular method. Astley also wrote an early conjuring book titled *Natural Magic*.

ASTRAL BODY

The incorporeal counterpart of the physical body, known in Egyptian belief as the *Ka*, and in Theosophical belief as the *Etheric Double*; often used as a dramatic premise in stage illusions, as for example the PRINCESS OF BAKHTEN.

ASTRO-BALL CABINET

A commercially marketed EFFECT in which a ball is placed in a small cabinet with a wineglass. The door is closed briefly; when it is opened, the ball has mysteriously jumped into the glass.

The effect was invented by STEWART JAMES, and used as part of his miniature spirit cabinet routine which he called SEFALALJIA; the ROUTINE appeared in THE JINX magazine and later in ANNEMANN's *Practical Mental Effects*.

AT A TENT IN THE DESERT
See MANACLE BOARD VANISH.

ATFUS

Acronym for *Any Time Face-Up Switch*, a utility sleight devised by ED MARLO. It involves the use of a face-down card secretly placed beneath a face-up packet; this face-down card screens the STEAL or exchange of cards between the packet and the face-down deck.

This move, which has spawned many variations, was published by Marlo in the February 1964 issue of TOPS Magazine.

ATKINS, JEFFREY (b. ?)

British amateur who specializes in ILLUSION magic and is noted for his re-creations of spectacular effects from magic's past greats. Most often Atkins's performances take place at magic conventions and organizational shows.

ATTABOY

An APPARATUS version of the STOP TRICK, this is an 18" plywood cutout of a bellboy holding a card HOULETTE; at his feet rests a similar houlette. After a card is chosen—and signed by the spectator, if desired—and replaced in the deck, the cards are put in the lower houlette.

One at a time they are transferred to the upper houlette; at any time a spectator may call, "Stop," and the card the performer is holding at that moment proves to be the selected signed card.

Attaboy was invented by JACK HUGHES.

AUBREY (b. 1931)

Born James Crabe, Aubrey began performing while still in his teens, presenting a highly-regarded ILLUSION act with many original features. He made numerous television appearances, including *The Colgate Comedy Hour, The Hollywood Palace, Dinah!*, and several appearances on *You Asked For It*. While best known as an illusionist, he is also an accomplished SLEIGHT OF HAND performer, noted in particular for his BILLLARD BALL work.

Crabe, for many years a professional cinematographer, has worked on many feature films and television shows.

AUDIENCE PARTICIPATION

The use of spectators from the audience, brought on stage to assist the performer; also, the use of the audience as a whole.

An example of the former would be a spectator who comes on stage to examine the rings in the course of a

LINKING RING routine; of the latter, a MENTAL MAGIC effect in which the entire audience is invited to call out a choice in response to a query from the performer.

The use of spectators from the audience will create both advantages and disadvantages for the performer. A positive aspect is that it gives the audience a chance to see how the performer reacts in an apparently unscripted situation; the magic seems more spontaneous and thus more legitimate. The related negative aspect is that the performer can never know exactly how the presentation is going to play.

In revue/variety venues, where the magician is one of several performers, it is usual for the acts to be timed to the second; performers specializing in such work, accordingly, either severely limit or entirely eliminate the use of spectators within these acts. Other venues often have considerably more latitude.

It is important that the performer keep in mind that, usually, the audience has paid to *see* the show, not to be a part of it—thus a spectator assisting the performer is, in effect, helping to do what the spectator's money is paying the performer to do. Spectators on stage, as representatives of the audience, obviously should not be made the butt of insulting humor; ideally they should view their time on stage as an enjoyable experience, and feel fortunate they were picked for the role.

AUDIENCE WORK

Performance of all or part of an effect within the auditorium rather than on the stage. While in the proper circumstances this can be very effective—as in the FLOATING LIGHT BULB performed by HARRY BLACKSTONE *pere et fils*—it should be used sparingly; visibility for a large part of the audience can be severely reduced, with a resultant loss of attention.

AUSTRALIAN DEAL

A procedure for eliminating cards from a PACKET of any size until only a single card remains.

The top card of the packet is dealt to the table, and the next card is moved to the bottom of the packet; these two steps are repeated until only one card is left.

When the first card is dealt to the table, the procedure is called a DOWN-UNDER deal (hence the name); when the first card is moved to the bottom of the packet and the next card dealt to the table, it is called an UNDER-DOWN deal. In the literature of card magic the two types of **Australian Deal** are usually abbreviated as D/U and U/D, respectively.

The **Australian Deal** procedure is also sometimes known as **Duck And Deal**.

AUTOMATA

Mechanical figures which perform complex tasks, in imitation of a living person. There are both true and false automata—a true automaton relying entirely on its mechanism, a false automaton being secretly controlled by a hidden assistant. Magicians have exhibited both kinds; an example of the former would be the writing automaton created by Pierre Jaquet-Droz, while examples of the latter kind would be MASKELYNE's **Psycho** (in which the controlling assistant was offstage) and ROBERT-HOUDIN's **Pastry-Cook Of The Palais Royale** (in which the assistant was concealed within the cabinet which held the automaton).

A thorough discussion of both types of automata can be found in *Automata* by Alfred Chapuis and Edmond Droz.

AUZINGER, MAX (1839-1928)

Inventor of the BLACK ART act, which he first performed as Maxistan A-Uzinger in Berlin, Germany in June of 1885. A year later a similar act using the same principle was created by BUATIER DE KOLTA and presented at London's EGYPTIAN HALL. (This may have been independent invention, but there is an indication that De Kolta may have seen Auzinger's act prior to creating his own.)

Auzinger, who performed in the long robes and conical hat of a bygone era, later used the stage name BEN ALI BEY.

AVIATOR BACK

A standard symmetrical back design used by the U.S. Playing Card Company for BRIDGE-SIZE CARDS; it is of interest to magicians because a number of MECHANICAL DECKS and various faked cards using this back design are available from HAINES' HOUSE OF CARDS, where they are called FOX LAKE backs. Outside the U.S. this brand is known as Caravan.

It should be noted that the POKER-SIZE Aviator deck is of an entirely different back design.

AVIS, JACK (b. ?)

Born in Britain; highly regarded as an inventor, particularly of CLOSE-UP MAGIC. He is the creator of the SIVA COUNT and many other SLEIGHTs and EFFECTs; these have appeared in PALLBEARER'S REVIEW, EPILOGUE, PENTAGRAM, and other publications.

BABY SPOT

A small spotlight used to illuminate a relatively small area, often just the face or hands of the performer. It is sometimes used effectively in MANIPULATION acts.

BACK COUNT

Also known as a FLUSHTRATION COUNT, under which name it was devised by BR. JOHN HAMMAN, it is used to apparently display the backs of several cards in a small PACKET as being the same color, when this may not be the case.

The face-up packet is held from above in the right hand; the left thumb draws a card into its palm and the right hand pivots momentarily, showing the back of its bottom card. This is repeated for the rest of the cards and creates the illusion that the backs of all the cards have been shown, rather than just one.

This principle has been combined by PHIL GOLDSTEIN with the techniques of several other COUNTS:

1. The **Jorback**—a combination of the JORDAN COUNT with the back count.
2. The **Elmback**—ELMSLEY COUNT and back count.
3. The **Haback**—HAMMAN COUNT and back count.

In combination, these counts can conceal faces and backs of several cards in a packet.

BACKING THE DECK

Turning half the deck so that the two halves face outward, faces of cards showing on both sides of the deck. The opposite of BOX THE DECK.

BACK PALM

To conceal an object (most often a card or coin) by clipping it between the fingers at the back of the hand, the palm of the hand being toward the audience; also known, confusingly, as a REAR PALM. The object is usually held by its edges between the first and fourth fingers; when only one edge of the object is held, this is usually referred to as a **back clip** or **rear clip**.

The back palm is used in the classical versions of the MISER'S DREAM, and many other coin effects. The back palm with coins is described in BOBO's *Modern Coin Magic*, DOWNS's *Modern Coin Manipulation*, BUCKLEY's *Principles And Deceptions*, and GAULTIER's *Magic Without Apparatus*, as well as many other books on basic sleight of hand.

In card manipulation it is often seen in the continuous production of fans of cards at the fingertips; this is known as SPLIT-FAN production. This name comes from the technique of dividing the fanned cards into two portions and dropping the smaller portion into a container (hat, bucket, etc.) while back-palming the remainder, creating the illusion that *all* of the cards were dropped into the receptacle. A group of cards in back-palm position may also, of course, be produced singly, or in alternation with fans of cards. The back palm with cards is extensively covered in Gaultier's *Magic Without Apparatus* (which dates the inception of this sleight in the late 1880's); however, no mention is made in that work of card fan productions, which constitute the major use of the sleight at present. The most complete work on split-fan productions is GANSON's *Expert Manipulation Of Playing Cards*; MARLO's *Card Fan Productions* is an excellent early work on the subject, and it is also discussed in Buckley's *Card Control*.

It is only moderately difficult to learn the basic

technique of split-fan card productions; however, it is *extremely* difficult to perform these techniques with the level of skill and presence that creates a sense of pure magic rather than simply an exhibition of skill.

The basic Back Palm technique with cards was introduced by a magic dealer named Otto Maurer in 1887; Maurer said he had learned the technique from a Mexican performer. (Some believe the sleight was invented by DR. JAMES WILLIAM ELLIOTT.) The split-fan technique is said by DAI VERNON to have been invented by a side-show performer known as "Ardo, The Frog Man."

BACK-ROOM BOYS

Magicians' parlance for the behind-the-scenes creators of magical effects, who are also quite often skilled craftspersons and technicians. The term formerly was applied primarily to technicians and mechanicians, such as JON MARTIN, but is now used in a more general sense. In the past it was the custom for such people to work exclusively for one performer, as in the case of DAVID J. LUSTIG's work for DUNNINGER; now they more usually are independent contractors, hiring on for development of a specific stage show or television special as TECHNICAL ADVISORS or CONSULTANT.

See CHARLES REYNOLDS; JIM STEINMEYER; ALAN WAKELING; DON WAYNE.

BACKSTAGE ILLUSION

First made famous by DANTE's excellent presentation of it, this ILLUSION is still popular today. The premise is that the magician is performing for another audience, thus the real audience gets a rear view and is able to observe what is really happening.

In the action of the illusion, the audience sees a woman assistant creep from one box to the other as each is shown empty, and then sneak into one of the boxes through a panel before the two boxes are nested together. The tables are suddenly turned on the audience when the boxes are opened and a *male* assistant makes his appearance—the woman having vanished completely.

In Dante's presentation, he used a painted backdrop to represent the imaginary audience; at the conclusion of the effect real hands came through slits in the drop and applauded.

BAG ESCAPE

The performer is placed in a large bag, the mouth of which is tied shut and/or otherwise secured; under cover of a screen or curtained cabinet a rapid escape is made.

In the most elementary version of this feat, the performer inside the bag shoves the neck of another bag, previously concealed, up into the neck of the visible bag; the assistant outside adjusts matters so it is this bag which is sealed, the juncture of the two bags being concealed by a tied rope or handkerchief. Behind the screen, all the performer has to do is peel away the bag in which he stands, and come out with the duplicate bag. This technique allows the spectators to seal the knots with wax, markings, etc., since the bag they seal never need be opened.

A more complex version of this is the MAILBAG ESCAPE; the performer is sealed inside a heavy canvas mailbag by means of a metal bar which passes through grommets at the mouth and is secured with padlocks. Escape from a legitimate bag is made by passing a lockpick (secured by a string) out through the top of the bag and then picking the padlock open—a difficult feat for any but the most expert performer. A simpler version requires the performer to switch the legitimate metal bar for another which appears identical but which can be unscrewed into two sections from within the bag.

Bag escapes may also be used in conjunction with more complex escapes. If, for example, the performer is first secured with several pairs of handcuffs, placed in the bag, and this in turn is sealed and placed in a box (*see* BOX ESCAPE), the bag actually works to the performer's advantage in giving him time to work on the handcuffs or manacles unobserved. The magician is then ready to escape from the bag as soon as the lid is placed on the box, and proceed with whatever technique is employed to get out of the box.

A bag is also often used as an adjunct to the METAMORPHOSIS illusion.

BAGS OF EVERYTHING

One of the many variations on the CUPS AND BALLS, this routine was created by LEWIS GANSON and appeared in the British magical publication THE GEN. It uses three large felt bags and ping-pong balls for high visibility, and the climax of the routine is the production of a liquid-filled wine glass from one of the bags. The routine was marketed by the UNIQUE MAGIC STUDIO.

BAILEY, SAMUEL W. (1875-1935)

Performer, briefly associated in his youth with CHUNG LING SOO, later a dealer and manufacturer (Bailey & Tripp) of magical APPARATUS.

Bill Baird (*photo courtesy GENII Magazine*)

BAIRD, BILL (1914-1978)

Born William Keckritz, Baird was for many years a noted professional, specializing in the difficult art of BILLIARD BALL manipulation, for which he had a worldwide reputation.

BAKER, AL (1874-1951)

Legendary magician noted both for his subtle inventions and methods, and for his stage presentations; Baker relied more on wit than on broad comedy. He began his career with a medicine show, and worked as magican, ventriloquist, and master of ceremonies in most phases of show business.

Baker's work is described in his *Al Baker's Book One*; *Al Baker's Book Two*; *Pet Secrets*; *Magical Ways And Means*; and *Mental Magic*.

Baker also put a number of items on the magical market, including his **Dictionary Test** and his version of the RICE BOWLS (an excellent description of the latter is in BRUCE ELLIOTT's *Classic Secrets Of Magic*).

BAKER, ROY (b. ?)

Versatile British professional magician who has worked also as a hypnotist and MENTALIST, but is primarily known for his excellent comedy magic. A regular contributor to ABRA and other magic magazines, he has many inventions and routines to his credit. A selection of these is found in his *Baker's Bonanza*, edited by Hugh Miller.

BAKER SLATE

A name often (erroneously) used to denote an ADDITION SLATE; actually invented by JOSEPH DUNNINGER; the contribution of AL BAKER was a device to lock the hinged flap in position.

BAKING A CAKE IN A HAT

A comedy effect, now rarely seen, in which the performer dumps various ingredients into a borrowed hat—flour, water, eggs, etc.—and then "cooks" the mess over a lighted candle. A cake is then removed from the hat, which is returned to its owner unharmed.

Al Baker (*The Mulholland Library of Conjuring & the Allied Arts, Los Angeles, California*)

BALABREGA (1857-1906)

Born John Miller in Sweden, he emigrated to the U.S. as a boy and immediately began performing, billed as The Swedish Wonder and The Boy Magician; he was assisted by his father, who was also a magician of considerable skill.

Later in his career he toured throughout the U.S. and Central and South America with a FULL EVENING SHOW; one of the most popular features of his performance was a TWO-PERSON MENTAL ACT presented with Emily Linderm, his wife. Balabrega died onstage in Brazil when a tank of stage-lighting gas exploded.

BALDUCCI (?-?)

Italian performer who exhibited automata in London in the early 18th Century; among his figures were a **Druggist** who brought out requested spices (a forerunner of ROBERT-HOUDIN's **Pastry-Cook)** and a **Blackamoor** who revealed thought-of numbers by striking a bell (clearly a praecursor to the SPIRIT BELL).

See also AUTOMATA.

BALDWIN, SAMRI S. (1848-1924)

Performer who began his career as a magician, doing card magic and ILLUSIONs. He achieved his greatest success, however, performing MENTALISM, and is generally credited with creating the ROUTINE in which questions thought of by members of the audience are mysteriously answered by the entranced mentalist. Baldwin called this act Somnomancy and billed himself as The White Mahatma; it should be noted that while he began his performances by identifying himself as a magician and disclaiming supernatural powers, most of his audience credited him with occult powers.

Baldwin wrote an interesting and revelatory book on strange phenomena titled *The Secrets Of Mahatma Land Explained*.

BALL AND BOWL

A variation of CUPS-AND-BALLS, this ROUTINE was created by ROY BENSON and described by him under the title *It's Magic* in the PHOENIX. In place of the usual cups and balls it used a single brass bowl, large spherical sponges, and a wand.

A later version of this routine, incorporating the production of a bagel or other large object under the bowl at the conclusion of the routine, was created and marketed by DON ALAN.

Don Alan in 1952 (*photo courtesy of GENII Magazine*)

BALL AND CONE

In some ways a variant of the CUPS AND BALLS, this EFFECT uses a cone made of composition or leather, and a ball which the cone can cover completely. The ball is taken in the hands and vanished in a variety of ways, always reappearing under the cone.

A ROUTINE for this effect was marketed by RALPH HULL under the name of **The Homing Ball**, and described in *Smart Magic* by Hull and GEORGE McATHY.

A much more elaborate presentation, originated by DAI VERNON and featured by him in his nightclub act, is described in the *Dai Vernon Book Of Magic*.

BALL AND TUBE

A classic pocket EFFECT using a steel ball and a brass tube; the tube is just a bit too small for the ball to fit. Nonetheless, as the performer holds the tube the ball slowly sinks out of sight, and then rises back into view—after which both ball and tube may be passed for examination.

BALL AND VASE

An EFFECT involving a small vase, similar to an egg cup with a matching lid. A ball removed from the vase reappears in it, then vanishes and reappears in other places at the will of the performer.

In a small version, it is a popular pocket trick, and

was the first magical effect for a considerable number of magicians.

BALLANTINE, CARL (b. ?)

Born Meyer Kessler; Performer with long professional career whose madcap satire of a magic act has brought him international acclaim. He has performed in venues throughout the U.S., and has made a number of television appearances.

He is also known as an actor, and was featured for many years on the television series *McHale's Navy*.

He is the recipient of a Performing Fellowship from the ACADEMY OF MAGICAL ARTS.

BALL BOX

A wooden box with two compartments into which a ball is placed; after byplay similar to that used with the DIE BOX (which see), the ball is shown to have vanished.

This term is sometimes used in Great Britain to refer to the BALL AND VASE.

BALL CLIP

A holder, usually made of rubber-covered spring steel, which can be pinned under the coat; it holds a ball in position for a STEAL and is used in BILLIARD BALL routines.

BALLED

Rolled into a roughly spherical shape for easier handling; the term most often refers to a silk handkerchief, which may be formed into a tight ball with a SILK WINDER for subsequent production.

To roll a silk into a ball in performance, a corner of the silk is placed between the palms which are then moved against each other in a rotary fashion; properly done, this will roll the silk into a reasonably compact ball which may then be palmed.

The term is also used to denote the crumpling of a sheet of paper into a ball; this may be either a full-size sheet (as in SLYDINI's classic FLIGHT OF THE PAPER BALLS) or a much smaller sheet such as a cigarette paper; in the latter case the ball is called a PELLET.

BALL GLASS

A clear tumbler (now usually of plastic) with a circular hole on one side at the bottom. A ball may be dropped into the glass; then, after the glass is covered with a handkerchief, a slight tilt will allow the ball to fall into the hand where it may be palmed.

BALL OF WOOL

A classic EFFECT in which a borrowed and marked coin vanishes and is found in the center of a large ball of wool; it is accomplished by means of a thin flat tube through which the coin may slide to the center of the ball, the slide then being removed.

Any object of correct size—such as a key or finger ring—may be used instead of a coin. To facilitate the winding procedure, carpet wool is usually employed.

BALLOON MODELING

Though not magic, the twisting of balloons into various shapes which theoretically represent animals has been a popular sideline with magicians, particularly those who specialize in children's shows or bar magic. It is often referred to as **Balloon Sculpting**.

Among the many books describing the techniques of balloon modeling are DON ALAN's *Rubber Circus*, *Balloonatrix* by Dwight Damon, the *Encyclopedic Balloon Modeling Course* (two volumes) by George Sands *Rubber Magic* (two volumes) by Roger Siegel, and *One Balloon Zoo* by Jim Sommers.

BALLOON PENETRATION

See NEEDLE THROUGH BALLOON.

BALLOON PRODUCTION

The production of one or more inflated balloons is sometimes included in PRODUCTION routines. It is usually accomplished by placing a corked capsule of water in the balloon, along with a chemical that will produce gas on contact with the water; the balloon is then sealed.

The inflation is accomplished by working the cork out of the capsule, which is then tilted slightly to make sure the water comes in contact with the chemical. Magician's logic dictates that the balloon should not be produced from a container too small to hold it fully inflated.

BALLS FROM MOUTH

See EGGS FROM MOUTH.

BALLS OVER THE HEAD

See FLIGHT OF THE PAPER BALLS.

BALL TO CUBE

A specially manufactured SPONGE BALL effect in which a sponge ball, poked into the hand, changes into a sponge *cube*; in a variant version a sponge cube poked into the hand changes into two sponge balls.

BALLY

In carnival slang, a magical EFFECT or stunt performed on the platform outside the tent to attract a crowd of customers (usually called a 'tip'); also, the spiel or dialogue that accompanies the performance.

The term has more recently been used in the context of television magic specials to denote the effect which is featured in advertising and other publicity; such a **Bally Effect** is usually spectacular, dangerous or both. Examples are DOUG HENNING's presentation of the WATER TORTURE CELL and DAVID COPPER-FIELD's version of WALKING THROUGH A BRICK WALL (performed at the Great Wall of China).

BAMBERG, DAVID (1904-1974)

Son of THEO BAMBERG, and last of the seven-generation family of magicians. Born in Great Britain but raised in the United States, he toured with the RAYMOND show (in which his wife was an assistant) doing his SHADOWGRAPHY act.

After the show toured parts of South America, he decided to remain there and create his own show; like his father, he performed in oriental guise under the name of FU MANCHU. (This choice of name brought problems of copyright infringement with the Sax Rohmer estate—Rohmer having authored the *Fu Manchu* series of novels—when Bamberg visited the U.S., so for that engagement he used the name *Fu-Chan.*) The show was very successful, with elaborate sets, broad comedy, beautiful women, and incredible illusions, and played in many areas of South America for several years. The chief mechanic and illusion builder for this show was EDMUND SPREER.

David Bamberg's approach to stage magic is described in his "Stage Presentation" chapter in HILLIARD's *Greater Magic.*

BAMBERG, DAVID LEENDERT (1786-1869)

The son of ELIASER BAMBERG, he began his career as his father's assistant before becoming a performer in his own right. He achieved considerable fame and in 1834 was named Court Magician to the royal family of Holland.

He is particularly noted for his EGG BAG routine, which involved the production of several eggs and climaxed with the appearance of a live hen within the bag.

Father of TOBIAS BAMBERG.

BAMBERG, DAVID TOBIAS (1843-1914)

Son of TOBIAS BAMBERG, and known to magical historians as "Papa Bamberg," he—like his father and grandfather—became Court Magician to Holland's royal family. He also maintained the family reputation for excellence in pure sleight-of-hand.

He toured extensively through Europe and Asia assisted by his son, THEO BAMBERG, finally returning to his home in Amsterdam.

BAMBERG, ELIASER (1760-1833)

Born in Holland, he became a well-known magician of his era, specializing in SLEIGHT-OF-HAND and the exhibiting of mechanical AUTOMATA. Losing a leg on board a warship, he replaced it with a wooden leg designed with secret compartments to accomplish various effects. The combination of the wooden leg and his impressive magic earned him the nickname of "The Crippled Devil."

BAMBERG, JASPER (?-?)

Magician of the early 18th century who, like many of the time, mixed the practices of "real" magic—alchemy and necromancy—with the

Jasper Bamberg (*The Mulholland Library of Conjuring & the Allied Arts, Los Angeles, California*)

chicanery of the performer. He is thought to have used a type of magic-lantern apparatus to produce images of spirits and other beings in columns of rising smoke. Father of ELIASER BAMBERG.

BAMBERG, THEO (1875-1963)

Son of DAVID TOBIAS BAMBERG, he developed a silent act after a swimming accident in his youth left him profoundly deaf. The act was designed in a rich oriental theme (originally of Japanese style, but later changed to Chinese). To perform it, Theo Bamberg took the stage name OKITO. The act was an immediate success in Holland, and with it he toured the world for many years. He was noted for his invention of many apparatus effects and for his OKITO COIN BOX. A feature of his stage act was his presentation of the Floating Ball (*see* FLOATING EFFECTS), developed from a routine for the effect taught to him by DAVID P. ABBOTT.

Father of DAVID BAMBERG. His work is described in *Okito On Magic* by ROBERT PARRISH; *see also* BAMBERG MAGIC.

Theo Bamberg as Okito performing the *Floating Ball* in 1928 (*photo courtesy GENII Magazine*).

BAMBERG, TOBIAS (1812-1870)

Son of DAVID LEENDERT BAMBERG, he performed in many countries and, like his father, was Court Magician in Holland. He was noted not only for his excellent SLEIGHT-OF-HAND but also for his exceptional education and knowledge, including fluency in several languages.

Father of DAVID TOBIAS BAMBERG.

BAMBERG MAGIC

Descriptions of the effects and methods of the Bamberg family can be found in Lesson 68 of the *Tarbell Course In Magic* by HARLAN TARBELL, and in *The Oriental Magic Of The Bambergs* by ERIC C. LEWIS.

BAND CALL

Rehearsal of the performer's act with the orchestra at the venue, to synchronize the music with the act and ascertain that cues for particular musical sequences or sound effects are clearly understood.

In some cases a **Band Call** will not be a rehearsal in the usual sense (i.e., the performer will ''walk through'' the effects with the orchestra leader or musical director to indicate cues and other information). Wherever possible, it is best to have at least one actual run-through of the act with the music.

BAND WRITER

A GIMMICK used for secret writing, consisting of a flesh-colored curved strip of metal with a piece of lead or crayon set in a small holder in its center. It is (usually) worn on the thumb, the lead or crayon beneath the ball of the thumb.

See NAIL WRITER.

BANG GUN

A comedy PROP looking somewhat like a pirate's pistol; when the trigger is pulled, the hinged barrel opens out to double its length and into view drops a hanging silk square bearing the word *bang*. The **bang gun** is so well known that it has little element of surprise, and thus now is rarely used except by a few performers specializing in CHILDREN'S MAGIC.

BANGKOK BUNGALOW

An ILLUSION invented by GUY JARRETT; it used a curtained platform on which the performer placed a small dollhouse. The curtains being drawn, the performer stated that there had actually been a person inside the little house and that person would now appear; the curtains opened to reveal a man standing on the platform. Announcing that the process would be reversed, the performer would close the curtains momentarily, opening them to reveal the disappearance of the man. The man had, claimed the performer, gone back into the little house; with this the performer picked up the house and handed it to an assistant who carried it offstage.

The audience, of course, did not believe any of this, and pointed to a suspicious bulge in one of the curtains. At this the performer pulled all the curtains from the cabinet, stripping it to a bare skeleton frame; the man had genuinely vanished.

Like many of Jarrett's illusions, this depended partly on technical subterfuge but primarily on the HONESTY PRINCIPLE.

BANG RING

A device used in conjunction with various faked coins, to separate the coin proper from a tightly-fitting SHELL. The ring has an inner ledge of the precise diameter of the shell; thus when a coin with shell is placed in the ring which is then tapped or 'banged' on a hard surface, the coin is caused to drop out of the shell.

It is possible to remove coins from tight-fitting shells by other means (shaking in a glass, for example), but the bang ring is the preferred method, being much less likely to damage coin or shell.

BANK

One of several identical groups of assorted cards within a MULTIPLE-BANK DECK. The term is also sometimes applied to a group of *duplicate* cards within a FORCING DECK.

BANK NIGHT

Usually credited to TOM SELLERS, this EFFECT uses a number of letter or pay envelopes, into one of which a large-denomination bill is placed. The envelopes are mixed, and several spectators choose until the performer is left with only one. At this point the performer usually gives various spectators the option of exchanging envelopes with him; needless to say, the performer invariably ends up with the envelope containing the bill.

The effect is popular with magicians, but not always with audiences, as the subtext is the performer using magical means to keep them from winning. For this reason, many performers have adopted more elaborate presentations in which each spectator wins some sort of prize.

The name comes from the Bank Night game played in theaters, where members of the audience won cash prizes.

In Great Britain the effect is generally known as *Just Chance*.

BAR ACT

An act specializing in liquid effects, almost always including some version of the INEXHAUSTIBLE BOTTLE; another major feature of such acts is the ability to pour any drink called for from a single container.

Abbreviated versions of such ROUTINES have been used by a number of performers; of those who made of it an entire act, the best known was undoubtedly THINK-A-DRINK HOFFMAN.

BARAN, JODY (b. ?)

Performer who, with wife and partner *Jennifer*, has performed in varied venues throughout the U.S., Europe, South America and the Far East. The Barans are winners of the World Championship of Magic competition held in Japan.

Jody and Jennifer Baran with their World Championship Trophy

BARBER POLE

A PRODUCTION item, now rarely seen, consisting of a roll of heavy red and white paper with a knob at its core; it may be produced in the form of a long striped pole from a Production Device (by pulling the knob upward to extend it into a spiral-walled tube); it may also be produced from the clothing of a spectator. It is humorous in appearance but not at all deceptive.

BAR MAGIC

A type of CLOSE-UP MAGIC performed by a magician/bartender for customers; also, effects which are suitable for performance in such a venue by a visiting magician.

BARREL MAGIC

Barrels have been used by magicians for a number of purposes—as objects from which to escape (as devised by HOUDINI and ROBERT STULL); as parts of an illusion (SELBIT's presentation of THROUGH THE EYE OF A NEEDLE, and DEVANT's *Barrel Of Diogenes* [see DRUM ILLUSION]); and even to produce liquids.

In this last category of EFFECT the barrel is usually shown empty and capped by heavy paper at both ends; a tap is inserted and any number of drinks of various kinds are poured; and finally a woman may be produced from the barrel.

BARTHOLOMEW FAIR

British fair established in 1133 and halted in 1855; except for its final few years the fair was held in Smithfield Plaza in London.

Over the centuries, countless magicians performed at Bartholomew Fair; of these perhaps the best-known is ISAAC FAWKES, due largely to his appearance in a popular print depicting the fair.

BASIC EFFECTS

It could be said that all of magic can be classified as one effect—that of change or alteration in seemingly impossible fashion. Such a broad definition, however, is less than useful, and there have been a number of attempts to classify the types of magical effect.

Of these, the best known is that of DARIEL FITZKEE, as given in his book *The Trick Brain*:
1. Production (appearance, creation, multiplication)
2. Vanish (disappearance, obliteration)
3. Transposition (change in location)
4. Transformation (change in appearance/character/identity)
5. Penetration (one solid through another)
6. Restoration (making the destroyed whole)
7. Animation (movement imparted to the inanimate)
8. Antigravity (levitation and change in weight)
9. Attraction (mysterious adhesion)
10. Sympathetic Reaction (sympathetic response)
11. Invulnerability (injury proof)
12. Physical Anomaly (contradictions, abnormalities, freaks)
13. Spectator Failure (magicians' challenge)
14. Control (mind over the inanimate)
15. Identification (specific discovery)
16. Thought Reading (mental perception, mind reading)
17. Thought Transmission (thought projection and transference)
18. Prediction (foretelling the future)
19. Extra Sensory Perception (unusual perception, other than mind)

A somewhat different system of classification is given by S. H. SHARPE in his *Neo-Magic*:
1. Productions (from not being to being)
2. Disappearances (from being to not being)
3. Transformations (from being in this way to being in that)
4. Transpositions (from being here to being there)
5. Natural Science Laws Defied:
    a. Anti-Gravity
    b. Magical Animation
    c. Magical Control (Psychokinesis)
    d. Matter Through Matter
    e. Multi-position
    f. Restoration
    g. Invulnerability
    h. Rapid Germination
6. Mental Phenomena
    a. Prediction
    b. Divination
    c. Psychometry
    d. Telepathy or Thought Transference
    e. Hypnotism
    f. Memorization
    g. Lightning Calculation

It is certainly possible to dispute these analyses, and in many cases the judgment of an effect's category must be a subjective one; also, it should be pointed out, a particular effect or routine can be presented in different ways.

The PENETRATION FRAME, for example, can be presented as (of course) a *penetration*—but it can also be presented as *matter through matter* (the solid rod passing through the solid glass), as *invulnerability*, as a *restoration*, and even as a *transposition* (the rod sequentially vanishing from one side of the frame and appearing on the other).

BASKET TRICK

Sometimes known as the **Hindu Basket Trick**, this ILLUSION actually is of East Indian origin. As it is now usually presented, the performer's assistant stands in a small round wicker basket and is covered with a cloth; the covered form sinks down into the basket and the basket-lid replaces the cloth.

Now the performer thrusts sticks or swords down through the lid and out the four sides of the basket, followed by one directly down through the center. These being removed, the performer replaces the cloth and removes the lid, and then steps into the basket and sits down in it to "prove" the absence of the assistant. The performer gets out and the cloth then rises; it is whipped away to reveal the assistant.

Such is the basic EFFECT and many variations have been added by various performers. In some ROUTINEs, flaming torches replace the swords; this idea was originated by THE PENDRAGONS. In other versions the assistant reappears in a different costume, or an entirely different assistant will appear. The illusion is popular because it has a strong and direct effect, and because it is ANGLE-PROOF.

A version of this effect which used the plot but not the traditional method was presented by COLONEL STODARE. In his routine a large chest-like basket was used; when the swords were run through the basket they exited red with blood; and the box was then tipped forward to show it empty, the assistant reappearing elsewhere. Stodare used the TIPOVER BOX principle.

BATHING BEAUTY

A comedy effect, invented by FREDERICK CULPITT, in which a picture of a pretty woman in a bathing suit, is shown; it is printed on oilcloth or light canvas. The picture is folded in half and various items seen in the picture—the woman's hat, shoes, and bathing suit—are removed from within the fold. When the picture is unfolded, however, the woman is now in water up to her chin—the tide has come in!

BATHING MACHINE

An ILLUSION invented by CHRIS CHARLTON in which a young woman was placed in a **Bathing Machine** (a wooden booth used for changing clothes at the seaside), which was then raised up into the air by ropes or chains. The woman was still visible, yet at a gesture from the performer the machine fell to pieces, these clattering to the stage; the woman had vanished.

BATTEN

A cross bar, usually of metal (wooden beams are sometimes used), which acts as a holder for a number of small floodlights; usually situated above and behind the PROSCENIUM, but may also be rigged at the sides of the stage.

In some venues—particularly those which have been converted into performance sites—battens may be fixed over the heads of the audience or otherwise located in full view.

B.D.V.

A SLEIGHT invented by DAI VERNON in which (for example) five cards, outjogged for two-thirds of their length from the deck, are switched for the bottom five cards of the deck.

With the deck held in the left hand, a break is held above the five cards at the bottom of the deck. The deck is spread and five cards are indicated by having a spectator point to them; the faces of the cards are not shown. This done, the right hand spreads the outjogged cards in a slight fan, and then moves back to hold the deck at the rear right corner *above* the break. The left hand, holding the five bottom cards, moves forward beneath the fan and strips out the outjogged cards. The left hand now moves back beneath the deck momentarily, presumably so the right hand can assist in squaring the cards. The right hand immediately moves forward and takes away all of the cards except the original bottom five.

In appearance the outjogged cards were simply removed and squared, and then the rest of the deck is set aside.

The sleight is most often used to switch five freely indicated cards for five known cards. The initials of its name stand for *By Dai Vernon*.

BEALE, KEN (?-1979)

Specialist in card magic who was noted for his work on mathematically based EFFECTs as well as STACKs. He contributed items to many periodicals, including PHOENIX, *Ibidem*, and ARCANE.

BEAM SHOT

An EFFECT created by BOB OSTIN in which a small pocket flashlight turns on and off by itself as desired by the performer; marketed originally by KEN BROOKE (and later by PAUL STONE and JOE STEVENS), the effect was widely copied under various names.

A more recent and similar effect, operating by an entirely different principle, is JOHN KENNEDY's **Magic Flashlight**.

A related effect, also marketed by Brooke and also copied by others, was Scotty York's **Lamp Trick**—in which a small bulb held in a handkerchief by a spectator would flash on and off to locate a chosen card, answer questions, etc.

BEAU BROCADE

An ILLUSION created by DAVID DEVANT (inspired by the Baroness Orczy novel) in which a young woman, having been wrapped in a cloth, is carried by the performer to the footlights, where she suddenly disappears, instantly reappearing elsewhere.

The illusion is accomplished by the exchange of the woman for a life-size inflated dummy, the air-valve of which is opened by the performer at the proper time.

BEAUFORT, DOUGLAS (1864-1939)

British magician noted as a society entertainer who appeared many times before royalty and also at the EGYPTIAN HALL. He was sent by the British government to Morocco to demonstrate the superiority of British magic to that of the native *marabouts*, a mission startlingly similar to one performed for the French government by ROBERT-HOUDIN a generation earlier.

Beaufort's life is described in his *Nothing Up My Sleeve*.

BECKER, LARRY (b. 1929)

Operator of a national advertising agency, Larry Becker is a long-time inventor of magical EFFECTS, many of which have been marketed or appeared in magazines. These include *Haunted House, Astronaut, Track Record, Psycho I* and *Supervision*. Latterly specializing in MENTAL MAGIC, on which he has written three books: *Larry Becker's World of Super Mentalism* (two volumes) and *Mentalism For Magicians*.

BEE

A type of POKER-SIZE CARDS manufactured by the U.S. Playing Card Company; these cards have a back design consisting of a diagonal cross-hatching which extends to the edge of the cards. Since there is no white border, such SLEIGHTs as the SECOND DEAL are usually more visually convincing with these or similar cards.

See SORT-EDGE DECK.

BEE, PERCY (1905-1973)

British professional magician noted particularly as a private party entertainer, and also for his thought-provoking and often controversial articles on magical presentation which appeared in the pages of ABRACADABRA magazine.

BEG-OFF

A speech used by the performer at the conclusion of a well-received act in which the audience is thanked and it is explained that the performer cannot continue—either because (a) he or she has no more performance material or (b) time will not permit it. The latter explanation is by far the preferable one.

Such speeches can be used in place of an encore, or after an encore has been performed.

BEHNKE, LEO (b. ?)

Performer who began as manager of two magic shops in California's *Disneyland*. He later worked for four years as a production assistant on MARK WILSON's television show *Magic Land Of Allakazam*, creating routines and story material.

Leo Behnke

Subsequently he has performed for many years at the MAGIC CASTLE, also working in television commercials and as a TECHNICAL ADVISOR for films and television.

In 1969 he founded Magic Touch, a sales promotion agency specializing in creating corporate presentations and special events. Among his books are *Entertaining Close Up, Entertaining With Cards,* and *Party Magic From The Magic Castle.*

BELL, SPIRIT

See SPIRIT BELL.

BELLACHINI (1828-1885)

Born Samuel Berlach in Poland, he performed in Russia and later in Germany, where he was Court Entertainer for Emperor Wilhelm I. A feature of his act was the production of several eggs from the mouth of an assistant; it is described in HOFFMAN's *Later Magic.*

BELLY SERVANTE

A GIMMICK originally worn inside the low-cut Victorian-age vests and now worn inside the trousers at the front, just behind the buckle. It consists of a flat pocket with a spring steel frame at the top into which articles may be secretly dropped. It should be noted that this device is best used by performers of reasonably slim build.

BELLY STRIPPERS

A type of STRIPPER DECK in which desired cards are tapered slightly at *both* ends on the long edges; the remainder of the cards are given a slight concave edge, or narrowing at the center.

Such a deck may be prepared to divide into any two groups (*see* DIVIDED DECK). An advantage **belly strippers** have over conventional stripper decks is their lack of one-way orientation (*see* ONE-WAY DECK); thus they may be shuffled freely by a spectator without the performer having to worry about a card being accidentally reversed end-for-end.

BEN ALI BEY

See AUZINGER, MAX.

BENDING GLASS

See FLEXIBLE GLASS.

BENDIX BOMBSHELL

A variant FLIPOVER WALLET designed by David Bendix so that a card or other flat item placed in an open pocket of the wallet can be found within a zippered compartment.

A collection of EFFECTs with this wallet entitled *Effects With The Bendix Bombshell* was compiled by ROY ROTH.

BENGAL NET

A miniature version of the DIZZY LIMIT illusion, this U.F. GRANT origination is a small net hanging in front of a banner; an object or animal of moderate size (dove, guinea pig) is placed into the net which is hooked closed. Suddenly the net falls open and the item placed within visibly vanishes.

Its operating principle is similar to some variations of the Dizzy Limit illusion, but not the original version created by OSWALD WILLIAMS.

BENNETT, DOUG (b. ?)

Inventor known for his highly visual approach to magic, as evidenced in his **Criss-Cross Cards** (which appeared in GENII Magazine), in which two decks of cards occupy the same space at the same time—and his **BewildeRing**, a marketed EFFECT in which a ring visibly penetrates a velvet cord.

He is the author of *Extra Sensory Deceptions.*

BENNETT, HORACE (b. 1925)

Known primarily as a creator of strong close-up magic, Bennett's work is described in *Horace Bennett's Prize-Winning Magic* by Hugh Miller and in *Bennett's Best, On Your Feet, Bennett's Fourth Book, Downs Palm Technique,* and *Alternate Handlings,* all of the latter books written by Bennett himself.

BENNETT, ZINA, DR. (1891-1965)

Though a physician by profession, Bennett achieved an international reputation as a magician, and was noted particularly for his manipulation of cards from a JUMBO DECK, at which he was unsurpassed. He was a member of countless magical organizations, inventor of several effects (including a deck of special manipulation cards called the **ZinaB Deck**). In 1959 he married the former SUZY WANDAS.

BENSON, ROY (?-1977)

Performer who was noted both as an excellent close-up magician and stage magical comedian. His stage work was distinguished by his bizarre comedic sense; he also created a highly regarded BILLIARD BALL routine, and was the originator of the *long-pour* finish for the SALT TRICK which has since been featured by many top performers.

Benson also created an elaborate act in ORIENTAL STYLE, in which he was assisted by his wife Connye; it involved manipulations and flourishes with **solid crystal balls**, many of his own originations, and some traditional magic of the Orient.

He is best-known for his creation of the BALL AND BOWL routine; it will be found, along with some of his many other contributions to the PHOENIX Magazine, in BRUCE ELLIOTT's *Classic Secrets Of Magic*.

BENYON, EDGAR (1902-1978)

Born Edgar Beynon in New Zealand, he went into vaudeville at the age of seventeen and toured many countries, including Great Britain, Australia and Africa; his act, billed as a "One-man revue," featured ventriloquism, juggling, rag pictures, quick-change, contortions and impressions. His FULL-EVENING SHOW was reputed to be one of the largest and most elaborate ever to play in several of the countries he visited.

In his memory, a "Benny" award was created for the winner of an annual vaudeville competition in New Zealand.

BENZAIS, JOHN (1940-1967)

Close-up magician who, in a tragically brief career, created approaches to CLOSE-UP MAGIC which continue to influence the field. His work is described in his *The Best of Benzais*, published just prior to his death.

BERG, JOE (1903-1984)

Magic dealer for over half a century, at first in Chicago and later in Hollywood. He invented numerous effects, of which perhaps the best known is the ULTRA-MENTAL DECK. His life and inventions are described in his *The Berg Book*, written with David Avadon and ERIC C. LEWIS.

BERGERON, BEV (b. 1930)

Born Bevely Bergeron, he started his career as an assistant on the show of HARRY WILLARD. Later he was featured as Rebo The Clown in MARK WILSON's long-running television series, *The Magic Land Of Allakazam*.

Bergeron is active in many phases of magic; in addition to many years as a regular performer at the Florida

Bev Bergeron

Disney World (featured in the *Diamond Horseshoe* show), he has worked as a TRADE SHOW performer and in many other venues.

He is also the author of a book on the life and magic of Harry Willard titled *Willard The Wizard*; he has also contributed to many magic magazines, including a regular column for M.U.M.

BERGLAS, DAVID (b. 1926)

Well-known British professional performer, who formerly did general magic but now specializes in MENTAL MAGIC. He has appeared in his own television series, both in Britain and Europe, and has drawn attention through a long career with his many ingenious publicity stunts.

Berglas is a former President of the BRITISH RING of the I.B.M. and also has served as King Rat of the Grand Order Of Water Rats (a British show business organization devoted to charitable causes).

BERGSON, SYD (1905-1980)

Born in England, Bergson came to the United States as a small child. A professional hotelier, he was quite active in the creation of magic (MENTAL MAGIC in particular); he held several offices in the I.B.M., including that of International President.

BERLAND, SAM (1907-1987)

Magic dealer and inventor, noted for his many marketed items; several of these, such as his three **Thimble Acts** and his **Dice Act**, are complete ROUTINEs of several EFFECTs.

He has written a number of books, including *The Magic Of Sam Berland, Amazing Tricks With Paper Cups, Book Of Routines, Tricks And Routines*, and *Tricks For Today And Tomorrow*.

In 1986 he was awarded a Creative Fellowship by the ACADEMY OF MAGICAL ARTS.

BERNARD, BOBBY (b. ?)

Born in Britain; highly respected as a teacher of magic and stage work. He has made numerous contributions to magazines including PENTAGRAM and many others. His approach is described in his *Coin And Card Magic*.

BERRY, JAY SCOTT (b. 1960)

Noted for his futuristically-themed act, he has performed throughout Europe, including appearances at the Folies Bergere in Paris, and in Monte Carlo. In addition to performances at FISM, he has also appeared at national magic conventions in France, Italy, and Holland.

He performed a FULL-EVENING SHOW with elaborate pyrotechnic EFFECTs and ILLUSIONs; using its own uniquely designed traveling theater, it toured West Germany and other European countries.

Within magic Berry is known for the several pyrotechnic and fog-effect devices he has created, many of which are described in his book *Magic For The New World*.

BERTRAM, CHARLES (1853-1907)

Born James Bassett; British performer who appeared at EGYPTIAN HALL on several occasions but made his reputation as a society entertainer; he appeared many times before King Edward VII. He was particularly noted for his performance of the CARDS TO POCKET and also the VANISHING LADY illusion invented by DE KOLTA.

Bertram wrote two books on his life and travels: *Isn't It Wonderful?* (a catchphrase he often used) and *A Magician In Many Lands*.

BERTRAM, ROSS (b. 1912)

Born John Ross Bertram in Canada, he performed in varied venues and was one of the first magicians to specialize primarily in TRADE SHOW work. Now retired, he is known for his excellent CLOSE-UP MAGIC, and is considered to be one of the greatest exponents of COIN MAGIC in the world.

His work is described in *Stars Of Magic* and in *Magic And Methods Of Ross Bertram*.

BETCHA

A type of challenge puzzle in the form of a bet, the resolution of which usually depends on a physical method, an understanding of odds or other specialized information, or a play on words.

A classic example is that in which the person is given a piece of string; the bettor says "I'll bet you can't remove the ice cube from your drink with that string without touching the cube with your fingers." After the person gives up, a loop of the string is allowed to rest on the upper surface of the cube and some salt is sprinkled on it; the ice melts slightly and the string is frozen into its surface, and may then be used to pull the cube from the glass.

Many such betchas may be found in MARTIN GARDNER's *Encyclopedia Of Impromptu Tricks*.

BETWEEN YOUR PALMS

A spectator holds an unknown card between his palms; three cards are then selected, signed, and returned to the deck. The first two selections are located and placed with the unknown card—which proves to be the third selection.

The effect, created by ALEX ELMSLEY, has spawned many variations in method and handling.

BEVAN, DONALD (b. ?)

British performer specializing in CHILDREN'S MAGIC. For many years he was associate editor of ABRA Magazine; on the death of FABIAN (E. Ray Griffiths) in 1965, Bevan became the editor of the magazine, a post which he still holds.

BEVEL BASE

Sometimes known as an **optical table**, the **bevel base** is the platform on which many illusions are constructed. It usually takes the form of a square or rectangular table with short legs; these legs are invariably equipped with wheels or rollers.

While from the audience's point of view the base appears to be only a few inches thick, the upper and lower surfaces of the base are slanted imperceptibly so that the central section of the base may be nine or ten inches thick—enough room for a person to lie concealed within. At the proper time the person makes his or her way in or out of the base as required by the illusion in progress. The opening in the upper surface of the base may be a trapdoor; more often it is simply elasticized cloth which can be pushed aside as required.

It should be noted that the **bevel base** is most efficaciously used in combination with other principles of ILLUSION construction; as a method in and of itself, the **bevel base** is not likely to be completely deceptive. It has been seriously suggested that the economy-minded illusionist can have several illusions by simply putting different kinds of boxes atop a **bevel base**; since this course of action will most likely result in illusions which have little if any magical effect, it is probably a false economy.

The **bevel base** is also sometimes known as a **wedge base**; this latter term may, however, be reserved for an illusion base which is thin on the DOWNSTAGE (audience) side and thicker on the UPSTAGE side. This kind of base is also called a **perspective base**.

BEVEL DECK
See STRIPPER DECK.

BEWILDERING BLOCKS

An EFFECT using two square wooden tubes, into each of which a set of four numbered blocks will fit. One set of blocks (stacked in numerical order) is covered with a tube. The other set is placed into its tube in a random order, or an order selected by the spectators. When both tubes are lifted, it is seen that the first set of blocks has rearranged itself to match the order of the other stack. The effect uses the SHELL principle as a part of its working method.

Depending on the routine, the effect may be repeated—and there are many variations in procedure and presentation.

The **bewildering blocks** (also known as the **sympathetic blocks**) is thought to have been invented by CONRADI, who was the first to manufacture it; a revised version of this effect was created by SELBIT.

BICYCLE

A back design for cards manufactured by the U.S. Playing Card Company; it is available in both BRIDGE-SIZE and POKER-SIZE CARDS and is quite popular with magicians.

BIDDLE COUNT

A counting maneuver, usually with a small PACKET of cards, which employs the technique of the BIDDLE MOVE to count a packet of cards as more or less than their actual number.

BIDDLE GRIP

A specific way of holding cards for certain COUNT and display procedures: the cards are held from above by the fingertips at the front short edge and the thumb at the rear short edge. The position is that naturally occurring when a packet or deck is picked up from the table.

The cards are usually held in the right hand, and counted by being drawn off into the left palm by pressure of the left thumb on the top of the held cards.

See BIDDLE MOVE; BIDDLE COUNT; HAMMAN COUNT; VEESER CONCEPT; VEESER COUNT.

BIDDLE MOVE

A card SLEIGHT invented by Elmer Biddle in which, as cards are counted from one hand to the other, a card or cards are indetectably stolen from the counted group. It is a utility move with many applications and is described in most modern texts covering the basics of card magic.

BIET, TED (b. ?)

Born in the former East Indies colonies of the Netherlands, he later moved to Holland. He specializes in card magic and has invented a highly popular GIMMICK for the RISING CARDS effect.

BIFF

The name given by DAVID DEVANT to a stage ILLUSION in which a motorcyle and rider vanished from a packing case suspended above the stage by chains.

Biff should not be confused with the motorcycle vanish featured by DOUG HENNING and more recently by SIEGFRIED AND ROY; these later presentations are adaptations of the DIZZY LIMIT illusion.

BILIS, BERNARD (b. ?)

Born in France and highly regarded for his approach to CLOSE-UP MAGIC, Bernard Bilis is the author of *French Pasteboards* and *Close-up Magic French Style*.

BILLET

A small slip of paper (usually about 2 inches by 3 inches) which bears the writing of the performer or a spectator; in feats of MENTAL MAGIC or MENTALISM, it will often bear a written PREDICTION made by the performer, or information secretly written by a spectator. Billets are usually folded once each way and then once again, to insure that the writing remains hidden.

The term, which came into common use in this sense through the message-reading tests of spirit MEDIUMS, comes from the French word for *letter*.

See also PELLET.

BILL FOLDING

A variant of ORIGAMI, using paper money to create various shapes. It is completely covered in *The Folding Money Book* (Volumes I and II), published by MAGIC, INC.

BILLFOOLED

A pocket-secretary type of wallet invented by RICHARD HIMBER, it often goes by the generic name of SWITCH WALLET or FLIPOVER WALLET. Himber's wallets, like the apparatus for other effects which he marketed, were noted for their elegant appearance and fine craftsmanship.

BILLIARD BALL

A term for the wooden or rubber ball used by manipulators in sleight-of-hand routines; the balls resemble real billiard balls in color (usually being red or white), but most often are appreciably smaller.

The classic effect of this type is the **multiplying billiard balls**, in which a number of balls are produced between the fingers of the performer's hands. The orginial version of this effect is said to be the invention of BUATIER DE KOLTA.

Major works on the subject are BURLING HULL's *Expert Billiard Ball Manipulation*, CAMILLE GAULTIER's *Magic Without Apparatus*, LEWIS GANSON's *Routined Manipulation (Part Two)*, and *Ron MacMillan's Symphony Of The Spheres*, GEOFFREY BUCKINGHAM's *It's Easier Than You Think*, ARTHUR BUCKLEY's *Principles And Deceptions*, and RICHARD KAUFMAN's *Balls—Lessons In Side-Arm Snookery*. Other sources include HENRY HAY's *The Amateur Magician's Handbook* and WALTER B. GIBSON's *The Complete Book Of Close-Up Magic*.

BILL IN LEMON

A classic effect in which a borrowed bill (identified by its serial number, the spectator's signature, or a torn corner) is vanished; a lemon which has been held by another spectator is sliced open to reveal the bill within.

The effect was a favorite of EMIL JARROW, who featured it in his vaudeville act. Performed in stage and platform acts, it is also used by many present-day closeup performers who depend on gratuities, as often the spectator will not really want the lemon-soaked bill returned.

BILL TUBE

A small tube, usually of brass, provided with a screw-on cap which is further secured with a bolt and lock. A borrowed bill is vanished in some manner, and is found inside the tube.

The tube is usually made to withstand rigorous examination, but does suffer from being a totally unfamilar object and quite obviously a magic prop.

See also LIPPINCOTT COIN BOX.

BINARELLI, TONY (b. ?)

Born in Italy; he is one of the best-known magical performers in that country. In addition to stage magic, he also is known for his card work, as well as his CLOSE-UP performances and his MENTAL MAGIC. He has made several national television appearances in Italy.

His approach is described in his *Playmagic* (two volumes).

BIRCH, MCDONALD (b. 1902)

Born George McDonald Birch, he began performing in his teens on the LYCEUM and CHAUTAUQUA circuits, and was an immediate and spectacular success. At first presenting a one-man show, he later trouped an elaborate FULL-EVENING SHOW with many illusions. Two of the many features of his show were the **Vanishing Pony** (a dwarf pony visibly vanished from a raised platform) and the **Silk Mirage** (in which he produced a stage-filling array of silks from a small tube).

A musical interlude in the show was provided by Birch's wife Mabel Sperry, who was a talented xylophonist; she also acted as her husband's chief assistant.

The Birch show toured throughout the U.S. for over thirty years; it was not only one of the most successful, but also was considered to be one of the very best.

Birch was noted for his dynamic yet charming manner, and the courtesy with which he treated volunteers from the audience. In the early 1960s Birch retired from performing.

Birch is (with his late wife Mabel) a recipient of the Masters Fellowship from the ACADEMY OF MAGICAL ARTS.

BIRD CAGES

In addition to the VANISHING BIRD CAGE, there are PRODUCTION cages, designed to fold into small compass and instantly expand to full size. Of these the most popular for many years was that manufactured by MERV TAYLOR.

Cages have also been devised which will reproduce vanished birds, exchange birds, or vanish them. There is also the popular DOVECOTE VANISH used in many DOVE ACTS and first presented by CHANNING POLLOCK; birds produced by the performer throughout his routine are placed in a large cage which is then covered with a cloth. The cloth is tossed into the air and the cage vanishes. While the effect *is* spectacular and some of the cages created for this feat are masterpieces of engineering, it has been performed so often that little mystery and less surprise can be created by it.

BIRD MAGIC

The great majority of bird effects in modern magic are done with doves (*see* DOVE MAGIC). Birds of all kinds have figured in magical feats for centuries, however, from the decapitated-and-restored geese of ancient Egypt's DEDI to the parakeets used in the acts of such performers as JACK KODELL (the first to create an entire act using this species) and more readily JOHNNY HART.

Most often, birds are produced or vanished in various ways. A classic of stage magic is W.J. NIXON's **Where Do The Ducks Go?**, in which several ducks are placed in a large box which is then shown completely empty; many variations on this basic effect have been created over the years.

In at least one case a bird is thought to have been part of the *method* of a magical feat; this was the SPIRIT BELL of *ALEXANDER HEIMBURGER*. According to reports, the bird was trained to stay hidden in a special table and watch for Heimburger's signal; on receiving it, the bird would jump up and down on a small perch, part of a mechanism which rang the bell on the table above!

BIRDS OF A FEATHER

See SYMPATHETIC ROUTINES.

BISEAUTE DECK

See STRIPPER DECK.

BIZARRE MAGICK

Phrase coined by Tony Raven to denote effects and presentations with occult and supernatural themes (witchcraft, ceremonial magic, ghosts and demons, etc.).

Among the many books providing **Bizarre Magic** presentations are *13!*, *Something Strange*, and *Daemons, Darklings and Doppelgangers*, all by TONY SHIELS; *Daemon's Diary*, *The Negromicon Of Masklyn*, and *Grimoire Of The Mages*, all by TONY ANDRUZZI; *The Book Of Thoth* and *Lovecraftian Ceremonies*, both by STEPHEN MINCH; *Devil's Diary*, *Witch's Brew*, and *Handbook of Horror*, all by Charles Cameron; and *Grymwyr*, by T.A. Waters.

A magazine devoted to this type of presentation was called *Invocation*; founded by Tony Raven, it ran for sixteen issues. Its successor, *The New Invocation*, is edited by Tony Andruzzi and was begun in 1979. The magazine has inspired a yearly convention, the Invocational, held in the Chicago area each October.

BLACK ART

A principle, developed for stage use by MAX AUZINGER, that under proper lighting conditions dead black against dead black is not visible, primarily because of the absence of shadow.

In stage black art acts, lights are usually arranged to "spill" toward the audience to some degree, thus making it nearly impossible to discern a black-draped object against the black background. Thus, when the object (always of a very light color) is suddenly revealed by the swift removal of the black cover, its instantaneous appearance seems very magical indeed. Among the performers who have specialized in stage acts of this kind are Omar Pasha, Emerson and Jayne, and The Black Art Theatre of Prague.

On a somewhat smaller scale the principle is often incorporated into ILLUSIONS, usually to make a table or cabinet wall seem thinner. Still smaller props which use the principle, most often to conceal a LOAD CHAMBER, include the SQUARE CIRCLE and the DAGGER BOX.

BLACK ART TABLE

A table with a black velvet top divided into squares by brightly colored ribbon; one of the squares thus created has been cut out of the top, the missing section being replaced by a black velvet bag. Because of the

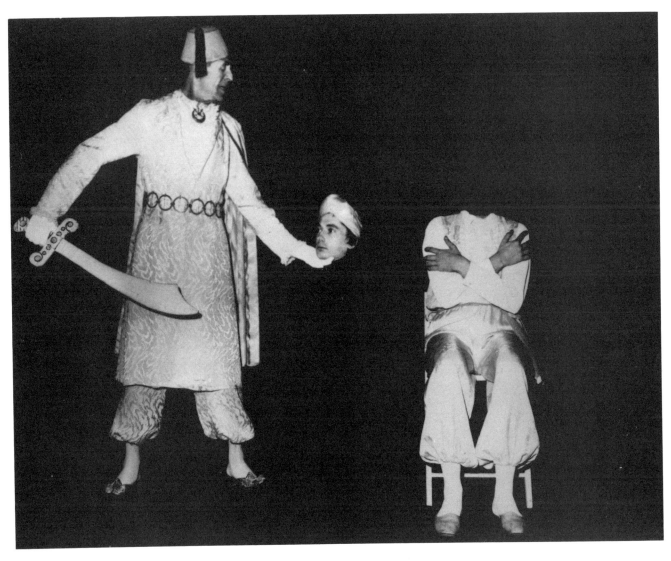

Black Art magic, as presented by *Omar Pasha* (*photo courtesy GENII Magazine*)

BLACK ART principle, the table appears solid. A short black velvet drape around the edges of the table conceals the bag from the audience's view. If an object is placed on the table directly in front of the well (as it is called), it may be allowed to drop into the well in the act of apparently picking it up. This type of black art table is believed to have been invented by HELLER and DEVERE.

Effects using this table are described in CHARLES MILLER's *Black Art Well Tricks* and PETER WARLOCK's *Black Art Well Tricks For the 80's*.

A more recent version, invented by E.H.C. WETHERED, uses a table with a white drape on which sits a tray with a black velvet surface. This extremely deceptive application of the principle may be found in TREVOR H. HALL's *Reading Is Believing*, and in the *Tarbell Course in Magic* (Vol. 6).

BLACKJACK DEAL

An exhibition deal of the game of Blackjack (or Twenty-One), sometimes incorporated into GAMBLING DEMONSTRATIONs (as in Glenn Haywood's use of the NIKOLA STACK) or as a plot for card location effects (as in FR. CYPRIAN's the "No-Name Game").

BLACK LIGHT

Ultraviolet (or UV) light; sometimes used in conjunction with BLACK ART acts. It is also used in the "blackout" portion of SPOOK SHOW, where among other effects it may be used to illuminate special makeup which is not visible in ordinary light.

BLACKOUT

The sudden elimination of all lights; usually done briefly to signal the end of a scene or particular performance sequence.

In a SPOOK SHOW, a climactic sequence (of a two-to-five minute duration) during which various luminous objects seem to float about in the theater.

In comedy, a type of short scene (or sketch) with a punch-line ending immediately followed by the lighting blackout.

BLACKSTONE, HARRY (1885-1965)

Born Harry Boughton; he began his performing career working in varied venues under many names. One act, performed with his brother Pete, was called **Straight And Crooked Magic**—Harry providing the straight magic and Pete delivering the comedy.

In 1918 he began performing as **Blackstone The Magician**, achieving great successs in the VAUDEVILLE of the 1920's; he continued to tour with a FULL-EVENING SHOW for over three decades and was, after the era of HOWARD THURSTON, the best-known magician in the country. He was noted for his unique performance of several EFFECTs, including the DANCING HANDKERCHIEF, the VANISHING BIRD CAGE, and the FLOATING LIGHT BULB; many who saw him feel that his performance of these and other effects will never be equalled. He was to many the quintessence of the word *magician*.

In the 1950's he ceased touring, but made a number of stage and television appearances.

Father of HARRY BLACKSTONE JR.

BLACKSTONE, HARRY JR. (b. 1934)

Beginning his show business career as a radio announcer, he later was associated with the Smothers Brothers in their television shows and Las Vegas act. After the death of father HARRY BLACKSTONE SR., he began performing in varied venues, including *Holiday On Ice*, with which he toured extensively.

Blackstone then began working the Playboy Club circuit, followed by appearances in Las Vegas and at hotels throughout the U.S.; he also appeared on *The Tonight Show, Merv Griffin, Mike Douglas* and *Dinah Shore* shows, and on his own *Magic, Magic, Magic* special.

With wife Gay (a former member of the *Golddiggers* television troupe), he created a FULL-EVENING SHOW which combined classic effects from his father's show with new EFFECTs and ILLUSIONs. The show toured throughout the U.S., including a 118-night run on Broadway—the longest such run for

Harry Blackstone, Jr. (*photo courtesy GENII Magazine*)

any magic-only show. He continues to perform throughout the country, and has been featured in television appearances as both magician and actor. He has also acted as TECHNICAL ADVISOR for television productions.

He is a recipient of the Star Of Magic from S.A.M., and has twice been named Magician Of The Year by the ACADEMY OF MAGICAL ARTS.

BLAKE, GEORGE (1893-1979)

British performer and creator of magical EFFECTs, of which perhaps the best known is UNCANNY HANKS. He also authored books, including his *Master Magic* series, his book on the ENDLESS CHAIN (*Loopy Loop*), and many others.

He was also a founder of the first British Ring of the International Brotherhood of Magicians, and for a time edited *The Budget*, a publication of the organization. Extremely knowledgeable and helpful, he was sought out for advice by many performers.

BLANEY, WALTER (Zaney) (b. ?)

Texas-born performer noted for his high-powered style of presentation and for his skill at magical invention; his best-known creation is his version of the SUSPENSION illusion, now being featured by DAVID COPPERFIELD.

Walter Blaney

BLANK DECK

Usually, a deck with a printed back but unprinted face; also, a deck with neither faces nor backs.

See also NUDIST DECK.

BLASTED

A commercially-marketed feat of COIN MAGIC, invented by Robert Swadling, in which a coin visibly appears under a downturned wineglass; sometimes presented as a PENETRATION effect. It makes use of the SHELL principle, as well as an ingeniously prepared tray.

BLENDO

A SILK effect in which a number of silks are tied together and visibly combine into a single, much larger silk. Variations include a version using red, white and blue silks which combine into a U.S. flag, and a MISMADE version of the same effect.

The best source of information on this effect is HAROLD R. RICE's *Encyclopedia Of Silk Magic*.

BLIND

A feint, or simulated action; also, an action taken as MISDIRECTION to remove attention or analysis from another action.

BLINDERS

In BLACK ART, the lights which—apparently illuminating the playing area—are actually directed outward to dilate the eyes of the audience.

BLINDFOLD DRIVE

A publicity stunt used by many magicians in which the performer is securely blindfolded and then drives a car through an obstacle course or (where permission can be granted) the streets of the town where the show is being given. The stunt is usually enhanced with various commercial tie-ins with town businesses (the auto dealer who supplies the car, the drugstore which provides the bandages for the blindfold, etc.).

BLINDFOLDS

Most often used in MENTALISM, where they may be the basis of entire acts (*see* KUDA BUX), blindfolds are sometimes used by magicians to add drama to particular effects.

Such blindfolds may be genuine—since many effects do not require the use of vision—or faked, either in the application of the material used or in the nature of the materials themselves. The primary sourcebook for blindfold work is WILL DEXTER's book *Sealed Vision*. Another source is *Intuitional Sight* by EDDIE JOSEPH.

BLIND SHUFFLE

A partial FALSE SHUFFLE in which a STOCK of cards is retained in order while the rest of the cards are genuinely mixed. *See* FALSE SHUFFLE.

BLITZ, SIGNOR ANTONIO (1810-1877)

Born Antonio van Zandt in Holland, he spent the early part of his career performing in Europe and the British Isles. After a brief tour of the U.S., he returned to Europe, but twenty years later moved to New York City, where he opened his own theater. Blitz was known as a very humorous and versatile performer, featuring not only the BULLET CATCH but also trained canaries and PLATE SPINNING.

His autobiography is titled *Fifty Years In The Magic Circle*. (Note: this has no connection with the British MAGIC CIRCLE.)

BLOCK

A cube, usually of wood and 3" square, used in such effects as the DIE BOX, BLOCK-GO, and BLOK-CORD; often, but not always, painted to represent a large gaming die.

Also, in card magic, a specific group of cards being controlled (also known as a **slue**), most often during a RIFFLE SHUFFLE, in which cards from the opposite half interlace above and below the block but not within it.

See STOCK; BLOCK TRANSFER.

BLOCK AND FRAME

An EFFECT using a wooden block with a hole drilled through its center and a wide frame (into which the block just fits) with holes in two of its sides that line up with those of the block. Ribbon or cord is threaded through frame and block, securing the latter to the former. The performer magically removes the block, leaving the ribbon or cord running through the empty frame.

A variety of methods have been devised for accomplishing this feat, ranging from a simple thread hookup which will reroute a ribbon around the block, to complex mechanical devices. It is a showy and puzzling platform effect.

BLOCK-GO

An apparatus PENETRATION effect in which two square wooden tubes are separated by a pane of solid glass; a block of wood dropped into the upper tube apparently passes through the glass and drops out of the lower tube. The effect is accomplished by an application of the SHELL principle.

BLOCKING

The sequence of stage movement and action in the course of a performance; also, the planning of such a sequence.

BLOCK PENETRATIONS

There are a truly surprising number of commercially marketed EFFECTs in which a wooden block is made to penetrate some solid barrier. *See*, for example, BLOCK-GO.

Other versions of the effect use a chimney-like wooden tube with slots in the center through which a slide of wood or metal may be placed, effectively blocking passage; the block goes through as usual.

Another type of effect in this category is that in which a block is secured within a chimney by a metal or wooden rod or sword passing through holes in chimney and block. The block releases itself and falls from the chimney. A version of this is known as the **vampire block**.

Another approach to the effect uses a skeleton frame into which the block is placed, remaining clearly visible; this is placed atop a borrowed hat and covered with a handkerchief, whereupon the block seemingly penetrates the crown of the hat and is found underneath—the frame, of course, being empty.

Still another class of effects are those in which blocks within a chimney seem to penetrate each other, rearranging themselves inside the wooden tube. Versions of this are known as **the obedient blocks, the patriotic blocks**, and the BLUE PHANTOM (which sometimes uses hockey-puck-shaped wooden disks, which may be impaled on a vertical metal shaft).

BLOCK TRANSFER

The movement of a BLOCK of cards from one half of the deck to the other, in the course of a RIFFLE SHUFFLE. This may be a **top transfer**, sometimes used to remove cards from above a selected card and thus bring it to the top of the deck at the completion of the shuffle; a **bottom transfer**; or a **center** or **general transfer**.

The subject is thoroughly covered in KARL FULVES' *Riffle Shuffle Technique*.

BLOK-CORD

Invented by Lyman Allen; a PENETRATION effect in which a wooden block with a hole drilled through its center is shown, and a rope is run through it twice, securely fastening the block to the rope. While spectators hold the ends of the cord the performer removes the block. Both block and rope may be given for rigorous examination as they are, in fact, quite ordinary—the effect being accomplished by a subtle and indetectable handling of the PROPS by the performer.

A variation of this has recently been marketed in which a clear plastic block with a "frosted" hole is used; this same basic idea was performed by BILLY MCCOMB on British television in the mid-1950's.

BLONDINO

A ball is made to roll back and forth along a rope or cord stretched between the hands in a feat of apparent juggling skill; it is accomplished by means of a supporting thread hidden behind the rope.

This feat, based on an earlier juggling stunt, is named after the noted French tightrope walker Blondin.

It is the invention of TOM SELLERS.

BLOOM, GAETAN (b. ?)

Born in France; performer specializing in highly visual effects, most often with a strong comedic slant. He is also noted for his inventiveness (including some unique applications of THREAD), and has created (among many other items) a startling version of the THREE-CARD MONTE routine called *Visible Monte*. In addition to performing throughout Europe, Britain, and the U.S., he has worked as a CONSULTANT to GERARD MAJAX and other performers.

His books include *Gaetan Bloom Series Number One* and *Gaetan Bloom Lecture Notes*.

BLOOMING BOUQUET

A large FEATHER FLOWER bouquet having been produced, the performer plucks the flowers one by one and tosses them to the stage where they stick upright (they are, in fact, flower darts); the bare bouquet is shown, and slowly buds appear which blossom into full-size flowers (usually roses).

The effect has been featured by many magicians, and for many years has been manufactured by HORACE MARSHALL, whose firm specializes in the creation and production of effects with feather flowers.

BLUE MATERIAL

Performance material, either PATTER or BUSINESS, with explicit sexual or scatological content, or containing strong expletives.

Gaetan Bloom (*photo courtesy GENII Magazine*)

It has been stated that in some venues audiences expect the performer to "work blue" and are dissatisfied if this is not done. This may be true in certain extremely limited situations, particularly if the performer presents himself as a comedian who performs magic rather than as a magician; in most cases, however, an audience will respond favorably to a well-performed act without pausing to assess the amount of off-color material.

It should also be noted that television exposure is an essential element in creating demand for the performer, and blue material is not acceptable on broadcast media; a performer, therefore, who is dependent on it to create audience response will find adaptation to the requirements of TV work that much more difficult.

All questions of taste aside, except at the very lowest levels of show business, the performer is likely to lose more work than he gains by using blue material. There are exceptions to this, but these are few; success in show business is difficult enough without creating unnecessary obstacles.

BLUE PHANTOM

An APPARATUS effect using several large puck-shaped wooden disks, or "checkers"; all are of the same color (e.g., yellow) except for a solitary blue disk. This blue disk is placed in the center of the stack, which is then covered with a cylinder.

When the cylinder is removed, the blue disk has risen to the top of the stack. A repetition of the actions reveals it at the bottom of the stack, and it finally returns to its original position.

In some models of the apparatus the disks have a central hole, and are stacked on a large chromed shaft. The effect is credited to OTTOKAR FISCHER.

BLUE ROOM

The name given by HARRY KELLAR to the METEMPSYCHOSIS ILLUSION.

BLUFF PASS

A card subtlety in which the deck is apparently CUT for the return of a selected card to the center; in actuality no cards are taken by the right hand, the action being merely simulated. The hand is held with the back flat on to the spectator's view to conceal its empty nature. At the same time, the deck remaining in the left hand is allowed to sink down into the palm somewhat to create the illusion that part of the deck has been taken.

The selected card is replaced on top of the deck in

the left hand and the action of replacing the upper half-deck on top of the selection is simulated; the deck is then squared.

The selection is now on top, and may be used as required by the performer.

In a variant technique, the performer takes a single card into the right hand, its back apparently that of the upper half of the deck. After return of the selection the single card is replaced, leaving the selection as the second card; this version of the SLEIGHT is described in HILLIARD's *Greater Magic*.

The original version can be found in *Westminster Wizardry*, by Frederick Montague (LORD AMWELL); an improvement in handling, by VICTOR FARELLI in his *Card Magic*.

BLYTH, WILL (?-1937)

British writer on magic; among his books are *Effective Conjuring*, *Impromptu Conjuring*, and works on paper, money, handkerchief and matchstick magic. He originated the **Sympathetic Blocks** effect (*see* BLOCK PENETRATIONS), and many others.

BOBO, J.B. (b. 1910)

He began as a LYCEUM and CHAUTAUQUA performer; later he began to specialize in school assembly programs and continues today in this type of show. He is noted for his work with coins and for his book *Modern Coin Magic*, which has long been accepted as *the* indispensable reference book on the subject.

Other books include *Watch This One* and, most recently, *The Bobo Magic Show*, which describes his school-show work.

BODY LOAD

A LOAD for a PRODUCTION which is concealed on the performer's body, often in a specially prepared pocket, clip, or container; also, the action of secretly moving the load from the body to the point where the production will take place.

The term is also sometimes used to denote the action of secretly loading objects into a spectator's clothing for subsequent production; techniques for this are described in EDDIE JOSEPH's *The Art Of Body Loading*.

BOFFO

Said of a performer or act which attracts large numbers of customers; from a contraction of *Box Office*.

BOGART TUBE

A cylindrical metal container, open at one end, which may be examined to prove its emptiness, after which the opening is sealed with a sheet of paper held in place by a metal ring. The cylinder is inserted in a holder consisting of a slightly larger cylinder affixed to a tripod stand. Breaking the paper, the performer proceeds to make a large production of silks or other objects.

The Bogart Tube operates on the same principle as the DRUMHEAD TUBE; the LOAD CHAMBER is held within the cylindrical stand by spring rods, and is automatically loaded into the tube as it is pushed upward through the cylinder.

BONGO, ALI (b. ?)

Born William Oliver Wallace in India, this British performer is well known for his **Shriek Of Araby** comedy act; he is also highly respected as a creator and inventor. In addition to his own performance work (which included his television series featuring CHILDREN'S MAGIC), he has acted as TECHNICAL ADVISOR and BACK-ROOM BOY for DAVID NIXON, PAUL DANIELS, and others. Also noted as an excellent artist, he has illusrated a number of books and magic catalogues. He is a past president of the BRITISH RING of the I.B.M. and is a winner of the British Ring Shield.

His straightforward approach to effect and method is well illustrated in his *The Bongo Book*.

BONUS GENIUS

This obscurely titled EFFECT is several centuries old, and is described in many early works on conjuring. It is usually presented with a fair-sized doll or wooden cutout figure which is placed under a cloth so that the head of the doll projects through a slit. With a flick of the cloth the doll is gone.

There are two basic methods; either the head is detachable, or a duplicate head is concealed in the cloth. The rest of the doll is allowed secretly to drop into a hidden SERVANTE behind a table; after the performer has moved away from the table he lets the visible head drop into a pocket in the cloth. The cloth may then be shown empty.

A model of this effect marketed by British dealer Burtini was called **Wandering Willie**; it featured legs which slid up into the torso of the figure, making a smaller object for disposal.

BOOK CARD

See ENVELOPE CARD.

BOOK TEST

A feat of MENTAL MAGIC, performed by magicians for at least three centuries, in which words or pages secretly selected by a spectator are divined and described by the performer.

BOOMERANG CARD

A card FLOURISH in which a card is thrown by the performer and returns to the hand. It is accomplished by the CARD THROWING technique of putting a spin on the card as it is released, and throwing the card upward at a 45-degree angle. Before doing this, the card should be given a slight bend by squeezing the ends; with the convex side downward a more aerodynamic surface is created. The move is fully described in RICKY JAY's *Cards As Weapons*.

BOOMERANGS

An optical illusion in which two boomerang-shaped wooden objects of different colors appear to change lengths; in actuality both remain the identical size, but whichever is held above the other (convex edge at top) will appear to be shorter.

Some presentations make use of a prepared boomerang with a section which can be indetectably removed, so that at the conclusion of the demonstration one boomerang actually *is* shorter.

BOOTH, JOHN (b. 1912)

Born John Nicholls Booth, he had a highly successful career as a nightclub performer throughout the U.S. and several other countries. In 1940 he retired from professional performing to become a Unitarian minister, but has remained active in magic to the present time.

Among his books are *Super Magical Miracles, Marvels Of Mystery, Forging Ahead In Magic* and—more recently—*Psychic Paradoxes* and *Wonders Of Magic*. He is also the author of the long-running LINKING RING Magazine column of history and reminiscence, "Memoirs Of A Magician's Ghost."

BORDER

Strip of canvas or other heavy material, suspended along the upper horizontal border of the PROSCENIUM, usually appropriately painted.

Also, the white margin on the back of a playing card; cards possessing such margins are preferred for effects in which a card is reversed in the deck, since the deck may be safely beveled or slightly spread without

John Booth as he appeared in the late 1930's, at the height of his performing career.

revealing the REVERSED CARD. With a borderless back, a reversed card is instantly detectable by a spectator.

BORROWED OBJECTS

Many magical effects depend on the audience's knowledge that the objects used are ordinary and unprepared; an example would be the LINKING FINGER RINGS, which appears miraculous when done with three borrowed rings, but would be only mildly interesting if done with three small rings from the performer's pocket.

Another aspect has to do with the uniqueness of an object; to tear up and restore a borrowed bill possessing a distinctive serial number which makes it one of a kind is a much stronger feat than would be the similar tearing and restoration of an anonymous napkin or sheet of tissue paper. There is also involved here the spectacle of a valued item being apparently destroyed, which is usually played for its comedic value, particularly when the destruction occurs as the result of an apparent mistake on the part of the magician. (It should be noted that this premise is only effective in the hands of an excellent performer/actor who can make it play believably; in most cases, the premise is not accepted for a moment either by the spectator who has loaned the object or the rest of the audience, who are thus resigned to waiting patiently for the unsurprising resolution of the effect.)

The advantages of using borrowed objects are considerable; indeed, the idea of doing an entire act with objects borrowed from the audience was once proposed by U. F. GRANT. An interesting manuscript on this premise, titled *Improv Magic*, was written by Kirk Charles.

Against this must be weighed the time taken in performance to locate a spectator with an object of the desired kind, who must then be persuaded to (a) loan the object and usually (b) come on stage to assist in the effect. Depending on the performer's skill and luck in this process, it may be accomplished briefly or may create a stage wait which runs a real danger of losing the audience.

It is probably a good general rule that no more than one effect requiring a borrowed object should be performed in any given show.

(Note: any object borrowed from a spectator should be returned in the same condition as when it was lent. If a bill has had a corner torn off, the performer should offer to replace it with a new bill if desired; this is best quietly done during audience applause, the performer saying simply, "See me after the show and I'll replace that bill with a new one if you'd like." This or similar verbiage can be said in a few seconds, and the flow of the act is not disrupted.)

BORSCHT BELT

Vacation resorts located in the Catskill Mountains section of the Appalachian range in southeastern New York state. These resorts cater to the nearby metropolitan centers and use many comedians, musicians, and variety acts.

BOSCO, BARTOLOMEO (1793-1863)

Italian magician noted as a performer of CLOSE-UP MAGIC and as an exceptional linguist; he spoke (and performed in) eleven languages. He is credited with the invention of the SAND FRAME and is best known for his excellent performance of the CUPS AND BALLS.

He is described (in a somewhat biased fashion) by ROBERT-HOUDIN in his *Memoirs*.

BOSTON, GEORGE (1905-1975)

Performer who worked in all phases of magic, but was best known as chief assistant or stage manager for numerous stage illusionists, including HARRY BLACKSTONE, SR., CHARLES CARTER, JACK GWYNNE, NICOLA and HARRY THURSTON. Boston wrote a book on his experiences with these shows; it was titled *Inside Magic*.

In later years he was noted as a technical advisor for feature films (including "Houdini" starring Tony Curtis) and television shows such as *You Asked For It*.

He is also noted as the inventor of the BOSTON BOX.

BOSTON BOX

Invented by GEORGE BOSTON, this variant of the OKITO BOX has a recessed bottom which will take a single coin, allowing for a number of subtleties. It is used both with the usual lid and without, most often for the effect of passing a stack of coins through the hand or table.

Effects and techniques with the Boston Box are discussed in *Modern Coin Magic* by J.B. BOBO and *Expert Coin Magic* by DAVID ROTH.

BOTANIA

An APPARATUS effect for a FEATHER FLOWER production, consisting of a flowerpot into which the performer drops a seed, and a tapered metal tube which is briefly placed over the pot. When the tube is lifted a large bouquet is seen.

The bouquet consists of feather flowers on spring-loaded stems which are attached to the leaf-decorated outer side of a cylinder which had formed the covering tube's inner wall; the tube is constructed along the lines of the PHANTOM TUBE, and may therefore be shown empty prior to the production.

BOTTLE

As a verb, a (now rare) slang term for making a collection of money when working as a BUSKER.

BOTTLE AND GLASS

See PASSE-PASSE BOTTLES.

BOTTLE IMP

British name for the IMP BOTTLE.

BOTTOM CARD

Lowermost card of the face-down deck; also known as FACE CARD. Within magic literature, the face card of the deck is sometimes referred to as the bottom card regardless of the deck's orientation, resulting in confusing descriptions which may puzzle the unwary student.

BOTTOM CHANGE

A card SLEIGHT in which a card held in one hand is exchanged secretly for the top card of the deck held in the performer's other hand; the originally held card is left on the bottom of the deck.

Like the TOP CHANGE of which it is a variant, the bottom change relies not so much on technique (which must be good) as on timing and MISDIREC-TION—which must be faultless.

BOTTOM DEAL

To deal cards from the bottom of the deck while apparently dealing them from the top in the usual manner. Like any false deal, it is difficult to deal in an indetectable manner—though the penalties for failure within a magical performance are less severe than those meted out at the card table!

On a theoretical level, the bottom deal can be more illusive than a SECOND DEAL simply because of the *sound* of the move; the sound of a card being dealt from top *or* bottom is perceptibly different to that of a card being dealt from between two others, as is the case with the SECOND DEAL.

Many descriptions of the technique of bottom dealing are in print; the seminal work is ERDNASE's *The Expert At The Card Table*. An excellent modern work is *ED MARLO's Seconds, Centers And Bottoms*.

See SECOND DEAL; CENTER DEAL.

BOTTOMLESS GLASS

A utility item used in countless effects, this is a glass or clear plastic tumbler from which the bottom has been removed; thus anything placed in the glass drops onto the performer's hand. The glass is usually covered with a handkerchief or opaque cylinder, after which the hand holding the object (which presumably is still in the glass) moves unobtrusively away.

BOTTOM PALM

With cards, to PALM the bottom (or face) card of the deck; the card is almost always palmed into the hand not holding the deck, and is usually moved into palming position by the fingers of the holding hand.

A full description of the technique may be found in ERDNASE's *Expert At The Card Table* and HUGARD and BRAUE's *Expert Card Technique*.

BOWL PRODUCTION

The production of a large clear bowl of water complete with fish has been popular with magicians for many years. Usually the bowl is produced under the cover of a cloth or a large array of previously produced silks. It was a traditional feat for Chinese performers; LONG TACK SAM was noted for his bowl production in the course of a somersault. A bowl production was also featured by ROBERT-HOUDIN, who describes his method in his *Secrets Of Conjuring And Magic*.

Some bowls are permanently sealed, and the fish seen swimming within are imitation; others have rubber covers to hold in the liquid, and these may be secretly removed before the production is made.

Large bowls can be produced by means of a special table; invented by Ernest Noakes, it is described in his book *Magical Originalities*. The bowl sits on the table proper and is hidden by a drape; to the spectators it appears to be a draped table with nothing on it. The performer apparently "catches" the bowl under a cloth and brings it toward the table (a water-filled sponge can be squeezed to simulate spillage). When the cloth conceals the table, a release drops the drape to the true table level and the bowl is revealed. Improvements on the basic idea are described in JARRETT's *Magic And Stagecraft—Technical* and in *Jack Gwynne* by David Charvet. An interesting touch described in S.H. SHARPE's *Conjurers' Optical Secrets* is to use an oval table and bowl, positioned so the audience sees the narrow dimension; in the act of production the bowl is turned sideways, and from the audience perspective seems appreciably larger than the tabletop on which it rests.

A drawback to this method is the table's apparent loss in height. Some tables have been manufactured with a locking spring-loaded piston or other device to raise the table to the correct height as the production is made.

A more complex feat along the same lines, not often seen, is that of producing a stack of several bowls; this was a feature in the performances of JACK GWYNNE, W. J. NIXON, and ROBERT HARBIN. The device which released the stack of bowls from their load bag whenever the stack was set down on a solid surface was invented by Nixon and Gwynne, and later considerably improved by Gwynne; it is thoroughly described, along with the technique for its use, in *Jack Gwynne* by David Charvet. Harbin's routine is described in his *The Magic Of Robert Harbin*.

BOWYER, TOM (1902-1949)

Born in Britain, he later moved to Canada. He performed semi-professionally under the name *Van*

Russell, but is best known to magicians for his inventions, notably the REPEAT DOLLAR BILLS effect.

BOX ESCAPE

The performer is placed in a wooden box and the lid is nailed down; chains and ropes may also be wrapped around the box in both directions. A screen or small curtained cabinet is placed around the box, and the performer immediately makes the escape; the box is still sealed and there is no sign of how the performer gained freedom.

This escape is usually done as a publicity stunt (the box being built by a local lumber yard) rather than as a regular program item. There are countless methods by which it may be accomplished, ranging from secret preparation of the box before the performance to special escape tools devised for the effect.

A sensational version of this escape has the box weighted with heavy chains and lowered or dropped into a body of water; the performer escapes from the box and swims to the surface. Part of the appeal of such stunts is explained by HOUDINI's comment that ". . . human beings don't like to see other human beings lose their lives—but they do love to be on the spot when it happens."

See ESCAPES.

BOX JUMPER

Magician's parlance for an ASSISTANT (usually female) who works in large stage ILLUSIONs.

BOX MAGIC

Phrase sometimes used in derogatory fashion to describe an act which relies too heavily on cumbersome standard APPARATUS; also pejoratively, an ILLUSION act which seems to consist only of people being produced from one box and vanished in another *ad infinitum, ad nauseum*.

In fairness, it should be noted that such acts can be highly entertaining and successful, when presented by a competent and dynamic performer.

BOX THE CARDS

See BOX THE DECK.

BOX THE DECK

To place the two halves of the deck face-to-face. This is sometimes done to facilitate an exchange, i.e., a group of cards are momentarily placed on "top" of the deck, which is then surreptitiously turned over; thus an entirely different group of cards is now removed from the new top of the deck.

It is also used with a deck consisting of two duplicate halves, where one half is prearranged; an excellent example of this application is found in Rupert Slater's version of MUTUS NOMEN, in HILLIARD's *Greater Magic*.

BOX TRICK

Term often used in Britain to denote the METAMORPHOSIS illusion.

Also, pejoratively, of any stage EFFECT using a large box or cabinet; the implication in the use of the phrase is that such effects are mechanical in nature and require no skill on the part of the performer. Indeed, a few such effects may be "operated" by almost anyone, but many (such as the **metamorphosis** mentioned above) require exceptional skill to perform, and all require the full range of stage skills to be effectively presented.

BOY, GIRL, AND EGGS

The name given by DAVID DEVANT to the production of a large number of eggs from a hat; the eggs were given to a young boy and girl to hold, and soon so many eggs had been produced that the children began to drop them.

It should be noted that Devant almost always used children of theatre employees and cast members for this effect, the two children "volunteering" from the audience or simply being brought out on stage from the wings. It was not considerate, Devant felt, to put an unsuspecting layperson—particularly a child—in a potentially embarrassing situation.

This routine was also featured by HOWARD THURSTON.

BRAINWAVE DECK

A MECHANICAL DECK which in its current form is the work of DAI VERNON; it enables the performer to show any card named as the only one face-up in a face-down deck—and to cap this by showing the card to have a back of an entirely different color from the rest of the deck (this final touch was created by PAUL FOX). The Vernon version employs the ROUGH-AND-SMOOTH PRINCIPLE; an earlier version, using beeswax, was created by Judson Brown, and a still earlier version was invented by Edward Bagshawe.

The progenitors of the modern version are described in *The History Of The Brainwave Principle* by KARL FULVES.

See INVISIBLE DECK; ULTRA-MENTAL DECK.

BRANCH, JUSTIN (b. ?)

Writer specializing in technical treatises on card magic; his works include *Cards In Confidence* (Volumes I and II), *Multiple Assemblies*, and *Progressive Card Magic*.

BRANDON (?-?)

British Court Magician to Henry VIII; he was a source of information for REGINALD SCOT's *Discovery Of Witchcraft*.

Brandon was noted for a feat in which he drew a sketch of a pigeon perched on a rooftop; when he stabbed the paper, the bird fell dead. Authorities forbade him to perform the effect again, fearing he might turn his powers against people. The trick, which used poisoned grain (or a thread in the hands of a confederate, which released a dead bird) is explained by Scot in his book.

BRASSIERE TRICK

An EFFECT, believed to have been invented by HOWARD BROOKS, in which two silk handkerchieves are knotted together and held by (or, optionally, tucked into the dress front of) an assisting lady from the audience. A third handkerchief is vanished and the performer announces it will be found tied between the two held by the lady. Instead, when the handkerchieves are shaken out, a brassiere (presumably the lady's) is found tied between them.

Though this often gets a laugh from the audience, it is usually sympathetic laughter at the plight of the embarrassed spectator; thus the effect is generally used only by comedy performers who specialize in making fun of their audiences, and never by magicians with any claim to competency or finesse. In the hands of an expert performer it might be possible to present this routine without offense, but an expert performer would hardly be likely to use it.

BRASS NUT TRICK

Sometimes known as the **Brema Nut Trick** (for its best known manufacturer CARL BREMA), in this EFFECT a small brass nut is threaded onto a string; while the ends of the string are held by spectators, the nut is mysteriously removed from it.

The effect is accomplished by a combination of an ingeniously-constructed nut with elementary SLEIGHT-OF-HAND.

Also sometimes known as the **spirit nut**.

BRAUDE, BENJAMIN G. (b. ca. 1935)

Dentist by profession; active in magic for many years, with numerous contributions to magazines. He is also noted for his work with various magical organizations, and his major editorial contribution to *Scarne On Card Tricks* by JOHN SCARNE.

BRAUE, FRED (?-1962)

A journalist by profession, he was noted for his many contributions to magic literature, primarily within the field of card magic.

His books include *Fred Braue On False Deals* and several collaborations with JEAN HUGARD: *Expert Card Technique*, *Royal Road To Card Magic*, *Tricks And Sleights*, the *Miracle Methods* series, *The Invisible Pass*, and others. He also contributed to many magazines, including a notable series on mental card effects which ran in *Hugard's Magic Monthly* (see JEAN HUGARD).

A series of books containing his previously published work are currently being published by JEFF BUSBY as the *Fred Braue Notebooks*.

BRAUE REVERSAL

A method of reversing a card in a deck in the course of a cutting action; invented by FRED BRAUE.

With the deck held in BIDDLE GRIP in the right hand, a break is held between the top card (which will be reversed) and the rest of the deck. The left hand cuts off the *lower* half of the deck and rotates it face-up onto the upper half; apparently this action is repeated with the new lower half, but only the cards below the break are taken, leaving the original top card face-down at the bottom of the face-up deck.

With a slight alteration in procedure—in the second phase, turning the half-deck face-up and replacing it on the bottom—the card is left reversed in the center of the deck.

The Braue Reversal is described in MENTZER's *Counts, Cuts, Moves And Subtleties*.

BRAUN, JOHN (b. 1896)

Mechanical engineer by profession; past president of the I.B.M. and for many years editor of LINKING RING Magazine (he is now Editor Emeritus).

He is the author (with STEWART JUDAH) of *Subtle Problems You Will Do*; he has edited books for others, and in some cases has done most of the writing involved. He has also contributed to a number of magic magazines.

He is a recipient of the *Literary Fellowship* from the ACADEMY OF MAGICAL ARTS.

BRAUND, GEORGE (?-1961)

British magician specializing in private party work, at which he was expert and for which he was one of the highest-paid performers of his time. He was physically imposing, and often used the billing "The Biggest Thing In Magic." Early in his career he would perform in the guise of a befuddled clergyman whose umbrella would produce a chosen card a la the CARD SWORD. During World War II he was commissioned with the rank of captain and entertained servicemen.

BREAK

In card magic, a secretly-held separation between two parts of a deck or PACKET; these parts can be composed of any number of cards from a single card upwards. The break is usually at the rear of the deck as it lies in the hand; it is most often done with the little finger or with a fold of flesh at the base of the fingers. Breaks may also be held by the thumb; here the cards are usually held from above in a BIDDLE GRIP with the thumb at the rear.

BREAKAWAY FAN

A comedy PROP which appears to be a normal fan, and can be used as such; when a spectator tries to open it, however, it separates into several sections. In the performer's hands again, it operates as usual.

See also BREAKAWAY WAND; CLATTERBOX.

BREAKAWAY WAND

A comedy prop, this wand may be handled by the performer in the usual fashion. When handed to a spectator, however, it collapses limply, draping over his hand. Returned to the performer, it regains its usual shape.

See also BREAKAWAY FAN; CLATTERBOX.

BREAK CARDS

Those cards most likely to be named by a spectator asked to call out any card; in RALPH HULL's NAME-O-CARD routine the cards are the Two, Three and King of Hearts, Jack of Clubs, Ace, Two and Jack of Spades, Ace and Two of Diamonds, and the Joker.

Over the years many such lists have been compiled; none of them agree completely, and there seems to be an interesting variance depending on the particular nation or geographical area in which the request is made.

BREESE, MARTIN (b. ?)

Born in Britain; he is noted for his series of Magicassettes, audiotapes containing interviews, reminiscences, and performance material of noted performers. His company, begun with the audiotape series, now offers several exclusive effects and routines as well.

He is the author of *The Harbin Book* and *The Magic Of Al Koran*.

BREMA, CARL (1864-1942)

Born Karl Brehmer in Germany; he emigrated to the U.S. as a child. He opened a magic shop and magic manufacturing plant in Philadelphia, Pennsylvania, which was noted for its precision-made APPARATUS—usually constructed in brass. Of the many items manufactured by Brema, undoubtedly the most popular was the NICKELS TO DIMES effect invented by his friend WALTER B. GIBSON.

Brema retired in 1932; his son Bill carried on the business for a time, and died in 1949.

An excellent account of the effects manufactured by Brema is *The Brema Brasses* by Richard Buffum.

BRENT, LU (b. 1904)

Born Boleslaw Lubrant, he had a long professional career in nightclubs and theaters. He is noted also for his many contributions to THE JINX, the PHOENIX, and other magic magazines.

BRESLAW, PHILIP (1726-1783)

German-born British magician noted as an exhibitor of AUTOMATA and also as the probable inventor of the modern form of the TWO-PERSON MENTAL ACT.

A book of simple tricks, *Breslaw's Last Legacy*, was published shortly after his death, but there is no definite indication that it was actually written by him.

BREWSTER, SIR DAVID (1781-1868)

Author of *Letters On Natural Magic*, a book which explained optical and acoustical effects, fire-resistance, and the mechanics of AUTOMATA.

BRIDAL CHAMBER

An ILLUSION in which a large, bare curtained cabinet was transformed into a **bridal chamber**—complete with bride and bride's maid. Variations of the basic illusion were performed by HERBERT ALBINI, HARRY BLACKSTONE SR., and many others.

BRIDGE

To bend a portion of a deck of cards downward, so that when it is replaced on the remainder of the deck there will be a break between the two sections. Slight pressure on the top of the deck will hold the cards flat and render the break invisible, but when pressure is released the performer can easily cut off the bridged portion. If the bridging is executed correctly, the performer should be able to use it without the bridge being "strong" enough to be visible.

BRIDGE DEAL

A GAMBLING DEMONSTRATION in which the performer deals a perfect bridge hand to a selected spectator. This may consist of all the cards of one suit, or a hand which will demonstrably win all the tricks.

BRIDGES, DR. MILTON (1894-1939)

Noted collector of magic books; his highly regarded collection is now part of the H. Adrian Smith library.

For many years he wrote on bibliographic subjects for the SPHINX Magazine, first as a historian of magic magazines and later as a book reviewer.

BRIDGE-SIZE CARDS

Cards of the same length as POKER-SIZE CARDS, but one-fourth of an inch narrower (two-and-a-quarter inches wide). Bridge-size cards are more popular with performers in Britain and Europe; in the U.S., the wider cards are preferred.

BRINDAMOUR, GEORGE (1870-1941)

Vaudeville performer who specialized in SLEIGHT-OF-HAND and ESCAPES.

BRITISH RING

Largest of the many local chapters (called *Rings*) of the I.B.M.; it holds an important convention each year, during which the British Ring Shield for performing excellence is awarded.

The British Ring (No. 25) was founded in 1928; it publishes a monthly journal called *The Budget* which contains news, reports of various activities, and columns of opinion and review.

An annual LINKING RING Magazine Parade is devoted to EFFECTs created by members of the British Ring; these Parades are noted for their consistently high quality.

BROADSIDE

A simple form of advertising consisting of an uncut sheet of paper printed on one side, and usually in one color only. These sheets were often used by showmen of the last three centuries, including magicians; many of these broadsides are extremely rare and highly prized by collectors.

BROAD TOSSER

In gambling parlance, the person who manipulates the cards in a THREE-CARD MONTE game. The word *broad* in this connection is an early term for the playing cards used, not—as is often thought—a reference to the Queen so often used in Monte games.

BRODIE

To give an unsuccessful performance; to flop.

Also, in fortune-teller's parlance, to make a strong and definite statement to the client based on the fortune teller's assessment and analysis of minimal clues.

Sometimes rendered as "To Take A Brodie." The term comes from the action of one Steve Brodie, who jumped off the Brooklyn Bridge and survived the fall.

BRODIEN, MARSHALL (b. ?)

Performer who specializes in TRADE SHOW work; also noted for his highly-successful mass-marketing of SVENGALI DECK and magic sets through television commercials.

BROKEN-AND-RESTORED OBJECT

A classic magic PLOT in which an object is apparently destroyed and then restored to its original condition. The most effective presentation uses a BORROWED OBJECT to eliminate the possibility of the performer simply showing a duplicate.

Rings and watches have been crushed, hammered and bent into pretzels in the service of illusion; the usual *denouement* for such effects, after causing the debris to vanish, is to discover the borrowed object in some seemingly inaccessible spot, such as the innermost of a NEST OF BOXES.

See also TORN-AND-RESTORED OBJECTs.

BROKEN WAND CEREMONY

A funeral ceremony for a magical performer, in the course of which a wand is broken over the casket. It was created by members of the S.A.M. on the occasion of HOUDINI's death in 1926.

''Broken Wand'' is also the title for obituary columns in the LINKING RING and M.U.M. magazines.

BROOKE, KEN (1920-1983)

Born in Britain, he began his career as a street pitchman, selling version of PIFF PAFF POOF, the DUTCH LOOPER, and a simple PULL. He later became the manager of HARRY STANLEY's Unique Magic Studio, his earlier experience making him a dynamic and highly successful demonstrator.

For many years he was a noted nightclub performer in the London area. Then, in 1965, he opened his own shop in London called Ken Brooke's Magic Place. It immediately achieved an international reputation for providing exclusive EFFECTS and thorough ROUTINES by some of magic's top names. These routines were widely copied and produced in un-authorized versions by others, including a major dealer who excused his thievery by saying that he had ''. . . to provide what his customers want . . .'' and who went so far as to photocopy the Brooke instructions with the originator's name whited out.

Partly due to this thievery, and partly because of health problems, Brooke turned the business over to partner Paul Stone in whose hands it continues.

A collection of his early routines and contributions to the GEN Magazine was published under the title of *Ken Brooke's Magic; The Unique Years*. More recent publications include *The Ken Brooke Series* (several manuscripts devoted to particular routines) *A Lifetime Of Joy* (a collection of tips and bits of business), and *Ken Brooke And Friends*, written by Derek Lever.

He was the recipient of a Special Fellowship from the ACADEMY OF MAGICAL ARTS.

BROOKS, HERBERT (1873-1923)

Born in Britain; performer who began his career in British variety, and then made a very successful tour of the U.S. He was noted for his excellent card magic, but is most famous for his invention of the BROOKS TRUNK. Featuring this EFFECT, Brooks made his seemingly impossible escape in only a few seconds. He became strongly identified with this effect, and successfully toured in vaudeville in the U.S., Britain, and Australia for many years.

BROOKS, HOWARD (1909-1984)

Performer with long professional career who performed throughout the world in varied venues. He appeared in films, and also performed at private parties. In addition to magic and comedy, he also performed as a silhouette cutter, and worked as a pitchman.

He is noted as the inventor of the BRASSIERE TRICK.

BROOKS TRUNK

An ESCAPE trunk designed by HERBERT BROOKS which could be carefully examined by a committee, after which the performer was locked inside it. A canvas cover was laced tightly around the trunk, yet the performer was able to quickly escape.

It has also been used by agile performers in the METAMORPHOSIS illusion.

BROOM SUSPENSION

See SUSPENSION.

BROWN, BOB (b. 1921)

Highly successful insurance salesman by profession (he has for over a decade been a member of the Million Dollar Club, restricted to those who sell over $1,000,000 worth of insurance annually). As a magician Brown has performed in nearly every major city in the world, and has been featured at numerous magic conventions in the U.S., Britain, Europe, and Japan.

Bob Brown and Brenda, here pictured doing their noted levitation, which requires no stage preparation.

He is noted for his businesslike approach to obtaining bookings, which includes what may be the largest press kit ever issued by an individual magician. Brown is also famous for his performance of the **Ultimate Levitation**, a SUSPENSION which requires no stage rigging whatsoever and may be performed under almost any conditions.

He is the author of *The Entertainmentalist* and *Six Hundred And Sixty Six Science Tricks*.

BROWN, EDWARD G. (1893-1947)

British bank manager and expert amateur magician who was particularly noted for his work with cards and his thoughtful and methodical approach to both presentation and method.

His card work is described in TREVOR HALL's *The Card Magic Of Edward G. Brown*; several of his other routines are described in WILLANE's *Methods For Miracles*.

BROWN, JONATHAN NEAL (b. ?)

Performer who has appeared in many venues in the U.S. and around the world; his fast-moving revue act with wife/partner Liane has been seen in Las Vegas and Atlantic City, and tours have included Japan and Australia.

He is a winner of the Stage Magician Of The Year award presented by the ACADEMY OF MAGICAL ARTS.

BRUSH, BAFFLES (?-1949)

Born Charles R. Brush, he was a noted amateur magician and columnist for both the SPHINX and

Jonathan Neal Brown and Liane

LINKING RING magazines, and contributed articles to a number of other publications.

BRUSH, EDWIN (1874-1967)

Performer who toured throughout the U.S. for many years on the LYCEUM and CHAUTAUQUA circuits in which he was one of the highest-paid acts. Most often he performed in the costume of an old-fashioned professor—knee-breeches, pumps and formal coat.

BUCHINGER, MATTHEW (1674-ca. 1740)

Born in Germany and known as the Little Man of Nuremberg, he was not only an excellent magician who featured a brilliant performance of the CUPS AND BALLS, but also an accomplished musician on several instruments and a master calligrapher and artist. His incredible breadth of accomplishment is even more remarkable when it is considered that he was born without hands or legs.

Buchinger's life and accomplishments are thoroughly described in RICKY JAY's *Learned Pigs And Fireproof Women.*

BUCKINGHAM, GEOFFREY (b. ?)

British magician noted for his brilliant pure SLEIGHT-OF-HAND act with BILLIARD BALLs, coins, and thimbles. He was a winner of the FISM's highest award, the Grand Prix.

Buckingham wrote a book describing his act in detail; the book was titled *It's Easier Than You Think*—but since few have followed in his footsteps, perhaps it isn't!

The Buckingham book was later republished in a three-volume softcover version containing additional material.

BUCKLE COUNT

A method of doing the FALSE COUNT with cards, used in a wide range of effects. The cards are taken one at a time from the left hand into the right; when there are, say, four cards remaining in the left hand, the left fingers buckle the bottom card downward. This enables the right fingers to take the three cards above it as a squared group with the appearance of a single card.

In doing this count the performer should display the cards full face or back to the audience, rather than showing the edges, so as not to betray the thickness of the multiple-card packet.

Geoffrey Buckingham performing the *Springing The Cards* flourish (*photo courtesy GENII Magazine*)

BUCKLE SPREAD

A display of a small PACKET of cards by fanning between the hands, in which the buckle is used to keep two or more cards squared as one. In the Multiple Buckle Spread technique of ED MARLO, this technique can be used when the cards to be concealed are in positions other than those required by the standard Buckle technique; this procedure is described in Marlo's *The Cardician.*

BUCKLEY, ARTHUR (1890-1953)

Born in Australia; noted for his SLEIGHT-OF-HAND act which featured BILLIARD BALL work and his approach to the MISER'S DREAM. Buckley toured professionally both with this act and with a TWO-PERSON MENTAL ACT presented with his wife, Helena. In the latter part of his life he became an executive working for a business firm in Chicago.

Buckley's work was described in his three books: *Card Control, Principles And Deceptions,* and (with JOHN BROWN COOK) *Gems Of Mental Magic.* It is worth noting that, while many readers of the first two books have felt the sleights were simply too difficult to perform, Buckley himself could perform them faultlessly and convincingly.

BUDDHA PAPERS

An ancient EFFECT, often used by magicians as a giveaway or "pitch" item, in which any small flat object placed in the paper (which is then folded closed) is seen to have vanished or changed into another object when the paper is unfolded.

Explained in many elementary conjuring texts, the secret lies in the use of two folded papers, glued back-to-back at their centers. A casual turnover of the folded packet so that the previously hidden packet may be opened accomplishes the feat.

BUDDHA TUBES

A variant of the ORGAN PIPES, this PRODUCTION device uses two wooden chimneys which are shown empty and then nested together; a production of various items is then made.

A feature of several models of this effect is a LOAD CHAMBER so designed (as a Chinese lantern, for example) that it can be produced as the final item.

BUDGERIGAR MAGIC

Generally refers to parakeets. *See* BIRD MAGIC; DOVE ACTS.

BUILD-UP

Term used to denote a type of STACK used in POKER DEALs and similar demonstrations, in which each deal not only produces a particular arrangement but also rearranges the cards for a succeeding deal.

Also called a **progressive build-up**.

BULLET CATCH

The catching of a marked bullet fired at the performer, usually from a rifle; the bullet is "caught" in the performer's teeth in most versions, though alternate targets have included the performer's hand, a china plate, a thin velvet cloth, and the point of a dagger.

Not surprisingly, it is known as the most dangerous trick in magic, and since its invention (probably in the 17th century, by a performer named Coullew) a number of magicians have been wounded, maimed or killed trying to perform it. It should be noted that such accidents and tragedies continue; no advances in technology are ever likely to make safe an effect in which a real bullet is fired from a real rifle at a human being. It should also be noted that HOUDINI, who performed many genuinely dangerous escapes without qualm, would not perform this effect (he had been advised against it by his friend HARRY KELLAR).

An excellent discussion of the bullet catch is contained in a book about its most famous victim—*The Riddle of Chung Ling Soo*, by WILL DEXTER. Routines and methods for this effect have been published by ORVILLE MEYER and JEAN HUGARD; both the Meyer and Hugard routines, and several others, will be found in *Twelve Have Died*, a book on this effect written by Ben Robinson with Larry White.

Experienced performers will know how to track down more precise references, and inexperienced performers are better off without it. (Indeed, the Hugard method had been worked out to make an accident or mishap all but impossible; yet Hugard was wounded during a performance of the routine.) *Caveat inventor.*

BURGER, EUGENE (b. 1939)

He began full-time professional performing in 1978, after a career as a teacher of philosophy and comparative religion. His first venture was a SEANCE-type presentation done for small groups in a private home, and later expanded for performance at the Playboy Clubs Resort Hotel and other venues.

Eugene Burger

Burger then began to specialize in CLOSE-UP MAGIC and was immediately successful, working in two exclusive restaurants in the Chicago area as well as many private engagements. He has also appeared at the MAGIC CASTLE several times; his lecture for the Castle membership has twice won him the Lecturer Of The Year award from the ACADEMY OF MAGICAL ARTS.

His highly regarded and clearly successful approach to close-up magic is presented in his books on the subject: *Secrets And Mysteries For The Close-Up Entertainer, Audience Involvement, Matt Schulien's Fabulous Card Discoveries, The Secret Of Restaurant Magic, Intimate Power, The Craft Of Magic and Other Writings* and *The Performance Of Close-up Magic.* He has also authored *Spirit Theater,* a book on seance presentations.

BURGESS, CLINTON (1880-1932)

Vaudeville performer, latterly collector, and writer. He is listed as "compiler" of HOUDINI's book on the collected magic of DR. JAMES WILLIAM ELLIOTT entitled *Elliott's Last Legacy,* but it is probable that most of the actual writing was done by Burgess.

BURLINGAME, H.J. (Hardin Jasper) (1852-1915)

Though for a brief time he essayed a career as a professional magician, specializing in society parties, Burlingame was most noted as a magic dealer and writer, at one time operating not only his own business but two others; one of these latter, specializing in APPARATUS and methods for stage mindreaders and fake MEDIUMS, was operated under the names of Ralph E. Sylvestre & Co.; the other, aimed at the general public, was operated as George L. Williams & Co. (These were undoubtedly the names of two Burlingame employees.)

Among the many books written by Burlingame were *Around The World With A Magician And Juggler; Hermann The Magician, His Life, His Secrets; Leaves from Conjurers' Scrap Books;* and *How To Read People's Minds.* He is also credited with compiling the first reasonably comprehensive bibliography of conjuring books, which he titled *Bibliotheca Magica.*

BURN

To observe closely; to keep under intense scrutiny. Example: "This SHIFT is so indetectable that you can do it with the spectators really *burning* your hands."

Possibly derived from gambling parlance.

Also, in many card games, to turn the top card face up and place it on the bottom of the deck prior to the deal.

BURNED ALIVE

See CREMATION.

BURNED-AND-RESTORED OBJECTS

A borrowed handkerchief or bill (currency) is burned and apparently destroyed; it is found in some seemingly inaccessible location in perfect condition. The handkerchief found in the NEST OF BOXES is one example; the BILL IN LEMON is another.

The *burned-and-restored bill* is a particularly popular feat, and there are dozens of routines to accomplish it in the magical literature. Of these the best known is that of ERIC WILLIAMS; it appeared originally in ABRA magazine and has been used extensively by TERRY SEABROOKE and many other comedy magicians.

See also BROKEN-AND-RESTORED OBJECTS; TORN-AND-RESTORED OBJECTS.

BURNING OF SHE

A once-popular title for the CREMATION ILLUSION, inspired by the H. Rider Haggard novel *She* in which Ayesha, the "She-Who-Must-Be-Obeyed," meets a fiery end.

BURTON, LANCE (b. 1960)

Performer who began his career in clubs and amusement parks near his native Louisville, Kentucky. He later moved to Los Angeles and appeared in MILT LARSEN's *It's Magic* stage show and at Hollywood's Body Shop nightclub. A television appearance on the *Johnny Carson* show led to repeat appearances; he has since moved to Las Vegas, and for many years has been a featured performer in the Tropicana Hotel's *Folies Bergère* show.

Specializing in DOVE MAGIC, Burton competed at the FISM Congress in Lausanne, Switzerland in 1982, and became the first U.S. performer to win the Grand Prix—its highest award. He is now considered by magicians and laypersons alike to be the preeminent performer of this type of act.

Burton continues to add new effects and illusions to his act, and has begun an acting career with appearances on television dramas.

BUSBY, JEFF (b. ?)

Magic dealer and writer of Oakland, California; noted for the thorough and sometimes controversial reviews of magic books and EFFECTs (written largely by himself) which appear in his house organ, *Epoptica.*

Lance Burton

BUTTERFLIES

Two small paper butterflies are torn from a sheet of tissue and float in lifelike fashion above a Japanese fan moved by the performer; though apparently a feat of pure skill rather than a mystery, it has often been performed by magicians.

Also known as the **Paper Butterflies** or the **Japanese Butterflies**.

BUTTERFLY

A very pretty visual effect created by KARL GERMAIN in which two silks are tied together and instantaneously change into a very large butterfly.

BUTT SHUFFLE

Identical in action to the FARO SHUFFLE, but without the necessity of a perfect alternation of cards from the two halves of the deck.

BUX, KUDA (?-1981)

Bux, a Pakistani, was best known for his X-RAY EYE act, in which he used a very complex blindfold consisting of bread dough, cotton pads, gauze and heavy

Kuda Bux (*photo courtesy GENII Magazine*)

Busby is also noted as the creator of a card routine called . . . **Into The Fourth Dimension**. A variation of the central effect of this routine, wherein a folded playing card seems to turn inside out, has been developed by ROY WALTON under the name of CARD WARP; it is one of the strongest and most popular effects in present-day card magic.

Busby's books include: *Back To Back, Shigeo Takagi's Coin Routine, The Epoptica Yearbook, Fred Braue On False Deals, Michael Skinner's Intimate Magic* and *Larry Jennings On Card And Coin Handling*.

BUSINESS

In stage performance, actions (and sometimes words) which, while not essential to the execution of an EFFECT or ROUTINE, serve to enhance the presentation.

BUSKER

Performer who works for gratuities in bars and saloons, theater queues, or wherever a crowd can be gathered; many magicians, notably MAX MALINI, have begun as buskers.

Derived from an earlier usage of the term meaning "to prowl or cruise about in search of gain."

See STREET MAGIC.

napkins—and for a series of "fire walks" he did in Great Britain and the U.S., but he also performed magic in his career.

Among his magical feats were the filling of several glasses with beer from a barrel drawn on a sketchboard, and a curious illusion (invented by a British magician named *Millington*) in which large tubes were pushed through a box containing two women.

Regarding his blindfold ROUTINE, it is interesting to note that while many magicians claimed to know its secret, to date it has never been exactly duplicated. Also of interest is the fact that in the last years of his life Bux suffered from failing vision—but was still able to do this "sightless vision" routine in his usual faultless manner.

BUZZSAW ILLUSION

A spectacular version of SAWING THROUGH A WOMAN invented by a man named Barbour, it was made famous by HORACE GOLDIN, and has been featured by many illusionists, notably HARRY BLACKSTONE SR., HARRY BLACKSTONE JR., ALDO RICHIARDI, and P.C. SORCAR.

Sorcar created a sensation performing this effect on British television; the show went off the air before the restoration of the woman, and the broadcasting company's switchboards were immediately jammed by viewers wanting to know if she was all right.

BYFORD, ARCHIE (?-1963)

British inventor of diabolically clever magic, many items of which were marketed. He also performed as a magical host and master of ceremonies.

BYPLAY

Stage business and dialogue not integral to the specific EFFECT being performed. In many cases such byplay if not overdone, is a better vehicle for expressing the performer's stage personality than the effect itself.

CABINET OF PROTEUS

An ILLUSION invented by Thomas Tobin in which people appeared and disappeared from a large cabinet in mystifying fashion. It operated by means of an application of the MIRROR PRINCIPLE similar to that used in the SPHINX illusion.

CAESAR GIMMICK

See TARBELL GIMMICK.

CAGLIOSTRO, ALESSANDRO DI, COMTE (1743-95)

European adventurer and occultist who most likely bestowed his noble title on himself. He traveled widely, and is believed to have used conjuring techniques to convince patrons of his powers as an alchemist.

He is often and erroneously identified as Joseph Balsamo because of a tract against him promulgated by the Holy Office in Rome. This was Dumas's source for his story, a liberal adaptation of which became the highly entertaining *Black Magic*, a film in which ORSON WELLES played Cagliostro; the film displays Welles' talents as magician as well as actor.

CAGLIOSTRO'S SPECTACLES

While wearing a pair of magical spectacles, a spectator is able to find three chosen cards in a shuffled deck. The effect, invented by BRUCE ELLIOTT, was originally accomplished by a switch of the regular cards for a BLANK DECK after the selections had been made and before they were returned to the deck. Various refinements of the general methodology have been developed.

CAKE BAKED IN A HAT

See BAKING A CAKE IN A HAT.

CALCULATOR MAGIC

EFFECTs most often of the MATHEMATICAL MAGIC or MENTAL MAGIC categories, performed with the aid of a pocket calculator.

While in the case of some Mathematical Magic effects the calculator can speed up the process and make it more interesting, their use in Mental Magic is more limited. This is because the calculator is a device not well understood in any technical sense by a layperson, thus it is under suspicion of having some special preparation to accomplish an effect.

Whether or not this is actually the case is irrelevant; when it *is* the case, as with some calculators prepared to produce a previously entered total to create a similar effect to the ADDITION SLATE, the result is not as convincing as with the less technological device of the **addition slate** or ADD-A-NUMBER pad.

Two interesting books on the subject of **calculator magic** are *The Conjurer's Calculator* and *The Circuited Sorcerer*, both by John C. Sherwood.

CALDWELL, MIKE (b. 1926)

Performer specializing in comedy magic who has appeared in nightclubs, hotels, conventions and many other venues throughout the U.S.. He also has done many television appearances, including *The Ed Sullivan* show.

Caldwell is famous for his "Caldwell Flip," a standing somersault that ends with Caldwell flat on his back.

John Calvert and Tammy (*photo courtesy GENII Magazine*)

CALVERT, JOHN (b. 1911)

Born Elburn Calvert, he created an elaborate and successful FULL-EVENING SHOW while still in his twenties. In the mid-1940s he established himself in a Hollywood film career; still later he produced another theater show, which, like the first, featured spectacular magic and equally spectacular women.

Calvert has traveled all over the world with his show, as pilot of a plane or skipper of his large yacht, *The Magic Castle;* he continues his adventures with a traveling magical extravaganza, featuring his wife and assistant *Tammy.* A highlight of this show is a large electric organ which levitates and floats out over the footlights, seemingly right into the audience.

A biography, *John Calvert,* has recently been written by William V. Rauscher.

CAMPBELL, LORING (1905-1979)

Born Alexander Loring Campbell; he began his career as a clown magician, later working in ORIENTAL STYLE. He then began working in CHAUTAUQUA and LYCEUM shows, working in hundreds of cities, towns and small villages throughout the U.S. By the time of his retirement in 1955, it is estimated he had given over 15,000 performances.

For many years he wrote a column for TOPS Magazine called "The Campbell Caravan"; he also wrote two books, *This Is Magic* and *Magic That Is Magic.*

He was the recipient of a Special Fellowship from the ACADEMY OF MAGICAL ARTS.

CANARY IN LIGHT BULB

A stage effect featured by HARRY BLACKSTONE SR. and HOWARD THURSTON, among others, in which a canary is "loaded into" a pistol which is fired at a floor lamp; instantly the lightbulb goes out and is seen to have something yellow within. When the bulb is removed from the lamp and broken, the canary emerges from within.

The effect is now rarely seen, perhaps because—contrary to the actuality—it appears to some that the bird is being mishandled. British magicienne June Merlin circumvented this problem by using a mouse, which is perceived as being less frail.

CANASTA, CHAN (b. 1921)

Born Chananel Mifelew in Poland, he came to prominence in the early 1950's with his highly individualistic style of MENTAL MAGIC, featuring DIVINATION effects with cards and a BOOK TEST. Canasta disavowed supernatural powers, saying his effects were achieved by psychological manipulation and analysis.

He made a number of appearances on British television, including his own series; he also appeared on a number of U.S. television talk/variety shows, and starred in his own network television special.

For many years he retired from the stage, achieving considerable success as a painter; recently, however, he has begun performing again, primarily in the service of various charities.

CANCEL

To perform an action which eliminates a method hypothesized by the audience to account for an effect.

In a performance of THE AMBITIOUS CARD, for example, spectators may suspect the existence of duplicate cards. The performer can cancel this suspicion by causing the selected card to REVERSE itself in the deck (by using the CENTER REVERSE or other method); to show this has happened, the deck is RIBBON SPREAD face-up on the table to show the single face-down card, which is then shown to be the selection. However, it also shows the faces of all the cards and thus establishes the absence of any duplicates.

As indicated by the above example, it is preferable that the canceling action be part of another procedure; to do it blatantly smacks of a "challenge" or "wise-guy" attitude which should be avoided.

The term was coined by DARYL.

CANDLE MAGIC

While candles are not the common household objects they once were, they are still quite often used in stage magic—partly because the audience recognizes the difficulty of conjuring with fire and flame, and partly because of the aesthetic appeal produced by candles in the appropriate setting and routine. Indeed, at least one pair of performers—the Gustafsons—do an entire act of candle magic. It is also featured in the act of LANCE BURTON.

The most often seen feat of candle magic is the **vanishing candle**. The MULTIPLYING CANDLES is also quite popular an effect; the original version, called the **nesto candles**, was invented by Earl Morgan and was a feature of his imaginative stage act. Other versions, differing in construction and technique of handling, are also available from magic dealers.

Much of the current interest in candle magic stems from the PRODUCTION candles marketed in the early 1960's by dealer James Rainho. A noted current manufacturer is FANTASIO, who specializes in magic with candles and walking sticks, and markets many of his creations; Fantasio's own professional stage act is an excellent advertisement for the effectiveness of the magic he sells.

Many commercially available items use candles; the **vanishing candle tube**, the **candle through Arm**, and the CHINESE FLAME CLOCK are only a few examples.

See also FIRE MAGIC.

CANDLE TUBE

See FIRECRACKER.

CANE, DANCING

See DANCING CANE.

CANE CABINET

An ILLUSION invented by P. T. SELBIT; a variation of the SWORD BOX, in which numerous canes are thrust through a cabinet after a female assistant has been placed inside. When the canes are removed, the assistant emerges unharmed.

In one version, with the canes still in place, a rope is lowered into the cabinet from above. When the rope is raised, it carries the assistant, who has apparently penetrated through the canes unharmed.

In a modern variant featured by DOUG HENNING, the cane cabinet is used in conjunction with a premise similar to the BACKSTAGE ILLUSION; the audience believes it sees Henning leave the cabinet and hide under a table, but when the canes are removed, he emerges from the cabinet.

In some presentations, the canes are pushed out by the performer or assistant inside rather than being removed by someone outside the cabinet.

CANE TO TABLE

A somewhat misleading title in that the cane does not transform into a table. Rather, when the cane is inverted, a small tripod drops out and locks in position; the performer's hat (which is fitted with a socket flange) is put on top of the cane to create a receptacle for the objects used by the performer.

This prop is used in all seriousness by many performers, and to excellent comic effect by JOHN THOMPSON.

CANNIBAL CARDS

A card effect in which Kings, representing cannibals, "eat" other cards—the cards are placed between the Kings and then vanish. In most versions, the vanished cards later reappear ("regurgitated") between the Kings in the deck.

The original plot was created and marketed by LIN SEARLES and achieved considerable popularity. Many subsequent variations have been devised and published.

CANNONBALL FROM HAT

At one time the PRODUCTION of a cannonball from a borrowed hat was a standard EFFECT. The cannonball was often hollow and hinged, and contained other production items. It is now rarely seen, partly because the few hats in fashion are not capacious enough, and partly because few people would recognize a cannonball.

A far more difficult feat along these lines is performed by JOHN THOMPSON as the closing effect in his Great Tomsoni & Co. act. From a few silk scarves he produces a very real (and very solid) *bowling ball!* A bowling ball production is also featured by DON ALAN.

CANNON ILLUSION

An ILLUSION invented (in varying versions) by WALTER CERRETTA JEANS and HORACE GOLDIN; a feature in the shows of half-a-century ago, it is still a favorite of many top performers. It is sometimes known as the *Triple Trunks*.

A female assistant is loaded into a cannon which is fired at a box hanging in the theatre's dome; the cannon is then shown empty. The box is lowered to the stage and opened, and a smaller box is found within; the process is repeated, and, from the third box, the same woman emerges. (Some performers will have the woman take a borrowed ring or watch with her on her mysterious flight, to prove that twins are not used—as indeed they are not.)

The woman vanishes from the cannon either by moving into a hidden compartment or by moving through a concealed tunnel and down through a TRAP in the stage. A number of methods exist to LOAD the assistant into the set of boxes after her secret removal from the cannon; some of these are quite similar to those used in the NEST OF BOXES, of which this effect is basically a larger version. The innermost box may be loaded upward through a stage trap (panels in the outer nest pivoting inward to permit this), or the assistant may move up into the boxes from a base or platform on which the set of boxes are momentarily placed.

The precise method used will vary with the performer's preference and the requirements of a particular venue.

CANTU (1896-1949)

Born Abraham J. Cantu in Mexico, he created a highly-regarded and influential act which featured DOVE MAGIC; it was the first successful commercial DOVE ACT.

Relocating to the U.S., he performed in theaters and nightclubs with considerable success for many years.

For a brief time he billed himself as "Professor Tucan."

CAP AND PENCE

British term for the STACK OF QUARTERS. A very old effect, described in *Hocus Pocus Junior* (1634), and countless later sources.

CAPPER

Term used to denote a sensational, or "punch" finish or climax to a routine, usually in the sense of an additional effect suddenly produced when the audience thinks the effect or routine has been completed.

Also, carnival slang for a "shill" or CONFEDERATE.

CARD AT NUMBER

A classic plot in card magic, in which a freely named card is found at a freely named number (position from the top of the deck). Ideally, the dealing and counting is done by the spectator.

There are a number of methods in print for achieving this effect, each with its own advantages and drawbacks. An early version is described in the *Nikola Card System* manuscript, reprinted in full in HUGARD and BRAUE's *Encyclopedia Of Card Tricks*.

CARD BOX

A small box (sometimes designed to look like a calling-card holder or cigarette case) which will produce, vanish, or switch a playing card.

Card boxes have been made in many models. Some use a loose flap which matches the interior top and bottom of the box and which can fall to conceal one card while revealing another previously hidden.

Others, called **locking card boxes**, have some means to hold the flap in place so that the box may be freely handled by spectators. Methods to accomplish this include magnets, clamps, and spring-loaded catches built into the walls of the box.

One model, manufactured by ROTERBERG and now rarely seen, had a tray hinged to the lid; when opened, this tray appeared to be the interior of the box proper, but, when the box was closed, the tray would lock up against the lid, and the box could then be looked over by a spectator with perfect safety.

The box has often been used in the CARD IN CIGARETTE routine, with tobacco appearing in place of a torn card. As with most such switching devices, however, it is best used in a more subtle manner, *secretly* to switch an item; for example, a card which has not been shown to the audience, thus executing a FORCE.

CARD CASE, SHRINKING

After the performer has extracted from it an ordinary and complete poker-size deck of cards, the card case is made to shrink to half its size, and will now accommodate only a Patience-size or other miniature card deck.

Versions of this effect have been developed by PETER KANE (Great Britain) and JOHN CORNELIUS (U.S.).

CARD CASE, VANISHING

In this effective OPENER for a card routine, invented by MILBOURNE CHRISTOPHER, the performer removes the deck from its case, and the case immediately vanishes. This is accomplished by means of a FAKE made from the back and flap of a card case to which has been glued a card from the deck.

The fake must be skilfully handled to create a convincing illusion of a complete card case; after the flap has been "opened" and the deck removed, the flap is bent back behind the attached card as the deck is fanned. The fingers of the hand holding the deck clip the fake against it; the case is shown to have vanished from the other hand, and the deck can be turned face-up and spread, the fake appearing as an ordinary card.

Later versions of this effect have been created by Canadian performer *Allan Lambie* and TOMMY WONDER.

CARD CASTLE

A deck of cards is spread on a tray, and under cover of a handkerchief is transformed into a multiple-tiered castle of cards. The effect was invented by LOUIS NIKOLA.

Though it can be visually appealing, the card castle is so obviously flimsy and collapsible that the mystery value of its appearance is negligible. It can, however, sometimes be effective as an element in a routine.

CARD DROPPER

A device which, pinned under the performer's coat, will secretly deliver any number of cards, from a few to a full deck, into the performer's hand.

CARD DUCK

Invented by L. L. IRELAND, this is an APPARATUS card effect originally marketed as **Otto the Duck** and now often known as **Joanne the Duck**; it consists of an angular wooden duck with movable neck and head, affixed to a wood or metal slat which also has a card holder (here called a "feed trough") at its forward end.

Cards having been selected and returned to the deck, it is placed in the holder. At the performer's command, the duck darts its head down to the "feed trough" and extracts one of the chosen cards. This is repeated with the other selections. Performed with ALPHABET CARDS or pictorial cards, this can be effective in shows for children. The card duck is a comedy effect rather than a magical one, and this distinction should be kept in mind.

In Britain a similar effect, invented by JACK HUGHES, is known as the **Dippy Duck.**

CARD FANNING

The spreading of cards into circular fan-like displays. Decks used for this FLOURISH have special varicolored back designs to enhance the visual impact of the fan.

Cards are usually fanned from left to right (clockwise), so that the indices will show. A right-to-left fan is called a **reverse fan** or **blank fan**, the latter term stemming from the fact that the indices are not visible and the cards appear blank. Often a blank-faced card is added to the face of the deck to further this impression.

A fan created by interweaving two halves of the pack with a FARO SHUFFLE (the cards being interlaced for only a small portion of their length) is called a **jumbo fan** or a **two-tiered fan**.

Decks used for flourish fans must be in good condition, and are usually treated with FANNING POWDER. Decks not so prepared can be fanned by means of a PRESSURE FAN; here the cards are held in one hand and fanned by the other. The fanning hand bends the cards and allows them to escape one-by-one as the fan is formed, resulting in a neat and even fan.

A book devoted entirely to this subject is Goodlette Dodson's *Exhibition Card Fans*. The subject is also dealt with in GANSON's *Expert Manipulation Of Playing Cards*, in a chapter in HILLIARD's *Greater Magic*, and many other places.

The **pressure fan** is described in HUGARD and BRAUE's *Expert Card Technique.*

CARD FAN PRODUCTIONS

See BACK PALM.

CARD FOUNTAIN

In this spectacular effect invented by BUATIER DE KOLTA, cards in a HOULETTE or glass suddenly shoot up and out in a continuous streaming cascade until the container is completely empty. The effect is often used to conclude a RISING CARD routine.

The effect can be accomplished by a thread hookup in which the thread is fed alternately under cards at front and back as the deck is assembled. The thread must be pulled from above, which limits this method to venues allowing for the necessary rigging. The rigging for the thread is described in the TARBELL COURSE (Vol. 2).

An alternate method, mentioned in *McComb's Magic* by BILLY MCCOMB, is to bring the rear of the deck into contact with a rapidly spinning rubberized wheel, brought up secretly behind the container—which, of course, must have an opening to allow the wheel to touch the deck. Other magical principles may be employed to render the mechanism invisible from the audience's point of view.

CARD FRAME

A small picture frame which, having been shown empty, is covered with a handkerchief; when the covering is later removed, a chosen card appears in the frame. This is accomplished by the secret removal under the handkerchief of a masking cloth which covers the card and which matches the backing of the frame.

The **sand frame** uses, instead of a cloth, a thin layer of sand which lies between two thicknesses of the glass; when the frame is inverted, the sand flows quickly into a secret receptacle in one end of the frame.

The **television card frame** consists of two sheets of glass which have been rubber-banded together and placed in a holder, whereupon the card visibly appears between them. A spring device propels the card from a hidden compartment in the holder. In a variant of this effect the two rubber-banded glass sheets are held between the hands; here the card is propelled from a special GIMMICK which is concealed in one hand.

There have been various versions of a card frame in which the card appears piece by piece, accomplished by the sequential withdrawal of thin black metal shutters into the border of the frame; one such model, marketed by RICHARD HIMBER, was called the **Fifth Dimension Card Frame**. The original version of this frame was invented by THEO BAMBERG.

CARDICIAN

A term coined by ED MARLO to denote a magician specializing in feats of card magic. It stems from the title of a book on this subject written in 1953 by Marlo: *The Cardician.*

CARD IN BALLOON

A small stand has a base on which a deck of cards may be placed, and a square metal column surmounted by two wire rings which hold an inflated balloon. At the performer's command, the balloon bursts and a previously chosen card appears in its place.

The original APPARATUS may have been invented by CLAUDE CHANDLER. In some versions, a duplicate card is used, while others (such as that designed by Hathaway (John Hathaway Butler) allow the actual signed card to appear. Later variations include apparatus and non-apparatus versions of a comedy routine (versions invented by JACK HUGHES,

Warren Stephens, and RUSSELL SWANN and MILBOURNE CHRISTOPHER) in which three balloons are used—in the most popular current routine, one deflating, another "escaping" before the final revelation; there are also a number of SLEIGHT-OF-HAND versions.

In a rarely seen variant of this general effect, a chosen card is made to visibly appear inside an *inflated* balloon; a spectator has to burst the balloon to remove the card.

CARD IN CIGARETTE

A classic card effect in which a chosen card is torn into several pieces, one of which is retained by the spectator who chose the card. The other pieces are wrapped in a handkerchief, placed in an envelope, or put in a CARD BOX.

The performer borrows a cigarette but has difficulty in smoking it. On breaking it open, he finds the chosen card, restored except for the piece held by the spectator—which fits perfectly! On examining the torn pieces, it is seen that they have vanished, leaving a small pile of cigarette tobacco.

The basic plot has spawned many variations, including versions of the routine in which the card is signed by the spectator; where the pieces change *visibly* into the tobacco in the performer's hands; where a cigar is eventually found to contain the card; and so on.

Though often done as a close-up or parlor effect, the routine can be performed for larger groups; FRED KEATING made it a feature of his stage act.

A simple version is described in HENRY HAY's *The Amateur Magician's Handbook;* many other routines are in print, including BILLY MCCOMB's strong version (described in his *McComb's Magic*) in which a thought-of card appears within the cigarette. An excellent routine in which the card is found in a cellophane-sealed cigar will be found in MIKE CAVENEY's *Magicomedy.*

CARD INDEX

A miniature card file, with projecting tabs, into which a deck of cards may be placed. (Usually two indexes are employed, each containing a half-deck.) With the index in the performer's pocket, he can produce any card named. (*See also* CARDS FROM THE POCKETS.)

A more subtle use is to secretly obtain a duplicate of a freely-chosen card which the performer PALMs while the deck is being shuffled by a spectator. Thus the performer may add this card to the deck and produce it in any manner he desires.

The ultimate performance using this principle was unquestionably that of ARTHUR LLOYD.

An interesting collection of effects made possible by this device is Max Andrews' *Sixteen Card Index Gems.*

CARDINI (1894-1973)

Born Richard Valentine Pitchford in Wales, he performed under various names—Valentine, Val Raymond, Professor Thomas—before achieving worldwide fame as "Cardini."

His pantomime act, in which he played the part of an elegant but slightly inebriated gentleman plagued by the mysterious appearance and disappearance of cards, billiard balls and other objects, was artistry of a very high level; with it, he was able to perform in many nightclubs and theaters which had never previously booked a magician. Cardini was paid the dubious compliment of having a great number of imitators, few of whom achieved any lasting fame on their own. Cardini was also known among magicians as a skilled craftsman; REELS made by him are highly prized as collector's items.

CARDOGRAPHY

A small piece of photographic paper is shown blank and initialed by a spectator. When later examined, it bears a photograph of a selected card.

The performer must FORCE the card, and the blank paper is SWITCHed for one bearing the card's photo; this is done prior to the initialing of the paper. There are many methods of accomplishing this switch; a popular one for many years used two half-dollar coins between which the paper was placed. The upper coin was momentarily lifted for the initialing; this action removed a SHELL from the lower coin, revealing the photo paper, while the blank paper was taken away with the shell and upper coin. Many other methods have been used, ranging from SLEIGHT-OF-HAND to various types of switching devices.

Two elaborate commercially marketed routines of this type are **Z-Ray** (created by Frank Kelly), and **Spirit Cartography** (invented by S. LEO HOROWITZ). In the Z-Ray routine, the spectator holds the chosen card between the hands; when the paper is removed from the Z-Ray box (actually a type of CARD BOX) it bears not only the image of the card but also an X-ray image of the spectator's hands.

The Horowitz routine uses a special wallet containing a clear window into which a white card is inserted, which the spectator is then allowed to initial on both sides—yet an image of the selected card appears on the card. This general type of effect is also sometimes known as **Cartography**—which should not be confused with the term meaning mapmaking.

CARD ON THE CEILING

A chosen card having been signed and returned to the deck, the performer suddenly tosses the deck up to the ceiling; the cards shower down—except for the chosen card, which remains stuck to the ceiling.

In some versions of the EFFECT there is no explanation as to why the card clings; in others, a thumbtack is apparently dropped into the center of the pack, and what appears to be this same tack secures the card to the ceiling.

Of necessity, the effect is usually the final one in a card routine, and serves this purpose admirably. There are many ROUTINES for it in print; one of the best is described in BRUCE ELLIOTT's *Classic Secrets Of Magic.*

CARD PUZZLE

A little-seen but intriguing card EFFECT invented by DAI VERNON (inspired by an earlier effect by CHARLES T. JORDAN); in it, sixteen cards are used—the Ace, King, Queen and Jack of the four suits.

The cards are dealt into four piles, segregated by suit and then a number of simultaneous transpositions occur to make each pile consist of cards of like *value*—i.e., the pile that held the Ace, King, Queen and Jack of Hearts now holds the four Aces; the pile that held the Clubs now holds the Kings.

A few different versions of the effect have been published, including RALPH W. HULL's **Intelligence Quotient Test** in *The Testament of Ralph W. Hull* and E.G. BROWN's improved version in *The Card Magic Of Edward G. Brown*, both books by TREVOR HALL; George Kaplan's "Royal Assembly" in his *The Fine Art Of Magic*; ROBERT PARRISH's "Quadruple Sympathy" in ALTON SHARPE's *Expert Card Conjuring*; S. LEO HOROWITZ's version, published in the PALLBEARER'S REVIEW; and by ED MARLO in *The Card Puzzle*, written by Marlo and JON RACHERBAUMER.

An interesting technical analysis of the above approaches, and additional material, can be found in JUSTIN BRANCH's book *Multiple Assemblies.*

Marlo makes the excellent point that, notwithstanding the title sometimes given to the effect, it should never be presented as an I.Q. test, but rather as a memory/observation test.

CARDS ACROSS

A major theme in PLATFORM and stage card magic, this plot involves the invisible passage of a number of cards from one packet to another, both packets being held by spectators.

There are many ways of accomplishing the effect, most by SLEIGHT-OF-HAND, a few by mechanical contrivances. Routines will be found in HUGARD's *Encyclopedia Of Card Tricks*, *Royal Road To Card Magic*, and *Modern Magic Manual*; also in HAY's *Amateur Magician's Handbook* and GIBSON's *Complete Illustrated Book Of Card Magic*.

Several versions cause *selected* cards to make the invisible journey; one of the best such versions is that of Michael Zens, and it is described in J. G. THOMPSON JR.'s *My Best*.

In a refinement of this, a few routines provide for the cards being *mentally* selected by various spectators. The classic routine of this type is DAVID DEVANT's *The Triangle*, which is described in JOHN NEVIL MASKELYNE & DAVID DEVANT's *Our Magic*. Other versions of this kind have been invented by E. G. BROWN and DAI VERNON. The Vernon routine, **Penetration Of Thought**, has in turn inspired many further variations.

CARDS AND PELLETS

An effect invented by AL BAKER in which cards are selected by spectators and their identities noted down on slips of paper. Holding each folded slip in turn, the performer is able to name the three cards.

Since the original Baker routine, many variations have been published; these are thoroughly described in a treatise on the subject by J.G. THOMPSON, JR., which appeared in the PALLBEARER'S REVIEW and was later reprinted in Thompson's *The Miracle Makers*.

CARDS FROM THE POCKETS

A shuffled deck having been divided into two halves and each half having been placed in one of the performer's front trouser pockets, he is able to instantly remove and show any card called for.

This is accomplished by means of a duplicate deck which has been placed into a CARD INDEX, a miniature file with tabs which will fit in the pocket. By touch alone the performer can find the correct card and extract it.

CARD SILK

A silk, usually 18 inches square, on which is depicted a playing card; most often used as a comedy revelation of a selected card after repeated "failures," the performer mopping his brow with the silk before opening it to show the picture of the selected card. This item was introduced by HARRY LEAT, but was also claimed by LEWIS DAVENPORT.

CARDS UP THE SLEEVE

A classic effect of card magic in which cards vanish singly from a PACKET held in the hand and apparently pass up the sleeve to the shoulder, where they are extracted from beneath the arm.

There have been many versions of the effect in print; an early version is described in C. LANG NEIL's *The Modern Conjurer*. One of the most technically sophisticated versions is that of DR. JACOB DALEY; it will be found in *Stars Of Magic*.

This effect is often confused with the CARDS TO POCKET.

CARD STAB

A dramatic way of revealing selected cards by locating them with a knife or dagger. This EFFECT can be performed in three basic ways:

1. The deck is wrapped in a sheet of paper and the knife inserted into the package from one side to the other; the deck being unwrapped, it is seen that the knife is next to the selected card (if two cards have been selected the knife is found *between* them). This version was a favorite of NATE LEIPZIG.

2. The deck is spread out over a table so that the backs of all the cards are exposed. The performer (usually blindfolded) stabs one of the cards; the impaled card proves to be the selection. MAX MALINI and DOUGLAS DEXTER used this general approach.

3. The performer plunges the knife into the squared pack as it rests on the table. When the knife is lifted up, the face card of the impaled portion of the deck is seen to be the selected card. One version of this presentation was created and performed by JACK AVIS.

Variations on the basic effect include stabbing any card named or stabbing a card merely thought of; using darts or arrows rather than knives; locating several selected cards in this manner; and so forth.

Routines for the card stab appear in nearly every book on general card magic. An entire chapter is devoted to this subject in Volume 3 of the **Tarbell Course In Magic**.

A stage routine using this plot is that of the CARD SWORD.

CARD STAR

A device usually in the shape of a wooden or metal five-pointed star; on these points appear visibly five previously chosen cards. The cards are concealed at the rear of the star and, a release being activated, jump out to the points by means of hidden springs or elastic cords.

CARDS TO POCKET

Cards travel one-by-one from a PACKET in the performer's hand to the trouser pocket; the EFFECT is similar to that of the **cards up the sleeve** with which it is often confused.

An excellent version will be found in HAY's *Amateur Magician's Handbook* (it is, however, given the "cards up the sleeve" title).

A marketed version invented by U. F. GRANT employs ingeniously-prepared cards from a JUMBO DECK.

CARD SWORD

A sword which apparently impales from one to three previously selected cards; this is done as the performer springs the deck of cards into the air and thrusts the sword into the falling cards.

See also CARD STAB.

CARD THROUGH HANDKERCHIEF

An old but still popular effect in which a deck of cards is wrapped in a handkerchief which is then held in bag-fashion; as the handkerchief is shaken, a previously chosen card seems to penetrate through the cloth and drop out the bottom of the "bag."

In some versions of the effect the deck is placed in its case before being wrapped in the handkerchief. A method for this version is described in *Blackstone's Modern Card Tricks* by WALTER B. GIBSON; another description of this same routine is in Greer Marechal's *The Complete Magician*.

Among the many other sources are ERDNASE's *Expert At The Card Table*, HUGARD's *Modern Magic Manual* and *Encyclopedia Of Card Tricks*.

CARD THROWING

The hurling of standard playing cards, for speed, distance, accuracy, or a combination of these. It was a popular feat with magicians of the past (and was featured by HOWARD THURSTON); many performers threw out specially-printed souvenir cards.

Undoubtedly the greatest present-day exponent of card throwing is RICKY JAY, who was also the first to be credited with the record for distance throwing in the *Guinness Book Of World Records*; his current record distance throw is 190 feet, 6 inches. Mr. Jay has described his card throwing techniques in his book *Cards As Weapons.*

CARD TO WALLET

A spectator's chosen card (usually signed for identification) vanishes from the deck and appears inside the performer's wallet.

There are many variations of this basic effect:

a. The card is found inside a zippered compartment of the wallet.

b. The card is found sealed in an envelope.

c. The card is found between steel plates which have been secured with rubber bands in every direction (a version created by BILLY O'CONNOR).

d. The card is found between two stapled pieces of thin cardboard. (In a version invented by JIM STEINMEYER, the card is found stapled inside an envelope—the staple going through the card and both sides of the envelope).

e. The card is found in a pocket of a smaller wallet inside the large one (as in the excellent version invented by TOM MULLICA).

There are literally dozens, if not hundreds, of methods and routines for this effect. It should be noted that most such routines use the wallet created by PAUL LE PAUL, or one of its later variations.

CARD TUNNEL

A term denoting a class of effects in which a card or cards, inserted crosswise in the center of the deck from the side, are made to change in some fashion by being pushed through the deck.

This change may be of identity; from a face-down to face-up condition; or another change in condition. Among those who have worked on this type of effect are NICK TROST, KEN KRENZEL and Howie Schwartzman.

Such effects may be indirectly inspired by the **Magic Tunnel** effect of S. LEO HOROWITZ, which will be found in HILLIARD's *Greater Magic.*

CARD WARP

A striking card effect in which a card folded along its length is pushed through a tunnel made by a card folded along its width. As the pushed card emerges, it has seemingly turned itself inside out—if the original fold has shown the back of the card, now the face is visible.

One of the most popular card tricks of the present day, **card warp** is the invention of ROY WALTON and is based on an earlier concept created by JEFF BUSBY.

CARGO NET ILLUSION

See DIZZY LIMIT.

CARLO, DR. (?-?)

Born Carlo Sommer; he performed in the Ohio area, and operated a magic shop in that state. He is noted as the inventor of **balls of fire** (production of fire-balls from a paper sack), the **Carlo glass production**, and the RUBBER DOVE.

CARLTON (b. ?)

Born Carlton Beck; performer specializing in spectacular ILLUSION magic who has appeared in the *Jubilee* show at Bally's Grand Hotel in Las Vegas and many other top venues. He co-starred with the PENDRAGONS in an edition of *Spellbound*, a FULL-EVENING SHOW which featured the two performers in a "Battle Of Magic."

CARLTON (1881-1942)

Born Arthur Philps in Britain; he began his career as a BUSKER, later performing in carnivals. He first achieved fame with his BOX ESCAPE when he won a case brought by JOHN NEVIL MASKELYNE (who felt Carlton was infringing on his version).

With his thin, tall form (accentuated by a makeup and headpiece which elongated his head), and a strange, high-pitched voice making humorous asides as he performed, Carlton became a major star of British variety. He also made highly successful tours of Europe, the United States, and elsewhere.

CARLYLE (b. 1906)

Born Lyle Laughlin, he performed throughout the U.S. in varied venues, including theaters, nightclubs, and hotels, and was noted for his highly sophisticated style of performance. He retired from full-time performing in 1954, but has made a number of appearances since then.

Within magic, he is noted as the inventor of the THREE-TO-ONE ROPES; he has also contributed effects to GENII magazine, Hugard's Magic Monthly (*See* JEAN HUGARD), and other publications.

CARLYLE, FRANCIS (1911-1975)

Born Francis Finneran, he became one of the world's greatest performers of CLOSE-UP MAGIC and was featured for many years at New York's exclusive Little Club and other elegant nightspots. Specializing in pure SLEIGHT-OF-HAND with cards and coins, he could make his onlookers believe they were seeing miracles.

His approach to magic is well indicated in his contributions to the *Stars Of Magic* volume; some useful information can also be found in Roger Pierre's *The Magic Of Francis Carlyle*.

CARMEN, VINCE (b. ?)

Illusionist who has toured throughout the world, including Spain, South America, New Zealand and Mexico; he has appeared on network television in eight countries. He has also appeared in Las Vegas at the Flamingo, and Reno at Harrah's.

He has toured as a featured performer with Circus Vargas, and with his own show, and also in TRADE SHOW appearances and acting work in film and theatre.

CARMO (1881-1944)

Born Henry Cameron in Australia, he worked as a minstrel, strong man and juggler before moving to Britain and becoming a magician. Though he performed in theaters, his major success was with his own circus; here he presented spectacular illusions. After the double catastrophes of a blizzard and a fire destroyed the circus, Carmo continued to perform in smaller venues and, during World War II, performed for soldiers in Britain and Europe.

Carlyle (Lyle Laughlin)

Vince Carmen

Charles Carter (*The Mulholland Library of Conjuring & the Allied Arts, Los Angeles, California*)

CARMO BEADS

An effect named for its inventor CARMO, in which beads cut loose from a necklace are magically re-strung. There are a number of methods for achieving this effect, several of which have been given the above title; properly, however, it should denote only the Carmo version—in which the beads are threaded on a single cord and never need to be re-strung.

See also ARABIAN BEADS.

CARNEY, JOHN (b. 1958)

Creator of a unique brand of visual comedy magic, he regularly tours the comedy clubs and other venues. Carney was recently named Close-Up Magician Of The Year by the MAGIC CASTLE.

Carney's approach to magic is described in his book *Carney Knowledge* and in his lecture notes titled *Conjuror's Journal*.

CARRER, CHARLES (?-1972)

Known to the public as one of the world's greatest jugglers, Carrer was known to magicians as a highly skilled builder of APPARATUS; he created nearly all of the PROPS used in the act of his wife DELL O'DELL.

CARTER, CHARLES (1874-1936)

Beginning his performing career while still a boy, he later worked in vaudeville for several years. Carter then created an elaborate FULL-EVENING SHOW with which he toured the world for many years, appearing in dozens of countries.

CARTOMANCY

DIVINATION or fortune-telling by means of playing cards or TAROT CARDS. The term is sometimes used loosely by magicians to denote magical effects with cards.

CASTRO, ERNEST (1905-1971)

British magician who specialized in entertaining children. In this field, he became quite successful, performing often for the families of royalty and the peerage.

CASUAL DATE

A performance engagement for one night only; also called (not surprisingly) a *one-nighter*.

CATO

In card magic, an acronym for "cut and turn over"—a procedure most often used with a small PACKET of cards; the packet is cut, the cut completed, and then the top card (or top pair of cards) is turned over.

The Cato procedure is often used in effects of a mathematical nature; it is the invention of BOB HUMMER, and many of his effects using this principle will be found in the card magic section of GARDNER's *Mathematics, Magic and Mystery*.

This acronym is occasionally rendered as "CATTO"—for "cut and turn two over."

CAULDRON, THE

An ILLUSION popular at the turn of the century, but rarely seen since that time; invented by CHUNG LING SOO. To begin the routine, a large cauldron is apparently filled with buckets of water and a fire lit beneath it. A lid is put on the cauldron; when it is removed the performer makes a large PRODUCTION of livestock and sometimes an ASSISTANT.

While, generally speaking, it was not very convincing, in Soo's presentation the illusion was quite effective.

CAVE

Term sometimes used to denote the performing area for a BLACK ART act.

CAVENEY, MIKE (b. 1950)

Performer who began his career with JOHNSON PRODUCTS, writing the firm's catalogs and instructions sheets; he also did some of the manufacturing work, and traveled to various conventions demonstrating the Johnson line of precision-made magical APPARATUS. During this time he became active as a performer, appearing in venues from Reno to New York City, from Canada and Britain to Japan. He also did considerable TRADE SHOW work.

Caveney is noted for his original approach to magic and comedy, and for his **linking coat hangers**, a routine based on the LINKING RINGS; other distinctive routines are his **three-handed juggling** and his presentation of the KNIFE THROUGH COAT.

After ending his ten-year stint with Johnson Products, he founded Magical Publications, which he operates with wife TINA LENERT. The company has published such books as *The Eric Lewis Trilogy* and *Martin's Miracles* by ERIC LEWIS, *Seabrooke's Book* by TERRY SEABROOKE, *Walter Jeans—Illusioneer* by PETER WARLOCK, and several others, including

Mike Caveney

Caveney's own *Magicomedy, Ideas*, and *The Great Leon: Vaudeville Headliner*.

Caveney is a member of Britain's Inner MAGIC CIRCLE.

CAZENEUVE, BERNARD MARIUS (1839-1913)

French performer noted for the many titles and honors bestowed upon him, and for his military exploits during the Franco-Prussian war. He specialized in SLEIGHT-OF-HAND with cards (at which he was considered expert) and also featured MENTAL MAGIC, the EGG BAG and the VANISHING BIRD CAGE.

CENTER CUT

With cards, a type of CUT in which the center portion of the deck is removed and placed on top.

Sometimes known in gambler's parlance as a **Scotch poke** or **Ginzburg poke**.

CENTER DEAL

To deal cards from the center of the deck while apparently dealing them off the top in the conventional manner.

The purpose behind this rarely used SLEIGHT is to

be able to bring desired cards to the top of the deck, offer the deck for cutting, and, after completing the cut, begin the deal without any necessity for a PASS or other method of nullifying the cut.

In any but the most expert hands, the center deal is of questionable use in card magic; it is generally better to do a good PASS and then deal the cards fairly than to use an extremely difficult sleight which is under continual scrutiny during the whole process of the dealing.

In a GAMBLING DEMONSTRATION a performance of the center deal can be impressive. It should be noted that there are several ways (FALSE CUTs, duplicate cards, etc.) of simulating the deal as part of a presentation.

CENTER REVERSE

A SLEIGHT which secretly turns a card face-up in the center of the deck without otherwise altering its position. It is believed to be the invention of ED MARLO, and is described in his book on the subject titled *Future Reverse*.

A description of this sleight is also available in ARTHUR BUCKLEY's *Card Control*.

CENTER-TEAR

A technique by which a folded slip of paper bearing a spectator's writing can be torn into small pieces and disposed of, the portion bearing the writing being secretly retained.

The basic technique is generally credited to MARTIN L. SUNSHINE. There have been many later variations and refinements, by AL BAKER, STANLEY JAKS, AL KORAN, ED MARLO, Richard Osterlind; also Bruce Bernstein, Tony Corinda, Al Mann, and T. A. Waters.

CENTER TEAR

Invented by NEIL FOSTER; a variation of the torn-and-restored newspaper (*see* TORN AND RESTORED OBJECTS) in which the center section of a folded newspaper sheet is torn away; this piece is torn into even smaller bits which are then dropped into the folded paper—which is immediately opened and shown to be completely restored.

In a version devised by ALI BONGO, the effect is immediately repeated several more times. This is best done in the context of comedy, and with some sort of final "payoff"; for example, a PRODUCTION of a bird or glass of liquid from the paper. (In some of Bongo's own performances, the repetitions are at the request of an audience heckler—actually a CONFEDERATE;

Scott Cervine

finally Bongo becomes exasperated at the offender and, producing a gun from the paper, shoots him!)

CERVINE, SCOTT (b. 1962)

Performer who began his career in a theatrical vaudeville production where, in addition to magic, he sang, danced, and juggled. He has appeared in a number of venues on the West Coast, and in Japan.

He has won numerous awards for his act, including Magic Entertainer Of The Year (two years in succession), Magic Olympics Gold Medal, and Achievement Award from the ACADEMY OF MAGICAL ARTS.

CERVON, BRUCE (b. 1941)

Born Andrew Bruce Cernava; highly successful close-up performer who has appeared in varied venues. He is a noted private party entertainer for Hollywood's elite, performing for dozens of leading entertainment, business, and political clients. He has appeared for Bob Hope, Sylvester Stallone, Sally Field, Milton Berle, Cary Grant, Dick Cavett, Woody Allen, James Stewart and many others. Cervon's television work in-

Bruce Cervon

cludes *The Tonight Show, Mike Douglas, Merv Griffin, That's Incredible*, and several other programs.

He has worked as a TECHNICAL ADVISOR for *One Flew Over The Cuckoo's Nest* and a series of Burger King commercials. He has also appeared as an expert consultant on gambling for the California court system.

Cervon has contributed numerous EFFECTS, ROUTINEs and SLEIGHTs to magazines, including GENII, PALLBEARER'S REVIEW, *Epilogue, Ibidem*, and others. His books include *The Real Work: Card Secrets Of Bruce Cervon, The Cervon Monte*, and *The Black Spot*.

He is a member of the Board of Directors of the ACADEMY OF MAGICAL ARTS. In past years he has won the Academy's Best Close-up Magician award twice, and also the Lecturer Of The Year award.

CHABERT, IVAN IVANITZ (1792-1859)

Born Julian Xavier Chabert in France, he performed as a fire-resister and magician throughout Europe, Britain and the U.S. In his later years he opened a drugstore in New York City where he purveyed elixirs of his own concoction.

He is discussed in RICKY JAY's *Learned Pigs And Fireproof Women*.

CHAIN ESCAPES

Escaping from a length of chain usually appears (and is) more difficult than a rope escape. The spectators know that a chain doesn't "give" and can't be cut or pulled loose as could a rope.

The **Siberian Chain Escape**, invented by P.T. SELBIT, was for many years a very popular version of this effect, and is still widely available; the chain, while specially made for this effect, is ungaffed, and any lock may be used, the secret being the way the performer is secured. The spectator must be clearly instructed in just how to chain the performer, and must follow these directions; this routine is not, therefore, recommended for the timid or uncertain performer.

In more elaborate chain escapes, where the spectators are free to secure the performer as they please, a faked lock may sometimes be introduced. When this is not possible, and the performer cannot gain a position from which he can pick the lock, the chain escape becomes a matter of endurance, technique, and sheer strength. Only a few performers have done this grueling feat on a regular basis, such as British **escapologist** ALAN ALAN; it currently is featured as part of an ILLUSION routine created by HANS MORETTI.

CHAIR SUSPENSION

See SUSPENSIONS.

CHALK TALK

Accompanied by appropriate (and usually humorous) dialogue, pictures are drawn on a blackboard; usually these are designed with some novel aspect, i.e., turning the drawing upside-down, or adding a few lines, transforms the picture into a new image. A dog-bone, for example, may become a dachsund.

Though not magic, this has been a featured specialty of many magicians, most notably HARLAN TARBELL. A series on the subject by Ed Harris is a long-running feature in the New TOPS Magazine; Harris has also authored several books on the subject. Another creator of this type of material was Harry C. Bjorklund, whose trick cartoons may well have inspired the "Droodles" of Roger Price.

CHANDLER, CLAUDE (?-1977)

British magician, ventriloquist, and actor noted both as performer and inventor. Named by DAVID DEVANT as his successor, Chandler played several times at ST. GEORGE'S HALL; he also appeared in theaters and music halls throughout the British Isles, and did a number of Royal Command performances. In addition to magic, he created many novelty ventriloquial routines, of which perhaps the most successful was billed as "On The Bust"—in which he played a tipsy gentleman who has a conversation with a statue—an act which became a favorite of music-hall audiences. He also often played the part of ABANAZAR in the *Aladdin* pantomime.

Chandler may have been the inventor of the still popular CARD IN BALLOON effect.

CHANG (1889-1972)

Born Juan Pablo Jesorum, this Chinese-Panamanian performer played in the U.S. and in many other parts of the world, achieving his greatest success in South America. His FULL-EVENING SHOW was spectacular and mysterious, reaping impressive rewards both artistically and financially.

CHANGEOVER PASS

A SLEIGHT which secretly transfers a PALMED object from one hand to the other. It is best performed as part of a visible movement, e.g., a ball held openly at the

Chang (*The Mulholland Library of Conjuring & the Allied Arts, Los Angeles, California*)

right fingertips is transferred to the left fingers, and as the hands come together for this purpose a ball hidden in the left palm is secretly transferred to the palm of the right hand.

CHANGING BAG

A UTILITY ITEM for producing, switching, or vanishing small items; in its original form the bag was affixed to a round frame which had a long handle. Turning this handle would move a cloth divider from one side of the bag to the other, thus effecting the exchange.

These bags were made in imitation of a then-common type of collection bag used in churches; since these are now rarely seen, modern versions of this device are often designed as simple drawstring bags, or to look like women's purses.

CHANGING TRAY

A tray, ordinary in appearance, which can exchange various small items. One model of this APPARATUS has a square or circular central section, deeper than the rest of the tray; this central section is actually one of two sliding compartments which can be brought into use by tilting the tray or moving a projecting stud.

Another type of changing tray has half its upper surface spring-loaded. If an article is placed on this section, pressure of the thumb will allow the article to slide into the tray's interior; at the same time a duplicate article will fall from a compartment at the end of the tray into the performer's hand.

The best design for this latter kind of tray is GEORGE ARMSTRONG's; it is described in the PHOENIX Magazine.

Still another kind of tray, best used by a performer working with an assistant, is simply double-sided, i.e., it looks the same no matter which side is up. The article to be switched is placed under the tray and held in position with the fingers; when the other article has been placed on the tray, it is held in position with the thumb, and the tray is simply turned over as the assistant returns to the stage. The assistant should be wary of holding the tray at revealing angles.

CHANIN, JACK (b. ?)

Magic dealer, inventor, and performer in ORIENTAL STYLE (variously as Chan-Jak and Chan-In. Many of the EFFECTS he marketed were original creations, Chanin's abilities as a performer/demonstrator enhancing their appeal. He was noted for his ability at SLEEVING, and wrote a book on the subject called *The Encyclopedia Of Sleeving*.

Other books by Chanin include *The Adventures Of Seven In One* (card routine), *J.C.'s Grand Finale* (silk production), and *Handle With Gloves* (coin manipulation).

CHAPEAUGRAPHY

Though not magic, this has been a feature of many magicians, and consists of folding a wide felt ring (somewhat like a sombrero with the crown removed) into a number of different hats and caps.

FELICIEN TREWEY made a reputation with chapeaugraphy over a century ago, calling it "Twenty-Five Heads Under One Hat"; it is still an effective routine for many present-day performers, and is currently featured by HARRY ANDERSON.

CHAPENDER, MARTIN (1876-1905)

Born Harold Jones, this British performer specialized in SLEIGHT-OF-HAND with coins, cards, and BILLIARD BALLS. He performed at a number of venues including EGYPTIAN HALL.

When Chapender died at the early age of thirty, THE MAGIC CIRCLE was formed in part as a memorial to him.

CHARLIER (?-?)

Believed to be a French amateur magician of the late 19th century who specialized in SLEIGHT-OF-HAND

Martin Chapender (*The Mulholland Library of Conjuring & the Allied Arts, Los Angeles, California*)

with cards. In the latter part of his life he may have been a busker, and he seems to have disappeared in 1884. Little is definitely known about him except for his invention of the CHARLIER PASS, a version of the FALSE SHUFFLE known as the CHARLIER SHUFFLE or *False Haymow Shuffle*, and a system of marking cards with pin-pricks.

Charlier is discussed by CHARLES BERTRAM in his book *Isn't It Wonderful?* and by WILL DEXTER in *This Is Magic*.

CHARLIER PASS

A one-handed CUT of the deck, invented by CHARLIER. Though it is most often used as a FLOURISH, it can in specific situations be secretly employed to bring about magical effects (sometimes in conjunction with a CRIMPed card, NARROW card, or some other types of KEY CARD).

It is described in HILLIARD's *Greater Magic*, HUGARD & BRAUE's *Expert Card Technique*, and many other places.

CHARLIER SHUFFLE

A FALSE SHUFFLE devised by CHARLIER, it is intended to imitate the action of the HAYMOW SHUFFLE.

The Charlier Shuffle is accomplished by pushing small PACKETS from the left to the right hand, as follows: a packet is pushed from the top of the deck into the right hand; a second packet is pushed from the *bottom* of the deck and placed on *top* of those in the right hand; a third packet, pushed from the *top* of the deck, is placed on the *bottom* of those in the right hand.

The procedure is continued, cards from the bottom of the deck to the top of those in the right hand, alternating with the opposite procedure, until the cards in the left hand are gone. This action apparently mixes the deck, but in fact has only the effect of a single completed cut; if a SHORT CARD or other KEY CARD has been placed on top of the deck at the outset, by simply cutting at this card and completing the cut, the deck is brought back to its original order.

This shuffle, with its casual, almost sloppy appearance, is ideal for those performers who do not wish to appear to be skilled card handlers.

CHARLIER SYSTEM

A method of marking playing cards by means of tiny pinholes which can be felt but not seen; said to have been invented by CHARLIER.

Modern versions of the Charlier system use tiny spots of clear glue in place of the pinholes. Marking can be done by a system of binary values (1-2-4-8) in an arc-like pattern; thus a sweep of the thumb across the card (held in dealing position) will reveal its identity.

The original Charlier system is thoroughly described in HOFFMANN's *More Magic.*

CHARLTON, CHRIS (1887-1963)

British magician who worked extensively in his own country and toured the world with great success, playing at the best theaters and other venues. His performing career lasted well over fifty years, and included a number of Royal Command performances.

He invented several effects and illusions, of which the best known is perhaps the BATHING MACHINE.

Charlton was also noted as a collector of magic books and magazines. His collection of periodicals, in particular, was one of the best in the world, and is now the property of the MAGIC CIRCLE.

CHARTS

In musician's parlance, sets of sheet music provided by the performer to the orchestra, providing both the music score and the necessary cues to integrate the music properly with the ACT.

While many performers (particularly those doing

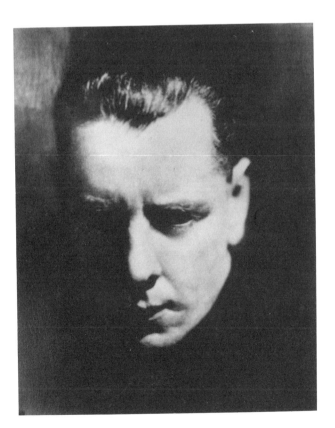

Chris Charlton (*The Mulholland Library of Conjuring & the Allied Arts,* Los Angeles, California)

PANTOMIME or SILENT ACTS) rely heavily on taped music, it is sometimes required that any necessary music be provided by the orchestra employed at the venue. In such situations, being able to provide the necessary charts (transposed from the act's music tape) is of major importance in presenting the most effective performance.

In Britain, charts are always known as "band parts."

CHASED

Usually rendered as *CHaSeD,* it is a mnemonic for a suit order of *C*lubs, *H*earts, *S*pades and *D*iamonds, used in many types of STACK.

See also SHOCKED.

CHAUTAUQUA

Originally begun as an educational service of lecturers who traveled from town to town throughout the U.S. on a "circuit" and spoke in large tents during the summer season; later in its development, a number of entertainers, including magicians, performed regularly on this tour.

The Chautauqua service began in 1874, and continued until the depression years. *See* LYCEUM.

CHAVEZ, BEN (?-1962)

Founder (with his wife MARIAN) of the CHAVEZ COLLEGE OF MAGIC.

CHAVEZ, MARIAN (?-1978)

Noted instructor of magic; with her husband Ben she founded the CHAVEZ COLLEGE OF MAGIC.

CHAVEZ COLLEGE OF MAGIC

Highly successful school founded by BEN CHAVEZ and MARIAN CHAVEZ; many top professional performers were graduates—including NORM NIELSEN, IRV WEINER and CHANNING POLLOCK).

The school continues operation as a private instruction/homestudy course under the direction of former students NEIL FOSTER and DALE SALWAK.

CHEATING THE GALLOWS

An ILLUSION (believed to have been invented by Britain's Stewart Lucien) in which the performer, on a gallows platform, is encased completely in a bag. A noose is then secured around the performer's neck. When the trap is sprung and drops open, the performer disappears, leaving only the empty bag to fall to the stage. In some versions, the bag also disappears. A version of this illusion using two nooses is currently featured by SIEGFRIED AND ROY.

Cheating the Gallows was also used as a title for an effect created by mentalist MAURICE FOGEL, in which he "influenced" a spectator to choose the one noose of five that would snap apart when Fogel, his neck through its loop, jumped off a chair beneath the gibbet.

CHECKER CABINET

A small (18-inch wide by 16-inch tall) cabinet has three doors fitted into its front wall; these are opened, and the cabinet is shown to have a stack of checkers in the central section. This stack is removed and covered by a cylinder; a glass containing rice is placed in the center of the cabinet. The two items transpose; the checkers are found back in the cabinet, the glass under the cylinder.

This effect was invented by THEO BAMBERG; a number of different versions have been made, with variations in the routine. The apparatus is often beautifully manufactured and decorated (particularly those sets made by Bamberg himself with the assistance of Don Redmon), but exceptional skill at presentation is required for effective performance of this feat.

CHEEK TO CHEEK

A card effect invented by ARTHUR FINDLEY (based on an earlier T. NELSON DOWNS effect called **Reverso**) in which half the deck is turned face-up and RIFFLE-SHUFFLED into the face-down half, which is then RIBBON-SPREAD on the table. While the performer's back is turned, a spectator turns any face-up card over to a face-down position.

Squaring the deck, the performer instantly spreads it to show the spectator's card is now the only face-up card in the deck.

The effect, marketed by U.F. GRANT (who gave it the present title) is still available, and relies on a MECHANICAL DECK utilizing the DOUBLE-BACK principle.

CHEFALO (1885-1963)

Born Ralfo Cefalo in Italy, he emigrated to the U.S. as a child. Chefalo developed an elaborate FULL-EVENING SHOW featuring ILLUSION (including one based on the principle used in the MILLION DOLLAR MYSTERY, the rights having been purchased from WALTER CERRETA JEANS), and

with it he successfully toured the world during a career that lasted well over fifty years.

Among magicians he is noted for the CHEFALO KNOT (although he claimed he had not invented it), the FLOATING TABLE, and for his remarkable stage routine with the LINKING RINGS.

CHEFALO KNOT

A fake rope knot erroneously attributed to CHEFALO, it consists of an open square knot which is further secured by having one end of the rope passed through both loops of the knot. In spite of this, when the ends are pulled the knot will vanish.

This knot is described in ABBOTT's *Encyclopedia of Rope Tricks*, edited by STEWART JAMES.

CHEMICAL MAGIC

At one time the use of chemicals in magical EFFECTS was quite popular. Perhaps the best known such effect was that of **wine and water**, where water poured into glasses assumed various colors and went through a sequence of bewildering changes.

With the exception of some pyrotechnic preparations and version of the **smoke vase** or similar effects (*see* SMOKE TRICK), few effects using chemicals are currently in use. There are three major reasons for this: the effect *looks* like a chemical effect (as with WINE AND WATER) it is known as such from school demonstrations; or it is simply not dependable enough to be used in a professional act.

An interesting book on the subject is *Modern Chemical Magic* by John D. Lippy, Jr.

CHEN LEE WATER SUSPENSION

A LIQUID EFFECT in which a metal tube is shown empty and unprepared, yet water poured in at the top does not come out the bottom. After a silk handkerchief and wand have been pushed through the tube, a glass is placed within; when the glass is removed, it holds the missing water.

The effect, created by U.F. GRANT, makes ingenious use of the SHELL principle. Many variations are possible, for example, the reproduced liquid may be wine instead of water.

An interesting presentation of this effect is featured in the historically themed act of MAX HOWARD.

CHERRY-COLORED CARD

A term used in PUMPING to discern the color of a selected card. The performer states that the spectator has chosen a cherry-colored card; if the answer is *yes* then the card is red, but if *no* the performer responds by saying, "Haven't you ever heard of black cherries?"

The theory behind this is that the performer's comments will be taken as a joke, the implication being that the performer knew the color all the time. In fact, the device is (to most laypersons) obvious and transparent, and calls attention to itself as a way of gaining information. It is, therefore, only advisable to use it as an *actual* joke—if at all—with the selected card clearly on display and the performer having apparently made a mistake.

CHESS PLAYER

A supposed mechanical automaton capable of playing chess, built in the 17th century by Baron Von Kempelen. It was actually controlled by a human player inside the chest behind which it sat. The technique for showing this chest empty was not unlike that later used in straightforward stage illusions.

See AUTOMATA.

CHIAROSCURO

A technique of painting a flat surface with effects of light and shadow to give the appearance of a three-dimensional object. Thus a disk may be made to appear as a ball, given convincing handling.

CHICAGO OPENER

A popular card EFFECT which begins with the selection of a card and its return to the deck, which is then shuffled. An odd-backed card is subsequently seen as the cards are spread face down; on examination this proves to be identical in suit and value to the previously selected card.

The odd-backed card is set aside and another card is selected; when the odd-backed card is turned face-up it is seen to have changed to now be identical to the new selection.

The effect, explained in many books on basic card magic, is usually credited to Frank Everhart.

CHICK PAN

Smaller version of the DOVE PAN.

CHILDREN'S MAGIC

A category of magic specifically designed and routined for performance for children. Many of the effects used are of the SUCKER EFFECTS category, to create loud and energetic audience participation in the party atmosphere peculiar to children's shows. Often effects will use characters known to the children from television and films, such as Muppet-like figures or beings from the *Star Wars* trilogy.

Except in performances for very young children, and/or in birthday party situations, many children's magic effects are neither necessary nor appropriate; indeed, many such effects seem structured simply to create a noisy response rather than to create a magical experience.

Most children of six years or older can appreciate "grownup magic" just as much as their elders, and are just as quick to be annoyed at the performer who talks—and performs—down to them.

Much information on children's shows will be found in the *Kid Stuff* series of books by FRANCES MARSHALL, and the works of DAVID GINN.

CHINATOWN QUARTER

A gaffed DOUBLE-FACE coin invented by KEN ALLEN, it can be shown either as a seemingly ordinary U.S. quarter or as a Chinese coin of the same diameter—but with a square hole in the center of the coin. This is accomplished by a clever application of the MASKING principle. Many intriguing routines are possible with this coin.

Similar coins have been made up using U.S. half-dollars and many other coins as their basis.

CHINESE COMPASS

A CLOSE-UP MAGIC effect using a small square or octagon of flat plastic with an arrow on either side; in the routine, the arrows appear to move around and change direction. The PROP is ungaffed and the deception is created by the handling and presentation.

A well-known stage version of the same basic EFFECT was created by MILBOURNE CHRISTOPHER, and is called HIGH SIGN.

CHINESE EGG BAG

Not actually a bag at all, but a folded mat into which an egg is placed; when the mat is allowed to drop open, the egg has apparently vanished. It may be reproduced and vanished as desired by the performer.

The mat is unfaked, but the egg has a small gut LOOP by which it may be suspended from the performer's thumb or finger, and can thus be hidden behind the mat while the hands are shown empty.

CHINESE FLAME CLOCK

A curious but effective APPARATUS invented by EDWARD O. MASSEY, which uses a small, chimney-style cabinet with three small doors at the front. The doors are opened to show a candle within, which is lit; the doors are closed and blades are inserted, dividing the cabinet into thirds. The cabinet doors are re-opened, showing that the central section of the candle has disappeared. The procedure is repeated and the whole and solid candle is removed from the cabinet.

CHINESE LAUNDRY TICKET

A popular version of the torn-and-restored paper effect (see TORN AND RESTORED OBJECT), this uses a long strip of paper decorated with Chinese characters.

CHINESE PRAYER VASE

A very old EFFECT using an opaque, narrow-necked bottle and a short length of rope. The rope is lowered into the bottle, but when the bottle is inverted the rope does not fall out; then the rope is grasped and the bottle is suspended from it and allowed to swing freely. To conclude, the rope is removed from the bottle and both items are handed for examination if the performer so desires.

There are a number of variations on the basic effect and method, some requiring GIMMICKS or FAKED materials. An excellent ROUTINE for this effect was created by Don White and may be found in HILLIARD's *Greater Magic*.

CHINESE SNOWSTORM

See WINTERTIME IN CHINA.

CHINESE STICKS

A cord apparently runs through holes at the ends of two sticks (or "wands"); it is cut between the sticks but continues to run through them as though nothing had occurred. After various other bits of business, the sticks are separated entirely; yet when the performer pulls down on the cord in one stick, the cord in the other stick goes up.

A variant of the earlier PILLARS OF SOLOMON (in which there were cords running through each end of a pair of sticks, and a similar cutting-and-restoring effect was produced), the **Chinese sticks** have been featured by many magicians. Methods have included threads, reels and sliding weights, and the PROP has been made in every size from a small pocket version to a huge stage model. Comedy versions of the effect, using *three* sticks, were great hits for ROY BENSON and FRED KEATING; it was later featured by FRED KAPS.

CHING LAU LAURO (?-?)

Performer in Germany and England for a decade beginning in 1828. Though his act was ORIENTAL STYLE and he performed as a Chinese, he is generally thought to have been an Occidental.

He is also believed to be the first performer to present a SUSPENSION in Europe as magical entertainment.

CHING LING FOO (1854-1922)

Born Chee Ling Qua in China, he became the first oriental magician to achieve an international reputation, which he established in numerous tours of Europe, Britain and the U.S.

He is noted in magic for the PRODUCTION of several unlikely objects (including bowls of water and small children) from a shawl; for his torn-and-restored paper ribbon (see TORN-AND-RESTORED OBJECT; well described in DAVID P. ABBOTT's *Book Of Mysteries*); for the probable invention of the FOO CAN; and as the reluctant inspiration for the career of CHUNG LING SOO.

CHINK-A-CHINK

A table effect in which four objects, arranged in a square and covered in turn by the hands, assemble under one hand. There are many routines for this effect; one of the best, created by S. LEO HOROWITZ, is described in *Stars Of Magic*.

The routine may be performed with balls, sugar cubes, dice, or such odd objects as bottle caps (AL GOSHMAN) or small sea shells (DOUG HENNING). In most (not all) versions, an extra object is needed, and this may be brought into play in any number of ways. In a commercially-marketed version, four truncated-cone-like objects are used, together with a SHELL which will fit over any of them.

See MATRIX ROUTINES; SYMPATHETIC ROUTINES.

CHINK CANS

An excellent (if unfortunately named) variant of the RICE BOWLS, this routine uses two decorated cans, one of which is filled with rice and placed mouth-to-mouth with the other can. The rice doubles in quantity. This excess rice having been removed, the can is wrapped in a sheet of paper, and the rice is then transformed to silks which are produced through a hole poked in the paper.

The routine is the invention of U.F. GRANT.

CHISLETT, THOMAS H. (1886-1979)

British amateur and writer who, with the assistance of correspondent DAVID P. ABBOTT, devised a ROUTINE of magic and spirit EFFECTs which he performed in his home for many years. His exceptional routine was described in his *Spirits in the House*; until the recent publication of *David P. Abbott's Book Of Mysteries*, by David P. Abbott, the Chislett work was the only existing record of many of Abbott's creations, including his famous FLOATING BALL routine.

CHOP CHOP (1901-1964)

Born Alvin H. Wheatley in Australia, he came to the U.S. as a child. His performing career lasted over four decades, and he toured throughout the world. In the early part of his career he performed in ORIENTAL STYLE as "Tung Pin Soo"; later, retaining the style, he changed his named to the more easily remembered "Chop Chop."

He appeared (with wife Charlene) in most of the top nightclubs in the U.S., including Chicago's Palmer House and New York's Latin Quarter; there were also a number of television appearances, among them the *Ed Sullivan Show*.

Chop Chop, an early photograph (*The Mulholland Library of Conjuring & the Allied Arts, Los Angeles, California*)

He is best known to magicians for his invention of the CHOP CUP.

CHOP CUP

Invented by Alvin H. Wheatley (CHOP CHOP) and popularized by DON ALAN, this well-liked effect is used for a one-cup-and-ball version of the CUPS AND BALLS. The cup contains a magnet which will attract one of the two balls used in the routine (the spectators are aware of only one ball). Thus that ball may be secretly retained within the cup; this, together with accomplished SLEIGHT-OF-HAND technique, make for an effective closeup ROUTINE.

Many routines for the Chop Cup are available; one of the most popular is that devised by LARRY JENNINGS. Several routines will be found in *The Chop Cup Book*, written by EARL NELSON and ALAN WAKELING.

CHOPPER

Term used to describe a class of illusions where a blade in a fixed frame is apparently passed through the neck of an assistant secured in a set of stocks.

See CHINESE CHOPPER; HEAD CHOPPER.

CHRIST, HENRY (1903-1972)

Inventor of many EFFECTS, ROUTINES and methods, primarily in the area of card magic. His best known effect is probably **Dead Man's Hand**, a dramatic card routine which appeared (as did other Christ creations) in THE JINX Magazine. He is also noted as the creator of the **Christ force** (also known as the **203rd force**), an exceptionally clean method of executing the FORCE of a card while the deck is in the spectator's hands; it will be found in THEODORE ANNEMANN's *Shh-h-h, It's A Secret*.

CHRISTIAN (b. 1945)

Born Christian Stelzel in Austria, he usually bills himself as "Magic Christian." He has performed throughout Europe and in many other countries around the world, including several appearances in the U.S.; while he performs in varied situations, he has become widely known for his work in TRADE SHOWS and INDUSTRIAL SHOWS throughout Europe.

In recent years he has worked with the Piatnik Card Company to produce an extensive product line of cards for magicians, including double face and DOUBLE-BACK cards as well as various MECHANICAL DECKS. He has won several awards in magic competitions. He also is known for his work in industrial and graphic design.

CHRISTOPHER, MILBOURNE (1914-1984)

Beginning his performing career in his teens, he received his first national publicity at the age of 21 when he performed at the White House for the Roosevelts. Later, specializing in nightclub work, he toured throughout the U.S. and Europe, and made several tours of South America. During World War II, he entertained military audiences, first with a USO show and then as serviceman himself, with a Special Services unit.

In the 1950's he created and starred in his own Broadway show, titled *Now You See It*; he also organized a television special called *The Festival Of Magic*, which featured magicians from several countries, with Christopher performing his version of the BULLET CATCH.

In 1961, he created another theater show, *Christopher's Wonders*, which played in New York and later toured Britain. He traveled widely in the course of his career, performing in over sixty countries.

In addition to acting as Editor for HUGARD's *Magic Monthly*, **M.U.M.** and *Magicol* (a journal for collectors of magic books and memorabilia), he wrote columns both as himself and as FRANK JOGLAR, and contributed effects and articles to many magic periodicals. He was particularly noted for his rope magic; STRETCHING A ROPE, one of his originations, has become a standard effect.

His books for magicians include *Conjuring With Christopher, Fifty Tricks With A Thumb Tip, One Man Mental Magic, Magic From M.U.M., Varied Deceptions,* and others. Christopher also wrote a number of books intended for lay audiences, describing the history and techniques of magic: *Panorama Of Magic, Milbourne Christopher's Magic Book, The Illustrated History Of Magic, Houdini: The Untold Story* and *Houdini: A Pictorial Life.* Christopher had a keen interest in psychic research, parapsychology, and other subjects long shrouded in mystery. His books in this area include *ESP Seers And Psychics, Mediums Mystics And The Occult,* and *Search For The Soul.* In recognition of his work, he was awarded a Literary Fellowship by the ACADEMY OF MAGICAL ARTS; among his many other awards was a Silver Wand presented by the MAGIC CIRCLE.

He was also noted as a collector, and his collection of items relating to magic—books, posters, playbills, paintings, etc.—is considered to be one of the largest and best such collections in the world.

Milbourne Christopher (*photo courtesy GENII Magazine*)

CHUNG LING SOO (1861-1918)

Born William Ellsworth Robinson, he worked for a time as ASSISTANT and BACK-ROOM BOY for ALEXANDER HERRMANN. At times he would fill in for Hermann, and so skillful was Robinson's makeup that the substitution was never noticed.

Robinson became interested in the TRICKS used by fraudulent spirit mediums, and in 1898 published a book still considered a classic on the subject—*Spirit Slate Writing and Kindred Phenomena.*

At the turn of the century, after being rebuffed by CHING LING FOO over a money challenge made by the latter, Robinson created the character and show of CHUNG LING SOO, and as an ORIENTAL STYLE magician was hugely successful. His career ended in 1918 when he was shot onstage in Britain during a performance of the BULLET CATCH; he died the next day.

A highly creative inventor, Chung invented several effects and illusions—among them GONE, THE CAULDRON, and the MANACLE BOARD VANISH. Chung was noted for the artistry of his performances and also for the unequalled quality and volume of his posters. An excellent account of his life is WILL DEXTER's *The Riddle Of Chung Ling Soo.*

CIGARETTE CATCHER

A flesh-colored device which, worn on a finger, enables a cigarette to be hidden behind the hand, and produced by bending the finger inward. It is rarely used by magicians who feature CIGARETTE MAGIC, as the same feat can be accomplished more convincingly by SLEIGHT-OF-HAND. Also, unlike manipulative techniques, it cannot be used in venues where the performer is surrounded.

CIGARETTE DROPPER

A device worn under the coat which delivers cigarettes singly into the performer's hand; these are sometimes dummy cigarettes which are decorated at the tip to appear lit.

There are also electric **cigarette droppers** which eliminate the necessity for such dummies; these use a hot coil to light each cigarette as it is taken from the dropper. Cigarettes which have had their tobacco treated with saltpeter (potassium nitrate) and will thus ignite quickly are often used in conjunction with this type of **dropper**. (Note: it is undoubtedly unwise to inhale the smoke from such cigarettes.)

These devices should not be confused with the CIGARETTE TANK.

CIGARETTE MAGIC

It is not surprising, given current opinion regarding smoking, that cigarette magic is seen much less than in past years; until quite recently, however, it was a standard feature of manipulative acts, usually in the form of continuous productions of lighted cigarettes. Such production sequences would often be capped with the production of a lit cigar, followed by a pipe.

Undisputed masters of this type of magic were CARDINI and JOSE FRAKSON; another performer who featured it was KEITH CLARK, who wrote the standard work on the subject, *Encyclopedia Of Cigarette Tricks*.

Among those currently featuring Cigarette Magic are LANCE BURTON, HARUO SHIMADA and ROCCO.

CIGARETTE PENETRATION

The passing of a lighted cigarette through a borrowed coat or handkerchief; in some versions this is a straightforward PENETRATION while in others the cigarette vanishes in the process. An excellent ROUTINE for this effect, by JARROW, may be found in *Stars Of Magic*.

See KNIFE THROUGH COAT.

CIGARETTE PULL

A specific type of PULL used for the vanish of a cigarette; it usually consists of a metal or wooden tube into which the cigarette will fit snugly, attached to a length of black elastic.

Some **cigarette pulls** are constructed in similar fashion to the CIGARETTE TANK, so that a cigarette placed within is not extinguished and may later be reproduced still lit.

Since the **cigarette pull** is quite small and narrow, it is often worn so that it will go up the sleeve rather than under the jacket as is usually done; this is *not* done with the tank-type pull, however, since it would be difficult to retrieve the cigarette from the sleeve in an unobtrusive fashion.

CIGARETTE TANK

This device is worn under the coat, and is designed to hold one to four *lit* cigarettes in clips surrounded by a protective grillwork through which air may circulate. Cigarettes placed in this tank will remain lighted for several minutes.

See also CIGARETTE DROPPER.

CIGARETTE THROUGH QUARTER

A commercially marketed EFFECT in which a cigarette is apparently pushed right through the center of a borrowed quarter. A common presentational touch is to then light the cigarette and puff on it while the quarter remains "impaled" on it; the cigarette is eventually removed and the quarter is seen to be solid and unharmed.

The effect has become quite popular, in part from its frequent performance on television by DAVID COPPERFIELD.

CIGARETTE VANISH

A cigarette (usually lit) is placed in the performer's hand or in a borrowed handkerchief, from which it disappears. The EFFECT may be accomplished with a cigarette PULL, or with a THUMB TIP.

CIGAR PRODUCTION

The performer produces a cigar from the air, takes it in his other hand, and places it in the pocket. As the performer does so, another cigar appears in the hand, and this sequence is repeated, usually at an increasing pace, for as long as the performer wishes.

The EFFECT was devised by G.W. HUNTER, and it has been applied to many other objects.

CIRCLE TO SQUARE

A startling EFFECT in which a metal hoop, held in the hands, instantly and visibly changes to a square. In a variant version, a triangle is transformed into a hoop which in turn is transformed into a square. The PROP is simply made and near-automatic in operation.

CLAIRVOYANCE

In Spiritualism, the ability to sense and converse with the souls of the deceased (*see* MEDIUM); in Parapsychology, the ability to obtain by extrasensory means information about an object not known to anyone else.

It is in this latter sense that the term is most often used by stage performers of MENTAL MAGIC. A basic example of an EFFECT in which the performer simulates clairvoyant perception would be SEVEN KEYS TO BALDPATE; clairvoyance by a spectator could be illustrated with a performance of OUT OF THIS WORLD.

CLARK, KEITH (?-1979)

Born Pierre Cartier, he was for many years a professional magician working primarily in night spots; his work is described in his *Celebrated Cigarettes*, *Rope Eternal*, and *Silks Supreme*, later issued together as *Keith Clark's Night Club Act*. He also authored the *Encyclopedia Of Cigarette Tricks*.

CLARK, OWEN (1877-1929)

Born Alfred Owen Clark in Britain, he began his performing career in his teens, specializing in ESCAPES. He later created an act of ILLUSION effects, and was featured many times at ST. GEORGE'S HALL and other venues. Clark toured throughout the U.S. as a vaudeville headliner, and also appeared in Australia and New Zealand.

He was noted as an inventor of intricate mechanical effects; an amusing story concerning one such invention is told by STANLEY COLLINS in J.B. BOBO's *Modern Coin Magic*.

CLARKE, HARRY (1892-1970)

British printer of magic books, notably those by LEWIS GANSON on the magic of DAI VERNON and SLYDINI.

CLARKE, SIDNEY W. (d. 1940)

British barrister (lawyer) and author of the ANNALS OF CONJURING; he also wrote (with Adolph Blind) *A Bibliography Of Conjuring* (1920), and was editor of the MAGIC CIRCLE's magazine, *The Magic Circular*. A biography of Clarke titled *The Barrister In The Circle* was written by DR. EDWIN A. DAWES.

CLASSIC EFFECT

Any long-popular standard EFFECT.

The usual use of the term implies an innate positive entertainment quality of the effect so designated. It has been suggested, however, that it may denote an effect requiring such basic skills that almost any performer can execute it in passable fashion. The reluctance of some spectators to sit through yet another performance of a feat already viewed dozens of times may lend some credence to this interpretation.

CLASSIC FORCE

A playing card FORCE which relies purely on technique—the performer having the desired card at the proper position as the cards are spread from hand to hand, and inducing the spectator to take that particular card without being aware that the choice was controlled.

In less than competent hands, this force is transparently obvious, the chooser feeling that the card has simply been shoved into his hand. Performed by an expert, however, the classic force will deceive even a magician who knows the technique. A few accomplished performers are able to execute this force with the cards held behind their backs.

CLASSIC PALM

A common form of PALM, in which the object is held in the apparently empty hand at the lower center of the palm, maintained in this position by a slight contraction of the hand.

A common mistake in classic palm technique is to stick the thumb out at an unnatural angle; this should be avoided.

CLATTERBOX

The box, a comedy PROP invented by Len J. Sewell, is handed to a spectator to hold. When the spectator opens the box as instructed to look for a vanished silk, the box falls completely apart—the silk hanging from the lid still held by the spectator.

CLEAN

A method or technique is said to be "clean" when it has no unnecessary aspects which might obscure the EFFECT or hint at the methodology used. To "finish clean" is to end an effect with nothing left in the way of evidence—the PROP can be examined, the hands are empty, and so forth.

CLEAR

Instruction by stage manager for all non-essential personnel to leave the stage area prior to the beginning of the show.

Sometimes given as "clear stage."

CLEVER, EDDIE (1904-1975)

Born Edward Rupp; a writer on magic and MENTALISM, he edited the Parades of magical EFFECTS which appeared in the LINKING RING MAGAZINE for many years.

He also authored a book on MENTAL MAGIC and MENTALISM titled *Thought Wings Onward.*

CLICK PASS

A coin SLEIGHT involving more than one coin; as these are placed by one hand into the other, the sound of a coin dropping on another strengthens the impression that the coin is really being placed into the hand. In actuality, the spectators hear the coin dropping onto another held in the same hand in FINGER PALM or being placed against a coin already in CLASSIC PALM.

Other versions of the pass employ a stack of coins.

A complete description of various click passes will be found in J. B. BOBO's *Modern Coin Magic*, and in ARTHUR BUCKLEY's *Principles And Deceptions.*

CLIMBING RING

A borrowed ring is dropped onto a pencil (or wand) held vertically at the lower end; at a gesture from the performer, the ring climbs back up the pencil and jumps off the top.

The feat is accomplished by a thread, one end of which is affixed to the top of the pencil—the other end fastened to a belt loop or buckle. When the ring is dropped on the pencil it is also dropped over the thread; an indetectable outward movement of the hand holding the pencil draws the thread taut and causes the ring to rise.

This very old EFFECT is explained in most elementary books on magic; properly presented, however, it can create a quite mysterious impression.

CLIMBING WAND

A magic wand is dropped into an empty bottle, from which it mysteriously rises. Similar in preparation to the CLIMBING RING, here the neck of the bottle acts as the ring and it is the wand that moves.

An excellent ROUTINE for this effect is a feature in the act of MAX HOWARD.

CLIP

To secretly hold an object (usually a coin or card) by its extreme edge between two adjacent fingers, the object often projecting out at an angle. The **rear clip** of a coin, for example, differs from a BACK PALM in that the Clip may hold the coin between the first and second fingers, projecting out from the back of the hand as the palm is shown empty—whereas in the **back palm** the coin would lie flat and be held by pressure from the sides of the first and little fingers.

CLIPBOARD

Once used in feats of MENTALISM and MENTAL MAGIC, the **clipboard** was made to exactly resemble the ordinary object available in stationery stores, but was prepared in such a way that anything written on a slip of paper clipped to its surface would leave a secret copy.

The earliest such boards, invented by SAMRI S. BALDWIN and used by Anna Eva Fay, used papers impregnated with an indetectable coating of candle wax on the rear surface; the impression thus left could be developed by sprinkling powdered charcoal on the **clipboard**. Later versions used carbon paper set into the board itself, hidden beneath a thin upper surface; the best of these was undoubtedly the **ultra perfect clipboard** developed by ROBERT NELSON.

There have been subsequent developments in the design and working procedure of clipboards, but they have been exposed so repeatedly—at one time even being marketed on television—that many members of the public are aware of their existence. Consequently, they are rarely if ever employed by stage performers.

CLIPPO

An ingenious EFFECT in which a strip of newspaper is folded and cut, yet is immediately unfolded and shown apparently unharmed; the process can be repeated a number of times. Originated and marketed by KOLAR in 1929, it was developed further by Will De Sieve (who gave it the present name).

Kolar's original presentation, which he called **Magic Shears**, will be found in J.G. THOMPSON JR.'s *My Best.*

CLOCK BACK

A card back design which incorporates a circular motif with twelve distinct points. Such a design may be created for purely aesthetic reasons, but is useful in a number of MARKED DECK systems. In such systems one value—usually the King or Ace—is left unmarked.

CLOCK DIAL

A clock hand, placed on a spindle at the center of a clear clock dial and spun freely, comes to rest at any number the performer desires.

The EFFECT is rarely seen at the present time. Even more rare is a variant version created by ROBERT STULL, in which the clock hand is replaced by a pendulum (of the kind found in old office clocks); while the rod of this pendulum could be made of clear glass—as there is no mechanism at the pivot-point—it, too, will stop at any number selected.

Variant versions of the dial have clips into which cards may be placed, the hand coming to rest pointing at a previously selected card; many similar effects are possible.

CLOCKING THE DECK

To add the values of the cards in the deck or a PACKET; the sum, subtracted from a known total, will indicate the value of a card removed from the group.

The basic principle has been known for several decades. Among those who have worked on it are CHARLES T. JORDAN, CHARLES H. HOPKINS and MARTIN GARDNER. Recent discussions include JAMES RANDI's article "Mathematical Discovery" in *Handbook of Mental Magic* by Marvin Kaye, and four books—*Epitome Location* by HARRY LORAYNE, and *Card Counting*, *The Parallel Principle* and *Parallel Lines*, all by KARL FULVES.

CLOCK MAGIC

Clocks and watches have been used in magical EFFECTs for many years. Though some such feats are little more than mathematical curiosities—relying on arithmetical properties of the clock face—there have been many full-blown effects of stage magic in which clocks of various kinds have played a central role.

In addition to the ALARM CLOCK PRODUCTION, there have been many versions of the **vanishing alarm clock**. Usually the clock is covered with a cloth—the alarm is set off—and then the clock is made to vanish as the cloth is tossed in the air, the ringing ceasing at the same moment. Special trays and/or stands are used to bring about the effect.

A watch may be made to display a time secretly selected by a spectator, through mechanical or electronic means. A borrowed watch may be smashed by the performer, to reappear unharmed in the innermost of a NEST OF BOXES. Nearly every kind of magical effect, has, in short, been applied to this item.

A British performer, GUS FOWLER, performed for many years an entire act using only watches and clocks. Currently, international star RICHARD ROSS features the barehanded production of large clocks and watches on chains.

See STULL WATCH.

CLOCK TRICK

A card EFFECT which gets its name from the circle into which twelve cards are dealt, one for each hour on a clock face. There are many effects accomplished within this general plot; the performer may determine a chosen card—a chosen card may appear at a designated position—the quantity of cards secretly taken by the spectator may be revealed; et cetera. Many such effects are given a Zodiacal theme.

Two books which deal exclusively with this effect are *On The Clock Effect* by JON RACHERBAUMER and *A World Of Clocks* by ROY JOHNSON.

CLOSER

Final EFFECT in an ACT or SHOW. The term implies an effect which has the necessary theatrical appeal and dramatic structure to serve as a climax to the performance.

CLOSE-UP MAGIC

EFFECTs performed for small groups of people in close proximity; often the performer will be seated at a table with the spectators all around.

The effects used in these situations should, of course, be ANGLE-PROOF; they can use smaller items—coins, dice, etc.—than would be appropriate in a larger venue; and they can be somewhat more elaborate in plot and subtle in effect than in less intimate performances. Most effects for such situations should directly involve the spectators as participants.

CLOSE-UP MAT

A special working surface, usually about 12 inches by 18 inches, used by many performers in presenting CLOSE-UP MAGIC. It is usually made of neoprene rubber with an upper surface of a smooth colored flocking; other versions may be thin slabs of foam rubber surfaced with green felt, or similar materials.

While **close-up mats** ease the working of a number of effects, such as for example MATRIX, there is some division of opinion regarding their advisability. Some performers feel that the mat establishes a "stage" and focuses the attention of the spectators; others feel that in the usual conditions of commercial close-up presentation (regarding space required and efficiency of working), the mat is just not practical. Performers therefore have to determine if a mat is really necessary for effective presentation of their repertoire and what venues will realistically permit its use.

CLOTH

A flat curtain, usually of canvas or oilcloth, mounted on a roller and suspended from the FLIES. It is often situated just behind the FRONT CURTAIN, and may have a realistic or fanciful scene painted on it.

Cloths such as these, once quite common, are rarely used in contemporary theatre except when it is specifically desired to create a nostalgic effect of the theatrical presentations of an earlier time.

CLUB DATE

The term does not (as often assumed) refer to nightclubs, but rather to organizations of various kinds—fraternal, business, religious, social—for which a performer may provide entertainment.

In most cases, a CASUAL DATE is implied—i.e., a single evening's performance.

COCONUT

An EFFECT featured by HOWARD THURSTON as part of his WATER FOUNTAIN ROUTINE and later by DANTE, it used a half-coconut from which the interior had been scraped out, giving it the appearance of a rough bowl.

Water was scooped from a large fountain with the coconut shell and then allowed to cascade back into the fountain; this was repeated a few times; and the final time the water continued to pour in a seemingly endless stream, rapidly causing the fountain to overflow.

The effect was accomplished by means of a jet of water within the fountain, aimed precisely at the center of the coconut-shell. The curved inner surface caused the water to flow out in a tube-like stream which completely concealed the incoming water jet.

CODE

A secret means of communication, either by verbal or silent CUES, used in TWO-PERSON MENTAL ACTS. Examples of these are given in the **Calostro Mind**

Reading Act by Ralph W. Read and **En Rapport** by THEODORE ANNEMANN.

Also (rarely) a mathematical Gray Code sequence generated in the course of a card effect.

COD MAGIC

Parody of a magical performance or EFFECT, in which an actual effect may or may not take place. Primarily used in Britain, from the slang term for hoaxing or humbug.

COFFEE VASE

Beans or other such items, filling a footed vase, are transformed into hot coffee after a cover has briefly been placed over the vase. Thoroughly described in *Modern Magic*, this mechanically complex but ingenious APPARATUS would probably not be convincing to audiences of today, particularly since far simpler means of obtaining the same effect have been developed.

COFFIN ESCAPE

The performer is sealed inside a regulation coffin which is then buried under several feet of earth; he then escapes.

In most such routines, the performer secretly escapes *before* the coffin is buried, and thus may reappear at the suitably dramatic moment.

Some coffin escapes are done without the burial; in these cases they are simply variants of the BOX ESCAPE, and use similar techniques.
See also ESCAPES.

COFFIN TEST

The performer is sealed inside an airtight coffin with, presumably, only enough air to sustain life for a few minutes. The coffin is then buried or submerged in a pool for a considerable time. When the coffin is unsealed, the performer is—usually—found alive.

Indian magician Rahman Bey performed such a feat, claiming occult powers; HOUDINI immediately duplicated the test, besting Bey's time by a considerable margin. Several decades later Houdini's record was broken in turn by RANDI, whose performance of it was shown live on the NBC-TV *Today* show.

COIL

Tightly rolled strip of paper used as a PRODUCTION item; depending on size it may be designated as a HAT COIL, **mouth coil**, or **tambourine coil**. When rolled up, the coil occupies a very small amount of space; allowed to cascade out to its full unrolled length, it can create a huge mass.

Quite often a LOAD is stolen from a chair, table, or the performer's pocket under cover of the mass of paper and produced as apparently coming from the paper itself.

Other coils include a mylar coil notable both for its metallic appearance and the fact that it may be rerolled and thus re-used, and standard throw-out coils used by ORIENTAL STYLE acts much as in the Japanese Kabuki theatre. Sometimes called "streamers" by Occidental performers, much of their current popularity is due to their use in the influential act of JEFF MCBRIDE.

COIN, FOLDING

See FOLDING COIN

COIN BOXES

See OKITO BOX; LIPPINCOTT COIN BOX; RATTLE BOX.

COIN CATCHER

A GIMMICK which holds a coin at the rear of the hand; the coin may be made to appear by bending the fingers.

A more elaborate version of this gimmick holds several coins, which may be extracted one-by-one.

See SPIDER.

COIN CLIP

A HOLDER pinned under the coat which will hold a stack of coins which the performer can secretly obtain.

This term is also sometimes applied to a flesh-colored device which the performer conceals in his hand (versions of which have been devised by DAI VERNON and TONY SLYDINI); a number of coins being placed into it, it holds them securely and thus the coins may be handled as a single unit, which allows for SLEIGHTS and moves not otherwise possible.

COIN CUT

An EFFECT in which a selected card is found by the vanish of a coin from the hand and its reappearance directly above the chosen card within the deck.

The effect was invented by Bob Driebeek, who called his version "Tosheroon"; later versions of the effect were created by LARRY JENNINGS, FRED KAPS and ED MARLO.

COIN DROPPER

A coin HOLDER which, pinned out of sight under the coat, will deliver coins one at a time into the performer's hand. Not to be confused with the COIN CLIP.

COIN EASEL

A stand which will hold coins (usually four) on display; it is so designed that the coins may be dropped into a secret compartment in the stand in the apparent act of removing them. Such a stand is often used in conjunction with other EFFECTs, as for example COPENETRO.

Some coin easels have the capability of reproducing the vanished coins, usually under cover of a handkerchief.

COIN FOLD

A method of wrapping a coin in a small square of paper so that it can secretly slide out into the fingers to be PALMED. The paper is later torn up or burned to show the coin has gone; in the latter case, for a showy effect, performers will often use FLASH PAPER.

COIN IN BOTTLE

A classic EFFECT which has been a feature of many stage and close-up performers; it consists of causing a half-dollar size coin to pass into an empty soda or beer bottle, in spite of the coin being obviously too large to pass through the bottle's neck.

Some versions of this require the use of a FOLDING COIN. Many modern performers make a point of using a borrowed coin which may be marked, and in some routines the spectator is given the bottle to keep with the coin still inside!

Excellent routines for this effect are *Coin In Bottle—Plus* created by JOHN THOMPSON, and BILLY MCCOMB's version to be found in his tape cassette (Billy McComb Magicassette Vol.2).

COIN LADDER

A structure made with "steps" consisting of slanted panes of glass, down which coins tinkle noisily after being produced by the performer; usually used in conjunction with the MISER'S DREAM. It is variously credited to CONRADI and ROBERT HELLER.

The **Coin Ladder** is rarely seen in its original version. However, a more practical version designed by OKITO (and described in his *Quality Magic*) had a strong influence on later designers. It has been brilliantly adapted by NORM NIELSEN into a "chime-coin-ladder," and as such is a feature of his famous act of "Musical Magic."

Other versions have been based on a design by JACK HUGHES in which the coins drop down a glass slide, bouncing against pins placed haphazardly in their path.

Nearly all **coin ladders** incorporate some form of COIN DROPPER in their mechanism.

COIN MAGIC

The attraction of money is universal, and from earliest times magicians have incorporated its appeal into their EFFECTs and ROUTINEs. Though there are a number of tricks with paper money, which is also used in demonstrations of ORIGAMI (paper folding), effects and routines with coins are far more common.

There are many stage effects with coins, such as the MISER'S DREAM and COPENETRO, but most coin effects are done under close-up conditions—at the table, or even in the spectator's hand.

Coins have a distinct advantage for many close-up specialists in that, while it sometimes seems that every layperson knows at least one card trick, very few are at all familiar with coin mysteries—and it is usually quite clear that the results the magician obtains are not simply from knowledge of a secret but from sheer skill.

This is not a mistaken impression; while there are a number of card tricks that can be done by non-magicians, even the most elementary of coin routines require a fair degree of skill. The more advanced effects, such as those performed by DAVID ROTH, call for a very high level of expertise.

It is not surprising, therefore, that the books written on coin magic are few in comparison with those describing card effects. Among the best of those currently available are J. B. BOBO's *Modern Coin Magic*, RICHARD KAUFMAN's *Coinmagic,* and DAVID ROTH's *Expert Coin Magic.*

For the stage performer, excellent material will be found in ARTHUR BUCKLEY's *Principles And Deceptions* and in *Ron Macmillan's Modern Art Of Coin Manipulation*, written by Walt Lees.

COIN ON STICK

Devised by FRED LOWE; a version of the RING ON WAND, using a coin having a hole through which the stick may be passed. This hole may either be natural to the design of the coin (as in the case of many Oriental coins, for example), or a coin specially manufactured for the purpose may be used.

COIN PAIL

Sometimes called the **coin bucket** (and designed to look like a Champagne bucket), this is used in the performance of the MISER'S DREAM. It is often equipped with hidden COIN DROPPERs for use in that effect.

COIN ROLL

A coin FLOURISH in which the coin is rolled back and forth over the fingers at the knuckles at the back of the hand; it is sometimes used in combination with coin PRODUCTION.

Some particularly adept performers do this flourish with several coins simultaneously, moving the coins along in single file and as a stack.

COINS ACROSS

Sometimes known as **the flying eagles** or **coins from hand to hand**, this EFFECT uses a small number of coins (usually four), which one by one travel from one hand to the other.

In some PLOTS, an odd coin (gold, foreign, etc.) is claimed to have influence over the other coins, magically attracting them through space. Similarly, a ring may be used for this purpose as it is in the HAN PING CHIEN MOVES.

There are countless methods for achieving this effect, many of which are described in J.B. BOBO's *Modern Coin Magic* and DAVID ROTH's *Expert Coin Magic.*

See also COINS THROUGH THE TABLE.

COIN SHELL

See EXPANDED SHELL; SHELL.

COIN STAR

A rarely seen feat which combines a magical EFFECT with a FLOURISH. In it, five coins are caused to vanish from one hand and appear in the other—balanced at the tips of the four fingers and thumb.

It was a favorite of T. NELSON DOWNS and is fully described in *Modern Coin Magic.*

COINS THROUGH THE TABLE

Also known as the **Magical Filtration of Four Half Dollars** (AL BAKER's title), this classic of COIN MAGIC is very popular with close-up performers. In effect, four coins pass one at a time from one hand down through the table into the other. In some versions the hand beneath the table may hold a glass, and as the coins "penetrate" they are heard to fall within; in variants of this routine the glass is placed under the table (gripped between the legs) and *both* hands are above the table when the coins are heard to fall into the glass.

There are many, many methods and routines for this effect, by such performers as Al Baker, J.B. BOBO, DAVID ROTH, DAI VERNON, and SLYDINI, to name only a few. *See* MODERN COIN MAGIC and EXPERT COIN MAGIC. The basic routine is generally believed to have been invented by Al Baker, but it is possible that it was first devised by GEORGE SANDERSON.

COIN TRAY

A small metal or wooden tray equipped with a secret channel which holds a number of coins; when coins on the surface of the tray are dumped into a spectator's hands, the hidden coins fall out of a slot at one edge of the tray and are thus secretly added to the others.

COIN WAND

A magic WAND at the tip of which coins may be made to appear. This is accomplished by means of a specially designed trisected coin, hidden within the wand which can be moved into view by sliding a projecting stud in the side of the wand, where the three sections spread out to give the appearance of a normal coin.

Variant **coin wands** have been invented by T. NELSON DOWNS, WELSH MILLER, and others.

COLD DECK

Gambler's parlance for a prearranged deck; a variant term often used is *Cooler.*

The cold deck is also the title of a book by FRANK THOMPSON (and a movie starring William S. Hart).
See STACK.

COLE, JUDSON (1894-1943)

Vaudeville performer noted for his elegant style and sophisticated sense of humor; his highly-regarded act played throughout the U.S. for many years.

COLLECTORS

A SANDWICH EFFECT created by ROY WALTON, in which three selected cards appear between four face-up cards which have been on top of the deck from the outset. Many variations of the basic effect have been published, including a complete book titled *Bottom Collectors* by FATHER CYPRIAN.

The term also refers to collectors of magical APPARATUS, literature and memorabilia. Conventions for such Collectors are held yearly in Chicago.

COLLINGS, HERBERT J. (1883-1958)

Born in Britain; he had a long performing career, working most often in ORIENTAL STYLE as *Col Ling Soo.* He was a member of the MAGIC CIRCLE from its inception and served as its president, and also held offices in many other magic organizations.

COLLINS, STANLEY (1881-1966)

A legend in British magic who, in addition to a long career as a professional performer, was also noted as a collector, researcher and writer on magical subjects.

Among his many books are *Original Magical Creations, Deceptive Conceptions In Magic,* and *A Conjuring Melange.* He also wrote a column called "Inconsequentialities" for LINKING RING Magazine and contributed articles on historical subjects to many other magazines.

Stanley Collins (*The Mulholland Library of Conjuring & the Allied Arts, Los Angeles, California*)

COLLUSIONIST

Pejorative term for a performer who makes extensive use of CONFEDERATES to achieve effects.

COLOMBINI, ALDO (b. 1951)

Born in Italy, Colombini performs under the stage name of *Fabian*. He is noted for his inventiveness and for his close-up magic, which won him a First Prize at FISM, as well as several other awards.

His work is described in *Colombini's Cups And Balls* by LEWIS GANSON, and in his own Spanish-language book on the PADDLE TRICK, titled *Magia Con Paletas*.

COLOR CHANGE

To change the color of an object—or, with cards, the identity.
See COLOR CHANGING CARD/KNIFE/ HANDKERCHIEF.

COLOR CHANGING CARD

A misnomer, in that almost always it is the card's identity that changes. The usual procedure is for the deck to be held face-up in one hand while the other hand is passed over it; as this gesture is made the change occurs.

It is often accomplished by depositing a previously palmed card over the one on the face of the deck, but other techniques have been used to produce the EFFECT. Methods and SLEIGHTS for this feat are described in HILLIARD's *Greater Magic*, HUGARD and BRAUE's *Expert Card Technique*, and most books on basic card magic.
See also FLAP CARD.

COLOR-CHANGING HANDKERCHIEF

Invented by HARLAN TARBELL, this is a handkerchief which may be caused to apparently change color instantaneously by simply passing it through the hand. It can be used as a sudden, "flash" EFFECT or incorporated into a silk ROUTINE. A full description of its construction and use will be found both in Tarbell's own *Tarbell Course In Magic* and in the *Encyclopedia Of Silk Magic* by HAROLD R. RICE.

COLOR CHANGING KNIFE

A pocket knife with each of its two sides a different color; it may be shown to be of one color only by means of the PADDLE move. A turnover similar to those used in PADDLE TRICKS is used to reveal the change.

Many different kinds of knives and knife sets are available from magic dealers, including those in which a stag handle changes to ivory; the change appears to happen as the knife passes behind two fingers (**Stanfield's Colorfusing Knife**); and many others.

There are many techniques and ROUTINES available for this EFFECT; works on the subject include *Merrill's Knife Book* by R.D. Merrill and *Ascanio's World Of Knives* by Jose de la Torre.

COLORED SANDS

See SANDS OF THE DESERT.

COLOR MONTE

A commercially-marketed PACKET TRICK invented by Jim Temple, in which a bewildering number of changes take place in the course of a THREE-CARD MONTE routine.

The EFFECT is one of the most popular packet effects ever sold.

COMP

Abbreviation for *Complimentary ticket*; also, as a verb, to admit a spectator without charge, e.g., "to *comp* them in."

In older theatrical usage, a comp is sometimes called an *Annie Oakley*, presumably because of the resemblance of the hole punched in the ticket to a bullet-hole.

COMPERE

In Britain and elsewhere, MASTER OF CEREMONIES. It derives from the French word for *godfather*.

COMTE, LOUIS (1788-1859)

Born in France; after many years of performing in the provinces, he was eventually successful at establishing himself in Paris. He performed for over forty years, also appearing in other European countries. A favorite of French royalty, Comte was made a Chevalier of the Legion Of Honor.

COMUS (1731-1807)

Born Nicolas Ledru in France, he had a very successful career in France and Britain as magician and exhibitor of AUTOMATA.

COMUS II (?-1820)

French performer who took the name of COMUS in the 1790s, after the latter's retirement. In addition to exhibiting AUTOMATA, he performed such EFFECTs as the BULLET CATCH, the NEST OF BOXES, and several feats of MENTAL MAGIC.

CONE

Usually rolled from a sheet of newspaper into a vaguely funnel-like shape. It may be unprepared, and used in combination with such APPARATUS as the MILK PITCHER or the FOO CAN, or prepared, usually with a secret pocket in which items may be concealed. Prepared cones are described in TARBELL COURSE IN MAGIC and in the MARK WILSON *Course In Magic.*

CONE AND BALL

See BALL AND CONE.

CONFEDERATE

Secret assistant who poses as member of the audience. They are rarely used by professional performers, for several reasons.

For one thing—there are surprisingly few EFFECTS which cannot, with a bit of ingenuity, be performed as well without confederates as with them; an effect which can *only* be performed by confederacy usually makes that fact self-evident. Also, it is not easy to act naturally onstage and thus the confederate is often an obvious "ringer."

Exposure of the confederate will often invalidate not only the specific effect involved but also the entire act. And—last but not least—the confederate represents one more check the performer must write.

BILLY MCCOMB has noted that a confederate should never be used on a cruise ship, as in the course of a voyage of even a few days the "helper" will almost inevitably reveal his or her secret role to other passengers.

Many performers do not even consider the points just mentioned; for them the use of a confederate is unethical, a breaking of trust with the audience. British magician/mentalist AL KORAN: "With stooges anybody can do it. That's not magic."

Other performers take a far different view; THEODORE ANNEMANN always insisted that "the effect is the thing" and often said that in a room of seven people he'd have no compunction about making confederates of six of them to convincingly fool the seventh.

Far more common is the practice of getting a genuine spectator to go along with the performer's secret directions, as described in the entry for IMPRESSMENT.

Other terms used to describe a confederate are STOOGE and PLANT; less commonly, SHILL, STICK, and CAPPER.

Two excellent books on the use of confederates are *Stooging Around* by JOE STUTHARD and *Magic With Human Gimmicks* edited by Walt Hudson.

CONFETTI VASE

A vase, usually of spun brass or copper, is filled with confetti and then covered with its lid. When the lid is removed, the confetti has been transformed into candy which fills the vase to the brim. Alternatively a bird or guinea pig may be produced.

CONJURER

Now, generally, a performer of entertainment magic; formerly, and in occultism, a sorcerer who uses necromantic means to summon supernatural entities and spirits of the dead.

CONJURER (Magazine)

There have been several magazines of this general title. The first was *Conjuror's Magazine,* which was published in Britain for two years beginning in 1791.

Conjurer's Monthly Magazine, edited by HOUDINI and published in New York City, ran for two years beginning in 1908.

Conjurer's Magazine, edited by Houdini's brother HARDEEN, began publication in New York City in 1945; in 1949 it was absorbed into GENII Magazine which continues publication as *GENII, The Conjurer's Magazine.*

The Conjurer was a U.S. magazine, edited and published by Michael Albright, which had a brief run in the mid-1970's.

CONRADI (1870-1944)

Born Conrad Horster in Germany, he became one of that country's leading magic dealers after opening a shop in Dresden. He invented or improved a number of EFFECTs, including a **vanishing lamp**, a **vanishing bowl of water**, and a version of the COIN LADDER. He also created specially-printed JUMBO CARDS.

He was also editor-publisher of *Der Zauberspiegel,* a magazine which began publication in 1895 and had a thirteen-volume run.

CONSULTANT

One who advises a performer on effects, techniques and methods, as well as presentational premises; a consultant may be retained to do anything from supplying a premise for an effect to working on the day-to-day construction of an effect to serving as technical director for an entire show.

Magic consultants include JIM STEINMEYER, CHARLES REYNOLDS, DON WAYNE, MAX MAVEN, and T. A. Waters.

This term should not be confused with TECHNICAL ADVISOR.

CONTACT MIND READING

A type of "thought-reading" based on the phenomenon of psychomotor response (formerly called ideomotor response), in which the performer, grasping a subject's wrist, locates a hidden object by interpreting the subtle muscular cues which are subconsciously given by the subject. The hidden-object test is, while not easy, one of the simpler feats of Contact Mind Reading; many far more complex and amazing tests have been accomplished by experts in this field, such as John Randall Brown, Washington Irving Bishop, Maud Lancaster, and C.A. GEORGE NEWMANN.

A still more difficult technique is known as *Non-Contact Mind Reading*; here, as the name implies, there is no physical contact with the subject. Experts in this difficult phase of the work included Newmann (mentioned above), his brother John Newmann, and Frederick Marion.

Among the works describing the technique are *Contact Mind Reading—Expanded* by DARIEL FITZKEE, *Master Mentality* by Stanton Carlisle, and *Practical Contact Mind Reading* by Dr. Edward H. Schatz.

Interesting accounts of performers of these techniques will be found in *E.S.P., Seers, and Psychics* by MILBOURNE CHRISTOPHER, *Learned Pigs And Fireproof Women* by RICKY JAY, *In My Mind's Eye* by Frederick Marion, and *Confessions Of A Ghost Hunter* by Harry Price.

CONTINUITY GAG

See RUNNING GAG.

CONTINUOUS BACK AND FRONT PALM

A repeated sequence of movements which show the hand empty while it actually contains a number of playing cards; the cards are shifted from a BACK PALM position to a type of front double-CLIP in the act of turning the hand over to show the back, and the process is reversed to show the palm again.

This technique, often used in conjunction with the production from the **back palm** of single cards or SPLIT FANs, is extremely difficult to do in anything like a convincing manner; most often the spectators know that the cards are somehow being hidden from them, and are impressed by the digital dexterity but do not perceive the occurrence of any magical effect.

CONTROL

In card magic, a method of keeping track of, or controlling the movement of, a specific card or cards. Also, FULL DECK **control** is sometimes used as a synonym for FALSE SHUFFLE.

In SEANCES, a discarnate entity who acts as intermediary between the medium and spirits with whom contact is sought.

CONTROL CARD

Another term for KEY CARD.

Also, a card which is the subject of a CONTROL technique.

COOK, JOHN BROWN (1908-1978)

A specialist in SLEIGHT-OF-HAND with coins, he created spectacular EFFECTs which are described in ARTHUR BUCKLEY's *Principles And Deceptions*. He also collaborated with Buckley on the book *Gems Of Mental Magic*.

COOKE, GEORGE A. (1825-1904)

Friend, performing partner and chief mechanic for JOHN NEVIL MASKELYNE, with whom he worked for thirty years. Though their billing was "Maskelyne and Cooke," in fact Cooke was Maskelyne's employee rather than legal partner.

COOKIE

A disc or strip, usually of metal, made to fit into a frame in front of a SPOTLIGHT; the **Cookie** has a pattern cut into it and thus throws a shadow of the pattern on a FLAT or curtain. **Cookies** can be effectively used in creating scenic effects and making a limited stage production seem more elaborate.

The term is an abbreviation of the older (and rarely used) term *cuckaloris*.

COOLER

See COLD DECK.

COOPER, TOMMY (1912-1984)

Highly successful British comedy magician, known as much for his considerable height, ever-present fez and bizarre laugh as for the feats of magic which never seemed to turn out as he expected.

COP

To secretly obtain; usually the term is in reference to an object, most often a playing card. However, it may also be used in regard to an action, for example, to Cop a GLIMPSE. The term derives from *copper*, criminal parlance for policeman, and in slang usage means to *capture, grab, lay hold of,* or *nab.*

More rarely, the term is used to refer to an adhesive fluid applied to the palm to allow gaming chips to be stolen away as a wager is pushed into the pot; the fluid is more generally known as *check cop.*

This latter term—*check cop*—may also refer to a mechanical device used to steal chips; an example would be a slightly larger SHELL stack of chips. Such devices are used most often by a dealer or croupier working in conspiracy with a player.

COPENETRO

A startling visual coin effect devised by BOB KLINE, this uses an ordinary shot glass which is placed on a small wooden pedestal and then covered with an inverted glass tumbler.

Coins taken one at a time are "thrown" at the glass; they vanish from the performer's hand and visibly drop, seemingly from nowhere, into the covered shot glass.

In the original version of this EFFECT, the pedestal is held in the hand of performer or ASSISTANT; later versions have incorporated clockwork mechanisms or electronic devices to enable the pedestal and glasses to sit isolated on a table with the effect occurring as usual.

Various models of this APPARATUS were designed and manufactured by British magic dealer JACK HUGHES under the title of **Visible Coins In Glass**; his first models used a tray, while later versions were similar to the Kline pedestal model. It is possible that these, like the Kline original, may have been inspired by a much earlier effect which used a special mechanical tray.

COPPER, GER (b. ?)

Dutch-born magician who has performed in Britain, Europe and the U.S.; his act is primarily SLEIGHT OF HAND of the manipulative variety. He has won several awards, notably the *Grand Prix* at FISM.

COPPER AND SILVER

The title most often given to a TRANSPOSITION of a half dollar and an old-style English penny (which is the same size as the U.S. half-dollar coin), one of the coins being held in a spectator's closed fist.

There are many methods available for this EFFECT; some involve pure SLEIGHT OF HAND, others combine sleights with specially prepared coins. Many versions are described in BOBO's *Modern Coin Magic.* A version credited to JOHN SCARNE is in *Stars Of Magic;* it is quite similar to a handling of this effect developed by DAI VERNON. Vernon is noted for his performance of this effect, as was FRANCIS CARLYLE.

COPPERFIELD, DAVID (b. 1956)

Born David Kotkin, Copperfield has had a career quite as astonishing as any of his illusions and—still a young man—is one of the best-known magicians in the world today.

Originally planning to be a ventriloquist, Copperfield was diverted to magic when he visited a magic shop to purchase a ventriloquial figure. He began taking magic lessons, learned quickly, and then achieved a major breakthrough when, while still in his teens, he was cast for the lead in the musical comedy, THE MAGIC MAN.

David Copperfield

David Copperfield (*photo courtesy of GENII Magazine*)

Then began the television specials which still continue, and appearances in the Las Vegas casinos and throughout the country on his frequent tours.

While perhaps best known for the spectacular feats used as publicity hooks for his television shows—vanishing a Lear Jet on one show, the Statue of Liberty on another; "flying" across the Grand Canyon for a third—he is at his best when he integrates television technique with music, choreography, and a story line in his ILLUSION sequences, making of them miniature fantasy dramas. At their best these sequences, reflecting David Copperfield's love of the musical theater, are first-class entertainment; they have become his unique trademark, and indicate a career of continuing success. He is a recipient of the Stage Magician and Magician Of The Year awards from the ACADEMY OF MAGICAL ARTS.

COPPER/SILVER COIN

A type of DOUBLE-FACE coin which shows a U.S. fifty-cent piece on one face and an (old-style) British penny on the other. It is used in many EFFECTs, of which COPPER AND SILVER is the most popular.

There are, however, a number of other effects using the c/s coin; many will be found in BOBO's *Modern Coin Magic* and in *The Coins Of Ishtar* by Jules de Barros.

(Note: there are many double-face coins of copper/silver in which the identities are other than those mentioned above. Usually, however, when a c/s coin is described with no further specification, it is the fifty-cent/British penny that is meant.)

See CHINATOWN QUARTER.

COPYISTS

Those who select EFFECTs—and sometimes ACTs—from the shows of current performers.

Copyists constitute a greater threat to magic than incompetence. When lay people see an incompetent magician they simply think that particular performer to be bad, but the effect of the copyist, showing them material they have seen before, is to make lay people think that *magic* is bad (or boring, which comes to the same thing).

Copyists are, for the most part, not censured by magical groups and societies and may continue for years without even realizing they are doing anything at all wrong. Some will attempt to excuse their actions with such lame and patently false rationalizations as "Well, so-and-so didn't invent it . . ." or, "Nobody really invents anything in magic." Thievery of performance material is rife in all areas of show business; magic, however, may be unique in viewing it as normal and acceptable behavior.

This point of view was answered elegantly by NEVIL MASKELYNE in *Our Magic*:

> Yet, one cannot help coveting the blissful ignorance and the sublime impudence which enable such a man to pose as an artist. The possession of an intellect so obtuse, and a hide so pachydermatous, must confer upon the possessor a self-satisfaction unknown to men of real ability.

CORDS OF PHANTASIA

Two ropes are tied at their centers to a cane; several silks are then tied at intervals along the double length of rope. At the performer's command, the cane and silks come free from the ropes, apparently having penetrated them. The method is almost identical in principle to that of the GRANDMOTHER'S NECKLACE.

This stage presentation was a high spot of DANTE's FULL-EVENING SHOW; it was titled *The Lazy Magician* and Dante performed it while seated in a chair, directing the proceedings in liesurely fashion.

CORNELIUS, JOHN (b. 1948)

Performer who began his career working in a magic shop, and later worked as a clown ASSISTANT to a

JOHN CORNELIUS

John Cornelius

traveling magician. Still later he sold SVENGALI DECKS at the Hemisfair in Texas.

Developing a unique approach to magic, he has given magic lectures throughout the U.S.; he has also appeared in Holland, Spain, Belgium, France, Japan, Mexico and elsewhere.

In 1979 he won the award for best CLOSE-UP MAGIC at FISM; at a following FISM Congress he won the award for best card magic. He has also received a number of other awards.

Cornelius specializes in performing at banquets and private parties; he has also done television commercials.

He has created and marketed a number of EFFECTs; the FICKLE NICKEL was used by DOUG HENNING to begin his first NBC-TV special. Other Cornelius effects include **Flash Die, FISM Flash, Pinnacle Slate, Pinnacle Pad**, and **Brainpower Board**.

He is the author of the *Cornelius Card System*; also, a full issue of PALLBEARER'S REVIEW was devoted to his effects.

CORNER CUT DECK

A deck which has been prepared by having one corner trimmed and rounded on all 52 cards. If a card is selected and the deck is then turned end-for-end, the card will in effect become a CORNER SHORT and thus easy to locate; also, of course, its untrimmed corner will project slightly at the trimmed corner of the deck.

See CORNER SHORT; ONE-WAY DECK; STRIPPER DECK.

CORNER SHORT

A type of KEY CARD made by trimming and rounding off diagonally opposite corners (usually upper left and lower right). It can be used in much the same manner as a SHORT CARD, but does not require the performer to SQUARE THE DECK precisely.

Effective use of the corner short is found in RALPH W. HULL's **tuned deck** routine, which is described in HILLIARD's *Greater Magic*.

CORRECTING A MISTAKE

A subplot to an effect in which things seem to have gone awry, but are then magically corrected by the performer. An elementary example might be a coin which slips from the performer's hand during a difficult MANIPULATION but then jumps back up to the hand; similarly, an INDIFFERENT CARD might be shown to a spectator as a previously selected card, and when this is denied the card changes into the correct one.

Such routines are vaguely related to SUCKER EFFECTS but have a more acceptable and appealing subtext.

COSSARI, JOE (1903-1980)

Performer who was noted for his highly-regarded MANIPULATION act which consisted almost entirely of CARD FANNING. He also marketed a deck of cards which he had designed specifically for producing intricate patterns when fanned.

COSTUME ACT

An ACT performed in specially made or selected apparel. The robes of a sorcerer or the period garments of an historically-based act would qualify as costumes, while the most sequin-studded set of tails or designer dress would not. Given current clothing styles, drawing this distinction is increasingly difficult.

COSTUME TRUNK

A classic ILLUSION, invented by SERVAIS LEROY, in which a large trunk is shown to be filled with several drawers of costumes. The trunk is closed and a costume is selected by a spectator.

Immediately the lid of the trunk is opened; the drawers of costumes have vanished, and in their place is a woman wearing the chosen costume.

In a version featured by AUBREY, the plot of the Costume Trunk was combined with a version of the DOLL HOUSE illusion.

COUNT

Within card magic, a method of displaying cards, usually in other than legitimate fashion; as, ELMSLEY COUNT; JORDAN COUNT; SIVA COUNT.

The term FALSE COUNT, while applicable to such counts as the above, usually refers to counts which show the group of cards to be a different quantity—less or more—than is actually the case.

See BUCKLE COUNT.

COUNTING FOUR AS FOUR

ALEX ELMSLEY's own title for what is popularly known as the ELMSLEY COUNT.

COURT CARD

A picture card of the royal "court"—Jack, Queen or King of any of the four suits.

With a Bicycle-brand deck of cards, the performer

can wager it contains *six* Kings—and proceed to prove it by showing the Jokers, both of which depict Kings of Spades riding bicycles!

COVER PASS

A type of SHIFT, believed to have been developed by ELLIS STANYON, in which the two halves of the deck are transposed beneath the top card, which acts as a screen to hide this movement. This sleight is also sometimes called the **top card cover pass**.

Variant procedures may involve the shift taking place beneath several cards in the top STOCK.

COW TRICK

An oddly popular effect created by U. F. GRANT in which two thin card plaques are used to produce two full glasses of milk.

CRACK

Slang term requesting a CUE from the prompter as to what comes next; it can apply to a line of dialogue or to a sequence of stage BLOCKING or BUSINESS.

Originated in carnivals; later used in vaudeville and other theater situations.

CRADLE

A framework, usually of iron or other extremely rigid material, on which the levitated ASSISTANT rests in the performance of the LEVITATION ILLUSION. It generally consists of a flat bar about 40 inches long which supports the back, with smaller side struts at two or three points along its length; some versions have an oval outer ring, and are covered with material which matches the costume worn by the assistant.

The **cradle** is attached to the lifting support at the UPSTAGE side, which may or may not have a GOOSENECK.

See GOOSENECK; LEVI COUCH; LEVITATION.

CRAIG, MYSTIC (1900-1987)

Born William Vagell, he began his career in carnivals. Later he worked vaudeville circuits with an act titled **Fashions In Magic**, and also performed in CHAUTAUQUA, appearing in venues throughout the U.S.

During World War II he appeared in U.S.O. shows in Britain, Europe, and the South Pacific. Retiring from show business, he later owned and operated a shop devoted to Lionel Model Trains.

Craig is noted for the many films he took of magicians; the collection now resides at the MAGIC CASTLE. He also created the Craig Trophy, given to outstanding female magicians. Craig is the author of *The Elusive Canary*.

He is the recipient of an Honorary Life Membership from the ACADEMY OF MAGICAL ARTS.

CRAMER, STUART (b. 1912)

A full-time professional before and after becoming a lawyer; he has continued to perform actively, doing three different television series in the northern Ohio area where he makes his home.

Cramer was for many years a friend and student of KARL GERMAIN, about whom he has written two books: *The Secrets Of Karl Germain* and *Germain The Wizard And His Legerdemain*.

CRANDALL, CLARKE (1906-1975)

Known as "Senator" Crandall, he performed in many different kinds of venues, primarily specializing in close-up work or BAR MAGIC, which was largely a vehicle for his acerbic and mordant wit.

His sense of humor was also a feature of his long-running column in TOPS Magazine titled *It's A Mystery To Me*. His books include *Crandall's Comments, How To Do The Dice Stack, Best Of Senator Crandall* and *Politicking Magic* (with JAY MARSHALL).

CRAWFORD, HARRY (b. 1924)

With wife and partner Gloria, he has performed at varied venues throughout the U.S. with his ILLUSION act, including the Steel Pier in Atlantic City, the Concord and Nevele resorts, nightclubs and fairs. Crawford and Gloria have also appeared for such corporations as Dupont, Bell Telephone, International Harvester, Kimberly-Clark, Sylvania and Westinghouse.

He has also contributed a number of EFFECTs to various magic periodicals.

CREDITING

In magic literature, the giving of information relating to precursors to the EFFECT under discussion. This may be as specific as an earlier identical effect for which a new method or routine is being provided, or as general as an inspiration which has led to the creation of a new effect.

Many performers and writers affect disinterest in the matter of crediting, thinking it of importance only to those with academic concerns. It should be noted, however, that performance material is real property

Harry and Gloria Crawford with Emily the sheepdog

(in the legal sense); it is thus sometimes necessary to know before performing an effect learned from a publication that the creator of the effect had a reasonably clear title to describe it without infringing on the rights of other inventors and creators.

Crediting is also useful in establishing the extent of the writer's actual contribution. It may well be that only a small detail has been changed, but this can sometimes be the difference between an impractical effect and one worth performing. Such contributions to the literature are far more valuable than some totally original effects which are essentially unperformable.

Another reason for crediting is to establish that in fact performance material is created by specific people who thus have the rights to that material, and does not simply appear out of the air. It is a very short philosophical step from not caring *who created an effect* to not caring *how you acquire it*, leading to the kind of COPYIST mentality which does considerable harm to magic as a performance art.

CREMATION

A spectacular illusion in which an assistant (usually a female) is placed into a large, open-top box and apparently set alight; as huge flames rise from the box its sides fall down, and with the lessening of the flame a smoldering skeleton is visible.

The original version of this illusion had the putative victim standing on a bare table, a large cone being lowered over her prior to the immolation. The effect was accomplished by means similar to those used in the SPHINX illusion. This version was the invention of HERCAT. A later version of this presentation was featured by ALDO RICHIARDI, whose method employed the principle of BLACK ART.

A thrilling and intense presentation of this effect was featured by Russian performer EMIL KIO.

CREO

Credited to an Herr Boelke, this rarely performed ILLUSION is one of the most beautiful in all of stage magic.

A plaster female head rests on a tall tripod, isolated on its own platform. The performer paints and "makes up" the head to give it a lifelike appearance, drapes a robe around it, and positions a wig on it. Then, slowly, the eyes of the figure open—it smiles—and she comes to life, stepping down from the platform.

Versions of this illusion are described in HILLIARD's *Greater Magic*, JARRETT's *Magic And Stagecraft—Technical*, and many other sources.

The illusion is also known as the **Vampire**, under which title it was presented by HOWARD THURSTON and others.

It should be noted that the specific effect of Creo is a TRANSFORMATION of the plaster head to the living person; thus similar presentations which involve large masks, headpieces and the like may be baffling and entertaining ways of apparently producing someone from nowhere, but they are distinctly separate effects from the one under discussion.

CRIMP

To bend a card slightly, usually only at a corner, so it can again be located; also, the bend thus made. In gamblers' parlance crimps are known as "bend work."

CROS, DANIEL (b. 1940)

Born in France, he began his performing career doing close-up magic in Paris's famed Lido de Paris. In 1964, along with many performers in the Lido show, he was brought over to Las Vegas. Shortly thereafter he became the resident close-up magician at the Desert Inn, where he continues to perform.

He is noted for the high quality of his effects and the charm of his presentations.

CROSS ESCAPE

A rarely seen ESCAPE illusion in which the performer's neck, wrists, and ankles are secured to a large cross with ropes—the ends of the ropes being held by spectators. Briefly concealed by a curtain or other cover, the performer instantly makes his escape.

CROSSING THE CUT

A very simple procedure to FORCE a card, for which the only preparation is to have the card at the top of the deck.

A spectator is asked to cut off a portion of cards (usually about half) and place them on the table; the performer then picks up the bottom half and places it crosswise on the former top portion. Later the new top portion is removed by the performer and the spectator invited to remove the top card of the lower portion—which is, of course, the original top card of the deck.

This force can be very deceptive, but only if there is a sufficient time lapse between the cutting procedure and the eventual showing of the forced card for the spectator to forget the specifics of the procedure. This is usually accomplished by preparing some other item to be used in the EFFECT; for example, showing the blank surfaces of a pair of SPIRIT SLATES on which the name of the card will later appear.

CROSS-REFERENCE

The principle used in the TWENTY-FIVE CARD TRICK.

CROSTHWAITE, ROGER (b. ?)

Clergyman by profession; performer who specializes in magic with a humorous slant, and who is also noted for his card magic and PICKPOCKET effects. He has contributed to many magic periodicals, including THE GEN Magazine (which published his excellent series on pickpocket routines).

He is the author of *Card Notes* and *The Commercial Card Magic Of Roger Crosthwaite*.

CRUSHING A WOMAN

A stage ILLUSION invented by P.T. SELBIT in which a woman lies in an open-topped box which has double doors at the front. A fractionally smaller box with an open front and top, usually containing two other women, is lowered into the other box until it is completely nested—the woman in the lower box having apparently been crushed flat—and the double doors are opened to show the two women. A reversal of the procedure restores the woman to her normal state.

Touches used in the performance of this illusion include having a number of balloons in the lower box, which burst as they (and presumably the woman) are crushed—and extracting from the bottom of the lower box a flat wooden slide, decorated to represent the woman in her "crushed" state. The slide is, of course, replaced before the woman is restored.

A striking modern version of this premise, in which one woman is apparently compressed to only a few inches in height, is featured by ANDRE KOLE.

CRYSTAL BALL

Technically, a sphere of quartz crystal; such crystals of any size are, however, quite rare, and thus most crystal balls in use today are of ordinary or leaded glass.

In occultism the crystal is used as a focus for visualization, usually for DIVINATION; this process is called scrying. A crystal ball is quite often used as a PROP in MENTAL MAGIC in simulation of the aforementioned process.

If a miniature card is held under the crystal ball by the performer, it will appear to be of normal size and *within* the ball—thus a spectator can be asked to gaze into the crystal and name the card he sees. A matching card has been previously FORCED on another spectator.

CRYSTAL BOX

An ILLUSION in which a large box with glass walls is seen to be empty; it is briefly covered with a cloth, which is then removed to show the appearance of a woman inside the box. It most often employs the BEVEL BASE principle.

It is sometimes called the CRYSTAL CASKET, but should not be confused with that smaller EFFECT.

CRYSTAL CASKET

A cubical box of glass, usually from three to eight inches on a side, in which an object visibly appears. Most often the object is a silk handkerchief or other compressible item, concealed behind a mirrored flap.

As with any PRODUCTION device using a mirror, care must be taken in lighting and staging to use this device to best effect.

CUE

Dialogue or action which serves as a signal for a succeeding action. Such a signal may be used between two performers onstage; to indicate an entrance; to communicate a lighting or scene change to the Stage Manager; to indicate a beginning or ending of a music sequence to the orchestra leader; etc.

Cues used by magicians, particularly regarding lighting and scene changes, may be critical to the success of an EFFECT; it is therefore important that such cues be clear and unmistakable.

CUFFING

A technique for secretly disposing of a palmed coin by allowing it to drop into the trouser cuff. Due to changes in men's fashions, the technique is little employed at present.

CULL

To secretly locate and collect desired cards, prior to moving them to the top or bottom of the deck in the course of an apparently legitimate SHUFFLE or while spreading the cards from hand to hand.

There are many **culls** described in card literature; interestingly, one of the best is also one of the oldest—the **Hofzinser Cull** invented by JOHANN HOFZINSER over a century ago, and described in *Hofzinser's Card Conjuring.*

CULLITON, PATRICK (b. 1944)

Performer who began his performing career by creating *The Houdini Mystery Show,* a presentation on the life and adventures of HOUDINI, which he toured through every state in the continental U.S., appearing at universities and colleges.

He now performs primarily as an actor, having appeared in stage productions and over a hundred television shows and films, including *Columbo, The Towering Inferno,* and a recurring role on the *Starman* series.

He has contributed historical articles to GENII Magazine and M.U.M.

Culliton was the recipient of the Best Lecturer award from the ACADEMY OF MAGICAL ARTS.

CULPITT, FREDERICK (?-1944)

Born Frederick Cull Pitt; British performer who was stage manager at EGYPTIAN HALL in addition to performing there. He traveled the world with an act consisting almost entirely of his own inventions. His best-known creation is the DOLL HOUSE ILLUSION, but he invented many other effects, including the BATHING BEAUTY.

His approach is described in his book *Laughter And Legerdemain.*

Patrick Culliton

CUMMINGS, CLARE (b. 1912)

Detroit-based performer who for many years had a television show in which he portrayed Milky the Clown, a character who was quite well-known throughout the upper midwestern part of the U.S.

CUPS AND BALLS

Quite possibly the oldest of magical EFFECTs; it may well have been performed in ancient Egypt, and accounts of it are found in the literature of Classical Rome and Greece.

In its usual form it uses three cups and three small balls. The balls penetrate the cups, gather, disperse, and multiply; the usual climax is the PRODUCTION of large balls, fruit, or even baby chicks from beneath the cups.

Most basic books on conjuring describe ROUTINEs for this effect; many modern routines are heavily influenced by those of DAI VERNON, published in *Stars Of Magic* and GANSON's *Dai Vernon Book Of Magic.* See also the relevant chapter in ELLIOTT's *Classic Secrets Of Magic.* Also of note are EDDIE JOSEPH's several books on this subject. Another notable recent routine is that of TOMMY WONDER.

An interesting historical work on the **cups and balls** is Kurt Volkmann's *The Oldest Deception.*
See BALL AND BOWL; CHOP CUP.

CURRY, PAUL (1917-1986)

Inventor whose best-known creation, OUT OF THIS WORLD, is quite probably the most popular card trick in modern conjuring. He also devised the CURRY TURNOVER CHANGE, TOUCH, and many other effects.

Some of these appeared in a column he wrote—''Curry Favors''—for the PHOENIX Magazine. Others appeared in his books for magicians—*Something Borrowed, Something New, Paul Curry Presents, Special Effects*—and in his book for general audiences titled *Magician's Magic.*

CURRY TURNOVER CHANGE

A card SLEIGHT invented by PAUL CURRY in which one card is indetectably exchanged for another in the act of turning it from a face-up to face-down position, or vice versa.

CURSE OF SCOTLAND

A nickname for the *Nine Of Diamonds*. There are several stories of how the nickname was acquired, of which the most popular is that an execution order for wounded prisoners was written on this card by the Duke of Cumberland after the battle of Culloden.

Another explanation refers to the Glencoe Massacre, of which an instigator was Sir John Dalrymple, whose coat of arms contains nine diamonds (lozenges).

CUT

To remove a portion of cards from the deck. A cut is *completed* by placing the remainder of the deck on top of the cut-off portion; it is *replaced* by returning the cut-off portion to its original position.
See FALSE CUT.

CUT-AND-RESTORED ROPE

The cut and restored rope shares with the CUPS AND BALLS the distinction of being one of the very oldest tricks in magic; it has been performed for centuries, and a version is described in REGINALD SCOT's *Discoverie Of Witchcraft.*

It is still a popular feat, and methods for its accomplishment are many. Abbott's *Encyclopedia Of Rope Tricks* (edited by STEWART JAMES)devotes several chapters to this single effect.

Thus, while the effect on the audience is (obviously) that a length of rope is cut in half and restored, there are so many ROUTINES and methods that no typical performance could be described.

Variations on the basic effect have employed everything from thread to turban-cloth to microphone cords to bicycle tires (the last-named item used in a routine devised by BILLY MCCOMB).

CUT FORCE

There are many means of forcing a spectator to CUT the deck at a certain point—by means of a BRIDGE or CRIMP, for example—but this term most often refers to the CROSSING THE CUT FORCE.

CUT-OFF

A sudden cessation of music, the signal for which is the hand drawn sharply across the neck in a throat-cutting gesture; used by performers both for dramatic and comedic effect.

CYCLICAL STACK

A STACK in which the cards follow a set progression, the values repeating every thirteen cards; thus the stack is an endless loop and has no set beginning or end. (In most cases the four suits also cycle, e.g., C-H-S-D-C-H-S-D, etc.)

The term is properly used only for arithmetical progressions such as the SI STEBBINS STACK, since, while certain types of mnemonic stack such as the EIGHT KINGS do repeat values every thirteen cards, the last value of the set does not lead into the first by a set rule. In practice, however, the term is often applied to this latter kind of stack as well.

Also known as a **cyclic stack**.

CYCLORAMA

A very large curved backing which is usually the scenic element furthest UPSTAGE. Most often the **cyclorama** (or **cyc**) is either left white or painted in a light blue shade (to represent sky) or other neutral color.

Some stages are fitted with permanent or semipermanent cycs built on a rigid structure; a virtual wall between the stage and backstage area is thus created, which can sometimes render the use of particular ILLUSIONS unfeasible.

CYPRIAN, FATHER (b. ?)

Capuchin monk by profession; noted for his inventiveness in the area of card magic. He has contributed many effects to magic periodicals, in particular the PALLBEARER'S REVIEW.

His books include *Bottom Collectors, Fr. Cyprian On The Hofzinser Card Problem, Nostalgia Torn And Restored Card,* and *Stand Up Close.* He has also written several sets of lecture notes under the series title of *You Are Magic. See also The Elegant Card Magic Of Father Cyprian* by FRANK GARCIA.

DACRI, STEVE (b. ?)

He began his career with the television show *Bozo's Circus*, for which he wrote material in addition to performing for four years. He then became the host of a weekly variety television series titled *Magical Mystery Tour*.

Since then he has made a number of television appearances on such shows as *That's Incredible, Evening At The Improv,* and *Candid Camera*. He has also

performed with Bob Hope, Tony Orlando, Rodney Dangerfield, Susan Anton and Barbara Mandrell.

He has worked as an actor on *TV's Bloopers and Practical Jokes* and *The Fall Guy.*

DAGGER BOX

A smaller version of the SWORD BOX, it is placed on the ASSISTANT's head and then a number of daggers are run through the chest from side to side. In most models the front door may then be opened to show the head has vanished (this may be accomplished by the SPHINX or other MIRROR PRINCIPLE, or by BLACK ART). The door being closed and the daggers removed, the chest is lifted off the unharmed assistant's head.

DAGGER CHEST

A device most often used for vanishing various items, this is a box with an open top and grillwork or slotted front, through which the interior may be seen. A wooden or metal dagger goes through the box from side to side. An opaque slide is put in place at the front and the dagger is removed; the item to be vanished is placed within and the dagger is then reinserted. When the slide is removed, the box is seen to be empty (except for the blade of the dagger) and may be freely shown both through the front and open top. The box operates on the BLACK ART principle, the dagger holding a movable black partition in position; the vanished item is hidden behind the slide.

The **dagger chest** by also be used to produce items by a simple reversal of the process.

Steve Dacri

DALEY, JACOB, DR. (1903-1954)

Famous as a top plastic surgeon, Dr. Daley was also noted in the world of magic for his expert SLEIGHT OF HAND card magic. Several of his technically sophisticated card ROUTINEs may be found in the book *Stars of Magic*.

DALEY'S LAST TRICK

A card EFFECT, so titled because this origination of DR. JACOB DALEY's was supposedly the last he was seen to perform. In it, only the four Aces are used, the red Aces transposing with the black Aces.

The effect was originally published in M.U.M. Magazine; there have been many later versions.

It should be noted that, according to some reports, the last effect actually performed by Daley was his **cavorting aces**, which will be found in *Stars Of Magic*; this effect also involves a transposition of red and black Aces—here, within the deck—hence the misunderstanding.

D'AMICO, CARMEN (?-1973)

Highly respected specialist in CARD MAGIC; inventor of the D'AMICO SPREAD. Within card magic, his name is often associated with that of ED MARLO.

D'AMICO SPREAD

A technique for showing three cards as two by drawing back the top card slightly with the thumb and pushing the two lower cards forward in alignment as one.

This move, created by CARMEN D'AMICO, is useful in many different kinds of card routines; it is in some respects a mirror-reversal of the basic move of the E.Y.E. COUNT.

DANCING CANE

A cane which floats about the performer, moving back and forth and circling his head as the performer moves about the stage. It is said to be based on an earlier routine invented by *R. C. Buff* which used a long wand.

The EFFECT has been a feature in the acts of many magicians; it was the major effect in the early career of PETER PIT, and his stunning routine with the cane gained him an international reputation.

A book devoted entirely to this effect is *The Dancing Cane* by Al Hegmann.

DANCING HANDKERCHIEF

A handkerchief borrowed from a spectator seems to come to life, crawling in and out of a small cabinet, hopping about and dancing in time to the music.

The routine, billed as "Cassadaga Propaganda" was a feature in the show of HARRY BLACKSTONE SR.; he is said to have been inspired by seeing Anna Eva Fay present a similar EFFECT as a genuine spirit manifestation.

A routine for the Dancing Handkerchief appeared in AUGUST ROTERBERG's 1895 book *The Modern Wizard*; it has since been discussed in many books and other publications.

DANIEL, JOHN (b. ?)

Performer who began his career with ROBERT TOWNER performing SPOOK SHOWS. He later operated several magic shops, and for a time was associated with CARL OWEN. He created several ILLUSIONs for Las Vegas revues, and later created his own show called *ShaZzam* which appeared at the Carrillon in Miami Beach, and other venues. Daniel has since created a number of other shows. He has also been associated with the company of Owen Magic Supreme.

DANIELS, PAUL (b. 1938)

Born Newton Edward Daniels in Britain, he began his performing career in his teens; after a term in the Army (during which, in Hong Kong, he did numerous performances for servicemen), he began playing workingmen's clubs and other venues, at first with his brother Trevor, and later with his wife under the billing of "The Eldanis."

An appearance on Britain's Granada Television brought him national attention; many further television appearances followed, as well as bookings at the Savoy Hotel and the London Palladium, and a featured spot in the Royal Charity Gala. Later engagements included acting as host for several B.B.C.-TV shows.

For several years his partner and featured assistant has been *Debbie McGee*.

Now the star of his own television show and numerous international specials (as well as appearances in Las Vegas), Daniels is perhaps the best-known magician in Britain. He is a member of the Inner MAGIC CIRCLE with Gold Star.

DANTE (1883-1955)

Born Harry Jansen in Denmark, he emigrated to the U.S. as a small child. His first involvement in magic was as an ILLUSION builder. Turning to performing, he was eventually chosen by HOWARD THURSTON to run the Thurston Number Two show, and it was Thurston who gave him the name Dante.

Dante toured the world with the show, now calling it SIM-SALA-BIM, performing everywhere from Australia to Russia and Africa to Britain with great success. Returning to the U.S., he opened his show on Broadway to rave reviews.

He continued performing for many years, both on stage and on such television shows as *You Asked For It* and films including *A-Haunting We Will Go, Bunco Squad,* and *Racket Busters*.

He was noted for his distinctive presentations of such EFFECTS as CORDS OF PHANTASIA and his own BACKSTAGE ILLUSION.

(An earlier performer also used the name Dante; *see* DANTE, THE MORMON WIZARD.)

DANTE, THE MORMON WIZARD (1869-1899)

Born Oscar Eliason, he began his performing career in his early twenties with a tour of the U.S., and then appeared in New Zealand and Australia. In the latter country he was killed as the result of a shooting accident during a hunt.

Daryl

DARWIN, GARY (b. ?)

Performer based in Las Vegas who is most noted for his books on the THUMB TIP: *Thumb Tip Secrets, Thumb Tip Thinking,* and *Thumb Tip Miracles*.

DARYL (b. 1955)

Born Daryl Martinez, he is a specialist in close-up magic. He has performed at the Aladdin and Caesar's Palace in Las Vegas; on several television shows and specials, including *The Today Show;* for TRADE SHOWS, in hospitality suites, and other corporate functions, and for private clubs and engagements.

He has won numerous awards, including twice being honored as Close-Up Magician Of The Year by the ACADEMY OF MAGICAL ARTS, First Place for Close-Up Magic at FISM, and First Place at the Las Vegas Desert Seminar Close-Up competition.

He has invented numerous effects, including **Ultimate Ambition, Jumping Knot Of Pakistan,** and **Cardboard Chameleons**.

His books include *Something For Everyone* and (with STEPHEN MINCH) *Secrets Of A Puerto Rican Gambler*.

DAUB

A colored, pasty substance which may be applied to cards by the performer's finger tip, marking them for later location; it is also used (but rarely) in crooked gambling.

Commercial daubs are available both from magic dealers and gambling supply houses; many performers, however, use instead an appropriately colored eye-shadow which will serve the purpose as well or better.

DAVENPORT, BETTY (b. ?)

Daughter of GEORGE DAVENPORT; current proprietor (with her husband Fergus Roy) of L. Davenport & Co.

DAVENPORT, GEORGE (1906-1962)

Son of LEWIS DAVENPORT; known to many by his nickname of "Gilly." Entering the family business, he rarely performed professionally but was legendary as a behind-the-counter demonstrator/performer of magic.

DAVENPORT, LEWIS (1883-1961)

British magician who achieved success both as performer and inventor, but is best known as the founder of **L. Davenport & Co.**, the company which still bears his name.

Davenport's stage act had several original features; of these, one legendary item was his color-changing vest, which altered its appearance several times in the course of the act. His most popular creation for the magical marketplace was his version of the MUTILATED PARASOL.

DAVENPORT BROTHERS

Professional spirit mediums, Ira (1839-1911) and William (1841-1877) Davenport began their careers in 1855; a decade later they performed in Britain, where participating in an exposure of their methods led JOHN NEVIL MASKELYNE into a performing career.

Their demonstration consisted of being secured with ropes inside a large wooden cabinet; musical instruments, also inside the cabinet, would then begin to play—apparently by spirit aid. This was the first version of the popular SPIRIT CABINET routine. An excellent account of the brothers and their routine can be found in HARRY HOUDINI's *A Magician Among The Spirits*.

DAWES, EDWIN A., DR. (b. ?)

Noted Scottish collector, historian, and writer; author of *The Great Illusionists* and many articles on historical subjects for THE MAGIC CIRCLE. He has also for many years been the book reviewer for the BRITISH RING's publication, *The Budget*.

DAYLIGHT SEANCE

A number of objects are shown on a table—bell, tambourine, paper plates, etc.—and the performer then holds a square of cloth in front of the table; the cloth is grasped at the two upper corners. The tambourine and bell then make noise, and the paper plates come flying over the top of the cloth.

In actuality, the performer only holds the cloth at one corner; a rod is sewn within the upper border, and a set of fake fingers are affixed at the end of this rod. Thus while the performer appears to be holding the cloth with both hands, it is actually supported by one hand, while the other—concealed by the cloth—is free to ring the bell, etc.

The term "daylight seance" has come to mean the principle as much as the specific original ROUTINE described above. The principle has been widely ex-posed, usually as part of a comedy routine, but in a carefully thought-out application can still be quite useful.

DAZZLE CURTAIN

See GLITTER CURTAIN.

DEAD MAN'S HAND

A dramatic card EFFECT created by HENRY CHRIST in which the revelation of a selected card is combined with a SPELLING TRICK and a gambling theme, involving the "Aces and Eights" poker hand supposedly held by Wild Bill Hickok at the moment of his murder.

The effect will be found in THE JINX and also in *Annemann's Card Magic*.

DEALER

Within the context of this encyclopedia, a seller of magical apparatus, books and manuscripts. *See* Magic Novelty Co. (PERCY ABBOTT); TANNEN; SUPREME MAGIC COMPANY; UNIQUE MAGIC STUDIO; L. Davenport & Co. (LEWIS DAVENPORT); MAGIC, INC.

There is a fairly high mortality rate for magic dealerships. It is usually a good idea to ascertain that a shop is still in existence before sending off an order.

DE BIERE, ARNOLD (1878-1934)

Born in Germany, he emigrated to the U.S. as a small child. His career began in small variety venues and theaters. Later he toured Britain, Europe, and Australia with considerable success, settling finally in Britain.

During part of his career he had a large FULL-EVENING SHOW with many ILLUSIONs and elaborate scenery, but he is best remembered for the smaller magic he performed, particularly his routine for the EGG BAG. This routine is described by WILL GOLDSTON in his *Tricks Of The Masters*.

DECAPITATION

An ILLUSION in which a person's head is apparently removed from his or her body. It is one of the oldest illusions extant; a version of it is described in REGINALD SCOT's *Discovery Of Witchcraft*, published in 1584.

Various versions of this illusion have been developed over the years; some incorporate aspects of the SPHINX or GUILLOTINE, while others may use the principle of BLACK ART. Still other versions work on a variety of principles and techniques.

See DAGGER BOX.

DECK SWITCHING

The secret exchange of one deck of cards for another, usually identical in appearance. It is most often used to replace a MECHANICAL DECK with an ordinary one, or vice versa, depending on the routine.

Deck switches can be accomplished in a variety of ways. The most blatant approach is simply to put one deck into a PROP case and later, without comment, take out the other. There are a number of SLEIGHT OF HAND switches in the literature; most are quite difficult and nearly all require the performer to be seated at a table. Of course, any piece of APPARATUS designed to switch one object for another—a CHANGING BAG, for example—can theoretically be used, but in practice such devices used for this particular purpose are obvious.

There are no books available devoted only to this subject; however, an excellent discussion of deck switches may be found in GEORGE SANDERSON's *The Concealed Art Of Magic.*

DE COURCY, HOWARD (b. ?)

Born Martin Veglio in Switzerland; performer with long professional career in British variety. He primarily performed manipulative magic, but was also noted for his exclusive effect GARBO.

DE COURCY, KEN (b. 1922)

Born in Britain, he began his performing career in an ENSA unit after World War II. He is best known as a writer and creator of magical effects; his first book was *Genial Improbabilities,* followed by over 50 more, including *Cards In Cabaret, Luck Of Lucretia, Pentertain, Sequacious Aces,* and *Troublewit Routines.*

He has made countless contributions to such magazines as THE GEN, ABRACADABRA and MAGIGRAM (for the latter magazine he is also managing editor). In addition to providing a large number of the items marketed by SUPREME MAGIC COMPANY, De Courcy has proved an indispensable element of their business as the writer of many of the instruction sheets and ROUTINEs provided with Supreme APPARATUS.

DEDI (?-?)

An Egyptian magician (ca. 3700 B.C.), his is the earliest recorded magical performance. He is described as removing the head of a goose and restoring it, repeating this EFFECT with other kinds of birds, and finally passing a blade through the neck of a bull calf without harming the beast.

The manuscript describing this performance was first obtained by Henry Westcar in 1823 and is known as the WESTCAR PAPYRUS. It was on exhibit for some years at the Berlin State Museum, but disappeared at the end of World War II. The manuscript is now generally believed to be in the Soviet Union.

DE GRISY, EDMOND (1760-1829)

French physician and amateur magician who became a professional performer after a conflict with PINETTI. He toured Europe for many years with considerable success, but in 1826 was imprisoned after the death of his son during a performance of the BULLET CATCH.

Leaving prison penniless, he took the name *Torrini* (his wife's maiden name) and became a vagabond conjurer with a wagon caravan; it was here, while traveling through France, that he met and inspired the young ROBERT-HOUDIN.

It should be noted that all the above information is from Robert-Houdin's *Memoirs,* and there is no independent evidence of De Grisy's existence. Most modern historians consider the De Grisy story to be a complete fabrication.

DE KOLTA, BUATIER (1848-1903)

Born Joseph Buatier in France, he achieved great success as a performer throughout Europe and the eastern United States. He was reputed to be one of the greatest of SLEIGHT OF HAND performers but is chiefly remembered by magicians for his many inventions: the VANISHING BIRD CAGE, the VANISHING LADY, the EXPANDING DIE, SPRING FLOWERS, an early version of the MULTIPLYING BILLIARD BALLS, and many others.

While MAX AUZINGER is generally credited with the creation of the BLACK ART ACT, it is *possible* that De Kolta developed it independently around the same time. In any case he presented an act of this kind at EGYPTIAN HALL in 1886.

DELAGE, AL (b. ?)

Performer who has appeared in nightclubs, resorts and many other venues throughout the U.S.; his television appearances include the *Ed Sullivan* show.

He is particularly noted for his extremely fast-paced style, and was for many years identified with an EFFECT of his own invention called the FASTEST TRICK IN THE WORLD.

Buatier de Kolta (*The Mulholland Library of Conjuring & the Allied Arts*, Los Angeles, California)

Clement de Lion (*The Mulholland Library of Conjuring & the Allied Arts*, Los Angeles, California)

DE LAND, THEODORE L. (1873-1931)

Noted as inventor of many EFFECTS using specially-printed cards, including TWO CARD MONTE, a complex MARKED DECK called the **Deland DOLLAR DECK**, and several others.

DE LION, CLEMENT (1874-1963)

Danish professional performer of the early part of this century; he was considered to be one of the very best SLEIGHT OF HAND performers, specializing in the difficult field of BILLIARD BALL MANIPULATION.

DE LA VEGA, MICHEL (b. ?)

Born in France; highly-successful performer who has appeared throughout Europe. He is noted for his effective variation of the METAMORPHOSIS illusion in which, instead of a trunk, De la Vega uses a large hatbox-shaped container which is roped shut.

DELIRIUM TREMENS DECK

A MECHANICAL DECK created by RALPH W. HULL; it changes from an ordinary-looking deck to one entirely covered on both sides with pictures of snakes, toads, spiders, and other creatures. It operates on an application of the ROUGH-AND-SMOOTH PRINCIPLE.

An excellent ROUTINE in which this deck plays a part is called **An Ancient Chinese Legend**; it will be found in TREVOR H. HALL's *Reading Is Believing*.

DE MANCHE, HENRI (?-?)

Pseudonym of a British performer of the turn of the 20th century about whom almost nothing is known. His legacy to magic consisted of a number of contributions to C. LANG NEIL's *The Modern Conjurer*, of which the best-known is the DE MANCHE CHANGE.

DE MANCHE CHANGE

A technique for a SLEIGHT OF HAND switch of two coins, or objects of similar size. With one coin in FINGER PALM position, the other coin is exhibited at the fingertips. In the course of a movement of the hand and arm, the coin at the finger-tips is taken into a

THUMB PALM, and the finger-palmed coin is then pushed up to the tips of the fingers.

At this point, the performer may allow the coin in thumb palm to slip down into a more natural finger-palm position. If the SLEIGHT has been executed correctly there is no chance that the coins will strike each other—an important consideration.

The sleight is thoroughly described in C. LANG NEIL's *The Modern Conjurer* and HENRY HAY's *Amateur Magician's Handbook*.

DEMON HANDKERCHIEF

British term for the DEVIL'S HANDKERCHIEF.

DEMON WONDER BOX

A small metal PRODUCTION box with doors at front, back, and top; it can be convincingly shown empty, and then from it a large number of silks can be produced. It is so constructed that the LOAD CHAMBER can be removed, leaving the box completely examinable.

The box was first marketed by L. Davenport & Co. (*see* LEWIS DAVENPORT) as one of their Demon Magic products.

An interesting use of this box is described by DAVID BAMBERG in TARBELL COURSE IN MAGIC (Volume 6).

DE PAULA, PETER (b. 1953)

A professional performer while still in his teens, he worked in nightclubs and on cruise ships. Later he studied mime with Marcel Marceau and acting with Lee Strasberg.

He has appeared in many countries throughout the world, primarily with a SILENT ACT which incorporates MIME techniques in its presentation; he was also featured in the starring role in the national touring company of *The Magic Show.*

DESFOR, IRVING (b. 1907)

Photographer by profession; known for his "Photo-Magic" act, and for his countless photographs of magicians over the years, which have appeared in many magic magazines.

Many of these photographs are collected in his *Great Magicians In Great Moments.*

DEUCE

With cards or dice, a value of two.

Peter DePaula

DEVANO DECK

A MECHANICAL DECK invented by Harry Devano for the classic feat of causing one or more chosen cards to rise from the center of the deck. The deck uses no threads or motors, is self-contained, and can make as many cards rise as desired by the performer, either in his hands or while standing alone. It is, not surprisingly, one of the most popular ways of achieving this effect.

DEVANT, DAVID (1868-1941)

Born David Wighton in Britain, he is generally considered to be one of that country's greatest magicians. He performed for over a decade at EGYPTIAN HALL, and for a like amount of time at ST. GEORGE'S HALL, in partnership with JOHN NEVIL MASKELYNE. After that he performed in various venues for about five years, then falling victim to an illness which left him an invalid for the last twenty years of his life.

Devant created a number of ILLUSIONS, including the ARTIST'S DREAM, BEAU BROCADE, HAUNTED WINDOW, MASCOT MOTH and many others.

Devant was noted for his pleasing personality and

David Devant (*The Mulholland Library of Conjuring & the Allied Arts*, Los Angeles, California)

charming presentational style, indications of which can be found in his books: *My Magic Life, Secrets Of My Magic*, and *Our Magic*, the last written in collaboration with John Nevil Maskelyne.

DE VEGA (1892-1971)

Born Alexander Mackay Stewart, this Scottish magician toured a FULL-EVENING SHOW through his country for many years. He was a founding member of the Scottish Conjurer's Association, and was also known for his many contributions to magical magazines.

In collaboration with CHRIS VAN BERN, he wrote *A Whirlwind of Wizardry*. He also produced a series of manuscripts on various subjects—many of them, as for example *The Devil's Whisper And Its Development*, having to do with FIRE MAGIC and other pyrotechnic effects.

An ILLUSION titled The Divided Lady, invented by De Vega, is said to have been ROBERT HARBIN's inspiration for his famous ZIG-ZAG GIRL.

DE VERE, CHARLES (1843-1931)

Born Herbert Williams in Britain, he became a professional magician while still in his teens. After briefly operating a magic shop in London, he toured throughout Europe for some time.

Settling in France, he opened a new magic shop in Paris, which stayed in operation for over thirty years. His wife Julia (*see* OKITA) and daughter (see IONIA) were both magical performers of note. Another daughter, Elise, was well known as a singer.

DEVIL OF A HAT

Name given by JOSEPH HARTZ to his HAT PRODUCTION, which was undoubtedly the most elaborate such ROUTINE ever devised. It is thoroughly described in the second and later editions of PROFESSOR LOUIS HOFFMANN's *Later Magic*.

DEVIL'S FIRE

A small GIMMICK with which the performer is able to make a large stream of fire erupt from a candle flame. The gimmick consists of a small plastic squeeze bottle (often attached to a flesh-colored metal clip to grip it between the fingers) containing a powder which will ignite in air; various chemicals have been used, including sulfur and lycopodium.

As with any pyrotechnic device, care must be taken in its use, and it should be well rehearsed and tested.

The gimmick has also been marketed as **Dragon's Breath**, among other names.

Greatly improved gimmicks making use of this general principle have been created and marketed by JAY SCOTT BERRY; they are also described in his book *Magic For The New World*.

DEVIL'S HANDKERCHIEF

An innocent-looking handkerchief which has a hidden pocket, usually comprising a full quarter of the surface area. With the handkerchief folded into quarters to form a bag of sorts, the performer can place his hand into the handkerchief proper or into the secret pocket with equal ease. It is sometimes used for PRODUCTIONs but more often for vanishing of small objects.

DEW, DANNY (b. 1906)

Performer who entered show business in his twenties as part of a song-and-dance act. Switching to magic, he toured extensively through the U.S., at first by himself and then with his wife Melba (whose own novelty act eventually included SAND PICTURES and RAG PICTURES, as well as "lightning sketches").

Later settling in Arizona, he operated, at various times, a magic shop and a booking agency, continuing to perform throughout the state. He also worked as a master chef for various hotels and with his own catering service.

Dew is highly regarded as a performer by both the public and magicians; of particular note are his LINKING RING and CUPS AND BALLS routines.

In 1976 he was the recipient of a Special Fellowship from the ACADEMY OF MAGICAL ARTS.

DEXTER, DOUGLAS (1878-1937)

Born Bernard Douglas Marks, this British magician was noted not only for his extremely baffling and meticulously routined magic, but also for his fencing expertise; he was on the British Olympic fencing team *four times*. In 1934, while in the U.S. to compete in the American open *epee* Championship—which he won—Dexter gave a performance for the New York City S.A.M. members; his CARD STAB, among many other feats, thoroughly baffled many well-informed magicians.

A schoolmaster by profession, Dexter also played many professional engagements, including a Royal Command performance and an appearance at EGYPTIAN HALL; he also performed and lectured for the MAGIC CIRCLE, which awarded him its Gold Star.

Regrettably, little of Dexter's work survived him; his SILK DYEING routine is described in DAVID DEVANT's *Secrets Of My Magic*, and a few of his routines (including the fabled card stabbing effect) were published in PETER WARLOCK's PENTAGRAM Magazine. A few other items were published in Percy Naldrett's *Collected Magic* and *Expert Magic* series of books.

DEXTER, WILL (1906-1985)

Born William Pritchard, he was the author of a number of books on magic; a few were directed within the profession, but most of his writing was for the public at large.

In his books Dexter was able to get across to the public the idea of magic as an art, disclosing a bare minimum of technical information to do so. Titles include *This Is Magic*, *Everybody's Book of Magic*, and *The Riddle Of Chung Ling Soo*.

His books for magicians include *Feature Magic For Mentalists*, *Identity Parade*, and *The Uncanny Power*. He also wrote two notable series of articles (on MENTALISM and publicity) which appeared in the British magic magazine THE GEN but have not as yet appeared in book form. In addition, he contributed many effects to various periodicals and was the editor of the book *Magic Circle Magic*.

DHOTEL, JULES (1879-1967)

Born in France; a doctor by profession, he was noted in the fields of music and sculpture as well as magic. He chaired the FISM congresses in 1947 and 1951; he also was involved in several magical societies.

He wrote several books on magic; one of these, *Magic With Small Apparatus*, was translated into English by PAUL FLEMING.

DIACHYLON

An adhesive, of the kind once used on bandages, formerly used in card magic to make one card temporarily adhere to another; this is now usually accomplished with a tiny ball of beeswax or a small square of double-stick cellophane tape.

DIACONIS, PERSI, DR. (b. 1945)

A noted professor of statistics, within magic he is considered one of the half-dozen top SLEIGHT-OF-HAND performers with cards, a level he had reached in his late teens.

Diaconis is also noted for his book collection, covering not only magic, but also several related areas. He has originated a number of EFFECTS, only a few of which have seen print, usually under pen-names; an exception is *Les Cartes Diaconis*, which can be found in *Dai Vernon's Ultimate Secrets Of Card Magic* by LEWIS GANSON.

He is the first magician-recipient of the prestigious Macarthur Foundation grant (the first *professional* magician to receive this award is JAMES RANDI).

DIAGONAL PALM SHIFT

A card SLEIGHT invented by S. W. ERDNASE in which a card pushed into the deck is moved into a diagonal position, and then out of the deck and into the palm of the deck-holding hand under cover of a forward-and-back SQUARING action.

It is not a SHIFT as herein defined, but is akin in its action to the SIDE STEAL.

The sleight is described in Erdnase's *Expert At The Card Table*.

DIAMOND CUT DIAMOND

A card EFFECT invented by ALEX ELMSLEY in which, a card having been previously selected, the performer shows the thirteen cards of the Diamond suit arranged in numerical order. The cards are turned face down and the spectator is asked to name a value; as the cards are dealt out in order, it is seen that the Diamond of the named value has vanished and has been replaced with the selected card, all other cards being in their proper order.

DICE STACKING

This FLOURISH using a dice cup and (usually) four dice looks more like magic than dexterity; the cup is held mouth down and the dice are scooped into it one by one. When the cup is lifted, the dice are stacked up in a single column.

A number of books on this subject are available, including ED MARLO's *Shoot The Works*, AUDLEY WALSH's *Dice Dexterity*, and CLARKE CRANDALL's *How To Stack Dice*; others are *Diversions with Dice* by Treborix and *Zach Stacks* by Jim Zachary.

DI-CIPHERING DICE

A commercially-marketed EFFECT of MATHEMATICAL MAGIC using five dice, the sides of each bearing two-or-three digit numbers; the dice may be fairly thrown, but the performer is instantly able to ascertain the total of the upper faces.

The effect, invented by Royal V. Heath (after an earlier effect by Edmund Balducci) is thoroughly described in MARTIN GARDNER's *Mathematics, Magic, and Mystery* and also in J. G. THOMPSON, JR.'s compilation, *My Best*. In the latter book, there is an interesting article by VERNE CHESBRO exploring further possibilities with the dice.

A later version of this effect was described by D.R. Kaprekar in *Mantra* (an Indian magazine published by Sam Dalal); in Kaprekar's version five- and six-digit numbers are used, making the effect even more impressive.

DICKSON, ABB (b. 1948)

Born Abner Dickson, he began his performing career in amusement parks including Six Flags Over Georgia, first as a magician and later as writer and producer of stage shows. He then entered the INDUSTRIAL SHOW and TRADE SHOW field, and created special effects for films.

In 1975 he wrote, directed and starred in his production of *Presto!*, a FULL-EVENING SHOW which

Abb Dickson and friend

toured extensively and was very favorably received. Dickson later created a shorter show, *Abnercadabra*, which was featured as the entire second half of MILT LARSEN's *It's Magic* production in Los Angeles. He also wrote and starred in a cable-television special with ORSON WELLES titled *Orson Welles At The Magic Castle*.

DIDO

An ILLUSION in which a large glass box filled with water is shown and covered briefly with a cloth; when the cloth is removed a woman has appeared in the water. The effect is repeated to produce a second and, sometimes, a third person.

This illusion was featured for a season in the show of HOWARD THURSTON; it was then eliminated, perhaps because of an incident related by GEORGE BOSTON in his *Inside Magic*, in which an ASSISTANT concealed in the water-filled secret compartment nearly drowned. However, the basic premise of the story is flatly contradicted in GUY JARRETT's *Jarrett Magic And Stagecraft—Technical*; Jarrett's description of the illusion (which he disliked) indicates the assistants entered the water-filled box from a dry secret compartment behind it in the supporting base.

DIE

A small cube, usually with spots indicating values from one to six on its sides. The spots on opposite sides of a die will always total seven (six and one, five and two, three and four). European and U.S. dice are numbered in a slightly different pattern; with the die set so that the one, two, and three faces are visible, the European die will show the one, two, three order in clockwise pattern, while the U.S.-manufactured die shows the same sequence in a counterclockwise pattern.

Some magical writers have seriously suggested the use of LOADED DICE to FORCE a number, but this strategem is generally neither advisable nor practical. Most, if not all, laypeople have heard of loaded dice and will immediately consider this possibility; also, most professionally manufactured loaded dice only come up on their specific number a high percentage of the time, since a die weighted heavily enough to produce a certain result would also be very obvious in operation.

In many magical effects (such as the DIE BOX) the term *die* simply refers to a large (usually about 3-inch square) appropriately decorated BLOCK.

DIE BOX

A classic EFFECT of APPARATUS magic believed to have been invented to JOHANN HOFZINSER; it uses a large (3-inch square) DIE and a double-doored box twice as wide as the die. The die is placed within the box and a SUCKER EFFECT routine is gone through, the performer opening one door at a time after apparently having slid the die to the other half of the box. Finally, both doors are opened to show the die has vanished, to reappear in a hat or other receptacle. The effect is accomplished by an application of the SHELL principle.

There have been many models of die box, varying both in size and complexity; many have incorporated additional principles to allow the die to be shown in the box after it has been removed.

See SUCKER EFFECTs.

DIETRICH, BUD (b. 1923)

Born Carl Dietrich, he began his performing career working in varied venues as a dinner entertainer, for various fraternal and business organizations, and in nightclubs. In 1962, he was one of the first magicians to break into the INDUSTRIAL SHOW field, working as a corporate entertainer for Westinghouse for over a decade.

He then began performing in TRADE SHOWS for

Bud Dietrich

General Motors and many other clients, including Faberge and the shows for which he is best known in magic—Hoyle Playing Cards, for whom he became "Mr. Hoyle." He was the MASTER OF CEREMONIES for the Omar Sharif Bridge Circus, and he has also performed on the state fair circuit throughout the U.S.

Dietrich is the author (with Dick Jarrow) of *The Trade Show Handbook.*

DIME AND PENNY

A standard POCKET TRICK using a special dime and penny set which permits the dime to apparently vanish without trace. It uses an application of the SHELL principle in conjunction with a DOUBLE-FACE coin.

Several routines for this coin set will be found in *The Dime And Penny Book* by LLOYD JONES.

DIMINISHING BALL

A BILLIARD BALL of the standard size for MANIPULATION is caused to shrink to half its size, then to one-fourth, and finally to a tiny ball which disappears. Often presented as an interlude in the MULTIPLYING BILLIARD BALLS or other ball routines, the effect uses a combination of a specially

FAKEd set of balls and manipulative skill. It is possible to perform the EFFECT with a set of balls graduated in size but otherwise unprepared.

It has also been marketed in a set of rubber GOLF BALLS.

DIMINISHING CARDS

A group of cards (generally a half-dozen or so) shrink to half-size; this process is repeated several times until the cards are almost too small to see clearly, at which point they vanish.

Although there are SLEIGHT-OF-HAND methods for creating this EFFECT with a full deck of fanned cards, it is usually accomplished by means of specially prepared sets of cards; a number of different versions are available for use in a variety of performing conditions.

DIMINISHING SILK PRODUCTION

A very popular EFFECT of SILK MAGIC invented by ERIC C. LEWIS in which a silk is snapped by one corner, and a slightly smaller silk appears tied to it. The silks are untied and the smaller one is snapped, and a still smaller silk appears; the procedure can be repeated several times.

In an oft-used variant the silks are all of the same size; this is best done in stage situations where the performer is distant enough from the spectators that the bulk of the prepared silks will not be revealed. The effect is described in HAROLD R. RICE's *Capers With Color*.

DIMMER

A type of rheostat which controls the amount of electrical current running to stage lighting, and thus the brightness or intensity.

DINGLE, DEREK (b. 1937)

Born in Britain, he emigrated first to Canada and then to the U.S.; he is a highly regarded CLOSE-UP performer, and has appeared several times on national television as well as TRADE SHOWS and private party work. He is noted for his invention of the ROLLOVER ACES, a showy revelation of the aces after they have apparently been lost in the deck.

His work is described in his *Derek Dingle Book*, in HARRY LORAYNE's *Dingle's Deceptions*, and in RICHARD KAUFMAN's *Complete Works of Derek Dingle*.

DIPPY DUCK

British name for an EFFECT designed and marketed by JACK HUGHES which was similar (but not identical) to the CARD DUCK.

DISAPPEARING HEAD BOX

A small bottomless cabinet which is placed over an ASSISTANT's head; the front doors are opened and the head has apparently vanished.

This EFFECT has been accomplished by a number of methods; simply having the assistant tilt his or her head backward through a swinging rear flap; use of BLACK ART; or sophisticated applications of the MIRROR PRINCIPLE.

See DAGGER BOX.

DISCOVERY

A particular way of revealing a selected card; both the CARD STAB and the RISING CARDS are types of discovery.

It has been observed by J.G. THOMPSON, JR., that if a performer knows a hundred ways of locating a selected card but only one discovery, the impression on the audience is that the performer knows one EFFECT; if, contrariwise, the performer knows only one way of locating the selection but a hundred different discoveries, the audience thinks the performer knows a hundred effects.

A book by Thompson which neatly illustrates this thesis is *The Living End*, which consists entirely of ways of revealing a selected card.

DISECTO

A variant of the CHOPPER effect, this APPARATUS uses a blade in a pivoting frame and a vaguely stocklike arrangement into which the spectator places his wrist; when the blade descends, carrots or similar items placed in adjacent holes are cut in half, but the spectator's wrist is unharmed.

The effect was first marketed in the 1930's by Abbott's Magic Co. (*see* PERCY ABBOTT).

DISEMBODIED PRINCESS

See GIRL WITHOUT A MIDDLE.

DISSOLVO PAPER

A type of paper, usually blue in color, with the property of instantly dissolving in water or other liquid. Though it is now used often in criminal circles to keep records that may have to be destroyed rapidly, magicians are beginning to develop ways of employing it in more benign areas of deception.

DISTRACTION

Diversion of the audience's attention by a strong stimulus, usually sudden and often apparently accidental. A classic example of distraction was used by HARRY BLACKSTONE SR. in an effect where the audience's attention had to be briefly drawn away from a DUCK VANISH box at upstage center. This was accomplished by the entrance of an ASSISTANT carrying a pistol on a tray; the assistant momentarily stumbled, instantly catching himself—but for that instant all attention had centered on him, and the necessary procedure at the box had been executed.

Distraction differs from MISDIRECTION in that an audience may realize that their attention has been distracted, but are unaware of the misdirection of their attention. Also, **Distraction** as a principle is best used very sparingly, whereas misdirective technique can be used not only through an entire act but also in creating its basic concept.

DITCH

To secretly dispose of an article; if the article has been on view, *ditching* can take place either before or after the article vanishes from the spectators' point of view.

DIVIDED CARD

Another term for DOUBLE-ENDER.

DIVIDED DECK

An elementary variety of stacked deck (*see* STACK), in which the cards are sorted into two approximately equal halves by some criterion (red/black, odd/even, high/low).

A card taken from one section and replaced in the other will be easy to locate, but there are many more subtle applications of the principle.

DIVINATION

The discernment and revelation of information in the mind of a spectator, as for example the identity of a selected card. The term within stage magic does not imply prophecy or PREDICTION. In occultism, however, it pertains specifically to foretelling the future.

DIZZY LIMIT

An ILLUSION created by Oswald Williams in which a net containing a person in its fold is suspended above the stage by ropes or chains. Suddenly the net falls open and the person visibly vanishes. The EFFECT, used by many present-day magicians, operates by means of a sophisticated technical application of the principle of BLACK ART.

Also known as the **Cargo Net** illusion.

DOBLER, LUDWIG (1801-1864)

Born in Austria, he toured throughout Europe and the British Isles with considerable success and spawned many imitators. He was noted for his skill at SLEIGHT-OF-HAND, his elaborate APPARATUS effects, and his many command performances for European royalty.

DOBRIN SLATE

Term sometimes used to refer to a particular model of the ADDITION SLATE which was manufactured by Harry Dobrin; it should be noted that Dobrin also manufactured another slate called the Periscope Slate, which had a concealed mirror which could be used to gain a reflected peek at writing on a spectator's slate.

DODSON, GOODLETTE H. (?-1970)

Expert on CARD FANNING; author of *Exhibition Card Fans*, considered by many to be the definitive work on the subject.

DOLLAR DECK

A type of MARKED DECK devised by THEODORE L. DELAND; it is used in conjunction with a version of the SI STEBBINS STACK, and is undoubtedly the most complex marked deck ever manufactured and commercially marketed. Deland claimed the deck had over 14,000 separate markings.

Not only does the back of each card reveal the identity of its face, but also the location of every other card in the deck! The top card of the deck will also indicate the bottom card; if the deck has been CUT into two portions, a special set of MARKS will indicate how many cards are in each portion.

Most versions of the deck are also prepared as STRIPPER DECKS.

DOLLAR THIRTY-FIVE TRICK

A set of coins consisting of two half-dollars, a quarter and a dime; all are placed within the hand and one of the half-dollars is removed. When the hand is opened, the remaining coins have vanished.

The effect is accomplished by an extended application of the SHELL principle.

An excellent routine for this set of FAKE coins is Rolland Hamblen's **85 cents through the table**; it appears in BOBO's *Modern Coin Magic*.

See also TWENTY-ONE CENT TRICK; TWO-EIGHTY-FIVE TRICK.

DOLL HOUSE

An ILLUSION invented by FREDERICK CULPITT in which what appears to be a child's Doll House on a small platform is shown empty by the opening of hinged double doors at one end; the doors being closed, an ASSISTANT makes her appearance from within by pushing open the hinged roof.

A variant, invented by JACK GWYNNE, is known as the **Temple of Benares** (Gwynne's own name for the illusion was the **Temple of An-Gee**, named for his wife, Anne). In this version, the woman gets into the Dollhouse (usually decorated in quasi-Oriental fashion), which then has swords thrust through it at various angles a la the SWORD BOX. The front doors are opened to show an interior crisscrossed with sword blades but otherwise apparently empty. When the swords are removed, the assistant is reproduced unharmed from within. Both versions of the illusion employ the principles of the FALSE WALL and the BEVEL BASE.

Aubrey's presentation of the *Doll House* illusion, which incorporated aspects of the *Costume Trunk*

DOMINIQUE (?-?)

Born in France, he began his performing career as a MANIPULATOR, later performing an act of general magic and ventriloquism. In the 1950's he developed his PICKPOCKET ACT which he has performed ever since. He has been featured in many Las Vegas clubs including the Sands, New Frontier, Sahara, Flamingo, Desert Inn and Stardust; he has also appeared in Monte Carlo, in Paris's Lido show, and many other venues.

DORNFIELD, WERNER C. (1892-1982)

Known throughout the magical community simply as *Dorny*, he began his performing career while a soldier in World War I, attached to a show unit. Later he appeared in Vaudeville and worked in nightclubs, first as a magician and then as the "Magical Master Of Ceremonies"—a billing and concept he originated and which was heavily copied by others. Still later, he made a specialty of business conventions, being introduced at banquets as a visiting executive. After a very serious beginning he would gradually move into his comedy and magic.

He is noted as the first person to suggest a magic

Werner C. ("Dorny") Dornfield (*photo courtesy GENII Magazine*)

convention (in his book *Trix And Chatter*), and was very active in the production of various conventions throughout his long career. He was the recipient of a Masters Fellowship from the ACADEMY OF MAGICAL ARTS.

His books (in addition to the previously mentioned *Trix And Chatter*) include *Comedy Blackouts* and *Dorny On Trix*.

DOUBLE

A person attired and made up to resemble the performer or an ASSISTANT. **Doubles** may be used in many different kinds of ILLUSION, particularly those involving TRANSPOSITION; one example is the THREE GRACES.

In the elaborate presentations of KIO, several sets of doubles were used in a single performance. On a more modest scale, several illusionists have used identical twins as assistants.

W. E. Robinson, later to achieve fame as CHUNG LING SOO, often doubled for his employer ALEXANDER HERRMANN—and at times did the entire show as Herrmann, the audience being none the wiser.

The idea of using **doubles** or twins in magic is one that often occurs to lay persons; thus, in some EFFECTs for which this is an obvious (and incorrect) explanation, the performer must so arrange the presentation that this possibility is discounted.

DOUBLE-BACK

A playing card printed with a back on both sides. Though such a card would seem useless to a lay person, in fact there are many ingenious EFFECTs which can be accomplished by its use.

The double-backed card is believed to have been first employed by HOFZINSER. It was used by THEODORE L. DELAND in his marketed TWO-CARD MONTE effect, and was brought into modern use in card magic by DAI VERNON.

DOUBLE CARD

See THICK CARD.

DOUBLE DOVE PRODUCTION

A special set of two DOVE HARNESSes, connected by a gut line and worn in pockets behind each lapel; invented by CHANNING POLLOCK.

The usual procedure for the **double dove production** is to knot two silk handkerchieves together and place the knot in the mouth; the two silks hang down in front of the chest. The line which connects the two harnesses has been secured in the knot, and as the performer lifts his head up the harnesses are drawn from the lapel pockets and grasped by the performer behind the hanging silks. With the knotted silks held out at arm's length, the performer grasps the outer side of each harness and pulls outward; the gut line holds the inner side of each harness, and thus both open simultaneously.

The double dove production is beautiful and effective when done properly; it is, however, far from easy to do cleanly and deceptively, and is an effect unlikely to be correctly performed without tutoring from a performer who knows it well.

DOUBLE-ENDER

A specially printed playing card which can show one of two identities. A Jack of Spades, for example, can have one INDEX altered to indicate the Jack of Clubs; when showing the card the performer's fingers conceal the lower index.

Usually the two cards represented will be fairly close in value, so that most of the card's surface can be shown. In some EFFECTs, however, the card is placed in a stand which conceals half its length; in such cases the double-ender can be made from two half cards glued to the FACE of a full-size card.

At one time, a FORCE deck known as the Monte Cristo Cards was marketed; this consisted of a regular card at the face of the deck and 51 double-enders. The cards at one end were all different, at the other end was the force card.

DOUBLE-FACE

Used to indicate an item which can be made to represent two different identities, depending on which side is exhibited. The most common use of the principle is with cards printed to show a different face on each side. It is also extensively used in the design of various mechanical effects of COIN MAGIC; see, for example, COPPER/SILVER COIN and CHINATOWN QUARTER.

DOUBLE LIFT

A basic card SLEIGHT in which two cards are taken from the deck as one and shown as a single card. It is useful in many effects, notably AMBITIOUS CARD routines, and is believed to be the invention of CLIFF GREEN (who was the first to use it in present-day card magic).

There are many techniques for accomplishing this sleight; with any of them, the most important factor is

a casual handling which replicates the way the performer would lift a single card.

Triple and **quadruple** lifts use the same basic techniques with three and four cards.

The double lift is described in HUGARD and BRAUE's *Expert Card Technique* and most other books on basic card magic.

DOUBLE SAWING

Created by BILLY MCCOMB, this is an elaboration of the SAWING THROUGH A WOMAN routine.

DOUBLE UNDERCUT

A technique worked out by both ARTHUR BUCKLEY and DAI VERNON to move a card or cards from the top of the deck to the bottom, or vice versa.

Presuming the top card is to be moved to the bottom, a BREAK is held beneath it by the right hand as it holds the deck from above in a position similar to that used for a BIDDLE COUNT. The left hand under-cuts about half the deck and places it on top; another cut is made by the left hand, this time removing all the cards below the break and placing them on top.

The deck has apparently been fairly cut twice, but in fact the only change has been the movement of the top card to the bottom.

This move is excellently applied by Vernon in his **Cutting the Aces** routine which appears in *Stars Of Magic*.

DOUBLE WALL

Just what it sounds like—an apparently single wall which is actually two very thin walls with a space between. It is used in a number of very diverse items, from the MILK PITCHER to the JAP BOX.

The principle is also employed in a number of illusions, such as the DOLL HOUSE; here, however, it must be carefully designed and decorated to be deceptive, since a double or false wall is often the first solution considered by a spectator.

DOVE ACT

Act in which the primary EFFECT is the continuous production of live doves, usually from silks or bare-handed. The major early exponent of dove magic (and originator of the Dove Act as such) was CANTU; the performer who first achieved world-wide recognition with this type of act was CHANNING POLLOCK.

At present the premier exponent of the serious approach to this act is LANCE BURTON, who performs in a dramatic style; a lighter touch is taken by

JOHNNY THOMPSON, who as The Great Tomsoni & Co. performs a brilliant comedy version of the "classical" act.

DOVE BOTTLE

A bottle which, having been used to pour a few drinks, is broken open to reveal a live dove.

Dove bottles are of two basic kinds. The first is made entirely of metal; an upper compartment may contain liquid, a lower section (with ventilating holes) the bird. It is so constructed that it will break into two jagged-edged pieces.

The second variety uses only an upper half of metal; the lower half is cut from an actual bottle and is of glass.

The effect is rarely performed, in part because its mystery value is not that great, but primarily because to some audience members it has the appearance of cruelty to the bird.

DOVECOTE VANISH

A large square cage sits on a table just large enough to hold it; within it are several doves which the performer has produced in the course of the act. The cage is covered with a large cloth and brought forward. Suddenly, the cloth is snapped in the air and shown empty, the cage and birds having vanished.

The effect makes use of a VANISHING CLOTH with a wire frame sewn within it which will simulate the top of the cage, and a cage which is designed to collapse into the table without harm to the birds. There are many different models of the APPARATUS available, and they vary widely in quality.

The effect is quite popular as a CLOSER for performers specializing in DOVE MAGIC. Indeed, it is so popular that it has largely lost the element of surprise; many lay persons recognize the PROP the moment it is shown on stage.

In performing this effect, it is usually preferable to have an assistant remove the table from beneath the cloth before moving forward with the cloth; a kind of "psychological retention" is created in the spectator's mind which heightens the final vanish.

DOVE HARNESS

A small tube of cloth, open at each end, and held closed along its length by velcro or snap fasteners; the dove is placed within, the head and tail projecting from the ends of the tube.

At the head end, the **dove harness** is fitted with a rigid loop, usually of piano wire but sometimes of stiff gut; with the dove harness placed within a special pocket in the performer's clothing, this loop projects unseen from the clothing and can be caught by the thumb or finger.

The usual application of such harnesses is to produce a bird from a silk handkerchief; the harness is made of material which matches the silk to be used, and harness and silk are put aside as one after the production of the bird. If a bird is to be produced from a newspaper, the cloth for the harness will have a newsprint design.

Various types of dove harness are discussed in IAN ADAIR's *Encyclopedia Of Dove Magic.*

See DOVE MAGIC; DOUBLE DOVE PRODUCTION.

DOVE MAGIC

Usually consisting of several productions of birds, this is a popular element in many silent acts, including those of LANCE BURTON, JOSEPH, JOHN THOMPSON, HARUO SHIMADA and others.

Though productions are the mainstay of such acts,

Silvan performing a feat of *Dove Magic* (*photo courtesy GENII Magazine*).

many other effects have been created using doves or similar birds; among the many sources for information on this subject are IAN ADAIR's *Encyclopedia Of Dove Magic* in five volumes and the *Dove Worker's Handbook* (two volumes) by Hutton and HADES.

DOVE PAN

A large pan designed like a chafing dish (which it is sometimes called). The contents of the pan briefly covered with the lid, and on its removal are seen to have transformed into whatever the performer desires to produce—cake, doves, etc.

The LOAD is concealed in the lid and is automatically released when this is placed on the pan.

One version of this effect uses, instead of the pan, a FIRE BOWL. The lid is placed on the bowl to extinguish the flames, and the production follows.

A book devoted entirely to this device is BRUCE POSGATE's *Dove Pan-Orama.*

DOVETAIL SHUFFLE

Technically, a synonym for the BUTT SHUFFLE, but now also widely used as a synonym for the RIFFLE SHUFFLE.

DOVE TO SILK

An effect invented by CHANNING POLLOCK (inspired by earlier effects of KARL GERMAIN and ARNOLD DE BIERE), and featured by many performers specializing in DOVE MAGIC, in which a dove tossed into the air seemingly changes visibly into a white silk handkerchief.

The dove is actually left in the PROFONDE at the bottom of the downward movement before the toss, and a previously palmed silk is thrown into the air. This bald description may indicate the effect is a simple one; in fact it is one of the most difficult effects to perform convincingly, since it depends primarily on timing and acting—abilities which are difficult to teach.

DOWLER, ARTHUR (?-1953)

British magician who became a full-time professional in late middle age and achieved considerable success with his unique brand of comedy magic.

DOWNS, T. NELSON (1867-1938)

Born Thomas Nelson Downs, he created an act consisting entirely of COIN MAGIC. It was thought that coins would be too small to be effective on the variety

Arthur Dowler, a publicity card (*The Mulholland Library of Conjuring & the Allied Arts, Los Angeles, California*)

T. Nelson Downs (*The Mulholland Library of Conjuring & the Allied Arts, Los Angeles, California*)

stage, but from the very beginning of his career Downs was successful, eventually becoming one of the highest-paid acts in vaudeville. Billed as the "King Of Koins," he was equally successful in Britain and Europe, where he performed before several reigning monarchs and heads of state.

Downs' act was built around the MISER'S DREAM (his name for the EFFECT of producing coins from the air), but included many other effects, for example, the COIN LADDER.

His work is described in his two books (largely written by their respective editors), *Modern Coin Manipulation* (edited by WILLIAM J. HILLIAR) and *The Art Of Magic* (edited by JOHN NORTHERN HILLIARD).

DOWNS CHANGE

A method of switching a card in the act of dealing it to the table.

The deck is held face-up across the palm with the two face cards jogged about an inch outward toward the fingers; the thumb holds the cards in place. As the hand is turned over the thumb draws back the FACE CARD of the deck and the fingers push the second card outward, placing it on the table as the front card is drawn square with the rest of the deck.

There are many variations in handling and technique.

DOWNS PALM

A coin palming technique invented by T. NELSON DOWNS in which the coin is held horizontally in the fork of the thumb; with the hand held facing the audience and the thumb parallel to the first finger, the hand will appear empty when one or more coins are palmed in this manner. It is thoroughly described in BOBO's *Modern Coin Magic*. A book devoted entirely to this subject is *Downs Palm Technique* by HORACE BENNETT.

An excellent application of this PALM to a MISER'S DREAM routine is that of Lee Noble; it will be found in BRUCE ELLIOTT's *Classic Secrets Of Magic*.

DOWNSTAGE

That part of the stage nearest the audience.
See also UPSTAGE; STAGE LEFT/STAGE RIGHT; PROMPT SIDE; OPPOSITE PROMPT.

DOWN-UNDER DEAL

See AUSTRALIAN DEAL.

DRAGON'S BREATH

See DEVIL'S FIRE.

DRAW BACK

With cards, another term for the GLIDE.

DRAWER BOX

A box which may be shown empty by pulling out the drawer which occupies the whole of the interior; a PRODUCTION of various items may then be made. The box can also be used in reverse to VANISH an item. It operates by means of an ingenious version of the SHELL principle.

DRAWING-ROOM MAGIC

See PARLOR TRICKS.

DRESS

In theatrical parlance, short for dress rehearsal; a rehearsal done with all costumes, music, etc., and usually done in the manner and at the pace of a regular performance. Any questions of BLOCKING, CUEs, etc., should have been resolved before the commencement of the dress rehearsal.

DROP

A flat sheet of material, often canvas or muslin, and usually painted to represent a particular scene; the drop may be drawn up into the FLIES when not needed.

Drops are also made of semi rigid materials, and may include such structural elements as doors and windows. Conversely, a drop can be made of a thin gauzy material; a scene painted on such a drop will be visible when the area in front of the drop is illuminated; when the area to the rear of the drop is lighted, however, the drop becomes transparent.

This latter type of drop is termed a *scrim* when the thinnest linen (rather than the theatrical gauze) is used in its construction.

DRUMHEAD TUBE

A PRODUCTION device, this is an ordinary metal tube (examinable by the spectators) which is sealed at each end with paper secured by metal rings or rubber bands (this also may be done by the spectators). The performer then pokes a hole in the paper and makes a sizable production of silks.

The unseen adjunct is a small LOAD container, capped at one end with paper and slightly pointed at the other. On receiving the sealed tube, the performer sets it down on this container (which has been concealed behind other objects) for a moment. When it is picked up the tube appears the same, the paper capping the container taking the place of the paper seal it destroyed. Now, of course, the production may be made.

Drumhead tubes come in sizes ranging from very small, for POCKET or PARLOR, to quite large, for full stage use. The drumhead LOAD principle is sometimes used in conjunction with the PHANTOM TUBE.

DRUM ILLUSION

A drum-like cylinder is shown empty and capped on both sides with paper; it is then raised into the air on chains or cables.

Punching holes in the paper, the performer produces a number of silk scarves, streamers, and other items, climaxing with the appearance of an assistant who bursts through the paper drumhead.

Often billed or listed as "The Drum That Can't Be Beat," a title given by PAUL VALADON; he invented the first version of the effect, in which silks and other items were produced from a small suspended drum. The illusion version, featured by RALPH CHEFALO, HARRY BLACKSTONE, and many others, may have been based on an earlier illusion called the **Barrel of Diogenes**, devised by DAVID DEVANT. The Devant illusion, it should be noted, worked on a different principle than that used in the later versions.

Also known as the **Girl In The Drum**.

DRUNK ACT

A premise for an act, usually consisting of manipulative magic done in pantomime, in which the performer plays the role of a well-to-do but somewhat tipsy gentleman—presumably on his way home after an evening of drinking.

The most successful and sophisticated exponent of this type of act was CARDINI. There were many other notable performers who used this premise, including BERT EASLEY, CLARENCE SLYTER in "A Magician's Night Out" and WILLANE as "The Immaculate Inebriate."

This premise was most popular in the 1930s and the following decade, perhaps as a reaction to the repeal of Prohibition. The social climate of the 1980's is such, however, that the premise of the **drunk act**, even in the service of comedy, may possibly not at present be an attractive one to some audiences. Thus, few acts of this type are currently being performed. It is, however, one of many acts featured by BEV BERGERON.

DUAL CONTROL

An EFFECT of ANIMAL MAGNETISM in which pencils cling to the hands in various positions. Most recently marketed under the Dual Control title (with a routine by LEWIS GANSON), the GIMMICK—consisting of a thin gut loop attached to a length of elastic—has been marketed under many other names, and is described in the Rupert Howard course in magic published in the early 1930's.

The gimmick can be used not only for the effect first mentioned, but also as the motive power for the ACROBATIC MATCHBOX, the RISING CARDS, the MAGNETIZED CARDS, and many other effects. An expert in the use of this gimmick is British performer and dealer ALAN ALAN.

DUCK AND DEAL

See AUSTRALIAN DEAL

DUCK BUCKET

A large wooden bucket with a two-sectioned lid which is hinged at the center, in the fashion of antique dairy buckets. It may be used to PRODUCE a duck, after it has been shown empty, or to exchange two objects of the requisite size. It operates on an application of the MIRROR PRINCIPLE.

DUCK VANISH

A feature of many illusionists, this EFFECT was invented by SERVAIS LEROY; it is often referred to by the title given to it by W. J. NIXON, who billed it as **Where Do The Ducks Go?**

One or more ducks are taken from an openwork basket and placed in a large box which sits on a draped table. The box is then rapidly taken apart to show the ducks have vanished, but suspicion is directed to the draped table with SUCKER EFFECTS byplay. Finally the drape is whisked from the table, which is shown to be simply an empty frame.

There are many versions of the basic EFFECT, with varying methodologies; Nixon's own routine is described in JOHN NORTHERN HILLIARD's *Greater Magic*.

DUCROT, FRANK (1872-1939)

Born T. Francis Fritz; performer in vaudeville and CHAUTAUQUA; latterly magic dealer in New York

Frank Ducrot (*The Mulholland Library of Conjuring & the Allied Arts, Los Angeles, California*)

DUNN, RICKI (b. ?)

Performer who began his career as a fire-eater in a side-show, and later worked in a carnival. He worked briefly as a magician, but it is with his PICKPOCKET ACT that he has become an internationally-known performer.

Making a point of not using CONFEDERATES, he gets a quartet of male spectators onto the stage; then, in the course of a BILL IN LEMON routine, extracts without their knowledge several items from their pockets and clothing—including, in some cases, the clothing itself!

He has appeared at the Flamingo, Aladdin and Hacienda in Las Vegas, at the Americana, Eden Roc and Carrillon in Miami Beach, and many other top nightclubs throughout the U.S. He has also been a featured entertainer on several cruise lines.

DUNNINGER, JOSEPH (1892-1975)

Though best known for his exploits in MENTAL MAGIC, which he featured on his popular radio and television shows, he began his career in show business as a magician specializing in SLEIGHT OF HAND with cards. Later he toured with an elaborate FULL-EVENING SHOW with considerable success, if less than the worldwide fame he achieved as a mentalist.

City, noted for buying the businesses of many other dealers.

Inventor of the TWENTIETH CENTURY SILK effect; he was also for a time the editor of MAHATMA.

DUMMY

An object which simulates a specific article but is specially constructed for the requirements of an EFFECT or ROUTINE. An example would be a **dummy cigarette** made to look like a genuine lit cigarette, the performer switches the genuine article for the dummy in the act of throwing it into a container or to the floor. The advantage of the dummy in this example is that it can be more easily handled and needs no CIGARETTE TANK or other special holder.

A dummy may also be used when the real item would be impracticable for the conditions of trouping; a metal bottle, for example, replacing one of breakable glass.

The term *dummy* is also used to indicate an item, identical in appearance, switched for the actual object; this may be anything from a slip of paper (in a feat of MENTAL MAGIC) to a dollar bill (for a BURNED-AND-RESTORED routine) to a horse or elephant (which is then made to vanish).

Ricki Dunn

Dunninger is listed as author of a number of books, including *What's On Your Mind?*; *Inside The Medium's Cabinet*; *Monument To Magic*; *Complete Encyclopedia Of Magic*, some of them ghost-written for him by WALTER B. GIBSON. Gibson also collaborated with Dunninger on his final book, *Dunninger's Secrets*.

DUNNINGER SLATE

See ADDITION SLATE.

DURBIN, W. W. (1866-1937)

Lawyer by profession; briefly a professional performer. First elected president of the I.B.M. (International Brotherhood Of Magicians).

DUTCH LOOPER

A version of the THREE-CARD MONTE routine which uses a special set of prepared cards.

DUVAL, ADE (1898-1965)

Born Adolph Amrein, he created an ACT specializing in SILK MAGIC; with it, and the assistance of his wife True, Duval achieved great success in vaudeville, nightclubs and other venues. The act was known as **A Rhapsody In Silk**—a title given to it by Ruth Waters (mother of the author) during a magic convention in Ohio.

Duval created many original EFFECTs and approaches for the act; of these the best known is his version of the SILK DYEING effect, in which the silks appeared to change color as Duval *blew* them through a paper tube. This effect is described in HILLIARD's *Greater Magic*.

DUVIVIER, DOMINIQUE (b. ?)

Born in France; performer specializing in CLOSE-UP MAGIC, primarily with cards. He also teaches magic.

Duvivier is noted for his unique and sometimes controversial style of performance.

DYE BOX

A commercially marketed device created by TOMMY WINDSOR, in appearance it is a standard cardboard popcorn box; in actuality it has a DOUBLE WALL in the form of a pocket open at one end, and with it many types of productions, vanishes and exchanges may be effected.

Many of these applications are described by Windsor in his *Dye Box Book*.

DYE TUBE

A GIMMICK for use in the SILK DYEING routine. It is usually made of plastic or metal and is about an inch in diameter by three inches in length; within, there is either a sliding disk or a loop of cloth tape affixed. Silks of various colors are placed in the tube which in performance, is secretly obtained and rolled up in a tube formed from a sheet of paper. White silks are poked into the paper tube, actually going into the **dye tube** and forcing the colored silks out the other end. The gimmick with the white silks within is secretly stolen away, and the paper is then shown empty.

A smaller version of this same gimmick is used to change the color of a silk as it is poked through the hand.

Full descriptions and handling for such ROUTINEs can be found in RICE's *Encyclopedia Of Silk Magic*.

EASLEY, BERT (1904-1987)

Performer who was noted for his comedy DRUNK ACT. Billed as "The Tipsy Trickster," he performed in varied venues for many years. He later retired from show business and opened a magic shop in Arizona.

He is a recipient of the Performing Fellowship from the ACADEMY OF MAGICAL ARTS.

ECKAM, ELMER (1891-1963)

For some time a professional performer, in later years he became a semi-pro; his ornate, ORIENTAL-STYLE ACT performed with his family was a great favorite of magic conventions for many years.

ECLIPSE

Rarely-performed stage effect invented by Hampton McLaughlin in which a large solid metal disc travels from one paper frame to another on the far side of the stage. The most interesting feature of the effect is its invisible passage in front of a lighted frame at center stage; while the disc is not seen, its *shadow* passes across the lighted surface in a simulacrum of an astronomical eclipse. The effect is now owned by Peter Tappan.

EDGE MARKING

A system of marking cards by the placing of dots or other indications (pin-scratch, razor-scrape) at a particular position along the edge of the card.

It is most often used to mark a KEY CARD so that the performer may locate it quickly. There have been FULL DECK marking systems; one such is described in *Between Two Minds* by J. G. THOMPSON, JR. and Ned Rutledge. Such decks have also been marketed; a deck created by Harry G. Franke was designed to permit the performer to ascertain which card was missing from the shuffled deck by a study of the markings.

To effectively use this principle, the performer must be expert at reading the **edge marks**, and at presenting EFFECTs using them without appearing to study the deck; otherwise, however ingenious the system of marking, the method may well become obvious to the audience.

EDGE PALM

A coin PALM in which the coin is gripped much as in the CLASSIC PALM, but by its edge so that it projects outward from the palm at an angle of about 45 degrees. Though it can be performed with smooth-edged coins, those with a milled edge are preferred.

It is particularly useful when more than one coin is being palmed, as the performer can draw off a single coin from this position without disturbing those remaining.

This palm is described in BOBO's *Modern Coin Magic* and many other basic texts.

EDUCATED PENCIL

A pencil or pen, held between the fingers and thumb in a vertical position, rises slowly upward in very eerie fashion. Though a standard POCKET TRICK, it can be very effectively employed as a THROWAWAY item.

Some versions operate in a manner similar to the CLIMBING WAND; others use an interior length of elastic which may be drawn out and clipped between the fingers behind the pencil, a gradual relaxation of the performer's grip allowing the pencil to rise through the hand.

EFFECT

In magical parlance, a TRICK or ILLUSION; also used to indicate what happens from the spectator's point of view. Descriptions and instructions in the literature are most often divided into two parts; the EFFECT as seen by the viewer—and the METHOD employed to bring it about.

EGG BAG

A classic EFFECT, performed for over three centuries, in which an egg placed in a small cloth bag disappears and reappears in seemingly impossible fashion.

Most egg bags have a secret pocket, but this is only a very small part of the method, the greater part consisting in the performer's skill in handling the bag. It has been a feature in the acts of far too many performers to list, but its best-known exponents in the past were ARNOLD DE BIERE and MAX MALINI; of the present day, CHARLES EARLE MILLER and JOHN THOMPSON.

The most popular design for the egg bag is that used by Malini. Other versions are the **TARBELL bag** (see HARLAN TARBELL) and the **Sterling bag**, which differ in construction and placement of the pocket.

There are many brands of egg bag on the magical market, but the best ones are those made specifically to the performer's hand size; this makes MANIPULATION of the bag much more convincing. The most highly-prized such bags, used by many top professional magicians, are those made by San Francisco magicienne LYNN HEALY.

EGG IN PAPER

A broken raw egg is poured into a folded newspaper, from which it vanishes when the paper is opened. A self-sealing plastic bag in a secret pocket is the means of accomplishment.

This EFFECT is rarely used on its own, but usually as a follow-up to a ROUTINE such as the SILK TO EGG or the EGG ON FAN, which ends with a raw egg being broken.

EGG ON FAN

In this, one of the most aesthetically pleasing EFFECTs in the whole realm of magic, a moistened bit of white paper is bounced on a Japanese fan. Slowly it seems to enlarge and become rounded, and forms itself into the shape and appearance of an egg. The performer removes it from the fan and breaks it into a glass, demonstrating that it is, in truth, a real egg.

The original (and still superior) version requires a painstakingly prepared egg-skin; a more popular version uses a thin rubber simulated egg (usually called a **Weller Egg** after the person who manufactured the most popular model). In a variant presentation the TRANSFORMATION takes place in a large, clear brandy snifter; this is less prone to disaster, but also less visually effective. Once expanded to its full size, the egg is switched by sleight-of-hand for a real egg.

It was first popularized by MAX STERLING (thus the effect, or the egg FAKE, is sometimes known as a **Sterling egg**), and has since been featured by many performers, notably TOMMY MARTIN in the 1930's and JONATHAN NEAL BROWN in the present day.

EGGS FROM MOUTH

An egg makes its appearance between the teeth of the performer or an ASSISTANT; it is removed, and several more appear in succession.

The egg which is seen in the mouth is actually a half-SHELL, and sometimes has a pink inner surface so the mouth can be shown apparently empty by positioning the shell with its open side outward. The shell egg is pushed out between the teeth with the tongue; as the performer's hand approaches, holding a real egg in PALM position, the shell is allowed to slip back into the mouth and the solid egg is shown, apparently having been just taken from the mouth. This egg is then put into the pocket or a container; once out of sight it is again palmed and the process is repeated. Finally the shell is actually removed from the mouth, being handled like a BILLIARD BALL shell to conceal its true nature, and placed in the pocket or container.

The effect is also performed with billiard balls or ping-pong balls.

EGYPTIAN HALL

British theater (originally a museum) built in 1812, which for the last three decades of its existence was known as "England's Home Of Mystery." It was managed by JOHN NEVIL MASKELYNE and GEORGE A. COOKE, and during their tenure many of the greatest names in magic performed there.

It was demolished in 1905, and Maskelyne moved to ST. GEORGE'S HALL. A history of the Egyptian Hall and its performers is *Maskelyne And Cooke: Egyptian Hall* by George Jenness.

EGYPTIAN HALL MUSEUM

Museum of magic memorabilia located in Brentwood, Tennessee; it is the collection of David Price who has used it as the major resource in the writing of his *Magic: A Pictorial History Of Conjurers In The Theatre.*

EIGHT KINGS
See STACK.

ELASTIC LADY

An ILLUSION invented by P. T. SELBIT in which a woman is placed into a cabinet with her head, hands and feet projecting through slots or holes. The hands and feet are then moved outward to the edges of the cabinet, apparently "stretching" the arms and legs well beyond their actual length; the woman's head moves in its slot from the center of the cabinet to both top and bottom. Finally the woman's body is restored to its proper form and she steps from the otherwise empty cabinet.

There have been many variations on this illusion, which is sometimes billed as **Stretching A Woman.**

ELECTRIC DECK

A deck of cards used for fancy flourishes such as the WATERFALL, it consists of cards strung together with threads which cannot be seen when the deck is spread.

Often a performer will do a few flourishes and then expose the construction of the deck.

Awareness by lay persons of the existence of these decks has meant that most performers who do genuine FLOURISH work with cards must first establish, by SHUFFLES or other means, that the deck they are using is not so prepared.

ELECTRIC GIRL

A sideshow ILLUSION in which a girl or woman seated in an "electric chair" or standing on a special platform is able to produce various EFFECTs such as arcs of electricity, lighting of FLASH PAPER and torches, illuminating of flourescent bulbs, etc. The effects are brought about by means of a static electricity generator hidden in the chair or platform apparatus.

ELEVATOR

Term for card EFFECTs in which cards invisibly move from a lower position in a deck or PACKET to the top thereof; the routine usually involves the passage of several cards (e.g., the four Aces).

There are many variant routines, e.g., a **Progressive Elevator** is a routine in which a card "passes through" an ever-increasing number of cards in repeated trips to the top.

Effects where a single card is made to come to the top (e.g., the AMBITIOUS CARD) are generally not considered to be **elevator** effects.

Elevator is also used to denote an ELEVATOR TRAP.

ELEVATOR TRAP

A type of TRAP mounted on a platform which lies flush with the rest of the stage floor, but can be raised or lowered as required. Some **elevator traps** are designed to rise a considerable distance above the floor proper, to INTRODUCE a person into a container or other ILLUSION structure; this is usually done in conjunction with an application of the SPHINX or other MIRROR PRINCIPLE.

In many cases a secondary **trap** (consisting of two hinged sections) is set to swing closed and lock in position, filling the gap left by the **elevator trap**, once that **trap** has descended beyond a certain point; this minimizes the time during which the **trap** area must be concealed.

In former theatrical parlance the **elevator trap** was sometimes called a **skip** (a term originally derived from the mining industry.)

ELEVEN CARD TRICK

A routine created by EDWARD VICTOR in which a group of eleven cards, dealt into the performer's hand by a spectator, change in quantity a number of times. The ROUTINE, which requires faultless technique, is described in WILLANE's *Methods For Miracles.*

The suggestion was made by GENE GORDON that this routine could effectively be performed with currency (bills); done this way, it was a feature in the performance of FRED KAPS and many others.

ELIMINATION

A method of determining which of a group of cards is a spectator's selected card. In such techniques, the spectator should not be aware of the process.

As an example: the spectator is thinking of one of six cards (three of each color), which have apparently been shuffled back into the deck but which the performer has controlled to the top (*see* CONTROL). The performer states the card to be (let us say) of a red suit; whether right or wrong, three cards have been eliminated; the remaining three are positioned by a SHUFFLE so that one is near the top, another near the center, the last near the bottom of the deck.

Spreading the cards from hand to hand, the performer shows about a third of them and asks if the spectator has seen the thought-of card; if the answer is "yes" it is of course the first of the three cards. If not, the performer continues the SPREAD until all but the card near the bottom have been shown, and the question is asked again; if "yes," it is the card in the middle of the spread; if *no*, the card near the bottom.

This is a very elementary and basic example of the technique—which first attracted attention with the publication of RALPH W. HULL's *Mental Discernment*—but many refinements have been developed over the years by DAI VERNON and others.

See the relevant section in DAI VERNON's *Inner Secrets Of Card Magic* series.

See also PUMPING.

ELLIOTT, BRUCE (1914-1973)

Professional writer with long involvement in magic magazines, first as a contributor to the JINX, later as co-founder of the PHOENIX (with WALTER GIBSON). Many of Elliott's own effects appear in the pages of his magazine.

Among his books are *Classic Secrets Of Magic, The Best In Magic, Magic As A Hobby,* and *What's New In Magic.*

ELLIOTT, DR. JAMES WILLIAM (1874-1920)

Physician who left medicine to become a professional performer. He worked with SERVAIS LE ROY and Felix Herrmann, and also as a solo performer, never achieving any major success.

He was, however, one of the greatest exponents of pure SLEIGHT OF HAND with cards. At one time he issued a money challenge to any who would dispute his claim as *World's Champion Card Manipulator,* and there were no takers. Elliott is believed by many to be the inventor of the BACK PALM with playing cards; he taught this and other sleights to LE ROY, T. NELSON DOWNS, and THURSTON.

Some of his work is described in *Elliott's Last Legacy,* attributed to HOUDINI.

ELLIS, JARDINE (?-1923)

Born Duncan Loren Campbell, he was a highly respected British magician known for his many in-

Dr. James William Elliott (*The Mulholland Library of Conjuring & the Allied Arts, Los Angeles, California*)

ventions, notably his ELLIS RING. He also created a popular method for duplicating a design secretly drawn by a spectator, and the PRODUCTION of a filled wineglass from beneath a handkerchief. (This latter EFFECT is described in BRUCE ELLIOTT's *Classic Secrets of Magic.*)

Many of Ellis's creations have been lost; some of his work, however, is described in the MAGIC WAND Magazine and in *A Few Jardine Ellis Secrets* by Stanley Norton.

ELLIS RING

A metal or brass ring, usually slightly larger than one-and-a-quarter inches in diameter, which is used for RING ON WAND effects. It employs the SHELL principle, and is the invention of JARDINE ELLIS.

ELMSLEY, ALEX (?)

British patent investigator, later a computer specialist; best-known for his ELMSLEY COUNT, but also creator of a great number of excellent effects and concepts—primarily in the field of card magic, where his work is of considerable importance.

His work will be found in various magazines, including THE GEN, IBIDEM, and PENTAGRAM; to the latter he contributed (among many other articles) an influential treatise on the mathematics of the FARO SHUFFLE.

ELMSLEY COUNT

A specialized FALSE COUNT invented by ALEX ELMSLEY, in which a four-card PACKET is counted from one hand to the other in apparently fair fashion; however, one card is counted twice and another card is never seen at all.

With the card to be concealed third down in the packet held in the left hand, the first card is pushed off into the fingers of the right hand, which then comes back to take the second card. At this point two things happen; the upper two cards in the left hand are pushed to the right and taken by the right hand, and the card in the right hand is left beneath the card remaining in the left hand. These last two cards are taken one by one into the right hand, in a seeming repetition of the previous motions. The apparent action is that four cards have been counted one-by-one from the left hand to the right.

(Five and six cards can also be counted as four using this procedure; when using the Elmsley Count in this fashion, it is best to have the cards flat-on to the spectator's view, so that the additional thickness of the pushed-off group of cards is not noticed.)

Elmsley originally called this the **Ghost Count**, and it was described in a marketed PACKET TRICK called The Ghost Cards.

This count has a family resemblance to the JORDAN COUNT and also to EDWARD VICTOR's E.Y.E. COUNT used in his marketed E.Y.E. routine (also a "Packet Trick," with a THREE-CARD MONTE premise).

The Elmsley count is described in *Counts, Cuts, Moves and Subtleties* by JERRY MENTZER and many other books. The Edward Victor E.Y.E. COUNT and routine is described in *Ken Brooke's Magic*.

See TWISTING EFFECTS; OPEC; VEESER COUNT.

EMCEE

See MASTER OF CEREMONIES.

ENCORE

Additional material performed after the conclusion of the formal ACT in response to a favorable reception by the audience. While encore material should appear unplanned—so as not to give the impression an encore was expected—it is arguable that this must be the most carefully prepared part of the act.

The magician has an interesting advantage over other performers in this situation, in that an apparently impromptu miracle can register much more strongly than those which are "part of the act," since it will sell the idea that the performer can create magic with anything. It follows, therefore, that the most effective encore should use an item unconnected with the performer, e.g., a napkin from a ringside table. (Note: in most cases it is probably unwise to borrow something from a spectator which must be returned, since this will interfere with the flow of the applause and the performer's final exit.)

The encore EFFECT must be at least as strong as the concluding effect of the regular act; ideally, of course, it will be far stronger.

ENDLESS CHAIN

A close-up GAMBLING DEMONSTRATION effect in which a three-foot loop of chain is placed on the table in a pattern of two loops. A spectator attempts to place his or her finger in the loop that will "catch," but the performer always draws the chain free. In one version, the spectator is left with a small solid loop of chain around *the* finger when the larger solid loop is drawn away.

The chain is unprepared, and the effects are brought about by specific patterns of "throwing" the chain and methods of handling; there are many such patterns and methods.

Several ROUTINEs for the use of the chain are in print in books and magazines, or available from dealers. A notable example is FRED LOWE's "Super Chain." A book devoted entirely to this EFFECT is GEORGE BLAKE's *Loopy Loop*.

END SHUFFLE

Term sometimes used to denote the HINDU SHUFFLE.

END STRIPPERS

A kind of STRIPPER DECK in which the beveling is done along the short edges of the cards instead of the long edges. With such a deck, it is a simple matter to bring reversed cards to the top of the deck in the course of an OVERHAND SHUFFLE.

ENGLISH PENNY

Within magic, this almost always denotes a coin no longer in circulation in the British Isles—a copper coin of exactly the same size as a U.S. half-dollar. (The currently circulating English penny is of much smaller size.)

The older English penny is still used extensively in COIN MAGIC, particularly in the classic COPPER AND SILVER transposition routine.

ENSA

Acronym for Entertainment National Service Association, a British organization for entertainers who performed for the military. Similar in function and purpose to the U.S.O.

The Northern Ireland branch was designated NIENSA.

ENTERTAINMENT

The intended purpose of all facets of show business, including magic.

Magicians sometimes tend to think the word *Entertainment* is synonymous with "comedy," and that the worth of an EFFECT can be measured by the number of laughs it produces. This is clearly a rather limited view, since serious drama and many other facets of performance work can be considered as entertainment without containing any element of comedy whatsoever.

This limited concept of entertainment often leads to a performer making the statement: "I don't care what I do, as long as I entertain them." Such a statement, indicating a need for approval rather than a desire to create, reflects a basic misunderstanding of both performance work and any creative art. As noted above, the end purpose of most show-business arts is to entertain, but the serious artist attempts to do this by creating new and unique experiences for the audience rather than pandering to already established appetites. This is particularly important in magic, which by its very nature is supposed to be special and mysterious; obviously, the hackneyed cannot be special, the common cannot be mysterious.

ENVELOPE CARD

Actually two cards, hinged at one side with thread or scotch tape so they can open book-fashion.

Such cards are sometimes used in commercially-marketed versions of the SIX-CARD REPEAT.

Another use for the **envelope card** is as a "holder" for a selected card which is returned to the deck so that it goes into the envelope. The deck may now be freely overhand shuffled, and at any time the **envelope card** can be instantly located in much the same manner as a THICK CARD—which, in effect, it is.

Envelope cards used in this latter fashion have been described in print and marketed. An early version was Xkwizit, sold around 1920 and later described in the JINX; a later version was called Card-Assyst, created and marketed by Ed Mellon.

EPILOGUE

Magazine published by KARL FULVES which had twenty-four regular and five special issues, beginning in November 1967; it was primarily devoted to advanced card magic, but also covered certain areas of MATHEMATICAL MAGIC, betting propositions, and various other subjects.

EQUIVOQUE

The interpretation of a spectator's choice in a positive or negative fashion to execute a FORCE. An excellent book on the subject is PHIL GOLDSTEIN's *Verbal Control*.

ERDNASE, S.W. (?-?)

Author of *The Expert At The Card Table* (published in 1902), a book on pure SLEIGHT OF HAND with cards which still stands among the very best works on the subject.

Much is speculated about its author but almost nothing is known for certain; the name reverses to *E.S. Andrews*, and some believe this to be the writer's real name; another possibility is Milton Franklin Andrews. Though Erdnase's personal history is uncertain, his work occupies a secure niche in the history and technique of card magic.

ESCAPES

Release from various types of restraint, container, or structure, such as strait jackets, packing cases, and jail cells. The best-known specialist in escapes was HOUDINI, and his record in this field has not been surpassed since his death in 1926.

Escapes are not as popular now as they were in Houdini's time, the pace of stage performance having greatly accelerated in the interim. By their very nature, escapes usually require a number of preliminary steps—checking of the locks or other properties, explanation of the procedure, and the actual securing of the performer in the restraint—before the escape can take place, and all these steps take time.

It is *possible* to present escapes effectively before today's audiences; it is, however, far from easy, and few performers find this challenging area of magic attractive. Performers currently specializing in escapes include *Steve Baker, John Novak* and *Norman Bigelow* in the U.S., and *Alan Alan, Howard Peters, De-*

Val (David Littler) and *Shahid Malik* in Great Britain, among others.

John Novak edits *Escape*, a magazine on this subject, and he has also written an eight-volume series of books collectively titled *The Art Of Escape*; he is also the author of *How To Make Your Own Trick Handcuffs*, and *Challenge Rope Escape*. De-Val has authored *The Key To Escapes* and *The Key To Lock Picking*. Other books on the subject include *Rope, Chain And Box Escapes* by U. F. GRANT, *Modern Handcuff Secrets* by *Dick Norman*, and *Houdini's Escapes And Magic* by WALTER B. GIBSON.

See BAG ESCAPES; BOX ESCAPES; CHAIN ESCAPES; STRAITJACKET ESCAPES; THUMB TIE.

ESCAPOLOGIST

Term used to describe a performer specializing in ESCAPES. The invention of this word was claimed by HOUDINI but it is most probably the creation of the Australian performer MURRAY.

ESCORIAL

Popular name for the *Journadas de Cartomagias*, held each year in Escorial, Spain (a town about twenty miles west-northwest of Madrid which formerly served as the residence of Spanish kings).

The Escorial convention is devoted, as its title indicates, to card magic only. And each year one particular effect, move or sleight is the primary subject of discussion. This often results in a publication documenting the discussion and related matters; see, for example, the following ESCORIAL 76.

ESCORIAL 76

A card EFFECT in which a spectator is able to sort the deck into its four suits without ever seeing the face of any card. Inspired by PAUL CURRY's OUT OF THIS WORLD, it is a PROBLEM effect to which a number of solutions have been proposed, by (among others) BROTHER JOHN HAMMAN (in PALLBEARER'S REVIEW) and REINHARD MULLER (in ARCANE).

The title comes from the ESCORIAL convention; this particular effect was discussed at the 1976 meeting and was the subject of a book later published under the *Escorial 76* title and containing solutions proposed by a number of performers.

ESP

An abbreviation for extra-sensory perception, a term popularized by parapsychological researcher Dr. Joseph Banks Rhine. The term is often used by magicians in presentations of feats of MENTAL MAGIC.

ESP CARDS

A deck of twenty-five cards consisting of five each of a *Circle, Cross, Wavy Lines, Square* and *Star* design; they were designed by Dr. J. B. Rhine and Dr. Karl Zener for testing the ESP abilities of test subjects.

The cards are used by many performers in feats of MENTAL MAGIC, and several books have been written on such EFFECTs, including *Magic with an ESP Deck* by Sam Dalal, *ESP Card Session* by Nick Trost, and *Mind Novas*, by STEPHEN MINCH.

A series of books on this subject, under the continuing title OICUFESP, have been published by H. A. Adams; the effects therein rely primarily on a STACK and/or mathematical principles.

EVANION, HENRY (1832-1905)

British performer who had a solid professional career for many years but never achieved major prominence; he is, however, noted as a collector. A wonderful account of his meeting with Evanion is given by HARRY HOUDINI in his *The Unmasking of Robert-Houdin*; much of the Evanion collection was purchased by Houdini over a period of time.

EVANS, HENRY RIDGELY (1862-1949)

Lawyer, and journalist by profession, known to magicians as historian and writer. His books include *Hours With The Ghosts* (also published as *The Spirit World Unmasked*), *History Of Conjuring And Magic*, *Magic And Its Professors*, *A Master Of Modern Magic*, and *The Old And The New Magic*.

EVANS, VAL (1896-1981)

Performer with long professional career and highly creative approach; among his many ROUTINEs are "An Invitation To Lunch" (described in THE JINX and later marketed), and his versions of the RISING CARDS and the STOP TRICK, both commercially marketed.

EVAPORATED MILK JUG

British name for the MILK PITCHER.

EVERYWHERE AND NOWHERE

A card EFFECT invented by J. N. HOFZINSER in which three displayed cards are transformed into a previously selected card in a complex sequence of changes. Unlike many card effects, it can effectively be presented as a platform or nightclub effect; it was a feature in the shows of PAUL ROSINI.

Hofzinser's version of the effect is described in OTTAKAR FISCHER's *Illustrated Magic*, Rosini's in *Greater Magic*; other versions may be found in T. NELSON DOWNS's *The Art of Magic* and in JEAN HUGARD's *Card Manipulations*.

EXAMINABLE

Said of APPARATUS which may be handled by the spectator without revealing its secret—either because its preparation is indetectable or because the FAKE or GIMMICK which is used may be secretly removed by the performer.

Unless there is a compelling reason for it—as for example with ESCAPES—having PROPS examined by the spectators is generally a bad idea, since it causes them to think (a) that the prop *is* faked, but too cleverly for them to discover, and (b) that anything the performer *won't* pass for examination *must* be faked!

However, if a spectator is allowed to hold a PROP, faked or unfaked, and is carefully controlled by the performer, it may leave both the assisting spectator and the audience with the impression that the prop has in fact been examined.

EXCELSIOR CLIP

A very small bulldog-type spring clip, fitted with a hook. A standard item in stationery stores, it can be very useful to the performer as a way of secreting small LOADS (particularly a playing card or PACKET thereof). It also has applications to COIN MAGIC.

EXPANDED SHELL

A variety of SHELL coin which appears of normal size, but which is fractionally larger and thus may be placed over a standard coin of the same denomination (or a different coin of the same diameter as that represented by the shell).

EXPANDING DIE

An ILLUSION created by BUATIER DE KOLTA in which a five-inch DIE, placed on a bare platform, suddenly enlarges to a die a yard square in size, which is immediately lifted to disclose a young lady.

The EFFECT is brought about by complex mechanical means—so complex, in fact, that this illusion has not been seen on a regular basis since De Kolta's time. A variation on the original model was devised by JOSEFFY, and is described in DAVID P. ABBOTT's *The Marvelous Creations of Joseffy*.

EXPANSION OF TEXTURE

A classic coin EFFECT invented by L'HOMME MASQUE in which a vanished coin reappears in a handkerchief held by a spectator. Another coin has been left in the handkerchief, thus the vanished coin is *heard* to arrive.

The effect is described in T. NELSON DOWNS's *Art Of Magic*, J.B. BOBO's *Modern Coin Magic*, and many other standard works.

EXPERIMENT

Synonym for EFFECT formerly used by magicians, and still occasionally by performers of MENTAL MAGIC.

See PROBLEM.

EXPOSURE

Revelation of the secret means by which an EFFECT is accomplished, either by design, accident or incompetence.

Methods are almost never as interesting as the effects accomplished by their means; exposure of these methods, therefore, can only diminish the audience's respect for the performer.

Some performers take the view that exposure is permissible in certain SUCKER EFFECT routines—where the exposure is followed by a mystifying finish—but such routines often create in the spectator the perception that *all* of the performer's feats are accomplished by equally simple methods, and thus the magician is no more than a possessor of a few secrets.

A conservative position is that *any* book on magic written for or marketed to the general public (rather than being exclusively distributed by magic dealers and publishers) constitutes an exposure. Such an extreme view would pillory many of the major figures in magic, from ROBERT-HOUDIN to DAVID DEVANT to HARRY BLACKSTONE, and several others. Since virtually anyone can go into a magic shop and purchase a book containing the most advanced secrets and routines, clearly this is not a workable standard.

Perhaps a clear definition of exposure would contain the element of *non-solicitation*; in other words, that the exposure is being presented to an audience—in newspapers, general magazines, films or television—which had not specifically sought it out. Another element might be serious intent on the part of the recipient, the revelation of magical information not being given simply to satisfy idle curiosity.

In any case, there exists within magic a diversity of opinion on this subject, ranging from the person who thinks revelation of even the simplest trick is harmful to the person who holds that exposure of any magnitude is unimportant and soon forgotten. It is, however, fairly safe to say that blatant exposures of magic rarely do any good, and often do harm.

EXTRACTION OF SILVER

A commercially-marketed EFFECT in COIN MAGIC created by Dr. Boris Zola, in which a half-dollar held by a spectator has its silver removed through the spectator's hand and produced by the performer as a silver nugget; the coin the spectator finds in his or her hand is an accurate representation of a half-dollar made of clear plastic.

E.Y.E. COUNT

The counting method used by EDWARD VICTOR for his E.Y.E. EFFECT using three lexicon cards, similar in effect to a THREE-CARD MONTE routine. It is based on an earlier count devised by CHRIS CHARLTON for his "Modern Monte" routine, published in THE JINX magazine.

In the Charlton/Victor count, the three cards are held in a PINCH GRIP at one side; two cards are pushed off as one, taken by the other hand and displayed, and then replaced beneath the single card. To spectators it appears that a single card has been shown and replaced.

The E.Y.E. routine was commercially marketed for some time; KEN BROOKE's handling of it is described in a collection of his routines, *Ken Brooke's Magic*.

EYELESS VISION

Title used by HARLAN TARBELL, and many others, for a routine of effects during which the performer is wearing a BLINDFOLD.

FABIAN (1912-1965)

Born E. Ray Griffiths in Britain; under his pen name of Fabian, he was for many years the associate editor of *ABRACADABRA* magazine. Griffiths also edited the *Journal of the British Magical Society* and served as its president.

FACE

The side of a playing card which shows its identity by PIP and INDEX.

FACE CARD

The bottom card of the deck, i.e., the only card whose FACE is visible.

The term is also to denote COURT or *picture cards*.

FAKE

A device, used to bring about a magical EFFECT, which is visible to the audience but not recognized for what it is; examples are the THUMB TIP and the mirror in the MIRROR GLASS.

FAKIR

An East Indian performer of various supposedly miraculous feats, such as fire-resistance, snake-charming, and immunity to pain (the well-known *Bed Of Nails*). Some fakirs are associated with religious sects.

The Fakir is often confused with a magical performer; the latter is known as a JADOO-WALLAH.

Demonstrations of a fakiristic nature are described in *Miraculous Hindu Feats* by JOSEPH OVETTE,

Stranger Than Fiction, by Derek Lever, and *Thrilling Magic*, by Clettis V. Musson.

The philosophical/religious aspects of Fakirism are discussed in *Mysticism And Magic Of India*, by ORMOND MCGILL and *A Search In Secret India*, by Dr. Paul Brunton.

FAKO DECK

A deck of cards, in its original version devised by SYL REILLY, which consisted of several sets of faked cards, each set prepared for a different effect in the routine supplied with the cards.

The term now is generally used for any deck-sized collection of various faked cards.

FALSE BOTTOM

The apparently solid bottom of a box which is actually constructed to give access to an area beneath it, either by hinging of its entire area or a section thereof.

In an ILLUSION, a false bottom is often constructed of two overlapping pieces of elasticized fabric, permitting quick passage in either direction.

Similar to FALSE WALL.

FALSE COUNT

With cards, to count a PACKET as being less or more than its actual number; see, for example, BUCKLE COUNT.

An excellent false counting routine is the ELEVEN CARD TRICK created by EDWARD VICTOR, which will be found in WILLANE's *Methods For Miracles*.

More generally, to count a Packet of cards in any way that conceals the true condition and composition of the packet; see, for example, ELMSLEY COUNT; JORDAN COUNT; HAMMAN COUNT.

Some of these counts can, of course, be adapted to other objects. FRED KAPS used an adaptation of the above-mentioned Victor routine to bills ("Dizzy Dollars" created by GENE GORDON); in Kaps's hands, the routine was very effective.

FALSE CUT

A simulated cutting of the cards in which something other than the supposed action takes place. In some false cuts the order of the cards in the deck is not changed at all. In others, such as the SLIP CUT, the top card may be moved to the center. And in still others a certain portion of the cards (usually near the top or bottom) may be kept in position while the remainder of the deck moves around them.

False cuts are described in HUGARD and BRAUE's *Expert Card Technique*, HILLIARD's *Greater Magic*, and countless other books.

FALSE DEAL

See BOTTOM DEAL; MIDDLE DEAL; SECOND DEAL.

FALSE FINGER

A hollow FAKE, invented by CHARLES MORRITT, that is usually placed between the second and third fingers; if its color is a close match and the hand is kept in motion, it will not be noticed. Used most often to produce a silk handkerchief, it can also be used to produce coins—if they are FOLDING COINs.

FALSE SHUFFLE

An apparent mixing of the cards—which, however, retains them in their original order.

As there are two general kinds of legitimate shuffle, so there are two basic types of false shuffle—the false OVERHAND SHUFFLE and the false RIFFLE SHUFFLE.

In a false overhand shuffle, the performer may RUN the cards from hand to hand in a predetermined order; a repeat of this action, reversing the sequence, brings the deck back to its original state (an invention of G. W. HUNTER). In doing this the performer may employ an IN JOG or OUT JOG to mark the position of particular blocks of cards. Another approach to this type of shuffle is a sequence of repeated cuts so executed as to give the appearance of a shuffle (a straight CUT of a deck will not disturb the sequence of the cards, only alter its starting point).

In a false riffle shuffle there are two basic approaches: known as the *push-through* and the *strip-out*.

In the *push-through*, the cards are genuinely interlaced; in the act of squaring, however, the two interlaced halves are angled slightly and are pushed past each other so that they now interlace for only part of their length. In the act of apparently cutting the deck, the projecting half is pulled out and placed on top of the deck. (Note: the *push-through* is referred to by some writers as the *pull-through*.)

In the *strip-out*, the cards are interlaced at their outer edges. In the act of pushing the two halves together, the two halves are stripped apart and placed one on top of the other. This is the general approach taken in the ZARROW SHUFFLE and the V-SHUFFLE (also known as the HUGH JOHNSTON SHUFFLE, after its inventor).

A RUN-UP SHUFFLE is used to position cards at particular locations; a *cull shuffle* is used to locate particular desired cards, and possibly also to position them at particular locations. As these actually change relative positions of cards, neither is technically a **false shuffle**, though they are sometimes considered as such.

Other shuffles include the SLOP SHUFFLE, in which cards are apparently mixed face-up and face-down (invented by SID LORRAINE); and the CHARLIER SHUFFLE, also know as the **false HAYMOW SHUFFLE**, in which cards are pushed in packets from the top STOCK of the dealing hand to the bottom stock of the receiving hand, and vice versa, which results in the cards being cut but not mixed.

The literature of the false shuffle is immense; following the seminal work of S. W. ERDNASE's *The Expert At The Card Table*, literally thousands of pages have been devoted to the technique of this SLEIGHT. Important early work on the false riffle shuffle was done by DAI VERNON and DR. JACOB DALEY. Notable recent contributors to this literature are KARL FULVES, Herb Zarrow and ED MARLO; their work should be consulted by the interested student.

See CHARLIER SHUFFLE; IN JOG; OUT JOG.

FALSE TURNOVER

A maneuver in which a card is apparently shown on both sides, while in actuality only one side is shown. The usual manner of accomplishing this is to have the card resting on the palm with the thumb beneath it; as the hand turns over the thumb levers the card outward so that the same side remains visible.

This technique was devised by FRANCIS CARLYLE, and is described in the PHOENIX

Magazine; there were earlier versions of the move but the Carlyle method is the most popular.

The move can also be done with a full deck, and is sometimes employed in the course of an ALL BACKS routine.

See also PADDLE TRICKS.

FALSE WALL

A principle used in many ILLUSIONs such as the DOLL HOUSE and the MODERN CABINET, this is exactly what it sounds like—a fake inner wall behind which a person or object is concealed.

It is a useful device, but only in conjunction with other aspects of design and presentation; since it is the first thing many viewers will suspect as a possible method, it must be well executed to be viably deceptive.

FAN FORCE

See CLASSIC FORCE; also, rarely, to denote a type of PSYCHOLOGICAL FORCE in which the spectator is shown a fanned deck with a particular card in an optimum position for mental selection.

FANNING POWDER

A formulation of zinc stearate which may be applied to playing cards to make them fan smoothly and evenly.

See CARD FAN PRODUCTIONS.

FAN SHUFFLE

A technique of shuffling the deck by making a fan in each hand and then interlacing them. Interestingly, the action can be simulated to create a FALSE SHUFFLE which is visually identical to the genuine procedure.

FANTASIO (b. 1936)

Born Ricardo Roucau in Argentina, he has achieved considerable success both as performer and as a manufacturer of magical APPARATUS.

As a performer he has (with wife Monica) performed at the Latin Quarter, Desert Inn, Hollywood Palace and many other nightclubs and theaters in the U.S. and elsewhere. He has also appeared numerous times on television, beginning with a number of spots on the *Ed Sullivan Show* at the start of his career.

As a manufacturer he is best known for his APPEARING CANE, VANISHING CANE, and appearing and vanishing candles—all made from a special plastic. Effects with the Fantasio apparatus are described in the *Cane And Candle Book* (four volumes), written by DAVID GINN.

FARELLI, VICTOR (1888-1955)

British writer of a number of books, primarily on SLEIGHT OF HAND. Among them are *Farelli's Card Magic* (two volumes), *Lend Me Your Pack*, *The Odin Rings*, *John Ramsay's Cylinder and Coins*, and several others. Farelli also translated a book by French writer Maurice Sardina titled *Where Houdini Was Wrong*.

FARMER AND THE WITCH

An ILLUSION created by U.F. GRANT in which a boy and girl from the audience are dressed respectively in farmer and witch costumes. After some byplay, they are found to have changed places—i.e., the boy now wears the witch outfit and the girl is dressed as the farmer.

The illusion is described in *Volume 3* of the TARBELL COURSE IN MAGIC.

FARO CHECK

A technique devised by ED MARLO which uses the interlacing procedure of the FARO SHUFFLE to ascertain that the cards (usually the full deck) have been divided into two exactly equal packets. In most applications of this technique the shuffle is not completed.

FARO SHUFFLE

Also known as the **weave shuffle**, it does not have the randomness the word "shuffle" usually implies. The deck is divided into two exactly equal halves, which are then interlaced in perfect alternation. Eight out-shuffles will bring the deck back to its original order.

The faro shuffle has many complex mathematical properties, some of which can actually be adapted to magical EFFECTs. There are three basic varieties of faro shuffle: the **out-shuffle**, in which the top card of the deck remains in place—the **in-shuffle**, in which the top card of the deck goes below the upper card of the lower half of the deck; and the **straddle faro**, in which there is one extra card in one "half" of the deck, and the cards at top and bottom of this half end up as top and bottom cards of the deck.

Use of the term *Faro Shuffle* almost always implies the perfect interlacing as described above, and such a shuffle is sometimes called a **perfect faro**; it should be noted, however, that in a few applications of this technique it may not be necessary to use a perfect faro, as long as the necessary STOCKs of cards are interlaced. Such an application may be referred to as a **partial faro**.

The **incomplete faro** is just that—a faro shuffle in which the cards are interlaced, but not squared. This technique may be used in something as simple as a two-tiered CARD FAN, or as complex as a selection process in which a card PEEKed at in one half possesses a relationship to a BREAK held in the other half, after the two halves have been separated.

Butt shuffle (from the action of the two halves being "butted" together) is sometimes used as a synonym for the faro shuffle; in general, however, its usage does not imply the mathematical exactness of the faro.

To have the effects created with its use play as magical, the faro shuffle has to be done *casually*; few performers are sufficiently adept at executing it to bring this off. Indeed, it is not unusual to see a performer miss a perfect interlacing on the first try—and unlace the halves to try again, which inadvertently creates a *de facto* exposure of the principle.

A great deal of research and development of the Faro shuffle has been done by ALEX ELMSLEY in Great Britain and ED MARLO in the U.S.; see Marlo's *Faro Shuffle* and *Faro Notes*, among many other books. Another work of considerable importance is Paul Swinford's book on the subject, *Faro Fantasy*.

FASTEST TRICK IN THE WORLD

Title of an APPARATUS effect invented by AL DELAGE in which a flowerpot holding a bouquet of FEATHER FLOWERS is shown on an undraped table. The performer fires a pistol at it, and both pot and flowers disappear instantaneously.

Not to be confused with the WORLD'S FASTEST CARD TRICK.

FAUST, BOB (b. 1929)

Born Robert James, he began his career as an assistant to VIRGIL. He has performed in such nightclubs as the Latin Quarter in New York and the Dunes in Las Vegas, as well as a series of appearances in the Terrace Rooms of the Statler Hotel chain. He has also appeared in other nightclubs and theaters throughout the U.S, and on numerous television shows, including *Ed Sullivan*, *Jack Paar*, and *Kate Smith*.

FAWKES, ISAAC (ca. 1675-1731)

Highly successful British performer who left a sizable fortune at his death. He performed often at BARTHOLOMEW FAIR, and is noted for his EGG BAG routine, which he climaxed with the production

Robert Faust

of gold and silver coins and a live hen, and for his "Growing Apple Tree."

FAYNE, CHUCK (b. 1940)

Born Charles Fayne, he is a Hollywood-based performer who specializes in private party work in the Beverly Hills area. He has also toured the comedy club circuit throughout the U.S.

FEAT

A magical EFFECT, ILLUSION or demonstration of skill.

FEATHER FLOWERS

Feathers attached to a wire framework to simulate the look of flowers; used in PRODUCTIONS. Their advantage is that bouquets constructed of feathers can be compressed into very small diameter, and can thus be concealed in a sleeve or in the interior of a VANISHING CANE; their chief disadvantage is that even the best of them look nothing at all like real flowers.

They can, however, be used effectively for visual flash and are generally used in commercial APPARATUS effects such as BOTANIA and the BLOOMING BOUQUET. A manufacturer noted for excellence in these products is HORACE MARSHALL.

FECHTER, EDDIE (1916-1979)

A noted bartender-magician, he bought the Forks Hotel (actually a restaurant located in a suburb of Buffalo, New York) in 1958 and hosted the first CLOSE-UP MAGIC convention there in 1969. These conventions (known as F.F.F.F.—Fetcher's Finger Flinging Frolics) have attracted the best close-up performers in the world. Fechter's work is described in *Magician Nightly: The Magic of Eddie Fechter* and *Eddie Fechter's Dice Holdout Methods for Magicians*, both by JERRY MENTZER.

FEINT

Generally, the simulation of a genuine action or process (e.g., a FALSE SHUFFLE).

Also, a legitimate action which is made by the performer's manner to appear suspicious. Attention is therefore focused on this aspect, which can be a useful technique of MISDIRECTION.

FEKE

Obsolete and affected spelling of FAKE, still used by some writers.

FETSCH, "HEN" (1912-1961)

Noted creator of many marketed EFFECTs and several books. Among his many effects are **Silk Epic, Breaking the Sound Barrier, Mental Epic,** and **Wallet Wallop.** His books include *Five O'Fetsch, Milk Pitcher Magic, Magic With Canes,* and several others written in collaboration with MILBOURNE CHRISTOPHER.

FIAHLO, PHILIPPE (b. ?)

Born in France; specialist in CLOSE-UP MAGIC who is noted for his bizarre routine in which varied effects are done with rocks.

Fiahlo is also noted for his collection of both broadcast and exclusive videotapes of magic performers, said to be the largest such in the world. It includes (among many other items) a complete collection of the the television appearances of FRED KAPS, with whom Fiahlo had a long friendship. Fiahlo is considered to be the leading authority on Kaps' work.

FICKLE FIRE

Pyrotechnic GIMMICK marketed by Yataka Kikuchi to create the appearance of flame in the performer's hand.

FICKLE NICKEL

A nickel placed in the performer's outstretched hand vanishes and reappears in an exceptionally straightforward fashion; this non-SLEIGHT effect invented by JOHN CORNELIUS and Ronnie Gann is noted as the first effect performed by DOUG HENNING in the first of his network television specials.

FIDLER, PAUL (b. 1950)

Performer who developed an award-winning ACT while still in his teens. Specializing in BIRD MAGIC, he created a Hawaii-theme act which featured an erupting volcano and the instantaneous PRODUCTION of a live ostrich. Billed as "The Magic Hawaiian," he has performed in numerous nightclubs in the U.S. and throughout the South Pacific.

FIEDLER, LUBOR (b. ?)

Born in Austria; chemist by profession. He has invented several EFFECTs, many of which are distinctive for their use of unusual scientific principles. His best known invention is probably his **Die Divination,** a feat of MENTAL MAGIC in which the performer is able to ascertain which face of a gaming die is that selected by a spectator.

FIFTY-FIFTY DECK

A type of FORCE deck which consists of twenty-six duplicate cards, comprising the top half of the deck, and twenty-six INDIFFERENT CARDS, which constitute the lower or bottom half of the deck.

The deck may be turned face-up and spread to show the cards all different; in this action only the cards from the face of the deck to a bit before the midpoint are shown. The deck is then turned face-down, and the upper half is spread for a selection.

Alternatively, a quarter of the deck may be UNDERCUT from bottom to top and the deck then RIBBON-SPREAD on the table, the central portion being more widely spread than the end portions. It is highly likely that the spectator will choose a card from the central section.

This deck is also known as a **Tarbell Forcing Deck.**

FIGURE EIGHT

See ENDLESS CHAIN.

FILM TO LIFE

An ILLUSION invented by HORACE GOLDIN (inspired by an earlier presentation by magician/filmmaker GEORGE MELIES) in which he interacted with a woman in a film projected onto an onstage screen. Objects were passed back and forth from the filmed woman to Goldin. He lighted her cigarette and at one point walked around behind the screen and appeared in the filmed sequence.

The climax of the illusion was the woman stepping visibly from the center of the screen, which was seen to be seamless and unbroken.

Modern versions of the illusion have used a video projection. This simplifies considerably the problem of synchronizing the actions; if videotape is used, it is a much simpler matter to produce a tape sequence precisely as required, and, if live video is employed, the performer can actually look to an offstage area and see the people whose images are being projected (who, in turn, can synchronize with the performer's actions).

The Goldin version is described in a number of books, including WALTER B. GIBSON's *Magic Explained*.

FINALE

Conclusion of an ACT or FULL-EVENING SHOW, of which it is arguably the most important part. *See* CLOSER.

FINAL LOAD

The last item to be produced in the course of CUPS AND BALLS, CHOP CUP, or similar routines. Usually this is a large ball or item of fruit (apple, orange), but it may be a small glass of liquid, a baby chick, or a small animal.

In his climax for the BALL AND BOWL routine, originated by ROY BENSON, DON ALAN caused a large bagel to appear beneath the bowl; the brilliant "two-cup" routine of TOMMY WONDER finishes with the production from one cup of the bag from which the cups were originally taken!

FINDLAY, JIMMY (1904-1973)

Internationally known collector of magic books, posters and playbills. He wrote a number of books on the subject, including *Conjurers Coins And Medals*, *International Guide To Posters And Playbills*, and over a dozen others. He also contributed a column to the SPHINX, and wrote historical and bibliographical articles for many other publications. His *Collectors Annuals* are essential reading for those interested in the field.

FINDLEY, ARTHUR (?-?)

Amateur magician of the 1930s who was a member of the "inner circle" of performers specializing in card magic; very little is known about him, even to the proper spelling of his name (which has been variously rendered as *Finley, Finlay,* and *Findlay*).

Among his inventions are the EFFECT later marketed by U.F. GRANT as CHEEK TO CHEEK; the TENT VANISH; and the RIFFLE FORCE. He also created a popular variation of the SPELLING TRICK, in which the spelled card is mentally selected.

FIND THE LADY

An ILLUSION invented by AMAC using the premise of the THREE-CARD MONTE game. A female ASSISTANT stepped up on one of three stools; a giant card was then hung on a batten in front of her, with a clear view of the stool's legs beneath the card. Two other cards were also hung from the batten, well separated from the first and from each other, and the woman would then vanish from behind one card and appear behind another. After this had been shown to occur several times, the woman would vanish completely.

A presentational variation, using cards decorated as jail cells and an assistant in convict uniform, was presented by NICOLA.

The find the lady illusion was so successful for Amac that for a considerable time it was his entire act. It was described in HILLIARD's *Greater Magic* with an incorrect explanation; and correctly by JIM STEINMEYER in his edition of *Jarrett Magic And Stagecraft—Technical*.

The title is also used to denote the standard THREE-CARD MONTE routine.

FINGER CHOPPER

An APPARATUS effect of CLOSE-UP MAGIC which duplicates in miniature the presentation of the stage CHOPPER illusion.

FINGER CLIP

To hold an object between two adjacent fingers, usually projecting from the back of the hand, which from the palm side appears empty.

Often used in COIN MAGIC and, less commonly, with playing cards.
See BACK PALM.

FINGER-FLINGER

Pejorative term for a performer who views SLEIGHT OF HAND and MANIPULATION as ends in themselves, rather than as means to accomplishing a magical effect.

FINGER PALM
See PALM.

FINGER TIP

A FAKE consisting of a SHELL which fits over the first joint of the finger, which it is made to resemble. It may be used in similar fashion to a THUMB TIP, but in many cases offers more natural handling. (It is a natural movement to poke with the finger; few people with normal motor skills use the thumb for this purpose.)

FINGERTIP CONTROL

A technique for holding the deck at the fingertips for a PEEK selection (rather than in the usual dealing position) and maintaining control over the selected card.

The standard work on the subject is ED MARLO's *Fingertip Control.*

FINNELL, GENE (b. ?)

Specialist in card magic who is best known for his formulation of the FREE CUT PRINCIPLE, described in his book of the same title; he has also contributed to magic periodicals.

FIRE AND WATER

An ILLUSION invented by LEON in which a woman standing on an isolated platform was wrapped in paper which was then set aflame; the woman disappeared from the paper and reappeared almost instantly in a water-filled tank on the other side of the stage.

FIRE BOWL

Usually made of copper or chrome-plated steel, this bowl is produced from under a cloth draped over the performer's arm; flames leap up dramatically from the interior of the bowl.

The bowl generally has an interior lined with some absorbent material which has been saturated with flammable liquid; this is ignited by any one of a number of means—a match affixed to a striking surface, the flint-and-steel from a cigarette lighter, or an electric hot coil. (An early method used chemical combination (e.g., potassium and ether plus water) to create the ignition; this was not very reliable and sometimes dangerous.)

In some models only half the surface of the bowl is ignited (though this is not apparent to the audience), and the release of a spring-mounted flap immediately extinguishes the flames while simultaneously releasing a bouquet of SPRING FLOWERS.

A fire bowl may also be used in conjunction with a DOVE PAN.

FIRECRACKER

Also known as the **Ching Soo Firecracker**; an APPARATUS effect using a wooden firecracker. The fuse of the firecracker is lit and the firecracker is then placed into a metal tube, which is capped. When the performer or a spectator opens the tube, the firecracker has vanished; in some presentations being replaced by a large silk handkerchief. The missing firecracker is found hanging on the spectator's back.

The effect is accomplished by a variation of the SHELL principle, along with a duplicate solid firecracker fitted with a hook in similar fashion to the HOOK COIN.

A variation of this effect uses a lighted candle in place of the firecracker.

FIRE EATING

An ancient skill sometimes incorporated by magicians into their performances. It has often been thought fire-eating was accomplished through the use of a special chemical in the mouth, and many "formulas" (some of them poisonous) have been published.

In actuality, it is merely necessary to keep the mouth moist and to continue to exhale while the torch is in the mouth. That said, it should be noted that even the best fire-eaters are sometimes badly burned and occasionally killed in the performance of this extremely hazardous routine. Often the heavier-than-air fumes will drift down into the performer's lungs; accidentally ignited by the torch in the mouth, the fumes will then explode in similar fashion to the combustion of an auto engine—the essential difference being that human lungs are not designed to withstand such explosions.

See Fire Magic by Clettis V. Musson and *Stranger Than Fiction* by Derek Lever.

FIRE MAGIC

EFFECTs with fire and flame have always been a part of the magician's repertoire and embrace a wide range, from the smallest of match tricks to the most spectacular of CREMATION illusions. At the present time fire is most often used as an added visual flash to enhance PRODUCTIONs and VANISHes, and in recent years a whole series of GIMMICKs has been developed to allow performers to produce fire in the hands.

Note, however, that even the best equipment can fail or be mishandled, and a potential for serious injury is always present. Also, special clearances or licenses may be required to use "live fire" in an enclosed theater.

FIREWALK

The feat of walking over a bed of hot coals or heated stones; it has been practiced in a religious or mystical context for many centuries in India, Malaysia, Africa, Fiji, China and the West Indies. The Hindu ceremony is called *treemiri*.

A series of scientific tests of this phenomenon were carried out in Britain in 1935 in which KUDA BUX performed the **firewalk**; many theories were advanced to account for his ability, but no conclusion was reached.

More recently, this feat has been the most highly publicized aspect of a self-help program, using elements of Neuro-Linguistic Programming, and developed by Anthony Robbins. Mr. Robbins's view (described in his book *Unlimited Power*) is that a person who can convince himself or herself to do the firewalk is then motivated to believe that anything can be accomplished if conviction is present. Robbins is said to have led several thousand people in performing firewalks.

If this is the case, the oft advanced theory that the extensively calloused soles of the feet of tropical firewalkers protected them from harm is clearly in error—as are other purported explanations involving secret chemical preparations, etc.

Another theory postulates that the ash on the bed of coals acts to some degree as an insulator; this factor, in conjunction with the extremely brief duration of the foot's contact with the coals during the brisk walk, may suffice as an explanation. However, neither the author nor the publisher accept any responsibility for injuries resulting to someone attempting to test this explanation!

The **firewalks** in Fiji are of a different nature; the ash is swept clear of the stones which are seen to be red-hot. The stones used in such walks are volcanic in nature, and as such are extremely poor conductors of heat; one end of a fairly short fragment may be held without discomfort while the other end has been heated to incandescence. Again, this factor may constitute a partial explanation (though it should be noted that the Fiji **firewalk** is traditionally done at a slower pace than those using hot coals)—and again, also, all those wishing to test this theory do so at their own risk.

FISCHBACKER, SIEGFRIED
See SIEGFRIED AND ROY.

FISCHER, OTTOKAR (1873-1940)

Born in Austria; performer, theater manager, and author of books on magic. Fischer was devoted to the creations of HOFZINSER and wrote two painstakingly researched books on Hofzinser's work; among his other books is an excellent general work titled *Illustrated Magic*.

For stage work he used the name *O.F. Marteau*, but Fischer was his real name, Marteau the stage name; not the reverse, as stated in some sources.

FISH CATCHING
See AERIAL FISHING.

FISH HOOK

A name given by DAI VERNON (in his *Select Secrets*) to a common flaw in PALM technique, i.e., to stick the thumb out and away from the hand in an unnatural and hooklike fashion.

Many beginners in palming technique think that spreading the thumb and fingers wide apart "proves" that nothing could be palmed; in fact, such an unnatural position only draws attention to the hand and accomplishes the opposite result.

FISHER, JOHN (b. 1945)

British television producer of the *Michael Parkinson Show* (which has featured many magicians), and of several magic specials, all for BBC-TV. He is also producer of the PAUL DANIELS Magic Show, and recipient of the Golden Rose of Montreux for his work on the show.

He is also noted as the author of *Body Magic* and *The Magic Of Lewis Carroll*, as well as other works in the entertainment field.

FISHING
See ELIMINATION; PUMPING.

FISM

The *Federation Internationale des Societies Magique* (International Federation of Magic Societies); founded by HENK VERMEYDEN in cooperation with several European magical organizations after World War II, it has held conventions in various European locations for over forty years.

Contests are held at these conventions, and many professional performers (FRED KAPS, RICHARD ROSS, and LANCE BURTON, to name only a few) have achieved major prominence through winning the top award (called the *Grand Prix*). A good showing at the FISM convention is often a major step toward a successful performing career.

FIT-UP

A temporary stage or, often, puppet theater which can be quickly erected for performance and dismantled for traveling.

FITZKEE, DARIEL (1899-1978)

Born Dariel Fitzroy, he was an acoustical engineer by profession; he is known to magicians as the author of a number of books—*Rings In Your Fingers*, *The Only Six Ways To Restore A Rope*, *Contact Mind Reading*, and others—and chiefly for the "Fitzkee Trilogy."

The trilogy consists of *Showmanship For Magicians*, *The Trick Brain* (on creativity), and *Magic By Misdirection*. These books cover their respective subjects in a manner rarely equaled, and are essential reading for any performer who takes the art of magic seriously.

For over a dozen years, Fitzkee also wrote "Paper And Ink," a highly-regarded column of book reviews, for GENII magazine.

FIVE-BY-FIVE

A term used for the cross-referencing principle employed in various versions of the TWENTY-FIVE CARD TRICK.

FIVE-CARD THOUGHT

Term for a general class of EFFECTs in which the performer discerns which of five cards is being thought of by a spectator. An example is DAI VERNON's "Five Card Mental Selection," which appears in *Stars Of Magic*. Other approaches which might fall under this classification (depending on the specific routine) are the PRINCESS TRICK and the FIVE BY FIVE principle.

Dariel Fitzkee (*The Mulholland Library of Conjuring & the Allied Arts*, Los Angeles, California)

FLAG BLENDO

See BLENDO.

FLAG STAFF

A telescopic staff, usually made of precision-machined brass, with tiny eyelets in each section to which a silk flag may be affixed. When the staff is swung outward, it extends to its full length and locks in position, creating the instantaneous appearance of a flag and pole.

Not to be confused with the BARBER POLE.

FLAP CARD

A card with a central flap which, depending on its position covering the upper or lower half of the card, will show one of two different identities. Also known as a **changing card**.

FLAP SLATE

See SPIRIT SLATES.

FLASH

To briefly reveal to the audience something they are not intended to see, for example, a glimpse of a palmed ball. A performer who is "flashing" is usually either using faulty technique or has not sufficiently checked the sightlines of the performance venue.

More generally, the strictly visual appeals which are used in an act to enhance its appearance or attention-getting qualities. It is preferable that such appeals seem integral to the magic being performed and not simply tacked on as an afterthought.

FLASH-APPEARANCE PORTAL

An archway, usually consisting of a small platform, two uprights and a crosspiece, in which the performer suddenly appears as a puff of smoke is fired from a FLASH POT at the front of the portal.

The ILLUSION is created by release of a spring roller blind, made to match the stage background, which conceals the performer (some versions use two blinds which move apart from a central point; these models are generally more deceptive than the single-blind version). Unless carefully timed and expertly lighted, the effect is not very mysterious. Some performers rig the blind release mechanism through the flash pot; thus the blind cannot release unless the flash pot ignites.

The illusion is also known as **Mephisto's Portal**.

FLASH BILL

A stage bill printed on FLASH PAPER to resemble currency; it is often used as a comedy adjunct in burned-and-restored bill routines.
See BURNED-AND-RESTORED OBJECTS.

FLASH COTTON

Chemically treated cotton similar in its effect to FLASH PAPER; it is often used as a primary ignition point in various kinds of pyrotechnic devices.
See FLASH POT; FLASH WAND.

FLASH PAPER

Chemically treated paper which, when ignited, will burn very rapidly with a bright flame. It is used in pyrotechnic devices such as the FLASH POT and FLASH WAND, and also in magical effects in which an object, apparently wrapped in the flash paper, is seen to have vanished when the paper is ignited.

In addition to its uses in magic, this paper was for many years quite popular with illegal "numbers" banks, as in the case of a police raid the evidence could be destroyed with the touch of a cigarette. In recent years, however, it has largely been replaced within the criminal professions by DISSOLVO PAPER.

FLASH POT

A pyrotechnic device used to create a flash and puff of smoke on stage. Electric current is passed through a thin wire in the pot, heating the wire and causing the ignition of flash/smoke powder placed adjacent to the wire. Sometimes the wire will be set to ignite FLASH PAPER, which will in turn carry out the secondary ignition of the flash/smoke powder.

As with all pyrotechnical devices, flash pots should only be used by those trained and experienced in their use. (Indeed, in some states of the U.S. a pyrotechnics license is required in order to operate these or similar devices.)

FLASH STRING

Chemically treated string which will burn instantly on ignition. It is often used to secure a PRODUCTION item or spring-loaded mechanism; thus, an item can be made to appear or change in a flash by the touch of a cigarette, candle, or torch.

FLASH WAND

A magic wand containing one or two electric heating elements which will ignite a wad of FLASH PAPER. Gases generated by the combustion shoot the wad out of the end of the wand where the paper then fully ignites, creating a ball of fire at some distance from the wand. A bit of flash or smoke powder is sometimes added to the wad of flash paper to enhance the effect.

As with any pyrotechnic device, caution must be exercised in the use of the flash wand.

FLAT

A basic element of stage scenery consisting of a wooden frame covered with a material which may be painted; this material is most often some type of cloth, but it may also be of paper or plastic.

FLEISCHER, ADAM (b. 1963)

Founder (in 1980) and editor of *Magic Manuscript*, a magazine that he later sold to TANNEN MAGIC COMPANY; and more recently of *Magical Arts Journal*, which he co-edits with MICHAEL AMMAR.

Fleischer is also the creator and producer of the New York Magic Symposium, a highly-regarded magic convention which, in spite of its name, has also been held in San Francisco, Los Angeles, and Tokyo. Each of these conventions has resulted in a *Symposium Collection* book containing effects from that convention's performers, and guest contributors.

Editor/publisher/producer Adam J. Fleischer

Fleischer is also a member of the Magic Hedonists (the other members: MICHAEL AMMAR, DARYL, and PAUL HARRIS) and wrote a book titled *Brainstorm In The Bahamas*, which described various effects and adventures of this quartet.

FLEMING, CARYL S. (1890-1940)

A well-known figure in U.S. magic, he was noted as a member of magical societies and clubs in several countries and for the many special chemicals he made available to magicians. Of these chemicals, the most famous is his IT'S A PIP liquid.

FLEMING, PAUL (1890-1976)

A Professor of economics, he was also a professional magician for many years, getting his start by taking over a tour for an ailing KARL GERMAIN.

He is also noted as the founder (with his brother *Walker*) of the Fleming Book Co., which published fine editions of classic magic texts, and for his thoughtful and incisive reviews of books on the subject; these reviews have been collected into a three-volume set.

FLESH GRIP

With playing cards, a BREAK held by a fold of flesh, usually at the base of the thumb or little finger. Most often the break will first be obtained with a finger tip and then shifted to a flesh grip position.

FLEXIBLE COUNT

See JORDAN COUNT.

FLEXIBLE GLASS

A rectangle of plate glass or mirror is placed in a hinged frame which is in turn wrapped in a sheet of newspaper. A large metal spike is then run through the bag (and presumably the glass) in several places; finally the frame is bent double. In spite of this, when the frame is straightened and removed from the bag the plate glass is shown to be unharmed.

This EFFECT was invented several decades ago by OSWALD RAE; not seen for many years, it is currently enjoying a resurgence of popularity—quite probably because it is a feature in DOUG HENNING's show. (Henning uses a loosely-woven cloth bag instead of the newspaper sheet; this simplifies and enhances the effect.)

FLIES

The area above the stage where scenery, curtains, and equipment are suspended, out of sight of the audience.

FLIGHT OF THE PAPER BALLS

Title given by SLYDINI to his routine in which a seated spectator is unable to determine how crushed tissue balls are being made to vanish by the performer; the spectator is unaware that the balls are being tossed over his head.

The routine is described in *Stars Of Magic* and in LEWIS GANSON's *The Magic Of Slydini*.

FLIP (b. ?)

Born Philippe (?) Hallema in Holland; creator of an intriguing SILENT ACT in which several of the items he uses mysteriously duplicate. He is also known for his innovative approach to magic, and for his highly regarded **flip-stick** routine in which a solid wooden stick of respectable size vanishes and reappears by pure SLEIGHT OF HAND technique.

He is the author of *Flip Quick Strip Trick* and *Some Manuscriptricks*.

FLIPOVER BOX

Invented by JACK GWYNNE, this piece of APPARATUS is used to vanish moderate-size objects or animals—most often two birds or a rabbit. The animal is placed in the box, which is then spun rapidly by means of two finger-holes in the sides; both top and bottom of the box drop down, affording a clear view of the empty interior. Though quick and effective, the box is not ANGLE-PROOF, and can only be used efficiently with the audience directly in front of the performer.

FLIPOVER WALLET

A variety of SWITCH WALLET, it is a sophisticated version of an old "magic money wallet" sold in children's magic sets.

Though the different makes of flipover wallet have their own specific designs, it is generally made as a Z-fold of three sections, though a spectator is aware of only two. Depending on which side of the wallet is opened, the performer has access to one of two sections which are identical in appearance. Leather strips at top and bottom borders, arranged in criss-cross fashion, hold the unseen third section of the wallet firmly against one of the other sections. In many such wallets a pocket in the central section is accessible from either side.

RICHARD HIMBER popularized the use of these wallets with his marketed BILLFOOLED wallet and other models of this item; he also induced HARRY LORAYNE to write *The Hundred Dollar Book*, which was entirely devoted to effects accomplished with these wallets.

FLOATING BALL

See FLOATING EFFECTS.

FLOATING EFFECTS

In magic parlance, the levitation of objects other than people; usually applied to small objects such as balls, corks, lightbulbs, etc.

The **floating ball** is a very old effect, and many routines have been devised for it. Like most floating effects it depends on the use of a horizontally strung thread, but the artistry of a performance of the effect consists of (among other things) proving to the audience that this cannot be so. A very sophisticated and baffling routine for the **ball** was devised by DAVID P. ABBOTT, and taught by him to OKITO, in whose hands it became a classic. More recent versions of this routine have been featured by DOUG HENNING and DAVID COPPERFIELD.

Another version of the same effect is known as the ZOMBIE BALL, invented by JOE KARSON. In the Zombie routine the ball floats behind and beneath a decorative FOULARD. No threads are used; a rod

Norm Nielsen performs his *Floating Violin*, an intriguing variation on the *Zombie Ball*.

operated by the fingers supports the ball behind the foulard, which makes it practical for many performers who work alone and without the advantages of a proscenium stage. In a brilliant variation of this effect created by NORM NIELSEN, a white violin floats—and plays—under Nielsen's influence.

(Note that the **Zombie** effect, used by many top-class professionals, is unfortunately so well known to laypersons that few are fooled by it. It is not unusual (at least in the author's experience) to have a spectator describe the effect as ". . . that ball on the stick thing . . ." While spectators may be impressed with a particular routine, the mystery element is either minimal or nonexistent.)

A floating routine which uses a thread in a unique way is FINN JON's highly regarded **silver stick**.

The above-mentioned effects and routines are for stage use, and until comparatively recently there were few, if any, convincing close-up effects of this type. Then FRED KAPS made famous the **floating cork** (invented by Bruno Hennig) in which the miracle takes place almost under the noses of the spectators; there have been many variations of this basic routine. Still other floating effects which can be performed at fairly close quarters are JOHN KENNEDY's **floating dollar bill** and Steve Dusheck's **WunderBar**.

A book which deals extensively with floating presentations is *Floating Routines For Table And Stage* by Ralf Wichmann-Braco.

See also SUSPENSION; LEVITATION.

FLOATING LIGHTBULB

A type of FLOATING EFFECT in which the object is apparently an ordinary light bulb, and which not only floats about mysteriously but does so lighted, apparently without benefit of electricity. The effect was featured by HARRY BLACKSTONE in his stage show and continues as one of the major feats in the full-evening performances of his son, HARRY BLACKSTONE, JR.

Routines and techniques are described in *Miracle Floating Light Effects*, written by BURLING HULL.

The Floating Light Bulb was also the title of a play written by comedian, filmmaker, and magic buff Woody Allen.

FLOATING TABLE

See TABLE LIFTING.

FLOODS

Abbreviation for *floodlights*; floods are unfocused lights, often arranged in vertical arrays in the wings, which are used to illuminate a wide area.

FLOSSO, AL (1895-1976)

Born Albert Levinson, he had a long career both as professional performer and proprietor of Hornmann-Flosso Magic Company, which, established in 1869 by FRANCIS J. MARTINKA at 304 West 34th Street in New York City, was the oldest magic shop in the United States.

Flosso began his career in Coney Island and later worked with several sideshows and circuses; still later he performed in vaudeville, theater, and on television. His performing style was unique, and his EGG BAG and the MISER'S DREAM were legendary masterpieces of magic and comedy.

As a magic dealer he knew most, if not all, of the major figures of twentieth-century magic; a very close friend was JOSEPH DUNNINGER.

Flosso was noted for his encyclopedic knowledge of magic and magicians, but even more for his patience and kindness with beginning performers; the stories of those he helped could fill a very large book.

Al Flosso (*photo courtesy GENII Magazine*)

FLOURISH

A showy demonstration of the performer's skill, meant to impress rather than mystify. Within the realm of card magic there are many such demonstrations: SPRINGING THE CARDS in a stream from one hand to the other, performing a ONE-HAND CUT, executing a one-handed RIFFLE SHUFFLE, fanning the cards into intricately perfect designs, and so on.

Some performers eschew the use of flourishes entirely, feeling they focus attention on SLEIGHT OF HAND prowess and take away from the magical aspect. In a closeup performance where the emphasis is entirely on mystery this view has some validity; on the stage, however, the visual appeal of a well-done flourish may add far more than is subtracted in mystery content. Of course there are exceptions to all rules—and this rule is no exception.

FLOWER GROWTH

The appearance of bouquets of flowers in previously empty pots. There are many ways of accomplishing the effect, from BOTANIA to the elaborate routine devised by KELLAR for the PRODUCTION of two large displays of real flowers; Kellar's routine is described in a book attributed to HOUDINI, *Elliott's Last Legacy*.

FLUENCE

A humorous or ironic term denoting hypnotic trance (or "influence").

FLUSHTRATION COUNT

See BACK COUNT.

FLY

To suspend an object or person from above by means of a strong but thin wire (usually piano wire). This is used not only for actual flying effects (as in the stage play *Peter Pan*), but also to counterweight an object so that it can be handled or carried as if it weighed much less. A version of this latter application was used in the BANGKOK BUNGALOW.

Also, in general theatrical parlance, to hoist a FLAT or other item of stage scenery up into the FLIES.

FLYING CARPET

A type of SUSPENSION illusion invented by JACK GWYNNE in which an ASSISTANT sits cross-legged on a small carpet supported by two screens. The screens are removed, leaving the carpet apparently floating in space, and a hoop is passed around it to show the absence of support.

Gwynne's version is described in *Jack Gwynne* by David Charvet; a later simplified version was marketed (with Gwynne's permission) by U.F. GRANT.

See SUSPENSIONS.

FLYING SORCERERS

Loosely knit international organization, founded by GOODLIFFE, of magicians who travel from Britain and Europe to the U.S. (and vice versa) to appear at magic conventions and similar functions.

Originally the organization was known as the Five Flying Sorcerers; the membership is now approximately three dozen, and prospective members do not apply but rather are invited to join.

FLYTO

An ILLUSION sequence believed to have been invented by CHARLES MORRITT. In the best known sequence, a woman entered a wooden cage on a raised platform; blinds were drawn down, and when released the woman had vanished, leaving a man in her place. The woman reappeared at the back of the auditorium.

A chain was lowered and the cage was raised above the stage, its blinds were again lowered. The woman entered a slightly smaller cage on the stage; this, too, had its blinds drawn down.

When the blinds of the cage at stage level were released, the woman was gone; the blinds of the suspended cage were now also released, revealing the same woman—the man having vanished.

FOGEL, MAURICE (1911-1981)

British performer who specialized in MENTAL MAGIC for the greater part of his career, but who also performed some spectacular feats of magic; examples are his versions of THROUGH THE EYE OF A NEEDLE and the BULLET CATCH (done with a firing squad!), and a publicity ILLUSION in which he was apparently blasted into orbit by magical means.

Fogel was a favorite in British variety for many years and was noted for his dynamic style of presentation. An indication of his approach may be gathered from an informative interview which appears in Tony Corinda's *13 Steps To Mentalism*, and also from a series of five booklets on particular routines (called the *Top Secret Series*) written by Fogel himself.

FOLDING COIN

A coin, usually made from a U.S. fifty-cent piece, cut into three sections which are then held together by a rubber band set into a groove in the edge of the coin. It is used in some versions of the COIN IN BOTTLE effect, in a routine where a coin passes through a borrowed finger ring, and also in conjunction with a variant version of the COIN WAND, where several **folding coins** are placed inside the wand to be secretly obtained by the performer.

In addition to the regular Folding Coin, there are available on the magical market more mechanically sophisticated models; these will withstand much closer scrutiny. (One example is the **profile cut**, in which the line of the cuts partially follows the profile of the head shown on the coin.)

The **folding coin** is over a century old; a description of its construction, and a routine for its use is in Edwin Sach's *Sleight Of Hand*. A recent book on the subject is *Folding Coin Secrets* by Peter Crush.

FOLLOW SPOT

See SPOTLIGHT.

FOLLOW THE LEADER

A card EFFECT which most often uses PACKETS of ten red and ten black cards; a "leader" card is placed face-up next to its packet. When the leader cards are transposed, the cards in the face-down packets seem to follow suit; as the cards are dealt face-up, they match the color of the leader cards no matter how often these are transposed.

An excellent ROUTINE for this effect by DAI VERNON (who is generally credited with its invention) is in HILLIARD's *Greater Magic.*

FOO CAN

An oddly shaped can which has an inner wall, open at the bottom and closed at the top. Water or other liquid poured into the can may then be poured out again, or retained behind the secret inner wall as the can is inverted. The can is supposedly named after CHING LING FOO.

FOOTLIGHTS

A shielded row of lights along the front of the stage, directing light upwards at an angle into the playing area. Many modern stages have no footlights at all; when available, they are often set flush into wells in the stage and covered with a sheet of a strong clear plastic such as Lexan.

FORCE

To cause a spectator to take a desired card or other item, while apparently giving him a free choice.

Many such forces are designed for use with cards; of these the most popular is probably the **Slip Force** (a variant of the SLIP CUT in which the performer riffles the deck and separates it at a point indicated by the spectator, actually slipping the top card of the deck to the top of the lower half). Another procedure is the CLASSIC FORCE, in which a spectator takes a card from a deck as it is spread before him. To do this without making the procedure obvious requires a good deal of skill.

The literature of forcing is immense; the primary work on the subject, *202 Methods Of Forcing* edited by THEO ANNEMANN, was first published over fifty years ago, and much has been accomplished in the field since then. In addition to development of various new techniques, many items of magic APPARATUS have been devised to force a particular item.

Often an array of cards is presented so that one card will be more appealing to the spectator than the others by virtue of its identity or position; such a technique is called a **psychological force**, but the term is a misnomer in that it may affect the probabilities of a particular selection but does not guarantee it.

In some cases, it may be necessary for a spectator to choose one of a group of objects within the apparent field of choice, rather than one specific item; for example, with a deck of cards where the choice is limited to a BLOCK consisting of the Heart suit, the performer so timing the spreading of the cards that the spectator makes a selection from this group. This general type of procedure is called a **Ranging Force**.

FORCING DECK

A variety of MECHANICAL DECK designed to FORCE a particular card on a spectator. This can be a deck containing fifty-two identical cards, a SVENGALI DECK, or a rough-and-smooth deck (*see* ROUGH-AND-SMOOTH PRINCIPLE) prepared with twenty-six pairs of cards, the upper being a force card and the lower an indifferent card; this latter deck is known as a POP-EYED EYE POOPER, **Nu-Idea** or **Mirage deck**.

FORESTAGE

Term sometimes used to indicate the area of the stage forward of the FRONT CURTAIN; see IN ONE. It may also indicate the APRON.

FORM

A wire frame which, covered with a cloth, simulates the presence of an object no longer there. In some cases the wire frame may be within the cloth itself (*see* VANISHING CLOTH.

In other EFFECTs such as the ASRAH, the thin wire form is hidden by a combination of lighting and background when the cloth is removed from it.

FORTON, PIET (b. ?)

Born PIETER DE BEAUFORT in Switzerland; teacher by profession. Known for his innovative approach to card magic, he is perhaps most noted for the **Forton Pop-Out Move**, in which half the deck is held in each hand; when the hands are brought together, a card suddenly appears "caught" between the two halves.

FOSTER, NEIL (b. 1919)

After studying at the CHAVEZ COLLEGE OF MAGIC, he toured throughout the U.S., appearing in supper clubs and hotels with an act of manipulative magic. He later toured Europe and Britain, where he was made a member of the Inner MAGIC CIRCLE.

Foster performed for several years through the north central U.S. for lecture bureaus; he then settled in Chicago for a time, working as a demonstrator for L.L. IRELAND's magic store. He was then offered a position at PERCY ABBOTT'S magic company, with whom he has been associated for many years. He was also the editor of the new TOPS for several years, and now is editor emeritus.

He is now a co-owner (with DALE SALWAK) of the Chavez College, operating its central branch.

He is noted as perhaps the greatest exponent of the ZOMBIE BALL since the invention of that effect. His books include *Tips On Zombie, Further Tips On Zombie, Tops Treasury Of Illusion, Tops Treasury Of Dove Magic,* and *Tops Treasury Of Cigarette Magic.*

Foster is a recipient of the Performing Fellowship from the ACADEMY OF MAGICAL ARTS.

FOULARD

A lightweight silk of plain or twill weave, often decorated with an intricate pattern. Foulards of slightly heavier weight are generally used in the ZOMBIE BALL routine.

FOUNTAIN

A cascade of a long ribbon, string of beads, or similar item from a PRODUCTION device. It is accomplished by loading the ribbon/beads into the LOAD CHAMBER in a zigzag fashion; once the end of the ribbon has been produced and a few feet have been pulled out, a sharp pull will cause the rest of the ribbon to flow out in a continuous stream, drawn by the weight of the ribbon already outside. For the most certain working, the production device should be held as high as possible.

See also CARD FOUNTAIN; WATER FOUNTAINS.

FOUNTAIN OF SILKS

A very visual EFFECT in which a huge mass of silk handkerchieves seem to well up one from within another in a gusher-like cascade. It is thoroughly described in RICE's *Encyclopedia Of Silk Magic.*

FOUR ACES

A classic PLOT in card magic, described by Ponsin in 1853, in which the four Aces are dealt separately onto the table, each Ace then having three indifferent cards dealt on it. At the conclusion of the EFFECT the Aces have transposed with indifferent cards so that all four Aces are now in the same pile.

Three popular variant plots are (a) the **Slow-Motion Aces**, invented by DAI VERNON (and described in *Stars Of Magic*), in which the Aces arrive in the "leader" packet one by one, (b) the **Red and Blue Backed Aces**, invented by LIN SEARLES, in which the Aces have backs of a different color than the other cards used, (c) **Progressive Aces**, invented by KEN KRENZEL, in which one Ace joins a second, the two join a third, and finally all gather to conclude the sequence, and (d) the **Reverse Aces**, invented by PHIL GOLDSTEIN, in which the four Aces begin in their own PACKET and distribute themselves among the other three packets in use.

There are hundreds of routines and variations of the basic effect; an entire chapter of HILLIARD's *Greater Magic* is devoted to it, and it is described in most basic books on card magic.

FOUR BURGLARS

A classic STORY EFFECT of card magic in which four like cards—usually the four Jacks—are placed in different parts of the deck, in illustration of four thieves going to different floors of a building. The four cards mysteriously come to the top of the deck.

An excellent version of this ROUTINE is that of S. LEO HOROWITZ; titled "The Mystery Of The Penthouse," it will be found in HILLIARD's *Greater Magic.*

FOUR-CARD BRAINWAVE

A PACKET version of the BRAINWAVE DECK, this effect, originated by DAI VERNON and S. LEO HOROWITZ, uses four cards of like value; one suit is named by a spectator, and that card is shown to be the one face-up card among the other three face-down cards. The effect is accomplished by applications of the ELMSLEY or JORDAN COUNT, in combination with other subtleties (as, for example, the THROUGH-THE-HAND flourish).

Though many handlings allow the named card to be shown to have a back of different color (as in the standard **Brainwave** effect), this touch is not often included, as it requires carrying extra cards.

A version using specially-printed cards, titled **Parade Of The Kings**, is marketed by the SUPREME MAGIC CO.; it allowed somewhat freer handling in showing the cards and is available in JUMBO (and larger!) sizes.

FOWLER, GUS (1888-1960)

British professional magician known as "The Watch King." His act of spectacular magic was done entirely with watches and clocks. He would, for example, pluck pocket watches from the air a la the MISER'S DREAM; from an empty hat he would do an ALARM CLOCK PRODUCTION of thirty ringing clocks; and clocks would vanish from his hands to visibly reappear at the ends of long hanging ribbons (this last a variant of Oswald Williams' **Homing Bells**).

This act, which Fowler created quite early in his career (the PROPS built by friend Bertram Evans), was very successful. With it, he toured the world for many years and became a major star of both British and U.S. vaudeville.

FOX, KARRELL (b. 1928)

Performer who began his professional career quite young, and was one of the first magicians to work in the TRADE SHOW field. From this he progressed to creating an INDUSTRIAL SHOW for the Ford Motor Company; called the Magic World Of Ford, it toured the U.S. for many years.

Fox has worked in every kind of venue from close-up to the *Ed Sullivan Show*, beginning with a comedy presentation and billing himself as the "King of Korn";

Karrell Fox

other characters include Milky the Clown and Wow The Wizard, and he has also presented MENTAL MAGIC for colleges and universities. In addition, he has had a successful career as a motivational speaker to sales groups.

Very active within the magic fraternity, Fox has been a regular feature at conventions, notably the Abbott's Get-Together held every summer in Colon, Michigan; he has also appeared at many I.B.M conventions, and recently served a term as International President of the I.B.M. Among his many trophies and honors are a SPHINX Silver Medal won at the age of 17 and a recently awarded Creative Fellowship from the ACADEMY OF MAGICAL ARTS.

His books include *Kornfidentially Yours, Comedy A La Card, Clever Like A Fox, Another Book, Abra K Fox,* and *For My Next Trick.*

FOX, PAUL (?-1977)

Highly-regarded creator and designer of magical EFFECTs. His versions of the SALT TRICK, the RISING CARDS and the CUPS AND BALLS have been featured by many top performers; of his many other creations perhaps the best known is the **Miracle Gimmick**, used in a popular feat of MENTAL MAGIC with cards.

FOX LAKE

Proprietary name used by first by John W. Snyder Jr., a manufacturer of specially-printed and prepared cards, his business was later sold to HAINES HOUSE OF CARDS, which now owns the rights to the name. The term is now most often used to denote the back design used in their MECHANICAL DECKS and various faked cards. It is the AVIATOR BACK BRIDGE-SIZE design used by the U.S. Playing Card Company.

FRAKSON, JOSE (1891-1981)

Born Jose Jimenez Seville in Spain, he was noted for his highly successful act featuring CIGARETTE MAGIC, with which he toured throughout Europe, the U.S., and elsewhere. He retired from performing in 1936, but lost everything in the Spanish Civil War. He eventually emigrated to the U.S., where he resumed his performing career with considerable success.

FRAME

Agent/booker's parlance for a week's booking; two frames equal two weeks, etc.

FRED

A card trick in which the performer states that he or she will name the spectator's card; the name, says the performer, is *Fred*. The spectator is asked to name any card, and says (for example) Four Of Hearts.

The performer removes the deck from its case and shows that the back of each card has a different name written on it—*Bill, Milt, Irene, Peter, David*, etc. The card bearing the name Fred is located; when it is turned over it proves to be the Four Of Hearts.

The original version of this EFFECT was FRED LOWE's **Christened Reverse**; ALI BONGO titled a later version Fred in honor of Lowe, and it is by that name the effect is now generally known. Variants have been marketed by KEN BROOKE and NICK TROST, and many versions of the effect have appeared in print.

The premise of the effect comes from an anecdote about Alexander Woolcott who—asked by a performer to name a card—pointed to one and said "I name this one Elmer."

FREDERICA (1919-1984)

Born Tommy Frederick in Scotland, he was a major figure in Scottish magic for fifty years. He was noted not only as a performer but also as a collector, magic dealer, active member of the Scottish Conjurer's Association, and TECHNICAL ADVISOR to theatrical productions.

He also contributed a number of EFFECTs to THE GEN Magazine, later collected in a book titled *The Magic Of Frederica*.

FREE CUT PRINCIPLE

A mathematical principle used in card magic, discovered by John P. Hamilton and later refined and further developed by Gene Finnell.

It states that, given two PACKETS, each containing an equal number of cards, if random portions of cards are CUT from the tops of the two packets—the cards cut to be noted—and then the two upper portions replaced on the *opposite* lower halves and the packets then placed together, the noted cards will be separated by the same number of cards as comprised one of the original packets.

For example: if a complete deck is used, being divided into two halves of twenty-six cards each, at the conclusion of the procedure the two cards will be twenty-six cards apart.

A book devoted entirely to this subject is Gene Finnell's *Free Cut Principle*.

FREEMAN, STEVE (b. 1951)

Born Mark Stephen Freeman; accountant by profession. He is considered to be one of the half-dozen premiere exponents of SLEIGHT OF HAND with cards in the world, and is highly regarded for his indetectable execution of difficult moves and his deliberate style of presentation.

He has contributed material to GENII Magazine.

FREER, WINSTON H. (?-1981)

Noted inventor of magical effects, many of which have become legendary. He marketed a few, including his **Half-Wit Deck**, through GENE GORDON, and others appeared in books and periodicals. Freer performed under the name of Doc Maxam. He was particularly noted for his LEVITATION effect, which could be performed with a spectator in almost any situation or venue; Freer achieved considerable publicity by demonstrating the ILLUSION in restaurants, offices, and other unlikely places.

Some Freer rope effects will be found in *The Encyclopedia Of Rope Tricks*, edited by STEWART JAMES. Freer's approach to the GEOMETRICAL VANISH was published in *Mantra*.

He is the author of *25 Rice Bowl Methods*.

FRENCH DROP

See TOURNIQUET.

FRESH FISH

A popular routine for the TORN-AND-RESTORED paper plot, devised by Arnold Furst (from a story told by comedian Fred Allen), in which the performer shows a strip of paper reading **Fresh Fish Sold Here Today**. With an amusing story, the words are torn one by one from the strip; at the conclusion the strip of paper is restored to its original condition.

FRIKELL, SAMRI

Pen name of FULTON OURSLER.
See also ANTHONY ABBOT.

FRIKELL, WILJALBA (1818-1903)

Born in Prussia; he began his career as ASSISTANT to a touring magician, and by his teen was performing his own show. He toured throughout Europe, Russia, Britain, and the U.S., and was quite successful. He is noted as the first magical performer to appear in evening clothes—i.e., dressed in the same way as his audience; prior to Frikell's creation of this style (by accident, when his wardrobe trunk was burned), magicians had traditionally worn long robes and conical hats. Frikell found this style of working so effective that he never returned to the old style—and in so doing set a long-lasting precedent for magicians.

Frikell was noted for the directness and simplicity of many of his effects, and for his closing HAT PRODUCTION effect.

FRONT CARD

Synonym for BOTTOM CARD or FACE CARD.

FRONT CURTAIN

The curtain nearest the front of the stage and/or footlights; also sometimes called the ACT DROP.

FUKAI, HIROMASA (b. ?)

Born in Japan; performer noted for his fast-paced act with parasols, performed with wife and partner Kimika. An award winner at FISM, he has appeared in Europe and the U.S., and has also made television appearances in several countries, including the PAUL DANIELS show in Britain.

He is also an inventor and dealer; his best-known effect is **Milk To Silk**, a startling visual change.

FULL DECK

The complete complement of fifty-two cards consisting of the thirteen values for each of the four suits (within magical use the phrase does not usually imply the presence of one or two Jokers).

For some EFFECTs, notably those employing **faro** techniques or other mathematically based principles, it is important that a full deck be used.

Also called a *complete deck*.

FULL-EVENING SHOW

Term used to denote a complete stage show, usually of not less than two hours duration, taking place in a theater. Most of the well-known magicians of the early part of this century—KELLAR, THURSTON, BLACKSTONE, and others—primarily performed this type of show.

FULVES, KARL (b. ?)

Writer, editor, and publisher known not only for the impressive volume of work he has produced, but also for the entertaining controversies and feuds carried on in his publications.

After editing the last four issues of THE NEW PHOENIX, he then created and edited the

PALLBEARER'S REVIEW Magazine (in which much of the material was his own, appearing under his own name and several others); in addition to the ten-year run of regular issues, there were over twenty folios published (ten devoted to particular magicians, the rest to CLOSE-UP MAGIC).

Following this was EPILOGUE, a magazine of twenty-nine issues in all, devoted almost entirely to card magic. A subsequent more general magazine called *Chronicles* has published thirty issues but is (as of now) in an extended hiatus.

Among his books are *Riffle-Shuffle Set-ups, Riffle Shuffle Technique I & II, Teleportation Notes, Jacob Daley's Notebooks, Charles Jordan Collected Tricks, Packet Switches I-V,* and *Methods With Cards* (three volumes), and many others.

For the lay public, he has written several books in his *Self-Working* series: *Card Tricks, Table Magic, Number Magic, Mental Magic;* other titles include *The Magic Book* and *Children's Magic Kit.*

FU MANCHU

See BAMBERG, DAVID.

FUNNEL

Ordinary in appearance, this is used in LIQUID EFFECTS and employs the DOUBLE WALL principle to conceal liquid—which may be released to pour from the spout by the opening of an airhole.

It has often been used in conjunction with the MILK PITCHER, to recover milk apparently poured into an assisting spectator's ear; usually the milk is "extracted" from an elbow while the other arm is moved up and down in pump-handle fashion.

FUROTA, M. (b. ?)

Born in Japan; editor for over two decades of *The New Magic,* a major Japanese magic magazine. He is noted for his stage act which consists largely of manipulative magic.

Furota also heads the *Tenkai Prize Committee,* an organization which each year recognizes the accomplishments of a particular performer/creator and publishes a book on the performer's work.

FUTAGAWA, SHIGEO (b. ?)

Born in Japan; well-known dealer and writer. He has marketed numerous effects, and is known for his off-beat approach to PACKET tricks. He is the editor of *Fushigi* magic magazine.

Futagawa has lectured widely, and also has written many books on magic; his *Introduction To Coin Magic* is available in English-language translation.

GAFF

Special preparation of an item which physically alters it to bring about a desired EFFECT. Thus a deck arranged in a STACK is not gaffed; a STRIPPER DECK *is* gaffed. The term comes to magic from carnival slang, and is derived from an Old English term for gambling and humbug.

GALI-GALI, LUXOR (b. 1902)

Born Mangous Mohammed Hanafi in Egypt, he toured the world for several decades, playing in the best nightclubs, before settling finally in Las Vegas.

He is particularly noted for his skill at CLOSE-UP MAGIC; features of his performance are the RING ON WAND and the CUPS AND BALLS. In the latter effect, his FINAL LOAD is of several live baby chicks.

GALLI GALLI

A phrase called out by Egyptian street magicians to gather a crowd; it is said to come from the singular *Galli* which referred to the emasculated priests of Cybele who wore women's dress and practiced occult arts.

The name Galli Galli was adapted for use as a stage name by Mangous Mohammed Hanafi, who is known as GALI-GALI.

Variations of the name have been used by other performers.

GALLOPING POST

A move in the CUPS AND BALLS ROUTINE in which the three cups stacked together are held mouth upward in one hand; the other hand removes the lowermost cup and, inverting it, places it mouth down on the table.

The lower of the two remaining cups is now taken, inverted, and placed on the tabled cup; the action is repeated with the last cup—with the effect that the stack, now in reverse order, is now mouth down on the table surface.

In effect this only seems to be a display—but since it may be done with balls in all of the cups without revealing their presence (during the turning motion they are held by centrifugal force), it can form a useful adjunct to various routines.

GAMBLER'S PALM

Not actually a palm in the technical sense; the card is held with its forward edge clipped between the bases of the thumb and little finger, and projects backward against the palm toward the wrist. An approach to this technique is described in HUGARD and BRAUE's *Expert Card Technique* under the title of the *Gambler's Squaring Palm*.

The term is also used to denote a type of BOTTOM PALM executed with the fingers of the hand holding the deck, which buckle the card away from the deck and retain it as the deck is removed by the other hand.

A book devoted to this subject is *The Gambler's Palm Revisited* by Dan McMillan.

GAMBLING DEMONSTRATION

Revelation of the SLEIGHTs, techniques and/or APPARATUS used by crooked gamblers, performed as a ROUTINE within an ACT or as an act in itself.

Usually such demonstrations center on card gambling, with demonstrations of POKER, BRIDGE, and

BLACKJACK DEALS as well as such sleights as the MIDDLE DEAL and BOTTOM DEAL.

Magicians are expected to be conversant with these methods and techniques; few are, but it is possible to present a very entertaining act along these lines without becoming an expert. Indeed, an entire act of this kind was once sold by ROBERT HASKELL; many "gambling" routines which give the appearance of great skill have appeared in print over the years.

However, most performers who have achieved any degree of fame with such demonstrations do so on the basis of real skill and knowledge. Among these are MARTIN NASH, FRANK GARCIA and RICHARD TURNER; the late FRED ROBINSON; and, of course, the premier exponent of this type of demonstration—the late JOHN SCARNE.

GANSON, LEWIS (?-1980)

Born in Britain; one of magic's most prolific and highly-respected writers. He was for many years the editor of the GEN Magazine; in addition to his editorial duties he often wrote the bulk of its contents, including painstakingly described routines and effects. He later contributed considerably to MAGIGRAM.

Among his many books are *Art of Close-up* (two volumes), *Card Magic By Manipulation*, *Dai Vernon's Book Of Magic*, *Vernon's Inner Secrets Of Card Magic* (four volumes), *Routined Manipulation* (three volumes), *The Magic Of Slydini*, *Magic With Faucett Ross*, and *The Ganson Book*.

Among his many awards was the first Literary Fellowship from the ACADEMY OF MAGICAL ARTS.

GARBO

An EFFECT invented by W. C. Vincent for HOWARD DE COURCY in which a cage is removed from a box and a bird in turn from the cage, the cage then replaced in the box. The bird is placed on a perch in front of a mirror and covered; it apparently passes through the mirror and into the cage within the box.

The effect is in some respects reminiscent of VANITY FAIR.

GARCIA, FRANK (b. 1927)

Performer who began his career as an employee of MAX HOLDEN's magic shop in New York; he later developed a manipulative act with which he toured the east coast theater circuit.

Garcia then began to specialize in a GAMBLING DEMONSTRATION which was quite successful, leading to numerous television appearances and TRADE SHOW work, as well as consulting work for a number

of law enforcement organizations. He used the billing "The Man With The Million Dollar Hands." His standing in this field was enhanced by his book *Marked Cards And Loaded Dice*.

He has written a number of books for magicians, including *Exclusive Card Miracles*, *Exclusive Card Secrets*, *Close-up Magic Of Frank Garcia* (two volumes), *Garcia's Billiard Balls*, *Wild Card Miracles* (a book of routines for PETER KANE's WILD CARD effect), and many others.

GARDNER, MARTIN (b. 1914)

Best known for his long-running column titled "Mathematical Games," which appeared for many years in the *Scientific American* magazine. Gardner has also had a long involvement with magic, and has contributed to the JINX, PHOENIX, PALLBEARER'S REVIEW, and many other magazines.

Gardner is considered to be an authority on close-up impromptu magic, and his *Encyclopedia Of Impromptu Tricks*, collected from his *Hugard's Magic Monthly* column, is the outstanding work on the subject. Other books with similar material include *Match-Ic*, *Twelve Tricks With A Borrowed Deck*, *Over The Coffee Cups*, and *After The Dessert*.

He is also the author of *Mathematics, Magic And Mystery* which discusses mathematically-based effects. His other books, written for the public and largely anthologized from earlier contributions to *Scientific American*, include *Mathematical Carnival*, *Mathematical Magic Show*, *The Incredible Doctor Matrix*. and several others.

GARRETT, TERAL (1914-1970)

Dealer in used and rare books and apparatus; he also published a monthly magazine called *The Corsair*, which began its run in 1942.

A later publication, devoted primarily to MENTAL MAGIC, was *Psycho-Gizmo*, which ran from 1951 to 1965, during which 48 issues were published. Garrett is also noted for his book *Twenty-Six Living And Dead Tests*.

GAUGHAN, JOHN (b. 1940)

Now one of the most highly respected builders of ILLUSION props in the world; among his clients are DOUG HENNING, DAVID COPPERFIELD, HARRY BLACKSTONE Jr., SIEGFRIED AND ROY, THE PENDRAGONS and many other internationally known performers.

His company has also created special items for the

John Gaughan supervising the finishing touches on an illusion to be featured by Peter Reveen (*photo courtesy GENII Magazine*).

Universal Studios Tour as well as props for film and television shows.

Gaughan is also noted for his restorations of AUTOMATA and antique magical APPARATUS.

GAULTIER, CAMILLE (1872-1943)

French physician who became a full-time professional magician. In 1914 he published his *La Prestidigitation Sans Apariels*; it was later (1945) translated into English by JEAN HUGARD and published by PAUL FLEMING as *Magic Without Apparatus*. This book has long been considered a classic on the subject of pure SLEIGHT OF HAND with cards, coins, billiard balls and thimbles.

GEL

Abbreviation for *Gelatin*; a sheet of clear plastic tinted any of a number of colors, usually fixed in a metal frame. It is placed in front of a SPOT, FLOOD or other item of lighting equipment to produce the appropriate color of illumination.

GELLER, URI (b. 1946)

Former stage performer who achieved worldwide prominence with his claims to the production of genuine ESP and psychokinetic phenomena. A primary EFFECT of Geller's has been the bending and breaking of spoons by apparent PSYCHOKINESIS. It is interesting to note that a similar effect appeared in ABRACADABRA Magazine some years prior to Geller's public performances.

Many magicians have been hostile to Geller's claims, viewing him as everything from a threat to their profession to a threat to western civilization; more than one has advanced the theory that Geller planned to become a "psychic healer" or to start a cult.

Geller has, in fact, stayed well away from such areas, and continues with much the same repertoire—key-and-spoon-bending, BLINDFOLD work, and design duplications.

It is probable that Geller's claims of ESP and PK are without merit; if this is the case, he is hardly the first person in the magical profession to make untrue statements to achieve publicity and fame. In any case, his claims have been a boon to many performers, whose challenges to him have created publicity and attention for themselves.

Geller has been the subject of two uncritical biographies: *Uri*, by Andrija Puharich, and *My Story*, ghosted for Geller by John Fuller. He is also the subject of JAMES RANDI's *highly* critical study, *The Magic Of Uri Geller*.

The most thorough examination of techniques to create Geller-type effects is *Gellerism Revealed* by Ben Harris.

GEN, THE

British magic magazine edited by HARRY STANLEY as a "house organ" for his UNIQUE MAGIC STUDIO; noted for the high quality of the magic it published, and also for excellent production values; it was the first magical periodical to feature extensive photographic illustrations of sleights and effects. It was begun in January of 1946 and ceased publication in the mid-70s.

Current holder of the rights to *The Gen* is the SUPREME MAGIC CO., which has already published several collections of material from the magazine.

GENERAL CARD

A classic feat of card magic in which a card held by the performer appears to change into a duplicate of several selected cards in turn. Also sometimes known as Everybody's Card.

GENERAL POST

A class of TRANSPOSITION effect in which three or more objects change places (for example, the RICE, ORANGE AND CHECKERS feat).

GENII Magazine

This monthly magic magazine began its run in September 1936 under the editorship of its founder, WILLIAM W. LARSEN, Sr., and continues today edited by his son, WILLIAM W. LARSEN, Jr., with wife Irene.

In its fifty-year history, *Genii* has chronicled the important events within the magic world; these reports, along with the many columns, reviews, descriptions of EFFECTs and much more, have made it indispensable. Though occasionally plagued by erratic publishing schedules, *Genii* today has a loyal readership of several thousand.

GENII TUBE

A variant model of the PHANTOM TUBE, divided into two lengthwise sections and hinged so the tube may be opened to show the empty interior.

The tube is then closed and a PRODUCTION, usually of silks, is made from one end of it.

GEOMETRICAL BACK

See PATTERN BACK.

GEOMETRICAL VANISH

An EFFECT in which two or more pieces of card (or other rigid material) may be arranged in two ways; both arrangements apparently occupy the same space, but in one arrangement an empty space has appeared.

Another version of this puzzle involves pieces which in either of two arrangements take up the same area, but one of a number of objects pictured on the card is seen to vanish or transform into a different object.

There are many variations in procedure and effect which fall into this general category. An excellent discussion of **geometrical vanishes** may be found in MARTIN GARDNER's *Mathematics, Magic And Mystery*.

Considerable interest in this type of effect was created by the publication of *Paradox*, by *Matsuyama*, in which a playing card cut into several pieces could be assembled with its back upwards as a solid card—but face-up assembly would produce a hole; this effect was published in KARL FULVES' *Chronicles*.

A much more complex effect (which preceded the Matsuyama Paradox) is Masao Atsukawa's *Fair Exchange* (described in *New York Magic Symposium Collection Five*); here *two* puzzles are used, which can be assembled face-down without difficulty; however, face-up assembly yields for each card not a gap but a final piece which will not fit—but when the two pieces are *exchanged*, each fits perfectly!

GERMAIN, KARL (1878-1959)

Born Karl Mattmueller, he began his professional career while still a boy. By the age of twenty he was performing throughout North America and continued to do so for several years; he then did equally successful tours of Britain and Europe. He was noted for his many original effects and his artistic style of presentation.

Retiring from the stage in 1911, he studied law and was admitted to the Ohio bar, but his eyesight failed soon afterwards and he was blind for the remaining half of his life.

He is noted as the inventor of the BUTTERFLY trick and numerous other creations; many of these are described by STUART CRAMER (one of his few students) in *Secrets of Karl Germain* and *Germain The Wizard And His Legerdemain*.

GERTNER, PAUL (b. ?)

Specialist in close-up magic; he works primarily in the TRADE SHOW field, in which he is highly successful and has many prestigious clients. He was the First Place winner at the Desert Seminar Close-up Competition. Gertner has made numerous television appearances, including *That's Incredible*.

Within magic, Gertner is particularly noted for his CUPS AND BALLS routine, in which the balls are actually *steel ball bearings*. He is also noted as the inventor of the *Reverse Matrix* effect, an added climax for the original MATRIX ROUTINE: in Gertner's finish for the routine, the four coins are suddenly found at their original separate positions.

GHOST COUNT

See ELMSLEY COUNT.

GHOST ILLUSION

An EFFECT created by DAVID DEVANT in which a ghost-costumed figure was surrounded with folding screens by a committee from the audience; when the screens were removed, the figure had mysteriously vanished.

The "ghost" had only to remove his light costume, beneath which he wore ordinary street clothes; then moving out at the rear of the screens, he helped to adjust them and was taken by the committee for one of their own.

The principle was later employed by HOUDINI and other magicians, and has cropped up on a number of television shows in recent years.

GHOST TRICK

See PEPPER'S GHOST; not to be confused with DEVANT's GHOST ILLUSION described in the above entry.

GHOST TUBE

See PHANTOM TUBE; GENII TUBE.

GHOST WALKS

In theatrical vernacular, *The Ghost Walks* meant the payment of salary—the obvious derivation being that the two events were rare and unusual.

GIANT CARDS

See JUMBO DECK.

GIANT FAN

A large card FAN created by giving the deck a *straddle* FARO SHUFFLE—interlacing the two halves only three-quarters of an inch—before executing the fanning action.

GIANT MEMORY

Term used primarily in Britain to denote a MNEMONIC demonstration in which a number of objects suggested by the audience are memorized by the performer, who is able to call them back in any order.

This feat is sometimes combined with the MAGIC SQUARE; among those who have devised such combined routines are ORVILLE MEYER and HARRY LORAYNE.

See MNEMONICS.

GIBICIERE

A French term originally denoting a bag used by hunters for carrying small game; also given, however, to the bag worn at the front of the waist by many early magicians, as a repository for PROPS and APPARATUS.

More recently, the term was applied to a small padded box which rested on a SERVANTE; palmed articles could be secretly dropped into this box by the performer.

GIBSON, WALTER B. (1897-1985)

Best known as the creator of *The Shadow* and the 282 books featuring that character (written under the pen name of Maxwell Grant, a name created from MAX HOLDEN and U.F. GRANT), he was also a prolific magical journalist. He was the editor of *Seven Circles* and CONJUROR MAGAZINE, associate editor of *Magic World*, and co-editor/co-founder of the PHOENIX Magazine; he was also the ghost-writer for several books for HOWARD THURSTON, HARRY BLACKSTONE, and JOSEPH DUNNINGER.

A complete bibliography of his works would be a book in itself; among his many magic titles are *The Book Of Magic*, *The Complete Illustrated Book of Close-Up Magic*, *Encyclopedia Of Magic And Conjuring*, *Houdini's Escapes And Magic*, *Houdini's Fabulous Magic*, *Magic Explained*, *The New Magician's Manual*, *Popular Card Tricks*, *Professional Magic for Amateurs*, *Secrets Of Magic*, *Dunninger's Secrets* and *What's New In Magic*.

He briefly operated a magic shop in Philadelphia which opened in 1924, and originated for CARL BREMA (another Philadelphia dealer) one of the most popular close-up effects of all time—NICKELS TO DIMES. Among his numerous contributions to magic magazines was his "Like Seeks Like," published in the JINX Magazine and now known as OIL AND WATER.

GIFT SHOW

A performance during which several or all of the spectators receive gifts from the performer; these may be inexpensive advertising novelties or they may be objects of real value.

Among the many performers using this type of show were Charles Andress and Wyman The Wizard; others who used it on occasion were ROBERT-HOUDIN, L'HOMME MASQUE, and ALEXANDER HERRMANN.

GILBREATH PRINCIPLE

A principle formulated by Norman Gilbreath concerning the mixing of alternating cards in a riffle shuffle.

Gilbreath's First Principle says that a deck arranged with red and black cards alternating, if cut into two parts—the bottom cards of the two parts being of opposite colors—and the two parts riffled together, each pair of cards will consist of one black and one red card.

Gilbreath's Second Principle—implicit in the first—states that if two groups of similar cards, one group in the reverse order of the other, are riffle-shuffled together, the upper and lower halves of the resultant larger group will each be similar to the original group.

It should be understood that the RIFFLE SHUFFLES referred to need not be perfect shuffles such as the FARO SHUFFLE; indeed, the strength of many EFFECTs using these principles is that the spectator is allowed to do the shuffle (the performer having divided the cards into two groups).

To give an example: if the deck is separated into its four suits, and is then stacked from top to bottom Ace to King, Ace to King, King To Ace, King to Ace—and is then separated at the center Kings and riffle-shuffled, the upper and lower halves will still have exactly two cards of each value.

There has been a considerable amount of work done on this principle; the most complete exposition in print is REINHARD MULLER's *Gilbreath's Principles*.

GIMMICK

A secret device, never seen by the spectators, which makes it possible for an EFFECT to be accomplished. A REEL, for example, is a gimmick.

Also, more generally within show business, a personal characteristic or unique aspect by which a performer can be identified (e.g., Telly Savalas' shaved head), or an aspect of an entertainment production which renders it unique and presumably more appealing.

The term derives from the earlier *gimcrack*.
See FAKE.

GINN, DAVID (b. ?)

Performer specializing in CHILDREN'S MAGIC; also a writer and publisher, he has authored a number of books on the subject. These include *Children Laugh Louder*, *Professional Magic For Children*, *Fifty Ways To Make Children Laugh*, *Comedy Warm-Ups For Children's Shows*, and others.

Other books by Ginn are *Cane And Candle Book* (four volumes), *Feather Flowers From Nowhere*, *Promoting Me And You* (two volumes), *Strictly Visuals* (two volumes), *Close-Up A-Ginn* and many more.

GIORDMAINE, JOHN (1898-1973)

One of Canada's best-known magicians, he was adept at all kinds of magic but was happiest working for audiences of children, at which he was unrivaled. His long professional career included appearances on *Captain Kangaroo* and the *Ed Sullivan Show* and performances for Canadian and U.S. dignitaries.

GIORGIO, TONY (b. ?)

Actor by profession; he has appeared in *The Godfather* and many other feature films, and countless television shows. He has also acted as a TECHNICAL ADVISOR on magic and gambling for film and television productions.

Within magic, he is best known for his close-up presentations, most often with a gambling theme; he is also noted for his version of the **Card in the Matchbox** effect.

John Giordmaine (*The Mulholland Library of Conjuring & the Allied Arts*, Los Angeles, California)

GIRL THROUGH GLASS PLATE

An ILLUSION in which a large wooden frame is shown; it contains a sheet of plate glass. Two smaller curtained frames are shown, and affixed to clips at the center of the sheet of glass. A woman is placed on a table level with the frames and apparently slid through the solid glass to a table on the other side; the frames are then removed to show the glass to be solid and undamaged.

This illusion is featured by MARK WILSON; it is in some respects a larger version of the PENETRATION FRAME, and is also influenced by the VANITY FAIR illusion.

GIRL WITHOUT A MIDDLE

Known familiarly, if disrespectfully as **no guts**, this striking ILLUSION invented by P.T. SELBIT has been a feature of large-scale magic shows for over half a century.

It consists of a large cabinet in three sections: a small upper compartment for the head, a larger central com-

partment for the arms and body, and two long and narrow lower compartments for the legs. Each compartment has its own door.

In effect, a woman is manacled into position within the cabinet and the doors are closed. Large blades are then pushed in from the sides at top and bottom of the central compartment, apparently trisecting the unfortunate occupant of the cabinet. When the upper and lower compartment doors are opened, the head and legs are seen in position as before; when the center compartment is opened, however, it is seen that the body has vanished! The visual aspect seems so impossible that the audience often suspects a mirror; to eliminate this thought, the back wall of the central compartment is lowered to show a completely clear space through the cabinet.

To conclude the illusion the doors are closed, the blades removed, and the woman is released from the cabinet—as complete as when she entered it.

In the original version, the woman left the cabinet completely through a TRAP beneath one of the legs; a dummy head and legs were left in place. Modern versions do not use traps, although the dummy head is still employed. Since this dummy head is under considerable scrutiny, it must be extremely convincing. It is usually best to add makeup touches to the

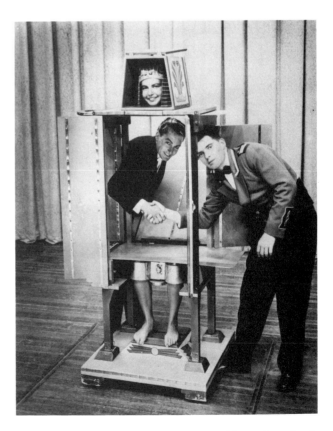

The *Girl Without A Middle*, as performed by Aubrey (looking through cabinet)

ASSISTANT so that she exactly resembles the dummy head, rather than vice versa. It should also be noted that skin reflects light in a very specific way; considerable care must be taken with the lighting. Sometimes a blindfold or similar item will be placed on the assistant to conceal part of the face.

Also known as the DISEMBODIED PRINCESS.

GLIDE

A card SLEIGHT in which the deck is held from above at the sides by the left hand, and the right fingers draw off cards from the bottom one at a time. The actual bottom card has been drawn back by the right little finger, thus the cards withdrawn by the right hand are taken from above it. At any point—a specified number, for example—the bottom card may be moved back into position and taken by the right hand.

GLIMPSE

See PEEK.

GLITTER CURTAIN

Term for a DROP made of strips of mirror-finish mylar hanging vertically. Used in conjunction with proper lighting, it creates a pattern confusing to the eye; THREAD or wire is almost impossible to see against a glitter curtain, and it is thus often used in presentations of various FLOATING EFFECTS and also the ASRAH version of the LEVITATION.

Also sometimes called a **Dazzle Curtain**, **Rain Curtain** or **Vegas Curtain**.

GLOVES TO DOVE

The performer removes his white gloves and tosses them into the air, where they seemingly visibly change to a dove. This effect, invented by BRUNEL WHITE, is accomplished by throwing the gloves into the PROFONDE on the "backswing" of the tossing motion, and producing the dove in the forward motion. The dove can be in the sleeve prior to the production, the foreward movement propelling it outward.

As with the DOVE TO SILK, this is far more difficult to accomplish convincingly than the description indicates, depending on timing and acting as much as magical technique. There are many variations in procedure; see IAN ADAIR's *Encyclopedia Of Dove Magic*.

An excellent version of this effect is featured by LANCE BURTON.

GLOYE, GENE (B. ?)

Writer on magic who has contributed to many magazines; for many years he has written a column titled "Our Magical Heritage" for LINKING RING Magazine.

He is the author of *Magic With Feather Flower Bouquets*, *Fantastic Tricks With Plastic Cups*, *More Fantastic Tricks With Plastic Cups*, *Glass-Ic magic*, *Table Book II*, and *Theatrical Magic*.

GODFREY, PETER (1900-1970)

British film director who had a long association with magic, first in his homeland and later in the United States. In Britain he had a long friendship with JASPER MASKELYNE; in the U.S., with many magicians living in or near Hollywood. Godfrey was well known in the magic community for the elaborate yearly shows he staged for various magical organizations.

GOEBEL, GEORGE (b. 1932)

Costumier by profession, he began his performing career while in the military, specializing in ESCAPES. He subsequently performed ILLUSION magic at state fairs, later appearing at movie houses and drive-in theaters.

In 1968 he debuted his FULL EVENING SHOW, and subsequently appeared at TRADE SHOWS; he also did regional television shows and commercials.

Goebel has appeared at several magic conventions; his *Goebel Magical Revue* is noted for its many illusions, large cast and elaborate sets, and for his performances in the grand style.

GOETIA

The kind of occult practice commonly characterized as black magic, usually involving the invoking of demons by means of ceremonies and rituals.

The simulation of such phenomena is one aspect of BIZARRE MAGICK.

GOLDFINGER (b. 1949)

Born Jack Vaughn, he began his performing career in his teens, combining magic with fire-eating and other spectacular feats. With his wife and partner Dove, he has performed all over the world, in nightclubs and theaters from Las Vegas to Paris; he has also appeared many times on television both in the U.S. and Europe.

Goldfinger and Dove have twice received the Stage Magician Of The Year award from the ACADEMY OF MAGICAL ARTS.

GOLDFISH BOWL

See BOWL PRODUCTION; AERIAL FISHING.

GOLDIN, HORACE (1874-1939)

Born Hyman Goldstein in Poland; he emigrated to the U.S. as a teenager. He began his performing career as a BUSKER and later worked in VAUDEVILLE, and first achieved real success during an extended tour of Britain, where he appeared at ST. GEORGE'S HALL and many other venues throughout the country. Goldin also toured through Asia.

He was noted for the fast pace of his performance and for his **Sawing a Woman in Half** ILLUSION, inspired by the P.T. SELBIT presentation of SAWING THROUGH A WOMAN. When too many other performers began featuring the Sawing illusion, Goldin presented the spectacular BUZZSAW version of the illusion.

Goldin is credited with the invention of FILM TO LIFE, and a curious illusion in which he appeared to thrust his hand right through a male assistant's body.

GOLDSTEIN, PHIL

See MAX MAVEN.

GOLDSTON, WILL (1878-1943)

British magician who, after a brief career as a performer, became a noted magic dealer and author. He wrote more than fifty books, of which the most famous are his three *"Locked Books"*—*Exclusive Magical Secrets*, *More Exclusive Magical Secrets*, and *Further Exclusive Magical Secrets*—which described effects from the smallest of pocket tricks to the most elaborate of stage ILLUSIONS; these books were fitted with hasps

Horace Goldin (*The Mulholland Library of Conjuring & the Allied Arts, Los Angeles, California*)

Will Goldston (*photo courtesy GENII Magazine*)

and locks. (The latter two are difficult to obtain; the first was reprinted in 1977 by Dover Books.)

Goldston also wrote *Sensational Tales Of Mystery Men*, which contained highly entertaining and very readable stories of various magicians—but it should be pointed out that his title is literally true; these *are* "sensational tales" and should not be taken as historical fact.

At various times Goldston was a booking agent, magic tutor, and editor of magic magazines. He also founded the Magician's Club of London.

GOLF BALLS

Sometimes used in preference to BILLIARD BALLs as appearing more natural, these are almost always rubber balls made to look like golf balls rather than the genuine article. An excellent MULTIPLYING BILLIARD BALLs routine can be done with the rubber golf balls; it was created and marketed by L. L. IRELAND.

GOLLIWOG BALL

An EFFECT featured by DAVID DEVANT, in which a wooden ball would roll up and down a slanted board in seeming defiance of gravity.

Devant first became aware of the effect while on a trip to the U.S., where HARRY KELLAR showed him a version depending on a series of electromagnets set into the board. Kellar was not happy with the method, and Devant offered to solve the problem if he was granted permission by Kellar to feature the effect in Britain. Kellar, thinking it impossible that a simpler method could be devised, agreed, and less than a day later Devant showed him a simple thread hookup which, with a cleverly-faked ball, would accomplish the effect.

A third method, described by WILL GOLDSTON, used a cup-like holder within the board to move the ball through a thin fabric covering.

GONE!

An ILLUSION created by WILLIAM ROBINSON in which a woman was secured to a chair with rope; the chair was then hoisted up into the air by a winch set into a large open framework. The woman was clearly visible in the chair, but at a pistol shot from the performer the chair fell to the stage and the woman vanished instantaneously.

The ILLUSION, accomplished by an application of the PEPPER'S GHOST principle, is described in *Magic* by Albert A. Hopkins and in S.H. SHARPE's *Conjurer's Optical Secrets*.

GOODLIFFE (?-1980)

Born C. Goodliffe Neale in Britain, he was by profession a supplier of church furniture; he is noted in magic as the creator and editor of ABRA Magazine (which see), which through his long stewardship never missed a deadline in spite of a gradually debilitating disease which finally took his life.

Many readers valued ABRA more for Goodliffe's trenchant editorials than any other feature of the magazine.

GOOD NIGHT BANNER

A large velvet square with rods in its upper and lower borders is folded in half, and a bright ribbon dropped into the fold. When the banner is allowed to drop open, the ribbon is seen to have attached itself to the velvet to spell out the words *Good Night* or a similar message.

The banner is constructed in similar fashion to a FLAP CARD, and the feat is performed as a CLOSER or ENCORE effect.

GOODSELL, DAVID (b. 1939)

Educator by profession; he has since 1977 been the editor of M.U.M., official organ of the Society Of American Magicians (*see* S.A.M.).

GOOSENECK

In a LEVITATION, the S-curved support immediately to the rear of the cradle which permits the HOOP PASS move.

See LEVITATION; HOOP PASS.

GORDIEN, HENRY (1890-1967)

Performer with long professional career; noted as a teacher of magic and for his many inventions, several of which are described in HILLIARD's *Greater Magic*.

GORDON, GENE (b. 1904)

Performer who began his career with school assembly shows throughout the southern U.S., and was one of the founding members of the INTERNATIONAL BROTHERHOOD OF MAGICIANS. A noted magic dealer, in collaboration with HEN FETSCH he invented and marketed many EFFECTs. His autobiography is titled *Gene Gordon's Magical Legacy*.

He is also the author of *Routines By Gene Gordon* (two volumes).

Gordon is a recipient of the Masters Fellowship from the ACADEMY OF MAGICAL ARTS.

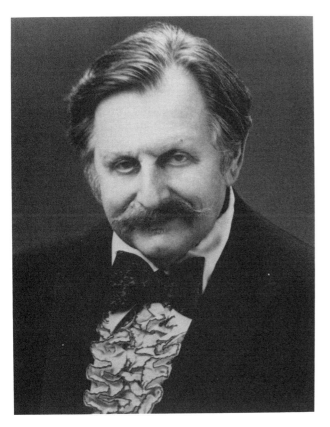

Albert Goshman

GOSHMAN, ALBERT (b. 1921)

Considered both by his peers and the public to be one of the very best performers of CLOSE-UP MAGIC in the world, he was originally a bakery operator in the New York City area. He moved to California and became a professional performer, honing his style in hundreds of shows at the MAGIC CASTLE.

Within magic, Goshman is also known for his line of SPONGE BALLS of various kinds, used by magicians all over the world.

His inimitable approach is described in his *Magic By Gosh*.

He is a winner of the *Close-up, Lecturer,* and *Magician Of The Year* Awards from the ACADEMY OF MAGICAL ARTS.

GO SOUTH

To secretly remove an item from its supposed location (and, in some cases, to dispose of the item in a specific way, so that the hands can be shown empty).

GOSPEL MAGIC

A type of presentation in which magical effects are used to illustrate biblical concepts (gospel magic is,

curiously, confined to Christianity). Some clergy-magicians find it very effective, while others feel it leads to confusion between events related in the Bible and the feats of stage magicians.

A number of books have been written on this type of magic, which is also the subject of a magazine—*The Christian Conjurer*.

GOZINTA BOXES

An effect invented by LUBOR FIEDLER; it uses two cubical boxes with nesting lids, either of which may be placed completely inside the other. This paradoxical effect is made possible because the boxes are not true cubes and because the lids do not nest completely.

GRABEL, LEE (b. 1919)

A professional performer while still a boy; after World War II, he created an elaborate FULL-EVENING SHOW with which he successfully toured the U.S. One of the features of this show was his famous **Floating Piano** ILLUSION.

In 1959, he retired from show business and began a second career in real estate investment; he has performed only occasionally since then.

Grabel's life and approach to magic are both thoroughly covered in *The Magic And Illusions Of Lee Grabel* by ORMOND MCGILL.

GRAND DAVID, LE

Stage magic company founded by Dr. Cesareo Pelaez which has been presenting elaborate FULL-EVENING SHOWS in their Cabot Street Cinema Theatre in Beverly, Massachusetts since 1977. The company owns and has completely reconditioned the theater; they have done the same for another Beverly theater, *The Larcom*, and present in that venue a completely different show. Both shows feature many ILLUSIONs and lavish scenery and costumes, for the most part in ORIENTAL STYLE.

The company is made up entirely of volunteers, many of whom are full-time professionals in other fields; the number varies, but usually more than sixty people are involved.

The show is billed as *Le Grand David And His Spectacular Magic Company*; in addition to the character of Le Grand David himself, other featured performers are *Marco The Magi* (played by Dr. Pelaez), *Seth The Sensational* and *Professor Besco*.

The Le Grand David company is noted not only for its lavish productions, but also for the high quality of its graphic and printed matter, including several multicolor posters; the Company has been the subject

The Le Grand David Company's featured players: (clockwise from top) Le Grand David, Marco, Seth, and Professor Besco

of countless news stories and features. They have also appeared several times at the White House Easter Celebration in Washington, D.C.

Dr. Pelaez has served as President of the SOCIETY OF AMERICAN MAGICIANS. As *Marco The Magi*, he is a recipient of the *Magician Of The Year* Award from the ACADEMY OF MAGICAL ARTS.

GRANDMOTHER'S NECKLACE

A very old EFFECT—described in the earliest conjuring books—in which several beads are magically removed from the two cords on which they are strung. The basic principle has been adapted to many platform and stage effects, including CORDS OF PHANTASIA.

GRANT, U.F. (1901-1978)

Magic dealer and inventor known to his friends as "Gen" Grant, he created and marketed countless EFFECTs during a long career in the business.

Among his many inventions are the TEMPLE SCREEN, the COW TRICK and the CHINK CANS; his

books include *Bodies In Orbit, Fifteen Great Illusions, Six Modern Levitations, Twenty-Five One Man Mind Reading Tricks, Victory Carton Illusions, Window Stoppers*, and many others. A number of the feats of MENTAL MAGIC he created and marketed are described in *Fabulous Feats Of Mental Magic* (edited by Don Tanner).

GRAVATT, GLENN (1899-1984)

Prolific author of magic books and articles whose first major book, *Encyclopedia Of Card Tricks*, surprised the magic community in general with its breadth and completeness—and many magicians in particular whose EFFECTs appeared in the book without permission. (A later edition, edited by JEAN HUGARD, sought and obtained permission from originators.)

He contributed effects of all kinds to magic magazines for many years; among his books are *Gold Mine Of Magic* and *Thayer Instruction Sheets* (three volumes).

GRAVITY PULL

A type of PULL in which the motive power is supplied by a weight moving in a vertically-mounted tube of cloth or other material; usually concealed within the performer's clothing. A THREAD is attached to the weight and may have a waxed bead at its other end, with which it may be affixed to the item to be vanished or otherwise affected.

This pull can also be used in some versions of the RISING CARDS.

GREAT DIVIDE

An ILLUSION created by DE VEGA in which a woman was placed in a tall cabinet and secured in position; the upper half of the cabinet was then slid to the side, apparently separating the upper and lower halves of the assistant. A reversal of the procedure restored her to normal.

The illusion was in some respects a precursor of the ZIG-ZAG GIRL illusion created by ROBERT HARBIN.

GREEK DEAL

Generally, any kind of FALSE DEAL, e.g., BOTTOM DEAL, MIDDLE DEAL, SECOND DEAL.

More specifically, in modern usage, to deal the card which lies *second* from the bottom, without disturbing the bottom card; an obvious advantage of this procedure is the ability to FLASH the bottom of the deck and show that the bottom card remains the same, thus eliminating to some degree the thought that a bottom dealing procedure is being used.

GREEK SHUFFLE

A type of FALSE SHUFFLE in which the cards are held as for an overhand shuffle and one half of the deck is apparently interwoven with the other; in actuality the cards are merely cut.

It is described in HILLIARD's *Greater Magic*.

GREEN, CLIFF (1896-1969)

Professional magician who worked in vaudeville for many years. He originated the INTERLOCKED CARD PRODUCTION and many other EFFECTs.

His highly visual approach to platform and stage card work is described in his *Professional Card Magic*.

GREENGAGE

Slang term which denotes the theatrical stage; of primarily British usage, it may derive from Cockney rhyming slang.

Sometimes the term is abbreviated simply to *"The Green"*.

GREEN ROOM

Place where performers wait just prior to performing; it is usually immediately adjacent to the stage, but may simply be a specified area rather than an actual room.

GRID

Abbreviation for *Gridiron*: the metal framework in the FLIES from which FLATS, DROPS and other items of scenery are suspended.

GRIFFITHS, E. RAY (1912-1965)

See FABIAN.

GRIFFITH, TONY (b. 1935)

Born in Britain; a teacher by profession, he has nevertheless had a very active performing career, appearing throughout Britain and Europe as well as several U.S. tours.

His books include *Griff On Cards*, *Griff On Close-Up*, and *An Invitation To Mystery*.

GRIPPO, JIMMY (b. ca. 1900)

Born in Italy; he moved to the U.S. and began working as a close-up performer in the 1930s, appearing at society parties in the New York City area. He also became known as a hypnotist, and received considerable publicity when he used hypnotic suggestion in an attempt to improve the abilities of boxers and other athletes.

Jimmy Grippo (*photo courtesy GENII Magazine*)

He became the close-up "magician in residence" at Caesar's Palace in Las Vegas in 1966, where he continues to perform, in addition to numerous private-party and television appearances. Grippo is considered to be one of the best close-up magicians in the world.

Some indication of his methods may be gained from his *The Magic Of Jimmy Grippo*.

GROSSMAN, DR. JOHN H. (b. 1914)

Physician by profession. He is a member of such organizations as the I.B.M., S.A.M., Inner MAGIC CIRCLE (with Gold Star), The Magic Collectors Association (for which he served a term as president) and many others.

He is noted as a collector of magic books and memorabilia, and for his long-running columns in the MAGIC CIRCULAR (Americana) and M.U.M. (Ask the Doctor).

GROUP DEAL

Dealing cards in groups of two, three, or more, rather than singly as is usual.

Also called MULTIPLE DEAL.

GROWTH OF FLOWERS

See BLOOMING BOUQUET; BOTANIA; FLOWER GROWTH; SPRING FLOWERS.

GUILLOTINE

A macabre ILLUSION in which a person (often an audience member) is locked in the stocks of a guillotine; when the release cord is pulled, the blade drops and apparently passes through the person's neck without harm.

In a variant version, usually performed with a stage ASSISTANT, a basket rests in front of the guillotine, and when the blade descends, the person's head (*not a* FAKE) is seen to drop into the basket. This version, sometimes called the **Monster guillotine** or **Will Rock guillotine** (Rock featured it in his show), was manufactured for many years by Abbott's Magic Novelty Co.

GUITAR, PRESSLEY (b. ?)

Manufacturer of precision magical apparatus, active primarily in the mid-1970s. He is noted for his introduction of the CIGARETTE THROUGH QUARTER.

GUN TRICK

See BULLET CATCH.

GWYNNE, JACK (1895-1979)

Professional performer whose long career began in vaudeville; later he starred in nightclubs throughout the U.S., where he was noted for doing ILLUSIONS and other spectacular feats, rather than the smaller EFFECTs usually performed in such venues. He also made a number of appearances on television, as a semiregular on *Super Circus* and on other shows.

He invented a number of effects, of which the most popular was probably his **Temple of An-Gee**, later to be known as the **Temple of Benares** (see DOLL HOUSE). Gwynne's most famous feat was the PRODUCTION from a bundle of silk handkerchieves of a stack of nine water-filled fishbowls, an effect which to date has not been duplicated by any other

Jack and Anne Gwynne, at the climax of his *Bowl Production* (photo courtesy of GENII Magazine)

performer under the same conditions. It is, however, thoroughly described in David Charvet's *Jack Gwynne*—which also gives the details of many Gwynne effects in addition to a full biography.

GYPSY CURSE

See WILD CARD.

GYPSY THREAD

Also known as the **Hindu Thread**; a type of TORN-AND-RESTORED OBJECT effect in which a length of thread is broken into a number of short pieces, which then join together to make one long piece again.

Several ROUTINEs for this EFFECT are described in *The Hindu Thread (Gypsy Thread)* by LEWIS GANSON.

HABACK COUNT

See BACK COUNT.

HADES, MICKY (b. 1927)

Born in Canada, he became a performer in his teens; he is best known, however, for his creation of **Micky Hades International** (MHI), a magic dealership specializing in mail order. It has become one of the largest magic book dealers and publishers in the world, producing hundreds of titles over the years. In addition, MHI operates magic shops in the U.S. and Canada.

In addition to publishing his *Hade-E-Gram* (1957-65) and editing several books (including the massive POTTER INDEX published by MHI), Hades has written several of his own, including *Hades Gone Wild, Just A Touch Of Hades, Out Of My Mind, Magic—The Way I See It, How to Make Flashes Bangs And Puffs Of Smoke, Bang,* and *The New Make-Up Of Magic.*

HAENCHEN, FRED (1903-1983)

A performer on the LYCEUM and CHAUTAUQUA circuits in the early part of his career, he later turned to the manufacture of magical APPARATUS of high quality and precision workmanship. Many Haenchen-produced effects are now collector's items.

The Haenchen business was sold to *Viking Magic Company,* which continues to manufacture some of the Haenchen effects as Viking-Haenchen Magic Company.

HAHNE, NELSON C. (1909-1970)

Illustrator for a truly astounding number of books and magazines. In addition to his many years association with the LINKING RING Magazine, for which he did not only "technical" illustrations but also many cartoons and column-head drawings, he illustrated *Modern Magic Manual, Modern Coin Magic,* and many magic catalogs and smaller books.

He also wrote *Modernism in Pasteboard* (with RALPH W. HULL) and *Here's Magic* (with JOE BERG).

HAINES, RONALD (1906-1973)

A past International President of both the S.A.M and I.B.M., noted as the founder of HAINES HOUSE OF CARDS, for many years the major supplier of MECHANICAL DECKS and various kinds of faked cards.

HAINES HOUSE OF CARDS

A company founded by RONALD HAINES (who bought out the business of John W. Snyder Jr., a manufacturer of faked cards); located in Norwood, Ohio (a suburb of Cincinnati), it supplies MECHANICAL DECKS and various faked cards to the magical profession.

HALF-PASS

An action which secretly turns over that part of the deck below a BREAK; see BOX THE DECK. It may be done with any number of cards from a single card to a PACKET to a full deck. The term comes from the SLEIGHT's resemblance in its initial action to that of the PASS (or, more properly, SHIFT).

HALF-ROUGHING

To apply ROUGHING FLUID to only half of a playing card's surface area. If two cards are thus prepared, and the roughed surfaces are placed together, the cards may be handled as a single card when held at the roughed end; when held at the opposite end, however, they can be handled and spread as single cards.

See SUPER-ROUGHING.

HALL, TREVOR H. (b. 1910)

Born in Britain; surveyor by profession. He is noted as a COLLECTOR and writer of works on magic and also as an investigator/author of books on psychic and supernatural subjects.

His books on magic include *The Testament Of Ralph W. Hull, Reading Is Believing, Nothing Is Impossible, The Card Magic Of E. G. Brown,* and *Bibliography Of Books On Conjuring 1550-1850.*

Hall's books on the supernatural include *Four Modern Ghosts, The Medium And The Scientist, The Strange Case Of Edmund Gurney* and *The Spritualists.*

HAMMAN, JOHN, BR. (b. 1927)

Now a Brother in the Catholic teaching order of the Society Of Mary, he is a strong influence in present-day card magic; he is best known for the COUNT which bears his name (*see* HAMMAN COUNT).

He has created a number of commercially-marketed items, including Micro-Macro, Haldeucination, and several others. His work is described in his *Seven Deadly Sins* and a book co-written with PAUL LE PAUL, titled *The Card Magic Of Brother John Hamman.* He has also published items in PALLBEARER'S REVIEW (including a Folio devoted entirely to his effects), M.U.M., and elsewhere.

HAMMAN COUNT

A counting procedure devised by BR. JOHN HAMMAN which conceals the identities of a number of cards in a packet. Most often an odd number of cards are used; held from above in the right hand, they are pulled off one at a time by the left thumb. When the central card is reached, the packets in the two hands are switched, and the first three cards are counted again, the three bottom cards of the packet never being seen, presuming (say) seven cards in the packet.

The count is fully described in MENTZER's *Counts, Cuts, Moves And Subtleties* and elsewhere.

HANDCUFF ESCAPE

A type of ESCAPE effect using police or military handcuff restraints. The handcuffs may be genuine, in which case the performer makes use of a duplicate key or a pick; or they may be secretly prepared so they may be opened without the use of any extraneous device.

HOUDINI had his first major success with an ACT of handcuff escapes. Such acts now are rarely seen.

HANDKERCHIEF BALL

A hollow, flesh-colored metal ball with an opening, in which one or more silk handkerchieves may be placed; this done, the ball can be palmed and the hands shown empty by means of BILLIARD BALL sleights, after which the silks can be produced. The ball may also be used for the vanish of silks by a reversal of the above process.

The handkerchief ball, invented by John Hamley, is sometimes known as a **Stillwell Ball**, after its popularizer; some of Stillwell's techniques are described in PROFESSOR LOUIS HOFFMANN's *Later Magic* and in many later sources.

A similar ball which had two openings was also invented by Hamley; now popularly known as a **palmo ball**, it could be used to create the effect of a COLOR-CHANGE by poking one silk into the ball and withdrawing a different one previously placed there.

HANDKERCHIEF FORCE

A method to FORCE a card by having a deck CUT underneath a handkerchief; invented by LORD AMWELL.

The card to be forced is on top of the deck; as the performer places the deck under the handkerchief, it is secretly turned face-up. The spectator cuts off a portion of cards by gripping them through the handkerchief, and as the cards are lifted away the performer again reverses the cards he holds, and extends them for the spectator to take the top card. This is apparently the top card of the lower half, but is actually the original top card. As the spectator notes the forced card, the performer retrieves the cards and handkerchief held by the spectator.

A variant version does not make use of the secret turnover; instead, the force card is on the bottom of the deck, and the performer uses a CHARLIER PASS to bring it to the top of the lower portion as the spectator is removing the upper portion of the deck.

HANDKERCHIEF GUN

This PROP has the appearance of an automatic pistol; a handkerchief draped over the barrel vanishes instantly when the gun is fired.

A spring-loaded roller with an attached hook is used; when the trigger is pulled it draws the handkerchief rapidly out of sight into the barrel of the gun, through an opening on the side away from the audience.

HANDKERCHIEF WAND

A now little-used method of vanishing a silk handkerchief which has been placed in a cone. The silk is actually draped over a thin dowel within the cone; the hollow wand is used to poke the silk further into the cone, and in this action is slid down over the dowel, trapping the silk inside the wand. The cone may then be shown empty.

HANDLING

The body of specific methods and techniques used to bring about an effect; also, the performer's level of execution of these procedures.

HAND MAGIC

Effects accomplished by SLEIGHT OF HAND; also, any small magic which takes place entirely in the hands.

HAND MUCKING

Gamblers' parlance for a SWITCH of cards during play; some of these switches may be adapted to magical purposes.

A comprehensive text on the subject is *Hand Mucking* by George Joseph.

HANDWASHING

Pejorative term used to describe excessive and repetitive movements of the hands in the course of an ACQUITMENT. Except when setting up for a SUCKER EFFECT, showing the hands to be empty should most often only be done once for the most convincing effect.

HANKY PANKY

A ROUTINE in which various objects are produced from a handkerchief draped alternately over each hand. An excellent routine for this effect was devised by AL KORAN and is described in LEWIS GANSON's *Routined Manipulation Finale*.

In gambling terminology, any small carnival game making its profit from steady play and inexpensive prizes.

Also, generally, any questionable or suspect deceptive activity.

HAN PING CHIEN (b. ?)

Born in China, he appeared in the U.S. in 1909 with his Peking Mysteries Troupe, performing feats of traditional Chinese magic. He toured in U.S. and British vaudeville for several years before finally returning to China.

He is best known within magic as the originator of the HAN PING CHIEN MOVE; his own version of this SLEIGHT, as well as a description of his paper-tearing effect, will be found in David P. Abbott's *Book Of Mysteries*.

HAN PING CHIEN MOVE

A coin sleight popularized in the Occident, and possibly invented by its namesake HAN PING CHIEN, in which coins apparently dropped from one hand are actually secretly dropped from the other. It is described in BOBO's *Modern Coin Magic* and many other books.

An interesting technical point is that, while the modern sources describe the sleight as being done with both hands palm *down*, Han performed it with the "dropping" hand palm *up*—as is shown in *Book Of Mysteries*, by DAVID ABBOTT.

Some excellent modern work on this move has been done by JAY SANKEY, and is described in KAUFMAN's *Sankey Panky*.

HANSON, HERMAN (1882-1973)

Born Herman Hansone in Sweden; emigrating to the U.S., he began working in vaudeville, eventually creating an act billed as "Mystic Hanson And The Burton Sisters," which combined his magic with the singing and dancing of the sisters. The act was particularly noted for Hanson's barehanded PRODUCTION of a huge number of flags.

He later worked on the staff of HOWARD THURSTON's show, and still later managed the Boston branch of MAX HOLDEN's magic shop. In the latter part of his life he was very active in the organization of magic conventions in the Boston area.

HAPNER, MAX (b. ?)

Performer who, with wife and partner Salli, specializes in school assembly shows, appearing in many other venues as well; he has toured throughout the U.S. The Hapners are noted for their bubble-

Max and Salli Hapner performing the Basket Trick.

Robert and Dolly Harbin in an early photograph, circa 1931 (*photo courtesy GENII Magazine*)

themed act titled **Bubbles, Bangles And Beads**, and for their excellent version of the BASKET TRICK.

HARBIN, ROBERT (1908-1978)

Born Edward (Ned) Williams in South Africa, he is considered one of the great creative geniuses of twentieth century magic. He emigrated to Britain as a young man, and had an uncertain career performing in music halls, cabarets, and at dinners, until he was offered a week at ST. GEORGE'S HALL, an engagement which stretched to three years. To avoid confusion with Oswald Williams he took the Harbin name of his grandfather, and continued performing in various venues with increasing success.

In addition to his theatrical work, he performed in several television series, including one in Bermuda where he performed *daily*; he also made appearances in the U.S., including New York's famed Palace Theater where he was very favorably received and reviewed.

He was also an expert at the Japanese art of ORIGAMI (paper-folding), which was featured in its own long-running television show; in this presentation, only Harbin's hands were seen, the show being titled *Mr. Left & Mr. Right*.

He is best-known, of course, as the inventor of several spectacular illusions, notably the ZIG-ZAG GIRL—but his creativity embraced the whole range of magic and related arts, as is evident from his *The Magic Of Robert Harbin* and *HarbinCadabra*—the latter a collection of effects from ABRA Magazine.

He is also the author of *Origami* and *More Origami*.

HARDEEN (1876-1945)

Born Theodore Weiss; brother of HOUDINI, with whom he briefly performed an act as the Houdini Brothers. He then went into retail selling for a time, but at Houdini's urging returned to performing, pretending to be his brother's rival and performing a similar act.

Hardeen later created a more elaborate show, and became a major vaudeville star in the U.S. and Europe. Again for a time he ceased performing to manage

Houdini's motion picture company, but after Houdini's death Hardeen returned to the stage.

He achieved another major success when he starred in the Broadway hit *Hellz-a-poppin* with comedians Olsen and Johnson; the show ran for several years in New York City and on tour.

HARDIN, HENRY (1849-?)

Born E.A. Parsons; professor of music, composer, and teacher by profession. He was noted as an inventor of numerous magical EFFECTs, many of which were sold as manuscripts.

Some of Hardin's effects were described in a special issue of JINX Magazine.

HARLEQUIN CIGARETTE HOLDER

A cigarette holder which is ordinary in appearance, but will cause a cigarette to appear or disappear from its end; this is accomplished by exhaling through the holder—which will cause the cigarette to be forced out of its hiding place within the holder—or by inhaling through the holder, which will reverse the process.

A **harlequin cigarette holder** was used to great effect in the act of CARDINI.

Paul Harris (*photo courtesy GENII Magazine*)

HARRIS, PAUL (b. ?)

Inventor and writer whose primary interest is CLOSE-UP card magic. He wrote a column for ADAM FLEISCHER's *Magic Manuscript*, and has also contributed to other periodicals.

His books, noted for their original approach and offbeat writing style, include *The Cardboard Connection, The Immaculate Connection, Close-Up Entertainer, Close-Up Fantasies* (three volumes), *Close-Up Kinda Guy, Close-Up Seductions, Las Vegas Close-Up, Paul Harris Reveals, Super Swindle, Supermagic, P.H. Breakthrough,* and *The Inner Circle.*

HART, CHRISTOPHER (b. 1961)

Born in Canada, he specializes in manipulative magic, and is noted for his highly original presentation of the TORN-AND-RESTORED effect using a music sheet.

Hart has performed in varied venues throughout the world, including appearances in Las Vegas, Japan, Canada and China; he has also made a number of television appearances.

HART, JOHNNY (b. 1945)

Born in Britain, he is a protege of HARRY STANLEY who in his teens was the first winner of the MAGIC CIRCLE's Young Magician Of The Year award. For many years his act featured effects with parakeets (in-

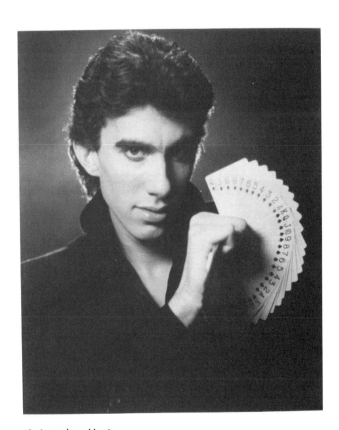

Christopher Hart

spired by JACK KODELL). His performances now include spectacular ILLUSION effects, and he has appeared at many major venues, including the MGM Grand in Reno and the Flamingo in Las Vegas.

HARTMAN, JERRY (b. ?)

Lawyer by profession; known for his inventions in the area of card magic, many of which he has contributed to PALLBEARER'S REVIEW and other publications.

His books include *Card Fare, Packet Magic, Means And Ends, Loose Ends*, and *Three Collected Works Of Jerry Hartman*.

HARTZ, JOSEPH (1836-1903)

Performer who began his career in Britain, and later toured the U.S. He is noted for his innovation of having all the APPARATUS used in his ACT made of glass, and for his elaborate HAT PRODUCTION routine in which the stage was filled with items taken from a borrowed hat. This ROUTINE is described in HOFFMANN's *Later Magic*.

HASKELL, ROBERT (?-1972)

Performer who appeared in nightclubs in the western U.S.; his act was noted for its many original features.

He is noted as the inventor of the SPLIT DECK and *Deep Freeze*, and also a GAMBLING DEMONSTRATION routine, and is the author of *The Magic of Haskell*.

HAT COIL

See COIL.

HAT PRODUCTIONS

The PRODUCTION of a rabbit from a hat is one of the archetypal EFFECTs of magic; curious, in that the effect was never all that popular and is almost never seen today. Hat productions of any kind are rarely seen today, primarily due to the changing styles in men's fashions.

The most effective such productions use a borrowed hat, and undoubtedly the most elaborate ROUTINE for this was created by JOSEPH HARTZ in his Le Chapeau De Diable (DEVIL OF A HAT) presentation. Beginning on a bare stage with a borrowed hat, Hartz drew from the hat an incredible succession of articles until the entire stage was covered. His routine is fully explained in HOFFMAN's *Later Magic*.

Few modern magicians have featured the hat production; of these the most notable is MACDONALD BIRCH.

HATTON, HENRY (1838-1923)

Born Patrick Cannon; co-author, with ADRIAN PLATE, of the influential book *Magician's Tricks: How They Are Done*. He was a founding member (and one of the first presidents) of the S.A.M. in New York, and is reported to be the first performer in that city to present the BASKET TRICK.

HAUNTED DECK

A deck of cards mysteriously cuts itself to reveal a previously selected card. Most versions of this EFFECT use a thread hookup of some kind. The effect was invented by AL BAKER (whose routine is described in his *Pet Secrets*); other routines have been devised by PAUL CURRY (in *Special Effects*), and FINN JON (his marketed *Esoteric*), among others.

This effect has also been accomplished with a MECHANICAL DECK created and marketed by LOUIS TANNEN; an elaborate version uses a takeup reel within the deck itself, so the performer need not be near the deck as the action takes place.

Other versions have used wire springs (*Oh-Wee-Gee*), rubber bands and sponge balls as the motive power.

A related effect is the Chop Chop deck invented by CHOP CHOP; here the upper half swivels to a 90-degree angle for the revelation. Also a mechanical deck, the Chop Chop deck is equipped with magnets to bring about the movement required.

The Haunted Deck is a primary subject of a book by EUGENE BURGER titled *The Performance of Close-up Magic*.

HAUNTED WINDOW

An ILLUSION devised by DAVID DEVANT from a principle invented by Julian Wylie, which used a large set of French windows set in a frame; the frame was mounted on legs, affording a clear view underneath it, and stairs were set at front and back to give access.

In performance a transparent scrim suspended from a square frame was raised around the window to further isolate it. In spite of these conditions, several people were made to appear and disappear within the window as a dramatic playlet was enacted.

The illusion was accomplished by an application of the MIRROR PRINCIPLE in conjunction with careful lighting.

HAY, HENRY (1912-1985)

Born (June) Barrows Mussey, he became interested in magic as a boy and began a professional career at the age of thirteen; during his first tour he met T.

NELSON DOWNS who remained a lifelong friend and influence.

Hay continued performing into adulthood, working a COSTUME ACT under the name of *Hadji Baba*. Later he devoted more of his time to writing, as ghostwriter, translator (of OTTOKAR FISCHER's *Illustrated Magic* and Kurt Volkmann's book on CUPS AND BALLS, *The Oldest Deception*).

His own books were *Magic* and *Learn Magic* (introductory texts), *Cyclopedia Of Magic* (an anthology culled from texts by many authors with much additional material), and *The Amateur Magician's Handbook* (considered by many to be one of the very best books ever written on magic; it has been the starting point for many professional magicians).

Hay relocated in Germany as a newspaper correspondent in 1952, where he spent the remainder of his life, working primarily as a leading advertising copywriter.

HAYMOW SHUFFLE

A method of mixing cards by pushing them in small groups or PACKETS from one hand to the other, placing the groups alternately at top and bottom. The FALSE SHUFFLE simulating this action is the CHARLIER SHUFFLE.

In Britain, this term is also sometimes applied to a mixing procedure in which the cards are divided into two halves, spread slightly, and then pushed together to interleave in random fashion. This latter procedure is said to be the oldest known method commonly used for shuffling cards.

HAZELL, PAT (b. ?)

Performer who specializes in comedy magic; he has appeared with Helen Reddy, Rodney Dangerfield, Sheena Easton and many others in such venues as M.G.M. Reno, Hollywood's Improvisation, and the MAGIC CASTLE.

He has also appeared on television many times, including *Thicke Of The Night*, *Merv Griffin*, and a *Nippon Television Special* in Japan.

HEAD CHOPPER

See CHOPPER.

HEADLESS WOMAN

An ILLUSION seen most often in carnivals and sideshows in which a woman's body apparently ends at the neck, from which several metal tubes and hoses

Pat Hazell

connect to complicated-looking machinery. It operates on a variation of the SPHINX principle, and is described in HILLIARD's *Greater Magic*.

HEADLINE PREDICTION

A publicity stunt often performed by magicians and MENTALISTs, in which a sealed PREDICTION is given to a dignitary some time in advance of a show date. On that date the prediction is brought to the stage and opened, when it is seen that the performer has correctly foreseen the headlines for this day of the show.

There are a number of methods for accomplishing this; several are described in DON TANNER's *How To Do Headline Predictions* and in *Super Prediction Tricks* by ROBERT NELSON & E.J. MOORE.

HEAD ON SWORD

An ILLUSION in which a sword rests across the arms of a massive throne; on the blade of the sword rests an apparently decapitated head (the audience can see the chair-back beneath it) which is nevertheless alive.

Often used as a sideshow illusion, it is dependent on a simple application of the MIRROR principle.

HEALY, LYNN (b. 1959)

San Francisco-based MAGICIENNE and magical seamstress noted for her highly regarded EGG BAG, used by many top performers. Her firm, Lynn's Sewcery, also tailors TOPIT devices into jackets and creates made-to-order magical props.

HEAP

Term sometimes used to denote a pile of cards; the number of cards in a heap may be anything less than the full complement of fifty-two, but the term usually implies a portion amounting to a quarter of the deck or less.

HEEL BOX

A small metal container, shaped somewhat like the heel of a child's shoe, open on the flat portion of the side; used for the PRODUCTION or VANISH of silks.

The **heel box** may also have serrated upper and lower edges, to assist in palming, and may be fitted with hooks so that it may be suspended under the performer's clothing; it is most often painted flesh color.

The **heel box** is described in HOFFMANN's *Later Magic*.

HEIMBURGER, ALEXANDER (1818-1909)

Born Johann Heimburgher in Germany; he began his career as an exhibitor of PHANTASMAGORIA along with his magic. He later toured the U.S. with considerable success for many years. He is most noted for his unique version of the SPIRIT BELL effect.

HEIROPHANT

A periodical published by JON RACHERBAUMER from 1969 to 1975; with contributions from many well-known creators, it was primarily devoted to card magic.

HELLER, ROBERT (1829-1878)

Born William Palmer in Britain; he began his career with an act which was said to be heavily based on that of ROBERT-HOUDIN; it was not successful there or in performances in the U.S., and for a time Heller worked as a music teacher.

Returning to performing with new effects, he was successful, and toured throughout the U.S., Britain, New Zealand and Australia. He was noted for his performance of the TWO-PERSON MENTAL ACT, which in his presentation was strong and convincing.

HEMINGWAY, DAVID (b. 1936)

Born in Britain, he is a performer, manufacturer, dealer, and writer who has also worked as a TECHNICAL ADVISOR for stage and television productions.

Among his marketed effects are **Triple Psychometry, Travel Trouble,** and **Third Time Lucky;** his books include *Exclusive Routines* (two volumes), *Professional Outlook, Comedy Teach-In,* and *How To Ensure A Full Date Book.*

HENNING, DOUG (b. 1947)

Born in Canada, he first came to public attention when he received a Canadian Council Grant to study magic with such masters as DAI VERNON and SLYDINI. Henning later created a show called Spellbound, which was hugely successful, breaking all records for Toronto's Royal Alexander theater.

The direct result of this was an adapted version, called *The Magic Show,* which played Broadway for four-and-a-half years (making it one of the longest running musicals in Broadway history).

Concurrent with the Broadway show, Henning began a series of yearly NBC television specials, in which brand new illusions were mixed with classic illusions which had not been presented for decades.

Doug Henning

These shows received an Emmy Award, along with seven nominations.

Henning returned to Broadway in 1982 as the star of the musical MERLIN which he co-created; it was said to be one of the most elaborate shows in the history of New York theater, and featured a number of original illusions. The show ran for several months, and set a Broadway box-office record for one-week receipts.

Henning continues to tour extensively, performing throughout the U.S.; he has several times appeared at the Las Vegas *Hilton* and the Lake Tahoe Sahara.

His company has also created illusions for musical groups Earth Wind And Fire and The Jackson Five, and for a musical extravaganza called Magic Mania in Japan.

Henning is the author (with CHARLES REYNOLDS) of *Houdini: His Legend And His Magic*). He is a recipient of the Magician Of The Year award from the ACADEMY OF MAGICAL ARTS.

At this time, Doug Henning is most probably the best-known magician in the world. It is fair to say that much of the present-day popularity of magic is due to the high visibility and positive image given the art by his performances.

HERCAT (1843-1914)

Born R. D. Chater in Britain; at first a journalist and actor by profession, he later became a magician and toured through Australia, the U.S., and Britain. He is noted as the inventor of **She**, more popularly known as the CREMATION illusion.

He wrote a number of books, including *Simple Tricks, More Conjuring, Chapeaugraphy, Latest Sleights*, and others.

HERRMANN, ADELAIDE (1854-1932)

Born Adelaide Scarcez in Britain; chief ASSISTANT in the show of husband ALEXANDER HERRMANN, she continued with the show after his death, at first in partnership with his nephew LEON HERRMANN, and later in vaudeville with her own act in ORIENTAL STYLE. (This act is believed to have been designed by William Robinson, later known as CHUNG LING SOO.)

HERRMANN, ALEXANDER (1843-1896)

Born in France; he began his career as an assistant to his older brother Carl. He began performing on his own in Spain and was immediately successful, giving a royal command performance during his appearances

Adelaide Herrmann (*The Mulholland Library of Conjuring & the Allied Arts, Los Angeles, California*)

there. He later emigrated to the U.S. where he had an equally successful career; he became, in fact, so well known that it is his physical appearance—the tall, narrow-faced man with dark beard and goatee—which is still associated with a magician in the popular mind.

Herrmann also performed in Britain at EGYPTIAN HALL and other venues throughout the British Isles; his tours took in most European countries, Central and South America. In 1875 he married Adelaide Scarcez, who was subsequently featured in his shows. A long-time assistant and BACK-ROOM BOY was W. E. Robinson (later to achieve fame as CHUNG LING SOO); Robinson also assisted Herrmann's nephew LEON HERRMANN.

His career was one of the most successful in the history of magic, with numerous royal command performances and many honors bestowed upon him. He created an image of the magician—not only in appearance, but also in style and manner—which continues to influence performers nearly a century after his death.

Alexander Herrmann (*The Mulholland Library of Conjuring & the Allied Arts, Los Angeles, California*)

HERRMANN, LEON (1867-1909)

Born in Paris; he began his performing career at the *Folies Bergere*, and later moved to the U.S. to continue the show of uncle ALEXANDER HERRMANN. Leon Herrmann performed this show for a few years, and later worked in vaudeville. Returning to France, he later toured Europe and Russia.

HERRMANN PASS

See TURNOVER PASS.

HERTZ, CARL (1859-1924)

Born Laib (?) Morgenstern; he began his performing career with an act which featured card magic and the VANISHING BIRD CAGE; the latter effect brought him considerable attention during a British tour, when he was twice accused of cruelty to animals, and later cleared of the charges.

In later years he did an elaborate ILLUSION act.

HIGH SIGN

A stage version of CHINESE COMPASS, this uses a directional highway sign; the routine was created by MILBOURNE CHRISTOPHER.

HILLIAR, WILLIAM J. (1876-1936)

Professional vaudeville magician and journalist, noted as the founder of the SPHINX Magazine; he also served as editor for T. NELSON DOWN's *Modern Coin Manipulation*. In later years he created the first column on magic for the theatrical paper *The Billboard*.

HILLIARD, JOHN NORTHERN (1872-1935)

Journalist by profession; writer on magical subjects who also served for a time as HOWARD THURSTON's advance man. His books include *Leaves from J.N.Hilliard's Notebook* (a compilation of articles which originally appeared in FLOYD G. THAYER's *Magical Bulletin*); *The Art Of Magic* (with T. NELSON DOWNS); and the monumental *Greater Magic*.

HIMBER, RICHARD (1907-1966)

Professional bandleader who got his start booking dates for Rudy Vallee and Russ Columbo before forming his own band. He had a successful radio show, and later an equally successful television show; he also performed a number of open-air concerts in the New York City area.

He is known to magicians for the many effects (several invented by him) which he marketed; all were expertly manufactured and produced with the best materials available. Of these perhaps the best known are the HIMBER RING and BILLFOOLED.

Himber staged a number of magic shows, some of them involving close friend ORSON WELLES. He also carried on a number of feuds (few of them serious) with various performers and magical writers. Another Himber interest, suffered and enjoyed by those around him, was his penchant for elaborate practical jokes, several of which have become legends.

Many of the instructional sheets issued with his effects have been gathered (with other material) in a collection titled *Richard Himber—The Man And His Magic* (edited by Ed Levy); there is also an interesting account of Himber in Maurice Zolotow's book on various show business personalities, *It Takes All Kinds*.

HIMBER RING

A specialized FAKE with which the performer can apparently link together borrowed finger rings. Marketed first by RICHARD HIMBER, it is the invention of DR. PERSI DIACONIS. (*See* LINKING FINGER RINGS.)

HIMBER WALLET

See FLIPOVER WALLET.

HINDU BASKET TRICK

See BASKET TRICK.

HINDU SHUFFLE

A genuine SHUFFLE used commonly throughout Asia, and in the Occident almost exclusively by magicians; it is similar in effect to a standard overhand shuffle, but the cards are held from above at one end by the long edges, the other hand stripping off packets from the top of the deck and allowing them to drop into its palm.

The hindu shuffle lends itself to a variety of sleights; against this, however, is its peculiar appearance to the Western lay viewer.

HINDU THREAD

See GYPSY THREAD.

HIPPITY-HOP RABBITS

Invented by British magician Norman, this SUCKER EFFECT is usually done for children; it uses black and white plywood cutouts of rabbits and wooden or metal covers for each. The two apparently change places, but the audience is led to believe that the performer is simply turning them around to show an opposite color; when the rabbits finally *are* turned around, one is red and the other is green.

See SUCKER EFFECTS; CHILDREN'S MAGIC.

HISTED, LOUIS S. (1897-1965)

British inventor of countless EFFECTs, of which perhaps the best known is the SQUARE CIRCLE PRODUCTION device used by thousands of magicians; he was, however, also noted for many effects involving hydraulic and hydrostatic principles. Among his other inventions were the JIFFY SLATE (a version of the SPIRIT SLATE) and the SAND AND SUGAR effect. Many of his effects are described in his *The Magic Of Louis S. Histed.*

HIVE

Also known as the **enchanted hive** or **beehive**, this was an ILLUSION created by DAVID DEVANT in which persons appeared, disappeared or changed while on an isolated platform when a bag-like cloth was drawn up around them.

It employed an application of the SPHINX principle.

HOCUS-POCUS

Now, commonly, a synonym for ILLUSION created by trickery or deceit; sometimes applied without any ironic sense to stage performers.

The derivation of the phrase is obscure. It is commonly thought to be a MAGIC WORD used by 17th century magicians, a corruption of the phrase *hoc est corpus* from the Latin Mass—but this theory, proposed by an early cleric named Tillotson, may not be correct. Another possibility is that it stems from a particular performer named *Hokos Bokos* (one of the many variant spellings of the name).

HODGES, JAMES (b. ?)

Highly regarded French magic illustrator, noted for his work in the *50 Grandes Illusions* book, *Mad Magic* Magazine, and numerous other publications.

HOFFMANN, PROFESSOR LOUIS (1839-1919)

Born Angelo Lewis in Britain, he was a lawyer and writer by profession. His series of magazine articles on magic for a boys' magazine was revised and expanded into the book *Modern Magic*, which was enormously successful and was published in a number of editions.

Subsequent books include *More Magic, Later Magic, Latest Magic, King Koko,* and *Magical Titbits.*

HOFZINSER, JOHANN NEPOMUK (1806-1875)

Born in Austria; at first a civil servant by profession, he later became a full-time performer, and for many years performed at his popular salon in Vienna.

Hofzinser created many effects and techniques, particularly in the area of card magic. He is believed to be the inventor of DOUBLE-FACE cards and other types of prepared cards, and also may have been the inventor of the CLOCK DIAL.

Little was known of Hofzinser's contributions prior to the researches of OTTOKAR FISCHER. Fischer wrote two books on Hofzinser's work, *Kartenkunste* and *Zauberkunste*; both are now available in English-language translation as *Hofzinser's Card Conjuring* (translated by S.H. SHARPE) and *The Magic Of J.N. Hofzinser* (translated by Richard Hatch).

HOLDEN, MAX (1884-1949)

Born William Holden Maxwell in Boston, he first achieved prominence as a performer in British variety; later he toured the U.S. vaudeville circuits with solid success. While magic was a part of his act, its major appeal was his colored-light SHADOWGRAPHY at which Holden was an acknowledged expert.

The last two decades of his life were spent as a magic dealer, at which he was equally successful; in addition to his New York City store he opened branches in Boston and Philadelphia.

A valuable work by Holden, based on his knowledge of British and U.S. show business, is his *Programmes Of Famous Magicians*.

HOLDER

GIMMICK which contains or retains an item in a place of concealment, usually within the performer's clothes.

See under specific object (e.g., BALL CLIP, CIGARETTE TANK).

HOLDOUT

A hidden device, or GIMMICK, secretly delivers an item into the performer's hand. Most such devices are **sleeve holdouts**, and operate in a number of ways: by pressure on a spring which operates a lazy-tongs arrangement—by pulling of a cord through a pulley system with some physical action (in the **Kiplinger holdout**, spreading of the legs); or by gravity, the holdout being weighted, and controlled by a cord fastened to the opposite arm (as in the JACK MILLER **holdout**).

Of these, only the **Miller holdout** was specifically designed for magical purposes; the others, used by crooked gamblers, are only practical for adding and removing cards.

Properly used (as, for example, the **Miller holdout** by its originator), this device can create what appear to be absolute miracles; it does, however, require considerable practice to attain that level.

The term *holdout* is sometimes erroneously applied to a CLIP or other device which holds a hidden item in position for the performer to obtain secretly; in the instance of cards, some such devices would more properly be called *bugs*.

HOMING

A class of EFFECTs in which an object—card, ball, etc.—magically returns to its original location after having been placed elsewhere.

See HOMING CARD; CONE AND BALL.

HOMING CARD

This title is used to refer to an EFFECT in which one odd card in a packet (one red among six blacks, for example) is repeatedly removed and yet returns to the packet; a routine for this is in HUGARD and BRAUE's *Show Stoppers With Cards*, and is based on an effect originated by TENKAI ISHIDA. An excellent stage version of this routine, in which an odd-backed card keeps reappearing, is GEORGE BLAKE's *Recurring Card*.

Less commonly, an effect in which a chosen card travels invisibly to the performer's pocket. An excellent routine by FRANCIS CARLYLE for this effect will be found in *Stars Of Magic*; it is quite possibly inspired by an earlier (unpublished) routine by JIMMY GRIPPO.

HONESTY PRINCIPLE

The actual working methods of some magical EFFECTs and ILLUSIONs are so unlikely that the performer can actually tell the audience how the effect is achieved, secure in the knowledge that the explanation will not be believed.

A prime exponent of this kind of presentation was GUY JARRETT, who used it in his routines for his BANGKOK BUNGALOW and TWENTY-ONE GIRLS FROM A CABINET.

Similarly, a performer of recent years would ask for a number from 1 to 1000 to be called out; a spectator was asked then to open a Manhattan telephone directory to that page and to concentrate on the first name. Before "divining" the name the performer would point out that he or she could know this name in one of only two ways: TELEPATHY—or by memorizing the telephone directory! Since the audience "knew" that no one could memorize the phone book, they were left with telepathy as the only explanation. (In this connection *see* MNEMONICS.)

HONG KONG COIN

A type of FAKE coin, made to simulate a Chinese coin of the type which has a central hole. The Hong Kong coin has a matching SHELL, and may thus be used in routines similar to those employing the ELLIS RING.

HONOR CARDS

The Ace, King, Queen, Jack and Ten of the four playing card suits.

HOOK COIN

A coin, usually of half-dollar size, with a small needle-point projecting inward and slightly away from the edge of the coin. Such a coin may be temporarily hooked to the clothing of the performer (or a spectator) while the performer shows his hands empty. Sometimes called a hoo coin.

See MAGNETIC COIN.

HOOKER, SAMUEL C., DR. (1864-1935)

Noted scientist and amateur magician, best known for his legendary RISING CARDS, a description of which is found in HILLIARD's *Greater Magic*; a more detailed account of the ROUTINE is given by JOHN MULHOLLAND in PALLBEARER'S REVIEW Magazine (Vol.2, No.6).

The few demonstrations of the routine took place only at Dr. Hooker's residence over fifty years ago; the APPARATUS used still exists.

HOOPER, EDWIN (b. ?)

British magic dealer; founder of the SUPREME MAGIC CO. He is a past president of the British Ring of the I.B.M. and is also a member of the Inner MAGIC CIRCLE with Gold Star.

Among his books are *Fun And Magic For Children* and *The Real Secret Of The Electric Chairs*.

HOOP PASS

Method of passing a solid hoop around a levitated or floating object which is being secretly supported (usually from the rear); see GOOSENECK; LEVITATIONS.

Less commonly, the legitimate passing of a hoop over a floating object; (*see* FLOATING EFFECTS).

HOPKINS, CHARLES H. (?-1948)

A printer by trade, he was an expert amateur performer who is best remembered for his book *Outs, Precautions and Challenges*, an invaluable collection of techniques to be applied when a card EFFECT goes awry.

HOPPING THE CUT

After the deck has been CUT by a spectator, to apparently complete the cut in legitimate fashion; in actuality, the original upper half of the deck is scooped up *above* the other half, and thus the deck retains its original order.

Far more often used by crooked gamblers (from whose parlance the term derives) than magicians.

See also RESTORING THE CUT.

HORN, ROY

See SIEGFRIED AND ROY.

HOROWITZ, S. LEO (1894-1971)

Professional whose long career began while he was still a teenager; almost immediately he became successful and remained so for many years. Performing first under the name of Leo Hartz and later as Mohammed Bey, he played in hotels, nightclubs, cruise ships and society parties and was highly regarded for his excellent close-up work.

Among magicians he was particularly noted for his skill at routining EFFECTs; examples of this can be found in *Mohammed Bey's Routines For The Okito Coin Box, Mohammed Bey's Routines For The Jardine Ellis Ring*, and in his contributions to the *Stars Of Magic* collection.

HORSTER, CONRAD

See CONRADI.

HOT BALL

A device which has the appearance of an ordinary 2-inch diameter ball; when held by a spectator it becomes too hot to hold. It is now rarely seen but at one time was used by hypnotists and magicians in dealing with troublesome spectators.

The ball is made of metal in two parts which unscrew, and the heat is produced by a chemical reaction which occurs when the ball is turned and the chemicals in two separated compartments are allowed to mix.

HOT BOOK

A comedy prop which in appearance is an ordinary book, but when opened produces flames; it is the invention of BILLY MCCOMB, and was described in his *The First Book Of William.*

HOUDINI, BEATRICE (1876-1943)

Born Wilhelmina Beatrice Rahner, she married HARRY HOUDINI in 1894, and replaced his brother in Houdini's act; for many years she appeared onstage with him.

After Houdini's death on October 31, 1926, Bess (as

she was known) held a SEANCE at Hallowe'en every year for a decade, in an attempt to contact his spirit. Though spirit mediums, notably Arthur Ford, claimed to have contacted Houdini and received the code phrase he had arranged with Bess, she remained unconvinced; the seances were terminated in 1936, after a final one broadcast from the roof of Hollywood's Knickerbocker Hotel, in which DR. EDWARD SAINT acted as medium.

HOUDINI, HARRY (1874-1926)

Born Ehrich Weiss in Hungary, he emigrated to the U.S. as a small child. After struggling in show business for several years, he went to Britain where his ESCAPE from Scotland Yard handcuffs brought immediate attention; over the next several years he became one of the greatest stars in show business, a position he maintained until his death.

Houdini is unquestionably the most famous magician who ever lived; his name (adapted from that of ROBERT-HOUDIN) is a part of the language, and is

Houdini and wife Beatrice, an early poster (*The Mulholland Library of Conjuring & the Allied Arts, Los Angeles, California*)

still used as a synonym for gaining freedom against all odds. While he is regarded by the general public as a magician, as such he was only of fair competence; as an ESCAPOLOGIST, however, he was the greatest of his time, and it is unlikely that anyone will ever eclipse his accomplishments in this field.

He was also a tireless crusader against the deceptions of fraudulent spirit mediums; a noted collector, whose library is now part of the Library of Congress; and, for a time, the editor of CONJUROR'S Magazine. Houdini also wrote a number of books—among them *The Unmasking Of Robert-Houdin*, *The Right Way To Do Wrong*, and *A Magician Among The Spirits*.

Insight into his methods may be gained from *Houdini's Escapes* and *Houdini's Magic*, both by J.C. Cannell, and *Houdini On Magic*, by WALTER B. GIBSON and Morris Young.

Biographies include *Houdini: His Life Story* by Harold Kellock; *The Man Who Walked Through Walls* by William Lindsay Gresham; *Houdini: The Untold Story* and *Houdini: A Pictorial Life*, both by MILBOURNE CHRISTOPHER; and *Houdini: His Legend And His Magic*, by DOUG HENNING and CHARLES REYNOLDS.

HOULETTE

A container, usually of wood, plastic or glass, to hold a deck of cards in an upright position; in some cases mounted on a stemmed base. Often used in performance of the RISING CARDS.

HOUSE LIGHTS

The lighting which illuminates the auditorium or area of a theater where spectators are seated.

Unless there is some compelling reason, house lights should be used as briefly as possible during an ACT or SHOW, since their use tends to remove the specific focus of attention from the performer (literally taking the performer from the spotlight); it also draws the spectator's attention to the mundane surroundings and disperses any magical atmosphere that has been created.

HOWARD, MAX

Emmy winning actor and performer with extensive theatrical experience; most noted for his stylistic re-creation (with partner Diane Bray) of a magic show as it might have been given by a performer of a hundred years ago. Howard performs in the character of Professor Gus Rich, the "Wizard of the Blue Ridge."

Max Howard and Diane Bray

HOY, DAVID (1930-1981)

Beginning his career as a minister, Dr. Hoy became interested in magic as a way to illustrate biblical concepts; he described this work in his *Magic With A Message*. Leaving the ministry, he became a full-time professional performer specializing in MENTAL MAGIC and performing under the stage name of *Dr. Faust*. A number of the EFFECTs he used in this guise are described in his *The Bold And Subtle Miracles Of Dr. Faust*.

Becoming more involved in psychic phenomena, Hoy gradually dropped the MENTAL MAGIC from his presentations and relied entirely on his intuitions and perceptions. During this latter phase of his career he wrote two more books, *The Meaning Of Tarot* and *Psychic And Other ESP Party Games*. He is the subject of an excellent biography by Brad Steiger titled *Super-Psychic: The Incredible Dr. Hoy*.

HUGARD, JEAN (1872-1959)

Born John Gerard Rodney Boyce in Australia; he began as a performer in vaudeville, working in ORIENTAL STYLE (featuring a spectacular version of the BULLET CATCH), and toured Australia, New Zealand and the South Pacific area. Settling in the

U.S., he performed in varied venues, including ten years at Coney Island, and retired from theatrical work in 1934.

He then began an impressive career as a writer, creating many of magic's most influential texts. In addition to the creation of his *Annual Of Magic* volumes, and the founding of Hugard's Magic Monthly in 1942, he wrote a number of books: *Modern Magic Manual, Close-Up Magic, Coin Magic, Encyclopedia Of Card Tricks, Mental Magic With Cards*, his *Card Manipulation* and *More Card Manipulations* series, and many others.

He also collaborated with FRED BRAUE on several books: *Expert Card Technique, The Royal Road To Card Magic, The Invisible Pass*, and others.

HUGHES, JACK (1906-1982)

British magic manufacturer noted for the many items of standard apparatus he produced over the years and for the high quality of workmanship; while specializing in woodworking, he built props in all kinds of materials.

His work is described in his *Jack Hughes World Of Magic*.

HUGS AND KISSES

A coin routine using three half-dollars with X's cut completely through their centers, and three British pennies similarly prepared with circular holes.

In the course of the routine the *holes*—not the coins—transpose, so that at the conclusion the half-dollars have the round holes and the British coins have the *X*'s.

The routine, which depends on the use of DOUBLE-FACE coins, was devised by AL SCHNEIDER; it is similar in some respects to a routine created by Jules De Barros which was called **The Coins Of Ishtar**, and which is described in De Barros' book of that name.

HULL, BURLING (1889-1982)

Born Burlingame Gilbert Gault Hull, he had a long career as a performer. He did many different acts, including BILLIARD BALL manipulation; MENTALISM; MENTAL MAGIC; an ILLUSION act; and a TWO PERSON MENTAL ACT.

He was, however, best known for his introduction of the SVENGALI DECK and MENETEKEL DECKS (which he is usually credited with inventing), for his many "feuds" with others in magic, and as a writer of instructional magic texts. His many books include: *Amazing World Of Mentalism, Expert Billiard Ball Manipulation, Gold Medal Showmanship, Miracle Floating*

Light Effects, Thirty-Three Rope Ties And Chain Releases, Encyclopedic Dictionary Of Mentalism (3 volumes), *Stage Illusions for the 1-2-3 Performer Show,* and many others.

He was the recipient of a Special Fellowship from the ACADEMY OF MAGICAL ARTS.

HULL, RALPH W. (1883-1943)

Professional performer in CHAUTAUQUA for only six years before the family business required his retirement from the stage; his strong interest in magic continued, however, and he devised a number of EFFECTs and ROUTINEs, notably in the area of card magic.

Many of his routines used MECHANICAL DECKS operating on the ROUGH-AND-SMOOTH PRINCIPLE, and several of these—the NUDIST DECK, POP-EYED EYE POPPER, and DELIRIUM TREMENS DECK—were commercially marketed. Other feats include his famous NAME-O-CARD and **Homing Ball** routines.

His books include *Eye-Openers, More Eye-Openers, Fifteen Minutes With A Rope, Modernism in Pasteboard,* and *Smart Magic,* the last two as co-author with NELSON C. HAHNE.

Several of his effects will be found in HILLIARD's *Greater Magic,* including an entire chapter devoted to his Tuned Deck routine. An excellent collection of Hull's routines, with much additional material, is TREVOR HALL's *The Testament Of Ralph W. Hull.*

HUMAN GASOMETER

A popular EFFECT in Great Britain, rarely seen elsewhere, in which the performer blows through a flexible pipe which has a gas mantle at its opposite end; the mantle stays alight, presumably due to the "fuel" provided by the performer's breath.

HUMMER, BOB (?-?)

Highly regarded inventor of mathematically-based effects, of which perhaps the best-known is his *Mathematical Three-Card Monte;* this and a number of other Hummer effects are described in *Mathematics Magic And Mystery* by MARTIN GARDNER.

Hummer marketed a number of his effects and manuscripts, including **Little Stranger, Whispering Spirit, The Little Moonies, Half-A-Dozen Hummers,** and others. The most complete collection of Hummer material is *The Collected Works of Bob Hummer* by KARL FULVES.

HUNTER, G.W. (1850-1936)

British music-hall performer (a comedian by profession) noted for his expertise at CLOSE-UP MAGIC; his inventions in this area (several of which are described in the books of WILL GOLDSTON) often baffled well-informed magicians.

He is the creator of the HUNTER KNOT, the ACROBATIC MATCHBOX, the GIMMICK for what is now known as DUAL CONTROL, the Red Snapper novelty, and also a repeat production of cigars from the hands. (*See* CIGAR PRODUCTION.)

HUNTER KNOT

The performer holds a short length of rope between his hands, and without letting go of the ends is able to form an overhand knot in the center of the rope. A spectator duplicates the performer's actions exactly, but is unable to produce the knot except when "helped" by the performer. Also known as the **puzzle knot,** this is the invention of G.W. HUNTER. It is described in *Abbott's Encyclopedia Of Rope Tricks,* edited by STEWART JAMES.

HURWITZ, ABRAHAM B., DR. (1906-1981)

Known in his professional appearances as Peter Pan, The Magic Man, Professor Hurwitz was designated the Official Magician for New York City. He was instrumental in organizing a junior magicians' club called F.A.M.E. (Future American Magical Entertainers).

His daughter is SHARI LEWIS.

HYDROSTATIC GLASS

This glass is filled with water and its mouth then covered with a card or napkin. The glass is inverted and the card or napkin is removed, but the water remains suspended in the glass until the performer commands it to fall—at which point the water immediately cascades into a waiting receptacle.

The water is retained by a glass or celluloid disk secretly placed over the mouth of the glass and held there by atmospheric pressure. A small air hole at the bottom of the glass is covered by the performer's finger; when this air hole is uncovered the pressure equalizes and the water falls into the bowl or bucket—the disk falling unnoticed.

Though a simple EFFECT, from a technical standpoint, this feat has been a feature of many top stage and nightclub magicians.

See also ANTI-GRAVICO.

HYPNOTIC OBJECTS

The term "hypnotic" is applied in magic to objects which take on a mysterious rigidity or balance in an unusual way; for example, the **hypnotic rope** which stands straight in the performer's hand, or the **hypnotic handkerchief** which behaves similarly.

Such effects are generally classed midway between SUSPENSION and ANTI-GRAVITY effects.

IASIA

An ILLUSION invented by CYRIL YETTMAH in which a curtained cage-like structure containing a female ASSISTANT was raised high above the stage. The assistant was seen to be in the cabinet almost to the last moment, but when the curtains were dropped away she was gone.

The illusion was featured by THURSTON; a popular copy line on his posters highlighting the illusion was "Vanished In The Theater's Dome."

I.B.M.

See INTERNATIONAL BROTHERHOOD OF MAGICIANS.

ILLUSION

Although all of performance magic can be said to consist of illusion, the word itself has a specific meaning within the profession; it almost always refers to a magical effect in which either people or large animals are involved.

ILLUSIONETTE

A small ILLUSION, usually performed with a child or animal of medium size.

IMPALING

An ILLUSION first conceived by LES LEVANTE; in its modern design the invention of Ken Whittaker. A woman is balanced on the point of a sword on a pedestal, the sword apparently touching the small of her back. She is spun on the sword and suddenly sinks down, seemingly impaled on the sword which juts up out of her midsection.

She then rises or is lifted up and off the sword, and is unharmed.

This illusion has become quite popular in recent years, most probably because of its dynamic performance by the PENDRAGONS. In lesser hands it can sometimes be ineffective, a standard presentation

The *Impaling*, as performed by Le Grand David.

leaving the audience confused as to whether they should react with horror or applause at the woman's impalement. Convincing performance of the **impaling** requires a very strong stage personality and dramatic presentation; it is probably not a good choice for the performers who consider themselves "just folks."

Also known as the **impalement**, this illusion is sometimes begun with the woman balanced on the points of three equidistant swords, the outer two being removed in the course of the presentation; this was a feature of the Levante routine (which, unlike the current Whittaker version, required elaborate belowstage rigging).

IMP BOTTLE

A very small opaque bottle with a long neck and rounded bottom; it will lie on its side at the performer's wish, but will refuse to do so for a spectator, rolling instead to an upright position. In most versions of this EFFECT, the GIMMICK is a small lead rod which fits into the neck of the bottle and may be secretly taken away by the performer. A more subtle version employs two similar-appearing corks; one is the genuine article, while the other is heavy painted metal.

Known in Britain as the BOTTLE IMP.

IMPECCABLE DOUBLE

A type of DOUBLE LIFT (and single-hand deal to table) devised by Howie Schwartzman. The two cards are held as one at the top of the deck by the pressure of the fingers against the outer edge of the pair of cards; this pressure is slightly increased to give the pair of cards a longitudinal CRIMP.

The hand is then turned over and with a very slight tossing action releases the two cards from just above the table. The crimp causes the cards to remain in perfect alignment as one, and the casual handling allays suspicion.

IMP PASS

A subtlety invented by SLYDINI, used by a seated performer in a close-up situation. One hand takes an object from the lap or elsewhere and secretly places it into a PALM position in the other hand, which has been shown empty and now rests casually at the edge of the table. It is described in *Slydini Encores*, (edited by Ed Levy).

IMPRESARIO

Promoter and/or sponsor of stage entertainments; also, manager or producer of an entertainment group or company.

IMPRESSMENT

More familiarly known as the **instant stooge** technique (the latter term probably coined by PHIL GOLDSTEIN), this is the art of getting the assisting spectator to secretly assist the performer to bring about a desired effect. An example might be to secretly show the spectator a card chosen by another member of the audience, which the spectator then "divines" by gazing into a crystal ball held by the performer.

The technique is rarely used, for if the spectator should refuse to cooperate and reveal the performer's request, the performer can be made to look very foolish. If used at all, it is best employed in such an effect as indicated above, where the spectator rather than the performer seems to accomplish the feat. In such a situation the spectator is far less likely to reveal his or her secret part in the proceedings.

IMPROMPTU

EFFECT which can be done without any special preparation; the major source for this kind of magic is MARTIN GARDNER's *Encyclopedia Of Impromptu Tricks*.

It should be noted that some performers go to considerable lengths to prepare for effects which will have the *appearance* of impromptu feats, if not the reality.

INCREDI-BOX

A sophisticated variation of the OKITO BOX routine, using a special box and accessories; invented by Sam Schwartz.

INDEX

The identifying numeral or letter and PIP in the upper left and lower right corner of a standard deck of cards (most European decks have indices in all four corners).

See also CARD INDEX.

INDIAN ROPE TRICK

A fabled miracle of East Indian magic in which a rope rises into the air; a small boy climbs to the top and vanishes. In variations of the tale, the magician climbs the rope after the boy, pieces of whom then come down; the magician descends and gathers the boy-fragments into a basket, from which the boy emerges restored.

As described, the trick almost certainly is a fable, and is said by JOHN MULHOLLAND to be based on an Indian tale not unlike Jack And The Beanstalk.

Nevertheless, stage versions of the EFFECT have been popular with Western magicians, and have been

The Indian Rope Trick, as featured in Thurston's show (*The Mulholland Library of Conjuring & the Allied Arts, Los Angeles, California*)

featured by many of them—from HOWARD THURSTON to DOUG HENNING.

INDIFFERENT CARD

Any card other than the significant card or cards in a given EFFECT; thus, for example, any other card than one chosen by a spectator, or the dozen cards used in addition to the four Aces in a FOUR ACES ROUTINE.

INDRAJAL

Name given by P.C. SORCAR to his elaborate FULL-EVENING SHOW; also a general Indian term for magic, deriving from the Vedic god Indra.

INDUSTRIAL SHOWS

Stage productions created for corporate sponsors; such shows are usually not open to the public, being presented for employees of the company.

Many magical performers have created and/or worked in Industrial Shows, notably MARK WILSON, who has created several shows for companies of every kind.

Not to be confused with TRADE SHOWS.

INEXHAUSTIBLE BOTTLE

Central EFFECT of the BAR ACT, this is a bottle or other container from which seemingly endless quantities of various liquids, usually liquor drinks, are poured. Models of this APPARATUS vary in size and complexity; they usually have one or more closed compartments, the flow from which is regulated by means of an air hole.

In the original version, the bottle was made of metal finished to look like glass; often the effect was climaxed by "breaking" the bottle to produce a dove from a separate section in the lower part of the bottle.

A later version of the effect, made by mechanician Henry Bate for DAVID DEVANT, was designed to look like a fancy teakettle; it is described in WILL GOLDSTON's *Great Tricks Revealed*.

INEXHAUSTIBLE BOX

Name sometimes given to the TIPOVER BOX.

IN-JOG

See JOG.

INK AND WATER

A glass, apparently filled with ink, is briefly covered with a cylinder or handkerchief which when removed reveals that the ink has changed to water, which may have goldfish swimming around in it.

The appearance of ink in the glass is created by a celluloid FAKE (removed with a cylinder) or a black cloth fake (removed with the handkerchief). The performer may "prove" the liquid to be ink by dipping a white card part way into it; this card has previously been painted black on half of one side, and in the dipping action the performer turns the card around.

IN ONE

Performance area of the stage between the FRONT CURTAIN and the first DOWNSTAGE curtain. Often used for the performance of smaller EFFECTs while the main stage area is being set for a subsequent ROUTINE.

INSTANTO DECK

A MECHANICAL DECK invented by BILLY O'CONNOR, with which any named card may be instantly located and cut to the top of the deck. The deck is arranged in a special STACK order, and certain of the cards are also trimmed in various ways to act as KEY CARDS.

The deck is thoroughly described in an article in the JINX Magazine.

INSTO-TRANSPO

A card EFFECT originated by THEODORE ANNEMANN in which two initialed cards change places under seemingly impossible conditions. There have been a number of later versions of this effect, varying in handling and method.

INSURANCE POLICY

A comedy card EFFECT invented by GEORGE MCATHY in which the performer's repeated failures to find a selected card are "covered" by his or her insurance policy—which on being unfolded reveals a giant picture of the chosen card.

INTELLIGENCE QUOTIENT TEST

See CARD PUZZLE.

INTERLOCKED CARD PRODUCTION

The PRODUCTION of playing cards, one at a time, from the hands while the fingers are interlaced. The SLEIGHT is generally credited to CLIFF GREEN, possibly inspired by Joseph Cottone; others influential in the development of this sleight are Dr. Victor Sendax, TENKAI and DAI VERNON.

A version of this sleight is described in INTERLOCKED CARD PRODUCTION by Mariano Palhinha.

INTERNATIONAL BROTHERHOOD OF MAGICIANS (I.B.M.)

Founded by GENE GORDON and LEN VINTUS in 1922; it was first headquartered briefly in Winnepeg, Manitoba, Canada, and then moved to Kenton, Ohio, where it has remained since. The I.B.M. is the largest magical organization in the world. It has over 10,000 members in local groups (called "Rings") in over 50 countries.

The I.B.M. is not a professional organization or guild; while many full-time professionals are members, the I.B.M. was founded by and for amateur performers, and they constitute the vast majority of its membership.

The I.B.M. has published a monthly magazine continuously for over 60 years (except for a brief interruption during World War II). It is called *LINKING RING*

and contains descriptions of magical effects, articles of historical or general interest to magicians, organizational news, and reports from Ring secretaries.

INTERNATIONAL MAGIC STUDIO

Well-known British magic company located in London for over a quarter of a century. It is operated by RON MACMILLAN, and publishes a house organ called *Magic Info*.

INTERSECTING SETS PRINCIPLE

A principle used most often in feats of MENTAL MAGIC, in which a spectator mentally selects an item from one set of several. After an apparent randomizing procedure the spectator is shown a series of groups of items; when he or she identifies a particular group as containing the item, the performer immediately knows which of the items is that selected by the spectator.

If, for example, five spectators are given groups of cards designated AAAAA, BBBBB, CCCCC, DDDDD and EEEEE, and subsequently a spectator is shown an ABCDE group and identifies it as containing a thought-of-card, it will of course be the only one from the set originally held by the spectator. In such effects the spectators are not aware of receiving specific groups in the primary phase, nor do they know that the groups presented later are not random in composition.

For an example of how this principle is used in practice, see the TWENTY-FIVE CARD TRICK.

INTRO

Abbreviation for Introduction; in theatrical usage, words spoken by the MASTER OF CEREMONIES to introduce a performer or ACT.

It is extremely unwise for a performer to leave the wording of this intro to the M.C. or anyone else, unless appearing in a revue or other fully-produced and scripted show.

The intro should be written on a small card which can be given to the M.C. It should be brief and to the point and, while it may mention the performer's most recent and future appearances—if appropriate, and if the dates are at noteworthy venues—statements about the performer's excellence are to be avoided; such remarks may inspire a defiant attitude in the audience, which prefers to make up its own mind about a performer's worth.

INTRODUCE

To secretly LOAD an item for a later PRODUCTION; also, to secretly add an item to be used in an EFFECT (for example, introducing a STRANGER CARD into a borrowed deck).

INVISIBLE CIGARETTE

See PHANTOM CIGARETTE.

INVISIBLE DECK

A presentational premise devised by Eddie Fields (possibly based on a prior J. B. BOBO presentation; see below) for the ULTRA-MENTAL DECK in which the spectator is handed an "invisible" deck, asked to remove a card and, after noting it, turn the imaginary deck around so as to replace the selected card face-down in the face-up deck. Returned to the magician, the invisible deck becomes visible and on being spread reveals only one face-down card in the face-up deck—which proves, of course, to be the selection named by the spectator.

It should be noted that some performers use this presentation with the BRAINWAVE DECK; since the presumed effect of that deck is that a named card had been previously removed from a deck of different back color and placed into the deck being used, clearly the premise of the invisible deck cannot logically be applied to it.

This flaw was *not* present in the J. B. BOBO version, which was marketed with a miniature deck and the invisible deck presentation. Bobo's deck, like the brainwave, revealed a face-up card in a face-down deck—but all the cards were of the same color.

Several methods have been devised to approximate the **invisible deck** effect by SLEIGHT OF HAND technique. Such methods almost always require a very high level of card-handling expertise to be deceptive.

A book devoted exclusively to the Invisible Deck presentation is *Invisible Secrets Revealed* by Fields & Schwartz.

See ULTRA-MENTAL DECK; BRAINWAVE DECK; ROUGH-AND-SMOOTH PRINCIPLE.

INVISIBLE PASS

Specifically, a type of SHIFT (which see) executed in the course of turning the deck over; it is described in HUGARD and BRAUE's *The Invisible Pass*.

More generally, any kind of SHIFT which can be executed with little chance of visual detection. The term thus used has a redundant ring, since the **shift** is presumed to be a secret SLEIGHT, and therefore any properly executed version of the sleight should by definition be "invisible."

INVISIBLE THREAD

See THREAD.

IONIA (ca. 1885-?)

Born Ionia Williams in France; daughter of CHARLES DE VERE and OKITA. She began performing in 1910, her show featuring many ILLUSIONs and other EFFECTs built by her father. The act was immediately successful, and she toured Britain and Europe for several years.

During a tour of Russia she was caught up in the Revolution in 1917, during which all her APPARATUS was lost and she had to hide in the cellar of her hotel for nearly three months. It appears that she survived this incident, but her fate is not known.

IRELAND, L.L. (?-1954)

Inventor, writer and creator of magic, and founder of Ireland Magic Company (now called MAGIC INC.). He was noted for his skill at SLEEVING; Ireland practiced by sleeving coins while standing over a subway grating, which, he said, motivated him to learn quickly!

Of his many inventions, perhaps the most popular is his **Multiplying Golf Balls**, an excellent adaptation of the BILLIARD BALLS ROUTINE; his books include *Lessons In Dishonesty* and *Ireland Writes A Book.*

ISIS

The goddess of magic in Egyptian religion; wife to Osiris.

Within performance magic, the name of an ILLUSION performed by DAVID BAMBERG in which a large model of a scarab-beetle moved across an alphabet board on an easel to spell out thoughts of members of the audience. The EFFECT was based on a DEVANT presentation called the A.B.C. FLY.

Also, the name of a zither-playing automaton of a woman seated on a large wooden chest (secretly controlled by a hidden assistant) invented by Cecil Nixon (*see* AUTOMATA).

IT'S A PIP LIQUID

Also known as **pip paint**, this was a mixture that could be painted onto cards or other smooth surfaces where it would give the appearance of solid black ink; it could, however, be easily removed with a rub of a finger, leaving no trace.

Formulated versions of it were combinations of lampblack (carbon) with rubber cement (or spirit gum), but the original material, marketed by CARYL S. FLEMING, was black rubber gasket sealer. It should be noted that in the later formulas chemicals such as Sodium Hydroxide and Sulfatate (a wetting agent) were incorporated to keep the carbon in suspension in the liquid.

Many of the EFFECTs which used this material are now accomplished with Velleda magic markers and erasable surfaces; for some applications, however, the original (now off the magical market but still available in some automotive stores) is clearly superior.

JACOBS (?-?)

Performer who toured Britain, the U.S. and Australia in the 1840s and 1850s, primarily with SLEIGHT OF HAND magic; he is also said to have performed the LINKING RINGS prior to their supposed introduction by PHILLIPPE.

JADOO-WALLAH

East Indian street magician and/or mystery performer; traditional EFFECTs for such performers include the CUPS AND BALLS, MANGO TREE GROWTH, and BASKET TRICK.

A discussion of their work is found in EDDIE JOSEPH's *Magic And Mysteries Of India.*

JAHN, VIGGO (b. ?)

Born in Denmark; performer who came to prominence in the late 1950s with his **Cane Knob** ACT, a manipulative act in which he used the knob from the top of his cane to perform various effects of THIMBLE MAGIC with his black-gloved hands. With this excellent adaptation he was able to overcome the visibility problem inherent in thimble work, and was very successful. He has performed throughout Europe; his appearances in the U.S. include the *The Ed Sullivan Show.*

JAKS, STANLEY (1903-1960)

Born Herbert Seigbert Jaks in Germany, he first performed as half of a comedy magic team called **Jax and Jax.** Moving to Switzerland, he specialized in CLOSE-UP MAGIC, at which he became very successful, appearing before numerous European royal families.

Emigrating to the U.S., he quickly established himself at New York's Savoy Plaza, The Versailles, and many other top venues. For the last dozen years of his life he specialized in stage demonstrations of MENTAL MAGIC; here too he was successful.

Jaks was noted for the exquisite PROPS and thoughtful presentations used in his close-up performances; his most famous stage feat was the duplication of a spectator's signature while blindfolded.

He contributed a number of EFFECTs to the PHOENIX, SPHINX and other magazines; many of these were collected in a book edited by an Austrian friend, Charles Epernay. The Epernay book is not currently available in an English-language edition.

JAMES, STEWART (b. ?)

Born in Canada; noted inventor whose EFFECTs have appeared in countless magic magazines for over sixty years. While it would be impossible to pick one of the hundreds of James originations as his best, he is perhaps best known for his miniature spirit cabinet routine called SEFALALJIA.

His *Case For Cards* was published serially in PENTAGRAM Magazine; other books include *Jamesosophy, First Call To Cards, Magic Mine No. 1, Quick Hypnotic Tricks, Sefalaljia Number Two, Three Star Special,* and *Remembering The Future.* He is the editor of the *Encyclopedia Of Rope Tricks.*

James is a recipient of the Creative Fellowship from the ACADEMY OF MAGICAL ARTS.

JAPANESE BOX

An item of apparatus magic, this "box" has only four sides—no top or bottom; a tray into which it just fits has a small finger-hole to hold the box in place. It is patterned after traditional Japanese rice boxes.

It is usually employed to PRODUCE or VANISH a silk handkerchief, and operates on the DOUBLE WALL principle; the inner wall on one side may be lowered (controlled by the finger) and a silk dropped in. Pressing the inner wall flush, the silk is concealed within the hollow wall and the box may be shown empty. A well-made model of this box can be extremely deceptive, and a number of very interesting effects can be accomplished with it.

A book on its uses, *Jap Box Tricks*, was written by GLENN GRAVATT.

JAP BOX

Term formerly used to denote the JAPANESE BOX.

JARDINE ELLIS RING

See ELLIS RING.

JARRETT, GUY (1881-1972)

Born in Ohio, Guy Jarrett became a legend in his own lifetime as a creator and builder of stage illusions, and also as author of the idiosyncratic work on the subject titled *Jarrett Magic and Stagecraft—Technical*.

Jarrett had the creative imagination to conceive an ILLUSION in visual terms and the mechanical ability to carry the conception to a finished reality. A number of his illusions depend on optical principles of design and construction so refined that it would seem impossible that an average-sized human being could be hidden in one of his apparently-empty boxes. Jarrett was proud enough of his abilities along this line that he often employed the HONESTY PRINCIPLE in his presentations—that is, he told the audience exactly how the illusion was performed, secure in the knowledge that he would not be believed.

Two prime examples of his thinking along these lines were his BANGKOK BUNGALOW and his TWENTY-ONE GIRLS FROM A CABINET.

The original edition of *Jarrett* was for many years almost unobtainable; it was republished in 1981 by MAGIC INC., with excellent annotations and additional explanatory material and illustrations by JIM STEINMEYER.

JARRETT PEDESTAL

Also known as a **Jarrett Base**, this is a slender pillar surmounted by a small platform, box, or whatever else is required by the specific presentation. Though it appears far too small for the purpose, it may be used as a passage from the platform to the below-stage area and vice versa. It is described by GUY JARRETT in his *Jarrett Magic And Stagecraft—Technical*.

JARROW, EMIL (1875-1959)

Born in Germany; after various jobs in show business, he became a magician, and was highly successful in vaudeville for many years. He is noted for his humorous performance of the BILL IN LEMON, but also featured an effect in which a penny held in a spectator's hand changed to a dime. This latter EFFECT would not seem the best choice for performance in a large theater, but Jarrow's presentation turned it into a small miracle.

Within magic, he was noted for his expert SLEEVING technique.

JAY, RICKY (b. 1948)

Performer and writer who began his professional career at the age of *four* (under the aegis of his grandfather MAX KATZ), and first appeared on television three years later.

Since that time he has appeared in virtually every kind of venue, from colleges to carnivals to cruise ships, from trade shows to the Tropicana and Caesar's Palace in Las Vegas. He has performed on television all over the world, including numerous appearances on such shows as *Johnny Carson, Dick Cavett, Mike Douglas, Merv Griffin*, and *Dinah Shore*; he has also starred in his own BBC-TV special.

In addition to being highly regarded for his innovative (and highly influential) approach to magic and comedy, he is generally considered to be an expert at SLEIGHT OF HAND magic, notably with cards.

He has been a TECHNICAL ADVISOR on several films, including *The Natural, The Escape Artist, The New Magic*, and *The Believers*. He also served in this capacity in the New York Shakespeare Festival production of *A Midsummer Night's Dream*, in addition to playing the part of Philostrate. As an actor he has also appeared in television shows (*Simon And Simon*) and features (*The New Magic; House Of Games*).

He is the recipient of the International Platform Association's Magician Of The Year Award.

In addition to his performing career, he is the curator of the Mulholland Library of Conjuring And Allied Arts in Los Angeles. He is noted as a lecturer on

Ricky Jay

entertainment (he has spoken at Harvard, UCLA, The Clark Library, etc.) and also as a collector of magic and show business memorabilia.

His books include *Cards As Weapons*, a definitive treatise on CARD THROWING (his skills in this area resulting in an entry in the *Guinness Book Of World Records*), and *Learned Pigs And Fireproof Women*, a best-selling history of unusual entertainers.

JAZZ ACES

A version of the FOUR ACES trick which uses only the four Aces and four INDIFFERENT CARDS. An indifferent card is dealt on the LEADER ACE, and one of the other Aces is put in the PACKET containing the three remaining indifferent cards—the Ace in the packet then changing places with the indifferent card dealt onto the leader Ace. This is repeated with the other two Aces.

The EFFECT is the invention of PETER KANE.

JEANS, WALTER CERRETTA (1877-1942)

Born Walter Janes, he aspired to be a professional performer; this, despite considerable SLEIGHT OF HAND skill, he was never able to satisfactorily

accomplish. As an inventor and creator of ILLUSIONS, however, he achieved considerable success. Of his many illusions, the most famous is un-doubtedly **The Silver Hat**, now known as the MILLION DOLLAR MYSTERY.

Jeans' life and inventions are described in PETER WARLOCK's *Walter Jeans, Illusioneer*.

JENNINGS, LARRY (b. 1933)

Plumber by profession; noted as one of the leading ex-ponents of sleight-of-hand magic with cards and coins. He has made a number of contributions to magazines, and is the author of *The Coin In The Beer Can*—an explanation of one of his featured routines.

Books on Jennings' creations include *Larry Jennings On Card And Coin Handling* by JEFF BUSBY and *The Classic Magic Of Larry Jennings* by Mike Maxwell.

JIFFY SLATE

A version of the SPIRIT SLATE invented by LOUIS S. HISTED (and described by him in PENTAGRAM) in which words appear instantly and visibly on a large slate. Words or messages can be made to appear on both sides of the slate.

The **Jiffy Slate** is intended for stage use and is not appropriate for close-up work; nevertheless, a tiny pocket-size slate using the Histed principle was marketed in recent years.

JIGGLE PASS

A type of SHIFT in which the two halves are transposed in the course of a sort of rough squaring motion as they are moved forward and back in the hand. Unlike the action of most shifts, in the **jiggle pass** the two halves move around each other at the *ends* rather than the sides; also, the upper section is not gripped but rather allowed to move by gravity.

Invented by Neil Elias and Robert Taylor, the jiggle pass is thoroughly described in EPILOGUE, and also in KARL FULVES' *Millennium Aces*.

JIMMY

A wire form which, under a cloth, simulates the presence of a human being; used in the ASRAH illu-sion. *See* LEVITATION.

JINX, THE

Begun in 1934 by THEODORE ANNEMANN, who not only edited and published it but wrote a great deal of its content, The Jinx ran for 151 issues—first as a monthly, then a fortnightly, and finally a weekly. Annemann himself called it an "information sheet" and that term is probably more accurate than "magazine"—it was produced by photo-offset and usually ran at four- or eight-page lengths (one or two large sheets folded over).

The Jinx was a major influence in the development not only of card and MENTAL MAGIC (at which its editor was expert), but all kinds of close-up and stage feats. Many of the classic EFFECTs of the present time first were revealed in its pages. In addition, the Editrivia column of editor-publisher Annemann is invaluable both for its colorful style and often biting content. Files (complete runs) of the original Jinx are difficult to find and expensive; fortunately, a reprint edition (in three volumes) is available.

The Jinx ceased publication in January of 1942 with the death of Annemann; the final issue was Number 151.

JOANNE THE DUCK
See CARD DUCK.

JOG

In card magic, the placing of a card slightly out of alignment, usually in the action of an OVERHAND SHUFFLE; if the card projects toward the performer, it is an IN-JOG; toward the spectator, an OUT-JOG. It should be understood that this is, properly done, a very minute projection, just sufficient for the performer to obtain a BREAK.

Jogs may also be created in the course of other deck-handling actions, such as counting and dealing.

Jog shuffles, used to position a number of cards, are often used in gambling and in demonstrations thereof; descriptions of early work in this area are included in *The Expert At The Card Table* by S.W. ERDNASE and in a reprint of that work annotated by DAI VERNON titled *Revelations*; excellent later developments by the Scalberts (Geoffrey and F. Leslie) are described in their *Scalbert's Selected Secrets*.

JOGLAR, FRANK

Pseudonym used by MILBOURNE CHRISTOPHER for his "Backstage" column which appeared in *Hugard's Magic Monthly*. The name derives from frank for "candid," and joglar, an early term for "magician"; thus Frank Joglar means "candid magician."

JOHNSON, GEORGE (1887-1962)

British editor-publisher, known for his thirty-year editorship of the MAGIC WAND (1914-45) and for his

publication of S. W. CLARKE's *Annals Of Conjuring* and *Bibliography Of Conjuring* (the latter compiled by Clarke and *Adolph Blind*).

He was also noted as a collector and bookseller.

JOHNSON, ROY (b.?)

Born in Britain; performer who has appeared in varied venues throughout the British Isles. He is the author of several books, including *The Roy Johnson Experience, Second Time Around, The Third Dimension, Feature Three, Everyman Cards, World Of Clocks* and *Final Call.*

JOHNSON PRODUCTS

California-based firm which specializes in the manufacture of precision made EFFECTs, primarily of metal and brass; they are noted for their many FAKE coins and coin sets.

JOHNSSON, RICK (b. ?)

Highly regarded writer/inventor, primarily in the area of CLOSE-UP MAGIC; his best-known EFFECT is perhaps his marketed **Wedlock** (in which a closed padlock vanishes from a wineglass to reappear locked around the stem). He has also written for several years a column in LINKING RING Magazine called "Come A Little Closer"; in addition, he is the reviewer of books and effects for that magazine.

His books include *Strike One* and *Practical Impossibilities.*

JOHNSTON, HUGH (1890-1956)

Inventor who specialized in card magic; his best known creation is the V-SHUFFLE.

He collaborated on a book with M.S. MAHENDRA titled *Modern Card Miracles.*

JOHNSTONE, GEORGE (b. ?)

Highly-regarded comedy performer who has performed at varied venues throughout the U.S.; he also has for many years written a column for the new TOPS and *Magigram.*

JOKER

Extra card in the deck, not belonging to any of the four suits (though it should be noted that the Joker of the Bicycle deck is clearly a King of Spades, a fact which can be used in various effect and bets); from the Latin word for Jester. The Joker is said to derive from *The Fool*—the unnumbered card of the Greater Arcana of the TAROT deck.

Most modern decks are supplied with two Jokers, which may or may not be identical. Jokers are often used in SANDWICH TRICKS; also, if left in the deck they can serve as a point of MISDIRECTION, the performer locating needed cards under the pretext of finding the Jokers and discarding them.

JON, FINN (b. ?)

Born Finn Hauser in Norway; he has appeared throughout Europe, including long runs at the Crazy Horse in Paris.

He is noted for his work with THREAD, and also for his inventiveness; he has created a number of EFFECTs. One of his earliest was **bolt of lightning**, in which a nut magically unscrewed itself from a bolt; perhaps his best-known ROUTINE is his **floating silver stick**. He is also the creator of **Esoteric**, his routine for the HAUNTED DECK effect.

He is the author of *The Magic Of Finn Jon*.

JONES, BASCOM (b. 1924)

Writer and editor who has specialized in MENTAL MAGIC but has also created EFFECTs of other kinds. For many years, with Frederick Shields, he wrote the ''Double Daring'' column in GENII Magazine; the two also collaborated on a marketed card effect, **Unbelievable**, which was the genesis of many similar routines.

In 1970 Jones created the biweekly magazine *Magick*, which he continues to edit and publish; it is devoted almost entirely to MENTALISM and MENTAL MAGIC.

JONES, CARL WARING (1887-1957)

Publisher of several excellently-produced books on magic, including the books of AL BAKER and HILLIARD's *Greater Magic*.

JONES, CHUCK (b. 1942)

Born Charles Jones, he began his career in his teens, with numerous television appearances; at the age of twenty he had his own daily television show which ran for several years.

He has since performed all over the world, also appearing on television in several countries. He has been very active in the TRADE SHOW and IN-DUSTRIAL SHOW field, for such corporate clients as A.T.& T., Honeywell, International Business Machines, American Motors, and many others.

Jones has created a number of magic shows for amusement parks, including Knott's Berry Farm. He

Chuck Jones presenting his version of the Sword Suspension.

has also worked as a TECHNICAL ADVISOR for numerous television shows and commercials.

He is the inventor of several ILLUSIONS, including the popular MIS-MADE GIRL (widely copied and imitated).

JONES, LLOYD (1906-1984)

Pharmacist by profession, he was a book dealer and publisher who also wrote a long-running book review column for GENII Magazine titled *Light From The Lamp*, and published two magical periodicals—*The Bat* and *S.O.B. Jr.*.

He served as President of several organizations, including S.A.M.; he was also noted for his extensive book collection, and for his reprints of classic works of magic literature.

He is the author of *The Dime and Penny Book*.

JONSON, WILFRID (1899-1974)

British performer and magical journalist known for his ''London Notes'' column which appeared in the SPHINX magazine for over twenty-five years, and for his highly-regarded books: *Let's Pretend, But Not To Play*, and *Mr. Smith's Guide To Sleight-Of-Hand*.

JORDAN, CHARLES T. (1888-1944)

A very prolific inventor and creator, known primarily for his contributions to card magic. He is particularly noted for his work in analyzing how a RIFFLE SHUFFLE does not actually destroy a STACK but separates it into interweaving chains.

A number of his card effects are described in his *Thirty Card Mysteries*; the most complete compendium of his work, however, is *Charles T. Jordan Collected Tricks*, edited and published by KARL FULVES.

See JORDAN COUNT.

JORDAN COUNT

A specialized FALSE COUNT invented by CHARLES T. JORDAN in which four cards are counted from hand to hand in apparently fair fashion; however, one card is never seen, and another is shown twice. In effect it is similar to the ELMSLEY COUNT; in that count, however, it is the third card down in the packet which is concealed—while in the **Jordan count** the *bottom* card remains unseen.

The four cards are held in the left hand by their left long edge at the center; the right thumb and fingers take the top card and move away. Returning, the right hand takes the second card on top of the first. As the hands come together for the third time, both the cards in the right hand are placed beneath the two cards in the left, and in a continuation of the same motion the three upper cards are pushed into the right hand. The remaining card is taken on top of those in the right hand. Properly done, it appears that four cards have been counted one at a time from left hand to right, reversing their order.

Since the action of the **Jordan count** shifts the concealed card from fourth to third position in the packet, and the Elmsley count does just the reverse, the two counts are often used together—so that, for example, the cards are counted twice and end up in the same order as at the outset.

The count is fully described in *Counts, Cuts, Moves, and Subtleties* by JERRY MENTZER and in many other books.

JOSEFFY (1873-1946)

Born Joseph Freud in Austria, he emigrated to the U.S. at the age of twenty-five and became a locksmith. In his spare time he began to construct original apparatus for an act; when it was ready, he became a professional on the CHAUTAUQUA circuit and continued to perform for nearly a quarter of a century. His act combined baffling magic with excellent musicianship on the violin, and was very popular throughout the U.S.

His mechanical creations became legendary; of these perhaps the most notable was **Balsamo**, Joseffy's version of the TALKING SKULL (which operated without threads, wires or electricity).

In later years, while he continued his interest in magic, he operated a laboratory where he designed and constructed devices for the military.

Many of his EFFECTs are described in DAVID P. ABBOTT's *The Marvelous Creations Of Joseffy*.

JOSEPH (b. 1958)

Born Joseph Gabriel Wierzbicki; now known professionally as *Joseph* or *Joseph Gabriel*. He was first noted as an illustrator, doing the explanatory drawings for HARRY LORAYNE's *Apocalypse* and a number of books.

Joseph then created an ACT of DOVE MAGIC which includes several unique effects, including a visible appearance of a bird on his shoulder and the production of two giant macaws. Assisted by partner and wife *Lucy*, he was almost immediately successful, an appearance at the Los Angeles club *The Body Shop* leading to television work and an extensive run in the *Lido de Paris* show at the Stardust Hotel in Las Vegas.

JOSEPH, EDDIE (?-1974)

Performer who for most of his life made his home in India; he performed under the name *Eddie Jason*, presenting varied EFFECTs, many of them in the category of MENTAL MAGIC.

He is the author of a large number of books, including *Card Bonanza, Dumbfounders With Cards, The Hindu Cups, How To Pick Pockets, Intuitional Sight, Magic And Mysteries Of India, Last Word On The Cups And Balls, Premonition*, and many more.

JOSOLYNE, SIDNEY (?-1965)

British performer who was the male half of the TWO-PERSON MENTAL ACT known as **La Celeste**; known within magic as the probable inventor of the version of WALKING THROUGH A BRICK WALL made famous by HOUDINI.

JUDAH, STEWART (1893-1966)

Performer with long professional career in every kind of venue. Within the profession he was noted as a creator of considerable ingenuity and an excellent teacher; he is named as one of the *Card Stars* in HILLIARD's *Greater Magic*.

Some of his creations may be found in his *The Magic World Of Stewart Judah* (edited by John Braun), and in a two-part PALLBEARER'S REVIEW Folio.

JUGGLER

From the 12th century to approximately the mid-19th, term used to denote a magical performer, or one who deceives by trickery while pretending supernatural powers.

Now, commonly, a performer who demonstrates feats of dexterity or equilibrium as demonstrations of skill.

JUICE

A preparation of (usually) red or blue ink diluted in a solution of alcohol, used to mark cards in a JUICE DECK.

JUICE DECK

A type of MARKED DECK, prepared by the application of JUICE. Instead of the usual minute markings, **juice decks** are marked with wide dashes and dots which cover the entire back surface of the card; however, if the **juice** has been properly prepared—so that it produces only a slight change in tone or sheen on the card—the marks will be unnoticeable to anyone not looking for them. A **juice worker**—card handler who uses this kind of marked deck—is judged by his ability to read very subtle **juice** markings.

In magic, such decks are generally used for GAMBLING DEMONSTRATION; their applications otherwise are limited, since they are most often marked for value only. Conversely, they do have an advantage over most other kinds of marked decks in that **juice decks** can be read from a considerable distance—often from several feet away.

JUMBO DECK

Oversize deck of playing cards (usually 4 1/2 inches by seven inches), often used by magicians in presentation of stage card magic. They were first produced by the Heraclio Fournier Co. of Spain; the first FAKE cards in jumbo size were made by CONRADI. The most commonly used Jumbo Decks are now manufactured by the U.S. Playing Card Company.

Books on their use include two with the title of *Magic With Giant Cards*, by REINHARD MULLER and Fred Castle respectively, *Gems With Jumbo Cards* by HARRY STANLEY, and *Jumbo Card Tricks* published by Abbott's Magic Co. A book of EFFECTs supplied with the set of special faked cards supplied with the Piatnik brand of Jumbo Deck was written by CHRISTIAN.

JUMPING GEMS

An excellent version of the PADDLE TRICK created and marketed by KEN ALLEN, using two small square black plastic rods into which sparkling "jewels" are set; the gems jump from rod to rod and change color, etc.

It is based on a ROUTINE of R. M Jamison's called **Spot Sticks**, which will be found in J. G. THOMPSON JR.'s *My Best*.

JUST CHANCE

British term for BANK NIGHT.

KABBALA

Periodical devoted primarily to CLOSE-UP MAGIC edited and published by JON RACHERBAUMER from 1971 to 1976 (with some later volumes published in book form in 1976 and 1981).

KALANAG (1903-1963)

Born Helmut Schreiber in Germany, he began his show business career in films, working on the productions of *Metropolis* and *The Blue Angel* among others. After World War II, he began performing an elaborate ILLUSION show as Kalanag (from the East Indian *kala nag*, meaning "black snake") using at times the SIM-SALA-BIM title; in this, he was assisted by his wife Gloria De Vos, and a company of over forty people. He performed in Europe, the U.S., and elsewhere.

His show made extensive use of CONFEDERATES, and featured a number of sets and costume changes. He was particularly noted for his presentation of the LEVITATION illusion.

KALIN, MARK (b. ?)

Performer who began his career while still in his teens, creating an act themed to pocket billiards and using cue-sticks, balls, triangle rack, etc.

He later created a fast-paced and spectacular ILLUSION act, which he has played many venues in Las Vegas, Atlantic City, and elsewhere.

He is a winner of the Achievement Award from the ACADEMY OF MAGICAL ARTS.

KANE, PETER (b. ?)

Born in Britain; specialist in card magic who has invented many popular EFFECTs, of which the best known is his **chase the ace**, now popularly known as WILD CARD (Kane has also created a new version of this EFFECT which uses Tarot cards and a different handling; it is called **gypsy curse**).

He is also the inventor of **shooting joker**, a card effect in which the deck is given a partial FARO SHUFFLE, the halves being angled to simulate a gun; the deck being "loaded" with a magazine, a previously chosen card shoots out of the deck. This effect has proved quite popular and spawned a number of variations. Also quite popular is Kane's **elongated lady**, in which a Queen placed between two other cards seems to stretch to nearly twice its length. This effect has been widely copied.

He is the author of *Card Session With Peter Kane, Another Card Session, Further Card Sessions with Peter Kane, Wild Card Plus*, and *Kane*.

KANE COUNT

A procedure to COUNT four face-down cards in the course of which only two backs are shown.

With the cards held in a BIDDLE GRIP in the right hand, the left thumb draws off the top card; as the left returns for the next card, the packet of three is exchanged for the single card; the left hand returns again, placing its three cards beneath the single card held in the right and with a continuous action MILKing off the top and bottom cards; and finally the two cards held in the right are placed as one on the two in the left.

Only the backs of the original top two cards have been shown; they are now at first and third positions. The count was invented by PETER KANE.

KAPS, FRED (1926-1980)

Born Abram Bongers in Holland, he performed for a time as Mystica before settling on the stage name of Fred Kaps.

Kaps was one of the most highly-respected magicians of recent times, noted for his smooth and sophisticated presentations of CLOSE-UP and stage magic. He was the only performer ever to win the *Grand Prix* (the highest award) at FISM three times. He appeared on the *Ed Sullivan Show* a number of times, and also gave command performances for both the Dutch and British royal families.

His approach to his work is indicated in his contributions to THE GEN and LEWIS GANSON's *Routined Manipulation Finale*, and also through a few routines which were marketed by KEN BROOKE.

KARDYRO, TONY (b. ?)

Performer with long professional career in all sorts of venues, including nightclubs, supper clubs and hotels throughout the U.S.

He is the author of a column called Kardyro's Magical Highway, which has appeared in the New TOPS; he has also written a number of books, including *Aces Galore, Kard Konjuring, Routine Supreme, Welcome Stranger*, and others.

KARSON, JOE (?-?)

Magic manufacturer and dealer who was most noted for his invention of the ZOMBIE BALL effect. He was also the creator of an ILLUSION called **no feet—some feat**, which was the precursor to the NO FEET illusion designed by ANDRE KOLE.

KATLYN

See KATLYN MILLER.

KATZ, MAX (1891-1965)

Creator of a number of ingenious EFFECTs, many of which he contributed to HUGARD's *Magic Monthly*, *M.U.M.*, and other magazines. Of these the most famous is his **Turning Aces**, which inspired a large number of similar PACKET TRICKS.

He is the grandfather of RICKY JAY.

KAUFMAN, RICHARD (b. 1958)

Writer and publisher of magic books; his own books include *Cardmagic, Coinmagic, Balls: Lessons In Side-Arm Sorcery, New York Magic Symposium Close-up Collection One, New York Magic Symposium Collection Four, Ron Wilson: The Uncanny Scot*, and others.

He is also the editor of *Richard's Almanac*.

K. B. GRIP

Former name for what is now known as the BIDDLE GRIP; named after Elmer Biddle and TONY KARDYRO.

KEATING, FRED (1898-1961)

Noted both as comedic actor and comedy magician, Keating became a great favorite of New York society in the 1930s and 40s. He scored a triple success by playing the fabled Palace Theater early in his career—being held over on that first engagement—and being brought back less than four months later; it was a rarity for a performer to accomplish any of these feats, and to accomplish all three was quite a triumph.

In the 1940s, Keating moved to Hollywood and

Fred Keating (*The Mulholland Library of Conjuring & the Allied Arts*, Los Angeles, California)

made a number of films without any major success; he returned to New York and appeared as actor and magician on stage with Cornelia Otis Skinner and Tallulah Bankhead, among others.

The feature effect of Keating's act was the VANISHING BIRD CAGE, with which he became famous; he also featured the CHINESE STICKS and the CARD IN CIGARETTE. His magic was always skillfully performed, but audiences responded most to Keating's pleasant personality and considerable charm.

KEENE, ROBERTSON (1880-1968)

Versatile British professional performer specializing in SLEIGHT OF HAND and CHAPEAUGRAPHY. He was noted for his expert handling of the PSYCHOLOGICAL FORCE.

He was also well known as a magical journalist, his "New Lamps For Old" column running in *The Magician* Magazine. His books include *Novel Notions, More Novel Notions, Ventriloquism For Beginners*, and (using the pen name Will Baffel) *Easy Conjuring Without Apparatus*.

KELLAR, HARRY (1849-1922)

Born Harold Keller; he began his career as an ASSISTANT to magicians, and later worked as assistant and then as agent for the DAVENPORT BROTHERS. With Fay (an associate of the Brothers), he toured as a magician in South America and Britain. He later made several tours of Latin America, and also appeared in Spain, India, Africa and other countries.

Returning to the U.S., he toured successfully for several years, his FULL-EVENING SHOW featuring many ILLUSION effects, and was for most of his life the nation's most popular magician.

KELLAR TIE

A ROUTINE featured by HARRY KELLAR in which the performer's hands are tied behind the back by spectators; the performer may then show a hand to be free and immediately thereafter show both hands still tied securely.

Kellar's own method for this involved secretly securing a loop of rope between the palms to gain slack; it is described in *Magician's Tricks* by Hatton and Plate. The method now most often employed is that described by HARLAN TARBELL under the present heading in his *Tarbell Course In Magic*; it involves a particular configuration of the tied rope.

KENNAUGH, ALAN (b. 1928)

British journalist noted as the feature writer for *T.V. Times*, he has had a long involvement with magic, specializing in CLOSE-UP performance.

For a time he was the editor of the British Ring's magazine, *The Budget*; he continues to write a long-running column for MAGIGRAM.

KENNEDY, JOHN (b. 1954)

Performer who began his career as a creator and manufacturer of original magic; his EFFECTs, including **the mid-air card stab, the floating dollar bill**, and **impossible matrix** attracted a great deal of attention for their strong effect and cleanness of working.

For two years he worked as a professional CLOSE-UP performer, and continued to create new effects. He now confines his activities to his mail order magic business, and has marketed a new series of effects, including *Visible Coins To Glass, Beyond Reach*, and the ANIMATED SELF-LIGHTING CIGARETTE—the latter effect on its own gaining for Kennedy a worldwide reputation.

Kennedy has appeared at magic conventions throughout the U.S., Britain, and Japan. He has contributed several items to GENII Magazine, and also has written a column for *Magical Arts Journal*.

KEY CARD

A card which marks the location of other cards, either by being immediately adjacent or a known number of cards away. Also known as a **locator card**.

A key card may be simply a card whose identity and position the performer has noted; it may also be a card which the performer can readily locate and cut to, either through previous preparation (such as trimming the edge) or in the course of handling the deck (such as a CRIMP).

There are literally thousands of card EFFECTs dependent on the use of key cards, including several complete routines; of these latter, among the best are RALPH W. HULL's **The Tuned Deck** and H. ADRIAN SMITH's **It's in the Bag**, both to be found in HILLIARD's *Greater Magic*.

KEY RING

In a set of LINKING RINGS, the ring with the opening or gap.

Some key rings have been designed so they will close, that they may be cursorily examined or briefly handled by spectators; in most cases, however, the linking technique itself is not as easily accomplished with such rings.

Often these rings are called **locking key rings**; this is a misnomer in that while the ring does close, it is not locked in the accepted sense and can be opened by a spectator who is unwisely given the time and opportunity. In most situations there is no compelling reason for the use of a locking key ring.

KICK CUT

With cards, a type of FLOURISH cut in which the forefinger of the hand holding the deck is used to propel the bottom half of the deck backward through the air where it is caught by the other hand, and placed on top of the half still held.

See CUT.

KING, CARLTON (1896-1977)

Born William Davison in Great Britain, he emigrated to the U.S. in 1930 and was briefly a partner with L.L. IRELAND in his magic company.

Moving to New York, he played at many prestigious nightclubs and other venues for the rest of his professional career.

KING, LIONEL (?-1958)

British performer with a long professional career, performing in many different kinds of venues. He was best known for his masterful presentation of the NAP HAND effect.

KING, MAC (b. 1959)

Born Paxson King, he specializes in comedy magic. One of the most popular performers on the comedy-club circuit, he appears at clubs throughout the U.S.; he has also toured with such performers as Jay Leno, Jerry Lee Lewis and Barbara Mandrell.

King has done a number of television commercials and corporate appearances for clients, including Kentucky Fried Chicken, The United Way, and Pillsbury.

KIO, EMIL (1898-1966)

One of the few Russian illusionists known in the West, he made several appearances with the *Moscow State Circus* on their tours of Europe, Great Britain, and the United States.

Working as he did in circus venues, Kio specialized in very large-scale illusions involving people and animals; he appeared as a ''director of magic'' rather than as a magician. On his death, he was replaced by his son Igor Kio.

Mac King

KIRKHAM, KIRK (b. 1925)

Performer who began his career as a performer in the U.S. Army Special Services division, doing hundreds of shows for servicemen throughout the Pacific and in Japan. He then worked for a year as an ASSISTANT on the touring shows of HARRY BLACKSTONE Sr. and VIRGIL.

In addition to numerous stage and television appearances, he became a noted TECHNICAL ADVISOR for television and films; his credits in this area are quite extensive, and include *The Donald O'Connor Show, You Asked For It, The Colgate Comedy Hour* and shows hosted by Jimmy Durante, Tennessee Ernie Ford, Mickey Rooney and many others. He also directed the magic sequences for the Ice Capades and has directed magic shows for Disneyland, Sea World, Knott's Berry Farm and Magic Mountain.

Kirkham is noted for his knowledge of ILLUSION magic, and has what is probably the largest private collection of illusions in the world.

KISSING

To bring two objects, usually cards, face to face.

Also, *Kissing The Deck* is an expression sometimes used in place of BOX THE DECK.

Kirk Kirkham

KITAMI, MAKI (b. ?)

Born in Japan; performer who has worked in many different venues. He is noted for his stage manipulative act which contains many traditional Japanese effects, and is highly-regarded for his performance of the THUMB TIE.

KLINE, BOB (b. ?)

Inventor noted for his creation of the COPENETRO effect; he is also the author of a book on the subject titled *Copenetro Tips and Routines*.

KLING KLANG

An egg is placed in a glass and covered with a cloth, and a silk handkerchief is poked into the hand. When the hand is opened the egg is revealed; when the cloth is removed from the glass the silk handkerchief is found within.

The EFFECT invented by COLONEL STODARE, is accomplished by means of a STODARE EGG, which is dropped into a BOTTOMLESS GLASS; the glass is covered with a cloth which has a duplicate silk handkerchief concealed within its folds. This silk is allowed to fall into the glass and the egg is stolen away as the glass is placed on the table. It only remains to poke the visible silk into the egg hidden in the hand, and then reveal the transposition.

The *Kling Klang* title has sometimes been erroneously used to refer to the SILK TO EGG effect.

KLINGSOR (b. 1929)

Born Claude Isbeque in Belgium, he became a performer and later a dealer. His studio, founded in Brussels in 1957, became a shop in 1966. Taking the stage name *Klingsor* (from the magical Lord in *Parsifal*), he has specialized in elaborately designed EFFECTs which employ electronics (and which are also marketed through his shop).

He was host to the 1979 FISM in Belgium; was editor of the magazine *Illusion* for several years; has written a book on the RISING CARDS (*Les Tours de Cartes Montantes*); and has translated other works.

KLONDIKE SHUFFLE

With the deck held in the left hand in the same grip as that used in the BIDDLE MOVE, the right fingers and thumb draw off the top and bottom cards simultaneously and place them as a pair on the table, the process then being repeated for the remainder of the cards. This procedure can also be executed from an OVERHAND SHUFFLE grip.

Sometimes rendered in the variant spelling of *Klondyke*, this shuffle is rarely used in present-day card magic.

See MILK-BUILD SHUFFLE.

KNIFE FORCE

The FORCE of a playing card by having a spectator insert a thin-bladed knife into the deck at the outer end—the card above the blade being the force card.

A BREAK is held below the selected card, which should be about a third of the way down in the deck; the performer must insure that the knife is inserted at any point *below* the break.

The spectator releases the handle of the knife and the performer tilts the front end of the deck downward, ostensibly to give the spectators a clear view of what is happening. All of the cards above the break are slid slightly forward by the right hand (if the left holds the deck). The right hand now grasps the upper portion at the front, pinching the knife blade against it, and draws the blade and cards forward and away from the rest of the deck. The knife is thus taken from its actual point of insertion and the blade ends up pressed against the face of the force card; card and blade are now shown to the spectators.

It is possible to use a knife in conjunction with other techniques used in forcing, such as the SLIP CUT—but these are methods which simply use the knife as a PROP, and should not be confused with the above-described technique.

KNIFE THROUGH COAT

A knife is passed partially or completely through a borrowed coat, leaving no trace of its passage.

One version of this EFFECT uses a pocket knife with a highly polished blade having smooth (but not sharp) edges; such a blade can be pushed into the weave of certain jacket materials and will simply push the threads aside. When the blade is removed, a bit of rubbing restores the weave to its proper position. The blade will not, however, separate the weave of most linings, which are much more tightly woven; care must be taken to perform this version of the effect with the unlined area of the coat.

Other versions, using large knives or scissors, may use SLEIGHT OF HAND techniques similar to those employed in the CIGARETTE PENETRATION. Such a version is featured by MIKE CAVENEY, who uses it as a lead-in to the comedy climax of his act.

Still other methods, several of which have been marketed, use specially-prepared knives or additional devices to bring about the effect.

KNIGHT'S TOUR

A feat of memory performed by HARRY KELLAR's wife Eva in the past and PETER REVEEN in the present, among many others. The blindfolded performer directs the movement of a chess knight around the board, beginning with a numbered square specified by a spectator, until the knight has touched every square, never landing on the same square twice. Since the knight has the most complex move in chess, to chessplayers this is a highly impressive feat and to lay spectators it is incredible.

Various MNEMONIC means have been devised to accomplish this demonstration; excellent versions are described in BERNARD ZUFALL's *Memory Trix #6*, and in DAVID M. ROTH's *Roth Memory Course*, as well as other works on mnemonics.

KNOT EFFECTS

Knot magic can be divided into two basic categories—those in which knots are made to magically appear in a rope or silk, and those in which securely tied knots are made to disappear.

There are countless techniques for such EFFECTs; those using silks are described in HAROLD R. RICE's *Encyclopedia Of Silk Magic* and his *Naughty Silks* and *More Naughty Silks*. Knot effects using rope will be found in the *Encyclopedia Of Rope Tricks* edited by STEWART JAMES.

Less common effects include those in which knots change color or jump from one rope to another; many such effects have been created by PAVEL. A popular effect of recent vintage is one in which a long rope is cut near one end and a knot tied; the knot is then *slid* to the other end of the rope *and there untied* to establish that the knot actually moved. This effect was invented by PAUL CURRY; later methods have been developed by PAVEL and JIM STEINMEYER.

See also SERPENT SILK; SYMPATHETIC SILKS; UNTYING SILK.

KODELL, JACK (b. 1930)

Born Jack Koudelka, he is noted as the first performer to feature parakeets in his act of BIRD MAGIC; he began performing professionally while still in his teens, and was highly successful, performing in nightclubs and supper clubs throughout the U.S.

His act had many original features, including the "multiplication" of parakeets on his fingers a la

Jack Kodell (*The Mulholland Library of Conjuring & the Allied Arts, Los Angeles, California*)

BILLIARD BALL manipulation; perhaps his most startling effect was a re-creation of the INDIAN ROPE TRICK in which a parakeet climbed to the top of a small length of magically-rigid rope and vanished in a puff of smoke.

KOLAR (1883-1949)

Born Joseph J. Kolar, he toured vaudeville and later played theaters with an act which featured not only magic but also ESCAPES, MENTAL MAGIC, juggling, FIRE-EATING and slack-wire walking. He was noted for his catchphrase, "Give my regards to the Chief of Police!" Kolar's father—and daughter Betty Jane—also had careers as professional performers.

In later years he retired from performing, but stayed active in magic with the creation of a number of EFFECTs, of which the best known are his **magic shears** (more popularly known under its marketed name of CLIPPO); an effect in which a soda straw is cut in half without harming a string threaded through it; and a feat of MENTAL MAGIC in which the performer discovers which of several keys will open a padlock (later popularized by THEODORE ANNEMANN as SEVEN KEYS TO BALDPATE).

He also wrote a column called "Chats By Kolar" which appeared in the SPHINX Magazine.

KOLE, ANDRE (b. ?)

Born Bob Gurtler, he first became known as an inventor of magic; among his originations are **spikes through balloon, helicopter cups**, and **atomic stack pile**.

Beginning his performing career, he won a number of magic competitions. He created a number of original ILLUSIONs, of which the best known is the TABLE OF DEATH; others include his **Bermuda Triangle** and very original approaches to the CRUSHING A WOMAN and LEVITATION effects.

For many years he has toured under the auspices of Campus Crusade For Christ, the first half of the show being a straightforward illusion show, the second half using magic to illustrate his religious views (see GOSPEL MAGIC).

KOORNWINDER, DICK (b. ?)

Dutch magician who has achieved an international reputation as an expert in card and CLOSE-UP MAGIC; he is also noted for his many marketed EFFECTs, of which perhaps the best known is the **Koornwinder Kar**—a toy car which mysteriously locates a selected card.

Andre Kole (*photo courtesy GENII Magazine*)

KORAN, AL (1916-1971)

Born Edward Doe in Britain, Al Koran became one of England's best-known magicians. He began his career as a close-up performer and gained a reputation for his incredible card EFFECTs—among them a CARD STAB which fooled well-posted magicians, and which was described in *Mastered Amazement* (written with Jack Lamonte). Though not an inventor of effects, Koran possessed the ability to see magic from a lay person's point of view; he was thus able to take long-neglected magical concepts and create with them strong presentations.

After a time he shifted the focus of his performances to MENTAL MAGIC, and here he achieved his greatest successes, including his own television series. Unlike many magicians who have specialized in mental magic, however, Koran often wove conventional magic into the presentation of his mental feats; he might, for example, divine the contents of a locked box—and then cause the box to vanish.

In 1964 a book titled *Bring Out The Magic In Your Mind* was published, supposedly written by Koran but actually ghosted; it was a combination of self-help positive-thinking advice with a number of publicity stories about Koran. The book has been described as the "world's thickest advertising brochure."

In 1969 Koran moved to Chicago, Illinois, and he began to build a new career in the United States; shortly thereafter he was stricken with cancer, however, and died two years later.

Of the many effects he invented, the best known is RING FLIGHT.

Some of his effects and presentations are described in three books: *Professional Presentations* and *Koran's Legacy*, both by Hugh Miller, and *The Magic of Al Koran*, edited by Martin Breese.

KORAN DECK

See ONE-O-ONE DECK.

The name is also sometimes (erroneously) applied to the MULTIPLE-BANK DECK known as the MAGICIAN'S DREAM DECK.

KORIM, FELIX, SIR (1905-1986)

Born Brewerton H. Clarke, he began his performing career as singer and actor. As a magician, he built an elaborate ILLUSION show (with many original effects) which he toured throughout the northeastern U.S. for many years. During World War II, he worked for the U.S. Army as a camouflage specialist, bringing to this work his knowledge of magical principles.

He was also a commercial artist; he contributed several illusions to GENII Magazine, illustrated in his distinctive style.

KORNHAUSER, MARK (b. ?)

Performer who began his career as a CLOSE-UP worker, later switching to nightclub work. Specializing in comedy magic, he has appeared with Dom DeLouise, Tony Orlando, Debbie Reynolds and many others in such venues as the Tropicana, MGM Grand, Dunes and Riviera in Las Vegas; he has also appeared in major clubs in Atlantic City (Resorts International), Reno (Harrah's) and Lake Tahoe (Sahara).

KORT, MILTON (b. 1913)

A pharmacist by profession, noted as a writer and inventor, primarily on card and close-up magic. He is also known for his creation of the O-KORT-O BOX routine. His name is the inspiration for that of MIKO, derived from the first two letters of his first and last names.

His books include *Kort Is Now In Session*, *Off-Color Card Tricks*, and *Kortially Yours*.

KOSKY, GERALD (1907-1987)

Not a full-time professional, he nevertheless had a long and very active performing career, either in his own persona or in two specialty acts he created—as

Mark Kornhauser

Mr. O'So, a Japanese magician, and Professor 'Iggins, a British performer.

Very active in a number of magical organizations (in many of which he served a term as president), he was also noted for his many contributions of effects to various publications, and for several marketed effects, primarily in the area of MENTAL MAGIC.

A varied collection of his creations is his *The Magic Of Gerald Kosky.*

KOVARI, GEORGE (b. ?)

British performer who specializes in shows for young people, and who has had a continuing theatrical show for over fifteen years. He is also noted as an inventor and dealer; his most popular effect is perhaps his *Codology*, an imaginative variant of the MONKEY BAR.

KRAMIEN, STAN (b. 1925)

Performer who began his career with extensive touring for the USO; he later developed a FULL-EVENING SHOW with which he played various venues, including schools and theaters.

For two years he starred in his own television show in Seattle, Washington; he then became the owner-operator of a circus which toured for over a decade. In 1970 he created another and more elaborate full-evening show titled *Magicazam*, which has toured through several states for many years.

He has also written several books on the booking of shows: *Making Big Money With Your School Shows*, *Making Money As A Part-Time Magician*, and *Professional Secrets Of Kramien*. He is also the author of the *Wonder Mouse Pitch*.

KRATKY-BASCHIK, ANTON (1821-1889)

Born in Bohemia, he began his performing career as a musician; at the age of thirty he worked with BELLACHINI, and this inspired him to take up magic.

For several years he appeared in Britain, including a Royal Command Performance and a tour with the circus of *P. T. Barnum*, and then performed throughout Europe. In 1875 he opened his own magic theater in Vienna; as his eyesight failed he permitted others to appear there, among them *George Heubeck* (a student of HOFZINSER), and OTTOKAR FISCHER.

KRENZEL, KEN (b. ?)

Child psychologist by profession; his primary interest is in card magic, and he is noted as the inventor of a SLEIGHT called the **mechanical reverse**, used for secretly turning over a card.

His approach is described in *Card Classics Of Ken Krenzel*, by HARRY LORAYNE. Krenzel has authored *The Incredible Card Tunnel* and (with RICHARD KAUFMAN) *On The Up And Up*.

KRUSKAL PRINCIPLE

A mathematical principle discovered by Martin Kruskal; it states that if a random card among the first ten in a deck is selected, and this card's numerical

Stan Kramien (*photo courtesy GENII Magazine*)

value is used to deal further into the deck, the process being repeated with the value of the cards thus arrived at until insufficient cards remain to complete a deal—then the last card successfully dealt to by this procedure will be the *same* card in repeated deals more than eighty percent of the time, given that the cards are not disarranged. (This presumes dealing the cards face-up from a face-down deck.)

The principle was first described in the PALLBEARER'S REVIEW.

LAFAYETTE (1872-1911)

Born Sigmund Neuberger in Germany; he was noted for his elaborate stage settings, and also for his devotion to his dog Beauty. His EFFECTs ranged from the PIGEON-CATCHING invented by CYRIL YETTMAH to his own LION'S BRIDE illusion. He was also known for his QUICK-CHANGE effects and ROUTINEs, and for his spectacular showmanship. For many years he was one of the highest paid entertainers in vaudeville. He was killed in a theater fire at Edinburgh, Scotland.

LA FOLLETTE, GEORGE (1886-1960)

Born George Reuschling; he began his career performing in ORIENTAL STYLE as Rush Ling Toy; like CHUNG LING SOO, he succesfully posed as an Oriental for many years. He toured throughout North and South America.

After his South American tours, he returned to U.S. vaudeville where he appeared both as Rush Ling Toy and as *La Follette*—under the latter name performing a QUICK-CHANGE act.

LAMP-CHIMNEY VANISH

See PULL.

LAPPING

Secretly disposing of objects while seated at a table by dropping them into the lap; less commonly, secretly obtaining objects therefrom.

In the right situation, and in combination with other SLEIGHT OF HAND techniques, lapping can be a very useful adjunct; it is, however, limited to those specific situations, and is thus not much used in professional CLOSE-UP performing. The undisputed master of this technique is SLYDINI, who applies it perfectly in concert with his unparalleled mastery of MISDIRECTION.

LARGE RING

In a LINKING RING set, a ring of fractionally larger size, through which the other rings of the set may be passed; used most often in techniques of counting the rings to show them as separate.

LARREVERSE

A card SLEIGHT invented by LARRY JENNINGS in which, in the action of righting a REVERSED CARD in the center of the deck held spread between the hands, a second card is indetectably reversed.

The sleight is described in Mike Maxwell's book *The Classic Magic of Larry Jennings*.

LARSEN, MILT (b. 1931)

With brother WILLIAM W. LARSEN, JR., he founded the MAGIC CASTLE, doing a good deal of the construction and decoration work himself. He is also the founder of the Society For The Preservation Of Variety Arts, for many years headquartered in Los Angeles in a downtown theater building.

He is noted for his comedy act in which a number of things go wrong in spectacular fashion.

LARSEN, WILLIAM W. (1905-1953)

Lawyer by profession; he contributed a number of items to the SPHINX (many with friend T. Page Wright), and in 1936 founded GENII Magazine. In

1942 he purchased the FLOYD G. THAYER magic company and operated it with wife Geraldine for the next five years. Larsen wrote a number of manuscripts during this time, many of which have been collected by son WILLIAM W. LARSEN JR as *The Mental Mysteries And Other Writings Of William W. Larsen Sr.*

He discontinued the practice of law and, in addition to editing GENII and running the Thayer operation, he performed in many venues throughout the West Coast area, as a single and with his family.

Many of his manuscripts have been published over the years in GENII; some of his other works include *Conjuring For Children, L. W. Card Mysteries, The Last Seance, Mental Mysteries With Cards, Puppetrix, Spook Show In Your Parlor,* and *Twelve Illusionettes.*

For many years Larsen had the dream of a meeting place for magicians—a dream which was brought to fruition by sons WILLIAM W. LARSEN, JR. and MILT LARSEN.

LARSEN, WILLIAM W., JR. (b. 1928)

An associate producer for the CBS television network, with mother Geraldine he took over the editorial duties for GENII Magazine in 1949. In 1963, with

The Larsens: (from top) Milt, Irene, and Bill Jr. (*photo courtesy GENII Magazine*)

brother MILT LARSEN, he founded the MAGIC CASTLE; shortly thereafter he retired from television work, and for many years has devoted his time to the operation of the MAGIC CASTLE and the ACADEMY OF MAGICAL ARTS (of which he is Life President), and continues (with wife *Irene*) to edit GENII Magazine.

William and Irene Larsen are recipients of the Literary Fellowship of the ACADEMY OF MAGICAL ARTS.

LAUNDRY TICKET

Also known as the Chinese Laundry Ticket; a torn-and-restored paper EFFECT (*see* TORN-AND-RESTORED OBJECT) using a strip of tissue bearing Chinese ideographs. The effect is usually done with a SUCKER routine, involving a supposed explanation of how the effect is done. It is credited to HARLAN TARBELL.

LAURANT, EUGENE (1875-1944)

Born Eugene Greenleaf, he became a highly successful performer on the CHAUTAUQUA circuit, for which his show was quite elaborate; he carried several illusions and full stage settings.

When Chautauqua came to an end, Laurant turned to school assembly shows and repeated his earlier success, becoming a great favorite throughout the U.S.

LAWTON, DON (b. 1922)

Performer with long career in which he has appeared in varied venues throughout the U.S. He was also for many years a dealer, during which time he began publishing his *Lines From Lawton* newsletter.

More recently he has appeared at the MAGIC CASTLE both as performer and as host; he is noted for his extremely corny comedy and the considerable charm that permits it.

He is now publishing his *New Lines From Lawton*—a potpourri of news, anecdotes, and comedy performance material.

Lawton is a recipient of the Best Stage Magician and Life Achievement Awards of the ACADEMY OF MAGICAL ARTS.

LAYMAN

More properly, *layperson*; one unacquainted with the principles and techniques of magic.

LEADER ACE

In a FOUR-ACE routine, the Ace to which the other three Aces are magically assembled.

LEAF

To look through a deck of playing cards by pushing them from one hand to the other without changing their order.

LEANEY, GIL (b. 1921)

Born in Britain; noted builder of APPARATUS and ILLUSION effects in wood and metal. His clients have included DANTE, FOGEL, HARBIN, LYLE, MURRAY, VOLTAIRE, and many others. He is currently on the staff of the PAUL DANIELS show.

He is the recipient of a Creative Fellowship from the ACADEMY OF MAGICAL ARTS.

LEAT, HARRY (1874-1949)

British performer, dealer, writer and publisher. He was first noted as a contributor to The Wizard; later he began to sell expertly-crafted PROPS to magicians and dealers, eventually setting up his own business.

His well-known house organ for this business was called *Leat's Leaflet*; among his many books are *Diversified Magic*, *Forty Years In And Around Magic*, *Magic Of The Depots*, and *Tragic Magic*.

LE BAS, ALBERT (1928-1972)

Noted Irish performer; though technically a semi-professional, he was considered Ireland's leading magician, and was constantly before the public in stage and television appearances.

Le Bas was equally at home with small magic or large illusions, but is best remembered for *Where The Money Is*—his presentation of the MISER'S DREAM.

LEDAIR, JACK (ca. 1885-1958)

Born in Britain; highly-regarded performer who had a long career in variety and music-hall venues.

He is the author of *Tricks Of A Trouper*.

LEECH, AL (?-1974)

Journalist by profession; noted for his inventive and direct approach to magic, particularly with cards.

His books include *Cardman Stuff*, *Super Card Man Stuff*, *Cardmanship*, *For Card Men Only*, *Handbook Of Card Sleights*, *Manipulating With Leech*, and *Don't Look Now*.

LEES, WALT (b. 1943)

Born in Britain; highly-regarded and versatile performer, noted particularly as a close-up and card worker; he also is known for his CHILDREN'S MAGIC and his PUNCH AND JUDY routines.

His many books include *Art Of The Grafter*, *Four Professional Card Tricks*, *Complete Cannibal Act*, *Immaculate Card Magic Of Walt Lees*, and others.

LEGERDEMAIN

Technically, SLEIGHT-OF-HAND or MANIPULATION, but often used as a synonym for performance magic; from the French *leger de main = light of hand*.

LEGS TABLE

A mechanical comedy PROP built by Yimka, in appearance a four-legged table. As the performer lifts it to move it forward, one of the front legs drops off; a moment later the other front leg also drops off. The performer is upset at this turn of events, but suddenly a plywood cutout of a pair of women's legs appears at the front of the table, which may now be utilized like any other table.

Featured by ARTHUR DOWLER, it is believed to have been invented by the Rigoletto Brothers.

LEIPZIG, NATE (1873-1939)

Born Nathan Leipziger in Sweden, he emigrated to the U.S. as a young man; at about the age of thirty he began professional performing, specializing in private engagements. Then he was booked for a tour on the Keith vaudeville circuit, and from that time on traveled the world with his act.

Leipzig's was essentially a CLOSE-UP act done on stage; a committee was invited up and the magic performed for them, their reactions "selling" the show to the rest of the audience. It is a testament to Leipzig's superb showmanship that he was able to make such an act not only play, but play extremely well.

His work is described in *The Leipzig Book* by DAI VERNON.

LENERT, TINA (b. 1948)

Born in Venezuela of U.S. parents; she began her career as a MIME, later incorporating magic into her work to create a unique act in which, as a mechanical doll, she would manipulate glass eyeballs and cause a giant eye to float a la ZOMBIE. Lenert has recently developed an entirely new act, in which a sleepy cleaning woman is romanced by a mysteriously animated coat on a rack.

Nate Leipzig (*The Mulholland Library of Conjuring & the Allied Arts, Los Angeles, California*)

Tina Lenert

She has appeared in a variety of venues, from the Los Angeles Music Center to Harrah's at Lake Tahoe. She has also appeared at numerous TRADE SHOWS throughout the country. She was a founding member of the L. A. Mime Company, with which she toured universities and colleges in addition to regular appearances on Dick Van Dyke's *Van Dyke And Co.*. She has also appeared in such television shows as *Man From Atlantis* and *Wonder Woman*, and commercials for such clients as Sears, Proctor & Gamble, and Kodak.

In addition to her performing career, she is actively involved with husband MIKE CAVENEY in the operation of their publishing company, Magical Publications.

LEON (1876-1951)

Born Leon H. Levy, he began his career as a boy performer in tent shows, carnivals, and medicine shows. In vaudeville he performed as Chunda Hula and later as Kadan Sami, working in ORIENTAL STYLE. His vaudeville turn was noted for its fast pace and spectacular ILLUSIONs, of which the most famous was his FIRE AND WATER.

He was also noted for his routine for WINE AND WATER, and for his Miniature Haunted House—a doll's house with one side removed, in which various spiritualistic effects occurred.

His work is described in *The Great Leon: Vaudeville Headliner* by MIKE CAVENEY.

LE PAUL, PAUL (1900-1958)

Born Paul Braden; professional performer who was, in the judgment of many experts, the greatest stage card MANIPULATOR of all time. He began the major part of his career in vaudeville, afterwards appearing in many top nightclubs and hotels as well as on Broadway (in Earl Carroll's *Vanities*).

For a time Le Paul acted as technical advisor to motion pictures; with the advent of World War II, he immediately joined the USO and performed on dozens of tours for the remainder of his career, often passing up highly lucrative engagements to do so.

In addition to his manipulative skill, he is known among magicians for his sophisticated version of the CARD TO WALLET, still used by many top performers. Other originations are described in his *The Card Magic Of Le Paul*.

LEROY, SERVAIS (1865-1953)

Born Jean Henri Servais Leroy in Belgium; he left home at a very young age, and began performing in Britain with considerable success in the mid-1880's.

Paul LePaul (*The Mulholland Library of Conjuring & the Allied Arts, Los Angeles, California*)

Servais Leroy (*The Mulholland Library of Conjuring & the Allied Arts, Los Angeles, California*)

He later toured Britain and the U.S., by himself and as Leroy, Talma, and Bosco, with wife TALMA and another performer named Leon Bosco (several performers took this role in turn, playing under the Bosco name). He also performed with FREDERICK EUGENE POWELL and Imro Fox under the billing of "The Triple Alliance."

Leroy is noted as one of the most inventive performers in the history of ILLUSION magic; among his inventions are ASRAH, THE PALANQUIN, THE THREE GRACES, THE COSTUME TRUNK, and other effects.

LESLEY, TED (b. 1937)

Born in West Germany, he began his career as an actor in a feature film, thereafter performing as a magician and mentalist at the Hanover Fair Show. Television appearances and nightclub work followed, including an eighteen-month run at the prestigious Berlin-Hilton Hotel.

Continuing as one of Germany's most successful performers, he has also created The Magic Productions Show Service, an agency that books many performers and produces shows.

He is known as the creator of The Working

Performer's Marked Deck, a highly readable MARKED DECK; it has been widely copied in unauthorized and inferior versions, and Lesley has undercut these counterfeits by marketing an inexpensive kit for marking a deck by his system.

He is the author of *The Kismet Connection.*

LESTER, LESLIE (1906-1968)

British performer noted for his skill at MANIPULATION; he performed throughout Britain in variety venues for several decades.

LEVANTE, LES (1892-1978)

Born Leslie Cole in Australia, he produced his first FULL-EVENING SHOW by the age of twenty; he thereafter toured the world a number of times. Among the many spectacular items he presented was his version of METAMORPHOSIS, using a thoroughly examined steel trunk, and the WRESTLING CHEESE.

He was the inventor of the effect of the IMPALING illusion which has become popular in recent years (it

Les Levante (*The Mulholland Library of Conjuring & the Allied Arts, Los Angeles, California*)

There are a number of methods and stage riggings for this effect; the most common uses a support through a slit in the curtains, connected by a GOOSENECK (S-shaped support) to the CRADLE on which the person reclines. The **gooseneck** allowed a hoop to be passed twice around the person—the first pass threading the hoop into the support, the second pass removing it. This version was originally known as the *AGA*; however, that term now usually applies to a version where the supporting/lifting rod comes up from beneath the stage behind the performer, engaging a socket in the supporting arm which curves around the performer's body. Both these versions are most often credited to JOHN NEVIL MASKELYNE, who also invented the **gooseneck** and **hoop-passing** procedure.

A later version, also used by J. N. Maskelyne, employed a complex fanlike arrangement of wires, one set fastened to a framework in the FLIES, the other set down through a slit TRAP in the stage to counterweights. These wires attached to a horizontal support rod behind the **gooseneck**, which allowed the person to float well away from any backdrop while the **hoop-passing** maneuver was executed. This methodology had previously been developed by DE KOLTA for his **cocoon** illusion.

A related effect, invented by SERVAIS LE ROY, was the ASRAH illusion. Here the assistant, lying on a

should be noted that Levante's method for this effect required a specially-rigged stage, and is not the method now used). He was also noted for his considerable personal charm, both on and off stage.

LEVI

Illusionist's parlance for the LEVITATION illusion.

LEVI COUCH

The couch or low table on which the ASSISTANT reposes in a supine position at the outset of the LEVITATION ILLUSION. It is constructed to conceal the presence of the CRADLE on which the assistant actually rests.

This term is also used to denote the BEVEL BASE table used in conjunction with the Asrah version of this illusion.

LEVITATION

An ILLUSION in which a person rises into the air without any apparent means of support; not to be confused with SUSPENSION.

Andre Kole performs his unique self-levitation (*photo courtesy GENII Magazine*).

The *Levitation*, as performed by Siegfried and Roy, featuring assistant Lynette Chapell

table, was covered with a cloth; the draped figure rose into the air, but when the covering was pulled away, she had vanished. A wire frame replaced the assistant, who dropped down into the table (actually a kind of BEVEL BASE); when the cloth was pulled away from the frame (usually supported by a simple wire rig), the wire frame was invisible on a properly lit stage. This illusion is still one of the most popular forms of the effect, since the mechanical requirements are considerably simpler.

A thorough discussion of various methods and techniques for this illusion will be found in *The Encyclopedia Of Suspensions And Levitations* by Bruce Armstrong.

LEWIS, ERIC (b. 1908)

Born in Britain; performer of long experience, and founder/operator of a magic manufacturing company known as MagiKraft. Emigrating to the U.S., he built APPARATUS for the Milson-Worth company; he later spent eighteen months with Dr. Robert Albo, constructing effects for the Albo collection and writing *The Oriental Magic Of The Bambergs*.

For some years he was associated with JOHN GAUGHAN, until his retirement.

Lewis's many creations would fill a book—or sixteen books (see below). Perhaps his best-known invention is his DIMINISHING SILK PRODUCTION, which has probably been used in one form or another by hundreds of magicians.

He is the author of *Well I Never!*, *Magical Mentality*, *The Magic of 1936*, *The Magic of 1937*, *Magic For Moderns*, *Studies In Mystery*, *Further Magical Studies*, *Modus Operandi*, *Magic To Entertain*, *Open Sesame*, *Opus Thirteen*, the afore-mentioned Bamberg book, and the *Eric Lewis Trilogy: A Choice Of Miracles*, *A Continuation Of Miracles*, and *The Crowning Miracles*. He is also the

Eric C. Lewis

Martin Lewis

author of *Martin's Miracles*, which describes the magic of his son MARTIN LEWIS.

He has received many awards. Lewis has twice been named Stage Magician Of The Year, and has also received the Literary Fellowship and Master's Fellowship from the ACADEMY OF MAGICAL ARTS.

LEWIS, MARTIN (b. 1946)

Born in Britain; he emigrated to the U.S. in his early twenties, and became interested in magic as a result of seeing close-up workers at the MAGIC CASTLE. Sharing father ERIC LEWIS's inventive turn of mind; he was soon creating a number of original EFFECTs, of which the best known is his marketed **sidewalk shuffle**.

While working as a close-up performer at Earthquake McGoon's Magic Cellar in San Francisco, he began developing a stage show, and since then has appeared in many venues; he has for many years primarily involved himself in cruise ship work.

His approach is described in *Martin's Miracles* by ERIC LEWIS. He is a winner of the *Visiting Magician of the Year* Award of the ACADEMY OF MAGICAL ARTS.

LEWIS, SHARI (b. ?)

Now known worldwide as an excellent ventriloquist, she began her career performing magic in combination with dance routines; at the age of 14 she had her own New York television show called *Facts And Fun*.

She has since had a spectacular career, with appearances all over the world. Her televisions shows have won several Emmys and a Peabody Award; she is also the recipient of a Kennedy Center Award.

She has written over twenty books, many of them intended for young readers, including *Magic For Non-Magicians*.

L'HOMME MASQUE (1835-1913)

Born Jose Antenar de Gago in Peru; he performed primarily in France, but occasionally appeared in Britain, Spain, Sweden and other countries. In public, including all performances, he always wore a mask (hence the stage name, which means *Man Of The Mask*). He also performed under the name of the Marquise d'O (for Orighuela).

Some of his methods are indicated in GAULTIER's *Magic Without Apparatus*.

Erhard Liebenow presenting one of his poker chip effects (*photo courtesy GENII Magazine*).

LIEBENOW, ERHARD (b. ca. 1937)

Born in Germany; he has performed throughout Europe, and made several tours of the U.S. He is particularly noted for the several effects he has invented using poker chips.

He is the author of *Liebenow On Cards*.

LIE DETECTOR

A PLOT in card magic in which the spectator calls aloud the names of cards as he deals them, miscalling his own previously chosen card as a totally different card. The performer is seemingly able to tell when the spectator lies.

As this is simply a presentational schema, methods for accomplishing it are as various as those to determine the identity of a selected card.

LIE SPELLER

Invented by MARTIN GARDNER, this is a variant of the LIE DETECTOR card effect; here the spectator is asked questions by the performer regarding color, suit, and value of his card; he may lie or tell the truth, spelling his answer by dealing one card from the deck for each letter. Regardless of the truth or falsity of the answers, the chosen card turns up as the last card dealt.

An excellent version of this effect was created by

BRUCE CERVON and published in PALLBEARER'S REVIEW under the title ''perfect Speller.''

LIFT TRAP

See ELEVATOR TRAP.

LIGHT-AND-HEAVY CHEST

An effect devised by ROBERT-HOUDIN in which he seemed to rob a man of his strength so he could not lift a small chest as he had done only moments before. The box had its bottom prepared with steel plate, and an electromagnet (little-known in Robert-Houdin's day) was under the stage.

With this effect and the BULLET CATCH, Robert-Houdin was able to easily win a ''battle of magic'' with the *marabouts* of Algeria when he was sent there by the French government for this purpose in 1856.

LIGHT CABINET

An ILLUSION created by CYRIL YETTMAH and featured by DAVID BAMBERG in which a square cabinet with translucent panels (usually of paper) is shown empty, and a light inserted through the top. The front door is closed, and the silhouette of a person gradually appears; suddenly the person bursts through the paper panel of the door.

This very pretty illusion is currently featured by DOUG HENNING; it is described in *Volume 6* of the TARBELL COURSE IN MAGIC.

LINE

A rope, wire or thread which is attached to a piece of scenery or other object; also, a sentence of dialogue.

LINKING FINGER RINGS

An EFFECT developed by DR. PERSI DIACONIS and marketed by RICHARD HIMBER in which three finger rings are borrowed from members of the audience and linked by the performer into a chain of three—the rings then, still linked, being identified by their owners. To conclude, the rings are unlinked and returned.

Many routines for this effect are described in *Routines With The Himber-type Linking Finger Ring* by Blake, deCourcy, and Himber, and in *Magic With Finger Rings* edited by Jerry Mentzer.

In the 1940's ORSON WELLES featured an effect in his *Mercury Wonder Show* in which a *dozen* borrowed finger rings were linked into a long chain. The method used by Welles has not been published, and is known to only a handful of magicians.

LINKING PINS

A ROUTINE created by JERRY ANDRUS in which safety pins link and unlink in various ways (without being opened, of course); it is an excellent and highly visual close-up EFFECT.

It is based on a FAKE created by L. VOSBURGH LYONS and described by him under the title of *Slip Snap Spoof* in an early issue of *The Phoenix* magazine. The Lyons version was in turn inspired by a routine in which two ordinary safety pins unlinked. Called PIFF PAFF POUF, it is described in HILLIARD's *Greater Magic*.

Andrus has also written a book on the subject titled *Safety Pin Trix*.

More recent versions of this effect have been developed by SLYDINI and GAETAN BLOOM.

LINKING RING (Magazine)

The official organ of the INTERNATIONAL BROTHERHOOD OF MAGICIANS, founded in 1922. In 1986 it began its sixty-sixth volume of continuous publication (except for a brief hiatus during World War II).

In addition to its Parades of magical effects, the *Linking Ring* also carries reports from Rings (member groups), columns on current and historical subjects, news and advertising. It is published monthly.

LINKING RINGS

Often called the **Chinese linking rings**, this may be a genuine oriental feat; its origins are vague, but it was first introduced to western audiences by a touring troupe of Chinese performers.

The PLOT of the EFFECT is simple and direct; showing a number of solid steel rings (usually 8 or 10 inches in diameter), the performer is able to link and unlink them in seemingly impossible fashion. Spectators may examine the rings continuously throughout the ROUTINE without, of course, gaining a clue to how the feat is accomplished.

Early performers used as many as a dozen rings in their routines; that of DAVID P. ABBOTT, described in his *Book Of Mysteries*, requires *fourteen*. For many years the "standard" set of rings consisted of eight in all—a chain of two, a chain of three, two singles and a key ring—and most routines in print assume the use of this set.

In the 1950's DAI VERNON released his **Symphony of the Rings** routine, which used only six rings; a few years prior, in 1948, BILLY MCCOMB had described his five-ring routine in ABRACADABRA magazine. JAY MARSHALL also created a comedy routine using

An interesting variation of the *Linking Rings*; Mike Caveney performs his *Linking Coat Hangers*

The *Linking Rings*, as performed by Marco of the Le Grand David company

only five. British performer AL KORAN developed a three-ring routine; a later routine with three rings created by RICHARD ROSS was a central part of his prize-winning act (Ross now does a routine in which a fourth ring is briefly used). A routine using only two rings is currently featured by JONATHAN NEAL BROWN.

These latter routines—using three rings or less—are usually done silently to music, and the rings are never passed for examination. Some critics, notably GOODLIFFE, argued that such routines, visually pretty though they might be, could have little real magic content since the rings were never proved solid by examination; others feel that the visual nature of the linking and unlinking obviates the necessity for this.

The literature of the **linking rings** is sizable; routines for the effect are in nearly every basic book of conjuring. Separately published routines include (in addition to the DAI VERNON and ROSS routines mentioned above) those by JACK MILLER and L.L. IRELAND among many others. A notable work on the subject is DARIEL FITZKEE's *Rings In Your Fingers*;

also important is *The Odin Count* of CLAUDIUS ODIN, edited by VICTOR FARELLI.

LINKING ROPES

A variant of the LINKING RINGS in which lengths of rope tied into loops link and unlink in various ways; the basic ROUTINE was invented by E.J. MOORE.

A very straightforward version of this EFFECT was marketed by PETER WARLOCK under the title **Red and White Ropes**.

LION'S BRIDE

This title in current usage is applied to an ILLUSION in which a woman is placed inside a large metal cage which is then covered with a decorative cloth; when the cloth is removed she has vanished, and in her place is a full-grown lion.

The title comes from an earlier illusion invented by LAFAYETTE, involving a complicated TRANSPOSITION sequence.

The illusion is sometimes called **lady to lion**.

Mark Kalin presenting the modern version of the *Lion's Bride* (*photo courtesy GENII Magazine*).

LIPPINCOTT COIN BOX

Invented by Jack Lippincott; a small wooden box, fitted with a hasp which may be secured with a small padlock, into which a coin may be secretly introduced. Most models will take coins up to half-dollar size.

The Lippincott Box may be used by itself, or as the innermost of a NEST OF BOXES. It may have been inspired by the WATCH BOX.

LIQUID EFFECTS

Those effects which have the PRODUCTION, VANISH or change of liquids as their primary feature.
See BAR ACT; FOO CAN; INEXHAUSTIBLE BOTTLE; LOTA BOWL; MILK PITCHER; WINE AND WATER.

LIVESTOCK

See ANIMAL MAGIC.

LIVING AND DEAD TEST

A feat of MENTALISM (first presented as a legitimate psychic test by fraudulent MEDIUMS) in which a spectator writes a number of names, one of which is that of a deceased friend or family member. The performer is able to discern which is the "dead name"; in some forms of the EFFECT the names are not shown to the performer, who is able to discern and reveal the name as a feat of DIVINATION.

Since—except as a recreation of a medium's demonstration—the test as described is not really appropriate for entertainment—most modern performers alter the presentation to discern between the name of a friend and those of strangers, etc., thus transforming it into a feat of MENTAL MAGIC.

An excellent collection of methods for this effect is TERAL GARRETT's *26 Living And Dead Tests.*

LOAD

To secretly place an object into or onto a location; as, to load a ball under a cup, or to load palmed cards onto a deck.

Also, the object or objects thus loaded.

LOAD CHAMBER

The area in a PRODUCTION device where the items to be produced are hidden, for example, the black central cylinder in a SQUARE CIRCLE.

LOADED DICE

Special dice weighted to consistently bring one face to the top; used for a number FORCE. These dice are, of course, adapted from those used in fraudulent gambling, but are far more heavily weighted; dice used in games are usually weighted to increase probabilities, but for a forcing procedure used in magic a certainty is required.

Dice weighted this strongly, however, can be very obvious in operation; their use as a forcing device is generally inadvisable.

LOCATION

Any method of finding a selected card which has been returned to the deck. Locations may be made by means of a CRIMP, DIVIDED DECK, KEY CARD, ONE-WAY DECK or many other methods.

LOCATOR CARD

See KEY CARD.

LONG CARD

A card fractionally longer than the rest of the deck, often used as a KEY CARD. In actuality this card is of normal length and the rest of the deck is trimmed slightly short.
See SHORT CARD; KEY CARD.

LONG TACK SAM (1885-1961)

Chinese magician and acrobat who performed in many parts of the world, the greater part of his career being in the United States. He was noted for his PRODUCTION of a goldfish bowl while performing a backward somersault!

LOOMIS, DENNIS (b. 1944)

Performer who has toured throughout the U.S., appearing in varied venues with a FULL EVENING SHOW featuring ILLUSION effects.

He is the author of the *Loomis Cups And Balls Routine* and *The Dennis Loomis Doll's House.*

LOOP

Circle of thread, wire, monofilament or gut line by which an object can be suspended. A loop may be attached (for example) to a DYE TUBE; with the loop over the thumb, the **dye tube** can hang suspended behind the hand. If the hand holds a sheet of paper, the

Long Tack Sam (*The Mulholland Library of Conjuring & the Allied Arts, Los Angeles, California*)

Dennis Loomis

looped item can hang behind the paper and thus both hands can be shown empty. This is the general methodology of the CHINESE EGG BAG.

Loops are used both on items which are unseen by the audience (such as the **dye tube** previously mentioned, or a DOVE HARNESS), or visible objects, for example, a BILLIARD BALL.

LORAYNE, HARRY (b. ca. 1930)

Performer who began his career doing CLOSE-UP MAGIC, appearing in nightclubs in the New York area. He then developed a memory act, performed with the assistance of wife Renee, in which he demonstrated instantaneous memorization of a deck of cards and many other feats. In addition to playing club dates and many other venues, he starred in two series of television shows based on his work. He is now internationally known as the foremost expert on MNEMONICS in the world, and has been brought in by many corporations to teach his systems; clients include General Electric, U.S. Steel, National Cash Register, Mobil Oil, Westinghouse, and many more.

His books on memory and mental techniques (several of which are best-sellers) include *How To Develop A Super-Power Memory, Secrets Of Mind Power,*

Harry Lorayne

Instant Mind Power, Miracle Math, Remembering People, Good Memory-Good Student, Good Memory-Successful Student, Memory Isometrics Course and (with Jerry Lucas) *The Memory Book.*

Within magic, he has invented countless effects and techniques which have appeared in a number of magic periodicals; he is the editor of the monthly magazine *Apocalypse,* and has also written several books. These include *Afterthoughts, Best Of Friends* (two volumes), *Close-up Card Magic, Deck-Sterity, The Epitome Location, My Favorite Card Tricks, Personal Secrets, Reputation Makers* and several others. He also was the editor for the final volume of the TARBELL COURSE IN MAGIC.

LORRAINE, SID (b. 1905)

Born in Britain, he emigrated to Canada. A commercial artist by profession, he has originated a number of EFFECTs, including **Snakes Alive, The Liquor Cards, Thumb Fun**, and many others, and is the inventor of the SLOP SHUFFLE. He has written a column for LINKING RING Magazine and is currently the book and effect reviewer for the New TOPS Magazine.

He is noted for his books on PATTER and comedy material, which include *Gags Routines And Patter, Patter, More Patter, Patter Pointers, Reference File, The Early Stuff,* and *Sid Lorraine's Scrap Book.*

He is a recipient of the Best Lecturer and Literary Fellowship awards from the ACADEMY OF MAGICAL ARTS.

LOST

Said of a selected card which has been returned to the deck, which has then been shuffled—the location of the card being unknown to the spectator and presumably the performer.

LOST ACE

An effect believed to be the invention of HOFZINSER, which begins with a chosen card being lost in the deck; the four Aces are shown in a fan, and the one corresponding in suit to the selected card vanishes, being replaced by the selected card. The lost Ace is found face-up in the face-down deck.

Many versions and variations of this effect have been published, notably a version by JACK AVIS in *Epilogue* which also introduced the SIVA COUNT.

LOST ACE PROBLEM

A card PROBLEM within the procedure of the LOST ACE effect—the problem in question being the determination of the proper procedure required to accomplish the effect when the exact order of the Aces is not known to the performer.

Since this has virtually nothing to do with the Lost Ace effect as perceived by a lay spectator, it is a purely academic problem; nevertheless, considerable effort has been expending in devising solutions for it.

LOTA BOWL

Originally, a brass vessel not unlike a spittoon in appearance; the water in it is emptied into a container, the bowl being completely inverted for this, yet a few moments later more water has appeared in the bowl. This process can be repeated several times.

The bowl is separated into two compartments by a central cylindrical wall; the flow of liquid into the central compartment from which it is poured is controlled by opening a small airhole.

Modern versions of the **lota bowl** are made of various metals, alloys and plastics, and come in a variety of shapes.

The **lota bowl** is believed to be of East Indian origin; however, a recent discovery indicates it may have been independently invented by Peruvian pre-Columbian cultures several centuries ago. There is considerable disagreement as to whether the artifact on which this supposition is based is in fact a lota-type bowl.

LOWE, FRED (?-1972)

British amateur, latterly a dealer, noted for the excellent craftsmanship of his marketed EFFECTs and

Fred Lowe (*photo courtesy GENII Magazine*)

for the high quality of the ROUTINEs he created, primarily in the field of COIN MAGIC. He is also noted as the creator of **Christened Reverse**, the progenitor of the popular card effect FRED.

In addition to his marketed items, he contributed effects to THE GEN, ABRA, PENTAGRAM and other magazines.

LOYD (1897-1968)

Born E. LLoyd Enochs; creator of a number of effects, including a popular version of the MULTIPLYING CANDLES. He was also the author of *Loyd's Master Manipulation Of Thimbles* and of a long-running GENII Magazine column titled *Loyd's Scrapbook*.

LUMINOUS PAINT

A phosphorescent paint which will glow in the dark after being exposed to bright light; this is usually accomplished by exposure to a light of average intensity for several minutes, but it may also be done quickly by exposure to a high-intensity photoflash device of either the electric or electronic variety.

Luminous paint is most often used in creating ghostly EFFECTs for SPOOK SHOWS and SEANCE demonstrations; it can, however, also be employed to mark stage equipment and positions to facilitate moves during a BLACKOUT.

LUMINOUS READERS

A variety of MARKED DECK which does not, despite the title, employ luminous paint; instead, a special ink is used to mark the back of the cards. Such marks can be seen with the aid of a pair of eyeglasses equipped with red-tinted lenses.

Unless prepared by an expert such decks are rarely practical, and are seldom used either by magicians or gamblers; their existence has, however, provided the PLOT for various comedy card EFFECTs.

This principle is used by JOHN CORNELIUS in his currently marketed **Dream Deck**; Cornelius has, however, developed a subtle and practical way of employing the principle, which does not require the use of special eyeglasses or lenses.

LUND, ROBERT (b. ?)

A professional writer for automotive publications for many years, he also wrote a long running and highly regarded column in ABRA Magazine.

He is noted both as a collector and for his creation of the American Museum Of Magic in Marshall, Michigan. The museum houses not only poster and apparatus but documentary information on thousands of magicians.

LUPO, VITO (b. 1962)

Performer who began his professional career (after winning several prizes for his ACT) appearing with RICHIARDI in New York. He then went to FISM, where (with his MIME-themed act) he became the first U.S. contestant to win the First Place award for Stage Magic.

Lupo then performed throughout Europe, including The Crazy Horse in Paris; he has since toured Japan, Italy, Austria, Britain, and Canada.

LUSTIG, DAVID J. (1893-1977)

Best-known as technical advisor to JOSEPH DUNNINGER, for whom he worked many years; Lustig devised many of the "brain-buster" tests with which Dunninger astounded his radio and television audiences.

Later in his career Lustig worked as a publicity and exploitation specialist for Columbia Pictures; in this capacity he set up tours, interviews and press conferences for several motion picture actors and actresses.

Vito Lupo with his FISM trophy (*photo courtesy GENII Magazine*)

Under the pen name of *La Vellma* he wrote a number of books, including *Vaudeville Mind Reading*, *Vaudeville Budget*, *Vaudeville Ventriloquism*, and *Vaudeville Magic*; also (under his own name) *Dunninger's Power By Hypnotism*.

LYCEUM

Associations which provided educational presentations and entertainments, usually in lecture halls, theaters or other auditoriums during the winter months. They were, in fact, the winter equivalent of CHAUTAUQUA.

LYLE, CECIL (1892-1955)

Born in Britain; he performed a highly original ILLUSION act as Magical Milliner. Among its features were the magical decoration of a number of hats, the appearance of several women in large hatboxes, and the vanish of a gramophone.

Lyle toured throughout the British Isles on the variety circuits, and also appeared at ST. GEORGE'S HALL; he later toured in Australia. Near the end of his career he undertook a world tour, passing through South Africa, India, and many other countries.

He is noted as the inventor of many EFFECTs, of which perhaps the best known is the PAPER HAT.

LYNN, DR. (ca. 1840-ca. 1900)

Born Hugh Simmons in Britain; he toured through several countries, including China, Japan, Australia and the U.S., finally returning to Britain where he performed at EGYPTIAN HALL.

Lynn was noted for his showmanship; among the EFFECTs he featured were his own creation of PALINGENESIA as well as a FLOWER GROWTH, a SUSPENSION, and the BASKET TRICK.

After some years in Britain he made another tour of the U.S., and also toured India. Returning to Britain he continued to perform, but with less success than formerly; he died in straitened circumstances around the turn of the century.

LYONS, L. VOSBURGH (1892-1976)

Physician by profession; noted for his invention of several magical effects and ingenious puzzles, many of which appeared in the JINX and PHOENIX Magazines, as well as many other publications.

LYONS, P. HOWARD (1927-1976)

Born in Canada; known in magic for his editorship of *Ibidem*, a periodical which appeared for several years on an erratic schedule. His magazine was noted for its highly specialized material, particularly in the field of card magic; methodologies were discussed in its pages which did not come into popular use until several years later.

The magazine was also noted for its wonderful cover illustrations by Lyons' wife, Pat Patterson Lyons.

MACCARTHY, E. BRIAN (1910-1968)

British amateur noted for his excellent SLEIGHT-OF-HAND work, including his versions of the MULTIPLYING BILLIARD BALLS and the CUPS AND BALLS, and many original effects.

His approach is described in his book *Sleights Supreme*.

MACDONALD ACES

A popular ROUTINE for the FOUR-ACES effect using DOUBLE-FACE cards, devised by Mac MacDonald; variants on the basic routine have been developed by DAI VERNON, JOHN THOMPSON, PHIL GOLDSTEIN and many others.

The use of double-face cards in the Four Ace routine is of considerable age; HOFZINSER's version (titled "The Four Kings") is described in *Hofzinser's Card Conjuring*.

MACMILLAN, RON (b. ?)

British performer specializing in SLEIGHT-OF-HAND and manipulative magic, with which he created a highly successful act—in 1957 he was the winner of the British Ring Shield at the British I.B.M. convention.

His work is described in his *Modern Art Of Coin Manipulation* and in *Symphony Of The Spheres* (on BILLIARD BALL manipulation) by LEWIS GANSON.

He is the operator of London's INTERNATIONAL MAGIC STUDIO.

MAGIC BAR

See BAR ACT.

MAGIC CASTLE

Located in Hollywood, California, it is the official clubhouse for the ACADEMY OF MAGICAL ARTS, a private club founded by MILT LARSEN and WILLIAM W. LARSEN, JR.

The Castle opened its doors in 1963 after an elaborate redecoration and alteration which transformed it from its previous existence as a private dwelling (known as the Lane Mansion). Over the years it has expanded to contain a number of showrooms—The Close-up Room, the Parlor Of Prestidigitation, the Pub Museum and the Palace Of Mystery—as well as several bars, a multiroomed dining area, and a magicians-only library. Other rooms include the Robert-Houdin Museum (containing AUTOMATA and other machines), Irma's Room (where an invisible pianist plays requests), and the Houdini Seance Room (where twelve guests are served a special dinner, after which the MEDIUM enters and conducts a SEANCE in which the spirit of HOUDINI apparently returns—twice nightly "for entertainment only").

There are usually a minimum of six performers on the bill for the various show areas, and the lineup changes each week.

See ACADEMY OF MAGICAL ARTS.

MAGIC CIRCLE, THE

Magical society founded in England in 1905; most of the leading lights in British magic are members. There are three degrees of membership: Member of the Magic Circle, Associate of the Inner Magic Circle, and Member of the Inner Magic Circle.

The society is located in London; the monthly magazine is *The Magic Circular*.

In recent years the Circle has been the object of some controversy due to its refusal to admit women as members—a policy which has been a source of embarrassment to many people both within the Circle and in the larger British magic community.

MAGIC CIRCULAR

The monthly periodical of the MAGIC CIRCLE; begun in June 1906, it is now the longest running publication devoted to magic. Among its many editors have been NEVIL MASKELYNE and S.W. CLARKE; it is now edited by John Young.

In addition to organizational news, the *Magic Circular* has carried a number of articles on general, technical and historical subjects, as well as descriptions of a great number of EFFECTs.

Several supplements were also published by the *Magic Circular*; these were most often transcriptions of lectures given at the Circle clubrooms, and were included with the magazine but separately bound.

MAGIC HANDS

Magic dealer and manufacturing company located in Herrenberg, Germany; founded in 1973 by MANFRED THUMM.

In addition to a wide range of products, the company is also known for its yearly convention, first held in 1978, called The Magic Hands Fachkongresse.

MAGICIAN

A practitioner of occult arts and possessor of supernatural powers; specifically, a sorcerer who uses rituals and ceremonies. The term is derived from the ancient Persian sect of the Magi (*see* MAGUS).

The term is now most often applied to a stage performer who simulates a magician for purposes of entertainment.

MAGICIAN'S CHOICE

See EQUIVOQUE.

MAGICIAN'S DREAM

A kind of MECHANICAL DECK invented by AUDLEY WALSH which severely limits the spectator's choice; Walsh first described the deck in the JINX Magazine, and it was later reprinted in *Annemann's Practical Mental Effects*. It operates on the MULTIPLE-BANK principle.

In recent years decks of this type have been called KORAN DECKS after their use was popularized by AL

KORAN, who did not claim to have invented the principle. The basic principle was created by Edward Bagshawe and, later, was further developed by Walsh.

MAGICIAN'S WAX

A specially formulated wax which can be used to adhere two objects together, but will allow them to be separated cleanly. For most purposes, a good grade of beeswax, softened with turpentine or a similar thinning agent if necessary, will work as well.

MAGICIAN VS. GAMBLER

Card ROUTINE done as a STORY EFFECT in which a magician is challenged by a gambler to cut four cards of like value; the magician succeeds on the first three (dealing them face down to the table in turn) but fails on the fourth. When the cards on the table are turned over, however, they have changed to match the value of the fourth card. The original cards are then produced from the performer's pockets.

The original PLOT for this effect was developed by DR. JACOB DALEY; a routine for it was developed by PAUL LE PAUL and is described in his *The Card Magic Of Le Paul*. An excellent modern version is that of HARRY LORAYNE, described by him in *Personal Secrets*.

MAGICIENNE

A female MAGICIAN; therefore, by extension, a female stage performer who simulates magical powers and abilities.

MAGIC, INC.

Manufacturing and publishing company located in Chicago; successor to the firm founded by L. L. IRELAND. It is owned, managed and operated by JAY MARSHALL and FRANCES (Ireland) MARSHALL. In addition to over-the-counter sales there is a large volume of mail-order business, and the company publishes several different catalogues of books and effects.

MAGIC MAN, THE

A stage musical production with magic first produced in 1975 in Chicago, Illinois; it is noted as being the debut vehicle for DAVID COPPERFIELD.

MAGIC NAPOLEONS

See NAPOLEONS.

MAGIC SHOW, THE

Broadway musical/magical production starring DOUG HENNING, which opened in New York City in 1974; its magical content was based on an earlier show called *Spellbound*, created and produced by Henning in Canada. *The Magic Show* was quite successful, and was of great importance in establishing Henning as a major performer.

MAGIC SQUARE

An ancient mathematical recreation consisting of a square divided into cells of equal rows and columns, each cell containing a different number; the numbers in any horizontal, vertical or diagonal row being added, they will produce identical totals.

Performers have often presented the construction of such a square for any given number as a demonstration of mind power and/or memory, often in combination with the memorization of a list of called-out objects. Presentations and techniques for such routines are described in ORVILLE MEYER's *Magic Square and Master Memory Demonstration*, HARRY LORAYNE's *Reputation Makers*, and CRAIGE SNADER's *Mind Square*.

General information on magic squares can be found in the relevant chapters of HILLIARD's *Greater Magic* and SIMON's *Mathematical Magic*, and in many books on recreational mathematics.

An excellent book-length discussion of the subject is *The Wonders Of Magic Squares* by Jim Moran.

MAGIC WAND, THE (Magazine)

British magic magazine begun as a monthly by George Munro in 1910; after a decade it became a quarterly and continued this schedule until it ceased publication in 1958. For over thirty years it was edited by GEORGE JOHNSON, who was succeeded by GEORGE ARMSTRONG for the final thirteen years of its run.

The Magic Wand featured not only excellent magic—in some cases entire magic books were run in serial form—but also many articles on the history of magic.

MAGIC WELDING

Separate metal links are shown by the performer; poured into a glass or other container, they are magically fused into a single length of chain.

This effect, invented by LOUIS NIKOLA, can be accomplished by any number of switching devices; a CHANGING TRAY is usually employed.

MAGIC WORD

Within occultism, a "word of power" or phrase, utterance of which is supposed to bring about magical effects. For a time stage performers emulated this procedure, the most common word for this purpose being *abracadabra*; few modern-day performers use magic words.

An amusing but not unusual lapse is for a performer to say, "We utter the magic words—and the ball vanishes!" The action occurs, but the performer has not actually uttered any magic words, merely stated his intention of so doing.

See ABRACADABRA; HOCUS POCUS; PRESTO.

MAGIGALS

Organization for female magical performers, founded fifty years ago by FRANCES MARSHALL (then Frances Ireland). The majority of its membership is based in the U.S.

MAGIGRAM (Magazine)

House organ of SUPREME MAGIC CO.; begun in 1966, it is edited by KEN DE COURCY. In addition to the many effects described in its pages, it has run a number of columns by ALAN KENNAUGH, BILLY MCCOMB, GEORGE JOHNSTONE, HAROLD TAYLOR, HARRY STANLEY, and many others.

MAGITAIN

A neologism coined by John McArdle to indicate magic performed as entertainment, rather than the occult connotation; the word has not come into common usage.

MAGNET COINS

Coins which have been FAKED by the insertion of small but powerful magnets (usually of the cobalt-samarium/rare earth variety). Since they will cling to any ferrous metal surface, some very baffling effects can be created with their aid.

Two books devoted entirely to this subject, both by Arthur and Frederick Kraft, are *Coin Magnetrix* and *Magneticoins*.

MAGNETIC COIN

Coin made of a ferrous metal which will be attracted by a magnet, or coin of non-ferrous metal which has been FAKED by the addition of a ferrous core; these latter are sometimes called SHIM coins.

No U.S. coin in current circulation is magnetic (with the exception of the 1943 penny); magnetic coins in some denominations are available from magic dealers.

In conjunction with magnets concealed within the performer's clothing or in variant versions of the OKITO BOX, magnetic coins can be used for a wide variety of EFFECTs. With a magnet in a trouser pocket, for example, the performer can duplicate many of the handlings possible with a HOOK COIN. *See MagnetiCoins*, by Frederick and Arthur Kraft.

See also MAGNET COINS.

MAGNETIZED CARDS

An EFFECT in which a number of playing cards are made to cling to the hand as though by a strange form of magnetism.

There are many methods to accomplish this feat, ranging from a toothpick beneath a finger ring (so that cards may be wedged between the toothpick and the fingers), to loops of THREAD, to techniques using no FAKES or GIMMICKS at all.

See DUAL CONTROL.

MAGUS

A priest of the ancient Persian religion of Zoroastrianism; more generally, any skilled occultist or sorcerer.

In modern times the term has been used to denote the stage performer, often as a convenient shorter word and sometimes ironically. It should be noted that Magi is the plural of Magus and should not be used when the singular form is intended.

MAHATMA

First U.S. magic magazine; founded by FRANCIS J. MARTINKA, it ran from 1897 to 1906; among its owners during this brief span were *George Little, Walter Peterkin* and FRANK DUCROT.

The name comes from the Sanskrit word meaning *Adept* or *Master*.

MAHENDRA, M.S. (?-1970)

Born Frank B. Sterling, at various times he performed magic and illusion, but for the most part specialized in MENTALISM and MENTAL MAGIC.

Among his books are *He Can't Read My Mind* (an adaptation of his routine for the Miracle Divination which appeared in HILLIARD's *Greater Magic*), *Mahendra's Mind Reading Dope*, and *Amazing Card Miracles* (a revised version of *Modern Card Miracles* which had been written with HUGH JOHNSTON).

MAILBAG ESCAPE

See BAG ESCAPE.

MAJA

Name used fancifully by some writers to denote the "Goddess Of Magic"; no such deity appears in the religious or mythological pantheons of the world.

Gods and Goddesses are by their very nature presumed to have magical powers; of these, the one most likely to be considered the *Goddess Of Magic* is ISIS.

MAJAX, GERARD (b. ?)

Highly successful French performer who has performed in a variety of venues, including his own national television show. Along with his magic (often with a comedy slant), Majax performs a PICKPOCKET ACT and does GAMBLING DEMONSTRATIONs.

In addition to *Magie Des Des* (on general magic) and a book on THIMBLE MAGIC, he has written two books for the lay public: *The Pickpockets* and *Secrets Of The Card Sharps*—both are highly entertaining reading and somewhat exaggerated regarding actual techniques.

MALDO, SENOR (1896-1960)

Born Abel Maldonado, he toured the southwestern U.S. for many years, and made a number of appearances for the USO. He was known for his **Burial Alive** publicity stunt, a variation on the COFFIN TEST; he also invented a number of items which were manufactured by THAYER.

MALINI, MAX (1873-1942)

Born Max Breit in Poland, he came to the U.S. as a child; in his teen years he performed as an acrobat before turning to magic. He became a BUSKER and saloon performer, learning to work under almost any conditions.

As a young man, Malini began to perform at private parties; his reputation grew rapidly, and in the course of his career he performed for several heads of state—including U.S. presidents as well as British and European Royalty. His odd and colorful personality, combined with his truly amazing magic, made him a favorite of the rich and celebrated.

Malini's trademark effect was the PRODUCTION of a large object under a borrowed hat; sometimes this would be a brick or paving stone, but often it was a block of ice. Many well-informed magicians were baffled by Malini's handling of this feat.

His work is described in *Malini And His Magic* by DAI VERNON.

MANACLE BOARD VANISH

A startling ILLUSION in which an ASSISTANT is manacled to a board which is then set into a tilted horizontal frame; there is a flash and puff of smoke and the board—*empty*—drops from the frame to the floor. The effect is created through sophisticated illusion mechanics allied with the MIRROR PRINCIPLE. It is described under the title *A Vanish In Mid-Air* in *Houdini On Magic* (edited by WALTER B. GIBSON and Morris N. Young.

WILLIAM ELLSWORTH ROBINSON is believed to have invented this illusion, which has no official title; it has been known as **At a tent in the desert** (from the tent in which the APPARATUS is set) and, erroneously, as STROBEIKA.

The mechanical working of this illusion must be precise in order to create a convincing effect; because of this, it has never been practical for a touring performer, and it is probable that no more than one or two have ever been built. Many illusion engineers believe that the **Manacle Board Vanish** cannot be constructed in a fashion that will make it a deceptive and workable illusion.

MANDRAKE (b. ca. 1910)

Born Leon Mandrake in Canada, he began his career with varied duties in a carnival, and later traveled as an ASSISTANT with the Ralph Richards touring magic show.

Developing his own FULL-EVENING SHOW and featuring a large cast (his first wife, Narda, was his chief assistant) and a number of spectacular ILLUSIONS, he toured extensively in the U.S. and Canada, appearing in every major theater in both countries. He had been performing for well over a decade as Mandrake The Magician when the comic strip of that title by Lee Falk & Phil Davis began to appear in newspapers, the title character bearing a strong resemblance to the real-life performer.

Mandrake later starred in two television shows, *Bag Of Tricks* and *Alexander The Great*—the latter featuring MENTAL MAGIC. At this time he also began appearing in hotels and nightclubs. Still later, with wife and partner *Velvet*, he made an extensive tour of the Orient. He was also a featured performer at the 1974 World's Fair.

He continues to perform, appearing at universities and colleges throughout Canada.

He is a recipient of the Performing Fellowship from the ACADEMY OF MAGICAL ARTS.

Mandrake the Magician (Leon Mandrake), 1939

MANGO TREE GROWTH

A traditional EFFECT of the street magicians of India, in which a seed placed in a mound of earth, and briefly concealed by a cloth, grows in stages to a height of a few feet.

It is thoroughly described in EDDIE JOSEPH's *Magic And Mysteries Of India*, Major L. H. Branson's *Indian Conjuring*, and *Oriental Magic And Conjuring* by Will Ayling and S. H. SHARPE.

MANIPULATION

EFFECTs performed by means of SLEIGHT OF HAND; also FLOURISHes. The term is often used to imply an absence of GIMMICK or FAKE, but this is by no means an inviolable rule.

MANIPULATOR

Performer whose ACT is wholly or largely based in SLEIGHT OF HAND magic. The term usually (but not always) implies a stage performer.

MANUEL (1883-1934)

Born Manuel R. Thomas; featuring COIN MAGIC, he performed for many years in vaudeville as Manuel,

Master Of The Mighty Dollar. He was thought by some observers to be the equal and possibly the superior of T. NELSON DOWNS at coin manipulation.

MARCONICK (b. ?)

Born Heinz Nikolas Stolk in Holland, he is a performer of long professional experience whose act has won several awards—including two First Place trophies (for manipulation and general magic) at FISM Congresses.

In addition to performing he has created and marketed a number of EFFECTs, including **silken bombshell, prisoner silk, flying silks, silken flash**, and dozens of others.

Many of his effects are described in his *The Magic Of Marconick* and in his Original Magic series.

MARDONI (1904-1987)

Born Clayton Hines; he began his performing career in CHAUTAUQUA, first by himself and then with wife and partner Louise, with whom he developed a TWO-PERSON MENTAL ACT. As Mardoni And Louise, they toured through several states, featuring magic, mindreading, and ESCAPES.

After several years of touring, playing school assemblies, universities, nightclubs and other venues, they were booked into the famed Los Angeles Trocadero; highly successful, they began appearing at the best nightclubs throughout the country.

During World War II they made several USO and War Bond tours. Later they resumed their appearances in nightclubs, also working on cruise ships and in the trade show field.

They received a number of honors, including election to the S.A.M. Hall Of Fame and the Performing Fellowship of the ACADEMY OF MAGICAL ARTS.

MARGERY (1886-1941)

Nickname of Mina Crandon, a MEDIUM who was investigated by HOUDINI when she attempted to win the *Scientific American Magazine* prize (which was to be awarded for the demonstrating of psychic phenomena under strict scientific controls).

The Margery SEANCES became quite famous and have been the subject of a number of books both pro and con, and the controversy continues. In his biography of Houdini, William Lindsay Gresham recounted a confession of Houdini's assistant James Collins, who admitted to planting evidence of fraud on Margery's part; this story was later refuted by MILBOURNE CHRISTOPHER in his own biography of Houdini, in which he stated that the source of the story, FRED KEATING, was angered at Houdini's assessment of him as incompetent at psychic investigation. It appears, however, that at the time Keating spoke with Gresham he was unaware of the Houdini comment, and it is unlikely that the questions regarding this accusation, and Margery's mediumship, will ever be completely resolved. It is probable that she was a fraud—but that can only be a theory, since the evidence for both sides of the argument seems to have been created in questionable ways.

MARK

In theatrical terminology, to make an indication on the stage surface of where a PROP is to be placed; this is most often done with strips of tape.

Marking of positions for many ILLUSIONS (particularly those using the MIRROR or SPHINX principle) is absolutely essential. If several EFFECTs require **Marks**, tapes of different colors may be used in a pre-set sequence; alternatively, wide-nibbed felt pens may be used to color-code the strips.

If a prop must be set on a totally dark stage, luminous tape should be used—not only to **Mark** an item's position, but also to indicate safe paths to and from the stage area.

MARKED DECK

Of all prepared decks, the marked deck is the one best-known to the general public; within magic, partly because of this suspicion, such decks are very little used.

Marking systems can be very simple—to discern red cards from black or high values from low—or very complex; an example of the latter is Deland's DOLLAR DECK, the back of which reveals not only its own identity but the position of any card in the deck, the identity of the preceding card, and the number of cards in a cut-off packet!

For simple systems, the performer may select decks from two different print runs, and find the back coloring noticeably different in intensity; he then makes up a complete deck from these two, sorting as required.

A deck used far more often by crooked gamblers than magicians is the SORT-EDGE; cards from the BEE diamond-pattern back are sorted by the presence of full or half-diamonds at top and side edges. Even here, such a deck will usually only indicate within a range of values, and thus is of little use for magical purposes.

Decks marked for suit and value are available through magic dealers and some gambling supply houses. The best such decks, however, are meticulously crafted and only available through the magic "underground."

As with other MECHANICAL DECKs, the reason marked decks are so rarely employed by performers is that such decks make possible few feats that can't be accomplished without them. Indeed, often the performer must make a point of proving he isn't using them.

One of the best marked decks created specifically for magical performance is that of TED LESLEY; it may be read easily with one brief glance.

See also DAUB; MECHANICAL DECKS; LUMINOUS READERS.

MARLO, ED (b. 1913)

Born Edward Malkowski, Marlo is one of the most influential figures in the history of modern card magic. A tool and die worker by trade, he nevertheless has found time to develop many entirely new concepts with cards.

In addition to privately circulated (and much-prized) manuscripts, and many contributions to magazines, he has written a large number of books, including *Acrobatic Cards, Action Palm, Card Fan Productions, The Cardician, Estimation, Faro Shuffle, Faro Notes, Multiple Shift, Seconds Centers and Bottoms* and *The Side Steal*—these and many others devoted entirely to cards, some of them being "chapters" in his *Revolutionary Card Technique* series.

Other books include *Coining Magic* (on, of course, COIN MAGIC), and *Shoot The Works* (magic with dice, including an excellent exposition of DICE STACKING).

He is the recipient of the first Creative Fellowship awarded by the ACADEMY OF MAGICAL ARTS.

MARSHALL, FRANCES (b. 1910)

For many years the wife and partner of L. L. IRELAND, she operated the business after his death. The business was later renamed MAGIC, INC., and she continues to operate it with husband JAY MARSHALL. She was a professional performer for many years, specializing in private parties and CHILDREN'S MAGIC.

In 1938 she founded MAGIGALS and was the first editor of its magazine. For several years she has written a column for the LINKING RING Magazine titled *Around Chicago With Frances*; she has also contributed numerous articles to other publications.

She is the author of *You Don't Have To Be Crazy, With Frances In Magicland, Kid Stuff* (five volumes), *The Success Book* (three volumes), *How To Sell By Magic, Those Beautiful Dames*, and many others.

MARSHALL, HORACE (1902-1976)

Builder of magical APPARATUS and PROPs; particularly noted for his FEATHER FLOWER bouquets and effects. For many years the FULL-EVENING SHOW of HARRY BLACKSTONE SR. opened with the **garden of flowers** sequence created by Marshall, which concluded with the stage seemingly filled with magically-produced flowers and bouquets. The company is now operated by Richard Hughes.

MARSHALL, JAY (b. 1919)

Born James Ward Marshall; he began his career as a magician, later incorporating ventriloquism and TROUBLEWIT into his act. His routine with glove puppet Lefty is world famous, and he has appeared on countless television shows (including several times on *The Ed Sullivan* show). Marshall has performed all over the world as "one of the better cheaper acts" (his own description). He appeared in Broadway shows, including the final edition of the Ziegfeld Follies.

Jay Marshall (*photo courtesy GENII Magazine*)

He is also the operator, with wife FRANCES MARSHALL, of MAGIC, INC. A noted collector, Marshall is reputed to have one of the most complete collections of magic literature in existence.

Marshall took over the editorship of the PHOENIX from BRUCE ELLIOTT and saw the *New Phoenix* through four dozen issues.

He is the author of *TV Magic And You, How To Perform Instant Magic, Jaspernese Thumb Tie,* and other books.

MARTIN, JON (1882-1968)

Legendary British mechanic whose fine workmanship was highly prized by magicians. Among the many items he constructed were models of the VANISHING BIRD CAGE, the REEL, and a GIMMICK used in conjunction with the RISING CARDS.

MARTINEAU, FRANCIS B. (?-?)

Magic illustrator and writer best known for the *Encyclopedia Of Silk Magic* (three volumes)—for which he executed thousands of illustrations and also *hand-lettered* the entire text!

He is the author of *Victory Bouquet*, which describes the manufacture of PRODUCTION bouquets from tissue paper; other books include *Miracle Silk, Rope Hectic* and *Walsh Cane Routines.*

MARTIN, TOMMY (b. 1910)

Originally a journalist by profession, he took up professional performing after tutoring by MAX MALINI. He was immediately successful, playing at top hotels, theaters, and supper clubs throughout the U.S., including appearances at the Empire Room of Chicago's Palmer House Hotel and in New York's Radio City Music Hall. He later performed in Britain and Europe with equal success. Still later he worked as a theatrical agent.

Martin was most noted for his presentation of the EGG ON FAN.

MARTINKA, FRANCIS J. (1843-1924)

Founder (with his brother Anthony) of a well-known magic shop called The Magical Palace in New York City in 1885; it remained open under his management for over thirty years.

MARTYN, TOPPER (b. 1923)

Born Victor Martyn in Britain, he began his performing career with ENSA at the commencement of World War II; at first he was billed as *V.C. Martyn, the Eton*

Tommy Martin, a publicity sketch (*The Mulholland Library of Conjuring & the Allied Arts, Los Angeles, California*)

Topper Martyn (*photo courtesy GENII Magazine*)

Topper, but to avoid confusion with a similarly-named act the billing was changed to *Topper Martyn*.

His performances mixed magic with comedy juggling and ice-skating; in addition to many tours of British variety, he has appeared throughout Europe, the U.S., Central and South America, and Africa.

He is also noted as a collector of various items with magical or occult associations.

Among his awards are a First Prize for Comedy at FISM and Visiting Magician Of the Year from the ACADEMY OF MAGICAL ARTS.

His work is described in *Topper's Mad, Mad Magic* (edited by GENE ANDERSON).

MARVELLO, HARRY (1879-1967)

Born Harry Hutchison in Scotland, he began his career as a pupil and apprentice to LUDWIG DOBLER. Specializing in private performances at parties and social events, he soon became a leading society entertainer, and performed for Queen Victoria and many other members of the Royal Family.

After four years at the Portobello Resort in Scotland, in 1910 he began a career as a variety performer; for a time he did an ILLUSION act (the effects being created by WALTER CERRETTA JEANS). Later he performed as "Harry Styles, The Racing Knut" in an act primarily of card magic. Eventually he retired from performing and became a journalist.

MASKELYNE, JASPER (1902-1973)

Born in Britain; grandson of JOHN NEVIL MASKELYNE, and briefly associated with ST. GEORGE'S HALL before touring with his own show.

During World War II, he became part of a special British military unit which applied his magical knowledge to military problems; Maskelyne was able to devise ways to seemingly move entire cities and hide the Suez Canal, among many other feats. The story of his wartime service is described in his *Magic—Top Secret*; a somewhat fictionalized account of the same events is David Fisher's *The War Magician*.

In his later years Maskelyne retired to a farm in Africa.

Maskelyne is also the author of *White Magic*.

MASKELYNE, JOHN NEVIL (1839-1917)

Born in Britain; he became a performer through seeing a "spiritualistic" demonstration given by the DAVENPORT BROTHERS, where musical instruments were played while the two men were bound hand and foot. Maskelyne discovered their secret and gave a public performance to duplicate their effects; in this he was assisted by his friend GEORGE A. COOKE, with whom he then created a performing partnership.

In London, after a successful season in *St. James Hall*, Maskelyne took a short lease on another theater; it was EGYPTIAN HALL, and he was to remain there for over thirty years.

Later, in partnership with DAVID DEVANT, he repeated earlier successes at the new venue of ST. GEORGE'S HALL.

Twice Maskelyne was involved in newsworthy lawsuits. The first involved *Archdeacon Colley* (an ardent proponent of Spiritualism), who claimed Maskelyne had not precisely duplicated a medium's feat as his money-backed challenge had claimed he would; the second involved Maskelyne's attempt to stop two other performers from doing a BOX ESCAPE similar to one Maskelyne was then performing.

This latter suit failed when Maskelyne refused to reveal to the court the secret of the box. This secret may well have been that the box was perfectly ordinary, and the escape, performed in the WILL, THE WITCH, AND THE WATCHMAN routine, was effected by means of an ingenious cabinet in which the box was placed. (This would explain, incidentally, NEVIL MASKELYNE's odd presentational suggestions for the box escape in *Our Magic*—clearly intended to mislead magical readers as to the real solution).

Maskelyne wrote *Sharps And Flats* (on gambling), *Modern Spiritualism* (on fraudulent mediums), and *The Fraud Of Modern Theosophy Exposed*.

Father of NEVIL MASKELYNE.

MASKELYNE, NEVIL (1863-1924)

Born in Britain; son of JOHN NEVIL MASKELYNE, he performed and also worked as stage manager at EGYPTIAN HALL and ST. GEORGE'S HALL.

With DAVID DEVANT, he wrote *Our Magic*—a classic book on presentation; Maskelyne's portion of the book has been reissued separately as *Maskelyne On The Performance Of Magic*.

MASKELYNE, NOEL (?-1976)

Born in Britain; son of NEVIL MASKELYNE. Originally an electrical engineer, he joined the board of the Maskelyne company on the death of his father. He began his performing career in 1927, and appeared at ST. GEORGE'S HALL hundreds of times over the next few years, presenting several ILLUSION effects associated with the family.

MASKING

A concealment principle with varied applications, usually accomplished by covering the object to be hidden with a material matching that directly behind it from the audience's point of view. Thus a picture frame might contain a photograph, but if a piece of red velvet covered the photo, and the frame was hung on a red velvet easel, the frame would appear to be empty.

This principle is effectively employed in every kind of magic from the smallest of close-up effects to the largest stage ILLUSIONs.

MASKLYN YE MAGE

See ANDRUZZI, TONY.

MASON, ERIC (1921-1986)

Born in Britain, he was a commercial artist for over three decades before retiring to become a full-time painter whose work is highly regarded. During much of this time he was a skilled amateur performer and creator of magic, specializing in close-up effects. His illustrations appeared in a number of magic texts including PATRICK PAGE's *Big Book Of Magic* and Tony Corinda's *Thirteen Steps To Mentalism*.

Several of his ROUTINEs, including **Boon, Legacy, Magnifique** and **Card In Picture**, were marketed; many were published in Pabular magazine (to which he has also contributed many excellent illustrations and artwork), and most of his work has recently been collected in a well-produced book titled *Stuff*.

(When Mason's **Card In Picture** was being sold, the dealer noted that several purchasers seemed to know little about magic; it turned out that they were totally uninterested in the effect and were buying it simply to obtain the Mason artwork that was supplied with the apparatus!)

MASONI (?-1977)

Born Eric Mason in Britain; performer with long professional career which began before World War I. His first venture was a short act which played in variety venues; he later achieved a national reputation with his FULL-EVENING SHOW titled *Out Of The Hat*, which toured Britain for many years. In 1950 he acquired much of JASPER MASKELYNE's show and presented it as *Maskelyne's Mysteries*, later incorporating it into his own show.

A special feature of his show was the GIANT MEMORY demonstration performed by his wife Shan; at times the couple presented this demonstration alone as an act.

His approach is described in his book *Showmanship Out Of The Hat*.

Note: Masoni should not be confused with ERIC MASON.

MASSEY, EDWARD M. (1889-1964)

Creator of several ingenious EFFECTs, including the SQUEEZAWAY BLOCK, SILK CABBY, *Duplex Slate, Commando Screen, Cardagger, Sawing Through A Cigarette,* and many others.

He is the author of *New Original Magic*.

MASTER CARD

Term sometimes used to denote KEY CARD; also in HILLIARD's *Greater Magic*, it denotes (in Chapter VII) a SLICK CARD prepared to act as a Key Card.

MASTER MOVE

A card SLEIGHT invented by JOSEPH OVETTE in which the FACE CARD of the cut off upper half of the deck is moved secretly to the bottom as the upper half is replaced on the lower; sometimes erroneously called the **Kelly Bottom placement** because it is described under that name in Volume III of the *Tarbell Course In Magic.*

MASTER OF CEREMONIES

The person who introduces the performers in a variety entertainment or other presentation, and acts as the show's host.

See INTRO.

MATCHED SET-UP

A type of STACK in which the MATE CARDS are exactly twenty-six cards apart. If, for example, the Ace Of Spades is thirteenth from the top, the Ace Of Clubs will be thirty-ninth. Most CYCLICAL STACKs have this property; it is, however, a simple matter to create a **matched Set-up** in which, except for this relationship, the cards are in random order.

There have been many EFFECTS employing this principle, of which perhaps the best known is a CARD STAB routine called the **encore card stab**, invented by AL KORAN; it is described in a collection of Koran's effects titled *Professional Presentations* by Hugh Miller.

An excellent series of articles on this principle, written by Douglas Hood, appeared in ABRA Magazine; a number of EFFECTs using the matched Set-Up will be found in GLENN GRAVATT's *Treasure*

Trove Of Tricks. Others who have worked on this principle include ALEX ELMSLEY and ED MARLO.

MATCH TO FLOWER

A match, on being blown out, immediately changes to a flower; various commercially-available GIMMICKs are made to create this EFFECT. Some models use artificial flowers, while others use real flowers which may be detached from the gimmick and tossed out to an audience member.

MATE CARDS

Cards of the same *color* and *value*—for example, Six of Diamonds and Six of Hearts; Queen of Spades and Queen of Clubs; etc.

MATHEMATICAL MAGIC

EFFECTs which are achieved by application of mathematical principles, either *openly*—as in the case of the MAGIC SQUARE—or *secretly*—for example, the AFGHAN BANDS.

Many effective card tricks are based on mathematical principles; several of this kind may be found in JOHN SCARNE's *Scarne On Card Tricks* and FULVES' *Self Working Card Tricks.*

More general treatments of mathematical magic are FULVES' *Self Working Number Magic,* GARDNER's *Mathematics, Magic And Mystery, Mathemagic* by Royal V. Heath, *Math Miracles* by Wallace Lee, and SIMON's *Mathematical Magic.*

See SELF-WORKING.

MATRIX

Term currently used for SYMPATHETIC ROUTINES, specifically in reference to coin assemblies. The term comes from AL SCHNEIDER's popular and influential routine of that name, first published in GENII Magazine and later marketed.

MATTER THROUGH MATTER

Any EFFECT in which one solid object appears to pass through another without harm; see PENETRATION.

MAURICE, EDWARD (1897-1964)

Born John Edward Maurice in Britain; he was a highly respected performer who received a number of honors in his career, including the Gold Star of THE MAGIC CIRCLE. He was also a Gold Medallist of the British Magical Society.

He is the author of one of the very best books on magical performance, titled *Showmanship And Presentation,* and is also noted for giving ABRA magazine its name.

MAVEN, MAX (b. 1950)

Born Phil Goldstein; performer specializing in MENTAL MAGIC, primarily accomplished by his use of psychological principles. He has appeared throughout the U.S., and also in Britain, Japan, and many other countries. He has made several television appearances as a performer, and has also worked as an actor in network television shows.

Maven has also been a CONSULTANT to a number of performers, including LANCE BURTON, DAVID COPPERFIELD, DOUG HENNING, THE PENDRAGONS, JEFF MCBRIDE, HARRY BLACKSTONE JR., MARK WILSON and many others. He has served as a TECHNICAL ADVISOR for several television productions, and is a coordinator for many magic specials on Japan's NHK television network.

Under the *Phil Goldstein* name Maven has marketed several EFFECTs, including **Masque, Tearable, Isolation, Ice Dice** and others. He has contributed over one thousand effects to magic periodicals, and has also written a number of books. These include *Classic Tackler, Gallery, Majorminor, Silentwe, Thequal, Thunday, Doth,* and others.

He is a recipient of the Lecturer Of The Year award from the ACADEMY OF MAGICAL ARTS.

MAY, E. LESLIE (1901-1980)

Born in Scotland; officer in the British Army by profession. He was noted for the many EFFECTs he invented, primarily in the field of MENTAL MAGIC. He contributed to THE JINX, PENTAGRAM, MAGIC CIRCULAR, LINKING RING and many other magazines.

MAYETTE, ANDRE (1900-1978)

French magic dealer for many years, proprietor of a magic shop first established in 1908. He was also the publisher of the magazine *Le Magicien* during its entire thirty-five year run.

M.C.

Abbreviation of MASTER OF CEREMONIES.

MCATHY, GEORGE (1910-1971)

Professional magician, magic clown, comedy magician and latterly specialist in children's shows. He wrote *Smart Talk* and *Smart Business* and (with RALPH HULL) *Smart Magic*; he also created the classic comedy card effect, **Mandroop's** INSURANCE POLICY, which he marketed through TOMMY WINDSOR.

McAthy was also famous (or notorious) for his formation of the Deceptive Order Of Prestidigitator's Society—known as the D.O.P.E.S.—of which he was, naturally, president, and for which he produced an excellent publication called *The Dope Sheet*. (Much of the material therein has since been collected in a book published as *Magic From The Dope Den*.)

In Hollywood he did a great deal of private party work for people in the film industry, and also served as technical advisor on a number of film and television shows. He was also a highly competent juggler and ventriloquist.

MCBRIDE, JEFF (b. 1960)

Performer who began his career while still in his teens, and has since created a unique ACT which fuses his skills in MIME, martial arts, Kabuki theater, and magic.

With this act McBride has been highly successful, appearing dozens of times in Atlantic City, Las Vegas, Japan and elsewhere; he has worked with Diana Ross, Tina Turner, Raquel Welch, Andy Williams, and others. He has performed in New York's Radio City Music Hall and in Tokyo's Mikado Theatre, as well as many concert dates.

In 1985 McBride was named Atlantic City Entertainer Of The Year; another honor he received was the Star Of Magic Award from the INTERNATIONAL BROTHERHOOD OF MAGICIANS.

He has lectured at magic conventions in the U.S. and Japan, and is the author of *Changing The Face Of Magic*.

MCCAFFREY, WILLIAM H. (b. 1899)

Business executive by profession; inventor of several EFFECTs (many of which will be found in HILLIARD's *Greater Magic*), of which the best known is his *Prize Winner*—which was the basis for the many succeeding PREMONITION effects.

He is also the inventor of **The Pedagogue's Nightmare**, a PADDLE routine with coins now commonly known as **The Money Paddle**; this effect (and the *Prize Winner*) are described in J. G. THOMPSON JR.'s *My Best*.

Jeff McBride

McCOMB, BILLY (b. 1922)

Born in Ireland, he began his performing career while still in his teens, not only performing magic but also working with Dublin's famous Abbey Theatre. Originally intending to be a doctor, he studied at Queen's University in Belfast and Trinity College in Dublin and received his medical degree.

Moving to London, he worked in every kind of venue, from theaters to radio and television to films; he performed a number of times for the royal family, at the London Palladium and elsewhere. He was the host and principal performer for the first BBC-TV primetime show devoted entirely to magic.

McComb invented the ILLUSION routine now popularly known as the DOUBLE SAWING in 1961, and presented it on British television the following year.

In addition to his own television series, McComb has guested on dozens of other television shows throughout the world, and performed live in a number of countries; he has also been a featured performer on many luxury cruise lines.

Among his many awards are *Honorary Life Member—MAGIC CASTLE*; *Inner MAGIC CIRCLE with Performance Gold Star*; and *Visiting Magician Of The Year* and *Performing Fellowship*, both from the ACADEMY OF MAGICAL ARTS.

Billy McComb

Ormond McGill (*photo courtesy GENII Magazine*)

His books include *The First Book Of William* and *McComb's Magic—25 Years Wiser*; in addition, he has done a number of audiotapes for MARTIN BREESE which are considered by many to be the best of their kind. He is also noted as the inventor of the popular **McComb-ical Card Trick** (a comedy card prediction).

MCGILL, ORMOND

While primarily performing as a hypnotist, McGill has also featured magic in his shows; one FULL-EVENING SHOW presented ILLUSION effects and other magic in the first part, and his *Seance Of Hypnotism* as the second act.

He is the author of *Atomic Magic, 21 Gems Of Magic, Psychic Magic* (six volumes), and two works on hypnotism: *The Art Of Stage Hypnotism* and *The Encyclopedia Of Stage Hypnotism*.

MCGUIRE, EDWARD (1891-1968)

Sometimes known as Tex McGuire; noted card magician and gambler, who was said to have "broken the bank" at Monte Carlo.

A book on his exploits is *Suppose You Lost Your $100,000 Overnight?* by E.S. Cannon.

McGuire is the author of *McGuire On Malini* and *The Phantom Of The Card Table*.

McMANUS, JOHN J. (1890-1955)

Lawyer by profession who gathered one of the world's largest collections of magical literature and memorabilia. This collection (combined with that of Dr. Morris N. Young) was donated to the Library of Congress.

McMILLEN, JACK (b. 1911)

Shipping agent by profession; noted for his many contributions to card magic, of which the best known is his PLUNGER PRINCIPLE.

MECHANICAL DECKS

Decks of cards prepared in some manner which physically alters them (without this being visually apparent) in order to bring about magical effects.

Such decks are almost never used by professional performers, if only because laypersons are so familiar with them through exposure by pitchmen and television advertising. Indeed, it is often necessary for the performer to clearly establish that his or her miracles are accomplished with ordinary cards.

See SVENGALI DECK; STRIPPER DECK; MENETEKEL DECK; DEVANO DECK.

MECHANIC'S GRIP

A method of holding a deck of cards in dealing position which facilitates various false deals. The forefinger is curled around the front of the deck, which is actually supported entirely by the tip of this finger and the base of the palm.

Thus in a BOTTOM DEAL, for example, the other three fingers may be moved away briefly to allow clear passage of the bottom card from the deck.

A thorough description of the Mechanic's Grip is given in ERDNASE's *The Expert At The Card Table*.

See BOTTOM DEAL; SECOND DEAL; CENTER DEAL.

MEDIUM

In **spiritualism**, a person who is able to contact the dead and through whom they are able to communicate.

Within stage magic the term is used to denote the onstage partner in a TWO-PERSON MENTAL ACT or the primary performer in the SPIRIT CABINET routine.

MELIES, GEORGE (1861-1938)

Born in France, he began his performing career after purchasing the Theatre Robert-Houdin, and was quite successful. He began presenting films at the theater which combined techniques of stage magic with special film effects. Melies is now generally considered to have been the father of special effects cinematography; an interesting account of his life and influence on film is described in *The Magician And The Cinema* by Erik Barnouw.

MELROSE

British cosmetic product similar to such U.S. lip balm products as Chapstick; it can be used to cause two playing cards to cling together and thus be handled as one.

Melrose or Chapstick can be used in many EFFECTs requiring a momentary adhesive which will wipe away.

MEMORY

See MNEMONICS.

MENETEKEL DECK

A MECHANICAL DECK which, apparently ordinary, consists of only twenty-six different cards; each has a duplicate, cut slightly shorter, just above it. Thus when the cards are RIFFLED they fall in pairs and so can be RIFFLE-SHUFFLED without breaking up a pair. When a spectator makes a selection it is a simple matter for the performer to CUT the deck at that point and complete the cut, thus having a duplicate of the selected card available for any of a number of denouements.

Some versions of the **menetekel deck** do not use trimmed cards, but instead rely on the ROUGH-AND-SMOOTH PRINCIPLE to hold the pairs of cards together.

The **menetekel deck**, like the SVENGALI DECK, is usually credited to BURLING HULL; it is possible, however, that it was invented by Donald Holmes.

MENNA, LISA (b. 1963)

Specializing in CLOSE-UP MAGIC she is the first woman to win the Texas Association Of Magicians Best Close-Up award. Primarily working for corporate clients, she has performed for American Airlines, Texas Instruments, Reiss Toys, Lord & Taylor, Hilton Hotels, Sheraton Hotels and many others.

Other appearances include varied venues throughout the U.S., and television shows in the U.S. and Japan.

MENTAL EPIC

A feat of MENTAL MAGIC favored more by magicians than MENTALISTS, this uses a large slate divided into six sections; the performer's predictions are written in three of the sections, and the choices of the spectators in the other three. Naturally, the performer's PREDICTIONS turn out to be correct.

An improved version of this EFFECT, **Final Epic**, was devised by ALAN SHAXON.

Mental Epic was invented by Hen Fetsch; it is based on an earlier effect called **The Taped Slate** which was created by PETER WARLOCK.

MENTALIST

Performer of MENTALISM or MENTAL MAGIC.

MENTALISM

Often erroneously classed as a branch of magic, mentalism is a separate performance art; its roots are not in conjuring but (for the most part) in the spiritualistic and psychic demonstrations of the 19th century. It is often confused with MENTAL MAGIC, but the two arts are different in that mentalism seeks to create a dramatic reality of belief in the performer's "powers," while mental magic is designed to baffle and mystify the onlooker.

MENTAL MAGIC

A branch of magic comprising demonstrations of apparent extraordinary or supernatural mental powers—lightning calculation, super-memory, TELEPATHY, clairvoyance, PRECOGNITION and PSYCHOKINESIS. Often included in this category are simulations of mediumistic phenomena, such as SPIRIT SLATE writing or demonstration SEANCES.

Primary sources for such effects are Tony Corinda's *Thirteen Steps to Mentalism* and *Annemann's Practical Mental Effects* (edited by John J. Crimmins, Jr.).

MENTZER, JERRY (b. ?)

Founder and operator of Magic Methods, a magic manufacturing and publishing company. He is the author of a number of books, including *Card Cavalcade* (five volumes), *Close-Up Cavalcade* (two volumes), *Counts Cuts Moves And Subtleties*, *Magic With Finger Rings*, *Effective Cups And Balls*, and many others.

MERLIN

Legendary sorcerer of Camelot, teacher and advisor to King Arthur; major figure in Arthurian literature. It has been speculated that the name *Merlin* is a corruption of *Merdwydd*—an ancient Gaelic term which translates roughly as "Oak-seer"—which in turn has led to further speculation concerning Merlin's connection with the Druids. *See Magic Arts in Celtic Britain* by *Lewis Spence*.

Recently Merlin was the eponymous hero of a Broadway musical show starring DOUG HENNING; at the time the show opened it was said to be the costliest Broadway theater production ever presented.

METAMORPHOSIS

An ILLUSION routine invented by HOUDINI, and known within magic as the SUB TRUNK, or substitution trunk; the effect of this illusion is the instantaneous exchange of one performer inside the trunk with another who stands outside.

In early stagings of the ROUTINE the exchange took place within a curtained cabinet similar to that used in the SPIRIT CABINET routine. Nearly all present-day performers have dispensed with the cabinet, using instead a rectangular or circular frame to which a curtain is attached. With the performer inside the trunk, the ASSISTANT stands on top of it and holds the frame above her head for an instant (both trunk and performer being out of view); when the frame is lowered the performer stands on the trunk, which is then opened to reveal the assistant.

The trunk is usually constructed to resemble a shipping trunk or packing case, as this natural appearance enhances the effect. Other versions have included clear plexiglas trunks (sometimes filled with water!), giant hatboxes, and other containers. Variations of the routine include handcuffing the performer and placing him in a sack before being locked in the trunk or box; also, quite often the assistant will undergo a costume change in the course of the routine.

The Metamorphosis was a mainstay of Houdini's act in his early career; it is currently a favorite of DOUG HENNING; and has served many magicians in the intervening years. Much depends on the rapidity with which the exchange takes place; currently, the fastest such exchange is performed by THE PENDRAGONS.

METEMPSYCHOSIS

A stage ILLUSION in which visible changes in form happened before the eyes of the audience—a man would change into a woman, a statue into a living person, an assembled suit of armor would come to life. Using a sophisticated application of the MIRROR PRINCIPLE, it was related in a general way to the PEPPER'S GHOST illusion; like that effect, it was created by John Henry Pepper, with a Mr. Walker.

A later version of this illusion was presented by HARRY KELLAR under the title of *The Blue Room*.

An excellent description of this illusion can be found in S. H. SHARPE's *Conjurers' Optical Secrets*.

MEXICAN JOE CRIMP

A specialized full-deck CRIMP in which an asymmetrical diagonal wave is put into the deck, making it into a kind of ONE-WAY deck. If a card is removed and the deck is turned around in the standard one-way handling, the returned card will create a slight BREAK from which a CONTROL can be begun. Beyond this elementary technique the Mexican Joe Crimp has several sophisticated applications.

The technique is sometimes referred to simply as **Mexican Joe**; also called a **wave crimp**.

The technique is thoroughly described by ED MARLO in The New TOPS Magazine, and by DAI VERNON in *More Inner Secrets Of Card Magic*.

MEXICAN TURNOVER

A card SLEIGHT in which one card is used to flip over another card which has been lying on the table; in this action, the two cards are indetectably exchanged. It is often used in routines for THREE-CARD MONTE.

The sleight is described in ERDNASE's *The Expert At The Card Table*, HUGARD and BRAUE's *Expert Card*

Technique, SCARNE's *Why You Can't Win*, and many other books.

MEYER, ORVILLE (b. 1911)

Performer who worked for many years in the Midwest as "The Wizard Of Ah's." He is noted as the inventor of the routine for the BULLET CATCH later used by TED ANNEMANN, and also of THINK INK.

He is the author of *Magic In The Modern Manner* and *Magic Square And Master Memory Demonstration*.

MIACO (1912-1949)

Born Stephen Frisbie, he became a performer while still a child; later he was noted for his smooth and sophisticated manipulative act, which was featured in New York's Rainbow Room and many other top nightclubs throughout the U.S.

MICRO-MACRO

A marketed effect created by BR. JOHN HAMMAN in which a deck of Patience-size (miniature) cards suddenly expands to the size of a regular deck, with the exception of a previously chosen card. It is a startling feat of visual card magic.

MIDDLE DEAL

See CENTER DEAL.

MIESEL, WILLIAM (b. 1935)

Noted for his interest in MENTAL MAGIC and card magic. In addition to many contributions to the LINK-ING RING Magazine and other publications, he has written several books: *Fork Full Of Appetizers, Seconds From The Forkers, Moe And His Miracles With Cards*, and *The Creative Card Magic Of William P. Miesel*.

MIKO

A novelty card feat using a small packet of cards and a DIE, with which a spectator determines that his card should be the Three-and-a-Half of Clubs; the card being shown, it proves to be just that. Invented by Harold Sterling, the effect is named after MILTON KORT.

MILK BUILD SHUFFLE

A type of overhand FALSE SHUFFLE in which desired cards are singly drawn off the bottom of the deck simultaneously with the top card in the course of the shuffle, to place them at a desired location. Most often this shuffle is used as part of a GAMBLING DEMONSTRATION; as a secret SLEIGHT, in any but the most expert hands it is less than deceptive.

MILK CAN ESCAPE

A stage EFFECT believed to have been invented by HOUDINI, in which a large container modeled on a milk can is filled to the brim with water; the performer submerges inside and the lid is locked on with several padlocks. A curtained cabinet is placed around the can, and the performer makes his escape.

Though a stage ILLUSION, this has the very real dangers of any underwater escape; it is currently a specialty of RANDI.

MILK PITCHER

A utility device for LIQUID EFFECTS, in appearance this is a glass pitcher from which milk is apparently poured into some opaque container (paper cone, hat, etc.); the milk then vanishes.

The pitcher is constructed with a DOUBLE WALL; at the outset the milk lies between these walls, giving the pitcher the appearance of fullness. When the pitcher is tilted, the milk goes through holes in the inner wall into the pitcher proper, and thus the visible level drops to less than a third of its former state.

The pitcher is most often used in combination with other EFFECTs such as the FOO CAN or the FUNNEL.

MILLER, CHARLES EARLE (b. 1909)

Known most often as Charlie Miller, Miller is considered to be one of the greatest experts in pure SLEIGHT OF HAND in the history of magic; he is particularly noted for his performance of the CUPS AND BALLS.

His performing career ranged from private parties to work in ILLUSION shows; he toured several times for the U.S.O., and appeared in several West Coast nightclubs. His act in these venues featured his highly-regarded routines for classic EFFECTs such as the LINKING RINGS, the RICE BOWLS, and the EGG BAG.

For many years he has written a column for GENII Magazine featuring routines by himself and others; he is also the author of *Charlie Miller On The Card Index, Black Art Well Tricks*, and *An Evening With Charlie Miller*.

He is the recipient of the Masters Fellowship from the ACADEMY OF MAGICAL ARTS.

Charlie Miller

Jack Miller (*The Mulholland Library of Conjuring & the Allied Arts, Los Angeles, California*)

MILLER, JACK (?-1962)

Performer who was noted for his expert use of a HOLDOUT; the model used by Miller, unlike the complex mechanisms employed by gamblers, relied on a simple weighted-cord arrangement. With this device Miller was able to accomplish seeming miracles.

He was also noted for his EGG BAG and LINKING RING routines, both of which have been commercially-marketed.

MILLER, KATLYN (b. ?)

Versatile performer who has done magic as a single act, and in partnership with PETER DE PAULA; has performed the ELECTRIC GIRL act; has worked as a fire eater (*see* FIRE-EATING); has performed a TWO-PERSON MENTAL ACT with LESLIE ANDERSON; has worked as ASSISTANT to illusionists; and has created her own three-person act involving magic, dance, fire and swords. She has performed throughout the U.S., and also in Japan, China and other countries.

She is also a sculptress whose magic-themed work has long been on display at the MAGIC CASTLE, and owner-operator of Mermade Magickal Arts, which supplies occult implements and accessories.

MILLER, WELSH (1864-1936)

Born Henry Miller, he achieved international fame with his act of coin manipulation, headlining bills in the U.S., Britain and Europe, and was often compared to T. NELSON DOWNS.

Miller was also a skilled mechanic and inventor (a version of the COIN WAND, a type of COIN DROPPER, many other items), and often in later years constructed REELS and other precision devices for magicians.

MILLION DOLLAR MYSTERY

An ILLUSION of this name was a major feature in the show of HOWARD THURSTON; since that time the principle, invented by WALTER CERRETTA JEANS for his **Silver Hat** effect, has generally been referred to by the same name.

A fair-sized container (in Jeans' version, the Silver Hat; in Thurston's, an 18" square box) is apparently completely isolated from stage floor or backdrop; yet anything which will fit in the container—and some things that won't!—may be produced, vanished or changed.

There have been several illusions which used this sophisticated application of the MIRROR principle;

where circumstances permit (it is not ANGLE-PROOF) it is still completely deceptive.

The principle is thoroughly discussed in PETER WARLOCK's *Walter Jeans: Illusioneer* and also in S. H. SHARPE's *Conjurer's Optical Secrets*.

MILTON, HERBERT (1897-1960)

British performer whose long career was primarily in after-dinner entertainment and private party engagements.

Milton invented a number of EFFECTs which have since become classics; a few examples are his SPELLING ROUTINE, the SALT LOCATION, SYMPATHETIC CLUBS, a BOOK TEST, and a now-popular card routine in which the Aces appear one at a time at the face of a deck in a clear glass goblet (the latter routine based on a KARL GERMAIN principle). All of these effects have at one time or another been erroneously attributed to others.

M.I.M.C.

Highest general level of membership in Britain's MAGIC CIRCLE; the initials stand for Member of the Inner Magic Circle.

A further distinction, awarded only to Inner Magic Circle members, is that of the Gold Star.

MIME

The expression of ideas or dramatic concepts by bodily movement and expression; also, one who performs this art.

The term is often (erroneously) applied to performers who present magic in the mime's traditional white-face makeup, and who may use some techniques of mime; true mime, however, uses no stage properties or external APPARATUS, and thus a performer of magic cannot properly be defined by this term.

A more appropriate term for the magical performer using concepts or presentational aspects of mime is *Pantomimist*.

See also PANTOMIME.

MINCH, STEPHEN (b. 1948)

Writer whose interests are primarily in the field of MENTALISM and MENTAL MAGIC but who has, however, written on a number of subjects. In addition to scripting work for television shows and *A Letter From Hades* (the monthly review newsletter from Micky Hades International), he has written several books. Among these are *Book Of Thoth, Creations Of A*

Magical Madman, Eyeless In Gaza, Mind Melds, For Your Entertainment Pleasure and *Secrets Of A Puerto Rican Gambler* (on the magic of DARYL), and *Any Second Now, Ever So Sleightly,* and *Sleight Unseen* (on the card magic of MARTIN A. NASH). He is also the author of a major work on the magic of DAI VERNON.

Minch was also for many years the General Manager of the U.S. branch of Micky Hades International, located in Seattle.

MIND READING

Sometimes, specifically, CONTACT MIND READING; more generally, MENTAL MAGIC or MENTALISM.

MINGUS, LEROY H. (1897-1979)

Owner and operator of the Mingus Magic Shop, he specialized in the production of FEATHER FLOWERS and APPARATUS employing them (such as BOTANIA); these EFFECTs were well-made and featured in the acts of many professional performers.

MIRASKILL

EFFECT devised by STEWART JAMES in which a spectator shuffles a deck and then deals the cards in pairs—separating them into red, black and mixed pairs. When this procedure is concluded the piles of all-red and all-black cards are counted, and the difference noted; this difference has been previously predicted by the performer.

The difference is created by secretly removing cards from the deck prior to performance; if two black cards are removed, for example, then the end result will be that there are two more red cards than black cards in their respective piles, regardless of any mixing or shuffling.

The James effect appeared in THE JINX, and later in THEODORE ANNEMANN's *Practical Mental Effects.* Many later variations, using beads, poker chips, etc., have appeared in print.

MIRROR GLASS

In appearance an ordinary drinking glass, it is divided down the center by a vertical mirror; the front of the glass (usually fluted) is reflected in the mirror and the glass thus appears empty, concealing whatever may lie in the compartment at the rear. The glass may be used to produce, vanish or exchange small objects; it is ideally used to secretly SWITCH one item secretly for another similar in appearance (as for example an unknown playing card or a balled-up handkerchief.

Such a glass should only be used when the performer cannot, for some reason, use a glass prepared with a MASKING partition, which is far more visually deceptive. If a mirror glass *is* used, the performer must check the lighting to make sure the glass appears empty—rather than simply *shiny*.

The Mirror Glass may have been invented by J. N. HOFZINSER or JOSEPH HARTZ.

MIRROR PRINCIPLE

Generally, the property of a mirror (the presence of which is unknown to the audience) to reflect one area to appear in a different location, and thus conceal the area directly behind the mirror itself.

More specifically, there are many different applications; in the ARM BOX, mirrors are used to make the arm appear to be in other than its actual location; in the SPHINX illusion, to make the area beneath a table appear empty.

Mirror principles are discussed in some detail in S. H. SHARPE's *Conjurer's Optical Secrets*; also, an interesting series of articles by PETER WARLOCK appeared in the LINKING RING Magazine under the title *Cause For Reflection*.

MISCALL

To apparently read aloud the identity of something not visible to the audience (e.g., a playing card or writing on a slip of paper), but actually to call out different information.

MISDIRECTION

The direction of the spectator's attention *away* from the critical or secret part of a trick or ILLUSION and *toward* some point or aspect which appears to have importance but actually has little to do with the actual methodology.

Misdirection is the cornerstone of nearly all successful magic; without it, even the most skilled SLEIGHT OF HAND or mechanical device is unlikely to create an illusion of real magic. Conversely, with its aid, the simplest of methods or devices can be used to create miracles.

The premier exponent of magical misdirection is TONY SLYDINI; his EFFECTs and routines are built almost entirely on this technique, and his application of it is so flawless that magicians of many years' experience find themselves quite as baffled as the most ingenuous layman.

The most complete work on the subject is DARIEL FITZKEE's *Magic By Misdirection*; an excellent smaller monograph is AL LEECH's *Don't Look Now*, as is JUAN TAMARIZ'S *The Five Points In Magic*.

MISER'S DREAM

The name given by T. NELSON DOWNS to the EFFECT of catching coins from the air, apparently plucking them into existence at the fingertips. Downs made his reputation with this effect, which at one time was his entire act.

It is considered to be the primary effect in stage COIN MAGIC, and is still a feature of many acts. Also known as **coins from the air, aerial mint, aerial treasury**.

MISHELL, ED (1896-1983)

A lawyer by profession, he was noted as a magical illustrator, much of his work being used in the LOUIS TANNEN INC. catalog and for EFFECTs marketed by RICHARD HIMBER. He was also the author of a long-running review column in GENII Magazine, ''Tricks Of The Trade,'' and a book on the use of the HOLDOUT called *Holdout Miracles*.

He was a member of several magical organizations, including the S.A.M., I.B.M., and Britain's Inner MAGIC CIRCLE.

MISMADE EFFECTS

Magical EFFECTs in which the magician apparently makes an error in the course of the ROUTINE which is reflected in the magical result.

The most common such PLOT is that of the **mismade flag**; here three silk handkerchiefs are poked into a tube made from a rolled-up square of paper, the performer announcing he will transform them into a U.S. flag. However, the blue silk falls from the tube, apparently unnoticed by the performer; when the flag is drawn from the opposite end of the tube, it has a blank white area where the blue field should be. Now the performer notices the fallen blue silk, and it is poked into the tube along with the mismade flag. This time a complete and correct flag emerges from the other end of the tube, which is then shown empty.

The ROUTINE is often preceded by a SILK DYEING routine in which two white silks are changed to red and blue; like that routine, the **mismade flag** uses the DYE TUBE gimmick.

See MISMADE GIRL.

MISMADE GIRL

An illusion invented by CHUCK JONES in which a woman is placed into a cabinet which then is disassembled in four boxlike sections—and then reassembled in a new arrangement. When the doors set in the front of each box are opened, the hips and

Chuck Jones performs his *Mismade Girl*.

thighs are visible in the top box; the second box shows the chest and stomach area; the third shows the woman's head and shoulders; and the bottom box shows the feet.

The doors are closed and the boxes are reassembled in the correct order, after which the woman steps out of the cabinet in her proper form.

In a variation of this final phase, the sections are numbered, and the performer merely transposes the numbers to bring about the final arrangement. This number-switching presentation was the invention of ORSON WELLES; Jones re-engineered the illusion to accommodate it.

MISSING CARD

A problem in MNEMONICS sometimes presented as a feat of card magic, in which a card is removed from the deck by a spectator and the performer, on hearing or seeing the remaining cards only once, is able to identify the missing card.

The mnemonic solution to this problem deals with the fact that each card has its own mnemonic picture; as the performer notes each card he pictures the mnemonic image, and alters it in some specific way. Later, as the performer mentally runs through the cards sequentially and recalls the pictures, he will note

one for which the picture has not been altered—and this is, of course, the missing card. This feat is quite often done with four or five cards.

An alternate method requires adding the values of the cards as the performer looks through the deck, and subtracting the total from the known sum of the complete deck. This is variously known as **summing** or CLOCKING THE DECK; two books which deal exclusively with this are HARRY LORAYNE's *The Epitome Location* and KARL FULVES' *Parallel Lines*.

M.M.C.

Abbreviation for Member of the MAGIC CIRCLE.

MNEMONICS

The art of systematized memory (after the Greek goddess of memory, Mnemosyne). It is used by magicians both openly, as in demonstrations of instant memorization, and secretly, as in (for example) knowing the order of a stacked deck (*see* STACK).

Briefly, mnemonics systems operate on two principles: association, and the table of fixed ideas. To take card memory as an example: the performer will have created pictures for each of the numbers from one to fifty-two, using a mnemonic technique for converting numbers into phonetic sounds. Likewise, he will have created a specific picture for each of the fifty-two cards—usually by combining the sound indicated by its value with that beginning its suit-name—e.g., the Ace of Diamonds might be symbolized by a *toad*, because a T or D sound has the mnemonic value of one (Ace) and the D is for the Diamond.

Thus if the performer wishes to recall that the Ace of Diamonds is in position seventeen, he or she recalls the picture for the number seventeen—which might be *tack*—and associates it with *toad*, making the mental image of a toad sitting down on a tack, for example. That done, the performer can "forget" the picture, because being reminded of either half of it will immediately bring the other half to mind.

The best general work on the subject is HARRY LORAYNE's *How To Develop A Super-Power Memory*; among the works more specifically aimed at the magical performer's needs are the *Memory Trix* series (six booklets) by Bernard Zufall, and a series of articles titled *Conjuring for the Cognoscenti* by Tom Harris (these articles appeared in GENII magazine beginning in January of 1959).

MODERN CABINET

A large cabinet, usually with a draw-curtain front, which may be used to produce two or three people; it operates on the DOUBLE WALL principle. The **modern cabinet** is often used in presentations of the THREE GRACES.

See also CABINET OF PROTEUS; MILLION DOLLAR MYSTERY.

MOE (?-?)

Born Morris Seidenstein, he achieved a national reputation among magicians in the late 1920s with his extremely baffling and unique card magic.

What little is known of his life, together with a collection of the EFFECTs sold by Moe, is described in *Moe And His Miracles* by WILLIAM MIESEL.

MONEY MAKER

A device consisting of two small rollers between which blank sheets of paper are fed, coming out the other side as genuine currency. Though apparently separate, the rollers are actually connected by a long fabric strip wound around them in an S-fashion; the blank paper is rolled around one of the rollers, concealed by the fabric, while the previously secreted bill is made to come out from its place of concealment in the fabric around the other roller.

A much improved model of this APPARATUS was marketed by U.F. GRANT as the **Flat Model Money Maker**. This apparatus had a tray in which the blank paper was placed; when a roller was passed over it, the paper apparently changed visibly to a dollar bill.

More recently, a plastic "money machine" has been marketed in which the paper appears to visibly change to the bill as it is withdrawn from a drawer-type apparatus.

MONGE SHUFFLE

See OVER-UNDER SHUFFLE.

MONKEY BAR

A SUCKER EFFECT in which three ropes pass through holes in a metal or wooden bar and hang down; at the end of one of the outer ropes is a ring, scarf, or other object. Claiming he will make the object jump to the other rope, the performer places the bar briefly behind his back; when the performer shows it, the object is on the other end, but the spectators assume that the performer has simply turned the bar end for end. After some byplay the object jumps to the *middle* rope.

An excellent stage version of this effect, with a nice visual finish, is GEORGE KOVARI's **Codology**.

MONTE

See TWO-CARD MONTE; THREE-CARD MONTE.

MOORE, E. J. (1881-1957)

Born Ernest Linebarger; for many years he was a leading vaudeville performer, featuring his **Tears Of Buddha**—a strange effect in which a bean placed in his mouth appeared from each eye in turn. His presentation of this effect was preceded by a film which showed the action in close-up. Moore was noted for his humorous presentations, often billing himself as "The Talkative Trickster."

He is the inventor of the **Instanto Rope** and **Linking Rope** effects, both commercially marketed.

MORA, SILENT (1884-1972)

Born Louis McCord, he performed for many years in CHAUTAUQUA, vaudeville, and other kinds of venue; his stage name notwithstanding, he did a silent act only in the early years of his career. He specialized in SLEIGHT OF HAND and is best known for his **Balls And Net** ROUTINE in which small white balls appeared, vanished and changed places, dropping from his hands into a net held by two spectators.

In addition to his regular act Mora did an ORIENTAL STYLE routine (which *was* performed in PANTOMIME), SHADOWGRAPHY, and juggling.

MORETTI, HANS (b. ?)

Born in Germany; performer noted for his many spectacular EFFECTs and ROUTINEs. In his SWORD BOX presentation, spectators are permitted to push the swords through a cardboard box where a chained-up Moretti is confined; not only does he emerge unharmed and free of the chains, but in full clown makeup! He has also devised an act featuring sharpshooting with crossbows, and another based on the RUSSIAN ROULETTE premise; these are performed both by Moretti and son Hans Pantar.

MORRITT, CHARLES (1861-1936)

Born in Britain; he began his showbusiness career as the manager of a music hall, and later became well-known for his many puzzling ILLUSION creations. In addition to his invention of the MORRITT CAGE, FLYTO and other ILLUSIONs, he is also credited with the **Morritt Grip**—a type of fingerpalming technique with a coin in which the coin is gripped between the folds of flesh at the base of the first and third fingers. With this grip—also known as a **PURSE PALM** from

Hans Moretti, at the climax of his *Sword Box* routine (*photo courtesy GENII Magazine*)

an EFFECT employing its use—the hand may be stretched out flat and the coin will remain in place.
See PURSE PALM.

MORRITT CAGE

An ILLUSION invented by CHARLES MORRITT in which a tall cage was isolated in a larger framework cabinet, the larger cabinet being fitted with spring blinds which could be raised or lowered as desired; persons could appear, vanish or change within the cage as desired. In Morritt's own presentation a man dressed as a prisoner was made to vanish from the inner cage; the illusion was called **The Convict's Escape**.

The illusion depended on a sophisticated application of the MIRROR PRINCIPLE; it is described in S.H. SHARPE's *Conjurer's Optical Secrets.*

MOVE

A single SLEIGHT OF HAND technique. Also, in gambler's parlance, to use sleights in crooked gambling.

MOVING PIP CARD

A playing card invented by OSWALD RAE, which shows (for example) the Three Of Clubs; it is displayed as the spectator's selection. The spectator states that his selection was the Two Of Clubs—and the center PIP is seen to move up the card to blend in with one of the end pips.

The extra pip, cut from another card, is affixed to a thread which runs in a loop from front to back of the card; a small button or knot on the thread at the rear allows the performer to control the pip's movements. There are many variations in construction and use.

MULHOLLAND, JOHN (1898-1970)

Leading magical authority of his time; among many other articles he wrote the entry on **Conjuring** for the *Encyclopedia Britannica*. He was the editor of THE SPHINX magazine for the last two decades of its existence.

Mulholland also gathered perhaps the finest collection of magical literature ever created. For a time after his death it was housed in New York's Players Club; it is now located in Los Angeles under private ownership, with RICKY JAY as Curator.

John Mulholland (*photo courtesy GENII Magazine*)

As a performer he was noted for his presentation of the TORN DECK and for his LINKING RING routine (often performed in Oriental guise); for many years he was a sought-after feature of New York society events.

Among his many books are *John Mulholland's Book Of Magic*, *Beware Familiar Spirits*, *Quicker Than The Eye*, and *The Story Of Magic*.

MULHOLLAND BOX

A type of OKITO BOX invented by JOHN MULHOLLAND; it is similar in some respects to the AL N' NATE BOX. A description of it will be found in BOBO's *The New Modern Coin Magic*.

MULLER, REINHARD (b. ?)

Born in Germany; professor of mathematics by profession. He is noted for his thorough technical explorations of card magic, exemplified in his *Gilbreath's Principles* and *Magic With Giant Cards: An Overview*. Muller has also done studies of the STACKED DECK and FALSE COUNT; these papers are not presently available in English-language translation.

MULLICA, TOM (b. ?)

He began his career as a demonstrator for Abbott Magic Company; moving to Atlanta, he began doing close-up magic while tending bar, and subsequently operated a bar called The Tom-Foolery. He then created his own Tom-Foolery Magic Bar Theatre, which has become one of the most successful bars in Atlanta. Mullica has so designed his performing space that lighting and sound effects can enhance his close-up presentations.

He has appeared on several television shows, including *Late Night With David Letterman*.

Mullica has contributed a number of articles to magic periodicals.

MULTIPLE-BANK DECK

A deck of cards which contains only a limited number of different cards, repeated several times. A **five-bank deck**, for example, would contain five each of ten different cards.

In many cases it is required that the cards within each bank be in the same order, so that no matter where the deck is CUT the next ten cards (in the five-bank deck mentioned) will be all different; the term *bank*, therefore, is usually taken to mean one of the discrete groups of different cards.

However, the *multiple-bank* term may simply refer to

a type of limited-choice deck, as for example the MAGICIAN'S DREAM DECK.

MULTIPLE CARD PASS

See MULTIPLE SHIFT.

MULTIPLE DEAL

See GROUP DEAL.

MULTIPLE SHIFT

A SLEIGHT invented by DAI VERNON in which several outjogged cards are apparently pushed down flush with the deck; in actuality the BLOCK of cards in front of the foremost projecting card is pushed upward to create this ILLUSION. The cards may now be stripped out in the course of a cut and brought to the top or bottom of the deck.

This sleight is sometimes referred to as the **multiple card pass**. It is thoroughly described in the TARBELL COURSE IN MAGIC (volume 3).

An early version of this sleight was developed by T. Page Wright, circa 1930.

MULTIPLYING BILLIARD BALLS

See BILLIARD BALLS.

MULTIPLYING BOTTLES

In the usual presentation, several bottles are produced from two metal tubes; this is done as a continuation of a PASSE PASSE BOTTLE routine.

In a variant ROUTINE, a large box is shown to have no top or bottom, and is placed over two bottles; these bottles being removed, two more bottles are seen. The process is continued until a large number of bottles (usually nine or more) have been produced.

The routine depends on an application of the SHELL principle. It should be noted that quality of manufacture for this effect varies widely, and in some badly made versions the principle is fairly obvious; given quality manufacture, the routine still requires careful handling and presentation to be deceptive.

MULTIPLYING CANDLES

An EFFECT in CANDLE MAGIC in which a single lighted candle held in the hands multiplies to four and then eight; it is the invention of Earl Morgan, who marketed his version as the **Nesto Candles**. A popular later version was manufactured by LOYD.

MULTIPLYING COINS

Coins counted onto a tray by a spectator are dumped into his hands; when the spectator counts them again it is seen that they have increased in number. The tray is of double thickness and holds extra coins in a hidden compartment; these slide out when the visible coins are dumped from the tray and are thus invisibly added.

MULTIPLYING RABBITS

A closeup variant of the SPONGE BALLS using small, vaguely rabbitoid rubber foam cutouts. The first commercial version of this, by ROBERT NELSON, was marketed as **Peter Rabbit Goes To Town**.

MULTUM IN PARVO

A LIQUID EFFECT using several clear glass or plastic containers of diminishing size. The largest is filled to the brim with milk; all the milk is poured into the next largest glass without overflowing. This process is continued until all the milk that was in the quart-sized glass now fits into a glass holding only a few ounces. The effect is believed to have been invented by Benson Dulay.

Variations of this effect include doing the ROUTINE in reverse, and in some cases concluding by filling *all* the glasses.
Like the MILK PITCHER, this effect employs the DOUBLE WALL principle.

The *Multum In Parvo* title is also used to denote a PRODUCTION effect using two nesting boxes; this effect was invented by OKITO and is described in his *Quality Magic*.

M.U.M. (Magazine)

Official organ of the S.A.M.; begun in 1911 as a separate periodical, it was later published as part of the SPHINX magazine and still later as part of GENII, The Conjurer's Magazine.

In 1951 it resumed publication as a separate periodical; for the past several years it has been under the editorship of DAVID GOODSELL.

MURRAY (b. 1901)

Born Leo Norman Maurien Murray Stuart Carrington-Walters in Australia, he took his middle name as a stage name, and embarked on a long and successful professional career. He played in dozens of countries for several decades, and is best known for the sensational escape stunts he devised. Many regard him as superior to HOUDINI in this branch of magic. One of

Murray (*photo courtesy GENII Magazine*)

his favorite publicity stunts was to be handcuffed to a railway track in the path of an approaching train!

Retiring in the 1950's, since that time he has operated *Murray's Magic Mart* in Britain; in addition he acts as advisor and producer to magical performers.

In 1986 he was presented with a Masters Fellowship by the ACADEMY OF MAGICAL ARTS.

MUSCADE

French term, often used in early magic books, for a small cork ball used in the CUPS AND BALLS routine.

MUSCLE READING

Term sometimes used as a synonym for CONTACT MIND READING; misleading in that much of the phenomena of **contact mind reading**, while psychophysiological in nature, is produced by a far subtler spectrum of cues than is implied by the phrase.

MUSE, RAY (1896-1965)

Longtime GENII Magazine contributor and indexer, noted for his several *Your New Act From Genii* features, and for his assistance to up-and-coming performers—of whom the most notable is MARVIN ROY. Muse was also an active performer, with a penchant for COSTUME ACTs, and appeared throughout the Southern California area.

MUSSEY, BARROWS

See HAY, HENRY.

MUTILATED PARASOL

A parasol is wrapped in a mat or stiff cloth; several silks are placed in a small bag. They transpose, the silks hang from the ribs of the parasol, and the parasol cover found in the bag.

Early versions of this required a faked mat which was used to switch the parasols; the version used almost exclusively today was invented by LEWIS DAVENPORT, and uses only one ingeniously constructed parasol. The bag, usually in the shape of a woman's purse, is a CHANGE BAG.

MUTUS NOMEN

Originally known as **the Pairs Re-paired**, this card EFFECT is now most often called by the first two words of the code phrase used in its method.

In effect, ten pairs of cards are dealt out, and spectators note and remember various pairs. The cards gathered, the performer deals them out apparently at random into four rows of five face-up cards each. On a spectator identifying the rows in which his cards lie, the performer immediately identifies them.

The method involves the visualization by the performer of a set of four words:

MUTUS
NOMEN
DEDIT
COCIS

The first card of the first pair is dealt on the position of the visualized M in MUTUS; the second card of the pair, on the other M, in the center of NOMEN—this process being continued with the remaining letters and cards. When the rows are specified, the performer has only to note which letter is common to the words in those rows and remove the cards in those positions; the second and fourth rows, for example, have only the letter O in common.

Magicians have amused themselves by coming up with other sets of words which would accomplish the effect, such as *bible/atlas/goose/thigh; fifth/troop/sheep/ rills; sheer/chaff/usual/color; Santa/timid/moron/reeds;* or *david/lovel/inyon/abbey.*

A later version, developed by STEWART JUDAH and published in the NEW PHOENIX, utilized a new set of words in conjunction with a sorting and shuffling procedure which allowed the performer to deal the cards in sequence into straight rows; a variant of this, developed by John P. Hamilton (and published in PALLBEARER'S REVIEW) used a different set of words and shuffling system to accomplish the same end. Other versions have been developed which use a larger number of cards, in pairs and in triplets.

Many variations on the original effect have been published; some excellent earlier versions will be found in HILLIARD's *Greater Magic.*

MYSTERIOSO

Term used to denote a genre or type of music used to accompany stage presentations of a mysterious or mystical nature.

NAIL NICK

With playing cards or similar objects, to make an indentation with thumb or finger nail which can be felt or seen and thus identify the object.

This technique works well with playing cards; with items of softer manufacture (such as some grades of paper), it is less reliable, as the nick can sometimes "fade out" in a very short time.

NAIL WRITER

Small GIMMICK which fits on the thumbnail, and to which a small piece of pencil lead is attached, enabling the performer to write secretly; used in feats of MENTAL MAGIC and MENTALISM.

Technique of the **nail writer** is thoroughly discussed in TONY CORINDA's *13 Steps to Mentalism*; other effects are described in *Twenty Stunners with a Nail Writer*, by Frank Chapman, and ERIC MASON's *A Boon for all Seasons*.

NAME-O-CARD

A card effect created by RALPH W. HULL in which the performer is able to reveal any card named in a surprising and interesting way. It involves the use of an ingenious stacked deck, and is described in the *Encyclopedia Of Card Tricks*.

See STACK; OPTIONAL DISCLOSURE; BREAK CARDS.

NAP HAND

Three spectators take part in a game of Nap (or Napoleon); of the three, one spectator has a very poor hand, but with the bids directed by the performer (who demonstrates his knowledge of the cards in all three hands dealt from the shuffled deck), the spectator is able to win all five tricks.

The EFFECT is very popular in Britain, where the game of Nap used to be well-known, but is not often seen elsewhere. This single effect for a time comprised the entire act of British performer LIONEL KING, who later gave permission for its use to AL KORAN and BILLY MCCOMB, both of whom featured it in their shows.

NAPOLEONS, THE

Japanese comedy team of "Bona" Ueki and "Parto" Koishi; they were formerly known as **The Magic Napoleons**, and have hosted a number of Japanese magic specials in addition to performing their own magic. They are among the best known comedians in Japan, and have starred in their own television series. They have also appeared in the U.S. and Europe.

NARROW CARD

A card fractionally narrower than those comprising the rest of the deck; most often used as a KEY CARD.

See also CORNER SHORT; LONG CARD; SHORT CARD; WIDE CARD.

NASH, MARTIN (b. ?)

Born in Canada; noted for his GAMBLING DEMONSTRATION performances and lectures, with which he has toured throughout Canada and the U.S. as an entertainer, and also as an instructor to police departments.

His books include *Colors On The March*, *Jacks Or Better*, *Ovation*, and his trilogy, written with STEPHEN

MINCH: *Any Second Now, Ever So Sleightly,* and *Sleight Unseen.*

NECROMANCY

Sometimes used as a grandiloquent term for stage magic; its actual meaning involves a process of DIVINATION by conversation with the spirits of the dead (e.g., Saul's consultation with the Witch of Endor).

NEEDLE TRICK

A length of thread and several needles are placed in the performer's mouth and apparently swallowed; presently the thread is pulled from the mouth and the needles are found to be strung along its length. Based on an earlier East Indian feat with beads, and apparently first performed with needles by Ramo Samee, this EFFECT was a feature in the act of HOUDINI, who made quite a production of it.

Later versions of this routine have replaced the needles with Razor Blades, which are both more visible and (seemingly) more dangerous (*see* RAZOR-BLADE SWALLOWING).

In a variant invented by British performer Cyro (Cyril Baker), the performer swallows a length of wire and several small lightbulbs; when the wire is drawn from the mouth, the bulbs appear at intervals along its length—*lighted*. Versions of this effect have been marketed by L. DAVENPORT & CO. and LOUIS TANNEN INC. An elaborate stage-filling version of this effect is a feature in the act of MARVIN ROY.

NEFF, WILLIAM (1905-1967)

A performer with a long professional career, he was most noted for his SPOOK SHOW; called Dr. Neff's Madhouse Of Mystery, it featured highly dramatic presentations and a number of exceptionally beautiful female assistants. Many considered it to be the best show of this kind ever done.

He invented a number of EFFECTs, of which the best known is his highly visual version of the CUT AND RESTORED ROPE known simply as the **Neff rope**.

NEIL, C. LANG (?-?)

Born in Britain; Victorian-era writer whose book *The Modern Conjurer* was notable for its clear exposition and for its use of photographs illustrating technique and presentation, posed by a number of well-known performers of the time. (These photographs are of con-

siderable interest in that in many cases they showed full-length poses, indicating proper body positioning for the most deceptive execution of the effect. Such photographs are extremely helpful, but nevertheless are rarely used in magic texts.)

Neil's wife performed under the name of *Mademoiselle Patrice,* and is featured in the above-mentioned book.

NELSON, EARL (b. 1950)

He began his performing career as an actor in regional theater. He is noted as an expert close-up performer, and is a featured entertainer at numerous Hollywood parties and film industry functions.

Nelson also has been a TECHNICAL ADVISOR for numerous television productions, and has also done many "hand inserts"—close-up shots in which his hands performed the magic apparently being done by a character in the show or commercial.

He is the author of *Variations* and (with ALAN WAKELING) *The Chop Cup Book;* he also created and edited a periodical called *West Coast Quarterly.*

Nelson has twice received the Best Close-Up Magician award from the ACADEMY OF MAGICAL ARTS.

Earl Nelson

NELSON, ROBERT (1901-1972)

Magic dealer in Columbus, Ohio for over fifty years, he also performed at various times during his life—usually presenting MENTALISM. He also created a number of ACTS for various performers, often acting as manager/producer as well.

Nelson wrote a large number of books on the subject of MENTALISM; he also wrote and edited several concerning MENTAL MAGIC. Nearly all of these titles are still available through their current publisher, Micky Hades International.

Nelson also created several kinds of horoscope readings, palmistry charts, etc.; this side of the business continues under the proprietorship of his long-time partner and wife, Betty Nelson.

NEST OF BOXES

A popular EFFECT for over two centuries in which a borrowed object (usually a ring, handkerchief, or marked coin) is found in the innermost of a set of several locked boxes of diminishing size. Versions range from those used on stage, where the largest box may be two feet square, to close-up ROUTINES using a set of tiny plastic boxes or rubber-banded matchboxes of graduated size.

There are many methods for accomplishing this effect; several versions use a slide, a flat tube which allows a ring or coin to be introduced into the innermost box. In other routines, the smallest of the boxes is loaded with the object offstage and the box is then loaded into the next larger box in performance, usually through a spring-loaded wall or bottom.

Other versions (invented by ROBERT HARBIN and PETER WARLOCK) use a Nest Of Boxes made of clear plastic; in the Warlock version the object appears *visibly* in the innermost box.

The **nest of boxes** concept is also used in the CANNON ILLUSION.

NEWSPAPER TEAR

The art of tearing bits and pieces out of a folded newspaper so that, when opened, the paper will show a specific design (a ship's wheel, a birthday greeting, etc.); though some such designs can be created by pure skill, others involve varying degrees of preparation and/or subterfuge—from lightly penciling the design on the folded paper to switching it for one previously prepared.

This should not be confused with the torn-and-restored newspaper (*see* TORN-AND-RESTORED OBJECT).

NEYHART HOULETTE

A special HOULETTE designed by A. P. Neyhart for the RISING CARDS; with the houlette and a special deck, any card named could be made to slowly rise from the houlette held in the performer's hand.

Few models of the Neyhart Houlette were made and, since it was a delicate piece of precision workmanship, it was reportedly difficult to keep it in dependable working order. Though several pages are devoted to its HANDLING and routine in HILLIARD's *Greater Magic*, the EFFECT is almost never seen.

NIBERCO, NIC (b. ?)

Holland-born magician who, with his partner Bob, has performed throughout the world with an act billed as The Niberco Brothers. In addition to top nightclubs in Britain and Europe, the act has been featured on television in many countries.

Among the awards won by Niberco are the *Visiting Magician Of The Year* Award (for the Niberco Brothers' act) presented by the ACADEMY OF MAGICAL ARTS, and a *Grand Prix* at FISM. He is regarded by knowledgeable critics to be an expert manipulator.

The Niberco Brothers (*photo courtesy GENII Magazine*)

NICKELS TO DIMES

A classic EFFECT, invented by WALTER B. GIBSON in which a brass cap is placed over a stack of nickels; when the cap is lifted the nickels have apparently changed into dimes, and everything may be examined.

Making use of an application of the SHELL principle, the APPARATUS is precision made, and there have been many variations of this basic effect.

NICKELS TO DIMES was undoubtedly inspired by the STACK OF QUARTERS or the earlier CAP AND PENCE.

NICOLA (1882-1945)

Born William Nicol, he began his professional career at the turn of the century; after performing at the Paris Exposition he returned to the U.S. and played the vaudeville and Chautauqua circuits for a number of years.

In 1910 Nicola embarked on the first of several world tours with his elaborate ILLUSION show; his last one, in 1939, was cut short when a mine in Singapore harbor sank the ship carrying all his show properties. He continued with a smaller show which he performed through the U.S. during the war years, and made many appearances at military hospitals.

NIELSEN, NORM (b. 1934)

Born Norman Nielsen. After a year's study at the CHAVEZ COLLEGE OF MAGIC (where he was later an instructor), and performances in Japan, he developed a new act while working as a manufacturer of magical apparatus. The act, titled "Musical Magic," and featuring his famous **floating violin**, is now one of the best-known and most successful acts in the world, having appeared at major venues in Las Vegas, New York, London, Paris, and in many other countries around the world. Nielsen has also appeared on television in several countries, beginning with a highly successful performance on *The Ed Sullivan Show*.

Within magic, he is also known as a manufacturer of high-quality apparatus, including PALMING COINS and special thin cards for manipulation, the DOVECOTE VANISH, and many other items.

He is a recipient of the Best Stage Magician and Magician Of The Year awards from the ACADEMY OF MAGICAL ARTS.

NIGHTCLUB TABLE

Not really a table in the conventional sense, when set up the **nightclub table** takes the form of a rectangular

Norm Nielsen

box on short legs. It is completely open at the back and has interior shelves to hold various PROPs. Most such tables consist of three hinged pieces forming the front and sides; the table top and inner shelves are removable, and thus the table may be disassembled easily for travel.

These tables are, from the performer's standpoint, convenient and practical; the props for an entire act can often be placed out of sight on the shelves, and the area can also allow for disposal of a GIMMICK, palmed object or other item. Nightclub Tables, therefore are quite popular with some performers.

However, these tables do have a major disadvantage in that many APPARATUS effects cannot be convincingly performed on them; the table is so massive and boxlike in appearance that the audience is likely to deduce that it contains mechanisms which bring about the effects. This is particularly true of PRODUCTION effects (e.g., the SQUARE CIRCLE), which become meaningless in this situation.

Another drawback is their appearance; as stage furniture, no matter how ingeniously decorated, **nightclub tables** are usually notably unattractive in design. An exception is a table redesigned to resemble something spectators recognize, as for example a small portable bar for use in a BAR ACT.

Despite these drawbacks performers continue to

use them; when this is necessary it is probably advisable to so decorate and position these tables that they will attract as little attention as possible.

NIKOLA, LOUIS (1878-1936)

Born William Smith in Britain; performer who featured at times several ILLUSION effects in his act, and performed SHADOWGRAPHY as his closing routine. He appeared at ST. GEORGE'S HALL and many other venues throughout Britain, but is best remembered within magic for his NIKOLA CARD SYSTEM.

NIKOLA CARD SYSTEM

MNEMONIC system devised by LOUIS NIKOLA for use with playing cards, and a specific arrangement of cards in a stacked deck (*see* STACK) which may be learned with the system; the particular card sequence makes possible a number of EFFECTs.

The Nikola System is available as a separate booklet; it is also included in HUGARD's *Encyclopedia Of Card Tricks*.

NIM

A mathematical game (sometimes called THE GAME OF THIRTY-ONE) using a number of piles of small objects—usually coins or matches—from which the performer and a spectator alternately take various amounts in accordance with the rules of the game.

The object of the game is to force the other person to pick up the last objects. The game is, in a mathematical sense, trivial, in that a particular consistent strategy will always result in a win by the first player.

Several magicians have become fascinated by this game, and have published strategies for its various versions in periodicals devoted to mathematical games and puzzles. A number of routines and variations are described in NICK TROST's *Expert Gambling Tricks*.

NIXON, DAVID (1919-1979)

Born in Britain, he began his career with performances for the military at the beginning of World War II, including several tours for ENSA. He later performed in various theatrical venues, and came to national prominence as a panel member of the British television edition of *What's My Line?*.

Shortly thereafter he began a long-running series of shows under the title *It's Magic*; these combined straightforward magic with complex camera trickery, which some critics thought unwise. The shows proved very popular, however, and Nixon was for many years Britain's best-known magician. He was also noted for featuring as guest stars top magical performers from around the world. The major CONSULTANTs for his television shows were BILLY MCCOMB and ALI BONGO.

NIXON, W. J. (1884-?)

Born William Nixon; he was noted for his performances in ORIENTAL STYLE under a number of different names (much of his apparatus bought from THEO BAMBERG); and also for his version of the DUCK VANISH effect which he titled **Where Do the Ducks Go?**.

His show was for many years billed as the "Hong Kong Mysteries," and played throughout the U.S. as well as in South America. In the late 1930s Nixon disappeared from sight, and his fate is unknown.

NO FEET

An ILLUSION, the original version of which was invented by JOE KARSON, in which a person stands inside a three-foot tall cylinder which is then raised up; though the person seems to be standing on solid ground, his feet are not visible. Spectators may assume that the performer has simply lifted up his or her legs within the cylinder but are then left wondering what holds the performer up.

No Feet has been featured by ANDRE KOLE, who has created a very popular version of this illusion; it is now commercially available. The illusion has also been featured by DOUG HENNING.

NO GUTS

Illusionist's nickname for the GIRL WITHOUT A MIDDLE illusion; also known as **The Disembodied Princess**.

NOTIS, PROFESSOR (?-1953)

Born Mario Amando Vigna in Argentina, he began his career as a circus performer; later he was a professional gambler; eventually he specialized in juggling and magic.

Though he did perform for a time in Europe, the bulk of his career was in South America. He is known for the **Notis Cascade**, a very pretty FLOURISH described by LEWIS GANSON in his *Dai Vernon's More Inner Secrets Of Card Magic*.

NUDIST DECK

A card EFFECT invented by RALPH W. HULL, in which an apparently ordinary deck suddenly becomes completely blank on both faces and backs. It is a MECHANICAL DECK, operating on the ROUGH-AND-SMOOTH PRINCIPLE.

Sometimes called the **mental photography deck**, in reference to a presentation supplied with some marketed versions.

NUDIST DECK ROUTINES

Also called all blanks or BLANK DECK routines, these are card routines which approximate the effect achieved by the MECHANICAL DECK known as the NUDIST DECK; here, however, an ordinary deck is used, and the effect is created with a few blank-faced cards and various sleights and subtleties.

NUMBER DECK

A deck of cards in which the usual playing card faces have been replaced by one-or-two-digit numbers; often used to FORCE a number for a BOOK TEST, or in situations where playing cards might not be appropriate.

NUMEROLOGY FORCE

A type of card FORCE based on a mathematical principle, in which the force card is the tenth card down from the top of the deck and the spectator is asked to name a number between ten and twenty.

The number being given, that number of cards are dealt off into a face-down pile; the performer invokes the principles of numerology and adds the two digits of the named number together (e.g., 14: 1 + 4 = 5). The dealt pile of cards is picked up and this new number is dealt; the card arrived at will always be the force card.

This force is often credited to BILLY O'CONNOR.

NUT

Operating expenses, or overhead; the difference between gross and net profits.

OBEDIENT BALL

A wooden ball (usually about 3 inches in diameter) has a small hole bored through its center, and a cord runs freely through the hole. When the cord is held vertically the ball slides downward, but will halt at the performer's command.

The hole through the ball is created by drilling into the ball at a very minute angle to the surface of the ball, from opposite sides; when the holes meet a shaft is thus formed which is not straight, bending at an obtuse angle. If, therefore, tension is applied to the cord, the ball will slow or stop as desired.

There have been many variations on the basic concept, including a bent-pipe device which could be secretly introduced into an orange in the course of threading the cord through it, thus giving the EFFECT an impromptu appearance.

A commercially-marketed item uses a small brass or plastic cube; these usually have a tiny interior rod which can be moved into position by tapping the correct side on a hard surface; tapping the opposite side "unlocks" the cube. A spectator can then be given the APPARATUS and will be unable to prevent the cube from moving freely on the cord.

Still other variations use rods rather than cords, the ball being operated by a thread; and balls with interior double-pulley systems. Such methods allow the ball to *rise* as well as fall.

The Obedient Ball designation is properly confined to balls threaded on rod or rope, and should not be applied to effects in which a free-rolling ball moves in accordance with the wishes of the performer (as for example the GOLLIWOG BALL).

O'BRIEN, "OBIE" (b. ?)

Teacher by profession; noted for his close-up magic, and as one of the organizers of Fechter's Finger Flinging Frolic (a convention devoted exclusively to close-up performing).

OBVERSE

The head or primary side of a coin. The term is sometimes used in descriptions of coin SLEIGHTs or EFFECTs.

O'CONNOR, BILLY (ca.1895-1974)

Born Eugene Devot in Britain, he began his performing career just prior to World War I. Specializing in card magic, he performed for over four decades as *Billy O'Connor And His Fifty-Two Assistants*; at one venue this billing was not completely understood, and O'Connor arrived to find twenty-seven rooms reserved—one for himself and twenty-six (double occupancy) for the assistants!

For a brief time he presented an act consisting of several P.T. SELBIT illusions, at Selbit's request. O'Connor invented a number of effects, of which the best known is his INSTANTO DECK.

ODD AND EVEN

A type of DIVIDED DECK in which the cards are sorted into groups of **odd and even** values (the Jack and King are considered Odd cards, the Queen as Even).

See DIVIDED DECK.

Billy O'Connor, a publicity card (*The Mulholland Library of Conjuring & the Allied Arts, Los Angeles, California*)

Dell O'Dell, an early photograph (*The Mulholland Library of Conjuring & the Allied Arts, Los Angeles, California*)

ODD CARD

A card unlike those with which it is grouped, for example, the single black card in a group of red cards. An **odd-backed** card is one with a back design and/or color not matching that of the deck in use.

Also, any card of an odd numerical value; Jacks and Kings are considered odd-value cards.

O'DELL, DELL (1902-1962)

Born Dell Newton, she became a highly successful nightclub performer, appearing in most major New York clubs and in other major cities; she was also a favored performer for society functions.

O'Dell featured for a time her version of the BAR ACT, the props made for her by husband CHARLES CARRER; at another point she bought the rights to the comedy act of FRANK VAN HOVEN, and was successful with her own revised version. The Dell O'Dell Fan Club was also quite successful, having one of the largest memberships for any such club devoted to a magician.

For many years she wrote a column titled "Dell-lightfully," which appeared in the LINKING RING Magazine.

ODIN, CLAUDIUS (1859-1969)

French street performer with a long career and several honors. He was especially noted for his LINKING RING routine; this routine was fully described in his *Les Anneaux Chinois*, translated into English by VICTOR FARELLI under the title *The Odin Rings*.

Odin was also an expert at handling the STRIPPER DECK; his book on the subject (*Les Cartes Biseautees*) was also translated by Farelli and ran serially in Hugard's Magic Monthly magazine.

ODIN COUNT

A method of counting LINKING RINGS to show them as eight solid and separate rings; invented by CLAUDIUS ODIN. It is described in *The Odin Count* by VICTOR FARELLI.

OGDEN, TOM (b. 1951)

He began his performing career with the circus, touring with Circus Kirk and later Clyde Beatte-Cole Brothers Circus; he then toured extensively on his

Tom Ogden

own, appearing at over 1500 universities and colleges throughout the U.S.

He has performed at several casinos in Atlantic City, including Resorts International, Bally's Park Place, The Sands, and The Golden Nugget. He has made a number of appearances on television as magician and actor: *Magnum P.I., Days Of Our Lives*, and several commercials for such clients as Sears and Kentucky Fried Chicken. He has also performed at comedy clubs and many other venues.

His books include *A Volunteer From The Audience, Mentalistrix For Kids*, and *The Stooge Book*; he has contributed items to a number of magic periodicals and has also written monthly columns for GENII, M.U.M., and *Magic Manuscript*.

He has twice received the Best Parlour Magician award from the ACADEMY OF MAGICAL ARTS.

OIL AND WATER

A card EFFECT in which a small group of red cards (usually four) are alternated with the same number of black cards; the four black cards (representing oil) assemble at the top of the packet, illustrating that oil and water do not mix. The effect is the invention of WALTER B. GIBSON, who published it in THE JINX magazine under the title *Like Seeks Like*; the **oil and water** title and presentation was provided by ED

MARLO, who has also created several methods and handlings for this effect.

A later version of this effect was created by ROY WALTON, and is known as **oil and queens**; here, after the original routine, the four cards of one color suddenly change to four picture cards.

The Gibson version may have been inspired by an earlier color-separation effect invented by HOFZINSER in which the entire deck was used.

OKITA (1852-1916)

Born Julia Ferrett in Britain; wife of CHARLES DE VERE and mother of IONIA. She performed a highly successful act in ORIENTAL STYLE, and was noted for her presentation of the LINKING RINGS. Okita toured through Britain and France for a number of years.

OKITO

See BAMBERG, THEO.

OKITO BOX

Invented by THEO BAMBERG in 1909, this is usually a small brass box of circular shape, of a size to take four half-dollars neatly. It is in fact ungaffed, and is used in combination with SLEIGHT OF HAND techniques to bring about various EFFECTs in the realm of COIN MAGIC.

Many ROUTINEs have been devised for the **Okito Box**, and may be found as chapters or sections in the books of J.B. BOBO and DAVID ROTH, or as complete books, such as S. LEO HOROWITZ's *Mohammed Bey's Routines With The Okito Coin Box*; further work on the subject is available in a number of books and magazines.

Over the years many new coin boxes have been developed, similar in appearance to the **Okito Box** but prepared in varying degrees. This may be anything from a recessed bottom—as in the **German coin box** (when used with a lid, known as a BOSTON BOX) which will take a single coin—to boxes equipped with internal magnets which are used in combination with magnetic SHELL coins.

Some (not all) of these later variants miss the psychology of Bamberg's original conception, which was that the box, while ungaffed, was somewhat unusual, and misdirected the attention of the spectators away from the sleight-of-hand that actually accomplished the effects.

OKITO GLASS

In appearance an ordinary fluted glass tumbler, it has a tapered glass cylindrical tube at its center, open at top and bottom. If the tumbler is filled with an opaque liquid, a small object (e.g., a finger ring) may be dropped into the inner cylinder; apparently the object is at the bottom of the glass, but actually it is in the hand which holds the glass. Conversely, a vanished object may be reproduced from the filled glass.

This utility device, now usually made in plastic, was invented by THEO BAMBERG.

O-KORT-O BOX

Actually a set of boxes for a routine devised by MILTON KORT; it consists of a regular OKITO BOX, a BOSTON BOX (without the lid), and a box with an interior too small to take a half-dollar size coin.

Kort's routine is described in J.B. BOBO's *Modern Coin Magic* (revised edition, titled *The New Modern Coin Magic*).

OLRAM SUBTLETY

A technique devised by ED MARLO (Olram = Marlo spelled backwards) to display a number of cards to be alike in a way they actually are not.

For example, in his or her left hand the performer holds a five-card packet face-up; the first, third and fifth cards have red backs, while the second and fourth are blue backed. One card is taken (face-up) into the right hand and both hands are turned at the wrist to show the backs of the cards (the left hand actually showing the bottom card of the packet).

The palms are turned up again and the face card of the left-hand packet is dropped (still face-up) to the table, along with the card from the right hand. The process is repeated with the next two cards; then the back of the remaining card is shown and it, too, is added to the cards on the table. To the spectator it appears that the backs of all five cards have been shown to be red.

The technique of the Olram subtlety is very simple but extremely deceptive, and finds applications in a wide variety of card effects.

OLSON, ROBERT (b. ?)

Performer who began his career as a comedy magician, co-authoring a book on the subject titled *Sick Sorcery* (with Bob Pearce); he also collaborated with John Hope on a *Column for Coin Men* which ran in *Hugard's Magic Monthly*.

He has for many years been a featured performer at Old Sturbridge Village in Massachusetts, where he recreates the shows of RICHARD POTTER.

OLSON, ROBERT E. (b. ?)

Writer on magical subjects who has contributed a number of articles to TOPS and other magazines; his books include *The Added Touch*, *Carl Rosini: His Life And Magic*, *A Tribute To Howard Thurston*, *Illusion Builder To Fu Manchu*, and *Two Hands-Three Pockets-Four Magic*.

OMBRAMANIE

A term for SHADOWGRAPHY; also sometimes rendered as *umbramanie*. It is of French derivation.

ONE-AHEAD SYSTEM

A technique used in feats of MENTALISM and MENTAL MAGIC, primarily in a ROUTINE where the performer answers questions sealed in envelopes—then opening each envelope in turn to determine if the question was correctly discerned.

In fact the first question answered has been written by a CONFEDERATE, whose envelope is at the bottom of the pile; any other envelope (purportedly the one holding the question just answered) is opened, and the performer notes the actual question while calling aloud the confederate's question. This information is used to read the next envelope, and the procedure is repeated for as many questions as desired.

The basic principle may be applied to other types of EFFECTs.

For further information see ANNEMANN's *Practical Mental Effects* and Corinda's *13 Steps To Mentalism*.

ONE-ENDER

See POINTER CARD.

ONE-HAND CUT

A transposing of the two halves of the deck while it is held in the hand, without assistance from the other hand or the use of a table.

There are a number of different **one-hand cuts**; the most popular by a considerable margin is the CHARLIER PASS.

ONE-HAND RIFFLE SHUFFLE

A type of FLOURISH in which the hand divides the deck into two halves which are gripped between the thumb and first finger, and the first and second fingers; the halves are angled in toward each other and allowed to interlace at the inner end.

The two halves are then pushed together and squared (*see* SQUARE THE DECK).

The action is accomplished without the use of the other hand or a table or other working surface.

This technique is said to have been devised by British performer *Jack Morrison*.

ONE-MAN EFFECTS

See ONE-PERSON EFFECTS.

ONE-O-ONE (1-0-1) DECK

A deck of cards in which INDIFFERENT CARDs alternate with four different FORCE cards. Thus (indicating indifferent cards with an *0*) an arrangement might be AH-0-3C-0-6D-0-9S-0-AH-0, etc. Since duplicate cards are eight apart, the deck may be dealt face-up without much risk of a previously dealt card being remembered.

The deck is often mistakenly credited to AL KORAN and called a *Koran Deck*; it had earlier been used by RICHARD HIMBER as part of his *Five-Star Prediction* routine provided with his FLIPOVER WALLET. The 1-0-1 Deck is actually based on principles developed by BURLING HULL (for the SVENGALI DECK) and AUDLEY WALSH (for his MAGICIAN'S DREAM DECK) and use of a very similar deck had been proposed by JEAN HUGARD.

ONE-PERSON EFFECTS

Those effects which can be accomplished by the performer without the need of a stage ASSISTANT, secret or otherwise—though they may employ spectators from the audience.

ONE-WAY DECK

A deck which has an asymmetrical back design. With such a deck, if all the cards are set with the design in the same orientation and one card is reversed end-for-end, that card can be easily located.

The asymmetry of the design can be very obvious, as for example, PICTORIAL BACK; magicians usually take more subtle approaches, relying on imperfection in the backs of standard decks which appear symmetrical to the casual observer.

Lacking such a deck, the performer may create the imperfection by dotting the cards or scratching them with a pin.

A one-way deck invented by THEODORE ANNEMANN is marked on the *faces*; his reasoning

was that in most situations it is more logical to look at the faces of the cards rather than the backs.

Hundreds, perhaps thousands of card EFFECTs can be accomplished with a one-way deck; a sizable chapter on these alone will be found in HUGARD's *Encyclopedia Of Card Tricks*.

See POINTER CARDS.

One-Way Deck is also sometimes erroneously used to refer to a one-*kind* deck, i.e., a FORCING DECK consisting of 52 identical cards.

ONOSAKA, TON (b. ?)

Noted figure in Japanese magic; founder of *Magic Land*, which markets its products (many invented by Onosaka) throughout the world. He is also the founder and publisher of *Fushigi*, a quarterly which is Japan's only independent magic journal, and also the monthly *Magic News*.

Onosaka has served as a CONSULTANT and TECHNICAL ADVISOR to performers on many Japanese television shows. He has also organized several magic conventions.

OOM

An acronym for "Oil Of Milk," a formula which, added to water, creates a liquid like milk in appearance, but which does not curdle and is far cheaper to use in various LIQUID EFFECTS. It is sold by magic dealers.

OPEC

An acronym for Out-of-Position-Elmsley-Count, a procedure used when the card to be concealed is second from the top rather than the third from the top position required for the ELMSLEY COUNT. The concept is credited to ED MARLO.

There are two basic methods of accomplishing the **Opec**:

The first is to remove a card from the *bottom* of the packet as the first card; the count then proceeds as if this first card had been taken from the top.

A more complex procedure is to push off *three* cards as one; leave them beneath the remaining card and take this card off in the same action (in effect switching the three-card packet for the single card); push off two as one onto the single card; and put the remaining card on top of all. This leaves the hidden card in third position, ready for a standard Elmsley Count.

OPENER

The first EFFECT done by the performer in his or her ACT or SHOW. In most situations, this effect is of critical importance, for the audience will often decide the performer's competence on the quality and performance of this first feat.

It is not necessary that an opener be brief and flashy; it can happen that the effect is over before the audience's attention is fully focused on the performer, an unfortunate but not unusual occurrence.

It *is*, however, important that the audience's attention be caught and strongly held until the effect is concluded. Other things being equal, therefore, the performer must make the opener as direct, CLEAN, and strongly-paced as possible.

The term opener is also used to denote the first performer in a presentation of two or more acts; most often it indicates the preliminary act before that of the show's star.

OPEN PREDICTION

A card PROBLEM proposed by PAUL CURRY, the conditions being these: a prediction is placed on the table "open"—i.e., anyone can read it, and note that the predicted card is (for example) the Nine of Clubs.

The performer then begins to deal the cards face-up from the face-down deck; at any point he is stopped by a spectator and the next card is dealt face down onto the face-up pile. The rest of the cards are dealt face-up, and no Nine of Clubs is seen; it proves to be the single face-down card.

Many solutions to this problem have been devised, by Curry himself, KARL FULVES, ED MARLO, ALEX ELMSLEY, PETER WARLOCK, and many others. One version which has attracted considerable attention is that of STEWART JAMES; it is called Fifty-one Faces North.

There are many variations in handling and presentation; the prediction in some cases is not written but takes the form of a card from another deck. Again, some versions stipulate that the spectator must do the dealing, while others use SLEIGHTs or MECHANICAL DECKS which preclude handling of the cards by the spectator.

OPPOSITE PROMPT

British stage direction traditionally corresponding to STAGE LEFT; the term is no longer in standard usage.

O. P. SIDE

Abbreviation for OPPOSITE PROMPT.

OPTICAL SHUFFLE

A type of FALSE SHUFFLE simulating the action of the overhand shuffle; it is described in HILLIARD's *Greater Magic*.

OPTIONAL DISCLOSURE

A technique or ROUTINE for the revelation of any of a number of possible selections, the manner of revelation depending on the specific choice made.

An elementary example would involve a spectator thinking of one of two cards; the performer leaves one possibility on the top of the deck, and secretly removes the other card and pockets it. Depending on which possible selection is made, the performer shows the appropriate card—the implication being that the effect would be concluded in this fashion regardless of the specific choice.

The most complex example of **optional disclosure** in card magic is NAME-O-CARD in which *any* of the fifty-three cards can be named and then revealed by the performer in an interesting way.

See ALTERNATIVE DISCLOSURE.

ORANGE TREE

A mechanical tree which gave the appearance of growing full-sized oranges in just a few moments. Sometimes exhibited as a purely mechanical device rather than an illusion, it would have to be classed as a *false AUTOMATON* as it was secretly operated by an assistant from below. Versions of this device were presented by PINETTI, JACOBS, ROBERT-HOUDIN and others. The very elaborate Robert-Houdin version is described in his *Memoirs*.

This tree may have been inspired by an earlier apple tree exhibited by ISAAC FAWKES.

ORBEN, ROBERT (b. ?)

Noted comedy writer who began his career in the New York City magic shop of STUART ROBSON; he later became a writer for Jack Paar and Red Skelton, and many years later was Chief of White House speechwriters during the presidency of Gerald Ford.

He now operates *Comedy Center*, which publishes biweekly and monthly newsletters with topical humor. He has also written humor books for performers, including *Patter For Standard Tricks, Blue Ribbon Comedy, Encyclopedia Of Patter, Magicdotes, Comedy Technique*, and many others.

ORDINARY

See EXAMINABLE.

ORGAN PIPES

Six or more metal cylinders or tubes are shown; they may be 14 inches long and are of progressively smaller diameter, the largest being about 6 inches across. Each tube is shown empty, first by direct exhibition and then by passing the next smaller tube completely through it. After all the tubes have been thus exhibited, a large production is made from them. (Originally this PRODUCTION consisted of a complete table setting, with food, wine, etc., and the EFFECT was known as **The Devil's Supper**.) The effect is quite old and is believed to have been invented by Antonio Molino of Austria.

All but the largest tubes have load bags hanging inside them by means of hooks over the upper edge; the action of passing the smaller tube through the larger transfers the load to the latter, and this process is repeated with all the tubes. At the finish only the smallest tube is empty, and during the production of various items a load can be secretly dropped into it.

Routines for the **organ pipes** are described in PROFESSOR LOUIS HOFFMAN's *Later Magic* and also in the TARBELL COURSE IN MAGIC.

The **Siamese Cylinders**, invented by THEO BAMBERG was a later variant of this effect; a later variant is called the **Kuma tubes**, after a performer who featured it. Still another variant combined in some models of this apparatus the basic Organ Pipe method with the BLACK ART principle as used in the SQUARE CIRCLE.

ORIENTAL STYLE

A form of presentation which was at one time quite popular, invoking as it did the associations of the then-mysterious East. Of the performers to adopt this style, undoubtedly the most successful was WILLIAM ELLSWORTH ROBINSON as CHUNG LING SOO. Among others who used oriental guise were THEO BAMBERG (OKITO); his son DAVID BAMBERG (FU MANCHU); Juan Jesorum (CHANG); Alvin Wheatley (Tung Pin Soo, later CHOP CHOP); and many others.

It should be noted that most occidental performers working in this style did not differentiate between Chinese, Japanese and various other Oriental cultures; thus OKITO (a Japanese name) performed in Chinese wardrobe.

Audiences having grown somewhat more sophisticated, few occidental performers adopt Oriental style today. However, it is unfortunately not unusual to find commercially-manufactured magical APPARATUS "decorated" with garish color schemes and vaguely Oriental ideographs. Such apparatus must usually be completely refinished to make it acceptable for professional performance—unless, of course, the performer is doing a comedy act.

ORIGAMI

The Japanese art of paper-folding, to create representations of various objects. Many magicians have become deeply engrossed in the art and have made contributions to it; Sam Randlett published a magazine on the subject called *The Flapping Bird*, and among other magicians taking an interest in it are Gershon Legman and Robert Neale.

A noted expert in this art was ROBERT HARBIN, who wrote two books on the subject—*Origami* and *More Origami* (these were also published as *Paper Magic* and *New Adventures In Origami*).

ORNAMENTAL SLEIGHT

Another term for FLOURISH.

ORRIN, J.F. (1897-1976)

Born in Britain; known as a highly creative inventor of numerous effects, including the SPIDER'S WEB. He is the author of *The Conjurer's Vade Mecum*.

ORTIZ, DARWIN (b. 1949)

He began his career as a magician, and later was a professional gambler—his knowledge of

Darwin Ortiz

MNEMONICS (he was an instructor for HARRY LORAYNE's memory school) giving him a considerable edge. He is now considered by many to be one of the foremost experts on crooked gambling in the world, and is a highly-regarded specialist in sleight-of-hand with cards.

Ortiz has conducted lectures and seminars for law enforcement groups, casinos, colleges and universities, and many other venues throughout the U.S. and in many other countries, including Britain and Japan. He has also done presentations for many corporate clients, including Purolator, Price-Waterhouse, Aetna Insurance, and several others.

His books include *Gambling Scams, Darwin Ortiz On Casino Gambling* and *Blackjack: Your Own Professional Program*. He has also contributed articles on gambling to many publications.

OSBORNE, PAUL (b. ?)

Beginning his career with an act of BIRD MAGIC, he later was the Ringmaster for the Dallas, Texas edition of the television show "Bozo Circus." Thereafter he was involved with the training of performers for the Bozo shows in various cities.

Osborne then began designing shows for theme parks; the shows featured many Osborne-designed illusions, and he continues in this work today.

He is noted for his long-running ILLUSION series in GENII Magazine, and also for his several *Illusion System* books on the design and performance of illusion magic. He is also the author of *Magical Mystery Time Machine*.

OSBORNE, TOM (1902-1963)

Performer and inventor of numerous EFFECTs; best known for his marketed version of the THREE-TO-ONE ROPE effect invented by CARLYLE (Lyle Laughlin). He also published a number of small booklets and routines, among them *Poker Dem, Passing The Buck*, and the *Torn-and-Restored Dollar Bill*.

OSE, JAY (?-1967)

Highly respected close-up performer who performed in nightclubs for many years, finally settling in Hollywood. In addition to his private party work, he was one of the first resident magicians at the MAGIC CASTLE.

He also worked as a TECHNICAL ADVISOR on several films, and appeared as an actor in many film and television dramas, including a supporting role in The Flim-Flam Man.

OSTIN, BOB (b. ?)

Born in Britain; noted inventor, primarily in the area of CLOSE-UP MAGIC. Perhaps his best known effect is BEAM SHOT (which see); he has also created the much-imitated **dice prediction**, a PACKET effect called **submarine card** (a card placed crosswise in a packet descends card-by-card), and many others.

He is the author of *Fingertip Fantasies* and *Slightly Surprising*.

OSWALD, OSCAR (?-1976)

Born Cuthbert Quantrill in Britain; former police officer (jailer) who became a magic dealer, operating the Magical Mart in London for many years. Noted for his skill with PUNCH AND JUDY, he was also the editor and publisher of a magazine called *The Magical Digest*.

OURSLER, (CHARLES) FULTON (1893-1952)

Well-known as an editor, playwright, and author, his most famous work is *The Greatest Story Ever Told*. Devoted amateur magician, he wrote several articles on magic—both for general publication and for magic magazines; not all of these articles should be considered as accurate history. Author of the play *The Spider*, which used magical principles. Among his pen names were *Anthony Abbot* and *Samri Frikell*.

OUT

A procedure which the performer can employ to bring an EFFECT to a satisfactory conclusion when, through error or accident, the original effect cannot be accomplished. Though such an out can sometimes be improvised, most prudent performers try to foresee every likely and unlikely problem and formulate a plan of action. An interesting book on this subject is *Outs, Precautions, And Challenges* by Charles H. Hopkins.

The term *out* is also used to denote one of several endings for an effect, depending on a spectator's action; one example of a *multiple-out* effect is NAME-O-CARD.

OUT-JOG

See JOG.

OUT OF THIS WORLD

A card EFFECT invented by PAUL CURRY, this is (outside the realm of take-a-card tricks) arguably the most popular effect with cards of the present day.

The spectator sorts the shuffled deck into two face-down piles, never looking at the face of any card, but attempting to separate the red cards from the blacks. When the two piles are turned over and spread, the spectator has succeeded with 100% accuracy!

Since Curry's manuscript was published, there have been many variations of his basic HANDLING and ROUTINE, including at least one by Curry himself. APPARATUS versions have also been marketed using specially prepared cards and/or stands.

OUT TO LUNCH PRINCIPLE

A principle which is now known by the name of a very popular pocket trick in which it is used. In that effect, a card showing a picture of a small East Indian boy climbing a rope (a la INDIAN ROPE TRICK) is initialed by a spectator; the boy vanishes, being replaced by a sign which says *Out To Lunch*.

The effect operates on the principle of MASKING; the particular application used here was invented by EDWARD BAGSHAWE, and will be found in his book *Twenty Magical Novelties*.

Also known as the O.T.L. PRINCIPLE.

OVERHAND SHUFFLE

One of the two standard techniques for mixing a deck of playing cards (the other being the RIFFLE SHUFFLE). The cards are held at the narrow ends between fingers and thumb of one hand, and the thumb of the opposite hand draws off PACKETS of various sizes and/or single cards and allows them to drop into its palm, succeeding cards falling on those already there.

See FALSE SHUFFLE; JOG; RIFFLE SHUFFLE; RUN.

OVER-UNDER SHUFFLE

Not actually a shuffle but a mixing procedure in which the cards are taken one-by-one in the right hand as they are dealt from the top of the left-hand group—the second card going above the first, the third card going beneath the first two, the fourth card above the three, etc.; the process is repeated for the rest of the cards.

This procedure, which shares some mathematical characteristics with the FARO SHUFFLE, is discussed in *Epilogue Magazine* and also in *Mathematical Recreations* by Maurice Kraitchik.

An excellent effect using an application of this shuffle is STEWART JUDAH's version of the TWENTY-FIVE CARD TRICK; it appeared in PALLBEARER'S REVIEW.

Also known as the "Monge Shuffle," after one of its analysts.

OVETTE, JOSEPH (1885-1946)

Born Joseph Olivo in Italy, he emigrated to the U.S. as a child. Beginning his career as a medicine-show performer, he later toured vaudeville and also played fairs and theaters. Often he was billed as *Great Ovette*, but he also performed an ORIENTAL-STYLE act as *Lung Chang Yuen* and performed MENTALISM under the name *Mar-Jah*.

Ovette also wrote a number of books and manuscripts; among these are *Fast Ones*, *Gambler's Paradise*, *Miraculous Hindu Feats*, *Tricks and Illusionettes*, and *Practical Telepathy*.

OWEN, CARL (CA.1890-1975)

Noted manufacturer of magical APPARATUS who began as an employee of THAYER, and in 1933 bought out the manufacturing part of the business (in partnership with his brother Emmett). As Owen Brothers, the business continued successfully, and in 1959 was bought by LES SMITH and continues as *Owen Magic Supreme*.

P. A.

An abbreviation which—depending on the context—stands for Personal Appearance, Press Agent, or Public Address (system).

PACING

Variations in the speed with which effects are performed, depending on (a) the nature of the effect itself and (b) the way in which the audience is responding to the performer.

Changes in pacing in the course of an act or show are helpful in maintaining the audience's interest. It is possible to do a whole act at the same pace; this usually requires a performer of exceptional energy or considerable charm.

PACK

Synonym for *deck* (of playing cards); usage of this term is more prevalent in Britain than in the U.S.

PACKET

A small group of cards, usually no more than six, and rarely more than a dozen.
See PACKET TRICK.

PACKET TRICKS

Card tricks done with a small group of cards, usually not more than a dozen at most. There are hundreds, probably thousands of such EFFECTs in the magical literature; many, requiring special printing or other preparation to the cards, are sold individually by magic dealers.

PADDLE TRICK

A small flat paddle held in the hand is shown to have a black spot on both sides; the spot can be made to vanish and reappear. Such is the most basic of paddle EFFECTs. of which there are a great number. They all depend, to greater or lesser degree, on the **paddle move**—in which, as the hand is turned to show the other side of the paddle, the paddle is secretly rotated a half-turn, so that the same side is shown twice.

Paddle tricks can range from those of the very elementary type indicated above to full routines, a notable example of the latter being EDWARD VICTOR's **Bat Trick**. The **paddle move** is also used in the JUMPING GEMS and the COLOR-CHANGING KNIFE.

PAGE, PATRICK (b. ?)

Scotland-born professional performer, writer and dealer. He is noted for his excellent CLOSE-UP and stage magic, and for his phenomenal skill with the TOPIT gimmick.

In addition to many manuscripts on various EFFECTs, Page has also created a line of instructional audiocassettes called *Trick-A-Tapes*; he is also the author of *The Big Book Of Magic*.

PAINTBRUSH CHANGE

With cards, a type of COLOR CHANGE made by passing a PACKET of cards across the FACE of the TALON remaining; in this action a card is STOLEN from the packet onto the face of the talon, and the packet is then passed back in the opposite direction to reveal the change. This is thought to be the invention of SID LORRAINE.

Another change sometimes referred to by the above title uses a single face-down card with a face-up card concealed beneath it. The two cards are placed as one on the face of the deck in an INJOG position; the cards are then slid square with the rest of the deck and the upper (face-down) card is immediately returned to the JOG position. The ILLUSION is that the FACE CARD of the deck changed instantaneously as the face-down card was placed over it. This is the invention of AL LEECH.

Still another change using the Paintbrush Change title and general effect has been developed by ROY WALTON. Early versions of this sleight were developed by STANLEY COLLINS and DAI VERNON.

PALANQUIN

An illusion invented by SERVAIS LEROY in which a palanquin (an enclosed couch supported on poles) is brought in by two assistants. The Palanquin is rested on sawhorses and the front and rear curtains are opened to show the interior empty.

The curtains are then closed; when opened, a woman has appeared within. She exits the palanquin, and a repetition of the process produces another woman.

The illusion employs an application of the DOUBLE WALL principle.

PALINDROMIC STACK

An arrangement, usually of cards, in which the lower half of the deck or packet is in reverse order to the upper half.

See REFLECTED STACK; STAY-STACK.

PALINGENESIA

The name given by DR. LYNN to one of his most effective (and gruesome) ILLUSIONs, in which a man tied to a door had an arm, a leg and finally his head removed by the smiling performer. The memorable line used by Dr. Lynn: "Another man cut up tonight!"

(In an alternate version also performed by Lynn, the man stood within an open-front cabinet; this version, invented by Lynn with the assistance of Tobin, used a variant of the SPHINX principle.)

It is said that watching a performance of this illusion inspired the young Ehrich Weiss to seek fame and fortune as a magician—which he later achieved as HOUDINI. Indeed, Houdini made a point of acquiring the rights to the illusion from Lynn's son, then presenting it in his own FULL-EVENING SHOW.

PALLBEARER'S REVIEW

An influential monthly periodical of magic edited by KARL FULVES which ran for ten years, beginning in 1965; in addition to the regular issues, there were also a number of Folios, many devoted to the work of a particular performer.

PALM

To conceal an object in the hand and to so hold the hand that from the back it appears to be holding nothing. Coins and other small objects are often held in the palm of the hand itself, by a slight contraction of the sides of the hand, and this is known as the CLASSIC PALM. However, they may also be held in the curled fingers or (cards and coins) concealed behind the fingers while the palm of the hand is shown; these maneuvers are given the somewhat paradoxical titles of, respectively, FINGER PALM and BACK PALM.

There are many ways of secretly gripping an object in the hand; while some (such as the EDGE PALM) actually use the palm of the hand, others (such as the TENKAI PALM or the DOWNS PALM) are finger or thumb grips like the finger and back palms, and do not employ the palm of the hand at all. They are, nevertheless, classed as palms.

A number of EFFECTs, particularly in COIN MAGIC, employ a classic palm as their only SLEIGHT; well executed, and with proper attention to MISDIRECTION and routing, this simplest of SLEIGHT-OF-HAND techniques can create effective mystery.

See BACK PALM; DOWNS PALM; FINGER PALM; GAMBLER'S PALM; TENKAI PALM.

PALMER, JAY (1899-1970)

Beginning his performing career as assistant to HOUDINI and LEON; later, with wife and partner Doreen (as "Lydy 'Awkins"), he toured the U.S., Britain and Europe with considerable success, featuring a magical teakettle with which he performed his version of the INEXHAUSTIBLE BOTTLE.

PALMER, TOM

See ANDRUZZI, TONY.

PALMING COINS

Specially-minted coins used in such EFFECTs as the MISER'S DREAM; they are the same diameter as fifty-cent pieces or silver dollars. However, they are much thinner and have a shinier finish, and a more deeply milled edge.

At one time such coins were widely used because they were cheaper than the equivalent "real money" coins; while this is no longer always the case, some performers prefer to use **palming coins** for their relative ease of MANIPULATION.

PALMO BALL

See HANDKERCHIEF BALL.

PALPITATOR

A GIMMICK consisting of a rubber squeeze bulb connected by a length of thin tubing to a small flat balloon which may be inflated by a squeeze of the bulb.

Though sold as a joke shop novelty (usually under the name **plate lifter**), the palpitator can often be applied as a secret motive power in various CLOSE-UP effects.

PANTOMIME

Performance without the use of spoken words, in which a dramatic idea or sequence is expressed entirely by gestures, movement and facial expression. Within magic, an undoubted master of Pantomime was CARDINI.

Also, a play without dialogue, as in the early versions of the British Christmas Pantomime of *Aladdin*; see ABANAZAR. (Though still often called pantomimes, these British shows now always have dialogue.)

A pantomime act should not be confused with a SILENT ACT (which see).

See MIME.

PAPER

Gambler's parlance for a MARKED DECK.

PAPER FOLDING

See ORIGAMI.

PAPER HAT

A PAPER-TEARING EFFECT invented by CECIL LYLE, in which the performer tears up two colored sheets of tissue and forms them into a decorative paper hat. In actuality the hat has been previously made and folded, and concealed in a pocket of one of the tissue sheets; these sheets, torn and crumpled into a ball, become the "rose" decoration on the hat.

In a variation on this, the performer may attempt to make another hat, but this time the torn sheets resolve into a pair of tissue panties; this version was marketed by both JOE BERG and L. L. IRELAND.

PAPER TEARING

The tearing of folded sheets of newspaper or similar material into various designs. This may be legitimate (as in the case of TOMMY WINDSOR's Showboat Paper Tear), or the paper first shown may be entirely cut away and a previously prepared and cut sheet unfolded and displayed (as with the PAPER HAT routine devised by CECIL LYLE).

Even in the case of legitimate paper-tearing, patterns are often lightly penciled on the paper to assist the performer.

Books on this topic include GENE ANDERSON's *Newspaper Magic* and Gerry Loe's *Capers with Paper*.

PARLOR TRICKS

Said of effects which are best performed for a group of people in a moderately-sized room; midway between CLOSE-UP and stage magic.

The phrase is also often used as a pejorative to imply that an effect under discussion is not suitable for professional performance.

PARRISH, ROBERT (b. 1918)

A highly respected creator and writer. His exceptionally well-written books include *For Magicians Only* and *New Ways To Mystify* (published in combined form as *The Magician's Handbook*). He has also written *You'd Be Surprised* (with John Goodrum) and *Do That Again* (with Oscar Weigle).

Among his other books are *An Evening With Charlie Miller*, *Okito On Magic*, *Paul Rosini's Magical Gems*, *Six Tricks by Tenkai*, and *Bert Allerton's The Close-Up Magician*. He is also believed to have been the ghostwriter for RUFUS STEELE's card books.

PARTNER ACTS

Acts in which the two people involved are of equal importance and work as a team, rather than as performer and assistant; examples include JOHN and PAM THOMPSON, JONATHAN and CHAR PENDRAGON, and SIEGFRIED AND ROY.

See also TWO-PERSON ACTS.

PASS

Generally, any SLEIGHT OF HAND move; specifically with playing cards, often used to denote the SHIFT.

Also, a mystical or mesmeric gesture which supposedly accomplishes a magical effect.

PASSE-PASSE BOTTLES

A bottle (beer,champagne,etc.) and glass, each covered with a metal or cardboard tube, change places at the performer's command. In a variant version, an ASSISTANT or STOOGE secretly steals the bottle out of the tube while the performer's attention is elsewhere, yet the trick then proceeds as usual.

The effect is accomplished by the SHELL principle, the bottles being made of metal; the inner bottle has a partition halfway down so it may contain liquid in the upper compartment and conceal a glass in the lower part, which is bottomless. When correctly made, the glossy enamel finish of the bottles renders them indistinguishable from the real thing.

PASS OFF

To secretly convey an object to the backstage area, usually to be loaded into a NEST OF BOXES or a production device such as a DOVE PAN. This phrase is no longer in common usage.

PASTEBOARD

A playing card; the slang term derives from a process used in their construction.

PATRIOTIC BALLS

A red container has three balls of the same color in front of it, as do white and blue containers. The balls are placed one by one into their respective containers, but at the denouement each container holds a red, white, and blue ball.

The effect is accomplished by a complicated sequence of PALMing and SWITCHes. It is described in several books, but is rarely performed because of the lengthy preliminaries required.

PATTER

The words spoken by the magician in the performance of an EFFECT.

Many magicians have an aversion to the word *patter*, feeling that it denotes a kind of mechanical and mindless blathering. It is certainly likely that use of this term does not create the best possible mind-set for the performer seriously involved in his or her art.

There are a number of "patter books," providing dialogue to accompany many standard effects; usually this is of an intended humorous kind. Such works may be briefly useful to the beginning performer, but may often tend to steer him into familiar and hackneyed approaches and presentations. It is essential for any performer to develop a unique approach and style; thus the use of standardized patter may lead into habits of thought which eventually create more problems than they solve.

PATTER IN RHYME

There have been a number of books on rhyming PATTER. Such patter was actually once featured by professional performer DELL O'DELL.

Sometimes rhyming patter can be "cute"—but generally it is dreadful; only when used by an excellent magician who is also a highly competent actor (as for example JOHNNY THOMPSON), can it be made to play successfully.

Rhyming patter is often used in children's shows, but there is little to suggest that children like it any more than adults.

PATTERN BACK

A geometrical design for the back of a playing card; it is usually an all-over pattern with no border or additional features. Examples of decks with the pattern back are STEAMBOAT and BEE.

Also known as a *Geometrical Back.*

PAUL, JOHNNY (b. ?)

He began his career as a comedy bartender, combining juggling and tap-dancing with the mixing of drinks. He began to specialize in CLOSE-UP MAGIC in the 1930s while working in the Gay Nineties room of Chicago's La Salle Hotel; later engagements included TRADE SHOW work and entertaining in company hospitality suites. In 1946 he opened Johnny Paul's Magic Lounge in the Chicago suburb of Cicero, and had his own half-hour television show.

After a stay in California, where he opened two supper clubs, Paul moved to Las Vegas to become the featured close-up entertainer at the Showboat Hotel, where he has performed for over two decades.

PAVEL (b. 1945)

Born Pavel Pomezny in Czechoslovakia, he developed a trophy-winning act while still in his teens. He has performed throughout Europe, Britain and the U.S. He is noted for his inventiveness (particularly in the area of ROPE MAGIC) and is best known for his **Jumping knot** effect; he won first prize for magical invention at a FISM congress.

His work is described in *The Magic Of Pavel.*

PAYNE, STAN (1916-1958)

Magic dealer of Portland, Oregon, and owner of Star Magic Products; noted for the quality of his products, several of which were made in aluminum (the cloth parts made by his wife *Hazel*).

Payne was highly regarded in the magic community for his organizational work in behalf of magic. He was also noted for his DRUNK ACT, a feature of which was his DANCING HANDKERCHIEF routine; a particular aspect of this routine, in which the handkerchief jumps in and out of a large bottle, has since been used by DOUG HENNING and many other performers.

PAY-OFF

Slang term for the climax of an EFFECT.

Use of the phrase has an unfortunate implication that the climax is the audience's reward for having sat through the preliminaries, rather than those earlier parts of the ROUTINE being entertaining in themselves.

PEA CAN

A theoretically humorous POCKET TRICK in which a pea is dropped into a small tube; when the tube is inverted over a spectator's hand, a small amount of liquid is poured out, the pea having vanished.

PEACOCK, VICTOR (1896-1968)

British amateur who operated a highly-regarded school for magicians. He was noted as a popular performer of CHILDREN'S MAGIC.

PEEK

This term is used in two ways: to denote a means of selection or to describe a technique for secretly sighting a card.

As a selection: the performer holds the deck in his left hand in dealing position, FACE of the deck toward the spectator; the spectator pushes back a portion of the cards at the upper-left-hand corner and notes a card, then allowing the deck to close up square. Alternatively, the performer may RIFFLE the corner with a finger of the other hand, stopping where the spectator indicates.

As a secret sighting technique: the performer apparently never sees the faces of the cards, but is able (by a variety of means) to note the identity of a particular card. Usually this card's location has been marked with a BREAK or JOG.

In this latter sense the term GLIMPSE is often used

in preference to *peek*; a chapter is devoted to the glimpse in HUGARD and BRAUE's *Expert Card Techniques*. Techniques for its use are described in most basic books on SLEIGHT OF HAND card magic.

PEEK DECK

A MECHANICAL DECK invented by Dr. Franklin V. Taylor; it may be freely shuffled, yet when a spectator merely peeks at a card, the performer instantly knows its identity.

A variation of this deck, the **Mirro-Peek deck**, was invented by JOE BERG.

PEEK MIRROR

A slightly larger version of a SHINER; used for card EFFECTs and in some feats of MENTAL MAGIC. It is often painted flesh color on its back to assist in concealing it when in FINGER PALM.

PELLET

A small piece of thin paper, crushed or rolled into a small ball, which bears writing done by performer or spectator; most often cigarette papers are used for this purpose.

Pellets are often used in feats of MENTAL MAGIC. A lengthy discussion of the **Cards and Pellets** routine, in which the identities of thought-of cards are divined by the performer, was written by J. G. THOMPSON JR.; it is described in the PALLBEARER'S REVIEW and was later reprinted in Thompson's book *The Miracle Makers*.

Pellets are also often used in PREDICTION effects.

PENCIL READING

A technique for learning what a spectator is writing by observing the motions made by the visible end of the pencil. The technique, employed in feats of MENTALISM and MENTAL MAGIC, is hardly ever used. A primary reason is that a spectator would be somewhat suspicious of a performer who stared intently at the pencil—or even in the spectator's direction—while the writing is done. Also, to use the technique with any accuracy at all requires a monumental amount of practice, even if the spectator is confined to printed letters; **pencil reading** of script is a skill which may take decades to acquire.

An excellent discussion of **pencil reading** technique will be found in *Mainly Mental: Volume One* by C.L. Boarde; additional information on the subject is contained in Step Two of Corinda's *13 Steps To Mentalism*.

PENDRAGON, JONATHAN (THE PENDRAGONS) (b. ?)

Born Claude Yarbrough; he began his career performing ESCAPES, MENTAL MAGIC, and close-up card effects. Later, with wife and partner Charlotte, he created an act of DOVE MAGIC, to which he gradually added ILLUSION effects. *The Pendragons* now do an act consisting almost entirely of lightning-fast ILLUSIONS.

In addition to magical performance, both Jonathan and Charlotte Pendragon have worked as *stunt persons*; Jonathan has doubled for a number of actors in such films as *Day The World Ended* and *The Blues Brothers*, and Charlotte has doubled for actors in *The Bionic Woman* and other shows. Both Pendragons are bodybuilders (Charlotte has been in national competition), and this adds a strong visual dimension to their act, as well as giving them the muscular power to perform illusions in a fashion that cannot be copied by others. One example of this point is their sword SUSPENSION, designed by Jonathan, which appears impossible even to other performers who are aware of the method; another is their presentation of METAMORPHOSIS, executed with the fastest exchange in the history of the illusion.

The Pendragons have appeared in venues all over the world, including Caesar's Palace, Holiday Casino,

Jonathan and Char Pendragon

Bally's Jubilee, and the Flamingo Hilton in Las Vegas, Trump's in Atlantic City, and many others in Monte Carlo, Austria, Britain, Spain, West Germany, Holland and Japan. They have been seen on television in many countries, their U.S. television appearances including *The Merv Griffin Show, Circus Of The Stars, P.M. Magazine* and many others.

They have twice been recipients of the Best Stage Magician award from the ACADEMY OF MAGICAL ARTS.

PENETRATION

A basic EFFECT in magic is that of penetration, or solid-through-solid, and it can take many forms—BLOCK PENETRATION, LINKING RINGS, COINS THROUGH THE TABLE, PENETRATION FRAME and many more. In some cases the presentation is that a hole or gap is created in one object through which the other can pass, the hole then being magically healed—but the effect is usually perceived as a penetration in any case.

PENETRATION FRAME

A wooden frame holds a piece of clear glass; clamps are affixed at the sides which hold a playing card in position over the central portion of the glass. A steel rod is passed through the playing card—and presumably the glass—yet when the card is removed the glass appears solid and unbroken. The most popular version of this EFFECT was invented by EDWARD M. MASSEY.

Some performers use a large feather in place of the metal rod, creating the illusion that a larger object is passing through the glass than is actually possible, given its construction.

The effect is probably inspired by an earlier ILLUSION called VANITY FAIR; a modern illusion, GIRL THROUGH GLASS PLATE, can be considered as a combination of the Penetration Frame and Vanity Fair.

A somewhat related effect is GARBO.

PENN AND TELLER

Penn Jillette and partner Teller first came to public notice as part of an act called the "Asparagus Valley Cultural Society"; a show featuring their talents had a very long run in San Francisco.

Moving to New York, the team presented their new show in an off-Broadway theater and were an immediate hit; the show ran for more than a year. They have also done two television specials.

Within the magic community there are some who resent the team because of their "exposes" of magical effects; in fact the exposure is done so fast and confusingly that it is unlikely that any layperson could follow it.

PENTAGRAM (Magazine)

British magic magazine founded and edited by PETER WARLOCK; it ran monthly from October 1946 to December 1959. It was noted for the very high quality of the magic published in its pages, much of it created by editor Warlock.

It has been succeeded by *The New Pentagram*, also under the editorship of Warlock, which began monthly publication in March 1969.

PEPPER'S GHOST

An elaborate stage ILLUSION invented by Henry Dircks and demonstrated by Dr. John Henry Pepper, in which live actors seemed to interact with skeletons and semi-transparent ghosts; also, the principle used in that illusion.

The actors performed behind a very large sheet of plate glass, angled to reflect to the audience images created in a pit directly in front of them but concealed from their direct line of sight by a low wall. This pit was painted black, and the people working in it were robed in black velvet. If, for example, a skeleton were held at a slight angle in the pit (feet toward the stage), its reflection would combine with the action taking place behind the glass to give the illusion of the skeleton appearing with the actors; the ghost was likewise created. Either image could be made to fade from view by a dimming of the pit illumination.

Using the Pepper's Ghost principle in combination with other stage techniques created some very mysterious and baffling presentations; the principle is still being used today.

Pepper's Ghost is thoroughly discussed in S. H. SHARPE's *Conjurers' Optical Secrets*.

A related illusion was METEMPSYCHOSIS.

PERSPECTIVE BASE

See WEDGE BASE. This term is also sometimes used as a synonym for BEVEL BASE.

PERVERSE MAGIC

Effects which, though magical and baffling, seem to be out of the performer's control; an elementary example is the ball or cigar which keeps reappearing in the performer's hand no matter how often he tries to get rid of it.

The term is also used to describe effects seemingly

other than intended; a pair of handkerchieves being cut and restored, but each with a part of the other, as in the SUN AND MOON effect.

The theme was formulated by CHARLES WALLER.

PETRICK (b. 1952)

Born Peter Krejcik in Czechoslovakia, he began performing in his teens, and won a Special Award at FISM; later, with wife and partner Mia, he performed throughout Czechoslovakia and at later FISM conventions.

In 1979, refused exit visas for a journey to the U.S. to appear in MILT LARSEN's *It's Magic*, Petrick and Mia made the momentous decision to defect. They now live in California and tour throughout the U.S.

Petrick has created a number of commercially marketed EFFECTs. of which the best known are his **straw through the card** and **linking razor blades**; he is also known for his many lectures to magical organizations. In 1983 Petrick and Mia were recipients of the Visiting Magician Of The Year award from the ACADEMY OF MAGICAL ARTS.

PETRIE, JOHN A. (1871-1954)

Manufacturer of magic apparatus who, with A.C. Gilbert, founded in 1909 the Mysto Magic Company; their partnership was later dissolved. In 1923, with Thomas C. Lewis as his partner, Petrie created the Petrie-Lewis Manufacturing Company, which became famous for the quality of its products, and for its distinctive logo; for decades the company has been referred to by magicians simply as "P&L."

When Lewis left the company in the 1920s, Petrie brought in his son Tod to help with the business; after John Petrie's death the business continued until 1968, when it went into hiatus.

The company has since been sold, and continues under the same name but with new staff and management; products and manufacturing techniques bear no relation to the earlier P&L line.

PETRIE-LEWIS MANUFACTURING COMPANY

See PETRIE, JOHN A.

PHANTASMAGORIA

Originally this term denoted the projection of pictures on thin gauze screens or on columns of smoke by means of a magic lantern. This was an improvement on the old technique of using concave mirrors for the same purpose (quite possibly the method used to create "demons" for Benvenuto Cellini in the Roman

Colosseum). A performer particularly noted for his Phantasmagoric demonstration was ROBERTSON.

In current usage the term indicates a constantly shifting complex succession of images either imagined or actually seen.

PHANTOM CIGARETTE

The performer MIMEs opening a bag of tobacco and rolling the invisible tobacco in an equally invisible cigarette paper; the invisible cigarette thus manufactured is placed between the performer's lips, and is then lit with a real match—whereupon the cigarette becomes visible as the performer puffs away on it.

The EFFECT is often used to begin a routine of cigarette manipulation.

PHANTOM TUBE

Used as a PRODUCTION device for silks, this is a large metal tube which can be shown empty; immediately a number of silk handkerchiefs may be taken from it. It is believed to be the invention of Curtis Dressen.

The tube has a secret inner wall is the same diameter as the outer tube at one end but which tapers gradually to create a DOUBLE WALL at the other end; between these two walls the silks are hidden.

Sometimes paper is placed over the ends, held in place with metal rings or rubber bands; holes are punched in the paper and the production is made.

A variant model, hinged so that it may be opened along its length, is the GENII TUBE.

The phantom tube is sometimes used in conjunction with the DRUMHEAD TUBE or the SQUARE CIRCLE.

Also known (particularly in Britain) as a Ghost Tube.

PHILLIPPE (1802-1878)

Born Jaques Noel Talon in France; he performed in the British Isles for most of his career. Philippe was known for his elaborately decorated costume of robe and pointed hat, and for his many spectacular feats. Among these were lighting a large number of candles with a pistol shot and the LINKING RINGS (the latter EFFECT taught to him by a Chinese magician).

He is also noted for his presentation of **Le Confiseur Galant**, a precursor to ROBERT-HOUDIN's **Pastry-Cook of the Palais Royale** (see AUTOMATA).

PHOENIX (Magazine)

A four-page offset periodical begun in 1942 by BRUCE ELLIOTT and WALTER B. GIBSON; Elliott later took over sole editorship. *The Phoenix* was published bi-weekly, and ran for 300 issues until 1954.

The New Phoenix, begun by JAY MARSHALL, ran for 100 issues, 48 of them under his editorship (two were never published). Forty-six issues were edited by Don Tanner and the final four by KARL FULVES.

PIANO TRICK

A card EFFECT invented by George Pugh which gets its name from the position of the spectator's hands on the table, pairs of cards being placed between spectator's fingers by the performer. This done, a card apparently passes from one hand to the other.

The effect is accomplished by a psychological subtlety; it has been used by a number of magicians including FRANCIS CARLYLE and DAI VERNON. A complete description of the Piano trick is included in RUFUS STEELE's *Card Tricks* and JOHN SCARNE's *Scarne On Card Tricks*.

PICKPOCKET ACT

A type of ACT often performed by magicians, in which the performer apparently indetectably removes various articles and property from a committee of onstage spectators—from wallets, watches and pens to belts, neckties and even shirts!

Usually a magical EFFECT is employed to act as a focus of the proceedings while the pickpocketing is going on; this can be any feat which reasonably requires the assistance of a few spectators.

Performers doing the pickpocket act today include Borra, Dominique, RICKI DUNN, GERARD MAJAX, and Mark Raffles.

It has also been employed effectively as a routine within a larger show by HARRY BLACKSTONE JR. and DAVID BERGLAS.

Although some performers, such as Ricki Dunn, make a point of working without CONFEDERATES (stooges), many others employ them very effectively.

There is little in print on pickpocketing; an early work is EDDIE JOSEPH's *How To Pick Pockets*,; much more recent books are *The Pickpocket Secrets of Mark Raffles* (by himself) and *Complete Course in Pick Pocketing* by Pierre Jaques. Aside from these, the only notable work is contained in a series of articles by ROGER CROSTHWAITE which appeared in *The GEN* magazine many years ago.

Gerard Majax's *Les Pickpockets*, written for the lay public, contains colorful background information which may be useful in presenting an act of this type.

PICKUP BUILD

A procedure used to STACK the deck by picking up cards or groups of cards from the table in a particular order.

An example: five poker hands have been dealt out face-up. The performer secretly notes a card in each of the five hands, the five cards constituting a favorable poker hand; in picking up the hands, each is CUT so that the desired cards are in the same position. After a FALSE SHUFFLE, the hands are again dealt out and the five noted cards are found in the same hand—usually the one received by the performer.

(The preceding example is from a routine by THEODORE ANNEMANN.)

PICTORIAL BACK

Playing cards with backs showing an illustration of some sort; many decks sold for Bridge play are of this variety.

While such decks almost always have a ONE-WAY back design, it is far too obvious for magical purposes; also, such decks are not always of the best quality. For these reasons, these decks are rarely used by performers—except occasionally in PACKET effects where the pictures can be incorporated into the presentation.

PICTURE CARDS

The Jack, Queen and King of the four suits in a standard deck of playing cards (which are more often referred to as *Court Cards*).

The term is also (but rarely) used to denote a deck of photographs or drawings used in feats of MENTAL MAGIC or in situations where playing cards might be inappropriate.

PIERCE, RAY (b. 1956)

He began his career as an actor, doing juvenile roles in productions of *Gypsy* and *Bye Bye Birdie* among others.

He subsequently performed as a magician in nightclubs and other venues.

Since then, creating a FULL-EVENING SHOW, he has appeared throughout the U.S., Canada, and Mexico; his show has been featured at venues in Lake Tahoe and Acapulco. He has also worked as a CONSULTANT for such clients as Olivia Newton-John, Steve Martin, and Bette Midler.

PIFF PAFF POOF

An EFFECT in which two ordinary safety pins, linked together, are visibly unlinked; a version of this routine, by Don White, is described in HILLIARD's *Greater Magic* under the variant spelling of *Piff Paff Pouf*.

See LINKING PINS.

Ray Pierce

Piff Paff Poof was also the name for a popular magic convention supervised by GENE GORDON; it was held for many years in upstate New York, beginning in the 1930s.

PIGEON-CATCHING

An EFFECT invented by CYRIL YETTMAH in which pigeons (or doves) appear in a long-handled net, from which they are dumped into an openwork wicker cage; the process is repeated until several birds have been caught.

It should be noted that many performers of this effect, knowing the "bird" which appears in the net is actually a fake, forget that the audience is unaware of this—and slam the net against the cage in a fashion that no real bird could survive; that the birds which simultaneously appear in the cage seem unharmed is not, in the audience's view, through any care taken by the performer.

PILE

With playing cards, synonym for HEAP.

PILLARS OF SOLOMON

An early APPARATUS method for doing the CUT-AND-RESTORED ROPE EFFECT; it used two wooden rods with holes drilled at each end, and two ropes passed through both rods, one at each end.

A rope was selected and the other was wrapped around the two sticks, holding them together; the selected rope was then cut between the two "pillars," yet when it was pulled it drew back and forth just as before, apparently restored.

In reality each rope passed down through the body of the pillars, which were hollow; thus the section of the rope between the pillars was at the opposite end from where it entered and exited the set of pillars. Therefore, the rope being cut was the one whose ends were wrapped around the base of the pillars; after the cutting the visible rope could be drawn back and forth as though it had never been cut—because it hadn't.

PILOT CARD

Term formerly used in Britain to denote a KEY CARD.

PINCHBECK, CHRISTOPHER (1670-1742)

Born in London; partner of ISAAC FAWKES who inherited many of Fawkes' EFFECTs. Pinchbeck was not primarily a magician but a creator and exhibitor of AUTOMATA; one magical effect he is known to have presented, however, is the *Apple Tree* (a forerunner of the ORANGE TREE).

He was also the creator of the copper/zinc alloy which still bears his name.

PINCH GRIP

The holding of a card or small PACKET of cards between the thumb and first two fingers; the cards are gripped at the center of one long side.

This grip facilitates certain card-counting procedures (*see* ELMSLEY COUNT; JORDAN COUNT; E.Y.E. COUNT), but is avoided by some card specialists who believe it is not natural in appearance. DAI VERNON, in fact, devised his TWISTING EFFECTS handling to give a reason for holding the cards in this manner.

It is also sometimes called an **Elmsley Grip**, because it is most often used with the ELMSLEY COUNT.

PINETTI, CHEVALIER GUISEPPE (1750-1800)

Born Guiseppe Merci in Tuscany, he toured through France, Britain, and Russia with a spectacular show, and is considered to be the major figure of eighteenth-century magic.

Pinetti is said to be the first recorded performer to do the THUMB TIE effect, though it is usually believed to be of Oriental origin; he also performed an early ver-

sion of the SECOND SIGHT (or TWO-PERSON MENTAL ACT) exhibited AUTOMATA, and presented the ORANGE TREE—feats later adopted by ROBERT-HOUDIN.

Two books exposing Pinetti's methods were written by Henri Decremps—partly, it is believed, because of Decremps' annoyance with Pinetti's occult pretensions; the exposures (though often incorrect) apparently damaged Pinetti's career severely. Shortly after their publication he ceased performing in European and British venues and moved to Russia, where he married and spent the remainder of his life.

An incident often recounted in histories of magic is of the encounter between DE GRISY and a jealous Pinetti; the incident is described in the *Memoirs* of ROBERT-HOUDIN, and is considered by most modern historians to be fictional.

PIN SPOT

See BABY SPOT.

PIP

On a playing card, a single SPOT (in the form of a Heart, Club, Diamond or Spade) used to denote the value of the card; the smaller pip at the corner index is not included in the count, thus (say) a Five of Diamonds has only five pips.

In a specific designation only (*corner pip* or *index pip*) is the smaller corner spot considered a Pip.

PIRACY

The stealing of performance material. Pirates differ from COPYISTS in that here *direct* espionage or thievery is implied—the method being anything from sneaking backstage with a tape measure and a camera to hiring the performer's knowledgeable assistants.

This type of behavior, while regrettable, is far from uncommon, and has been perpetrated by many well-known magicians of past and present. Court cases have, in fact, arisen out of such activities and, in some instances, resulted in the punishment of the offender—but such resolutions have been the exception rather than the rule.

PIT, PETER (b. ca. 1935)

Born in Holland, he began his performing career as a juggler in a Dutch circus. Becoming interested in magic, he perfected the DANCING CANE routine with which he won a number of competitions, climaxed by a first place award at FISM; shortly thereafter he appeared on the *Ed Sullivan Show* in New York.

Peter Pit

Pit performed throughout Europe and Britain in nightclubs and other venues; moving to the U.S., he worked on shows with Liberace, Jack Benny, Louis Armstrong and many others. He began working as an actor, appearing in *Combat, Garrison's Guerillas* and other shows. He has appeared as a MASTER OF CEREMONIES for television's Miss World pageant, and has also been a celebrity panelist on a number of game shows. He was also a featured performer in Ann-Margret's Las Vegas show.

He has since 1971 been the Secretary for the ACADEMY OF MAGICAL ARTS, and for over a decade he has been the Talent Co-ordinator for the *Palace Of Mystery* at the MAGIC CASTLE. He has also produced shows from San Francisco to Arizona to Hong Kong, and has served as a Master of Ceremonies at FISM, where his ability to speak five languages served the audience well. He continues to develop and perform new material, specializing now in comedic presentations.

He is a recipient of the Best Stage Magician award from the ACADEMY OF MAGICAL ARTS.

PIT AND THE PENDULUM

Poe-inspired presentation created by DAVID BAMBERG (as *Fu Manchu*) for his version of SAWING THROUGH A WOMAN. In the context of a dramatic playlet a scythe-like blade slowly descended and appeared to cut through the center of the woman's body as she lay chained to a thin supporting platform, Fu Manchu then using his magic powers to restore her to life.

PLANT

Specifically, an object (prepared or otherwise) to be used in an EFFECT, given to a spectator prior to the performance; an example would be a necktie to be used in a routine where it is cut up and burnt and a duplicate is produced.

Also, (as a verb) to *secretly* load an object on a person or in a particular location, for later discovery; the more common term for this usage is SALT.

The term is also used to denote a CONFEDERATE.

PLATE, ADRIAN (1844-1919)

Dutch-born performer who emigrated to the U.S.; he performed varied effects but was known particularly for his MENTAL MAGIC.

Co-author, with HENRY HATTON, of *Magician's Tricks: How They Are Done*.

PLATE SPINNING

A juggling feat in which the performer spins a plate by its rim on a tabletop with a one-or-two finger action; it is far more difficult than it looks. This was featured by a number of magicians, notably NEVIL MASKELYNE (who is shown performing it in Neil's *The Modern Conjurer*).

Less commonly the phrase is used to denote the act of spinning a plate on top of a thin rod, usually accomplished with the aid of a small groove or indentation in the underside of the plate.

PLATFORM ACT

An act which may be effectively performed on a raised platform, usually with spectators on all sides; in such a venue the performer must limit himself to ANGLE-PROOF effects. This kind of performance situation is not unusual in many circuses, carnivals, sideshows, amusement parks and malls.

The term is also used more generally to describe a theatrical act which uses APPARATUS and PROPs of moderate size.

PLATT, JOHN (b. ?)

Performer with long professional career in all kinds of venues including vaudeville, burlesque, nightclubs,

Johnny Platt

state fairs and carnivals. He has performed throughout the world, including the U.S., Canada, Europe, Japan, South America and Africa. While he has done many different kinds of magic, he is most noted as a close-up performer; one engagement, at Chicago's LaSalle Hotel, ran for a record-setting fifteen years!

He is a recipient of the Best Close-up Magician and Performing Fellowship awards from the ACADEMY OF MAGICAL ARTS.

PLOT

In stage terminology, the list of requirements for an ACT, SHOW, or scene. There are usually separate plot lists for lighting, sound and PROP.

Also, the dramatic premise and sequence of an EFFECT, ACT or show.

PLOUGH, ALVIN RICHARD (1891-1965)

Professional writer and public relations specialist, briefly a full-time performer. He had a long involvement with magic and was the executive editor of LINKING RING Magazine for thirteen years; his column, *Turned Up By A Plough*, was a regular feature of the magazine.

PLUG BOX

A small, straight-sided and flat-bottomed cup (usually made of brass) into which a flanged lid will fit, the flange being nearly as tall as the cup. An object placed in the cup may be secretly obtained by the performer, with the APPARATUS left for examination in the hands of the spectators. The **plug box** may also be used to SWITCH a small item.

The apparatus works in somewhat similar fashion to the DOVE PAN; when the lid (or "plug") is inserted into the cup, it forces an inner lining out into the performer's palm. When the lid is pushed fully into the cup, an outer SHELL of the flange is locked by friction fit into the cup and becomes the new interior, complete with bottom; if this section has been previously loaded with a duplicate object, a switch can thus be made.

There have been a number of differing models of the **plug box**; in some the original inner lining of the cup is dispensed with, and the performer conceals the fact that the cup is actually a cylinder with no bottom. Some models are made in the form of tubes and are used in conjunction with the BILL TUBE.

The term is also used to denote a solid brass or metal piece turned to resemble an OKITO BOX base, employed in some **okito box** routines.

PLUNGER PRINCIPLE

A principle in card magic developed by JACK MCMILLEN. In a basic example, two cards inserted partway into the deck above and below a particular card will, as they are pushed flush with the rest of the deck, push that card out the opposite end of the deck.

McMillen has applied this principle to a method for the RISING CARDS and it is also used in an effect called **fade away cards**, both to be found in HILLIARD's *Greater Magic*; the principle has also been used by HARRY LORAYNE in his PUSH-THROUGH CHANGE.

POCHETTE

In formal wear, a pocket under the coat at the side of the tail. It is described by PROFESSOR LOUIS HOFFMAN in *Later Magic* as of "doubtful utility".

Not to be confused with PROFONDE.

POCKET PASS

A technique for achieving the result of a SHIFT in the action of placing the cards in the pocket.

As an example, a BREAK is held above a chosen card, and the deck is placed into the side jacket pocket.

When the deck is just within the pocket, the portion of the deck above the break is released and allowed to drop to the bottom of the pocket; the remaining portion is now released, but in such a way that it becomes the top half of the deck. Thus the chosen card is now on top and may be produced as the performer desires.

This technique is the invention of LOUIS S. HISTED.

POCKET TRICK

Descriptive term for any small trick which may conveniently and reasonably be carried in the pocket (as for example the COLOR-CHANGING KNIFE).

While playing cards may be carried in the pocket, the present term usually implies the use of PROPs other than a deck of cards.

POINTER CARDS

Those cards in a standard deck which are asymmetrical on the faces and may, therefore, be used in effects employing the ONE-WAY DECK principle. The Ace, Three, Five, Six, Seven, Eight and Nine of Hearts, Clubs, and Spades are asymmetrical, as is the Seven of Diamonds; some COURT CARDs may also have this characteristic, depending on the particular brand and design.

See ONE-WAY; REVERSE.

POINTING

A theatrical technique for centering the audience's attention on an important aspect of a particular EFFECT or procedure.

It should be noted that this usually is accomplished by BLOCKING, PATTER and other elements; only in the rarest of cases is it to be taken literally, i.e., to indicate something by physically pointing at it. Procedures which create the strongest ILLUSION are those in which the audience feels it is making a discovery rather than simply being presented with information.

POKER DEAL

A type of GAMBLING DEMONSTRATION in which the performer demonstrates his ability to deal desired hands in the game of Poker. Such demonstrations may require only a STACK (**The Gambler's Rehearsal** in the TARBELL COURSE IN MAGIC) or a subtlety (**The Gambler in Person** in THEODORE ANNEMANN's *Book without a Name*), or highly difficult SLEIGHTs such as the RIFFLE STACK.

The title is also sometimes applied to an EFFECT in

which each of several spectators chooses a card from a hand dealt to him or her; on the next deal all the chosen cards turn up in the performer's hand. In some presentations of this latter effect the performer is blindfolded, thus it has come to be known as the *Bindfold Poker Deal*; it has been featured by NATE LEIPZIG, FRANCIS CARLYLE, DAI VERNON and CHARLES MILLER, among others.

POKER-SIZE CARDS

Playing cards measuring three-and-one-half inches in length by two-and-one-half inches in width. Poker-size cards are used by most professional magicians (in the U.S.) for all card effects except CARD FAN PRODUCTIONS, which employ thin BRIDGE-SIZE CARDs.

POLKA DOT PAINT

An EFFECT devised by PAUL STADELMAN in which the performer dips a paintbrush into a can and apparently paints a white board with a large polka-dot design by straight brush strokes; the board is turned over and a pattern of stripes is produced in similar fashion.

Both patterns are permanently on the board, and are covered with a removable white finish; the paint can is empty, and the brush is made of stiff wire bristles which will remove the white coating from the board.

This effect, once quite popular, is now seldom seen.

POLLOCK, CHANNING (b. ?)

Performer who, specializing in DOVE MAGIC, inspired many other magicians to develop similar acts. Features of his act were the DOUBLE DOVE PRODUCTION and the DOVE TO SILK, both of which he originated. His excellent technical skills, coupled with his handsome appearance and commanding manner, made him an artistic and commercial success in the 1950s. At the time of his retirement from magic he was the undisputed top performer of his kind.

Later he became a screen actor and made a number of films, of which the best known is *Judex*.

POLYCHROMATIC BALL

A small ball made of clear plastic, with an opening in one side into which a silk may be inserted. With the ball concealed in the hand, a spectator is asked to choose one of a number of differently-colored silks. The chosen silk being poked into the hand (and into the ball), the hand is opened to reveal that the silk has apparently changed into a ball of the freely-chosen same color.

PONTOON DEALS

Pontoon is the British name for the game of Blackjack, or Twenty-One; thus, *see* BLACKJACK DEALs.

POP-EYED EYE POPPER DECK

A FORCE deck credited to RALPH W. HULL; similar in construction to the SVENGALI DECK (force cards alternating with INDIFFERENT CARDs), but using the ROUGH AND SMOOTH PRINCIPLE instead of the SHORT CARD principle to conceal the force cards.

The deck has been marketed under various names, originally by RALPH W. HULL as the Nu-Idea Forcing Deck; one current name for it is the Mirage Deck. The Pop-Eyed Eye Popper Deck is described in JOHN NORTHERN HILLIARD's *Greater Magic*.

POSGATE, BRUCE (b. 1901)

Born in Britain; performer with long professional career in varied venues. Emigrating to Canada in 1947, he continued performing, specializing in CHILDREN'S MAGIC—a subject on which he is considered an authority; for The New TOPS Magazine he wrote a column called "Kid Show Forum."

Among his books are *Dove Pan-O-Rama, Kid Show Showmanship* and *Table Hopping*.

POST COIN

A variant of the SHELL principle, an example of which would be a half-dollar shell which fits over a double-faced coin showing a half-dollar on one side and a Chinese coin on the other—a hole going through the center of the coin. The interior center of the shell is fitted with a small circular section (or "post") which matches the missing center of the half-dollar side of the double-faced coin.

Thus the set may be exhibited as a half-dollar and a Chinese coin; when the shell is placed over the coin, however, it appears from either side to be a lone ordinary half-dollar.

This principle has been applied in various ways to sets of prepared coins, sometimes used in conjunction with variations of the OKITO BOX.

POTSHERD TRICK

See SUGAR CUBE TRICK.

POTTER, JACK (?-1978)

Born in Britain; television engineer by profession. For many years he wrote a column for LINKING RING Magazine called "Potter's Bar," in which he gave bibliographic references for many standard effects. Later, collected, revised, and updated, this work was published as the monumental *Master Index To Magic In Print*, consisting of fourteen large volumes and nine supplements. It is now generally known as the POTTER INDEX.

He was also the author of an excellent series on BLACK LIGHT which ran in ABRA Magazine.

Potter was awarded one of the first two Literary Fellowships of the ACADEMY OF MAGICAL ARTS.

POTTER, RICHARD (1783-1835)

First U.S.-born magician to achieve a national reputation in his own country. He had a highly successful career and settled in Andover, New Hampshire, in an area now known as Potter's Place.

For many years, present-day performer ROBERT OLSON has been presenting a re-creation of Potter's show in Old Sturbridge Village in Massachusetts.

POTTER INDEX

Term by which *The Master Index To Magic In Print*, compiled by JACK POTTER is more generally known. This index, comprising fourteen very large volumes, lists bibliographic and periodical references for most magic EFFECTs. It is an invaluable tool for those researching the genesis and development of particular effects, and is also very helpful to the performer needing additional information on an effect in his or her repertoire.

Originally published serially in the LINKING RING magazine under the title Potter's Bar, it was collected and published (along with several supplements) by Micky Hades International.

POWELL, FREDERICK EUGENE (1856-1938)

A teacher of civil engineering in the early part of his life, he turned to full-time professional performing and created a large ILLUSION show; with it he toured the U.S., South America, and the West Indies. For a time he performed with IMRO FOX and SERVAIS LEROY under the billing of the TRIPLE ALLIANCE. He was noted for his handling of both smaller EFFECTs such as the EGG BAG and spectacular illusions such as **She**—Powell's version of the CREMATION illusion. Twice his show was entirely destroyed—by a fire in 1915 and a flood in 1921—but he continued to perform a less ambitious show. In his

Frederick Eugene Powell (*The Mulholland Library of Conjuring & the Allied Arts, Los Angeles, California*)

latter years he was known as the "Dean Of American Magicians."

PRACTICE

Repeated performance of a SLEIGHT or other methodology of an EFFECT until it becomes automatic and little conscious thought is required for its execution. Acquiring this level of facility with an effect is not always done by performers, which is unfortunate, for even when the method is not visible the spectator will sense the performer's divided concentration and thus possibly be aware that some secret maneuver is taking place.

Not to be confused with REHEARSAL.

PREARRANGED DECK

See STACK.

PRECOGNITION

Literally, "knowing before"; it is generally used to indicate a faculty or power which gives awareness of a future event or occurrence which could not be acquired by normal means.

Often used as a premise in feats of MENTALISM and MENTAL MAGIC.

See ESP.

PREDICTION

Stated or written foreknowledge of a particular event; the documentary or other proof of the ability of PRECOGNITION. Within magic, an example in the area of MENTAL MAGIC with cards would be the written prediction of a card to be chosen from a FORCING DECK. PREMONITION and NAME-O-CARD are variant presentations of this theme in which the resolution of the effect appears to indicate the performer's foreknowledge of a card to be named.

PREMONITION

A feat of MENTAL MAGIC with cards in which a spectator names any of the fifty-two cards; the named card is found to be the only one missing from a deck which has been on view from the outset. (In some versions of the EFFECT the missing card is reproduced from a hat, the pocket or some other location.)

The effect was originally developed by BILL MCCAFFREY and will be found in HILLIARD's *Greater Magic* under the title "The Prize Winner"; a later version by EDDIE JOSEPH published as a manuscript under the *Premonition* title attracted a great deal of interest, and thus it is by this title that the effect is generally known. It has had countless variations in presentation and method, since the PLOT is intriguing to magicians. As STEPHEN MINCH and others have pointed out, the effect is somewhat less interesting to lay persons, who would find a straightforward prediction of the card to be named far more direct and understandable than this rather byzantine prediction-by-exclusion.

It should be noted that the word *premonition* does not imply prophecy but means simply a prior warning of an event; it is, therefore, wrongly used as a title for this general class of effect—though it might accurately apply to a specific incompetent performance of it!

PREPARATION

Setting and ordering of PROPs and APPARATUS prior to the performance of an effect; effects which do not require this are called IMPROMPTU.

PRESS, PERCY (1902-1980)

Well-known British PUNCH AND JUDY puppeteer (or "Punch man") and magician who worked as a street entertainer or society performer with equal aplomb. He was noted for his exceptionally baffling production of a glass of water from a borrowed hat. Press was honored with a plaque in the Actor's Church at Covent Garden.

His son Leslie has taken his father's name and continues the tradition of Punch And Judy performance.

PRESSURE FAN

A card fan made by applying pressure to the deck with the fingers of the hand not holding the cards, to bend the cards slightly forward; as the fingers make a rotary motion they allow the cards to be released one by one from the fingertips, resulting in an evenly spaced fan.

To execute such a fan requires practice; its advantage, however, is that it can be done with cards of almost any condition.

PRESTIDIGITATION

SLEIGHT-OF-HAND or, more generally, any performance magic; from the French for nimble fingers, it is a term coined by French performer Jules de Rovere in 1815.

PRESTO

Italian word often used as a MAGIC WORD; its literal meaning is "quickly," "immediately," "at once."

PRICE, HARRY (1881-1948)

British psychical researcher and writer who was also an amateur magician; noted for his immense collection of books on magic and psychical phenomena. This valuable collection, comprising over twenty thousand pieces, is now housed at the University of London.

Price wrote a number of books on supposed supernatural phenomena, including *Cold Light On Spiritualistic Phenomena*, *How To Go To A Medium*, and *Confessions Of A Ghost Hunter*.

PRICKING THE GARTER

A gambling game using a doubled belt, rolled up; the victim attempts to find the loop that will "catch" when the ends of the belt are pulled slowly away. The result is under the game operator's complete control.

See ENDLESS CHAIN.

PRINCESS OF BAKHTEN

The name for an elaborate presentation which used a principle similar to that employed in the METEMPSYCHOSIS illusion.

A woman in the dress of an Egyptian princess was swathed in mummy-like wrappings and placed within a standing, lidless sarcophagus. After a time her ghostly image (or *ka*) was seen to appear standing before the sarcophagus. The image moved away and faded from sight; when the wrappings were examined, they collapsed—empty.

PRINCESS TRICK

A spectator thinks of one of five cards; the performer places the cards in his pocket and withdraws four. The thought-of card being named, it proves to be the one remaining in the performer's pocket.

This EFFECT, devised by HENRY HARDIN, is one for which there are many methods and routines; it is a later development of a very old effect called **The Egyptian Pocket**.

In recent years, some magic writers have taken to describing *any* effect in which a card is thought of from a small packet or group as a "Princess effect"; this is unfortunate and confusing, as the title properly refers only to the specific approach and presentation described above.

PRINTED FAN

A set of (usually) just a few cards, each (except for the FACE CARD) printed to show several overlapping cards. At stage distance such a set appears to be a fan of a large number of cards, and thus a few such sets can be used to create a similar EFFECT to that of the SPLIT FAN technique.

These **printed fan** sets have been marketed under various names for many years, and may have been invented by THEODORE L. DE LAND, who is known to have used the principle in other effects.

PROBLEM

Formerly a term for an EFFECT used by the performer to the audience; similar in usage to "test," "experiment," etc.

Now generally used to describe an effect for which, as yet, no satisfactory method is available. HOFZINSER, VERNON and MARLO have used the term in this sense.

PRODUCE

Specifically, within magic terminology, to perform a PRODUCTION of any kind.

Also, in theatrical usage, to obtain and bring together the various elements of an ACT or SHOW.

PRODUCTION

A generic term for the bringing forth of any objects from a previously-seen-empty location; the location may be a box, the performer's hand, or the empty air.

Thus a piece of APPARATUS for producing this effect (such as a SQUARE CIRCLE or JAP BOX) is a **production device**; objects often used in such productions, or specifically made for them (such as SPRING FLOWERS or RUBBER GOODS) are **production items**.

See also LOAD.

PROFESSOR

An appellation used by many performers and magical writers of a century ago, e.g., "Professor Hoffman." At present, within magic "The Professor" is used only as a nickname for DAI VERNON.

PROFESSOR'S NIGHTMARE

See UNEQUAL ROPES.

PROFONDE

In formal wear, a pocket inside the coat at the bottom of the tails, from which an object may be obtained or (more commonly) into which it may be dropped. Described by PROFESSOR LOUIS HOFFMAN in *Later Magic*, it is still very much in use nearly a century later.

PROGRESSIVE ACES

See *FOUR ACES*.

PROMPT SIDE

British stage direction (rendered sometimes simply as **Prompt**) corresponding to **stage right**.

See STAGE LEFT/STAGE RIGHT.

Opposite prompt (sometimes rendered as **o. p. side**) is accordingly **Stage Left**.

(Actually, the direction refers to the side of the stage on which the prompter's box is located; this is usually **stage right** which—in the absence of a prompter's box—is assumed.)

PROP

An object required in the performance of an EFFECT. Sometimes a distinction is made between a prop (as unprepared) and an item of APPARATUS (prepared); thus, for example, in a performance of the RISING CARDS the DEVANO DECK would be apparatus while the ordinary glass into which it is placed would be a prop.

Standard theatrical abbreviation of the word property.

PROSCENIUM

The arch framing the front of the stage at top and sides; also called the **proscenium arch**.

PROTEAN ACT

See QUICK CHANGE.

PROTEUS CABINET

See CABINET OF PROTEUS.

PSI

General term used to denote paranormal powers; from a letter of the Greek alphabet.

Performers of MENTAL MAGIC should probably use specific terms such as TELEPATHY, CLAIRVOYANCE, etc. A technical term, Psi is a word little known outside parapsychological circles and conveys little to the usual lay audience; also, it is a homophone for the word *sigh*, which might further confuse listeners.

PSYCHO

One of the famous AUTOMATA exhibited by NEVIL MASKELYNE at EGYPTIAN HALL; it was a small human-like figure, Oriental in appearance and costume, which sat on a small box surmounting a clear glass pillar. In addition to playing whist (its specialty), Psycho could also (apparently) perform mathematical calculations by indicating numbers.

Psycho was a false automaton; for details on how it was operated, see *The Mystery Of Psycho* by JIM STEINMEYER, and *Automata*, by Chapuis and Droz.

See also AUTOMATA.

PSYCHOGRAPHY

Term used in psychic research to denote writing done by a discarnate entity, either through the MEDIUM's hand or directly, on paper or slates. This latter phenomenon is simulated by performers using the SPIRIT SLATES.

PSYCHOKINESIS

Term coined by parapsychologist Dr. J.B. Rhine to denote the power or ability to move or to influence the movement of objects by mind power alone.

Psychokinetic feats are often simulated by performers; one, URI GELLER, has made a world-wide reputation by apparently bending spoons and keys by this means.

An excellent compendium of such effects is STEPHEN MINCH's *Mind And Matter.*

The standard abbreviation for psychokinesis is PK; a synonym sometimes used is *telekinesis.*

PSYCHOLOGICAL FORCE

An oxymoron, this term indicates a procedure which will tend to influence a spectator to make a particular choice more often than simple probability would predict.

See FORCE.

PSYCHOMATIC DECK

A type of MECHANICAL DECK used to FORCE a card; in construction it is a combination of principles employed in the PEEK DECK and the SVENGALI DECK.

Its advantage is that it may be freely shuffled (the cards being shown different) before the force is executed, during which latter procedure the spectator holds the deck.

PULL

A device used for vanishing objects, usually consisting of a black elastic cord fastened at one end under the performer's coat (often through belt loops), and with a small container or clip fixed at the other end; the precise configuration of this container or clip is determined by the nature of the object to be vanished.

A **handkerchief vanisher**, for example, is roughly pear-shaped, with an opening into which the handkerchief may be poked; a **ball vanisher** may consist of two ring-like clips; and a **coin vanisher** may simply be a small spring clip.

Some pulls do not use elastic; they may employ mechanical take-up REELs, as in the case of ring or VANISHING BIRD CAGE pulls; with the latter, the reel is used to take up the slack in a cord. The actual vanish of the birdcage is executed in similar fashion to the **lamp-chimney** vanish, in which a system of pulleys draws a cord tight as the arms are extended, where a silk placed in a glass tube instantly and visibly disappears by being rapidly drawn up the sleeve.

More elaborate rigs are sometimes used for the **vanishing bird cage**.

Whatever the specific method, it is not enough to put the object in the pull and let it go; its effective use involves not only deceptive technique but first-class MISDIRECTION and acting.

PULL-DOWN

A card move in which the little finger pulls down the lower corner of the bottom card of a PACKET so that the cards above it may be taken as one; it is used for many of the same purposes as the BUCKLE COUNT.

The move was devised by JOHN BOOTH, and is discussed in Volume 3 of the *Tarbell Course In Magic.*

PUMPING

Gaining information from a spectator without their knowledge, through the use of remarks which appear to be statements but are actually questions. The spectator's response, which need not be verbal, conveys information which can be analyzed by the performer.

An example might be a spectator thinking of either the Eight of Diamonds or the Queen of Hearts. Since both cards are red (and presumably neither possibility is known to the performer), the first statement is that the card is red. When the spectator agrees, the further statement is made that it ". . . is a high card." If the spectator immediately agrees the card is obviously the Queen—but an Eight might or might not be considered a high value, so even a brief hesitation on the spectator's part will indicate the Eight, without the spectator having said a word.

An analysis of pumping technique, specifically related to cards, is found in *Trionic* by T. A. Waters. There is also an interesting section on the subject in ORVILLE MEYER's *Magic In The Modern Manner.*

PUMPKIN SEED VANISH

A technique for vanishing a small coin, so called because of the action involved; the coin, held between thumb and forefinger, is apparently placed in the other hand but actually is "squirted" up the sleeve of the receiving hand. This is accomplished by the sudden pressure of the thumb and forefinger coming together.

With practice, larger coins and other objects may be used. The SLEIGHT is described in J.B. BOBO's *Modern Coin Magic.*

PUNCH AND JUDY

The major figures in a centuries-old comic puppet show which continues to be seen in many parts of the world. A number of magicians have achieved notable reputations as "Punch workers", among them ELMER P. RANSOM, AL FLOSSO, JAY MARSHALL, PERCY PRESS, Les Nottle, John Styles, Sydney de Hempsey, and Eric Sharp.

PURSE PALM

Invented by CHARLES MORRITT, this is a method for gripping a half-dollar or quarter size coin with the hand held perfectly flat; technically it is not a palm at all.

The coin rests at the innermost joint of the second finger (on the palm side of the hand), and is gripped at the sides by folds of flesh from the first and third fingers. With the coin gripped in this manner, it is possible to hold the fingers together straight and flat in a manner that seems to preclude the concealment of a coin.

The palm gets its name from its use in Morritt's routine for an effect called the PURSE SWINDLE, in which two coins in small purses change places.

PURSE SWINDLE

A CLOSE-UP effect based on an old British con game, in which coins dropped into a small leather change purse are mysteriously transformed into coins of different values.

Several HANDLINGs for the effect have been developed, including those of AL BAKER and CHARLES MORRITT which can be found in J.B. BOBO's *Modern Coin Magic*.

PUSH-OFF

To hold the deck in dealing position and push two cards to the right (as in a dealing action); the cards are perfectly squared and appear as a single card. The technique is employed in some forms of the SECOND DEAL and in FALSE COUNTs.

PUSH-THROUGH CHANGE

An excellent SWITCH of four cards projecting as a group from the deck; invented by HARRY LORAYNE, it operates on the PLUNGER PRINCIPLE.

In placing the four cards part way into the deck, the upper and lower cards have one card each of the deck interleaved; the center two cards have two cards of the deck between them. In passing the deck from one hand to the other it is reversed end-for-end, and at the same time a finger pushes the four cards flush; this action causes the interleaved cards to project out from the deck which thus appears unchanged.

The move and its applications are thoroughly described in Lorayne's *Close-Up Card Magic*.

Q, DOCTOR

Purported subject of *The Life And Mysteries Of The Celebrated Dr. Q*, by C.A. ALEXANDER; also the pen name used by WILLIAM W. LARSEN SR. for several manuscripts.

Q—FORCE

A number of objects (usually coins) are laid out in the shape of a letter Q—i.e., a circle with a "tail". A spectator is asked to think of a number and then, beginning at the bottom of the tail, to count up the tail and around the circle in counter-clockwise fashion until the number is reached. Starting at this same spot, the spectator is now instructed to count to their number again, this time around the circle in clockwise fashion.

In spite of the free choice of number, the final point at which the spectator arrives is forced; it is determined by the number of objects in the tail, as the force position will be at that same number from the point where the tail joins the circle (counting clockwise). Depending on the objects used, the technique can be applied to many different presentations.

QUEEN OF THE AIR

A version of the RISING CARDS featured by HOWARD THURSTON in which the chosen card would rise clear of the deck and float through the air. A version is described in HILLIARD's *Greater Magic*.

QUICK CHANGE

There are few acts now working based on the premise of complete changes of wardrobe and character. Of these, two of note are Arturo Brachetti, a highly regarded European performer, and Michael McGiveney, who performs a scene based on Dickens' *Oliver Twist* in which he plays all the major characters (the act was developed by his father, Owen McGiveney).

Magicians have sometimes used the techniques of quick-change as a method, but rarely have used it openly; among those who have are Edgar C. Stowell and GEORGE LAFOLLETTE.

In many present day ILLUSION sequences a costume change will be included as an additional "kicker"; rapid and impressive as such changes may be, they do not technically fall within the category of quick-change.

Quick-change acts are sometimes referred to as Protean acts, after the shape-changing sea-god Proteus.

QUICK THREE-WAY

A sequence of moves devised by ED MARLO to show three different cards in a three-card PACKET to be identical, when they are actually three different cards.

The card on the bottom is shown by lifting up the packet, which is held in the left hand by the two long edges between fingers and thumb. The left hand slides back the top card an inch or so and then slides it forward again—but pressure of a left finger is exerted to move the second card outward; the left thumb stops at the rear of the bottom card, so that now the center card projects and the top and bottom cards are in alignment.

The left hand draws away the top and bottom cards as one (apparently only the top card) and lifts it to show the same FACE; the two cards (still held as one) are replaced on the single card held in the left hand and the three cards are immediately fanned. The center card is extracted and shown, displaying the same face for a third time.

Marlo's sequence is logical and, performed smoothly, very convincing.

RABBIT FROM HAT

The PRODUCTION of a rabbit from a hat, while a classic symbol of magic, is rarely performed except for publicity purposes. Indeed, the EFFECT is said to have been created by a British magician wishing to capitalize on the widely publicized claims of one Mary Tofts to have given birth to a number of rabbits.

There are many reasons for the decline of the effect (which was never very popular among magicians). A primary cause for its disappearance is changing fashion; few men now wear hats, and fewer still the type of hat that would be practical or appropriate for such a production.

Also, while few spectators may have actually seen the effect, it is such a well-known symbol of magic that it has become hackneyed without being performed, and thus is lacking in any element of surprise or uniqueness.

Rabbits *are*, however, often used in PRODUCTION effects; docile and relatively easy to care for, they are more practical for this purpose than more exotic animals.

See ANIMAL MAGIC.

RACHERBAUMER, JON (b. 1940)

Airline businessperson by profession; noted as a writer/editor/publisher whose primary interest is card magic. In addition to his magazines HEIROPHANT and KABBALA, he has also written a number of books.

These include *Arch Triumphs, The Ascanio Spread, At The Table, Card Finesse, Marlo Without Tears,* and several others.

RAE, OSWALD (b. ?)

Born in Britain; inventor and writer noted for his many ingenious EFFECTs, of which perhaps the best known is his FLEXIBLE GLASS. His books include *Original Magic, Sub Rosa, Wizardry With Watches, Practical Patter* and *More Practical Patter.*

RAG PICTURES

A specialty ROUTINE sometimes performed by magicians, in which pieces of felt are placed on a cloth easel to gradually form a recognizable picture. Sometimes the felt may be treated with special paints which fluoresce under ultraviolet light, and thus transform the picture to a greater or lesser degree.

Once popular, this specialty is now rarely performed.

RAKE

A slight upward slanting of the performing area of a stage, the upstage area being higher. The raked stage is rarely used in modern theaters, but may be found in those built in an earlier era. Also, such stages are in common use in the Soviet Union and other Eastern European countries.

Many illusions are impractical for performance on a raked stage unless the rollers or wheels at their bases can be securely locked off.

RAMSAY, JOHN (1877-1962)

Scottish amateur performer noted particularly for the excellence of his CLOSE-UP MAGIC and his ingenious use of MISDIRECTION; it was not unusual for Ramsay to completely baffle well-informed magicians.

His approach has been detailed by VICTOR FARELLI in several booklets—*John Ramsay's Routine For Cups And Balls; John Ramsay's Cylinder And Coins;* and *The Triple Restoration.* Ramsay's work is also the subject of three books by Andrew Galloway entitled *The Ramsay Legend, The Ramsay Classics,* and *The Ramsay Finale.*

RANDI, JAMES (b. 1928)

Born Randall Zwinge in Canada, he achieved early fame as a specialist in ESCAPES, not only from handcuffs and straitjackets but also from maximum-security prison cells. He has done a number of spectacular publicity feats, including walking through the solid wall of a partially-demolished building and performing an upside-down straitjacket escape while suspended over Niagara Falls. He is well known through his many television appearances in the U.S. and Britain.

In recent years he has become noted for his critical attitude regarding those claiming psychic abilities; a particular target is URI GELLER, about whom Randi has written a book (*The Magic Of Uri Geller;* a revised edition is titled *The Truth About Uri Geller*). A more general book is his *Flim-Flam: Psychics, ESP, Unicorns And Other Delusions.*

For his efforts in this latter area, he has recently been made a recipient of a sizable financial grant from the MacArthur Foundation; Randi is the first professional magician to be so honored (however, see also DIACONIS).

RANGING FORCE

FORCE of any of a specific group of items within a larger group—e.g., from among the Diamond suit cards within a deck.
See RESTRICTED CHOICE.

RANSOM, ELMER P. (1862-1942)

Performer with long professional career, both in CHAUTAUQUA and touring his large FULL-EVENING SHOW. He was noted for his excellent PUNCH AND JUDY routine, and also his exposures of fraudulent spirit MEDIUMs.

RAPP, GUS (1871-1961)

Born Francis Augustus Rapp, his long professional career was spent touring small towns and rural areas, at first working town halls and opera houses and later under his own large tent. In his later years he briefly managed a Nashville hotel, then for a time worked for PERCY ABBOTT.

In addition to magic, Rapp performed ventriloquism, puppetry and comedy. For many years he wrote a column for the SPHINX Magazine called "Comedy Write-ups Of A Rube." Rapp was noted for his excellent presentation of the classic SPIRIT CABINET act; a version of his routine (though not the one he actually presented) is described in his booklet on the subject published by Abbott's Magic Novelty Co.

His career is recounted in his autobiography titled *The Life And Times Of August Rapp, The Small Town Showman.*

RAPPING HAND

A wooden hand placed on a board or tray raps out answers to questions, much like the TALKING SKULL. While presumably a mediumistic effect, it has been used almost exclusively by magicians.

Many methods have been developed to make the hand move, ranging from the simplest of thread hookups to electromagnets.

RASHOMON PRINCIPLE

Taken from the Japanese film of that name and classic Asgatanaka story, this denotes a created situation in which the spectator's viewpoint is used to mislead him or her into a false conclusion.

If (to take an elementary example) the same card is FORCED on two spectators, and each is shown a pair of cards consisting of the force card and any other, each spectator will assume the indifferent card is *that selected by the other spectator.* A number of exceedingly subtle effects can be accomplished with the aid of this principle.
See SMITH MYTH for a further example.

The Rashomon title was first used in a magical context (although not in the sense indicated above) by PHIL GOLDSTEIN.

RATTLE BARS

A variant of the theme used in the SHELL GAME or THREE-CARD-MONTE, in which one of three small metal bars is shown to rattle while the other two do not. No matter what precautions a spectator takes, he or she is unable to keep track of the bar that rattles.

In actuality, *none* of the bars rattle; the performer has a small rattle device concealed in the hand or strapped to the wrist. The rattling will seem to come from the bar held in the hand; a bar can be demonstrated solid by shaking it with the other hand.

There have been many ways devised to hide the rattling GIMMICK, including the interior of a cigarette or a hollowed-out wristwatch. The most common version of the EFFECT uses three matchboxes, only one of which contains matches; the rattling is effected with a matchbox secured to the performer's arm within the sleeve by a rubber band. A totally different approach was taken with a marketed routine called the **Wandering Lipsticks**; here no external gimmick was used, and the three "lipstick cases" were so designed that the performer could make them rattle or remain silent.

RATTLE BOX

Used primarily in COIN MAGIC, this small box has a sliding lid which may be opened to allow a spectator to drop in a marked coin; the box is then set aside. At any time the performer may pick it up and shake it, proving by the rattle the presence of the coin—which has long since left the box.

The box is equipped with its own rattle, hidden beneath a false bottom; pressure of the fingers on the bottom of the box releases the rattle so that it may be heard when the box is shaken. When the pressure is released the box is, of course, silent.

One of the end walls of the box is attached to the lid; thus when the lid is moved aside, the deposited coin may slide directly into the performer's palm.

Other small objects, such as finger rings, may also be used, often in connection with the NEST OF BOXES.

RAWSON, CLAYTON (1906-1972)

A professional editor and writer, he also contributed to many magic magazines, notably the PHOENIX; he is best known, however, for his creation of the fictional magician-detective Merlini, who was featured in such novels as *Death From A Top Hat*, *No Coffin For The Corpse*, and *The Footprints On The Ceiling*. Another fictional magician created by Rawson (under the pen name of Stuart Towne) was Don Diavolo, who appeared in *Death Out Of Thin Air*.

Rawson also wrote *How To Entertain Children With Magic You Can Do, by The Great Merlini*.

RAY, DEL (b. ?)

Born Seymour Potowsky; performer with long professional career. After a brief period working in the show of HARRY BLACKSTONE SR., he left to work in the nightclub field with a PANTOMIME act featuring CARD FAN PRODUCTIONS and CIGARETTE MAGIC.

He has since created stage and closeup presentations with many original features, including several effects involving sophisticated electronics.

Generally considered to be one of the top closeup performers in the world, he is noted for his DICE STACK routine and highly skilled card work.

RAYMOND, MAURICE F. (1879-1948)

Born Morris Saunders, he began his performing career while still a boy; on his first trip to Britain he began to achieve success, and built an elaborate FULL-EVENING SHOW with which he toured the world. For most of his life he appeared throughout Europe and South America, performing in the U.S. only rarely.

RAZOR-BLADE SWALLOWING

A variant of the NEEDLE TRICK; many commercially-marketed routines are available, and there are also several described in the literature. Notable among the latter are the **Lee Noble** routine described in BRUCE ELLIOTT's *Classic Secrets Of Magic*, and that of TERRI ROGERS, described in her book *Secrets*.

READ, BOB (b. ?)

Born in Britain; textile executive by profession. Highly regarded for his very funny and extremely strong CLOSE-UP MAGIC; many of his EFFECTs are described in his *Thanks To Pepys, One Hundred Dollar Glass Through Table, Penultimate Cups And Balls* and *Transpo Tumbler*. He has also contributed effects to *Pabular* and other magazines.

READERS

Slang synonym for MARKED DECK.

REAR PALM

A type of playing card PALM technique in which the front (or outer) edge of the card is below the base of the fingers, and the inner edge projects toward the wrist—the greater part of the card being within the palm area proper.

An entire chapter is devoted to this palm in HUGARD and BRAUE's *Expert Card Technique*.

Not to be confused with BACK PALM.

RED-BLACK SHUFFLE

With the cards separated into red and black, an OVERHAND SHUFFLE is commenced; when somewhat less than half of the cards have been drawn off, the cards are RUN through the central section, and the shuffle then continues legitimately. While cards within each of the two halves may be mixed, this procedure keeps the two groups separate. It may be employed in any EFFECT using a DIVIDED DECK.

Sometimes known as the **Ireland shuffle**, after the person to whom it is credited—L. L. IRELAND.

REEL

A small GIMMICK, often flesh-colored, containing a length of thread or transparent gut on a spring-loaded take-up reel. The thread may be drawn out and held in position by pressure on the side of the reel; when pressure is released the thread is smoothly drawn inside. Some reels are equipped with locking devices which will allow the thread to stay extended; putting tension on the thread releases the locking mechanism.

Small reels are used most often for the UNTYING SILK (sometimes called the SERPENT SILK).

Larger, more powerful reels have been used to take up the slack in the cord attached to the VANISHING BIRD CAGE—the cage then being vanished by extending the arms, pulling the cage into the sleeve. More sophisticated hookups have been designed to pull the cage (once vanished) down into the rear of the trousers so that the performer's jacket can be removed.

Some reels are noted for exceptionally long thread, as was the case with the now-unavailable THORNTON REEL, and also an electrically-operated reel currently being manufactured by JOHN KENNEDY.

An excellent work on the use of reels is JOHN ALBENICE's *Reel Magic*. Methods of construction and use, including several new applications, are discussed in a section of JAY SCOTT BERRY's *Magic For The New World*.

REFLECTED STACK

Sometimes called a **mirror stack**, this denotes an arrangement of the deck where the top card is the MATE CARD (same color and value) of the bottom card; ditto the second from top and bottom; and so on to the two center cards of the deck (twenty-sixth from top and bottom).

The stack is often used in conjunction with the STAY-STACK principle, and also in various coincidence effects.

A variant of this stack uses duplicate cards, rather than mates.

See STACK.

REHEARSAL

A term often confused with PRACTICE; briefly, the difference is that a MOVE or SLEIGHT is practiced, while an ACT or SHOW is rehearsed.

In rehearsal, the performer does not merely "go through the motions" but says every word and makes every movement of the entire performance exactly as if it were an actual show. Ideally, this includes full lighting and music CUEs, and is done in the venue where the performance will take place. This is, of course, not always possible—but the closer the performer is able to approximate actual performance conditions in rehearsal, the less likelihood there will be of unpleasant surprises.

It should be noted that this confusion between the terms *practice* and *rehearsal* is more often found within magic than in the larger field of show business; undoubtedly this is due to the predilection of some (not all) magicians to initiate performing careers without any formal stage training.

REILLY, SYL (?-1959)

Dealer who for many years had a shop in Columbus, Ohio; he was also the founder of the Magi-Fest, a yearly convention held in Columbus. He created a number of EFFECTs, including **Stop-Light**, THE FA-KO DECK, **Dun-A-Trix**, and others; Reilly also invented a number of SEANCE effects, some of which used BLACK LIGHT principles.

His books include *Modern Fortune Telling*, *Hellstromism*, *Brain Control* and *Ghost Show Routine*.

REINCARNATION

The doctrine of the soul's rebirth in successive lives, a feature of many religious and philosophical systems.

Within magic, the name of an ILLUSION in which a small box rests on a cabinet or sectioned screen with a grillwork front through which the space beneath the box may be observed. The box is opened to reveal a mummified head, which slowly and visibly changes to that of a living person. The head may speak, smile, etc., and at the end of the routine is transformed back into the mummy-head.

The illusion is accomplished by a combination of the SPHINX and BLACK ART principles. Variant versions may employ PEPPER'S GHOST, DOUBLE WALL or other principles in place of the BLACK ART method.

REMOTE CONTROL

A card EFFECT in which the performer removes one card from a red-backed deck (for example) and places it in a blue-backed deck without letting the audience see the face of the card.

The blue-backed deck is now spread face-up and a spectator freely indicates any card; this proves to be the red-backed card from the other deck.

This plot was most probably devised by THEODORE ANNEMANN; there have been dozens of variations and methodologies, ranging from pure sleight-of-hand techniques to the use of MECHANICAL DECKS. An example of the latter approach is RALPH W. HULL's *Magnetic Mental Control* which will be found in HILLIARD's *Greater Magic*.

RENO, ED (1861-1949)

A professional performer for several decades, Reno appeared throughout the U.S. in his long career. He was a life member of the I.B.M. and during the latter part of his life was known as the "dean of American magicians."

REPEAT DOLLAR BILLS

The performer shows six dollar bills, then counts off three and discards them—but still has six; the EFFECT is repeated several times in the ROUTINE. Developed by TOM BOWYER, it is based on the classic SIX-CARD REPEAT effect.

It employs specially-prepared stage money, but some performers go to the trouble of making it up with real currency.

REPEAT EFFECTS

Feats in which the same magical EFFECT takes place several times; of these perhaps the best known is the SIX-CARD REPEAT, but many other ROUTINEs have been devised with this element—notably the CUT AND RESTORED ROPE.

It is usually advisable to have a strong conclusion to such routines, in which the climactic effect is quite different than the preceding repeat sequence.

RESET

To prepare again for performance a PROP or device as needed—for example, to re-STACK a deck which had been shuffled in the course of a ROUTINE, or to re-LOAD a PRODUCTION device.

CLOSE-UP performers in particular may not always have the time or opportunity to do such resetting; thus EFFECTs which do not require it, or routines which allow the props to end in the same situation as at the start, are highly favored as more practical for this type of venue.

Also, the name of a popular card effect invented by PAUL HARRIS in which a number of transpositions take place between a PACKET of four Aces and a packet of four Kings. Many variations of this effect have appeared in print.

RESTORING THE CUT

Any secret technique or SLEIGHT by which the deck is secretly restored to its original order while apparently completing the CUT, or immediately thereafter; *see*, for example, HOPPING THE CUT.

Among the many other techniques for accomplishing this are the SHIFT and the CHARLIER PASS (the latter being done under cover rather than openly).

RESTRICTED CHOICE

A technique to limit the spectator's choice to a smaller range of options than seems apparent.

With playing cards, the performer might request the spectator to call stop at any point while the deck is riffled—but the performer is riffling the deck as he speaks, thus the cards already passed cannot be selected. This technique is useful in limiting the choice to a card from one specific half in a DIVIDED DECK; replaced in the other half, the card is easily located.

Restricted choice can also be accomplished with a MULTIPLE-BANK DECK such as that used in the MAGICIAN'S DREAM effect.

RETENTION OF VISION

Term to denote the endurance of a visual image in the mind when it is no longer present to the eye; within magic, this phenomenon is most often used by briefly covering or concealing an object in a specific position and then secretly withdrawing it from that position. The spectator's mind, in the absence of any contrary information, will assume it has actually *seen* the object when the object is in fact no longer there.

See RETENTION VANISH.

RETENTION VANISH

A SLEIGHT-OF-HAND technique for the VANISH of a small object, usually a coin, which uses the phenomenon of RETENTION OF VISION. The spectator sees the coin placed into the palm of the hand and the fingers closed around it; though the fingers of the holding hand in fact never release the coin, and extract it in the course of moving the hand away, the visual impression of the coin remaining in the hand is very strong.

Several retention vanishes are described in J. B. BOBO's *Modern Coin Magic*.

REVEEN, PETER (b. ?)

Born in Australia; while he is primarily known as a hypnotist, Reveen has also toured one of the most elaborate ILLUSION shows of recent years. He appeared at the Shubert Theater in Los Angeles, and in Las Vegas at Caesar's Palace and in the Folies Bergère show at the Tropicana. His magic was also featured on several television appearances including *Merv Griffin*.

REVERSE

As a *noun*, this indicates an asymmetrical point or section of a generally symmetrical card back design, permitting a deck with that back design to be used in EFFECTs employing the ONE-WAY DECK principle.

The term is almost always used to refer to an asymmetric point which occurs naturally in the deck as manufactured, rather than a one-way marking added later.

Also, as a *verb*, to turn a card face-up in a face-down deck or vice versa, secretly or openly; in this connection see CENTER REVERSE; REVERSED CARD.

REVERSE ACES

See FOUR ACES.

REVERSED CARD

An unfortunately ambiguous term, it is generally taken to mean a card turned over in a deck—for example, a card face-up in a face-down deck. It should be mentioned that magicians commonly use this term in performing for lay persons who may not understand just what the performer means. It is probably better to specify "face-up," "face-down," or "wrong-way-around" as appropriate.

The term is also used to indicate a card in a ONE-WAY DECK which has been reversed *end-for-end*, and thus can be detected.

REVERSE FAN

A FAN of cards created in a reverse, or counter-clockwise motion; a fan thus made appears to be blank except for the face CARD, and if this card is blank it creates a very convincing ILLUSION of a completely blank deck. This fan is often used in NUDIST DECK routines.

With ordinary cards, the reverse fan is often used as an unsubtle force, i.e., a spectator is asked to remember "any card that he sees" and only the face card is visible. If, as will sometimes happen, the spectator reveals this situation to the audience, it can be passed off as a joke; in this event the spectator should immediately be given a free choice and another effect performed.

REVERSE FARO

To separate alternate cards of a deck or packet into two groups. This is often done by openly up-jogging and down-jogging alternate cards, and then separating the two groups.

The same result can also be accomplished by dealing the cards alternately into two piles; however, assuming the deck is face-down, the cards must be dealt into face-*up* piles, as otherwise the order would be reversed by the dealing procedure.

See FARO SHUFFLE.

REVERSE PALM

Term sometimes used in Britain to denote the CONTINUOUS BACK AND FRONT PALM.

REYNOLDS, CHARLES (b. ?)

Formerly an editor at *Popular Photography* Magazine; now a CONSULTANT and TECHNICAL ADVISOR. As a consultant he has worked with DOUG HEN-

Charles Reynolds

NING (for the Henning television specials and the Broadway production of MERLIN), HARRY BLACKSTONE JR. and many other clients; as a technical advisor he has worked for Alice Cooper, The Jackson Five, and Earth Wind and Fire. With his wife Regina Reynolds he has formed Illusion Associates, which supplies magic concepts and effects to corporate and individual clients, as well as theatrical productions.

He is a co-author of *100 Years Of Magic Posters* (with Regina Reynolds); *Houdini, His Legend And His Magic* (with Doug Henning), and *The Blackstone Book Of Magic And Illusion* (with Harry Blackstone Jr. and Regina Reynolds).

RIBBON SPREAD

To spread the cards across the table in a long, evenly spaced overlapping row; also, the spread of cards thus made.

RICE, HAROLD R. (1912-1987)

Educator by profession; noted as the founder of Silk King Studios, which for many years has supplied magicians with high-quality silks and SILK effects.

Rice is the author of *Naughty Silks, More Naughty Silks, Capers With Color, Selected Sympathetic Silk Routines* and others; also, most notably, of the *Encyclopedia of Silk Magic* (three volumes).

RICE BOWLS

A classic EFFECT of magic, possibly of genuine Oriental origin, in which a bowl is filled with rice and a second bowl is inverted on it mouth-to-mouth. The bowls are momentarily held above the performer's head and then replaced on the table; when the upper bowl is lifted rice cascades out, seemingly having doubled in bulk. The rice is leveled off and again the bowls are placed together; this time, when the upper bowl is removed, the rice has apparently changed to water, which is poured from bowl to bowl.

There are several ways of accomplishing the effect:

1. A bowl is filled with water and a clear plastic disc placed on it; if the bowl is inverted, atmospheric pressure will hold the disc in place. In performance, the two bowls are inverted as they are held up; thus the rice rests on the disc and gives the appearance of having doubled. When the rice is leveled off the disc is secretly removed.

The disc must, of course, be absolutely flat and an exact fit for the lip of the bowl, which must likewise be flat; several models of this APPARATUS are available from magic dealers.

2. In the AL BAKER method a white rubber cover replaces the disc; it perfectly matches the interior of the white china bowls used, and an indetectable move transfers the rubber cover from one bowl to the other.

3. In the **Brahman rice bowls** method, spun copper bowls are used; one of these is faked with an inner compartment which holds the water, which may be released by the unplugging of an airhole.

An excellent discussion of all these methods will be found in BRUCE ELLIOTT's *Classic Secrets Of Magic*.

RICE CUP

A cup or glass is filled with rice scooped from a box and is then wrapped in paper; a hole is then punched in the paper and a PRODUCTION of silks, bird, or other items takes place.

The box contains a LOAD CHAMBER which is made to fit the interior of the cup or glass, and is covered on the outside with grains of rice. After a few "trial" scoops of the genuine rice, the load chamber is scooped into the cup which is then shown apparently full of rice; the wrapping and subsequent production of items from the load chamber is then made.

There are many variations on this general type of APPARATUS. Instead of paper being used, the cup may be of opaque material and have a lid which, on being removed, will take away the rice-covered top of the load chamber to reveal the transformation. Sand or confetti may be used in place of rice.

A variant of this principle is used as part of the ROUTINE for the CHINK CANS.

RICE, ORANGE AND CHECKERS

An elaborate APPARATUS effect in which a stack of large wooden checkers and an orange are each

Peter Reveen presenting an elaborate variant of the *Rice, Orange, and Checkers* routine (*photo courtesy GENII Magazine*).

covered with a tube, and rice is poured into a large opaque vase and covered with a lid.

When the tube which contained the checkers is lifted, rice cascades out; the other tube (which formerly contained the orange) now holds the checkers; and the orange is discovered in the otherwise empty vase.

RICHIARDI, ALDO (1923-1985)

Born Aldo Izquierdo in Peru into a family of magicians. His grandfather, who toured only in South America, was the first to use the Richiardi name; his father, Ricardo Richiardi (1895-1937), toured the U.S., where he was killed in an auto accident.

Beginning his performing career as ASSISTANT to his father, he began performing on his own (as Richiardi Jr.) in Argentina in 1943; a few years later he came to the attention of U.S. magicians with a trophy-winning performance at a Texas magic convention.

With an elaborate ILLUSION show he toured through Europe and South America; he later appeared several times in the U.S, including a long run in New York and repeated bookings in Atlantic City. He was particularly noted for his presentation of the **broom suspension**, the VANISHING LADY, and the BUZZSAW ILLUSION.

He received a number of awards, including Magician Of The Year and a Performing Fellowship from the ACADEMY OF MAGICAL ARTS; Magician Of The Decade from the S.A.M.; and Variety Entertainer Of The Year from Atlantic City.

His son, Ricardo Richiardi, continues the family performing tradition with his BLACK ART act.

RIFFLE

With a deck of cards, to hold the deck in one hand and bend it back with the fingers of the other, then allowing the cards to escape the fingers in rapid succession; often used as a method of card selection, the spectator indicating where the performer should stop the riffle.

There are several methods of FORCING a card in the course of a riffle selection; see RIFFLE FORCE.

An alternate riffling technique, using only the holding hand, is to run the thumb down the outer left corner of the deck (presuming the deck is held in the left hand).

RIFFLE FORCE

To FORCE a card during the action of a RIFFLE; this can be accomplished in a number of ways.

1. A BREAK can be held above the force card, and the riffle timed to stop as the spectator calls "Stop!" (the usual procedure).

2. Also with a BREAK, the performer can riffle fairly but simply lift off all the cards above the break regardless of where the riffle is stopped; in doing this the deck should be tilted downward so that the front edge is not clearly visible. This technique is sometimes called a **rocking-chair force**, from the forward rocking action of the upper portion of the deck; it is the invention of DAI VERNON.

3. A SHORT CARD may be used, instead of a BREAK being held; the riffle will stop at the short card automatically. Care must, of course, be taken to time the action convincingly.

4. A SLIP CUT technique may be employed.

There are a number of other techniques available, but these will give an indication of possible approaches.

RIFFLE PASS

A type of SHIFT done under cover of the action of giving the deck a RIFFLE. In some versions of this SLEIGHT the action of the shift occurs halfway through the riffle (so that one half of the deck is actually riffled twice, the other half not at all); in other versions the riffling action is repeated a few times, and the **shift** is executed between riffles.

The theory behind the **riffle pass** is that the larger action and noise of the riffle covers the smaller action of the **shift**; an opposing view is that the riffle attracts attention to the deck at the precise moment a sleight is being executed.

RIFFLE SHUFFLE

The standard SHUFFLE used in card games, in which the deck is divided into two halves which are then interlaced by release from the thumbs in rough alternation, the interlaced halves being then pushed together to SQUARE THE DECK.

RIFFLE STACK

To STACK the deck in the action of a RIFFLE SHUFFLE, by letting the cards fall from the right and left thumbs in a controlled manner to allow them to interlace in the required order.

This very difficult SLEIGHT is described by ED MARLO in his *Riffle Shuffle Systems*.

RIG

In general theatrical usage, to prepare the stage, specifically scenery and lighting suspended above the playing area. Within magic, to secretly prepare a PROP or performance situation.

RING FLIGHT

An EFFECT invented by AL KORAN in which a borrowed ring vanishes from the hand and is found attached to a key loop in the performer's key case.

The effect, which has been manufactured in many different models and with varying routines, uses a REEL concealed within the key case. It is an outgrowth of an earlier routine, also employing a reel, for the vanish of a ring from the performer's hand.

RING IN/OUT

To secretly SWITCH one item for another; more generally, to secretly bring an object into play.

The phrase derives from **ringing the changes**, an expression used in campanology.

RING ON WAND

Sometimes known as the **ring on stick**, this CLASSIC EFFECT is very popular with magicians the world over. A ring (often a borrowed finger ring) held by the performer is passed onto a wand while both ends of the wand are being held by spectators.

There are many methods for accomplishing the general effect, from pure SLEIGHT OF HAND to such special devices as the ELLIS RING. In variations of the basic effect, the ring may be passed onto a ribbon, cord, or rope.

Interestingly, as a magical problem it is considerably more difficult to develop methodologies for taking a ring *off* a wand or rope, but magicians have devised several ways of accomplishing this feat as well.

There are numerous ROUTINEs for this effect, including *Ring On Stick And Ring On Rope* by Mohammed Bey (S. LEO HOROWITZ) and DAI VERNON's routine in *Stars Of Magic*.

See also ELLIS RING.

RINK (b. ?)

Born J. Van Rinkhuyzen in Holland, he is highly regarded in Europe as a creator and performer, having won several prizes. His work is described in his *Magic From Holland* and *Rope And Ring Penetrations*, as well as many contributions to THE GEN and other magazines.

RISER, HARRY (b. 1928)

A businessman by profession, but highly regarded as an expert SLEIGHT-OF-HAND performer, specializing in CLOSE-UP MAGIC. While he has lectured for many magical groups, little of his work is available in print; he has recently been writing a column called The Riser Repertoire for M.U.M. Magazine, and another recent source is an issue of JEFF BUSBY's *Arcane* Magazine devoted entirely to Riser's effects.

RISERS

Platforms of various sizes, used to create different levels on the stage.

RISING CARDS

A CLASSIC EFFECT of card magic in which several chosen cards rise almost completely out of the deck at the performer's command. In a variation known variously as QUEEN OF THE AIR and the *Aerial Cards*, the cards leave the deck and float to the performer's hand or across the stage.

There are several methods for accomplishing the effect, from pure SLEIGHT OF HAND to elaborate mechanical contrivances; JOHN NORTHERN HILLIARD's *Greater Magic* devotes an entire chapter to this feat alone.

In a variation of this effect, *any* card called for is made to rise from the deck; most solutions to this problem have been less than satisfactory, either requiring a special stage setup or using complex mechanics—factors which limited their usefulness and reliability.

The most baffling routine for this effect was undoubtedly that of DR. SAMUEL C. HOOKER, whose performances (described both in *Greater Magic* and in an issue of Pallbearer's Review magazine) baffled many magicians. Though Hooker's APPARATUS still exists, his routine has not been performed in over forty years, leading some magicians to be skeptical of the accuracy of the descriptions.

See CARD FOUNTAIN; DEVANO DECK; QUEEN OF THE AIR.

RISING PENCIL

A pencil is rested across the palm of the hand; it slowly rises to a vertical position.

The EFFECT is accomplished by means of a cap which matches the head end of the pencil; it is prepared with a needle-point affixed across its surface, so that the cap may be attached to the skin of the hand. As the hand is stretched out flat, the cap is drawn into a perpendicular position. The cap may easily be removed from the pencil in the act of handing it to a spectator.

The effect has been featured by a number of close-up performers, notably CHARLES EARLE MILLER.

ROBBERS AND SHEEP

A STORY EFFECT using seven objects (representing two thieves and five sheep) and two containers; though in the course of the presentation the objects seem to be placed into the containers in roughly equal amounts, at the end there are only two objects in one container and five in the other.

The basic effect is accomplished by the way in which the hands alternate in placing the objects in the containers; more elaborate versions, using colored blocks or wooden figures, have also been developed.

Also known as **thieves and sheep**.

ROBERT-HOUDIN, JEAN EUGENE (1805-1871)

Born Jean Eugene Robert in France, he added his wife Josephe's family name at marriage. Known as "The Father Of Modern Magic," he used his mechanical skill to produce many ingenious magical effects and AUTOMATA.

In 1856, at the request of the French government, he went to Algiers to engage the Arabian magicians (marabouts) in a magical contest which he easily won—using such feats as the LIGHT-AND-HEAVY CHEST and the BULLET CATCH.

Among the books authored by Robert-Houdin are his *Memoirs*, the *Secrets Of Conjuring And Magic*, and a book on crooked gambling titled *Tricks Of The Greeks*.

A biased but nonetheless interesting critical work on Robert-Houdin is HOUDINI's *The Unmasking Of Robert Houdin*. A response to this, *Where Houdini Was Wrong*, was later written by Maurice Sardina.

ROBERTS, WHITEY (b. 1902)

Born Alston Peterson, he has had a long career in vaudeville, primarily as comic and juggler, but also using magic in his performances. He was known for his long running ad in the theatrical paper *Variety* which stated "always working"—and he was.

In the course of his career he has performed in every kind of venue, including several national television shows as well as a number of films.

ROBERTSON (1763-1837)

Born Etienne Gaspard Robert in Belgium, he used his knowledge of optics to produce an exhibit he called PHANTASMAGORIA—which consisted of magic-lantern slides projected onto a column of smoke. He is also known to have presented an **invisible woman** ILLUSION, the woman's voice coming from an empty glass box (but actually through a hidden tube from backstage).

ROBIN, HENRI (1805-1874)

Born Henry Dunkell in Holland, he performed in France and Britain. In addition to magical effects he also presented a TWO-PERSON MENTAL ACT with his wife and exhibited various AUTOMATA.

Robin was noted for the great charm and sophistication of his performing manner.

ROBINSON, FRED (1910-1986)

Born in Britain, a railway worker by profession; regarded as one of the very best SLEIGHT OF HAND performers, he specialized in card magic and was expert in such sleights as the SECOND DEAL, BOTTOM DEAL and CENTER DEAL.

He was also noted as the editor of *Pabular*, a British magazine devoted primarily to CLOSE-UP MAGIC.

ROBINSON, WILLIAM ELLSWORTH

See CHUNG LING SOO.

ROBSON, STUART (1892-1946)

Born in Britain; stage manager for Florenz Ziegfeld, then theatrical producer of Earl Carroll's *Vanities*, and later of the acts of magical performers; still later, a magic dealer whose Conjurer's Shop in New York was very successful.

Among his books are *Tips On Thumbs*, *Tips On The Bill In Cigarette*, and *Flash Paper Tips* (with Ralph W. Read).

ROCCO (b. 1959)

Born Rocco Silano, he is noted for his moody and atmospheric act themed with long-stemmed roses. With this act, and a close-up presentation, he won the Complete Conjuror award at the Las Vegas Desert Seminar. Since that time he has appeared in various venues in the U.S. and Britain.

ROGERS, MIKE (b. 1938)

After a 20-year career in the Navy, he began professional performing, specializing in TRADE SHOW work. He is highly-regarded as a CLOSE-UP performer, and works primarily in the area of card magic.

His approach is described in his *The Complete Mike Rogers*.

Mike Rogers

Terri Rogers and her talkative friend Shorty Harris (*photo courtesy GENII Magazine*)

ROGERS, TERRI (b. ?)

Born in Britain; while she is primarily known as a ventriloquist, performing in Britain, the U.S. and Europe, she is noted within magic for her many original EFFECTs and ROUTINEs.

Among her marketed effects are *Word Of Mind* and *Star Gate*; she has also written a book called *Secrets—Original Magic Of Terri Rogers.*

ROLLOUT MOVE

A SLEIGHT usually performed with small balls of cork or rubber in which one ball is placed on top of the closed fist and apparently allowed to sink down into the hand; in actuality it moves down to a point at the base of the first finger.

Another ball is taken and apparently placed on top of the fist as was the first, but the ball already in the hand is levered back to its original position by the action of the thumb moving beneath it and rolling it out. At the same time the ball in the other hand is palmed.

The ball on top of the fist is again allowed to sink down, and the sequence of actions may be repeated to apparently place three or four balls in the hand. Needless to say, no more balls should apparently be put in the hand than could actually be held there.

The sleight was devised by Oscar Pladek, and is sometimes called the **roll-up** or **pop-up** move. A move which is similar in effect but different in technique was devised by SILENT MORA for his **Ball and Net** routine of manipulation with small rubber balls.

ROLLOVER ACES

A highly popular effect devised by DEREK DINGLE in which the four Aces are shuffled into the deck, half of which is then turned face up for continued shuffling.

The deck is then placed on the table and turned over, leaving behind a small PACKET with an Ace on its face; this action is repeated three more times to produce the other three Aces. The rest of the deck is shown to have magically rearranged itself so that all cards are now face down, and to conclude the four packets are spread to reveal that beneath each Ace are the King, Queen, Jack and Ten of the same suit!

The routine is fully described in RICHARD KAUFMAN's *The Complete Works Of Derek Dingle.*

ROLTAIR, HENRY (1857-1910)

Born in Britain, he emigrated to the U.S. while still in his teens. He was first associated with ALEXANDER HERRMANN, most probably as a builder of ILLUSION effects. Later he performed in vaudeville with his wife and daughter in what was described as a very elaborate act.

He is best known as the creator of various large illusion installations for permanent or semi-permanent exhibition; among these were his **Creation** and **Arabian Nights Up-To-Date**. Many of Roltair's illusions depended on optical principles of the PEPPER'S GHOST or METEMPSYCHOSIS type. He is also thought to be the inventor of SPIDORA.

An excellent account of his work is *Roltair, Genius Of Illusions* by John A. McKinven.

ROOKLYN, MAURICE (b. ?)

Australian magician who toured a large FULL-EVENING SHOW through his own country and New Zealand, and presented a smaller manipulative act in other countries.

He is particularly noted for his skill at BILLIARD BALL manipulation; he has described this work in his *Spherical Sorcery And Recollections Of A Pro*, which also contains autobiographical material and memorabilia.

ROPE, COAT AND RINGS

A variation of CORDS OF PHANTASIA; here doubled ropes are threaded through metal rings and the sleeves of a coat—coat and rings coming free at the performer's command.

ROPE ESCAPES

Not to be confused with ROPE TIES, these are ROUTINEs in which the performer is tied up with rope and then, either visibly or in the concealment of a cabinet, makes his escape.

There are many books on the subject; the classic work is BURLING HULL's *Thirty-three Rope Ties And Chain Releases*. Others include U.F. GRANT's *Rope, Chain And Box Escapes*, Lee Jacobs' *Real Methods And Secrets Of The Challenge Escape From 75 Feet Of Rope* and its "sequel," *What Lee Jacobs Didn't Tell You About The 75 Foot Challenge Rope Escape* by John Novak (published by Lee Jacobs!), *The Secrets Of Houdini* by J.C. Cannell, and *Houdini On Magic*, edited by WALTER B. GIBSON and Dr. Morris N. Young.

ROPE GIMMICK

See TARBELL GIMMICK.

ROPES AND RINGS

See ROPE, COAT AND RINGS; CORDS OF PHANTASIA; GRANDMOTHER'S NECKLACE.

ROPE TIES

Unlike ROPE ESCAPES, rope ties are designed so the performer can not only extricate himself but *return* to a secured condition; though now such ties are often played for comedy, they began as the central point in the repertoire of the Davenport Brothers, who caused "spirit manifestations" to take place while they were apparently securely tied (see SPIRIT CABINET).

The most commonly used rope tie at present is the KELLAR TIE (after HARRY KELLAR); it is currently featured by many performers, notably HARRY BLACKSTONE JR. Versions of it will be found in the TARBELL COURSE IN MAGIC, and many other places.

See ROPE ESCAPES.

ROPE TRICK

See INDIAN ROPE TRICK.

ROSARY DECK

British term for a deck arranged in a CYCLICAL STACK.

ROSINI, CARL (1885-1969)

Born Johan Rosen in Poland; he began his performing career as an ASSISTANT, first to a German magician and later to a Britsh hypnotist. Under the name *Carl Rosine*, he began performing in British vaudeville; his act featured the multiplying BILLIARD BALLS and the THUMB TIE (the latter effect taught to him by TEN ICHI).

As Carl Rosini he toured throughout Britain, Europe and South America. Emigrating to the U.S, he presented a fast-paced ILLUSION act in vaudeville, and made more tours to South America; during World War II he made several tours for the USO. In the late 1940s, he retired.

ROSINI, PAUL (1902-1948)

Born Paul Vucci in Trieste (now a town in Italy); he emigrated to the U.S. as a boy and began his performing career as the "receiver" in a TWO-PERSON MENTAL ACT created by Julius Zancig.

After being tutored by THEO BAMBERG, he began to perform stage and CLOSE-UP MAGIC under the *Paul Rosini* name, and was quite successful, his seven-month run at Chicago's famed Palmer House Empire Room setting a record. He was noted for his performance of such classics as the CUPS AND BALLS, the CARD IN CIGARETTE, the THUMB TIE, and EVERYWHERE AND NOWHERE.

Paul Rosini (*The Mulholland Library of Conjuring & the Allied Arts*, Los Angeles, California)

ROSS, FAUCETT (1900-1987)

He became a professional magician at about age 30, working at fairs and carnivals, schools and theaters; at the latter he presented SPOOK SHOWS. At around the same time he established a friendship with DAI VERNON, assisting him in the preparation of the latter's *Twenty Dollar Manuscript* and in the staging of Vernon's *Harlequin Act*.

His work is described in *Magic With Faucett Ross* by LEWIS GANSON.

ROSS, RICHARD (b. ?)

Born in Holland; performer who is noted for his prize-winning act featuring the production of watches and clocks (the only act to win the FISM Grand Prix award twice in a row), and also for his poetic and visual LINKING RING ROUTINE described in his *The Chinese Rings*. This routine uses only three rings; since publication of the book Ross has performed a routine using (in one phase) four rings.

While Ross is best-known for his stage act, he is also highly skilled at CLOSE-UP MAGIC, including sophisticated and technically-demanding card work.

ROTERBERG, AUGUST (1867-1939)

Born in Germany, he emigrated to the U.S.; establishing a store in Chicago, he became well known as a dealer, inventor, author, and manufacturer.

Among his many books are *New Era Card Tricks, Card Tricks And How To Do Them, Latter Day Tricks,* and *The Modern Wizard.*

ROTH, DAVID (b. 1952)

Born in New York City, Roth is considered by most magicians to be the top performer in the exacting field of close-up COIN MAGIC. His technique is faultless; indeed, when he lectures to magicians they often find it difficult to follow Roth's explanations—simply because even when they know precisely what he is doing they still can't see it.

Roth's *Expert Coin Magic*, which fully describes his creations, is an essential to any coin-magician's library.

ROTH, DAVID M. (1875-1972)

Expert on MNEMONICS who often gave public demonstrations and shows. He authored the *Roth Memory Course*, a best-selling book which influenced many later writers on the subject.

ROTH, ROY A. (b. ?)

Born in Britain; founder of R.A.R. Magic. He is a manufacturer of magical products who is particularly noted for the high quality of his leather goods, including the FLIPOVER WALLET and special cases for magic APPARATUS.

ROUCLERE, HARRY (1866-1942)

Born Harold Terhune; he began his performing career as a juggler and acrobat, working in various circuses. After working as an ASSISTANT to a magician, he began learning the art and adding it to his own act.

Later, with his wife Mildred, he briefly performed an act of spiritualistic effects; they subsequently added a TWO-PERSON MENTAL ACT to their show, which toured through several southeastern states.

For some years his daughter (also named Mildred) performed under the name *Rouclere Jr.*

ROUGE ET NOIR

A variation of OUT OF THIS WORLD, in which only ten cards are used—five reds and five blacks. The spectator freely chooses five from among the ten mixed cards as they are spread face-down, which prove to be the five cards of one color.

The EFFECT was invented by DR. JACOB DALEY and first appeared in the PHOENIX magazine.

ROUGH-AND-SMOOTH PRINCIPLE

If two cards are treated with ROUGHING FLUID, one on the FACE and one on the back, and the two roughed surfaces placed together, the cards will remain in perfect alignment and may be handled as a single card. A slight gliding pressure will separate the cards.

The principle is generally credited to DAI VERNON; it is employed in several MECHANICAL DECKS (such as the BRAINWAVE, ULTRAMENTAL, and MIRAGE decks) and also in many commercially marketed PACKET tricks.

The principle is discussed in Trevor H. Hall's *Nothing Is Impossible*; *Roughingly Yours* by Aldini; and *Rough And Smooth Possibilities* by TAN HOCK CHUAN.

See HALF-ROUGHING; SUPER-ROUGHING.

ROUGHING FLUID

A liquid, usually composed of Canada balsam dissolved in benzine, which can be applied to the surfaces of playing cards. It is used in applications of the ROUGH-AND-SMOOTH principle.

In preparing roughing fluid, it is advisable to add a few drops of bleach to remove the brownish hue.

ROUTINE

A sequence of EFFECTs utilizing the same PROP; e.g., an AMBITIOUS CARD or OKITO BOX routine.

Also, a number of discrete effects arranged in effective sequence into an ACT.

ROY, MARVIN (b. 1925)

Born Marvin Levy, he began performing as a boy, and in his teens developed a trophy-winning ACT of silk magic called **Marvin the Silk Merchant**.

In 1950 he developed the first version of the act featuring magic with lightbulbs, with input from ALAN WAKELING and Ray Muse; he also obtained the rights to some EFFECTs featured by British performer BOBBY VOLTAIRE. Learning to ice skate at the request of an agent, he presented the act in several ice shows. It was at this time he met his wife and partner Carol.

Booked into the Lido show in Paris, the act attracted considerable attention and was quite successful; several appearances on *The Ed Sullivan Show* followed,

Marvin ("Mr. Electric") and Carol Roy (*photo courtesy GENII Magazine*)

along with repeated bookings into the Lido show playing at the Stardust in Las Vegas.

Among the effects in the act are the production of lighted bulbs from the air à la MISER'S DREAM; the appearance of lighted bulbs from Roy's mouth in an adaptation of the NEEDLE TRICK; Carol's appearance inside a giant bulb; and the lighting of a huge bulb in Roy's bare hands.

Marvin and Carol Roy have appeared all over the world, and their Mr. Electric act, with its many original features, is considered one of the top specialty acts in magic. They have also developed two other acts—one features effects with jewelry; the other, billed as Mr. Puzzle And Carol, uses giant versions of familiar wire puzzles as PROPs for various effects.

ROYAL ASSEMBLY

See CARD PUZZLE.

ROYAL MARRIAGES

A card EFFECT invented by DAI VERNON and first described in his *Select Secrets*, in which through a seemingly random procedure the four Kings are magically paired with their respective Queens. There have been many later variations of the Vernon effect.

RUB-A-DUB-DUB

A marketed ROUTINE for a very simple version of the CUPS AND BALLS; it was supplied complete with PATTER IN RHYME.

It also refers to a card move in which the left hand apparently deals a card under the palm of the right hand as it rests on the table; in actuality the card is drawn back into alignment with the rest of the deck. The card is later shown to have vanished. This move is used in a number of routines, and is described in HUGARD and BRAUE's *Expert Card Technique* under the title of "Rub-A-Dub-Dub"; hence this SLEIGHT has come to be known as the **rub-a-dub move**.

RUBBER DOVE

Invented by DR. CARLO; a lifelike dove of collapsible rubber which is often used for vanish effects, and also in apparatus which might be unsafe for a live bird.

RUBBER GOODS

Items constructed of thin rubber which resemble real and presumably solid objects; these can be anything from eggs to chickens, from cakes to bleached skulls. They are usually employed in PRODUCTION effects.

Two such items, however, are far more often used in VANISHES; rubber doves, and rubber liquor or soda bottles (which are often called Weller bottles after an early and famous maker of such objects).

Excellent collapsible bottles (made not of rubber but of a special plastic) are now available from NORM NIELSEN.

RULLMAN, LEO (1875-1946)

Noted collector of (and dealer in) magic books, on the subject of which he was considered to be an expert. He wrote the *Magicana* chapter on magical literature which appears in HILLIARD's *Greater Magic*.

RUN

In the course of an OVERHAND SHUFFLE, to draw off cards one at a time (with the thumb) into the receiving hand.

See RED-BLACK SHUFFLE; RUN-UP SHUFFLE; FALSE SHUFFLE.

RUNDOWN

Ramp leading from the stage down into the auditorium. This term is used primarily in Britain.

RUNNING GAG

An EFFECT which is repeated several times during the performance, getting funnier and presumably more baffling with each repetition.

The classic example of a running gag is the LOTA BOWL; other effects which can be used in this way are the SIX-CARD REPEAT and a repeat version of the torn-and-restored newspaper (*see* TORN-AND-RESTORED OBJECT).

RUN, RABBIT, RUN

Well-known feat of CHILDREN'S MAGIC invented by HARRY LEAT. A flat tin cutout of a rabbit is placed in a thin cabinet having a door at each end, separated by a "garden wall"; the ears of the rabbit are seen above this wall as it is shifted from one end of the cabinet to the other. The byplay is similar to that employed in the DIE BOX; eventually the rabbit vanishes and is reproduced from another location.

RUN-THROUGH

An informal REHEARSAL of an ACT or SHOW, the primary purpose of which is to discover any actual or potential problems, and to ascertain the understanding of CUES.

RUN-UP SHUFFLE

A kind of FALSE SHUFFLE used to place cards in various positions, usually for GAMBLING DEMONSTRATIONS. Such shuffles are described in ERDNASE's *The Expert At The Card Table* and a number of later sources. *See* also MILK-BUILD SHUFFLE.

RUNWAY

A long, usually narrow section of the stage which projects out into the auditorium; it may or may not include at its end a ramp leading down to the audience level.

RUSDUCK (?-1959)

Born J. Russell Duck; law enforcement officer by profession. He was noted for his interest in BUILD-UP STACK routines; such stacks were a major focus of his magazine *Cardiste*, which ran for twelve issues under his editorship (a thirteenth memorial issue was later published).

Rusduck also contributed to PHOENIX Magazine and other periodicals.

RUSE

A subterfuge which serves to conceal a necessary action. A common (if unconvincing) ruse used to secretly dispose of a palmed object is that of reaching into the pocket for the "magic powder" known as WOOFLE DUST.

RUSSIAN ROULETTE

An EFFECT which combines the dramatic features of the BULLET CATCH with MENTAL MAGIC.

In the routine created by MAURICE FOGEL, half a dozen riflemen aimed at china plates—and Fogel would select by apparent ESP the one person whose rifle was loaded with a blank, and instruct the man to fire at him! Fogel was seriously injured more than once in the performance of this effect.

An earlier version, developed by Alan Milan (Alan Cracknell), used a single revolver as in "traditional" Russian Roulette—the performer guessing when the hammer was on a blank charge/empty chamber, and having the volunteer marksman fire at him. There have been many later variations on this version. A particularly striking and dramatic presentation is that of HANS MORETTI, also performed by his son Pantar.

SACK ESCAPE

See BAG ESCAPE.

SAFE ESCAPES

The performer is locked into an office safe of sufficient size, and from it makes his escape. Such escapes generally depend on the fact that safes are meant to keep people out—not in.

The office safes of HOUDINI's time were simple affairs on the interior, and escape could often be made simply by removing an interior metal plate and operating the tumblers manually. Modern safes are considerably more tamper-proof, and as a result such escapes are now rarely seen.

SAFETY PINS

The most well-known EFFECT with safety pins is the LINKING PINS routine devised by JERRY ANDRUS. In that ROUTINE a specially prepared pin is used, but there are many effects possible with unprepared pins.

See Andrus' *Safety Pin Trix*, and the relevant section of MARTIN GARDNER's *Encyclopedia Of Impromptu Tricks*.

SAINT, EDWARD, DR. (?-1942)

Born Charles D. Myers, he performed under several names before becoming business manager for BEATRICE HOUDINI after the death of her husband. Saint acted as "medium" for the final Houdini SEANCE held ten years after the performer's death.

He was also the originator of National Magic Day (October 31st).

SAINT GEORGE'S HALL

British theater bought by JOHN NEVIL MASKELYNE when he was required to move from EGYPTIAN HALL; it opened in 1905 and was London's mecca for magic until 1933, when it was purchased by the British Broadcasting Corporation. It was bombed during World War II; the site is now the location of St. George's Hotel.

ST. PIERRE, JR., LOUIS (b. 1926)

He has for many years been the owner and operator of Hollywood Magic, a well-known Los Angeles magic shop (and Hollywood Magic #2, located in the town of Costa Mesa, California). He is the son of Louis St. Pierre (d.1971), a former theater operator/manager who served on the governing board of the MAGIC CASTLE, and with whom St. Pierre Jr. opened the Hollywood Magic business in 1947, purchasing the Bert Wheeler store.

SALT

To secrete an object in some hidden location at the venue prior to the performance. A card, for example, might be hidden in a chandelier; a duplicate having been forced and then vanished, its mysterious reappearance in the chandelier is then revealed.

The term comes from the practice of salting meat so it could be stored safely and later used.

SALT LOCATION

After shuffling a borrowed deck, a spectator places it on the table and cuts off a portion; he notes the FACE

CARD of the CUT and then, at the performer's instruction, replaces it.

Picking up the deck, the performer with appropriate presentation causes it to cut itself at the selected card.

This is accomplished by simple means: when the performer instructs the spectator to replace the cut he points to the tabled half of the deck—and in so doing, releases a few grains of salt which fall invisibly onto the cards. When the upper half is replaced, the cards will automatically cut at the same location as before, the grains of salt acting like ball-bearings.

A marketed item for accomplishing this EFFECT was called the **radar pencil**; pressure on the pencil's clip would release a few grains of sand from a cavity within. Some performers who regularly use this effect have gone to the trouble of carrying small vials containing fine red and blue sand—the red sand, for example, being totally invisible on red-backed cards.

The principle was first developed by HERBERT MILTON; a book devoted entirely to this principle is *Salt Sorcery* by Dr. George E. Casaubon.

SALT SHAKER

In appearance the ordinary article, but FAKED to assist in accomplishing various versions of the SALT TRICK.

One type of shaker, invented by AL BAKER, operates on a similar principle to the MILK PITCHER, allowing most of the salt to apparently be poured into the hand from which it then vanishes. A more recent version by Vernet allows *all* of the salt to seemingly be poured from the shaker. A similar shaker is marketed by Aldini.

Another approach was devised by LOU TANNEN, whose salt shaker—while ordinary—is designed to secretly deliver a GIMMICK into the performer's hand which will serve as a repository for the salt; with the Tannen method, the salt may be reproduced in the traditional manner.

SALT TRICK

Salt is poured from a shaker into the performer's hand, from which it disappears; it then reappears in a long stream from either or both hands.

Versions of the EFFECT have been performed by many magicians over the years; JARROW featured it in his close-up work (onstage Jarrow used tobacco for visibility), and ROY BENSON used it effectively as a stage piece. Benson also originated the **Long-pour Finale**, in which far more salt than was originally vanished streams from the performer's hand in seemingly endless fashion. More recently the routine was a major sequence in the SILENT ACT of FRED KAPS.

Dale Salwak

Various GIMMICKs to hold the salt have been devised; the most popular design, which allows for many subtleties of HANDLING, is that of PAUL FOX. Some SALT SHAKERs have been designed for this effect.

SALWAK, DALE (b. 1947)

Professor of English by profession. He has appeared in supper clubs and hotels throughout the U.S., and has also performed in Canada, Europe, and the Orient. He has appeared in the MGM Grand and Caesar's Palace in Las Vegas, and on many cruise lines; his television work includes *The Merv Griffin Show* and many other appearances.

He is a co-owner and director of the CHAVEZ COLLEGE OF MAGIC, teaching at the school's West Coast branch. He is also a contributor to a number of magazines, including GENII and The New TOPS.

S.A.M.

Society of American Magicians; oldest magical organization in the U.S (and perhaps the world), founded in 1902 in New York City by Dr. W. Golden Mortimer and Dr. Saram R. Ellison. From a first meeting of two dozen members it has grown to several thousand, with branches in most major cities; each of

Peter Samelson

Fetaque Sanders (*The Mulholland Library of Conjuring & the Allied Arts, Los Angeles, California*)

these branches is called an Assembly, the founding branch in New York being known as the Parent Assembly.

Its monthly magazine is titled M.U.M. (Magic, Unity, Might); for a time the magazine was incorporated into the SPHINX Magazine, but for most of its life has been published separately.

SAMELSON, PETER (b. ?)

He began his career as a CLOSE-UP performer, working in venues such as New York's Magic Towne House. He then developed a stage production called *Theater Of Illusion*, which he has toured to many colleges and universities throughout the U.S.; he has also performed in Africa and the Orient, and has made numerous television appearances.

He is the author of *Theatrical Close-Up*.

SAND AND SUGAR

An EFFECT invented by LOUIS S. HISTED in which sand and sugar are mixed together in a canister, the sand then vanishes and leaves the sugar clean. This is one of several possible effects that can be accomplished with the APPARATUS.

SANDERS, FETAQUE (b. 1915)

Performer who has worked in venues ranging from sideshows to the World's Fair, from private parties and school assembly shows to the largest theaters.

For some years he was a featured close-up performer in Duke Ellington's New York nightclub. Later, he developed a specialized and unique SPOOK

SHOW which was designed to play at schools and colleges.

Sanders retired in 1958.

SANDERSON, GEORGE (?-1986)

British magician who made his home in Malta, noted for his three highly regarded books: *The Concealed Art Of Magic, Right Under Their Noses*, and *Price-less Magic*. He is also credited by some with the invention of the original routine for the COINS THROUGH THE TABLE.

SAND FRAME

See CARD FRAME.

SAND PICTURES

Sands of various colors are allowed to trickle from the performer's hand onto an inclined board, where they gradually create a picture. Like RAG PICTURES, this novelty routine has from time to time been employed by magicians. A noted performer of this ROUTINE is Melba Dew, wife of DANNY DEW.

SANDS OF THE DESERT

In its simplest form, this is a very ancient feat of magic; sand is mixed into a container of water, but when removed from the container, the sand pours from the performer's hand freely—completely dry.

The original version involved "cooking" the sand with wax or paraffin, so that each grain was surrounded by a waxy coating. This done, as the sand was placed into the water it could be squeezed into a solid lump which would be virtually waterproof. On being removed from the water, the lump could be broken and the loose grains allowed to cascade to the ground. An opaque container was used.

In later variations, three different colors of sand were used, and the performer removed the sands from the water in any order called for. Here a clear glass bowl was used; at the beginning of the EFFECT the water turned dark; and at the conclusion, the sand having been removed, the water was made clear again. A full description of the routine, and many techniques that were used in it, may be found in HILLIARD'S *Greater Magic*. This effect was a feature in the acts of (among many others) HARLAN TARBELL and JACK GWYNNE.

Unfortunately, there is now available in toy stores a sort of glass-bead sand which is not affected by water, and with which any small child may duplicate the basic effect. Whether this will spell an end to the performances of this classic of magic remains to be seen.

A version using three colors of confetti mixed in a box was marketed by Willard S. Smith as The Snows of Kimalatong; it was a variant of an earlier BILLY MCCOMB routine which used a JAPANESE BOX. A much earlier version was that of DOUGLAS DEXTER; it was called *The Obedient Colours* and was described in PENTAGRAM Magazine.

SANDWICH TRICKS

Card EFFECTs in which a card will appear, change, multiply or vanish while "isolated" between two other cards. In many cases the two outside cards are face-up (the center card or cards being face-down), and often these outer cards are MATE CARDS.

There are several variations of the basic idea, including **multiple sandwiches** (which could describe the COLLECTORS), and such effects as the CANNIBAL CARDS—in which the **sandwich** eats rather than being eaten!

SANKEY, JAY (b. 1965)

Born in Canada, he is noted for his offbeat and innovative approach to CLOSE-UP MAGIC. He has contributed to *Richard's Almanac* and other periodicals.

His approach is described in *Sankey Panky* by RICHARD KAUFMAN.

SARDINA, MAURICE (1891-1977)

French magician, author and translator; he is best known for his book *Where Houdini Was Wrong*, written in answer to HOUDINI's *The Unmasking Of Robert-Houdin*.

SATAN'S SEAT

An ILLUSION devised by Tom Palmer (*see* TONY ANDRUZZI), in which a person visibly appears seated in a large chair. The illusion is described in Palmer's *Modern Illusions*, and a version of it was used in the Broadway production of MERLIN, which featured DOUG HENNING.

See FLASH APPEARANCE PORTAL.

SAUTER LA COUPE

French gambler's phrase for RESTORING THE CUT; used in some early magic books to denote the SHIFT.

SAWA, DR. HIROSHI (b. 1941)

Born in Japan, a dentist by profession, he is highly regarded for his unique approach to CLOSE-UP MAGIC—much of which involves effects with natural objects such as leaves and sea-shells.

He is noted as the inventor of a routine in which a spoon is broken and restored; this routine has spawned many variations.

SAWING THROUGH A WOMAN

The above title was that of P.T. SELBIT, who originated the EFFECT—and in his version, where the woman was secured by ropes within a long box, the impression given was that the saw passed through her without harming her.

The version developed by HORACE GOLDIN was more properly described as **sawing a woman in half**; in Goldin's version, the box was separated into two halves, giving the effect that the woman had indeed been sawed into two parts.

Mark Wilson performs his *Train Illusion*, a visually striking variation of *Sawing Through A Woman*.

In a later development, the boxes were done away with entirely, and the woman's exposed midriff was apparently cut in half by a buzzsaw; this version has been featured by ALDO RICHIARDI, HARRY BLACKSTONEs SR. and HARRY BLACKSTONE JR. A variation of this, using a premise from the Poe story of "The Pit And The Pendulum," was devised by DAVID BAMBERG; here a scythe-like blade swung back and forth, slowly descending and apparently cutting through the woman's body. It should be noted that Bamberg made use of an original principle in constructing the table on which the woman rested; it appeared to be only a few inches thick.

The Goldin model of the ILLUSION had used a rather large box; the model most often used now employs a very small box and is known as the **thin sawing**. It is suggested by JIM STEINMEYER that this improved model *may* have been first devised by GUY JARRETT (*see Jarrett Magic and Stagecraft—Technical*); Turkish performer Zati Sungar has been suggested as another possible inventor of this version.

In 1962 a routine was featured on British television by its inventor, BILLY McCOMB, which used a boy, a girl and two boxes; after the sawing process the two lower halves were switched, and when the two assistants were restored, each apparently had the bottom-half of the other! The later performers of this presentation (now usually using two women in contrasting clothing) include CHANNING POLLOCK and DOUG HENNING.

SCALE

The minimum acceptable wage for a performance, as determined by the appropriate theatrical union.

In most cases performers of any competency work for appreciably more than scale; a notable exception is the television non-prime-time "talk" show, where all performers regardless of professional stature are paid scale.

It should be noted that an agent is not permitted to take a commission on an engagement which pays only scale.

SCARNE, JOHN (1903-1985)

Born Orlando Scarnecchia; he was for the greater part of his life one of the world's foremost authorities on gambling. He began his career, however, as a close-up magician; Scarne performed primarily at private parties and was considered to be an expert at SLEIGHT OF HAND magic.

His books include *Scarne's Magic Tricks* and *Scarne On Card Tricks*; his works on gambling include *Scarne On Cards, Scarne On Dice*, and *Scarne's Complete Guide To Gambling*.

SCHNEIDER, AL (b. ?)

Specialist in close-up magic most noted for his highly popular MATRIX effect, which has spawned many variations. He is the author of *Matrix* (the manuscript which describes that effect), and also *Al Schneider On Coins* and *Al Schneider on Zombie*.

SCHULIEN, MATT (1890-1967)

Proprietor of Schulien & Sons, a well-known Chicago restaurant, where he entertained the patrons with colorful CLOSE-UP MAGIC.

His work is described in *The Magic Of Matt Schulien* by PHILIP WILLMARTH and *Matt Schulien's Fabulous Card Discoveries* by EUGENE BURGER.

SCOT, REGINALD (1538-1599)

Author of *The Discoverie Of Witchcraft*, published in 1584, which he wrote to establish that the wonders performed by magicians—or "jugglers" as they were then known—were accomplished by SLEIGHTs and secret devices rather than by partnership with demons or devils.

In Scot's book are the first important and meaningful descriptions in the English language of how magical feats are accomplished; later writers borrowed liberally from his work.

Matt Schulien (*The Mulholland Library of Conjuring & the Allied Arts, Los Angeles, California*)

King James I, a believer in the powers of witchcraft, naturally did not agree with Scot's point of view—so he ordered the book destroyed. Few copies escaped immolation, thus the book is quite rare.

A facsimile of the text is available in an edition published by Dover Books.

SCOTCH AND SODA

EFFECT of COIN MAGIC in which a half-dollar and Mexican twenty-centavo coin are placed in a spectator's hands; the smaller coin changes into a quarter.

The effect is accomplished by a set of FAKE coins, and uses a sophisticated application of the SHELL principle in conjunction with other techniques. It may be replicated without difficulty by SLEIGHT OF HAND.

SEABROOKE, TERRY b. ?)

Born in Britain; highly-regarded comedy magician who has appeared throughout the world. He is best known for his marketed **Burnt Note in Wallet** routine, which has become a mainstay of many comedy performers.

He is the author of *Seabrooke's Book*.

SEANCE

A meeting, usually consisting of a dozen people or less, during which conversation is held with spirits or other discarnate entities, with a MEDIUM acting as the channel through which the entities speak.

Simulation of a seance has often been done for purposes of entertainment; an excellent book on the subject is EUGENE BURGER's *Spirit Theater*. Other sources include DAVID P. ABBOTT's *Behind The Scenes With The Mediums*, THOMAS H. CHISLETT's *Spirits In The House*, and *Step Nine* of Corinda's *13 Steps To Mentalism*.

SEARLES, LIN (1914-1972)

Born Lynn Searles, he worked as a writer for many years, producing Western novels and stories. During this time he was employed for three years by Owen Magic; later he wrote the scripts for MARK WILSON's *Magic Land Of Allakazam* television series.

He continued writing, working also in a magic shop; it was in this shop that Searles was murdered during a holdup.

He is best known in magic for his creation of the CANNIBAL CARDS plot. Some of his other creations were collected in a PALLBEARER'S REVIEW Folio.

SECOND DEAL

To retain the top card of the deck in position while dealing the cards beneath it; most useful in conjunction with a MARKED DECK.

Second dealing is a difficult SLEIGHT to do well; particularly troublesome is the fact that a card sliding from between two others makes a different sound than a card dealt fairly from the top.

A large number of books describe the technique of the second deal; primary sources are ERDNASE's *Expert At The Card Table*, L.L. IRELAND's *Lessons In Dishonesty*, and MARLO's *Seconds, Centers and Bottoms*.

SECOND SIGHT

Term used to denote CLAIRVOYANCE and, less commonly, PRECOGNITION; of Scots origin.

Within magical usage, a descriptive term for a TWO-PERSON MENTAL ACT.

SECRET

Term used by laypersons to denote the methodology or technique of magical EFFECTs.

The term is rarely if ever used in this sense between magicians, aware as they are that most worthwhile magical effects do not have *a* secret but rather a complex combination of various techniques.

SEFALALJIA

Originally the name given by STEWART JAMES to his miniature SPIRIT CABINET routine which was published in THE JINX Magazine, it has in later years become associated with a ring-on-string principle which formed a part of that routine. Several applications and variations of this principle are described in Volume Three of the *Encyclopedia Of Rope Tricks (ed. Stewart James).*

In 1982 a revised and expanded version of the original routine was published by James; its title is, not surprisingly, *Sefalaljia Number 2.*

The title comes from the word *cephalalgia*, a synonym for headache; James has replaced the *c,ph* and *g* with his own *SFJ* initials.

SELBIT, P.T. (1879-1938)

Born Percy Tibbles in Great Britain, he became well known as a creator and performer of ILLUSIONs. Of

P. T. Selbit (*The Mulholland Library of Conjuring & the Allied Arts, Los Angeles, California*)

these his most famous creation was undoubtedly SAWING THROUGH A WOMAN; others were CRUSHING A WOMAN, MAN WITHOUT A MIDDLE (now known as GIRL WITHOUT A MIDDLE), THROUGH THE EYE OF A NEEDLE, and the WRESTLING CHEESE. Other originations included versions of the TALKING SKULL, a stage presentation of THREE-CARD MONTE, and at least two routines for the SPIRIT PAINTINGS.

He began his professional career at the turn of the century, appearing shortly thereafter at the prestigious ST. GEORGE'S HALL; about ten years later he made a tour of the U.S. On his return to Great Britain he performed throughout the British Isles, appearing regularly at St. George's hall.

SELECTION

The specific card chosen by a spectator in the course of a feat of card magic.

SELF-CORRECTING SETUP

A principle invented by KARL FULVES in which two identically-stacked groups of cards are fairly RIFFLE SHUFFLEd; the identities of the resultant pairs of cards, if matching, will be a function of their position in the shuffled group.

The principle is described in EPILOGUE.

SELF-WORKING

Said of an EFFECT which requires no SLEIGHTs or secret maneuvers in performance (though it may require elaborate prior preparation).

The term is unfortunate in that inexperienced magicians may confuse its meaning, thinking self-*working* is synonymous with self-*performing*; though some effects fall into the former category, there are virtually none in the latter.

SELLERS, TOM (1890-1961)

Highly creative inventor; of the dozens of EFFECTs he invented, undoubtedly the best known is **Just Chance**, known in the U.S. as BANK NIGHT.

He was the author of numerous books. *Condensed Conjuring, Immediate Magic, Novel Necromancy* and *Subtle Sorcery* are just a few of his many titles; there is also a recently published collection of his magazine contributions titled *Best Sellers*, containing several dozen effects.

SERPENT SILK

Another name for the UNTYING SILK; sometimes used to specify performance of the EFFECT with a long, narrow, appropriately decorated green silk.

SERVANTE

A hidden shelf or bag at the rear of a table, from which articles may be secretly obtained and into which they can be secretly dropped. Present-day performance conditions, where a magician may often work with an audience on three or four sides, have led to a decline in the servante's use.

The **Invisible Servante**, marketed by Abbott's Magic, is a small open bag fixed in a wire frame which is cleverly concealed in a handkerchief; it can be used with any table, in situations where a standard servante would be unfeasible. It is generally credited to KARL GERMAIN.

The **belly servante** is worn in the trousers by the performer (usually just below the belt line at the front); it can be used to dispose of small palmed objects.

SET

To arrange and prepare APPARATUS and PROPs for performance.

SETUP

Particular pre-performance arrangement of an item of APPARATUS or PROP; for example, the order of cards in a stacked deck (see STACK).

SEVEN KEYS TO BALDPATE

Originally the title of an Earl Derr Biggers mystery novel, this was used by THEODORE ANNEMANN to name his version of a feat of MENTAL MAGIC using a lock and several keys; the name is now applied to most versions of the effect.

Originated by KOLAR, the effect uses a lock and several keys, only one of which will open the lock. The keys are mixed and selected by spectators, and the performer determines which person is holding the correct (working) key.

Many methods and ROUTINEs have appeared in print to accomplish the effect; there have also been several marketed versions, including KEN ALLEN's **Lock of Gibraltar**, **Key-R-Rect**, and STEWART JUDAH's **Keys Of Judah**.

SEVERN, BILL (b. 1913)

For many years a professional performer, specializing in CIGARETTE MAGIC and SILK effects, he is now noted for his many books on magic for the general public.

His books include: *Big Book Of Magic, Guide To Magic As A Hobby, Impromptu Magic, Magic Across The Table, Magic In Your Pocket, More Magic In Your Pockets, Magic In Mind,* and *The Magic Workshop.*

SEX DETECTOR

A pendulum, usually a small gold-painted ball of wood on a cord, is held by an expectant mother to discover what sex her child will be; if the pendulum moves in a circle it will be a boy, in a straight line it will be a girl.

In actuality, the pendulum's movement is caused by unconscious tremors in the hand of the person holding the cord; these tiny movements cause the pendulum to move as the person desires. The phenomenon was formerly referred to in psychology as ideomotor response; it is now known as psychomotor response.

The pendulum has often been used by magicians in feats of MENTAL MAGIC.

SHADE

From gambler's parlance: cover for a SLEIGHT or secret move. This cover may either be physical—in reaching for an object on the table the performer's arm blocks sight of the other hand, which may then execute a required move—or situational, where the performer employs MISDIRECTION to keep attention diverted from the move.

SHADE WORK

A particular technique for marking a deck, used far more often by gamblers than magicians. A dilute solution of ink of the same color as the back design is used to give areas of the card a very light tint; this is most often done in stripe patterns. Its primary use is to differentiate high and low value cards (as for the game of Blackjack); this technique is not used to mark for suit and value.

Within magic, its rare applications usually are combined with the DIVIDED DECK principle.

See MARKED DECK; JUICE; JUICE DECK.

SHADOW CABINET

See LIGHT CABINET.

SHADOWGRAPHY

The art of making lifelike pictures on a screen with shadows created by the positioning of the hands. Now rarely seen, it was in the past featured by FELICIEN TREWEY; its best-known current exponents are Prandra Rao and Sonny Fontana.

An excellent modern work on the subject is BILL SEVERN's *Shadow Magic*.

SHANK SHUFFLE

Term once erroneously used to denote the ZARROW SHUFFLE.

See also FALSE SHUFFLE.

SHARPE, ALTON (b. ?)

Performer who has appeared in varied venues with an act featuring manipulative magic. His highly-regarded books include *Expert Card Conjuring*, *Expert Card Mysteries* and *Expert Hocus Pocus*. He is also the founder and editor of *Olla Podrida* magazine.

SHARPE, S.H. (SAM) (b. 1902)

Born in Britain; most noted as a theorist and writer on magic. In addition to his voluminous contributions to magical periodicals (including a magic glossary which ran through several issues of the MAGIC CIRCULAR) he has written several books.

These include: *Neo Magic*, *Conjured Up*, *Good Conjuring*, *Great Magic*, *The Magic Play*, *Devant's Delightful Delusions*, *Salutations To Robert-Houdin*, *Conjurers' Optical Secrets*, *Words On Wonder*, and *Oriental Conjuring And Magic* (with Will Ayling). He also edited (clarifying and partially retranslating) the English-language edition of *Hofzinser's Card Conjuring*, and wrote the English-language edition of *Ponsin On Conjuring*.

He is a member of the Inner MAGIC CIRCLE and a recipient of a Literary Fellowship from the ACADEMY OF MAGICAL ARTS; he has also won several awards for his work in the LINKING RING Magazine.

SHARPSHOOTER

The most common name for an EFFECT devised by PETER KANE in which a toy gun is fired at a deck of cards, and a previously selected card is found to have a "bullet" hole in it.

The EFFECT can be accomplished by SLEIGHT OF HAND means, with one prepared duplicate card; also, a version using a MECHANICAL DECK is marketed under the above title by ALAN ALAN.

SHAW, ALLAN (?-?)

Born in Australia; he performed in vaudeville in the early decades of the 20th century, his act being pure SLEIGHT OF HAND structured around a masterly presentation of the MISER'S DREAM.

Some of his sleights are described in ARTHUR BUCKLEY's *Principles and Deceptions*.

SHAXON, ALAN (b. 1933)

Born Alan Howson in Britain; he began his performing career as a teenager and continued it through a stint in the R.A.F. An appearance on the DAVID NIXON show (now with his wife Anne) led to many dinner and cabaret bookings, and increasing success. He has performed in over thirty countries around the world and on many of the top cruise ship lines, as well as dozens of television appearances in Britain, the U.S. and elsewhere. Shaxon was described by GOODLIFFE as ". . . one of the top ten after-dinner acts in the world." He is a member of the Inner MAGIC CIRCLE with Gold Star.

Shaxon's approach is described in his books *My Kind Of Magic* and *Practical Sorcery*.

Alan Shaxon (*photo courtesy GENII Magazine*)

SHELLEY, TONY (b. 1939)

Born in Britain; pharmacist by profession. Noted for his colorful act featuring birds and silk productions, performed with wife and partner Elizabeth. He has appeared at venues in Britain, France and the U.S., and has also performed on numerous television shows. He is a winner of the BRITISH RING Shield, and has served as president for that organization.

SHELL

A hollow object made to simulate a solid object; usually it is constructed slightly larger to permit placing it over the "real" object.

A **shell ball** is actually a half-shell into which a ball will fit; it is used in many versions of the MULTIPLYING BILLIARD BALLS and the **Ball Through Silk**. Needless to say, the shell is always positioned with its convex side to the audience to simulate the existence of a real ball.

Shell coins are used in many routines of varying complexity; a simple application would be to show a shell and real coin in one hand, with another coin secretly palmed in the other. The shell is slipped over the coin; coin and shell together now appear as a single coin and the coin PALMed in the other hand is produced, apparently having traveled invisibly from hand to hand.

Complex applications of this principle to COIN MAGIC include sets made of several nesting shells of coins of different values; "locking" shells which when placed on a coin snap into place, so the coin may be freely handled by a spectator; magnetic shells; shells whose interior is made to match that of a special OKITO BOX; and much more. Specialists in the production of such coins include JOHNSON PRODUCTS in the U.S. and Eddie Gibson in Great Britain.

Shells, as a basic principle, are used in a large number of APPARATUS effects—from the DIE BOX to the PASSE-PASSE BOTTLES. In using such items, it is important that the performer handle the shell convincingly, as though it had the same weight and solidity as the real thing.

SHELL GAME

An ancient gambling game often performed by magicians, it usually consists of three (empty) walnut shells and a small pea (actually a pea-shaped object made of rubber). The pea is placed under one of the shells which are then mixed, and it is up to the spectator to find it. As a magical EFFECT, a point is made of the pea disappearing from under one shell and appearing elsewhere—rather than, as in the gam-bling context, so mixing the shells that the spectator really is not sure where the pea can be found.

Elaborations of the basic routine include having the spectator place his finger over the shell containing the pea, covering it with a clear glass tumbler, and so forth.

A number of books and articles are available regarding the shell game presented as entertainment; among them are *Hello, Sucker* by JACK CHANIN and *Encyclopedia of The Three Shell Game* by FRANK GARCIA.

SHERIDAN, JEFF (b. 1948)

Performer who began his career working in the New York shop of AL FLOSSO. While still in his teens he became a specialist in STREET MAGIC, and is now well known for his performances in New York's Central Park. He has also appeared in Carnegie Recital Hall, Lincoln Center, and other venues.

In 1975 he was the recipient of the Street Enhancers Award from the Municipal Arts Society Of New York.

SHIELS, TONY (b. 1938)

Born in Britain; he has for several years toured the country from Ireland to Cornwall with a tent show, mixing magic, MENTAL MAGIC, and MENTALISM, and PUNCH AND JUDY.

He is best known, however, for his work in the field of BIZARRE MAGICK. In addition to magazine contributions, he has written several books on the subject. These include *13!*, *Something Strange*, *The Shiels Effect*, *Entertaining with ESP*, and *Daemons, Darklings and Doppelgangers*.

SHIFT

A card SLEIGHT in which the upper and lower sections of the deck are indetectably transposed; it is most often used to bring a chosen card to the top or bottom of the deck, but has many other applications.

The technique of the shift is described in HILLIARD's *Greater Magic*, HUGARD and BRAUE's *Expert Card Technique*, and dozens of other books.

(*Note:* the Shift is often referred to as the PASS, which can be confusing, as the term pass is also used in a general way for many different sleights.)

SHIM

Generally, a thin strip of some hard substance such as wood or metal; within magical terminology, it usually denotes a thin strip of ferrous metal which can be imbedded in a card or coin to enable it to be attracted by a magnet.

In ESCAPE work, this term is both noun and verb. As noun it describes a thin strip of *very hard* metal (often spring steel); as verb it means to insert such a strip in a lock or handcuff to allow the shackle to be slipped from the holding ratchet.

SHIMADA, HARUO (b. 1940)

Born in Japan; he began his magic career at age thirteen as a demonstrator for the Japanese magic firm of Tenyo. Beginning his performing career two years later, his act featuring BILLIARD BALL magic, he worked in many venues and made several appearances on television, and also a royal command performance for Hirohito and his family.

Shortly thereafter, inspired by CHANNING POLLOCK, he developed an act of DOVE MAGIC which was quite successful. While appearing in Australia he met his wife Deanna; after their marriage she joined the act and they toured Australia for the next few years, also doing considerable television work. Later they toured through over twenty countries, and did a television series running several months while in Mexico. In addition to the dove act, Shimada began performing an act in traditional Japanese wardrobe; this featured the production of several parasols and fans of various kinds.

In 1975 Shimada and Deanna premiered the Dragon Act—a spectacular routine in which he battles a giant dragon, with the climax an instantaneous TRANSPOSITION. Like the dove act, it has been quite successful; Shimada and Deanna have performed it in venues from Las Vegas to Paris to London and throughout the world.

They are double winners of the Stage Magician award, and have also won the Magician Of The Year award from the ACADEMY OF MAGICAL ARTS.

SHINER

A small reflector which may be hidden in the performer's hand or concealed in or on an item on the card table; it allows the performer to learn the identity of a face-down card.

The device, adapted from one used by crooked gamblers, is usually a small convex mirror, but any reasonably reflective surface will serve as a shiner—a tack-head, the blade of a knife, even a spilled drink! Considerable practice, however, is required to use a shiner in deceptive fashion.

See PEEK MIRROR.

SHIRT REMOVAL

The performer requests an onstage helper from the audience to remove his tie and unbutton his shirt cuffs; this done, the performer grasps the shirt collar and pulls the shirt entirely free of the assistant, leaving the jacket in place. This stunt is done by many performers specializing in the PICKPOCKET ACT, notably DOMINIQUE and RICKI DUNN.

The person whose shirt is removed is a CONFEDERATE and the shirt is draped around him and buttoned; the hands and arms do not enter the sleeves. With a jacket and vest on over the shirt it appears to be worn in the usual manner.

It might be assumed that a stunt of this kind would seem obviously to require a STOOGE—but in fact most lay persons do not so regard it, and think it is somehow possible for the performer to do what he seems to do with an "unprepared" spectator.

SHOCKED

Usually rendered as *SHoCkeD*, it is a MNEMONIC for the suit order of *S*pades, *H*earts, *C*lubs and *D*iamonds, used in various types of STACK.

See CHASED.

SHOOTING THROUGH A WOMAN

A stage ILLUSION invented by CHUNG LING SOO in which an arrow with an affixed ribbon is put into a muzzle-loading rifle; the rifle is then fired at an assistant who stands between the performer and the target.

The arrow is seen to bury itself in the target, and the trailing ribbon is seen (apparently) to be threaded straight through the body of the assistant.

Later versions have used a bow and arrow, or a crossbow.

The Soo routine is fully described in HILLIARD's *Greater Magic*.

SHORT CARD

A card fractionally shorter than the rest of the deck, it can be instantly located by riffling the cards. Such cards are often used singly as KEY CARDS, or in MECHANICAL DECKS such as the SVENGALI DECK.

An entire chapter in JEAN HUGARD's *Encyclopedia Of Card Tricks* is devoted to effects using the short card.

SHOT

A single appearance on a show or television program.

SHOW

A performance or theatrical presentation.
See ACT; FULL-EVENING SHOW.

SHOWCASE

A performance done for the purpose of letting prospective bookers see the act; most showcase situations feature a number of performers, and even a small payment is the exception rather than the rule.

Unless the performer is using the showcase simply to practice in front of a real audience, caution should be exercised in such appearances; it should be ascertained that bookers do attend the performances and that the showcase is not simply a device for the club to avoid paying for entertainers.

SHOWER OF SWEETS

A charming and venerable EFFECT, now almost never seen, in which nuts and candies cascade onto a plate from the folds of a borrowed handkerchief.

It is described in many magic books of a century past, notably PROFESSOR LOUIS HOFFMANN's *Modern Magic* and *Later Magic*.

SHUFFLE

To mix the cards in a deck to produce a random sequence.

SHUFFLE OFF

In an OVERHAND SHUFFLE, to genuinely shuffle the remaining cards in the usual shuffle action into those in the receiving hand. Done after an earlier FALSE SHUFFLE action, such as a RUN, MILK-BUILD or JOG.

SHUFFLE REVERSE

To RUN the cards in the course of a SHUFFLE, specifically to reverse their order.

SHUTTLE PASS

With coins, a particular technique for the apparent transfer of a coin from one hand to the other; in actuality the coin is retained, and a coin already in the other hand is shown. This SLEIGHT, invented by DAVID ROTH, is described in his *Expert Coin Magic* and also in RICHARD KAUFMAN's *Coinmagic*.

SIDE SLIP

Term used by JEAN HUGARD and FRED BRAUE to describe the SIDE STEAL in the chapter on the subject in their *Expert Card Technique*.

SIDE STEAL

A card SLEIGHT which can in many cases replace the SHIFT, this consists of moving a chosen card out of the central area of the deck and into the right palm, which may then deposit the card on top. Many performers do not actually palm the card, preferring to clip it by the outer edge between the fingers for the move to the top of the deck. Correctly done it appears that the performer has simply SQUARED THE DECK.

Optionally, the card may be kept in the palm and loaded into a pocket or other location; see, for example, CARD TO WALLET.

The move is thoroughly described in HUGARD and BRAUE's *Expert Card Technique*, where it is referred to as the **side slip** (in a chapter by DR. JACOB DALEY added for the third edition it is called the **side steal**); it is also the subject of ED MARLO's *The Side Steal* book (part of his *Revolutionary Card Technique* series).

A variant devised by Dr. Daley was called the **incomplete side steal**; as the title implies, only the first part of the move was executed, to JOG the card out the side of the deck. At this point the performer could GLIMPSE the card, or put a CRIMP in it, then push the card flush with the rest of the deck.

SIEGFRIED AND ROY

Born Siegfried Fischbacker in Germany in 1943; and Roy Horn in Germany in 1945. They met when Siegfried was performing on the cruise ship *Bremen* in 1960, and met ship's steward Roy—who had a pet cheetah on board. Combining Siegfried's magical abilities with Roy's rapport with wild animals, they created an ACT which took them eventually to the Las Vegas *Tropicana* where they were featured in the Folies Bergere show. After a few more years of appearances in Puerto Rico and France, they returned to Las Vegas to star in the *Hallelujah Hollywood* show at the MGM Grand. From there they moved to the *Lido de Paris* show at the Stardust, and then to the Frontier with their own show titled *Beyond Belief*.

The *Beyond Belief* show is one of the most successful in the history of Las Vegas, playing to sellout crowds for every performance; it is also one of the most spectacular in the history of magic, with tigers, elephants, and many other kinds of animals featured in ILLUSIONs involving lasers, fire and fog—and also

Siegfried and Roy

featuring the talents of chief ASSISTANT *Lynette Chapell*.

(Born in Kenya and trained as a dancer, Miss Chapell was first involved in magic when she worked with the JOHN CALVERT show during its stay in Kenya; she was later a featured and principal dancer in many Las Vegas shows before joining Siegfried and Roy. In addition to her performance work, she is also their personal coordinator, assisting with all facets of their onstage and offstage existence.)

Siegfried and Roy have made several television appearances, including their own prime-time network specials.

Considered by many to be the most successful magicians in history, Siegfried and Roy have won the Las Vegas Show Act Of The Year Award many times; they have also received numerous other awards, including the Magician Of The Year Award from the ACADEMY OF MAGICAL ARTS.

SIGHT

To unobtrusively view an item, usually in the course of another action.

For example, in handing a deck of cards to a spectator, it might be tilted slightly forward for a brief moment during this action, allowing the performer to sight the bottom card of the deck.

Again, with the performer's back turned, a spectator might be asked to remove a card from a row dealt in front of him; in asking "Have you done that?", the performer might turn slightly toward the table, just long enough to sight the gap in the row of cards.

SIGHTLESS VISION

See BLINDFOLD.

SILENT ACT

Performance in which there is no dialogue; such acts are usually accompanied by a continuous musical score.

Unlike a PANTOMIME act, a **silent act** does not attempt to convey specific dramatic concepts, except by indirection; it is instead structured to create an impressive and satisfying sequence of magical EFFECTs. A dramatic line may be established through the integration of the magical presentations with appropriate music; the presence of such a line or plot is not, however, necessary to the definition of this term.

See MIME.

SILK

Term used to indicate a silk handkerchief; these are usually of very thin silk with the smallest possible hem. For stage use, silks are rarely smaller than 18-inches square; more often they are 24 inches and larger.

SILK BLOW

See SILK DYEING.

SILK CABBY

A utility item of APPARATUS used primarily in SILK MAGIC, this is a box (generally about 3 inches by 5 inches by 8 inches) with doors at front and back, hinged at the bottom; there are also 1 inch holes at each side.

The box may be used to PRODUCE, VANISH or exchange silks or similar items; these are inserted or extracted through the holes at the sides. The performer can open the front and back doors to show the box empty before or after any of these effects.

It is believed to be the invention of EDWARD M. MASSEY.

SILK CLIP

A holder which is clipped under the coat and contains a rolled-up silk handkerchief.

See SILK WINDER.

SILK DYEING

A presentation in which white silks are changed into various colors, usually by passing them through a tube made from a rolled-up sheet of paper; for this a DYE TUBE gimmick is used.

In a variation by ADE DUVAL, when the white silk has been poked into the tube the performer holds it to his lips and *blows* the silk with changed color out the other end of the tube.

A SLEIGHT-OF-HAND method for accomplishing the effect needs nothing more than the two silks and a PALMO BALL, or hand DYE TUBE gimmick.

Since the basic requirement of the effect is that one silk be switched for another, there are literally hundreds of ways of producing the effect; which method will be selected by an individual performer depends, naturally, on the specific nature of the presentation to be accomplished.

SILK MAGIC

EFFECT which uses a SILK handkerchief or scarf as its primary property. The most complete work on this subject is RICE's *Encyclopedia Of Silk Magic* (three volumes).

See BLENDO; COLOR-CHANGING HANDKERCHIEF; SILK DYEING; SYMPATHETIC SILKS; TWENTIETH CENTURY SILKS.

SILKS FROM NEWSPAPER

A small sheet of newspaper is shown, the performer's hands seen to be otherwise empty. A hole is poked in the paper and a silk withdrawn from it; this process is repeated several times.

The EFFECT is accomplished by a GIMMICK consisting of a flesh-colored metal tube equipped with a clip so that it may be easily concealed at the back of the hand. The tube is loaded with the silks and is clipped to the back of the hand as the paper is picked up; the hand appears empty, but the fingers of the other hand can reach through the hole in the paper and extract silks from the hidden gimmick.

The gimmick may be used in many other ways.

SILK TO EGG

A handkerchief poked into the closed hand is transformed into an egg; often presented as a sucker EFFECT, in which the hollow egg with the hole in its side (STODARE EGG) is shown to the audience in the course of a pretended explanation, the ROUTINE being concluded with the hole being apparently removed and the genuine egg broken into a glass. This sucker routine is credited to FREDERICK CULPITT.

Most such sucker routines require a SLEIGHT-OF-HAND SWITCH of the fake egg for the real one; however, at least one marketed version uses a compartmented plastic egg which can be "broken" to show its contents—a rubber yolk and vegetable syrup.

The STODARE EGG here used is also employed in the classic TRANSPOSITION effect called KLING KLANG.

SILK WINDER

A small dowel with a slot made through half its length, it is used to prepare SILKs for production. A corner of the silk is placed in the slot and the remainder of the silk wrapped around the dowel; removed from the silk winder, the silk has its outer end partially tucked into the center of the coil to keep it from unrolling—and now the performer may PALM it in readiness for a PRODUCTION. To do this, the outer end of the silk is clipped in the fingers and a sharp snap unrolls the silk instantly for a pretty and visual production.

Often the winder will be provided with a safety pin at the end opposite the slot, so it may be pinned under the coat and double as a SILK CLIP.

SILK WONDER BOX

See DEMON WONDER BOX.

SILVAN (b. ?)

Born Aldo Savoldello in Italy; he began his career with a manipulative act, then adding DOVE MAGIC. Since that time he has created a FULL-EVENING SHOW, has appeared in his own television series and in films, and has appeared in such venues as New York's Latin Quarter, the London Palladium, and the Moulin Rouge in Paris. One of the best-known magical performers in Europe, he was recently honored with a special award at FISM.

Within magic, he is noted for his **dove levitation**, now featured by a number of performers.

SIMMS, WARREN (?-1976)

Inventor noted for his many marketed effects, including versions of the RICE BOWLS, RAZOR-BLADE SWALLOWING, and many others.

SIMON, BILL (b. ?)

Noted creator of many ingenious and subtle sleights and effects, primarily in the area of card magic. He is the author of *Controlled Miracles*, *Effective Card Magic* and *Sleightly Sensational*.

For the lay public he has written a book with the title and subject of *Mathematical Magic*.

See DISPLACEMENT.

SIMON DISPLACEMENT

A subtlety created by BILL SIMON in which a business card bearing a PREDICTION written by the performer is placed into the deck by the spectator. When the business card is turned face-up, it is seen to bear the names of the playing cards immediately above and below its position.

The **Simon displacement** is executed by lifting all the cards above the projecting card and turning them face-up; the business card is now grasped by the thumb which holds the upper half at the underside, the hand then being turned back and the half-deck (with the business card above it) being replaced beneath the other cards. While it appears that the business card has simply been turned face-up, in actuality the deck has been cut around it; thus the cards next to the projecting business card are the original top and bottom card of the deck.

This move, which has many other applications, is described in Simon's *Effective Card Magic*. A slightly simpler version is described in SCARNE's *Scarne on Card Tricks*.

SIM SALA BIM

Phrase (adapted from a Danish children's song) used by DANTE as the name of his FULL EVENING SHOW, and also in performance as both MAGIC WORD and acknowledgment of applause.

Later also used as a show name by KALANAG.

SIMULATION

Though all stage magic is in a sense simulation, the term is used specifically within the context of SLEIGHT OF HAND; it is the act of creating the ILLUSION of a particular movement or situation. Even more specifically, it denotes not only (for example) the apparent placing of a ball within the hand, but also the appearance of the closed hand as though the ball were actually there. Effective and convincing simulation is crucial to convincing sleight of hand.

SIVA COUNT

A method of counting a small PACKET of cards; if five cards are used, four may be shown freely while the fifth is concealed, while if only four are used the order of the first two counted is secretly transposed. The Siva Count is the invention of JACK AVIS.

The technique, similar to that of the JORDAN COUNT and ELMSLEY COUNT, is to hold the cards in a pinch grip and take off a single card; this is replaced on the bottom as a two-card PUSH-OFF is done with the top two cards; these are replaced on the bottom and the three top cards are pushed off; and finally the single card remaining is placed onto those in the other hand. If a fifth card is to be concealed it is in the center of the packet, and in the second stage three cards are pushed off rather than two; at the conclusion of the count the unseen card will be at the bottom of the packet.

A full description of the SIVA COUNT is found in JERRY MENTZER's *Counts, Cuts, Moves & Subtleties*.

SIX-CARD REPEAT

A stage card EFFECT invented by TOMMY TUCKER in which the performer shows that he has six cards; three are discarded and yet when the cards are counted the performer still has six. The effect is repeated several times, usually to illustrate a humorous story.

There are several SLEIGHT OF HAND methods for accomplishing the effect; also, marketed versions are available making use of specially prepared cards.

SIXTEEN DIGIT TEST

A feat of MENTAL MAGIC in which four spectators each think of a four-digit number, after which the performer writes something on a slate which is placed aside without being shown.

The spectators write down their numbers on a pad or slate and these are totaled by another spectator. When the performer's slate is shown, it bears the identical number.

A variant in presentation has the performer do the writing before having any numbers thought of—which changes the effect from TELEPATHY to one of PREDICTION.

The effect is accomplished through the used of an ADD-A-NUMBER PAD or an ADDITION SLATE.

Despite its name, the EFFECT is often performed with *three*-digit numbers, as this somewhat speeds the process of addition.

Later variations of this effect involve the use of a gimmicked pocket calculator; most such versions are less than convincing, since spectators are likely to believe (in this case, correctly) that the effect is accomplished by electronic gimmickry.

SIXTH FINGER

See FALSE FINGER.

SKINNER, MICHAEL (b. ?)

Performer specializing in CLOSE-UP MAGIC; he is considered by magicians and lay persons alike to be one of the best such performers in the world. He has performed in varied venues, including private parties and national television. For many years he has been the featured resident magician in the Lily Langtry Restaurant of Las Vegas' Golden Nugget casino.

He is legendary for many accomplishments, one of which was a week's worth of performances at the MAGIC CASTLE—28 shows—without ever duplicating an EFFECT.

Skinner has contributed a number of effects to such magazines as GENII and *Arcane*; also, several of his ROUTINEs are described in *Michael Skinner's Intimate Magic* by JEFF BUSBY.

SKULLO-CATION

A charming close-up card EFFECT created by Bill Nord in which a small packet of cards, none of which are a spectator's previously chosen card, is placed in the jaws of a small plastic skull hanging on a chain. The chosen card vanishes from another packet and when the performer taps the hand of the person holding the chain all the cards fall but one—the spectator's card.

This effect may have been inspired by an earlier card effect in which the spectator held the deck between thumb and finger and the performer knocked the cards away; the bottom card (the spectator's selection, positioned there by SLEIGHT OF HAND technique) would be the only one left in the spectator's hand.

The effect was commercially marketed. Later variations have used tie-clips and other items to hold the cards.

SLAT FRAME

A frame (usually of wood) with a number of slats across its face and back; these slats are separated by gaps slightly less wide.

The *Card Slat Frame* employs a card with gaps cut out to match those in the frame. When the card is resting at one end of the slightly longer frame, its uncut portions show through the gaps in the Slat Frame which thus appears to be holding a complete card; if the frame is turned over the card shifts slightly so that its cut-out portions match the gaps in the frame, which then appears empty.

Variations of this principle have been applied to STAGE illusions, as for example two slatted fences which meet at a point nearest the audience, and behind which an object or person is visible. Mirrors hidden behind the slats can move to fill the gaps (in an application of the SPHINX principle) which causes the object to apparently vanish. Movement of the mirror-slats is usually covered by use of one or more FLASH POT devices.

SLEEVE ACES

Term given by ED MARLO to a card sequence in which the indifferent face cards of two halves of the deck change to Aces, when rubbed on the sleeves.

The basic premise and technique, which may also be used as a REVELATION for chosen cards, is the invention of AL LEECH, and will be found in his *Super Card Man Stuff*.

SLEEVING

Secretly disposing of an object into the coat sleeve, or obtaining it therefrom. Far more rarely employed by magicians than laypersons generally suppose, it is nevertheless an effective technique in the hands of a master such as EMIL JARROW or JACK CHANIN. Chanin's book, *The Encyclopedia Of Sleeving*, is one of the very few sources for information on this difficult, but useful methodology.

SLEIGHT

Any move or action accomplished with the hands to bring about a magical EFFECT; the term implies a deceptive technique being employed with an ordinary object (card, coin, etc.), but this is by no means always the case.

Such actions as defined by this term are, of course, distinct from actions performed with the hands to operate an article of magical APPARATUS.

This term is also not to be confused with those openly skillful actions of the hands used to execute a FLOURISH.

SLEIGHT OF HAND

A SLEIGHT (or sequence of sleights) which, in conjunction with other performance skills, brings about a magical EFFECT.

SLICING IN FOUR PARTS

An ILLUSION in which an ASSISTANT is chained to a long table and a three-sided cover is placed over him or her, completely concealing the assistant from view except for the hands, which are brought up through an opening at the top of the cover and fastened in position.

Large blades are then passed down through slits in the cover, dividing it into four parts. When the blades are removed and the cover is lifted off, the assistant is unharmed.

SLICK CARD

A card specially prepared by waxing and polishing, either on face or back; such a card may easily be located by a sliding pressure on the deck, which will divide at the slicked card.

Such cards can be prepared with some commercial waxes, or special pastes available from gambling supply houses may be used.

Card slicking is often used in conjunction with the ROUGH-AND-SMOOTH principle, making the action of cards thus prepared more certain than would either preparation used alone.

SLIDE

A small GIMMICK consisting of a flat rigid tube, usually of metal, which is used to secretly introduce an object into the interior of a container. A **coin slide** is used to get a marked coin into the center of the BALL OF WOOL; other slides may be used in conjunction with the NEST OF BOXES and similar effects, as well as some versions of the CARD TO WALLET (as where the card is found sealed between rubber-banded metal plates within the wallet).

SLIP

To secretly move a card from the top of one portion of the deck to the top of another.
See SLIP CUT.

SLIP CUT

A card SLEIGHT in which the top half of the deck is cut off and the card on the lower half taken; in actuality the left thumb retains the original top card of the deck as the upper half of the deck is removed, and this card becomes the top card of the lower half.

The sleight may be used not only to simulate a genuine CUT (only the top card is displaced), but may also be used to FORCE a particular card. There are many variations in technique and HANDLING (e.g., doing it as a table cut, using only one hand), and so on.

A brilliant routine using this sleight is DAI VERNON's **Cutting the Aces** which is described in *Stars Of Magic*.

SLIT GLASS

A glass with a horizontal slot cut in one side at the bottom; a coin dropped into the glass can be easily retrieved by tilting the glass slightly.

Glasses thus prepared should be heavily fluted or have a cut-glass design.

Also known as a **slot glass**.

SLOP SHUFFLE

Devised by SID LORRAINE, this is not technically a shuffle, though it appears to mix the cards not only in the usual way, but also face-up and face-down.

The left hand pushes a group of cards into the right; the left hand then turns and deposits another group on top of these, but facing the opposite way. The left hand turns again and the process is repeated ad lib until all the cards have been put in the right hand; often the procedure is varied by turning of the cards held in the right hand, to add to the confusing appearance.

Though it would appear that the cards are thoroughly mixed, in fact they are separated into two halves facing in opposite directions; in each half all the cards face the same way.

The shuffle may be used not only for the basic effect of suddenly righting the cards, but also to openly sort the deck into two halves (red/black, high/low) for a subsequent effect.
See DIVIDED DECK.

SLOW-MOTION ACES

See FOUR ACES.

SLYDINI (b. ca. 1900)

Born Quintino Marucci in Italy, he moved to Argentina as a youth. In 1930 he left that country, coming finally to the U.S., where he performed in various venues, including two seasons with a carnival.

He became best-known for his flawless CLOSE-UP MAGIC, in which he applied the art of MISDIREC-TION on a level few had seen before; Slydini's name has now almost become synonymous with misdirection.

In addition to his performing, Slydini became highly respected as an instructor when, in New York, MAX KATZ formed a group of students for private lessons; in the ensuing years many famous performers have come to Slydini for personal instruction.

Slydini's work is described in his three effects described in the *Stars Of Magic* book, as well as in *The Magic Of Slydini* by LEWIS GANSON, *Slydini Encores* (edited by Levy), and *The Magical World of Slydini* and *The Best Of Slydini. . .And More*, both of which are two-volume sets written by KARL FULVES.

SLYTER, CLARENCE (?-?)

Performer who specialized in a distinctive version of the DRUNK ACT; billing the act as A Magician's Night Out, he performed in nightclubs, hotels and similar venues on the west coast and in the midwest. During the late 1930s and early 1940s he was quite successful.

SMALL RING

In a LINKING RING set, a ring fractionally smaller in diameter which may therefore be passed through the larger rings; it is employed in various counting methods to show the rings to be solid and separate.

SMITH, H. ADRIAN (b. ?)

Engineer by profession; highly regarded COLLECTOR of magic publications and memorabilia (the Smith collection is reputed to be one of the very best ever assembled).

Smith is also noted as an expert in the field of MNEMONICS, and has contributed an article on the subject to HILLIARD's *Greater Magic*. He is the author of *It's In The Bag*, an influential ROUTINE of card effects accomplished while the performer is genuinely blindfolded; this routine, originally published as a booklet, will also be found in the Hilliard book cited above.

SMITH, LES (b. 1915)

Owner since 1963 of Owen Magic Supreme, the magic manufacturing company founded by CARL OWEN. He is a noted builder of ILLUSIONs, and has supplied many of the illusion effects used by SIEGFRIED AND ROY, DOUG HENNING, and countless other magicians.

SMITH MYTH

A seminal card effect invented by HEN FETSCH and Fred Smith in which two spectators are made to choose the same card from a packet by means of a mathematical procedure. Both spectators then shuffle the packet, after which it is cut into two smaller packets.

Instructing the spectators to call "stop" when their cards are seen, the performer deals cards face-up from both packets simultaneously. Of course, both spectators call "stop" at the same time, and the effect of an amazing coincidence is thus created.

Others who have worked on the underlying principle include STEWART JAMES and Ronald Wohl.

See RASHOMON PRINCIPLE.

SMOKE PICTURES

Like SAND PICTURES and RAG PICTURES, this was a novelty sometimes featured by magicians. A white surface, usually ceramic tile, was blackened with the soot from a bundle of burning tapers, and then the performer rubbed away areas of the soot to rapidly produce a picture.

Smoke pictures were featured by MAX HOLDEN in the vaudeville act of "Holden and Graham."

SMOKE TRICK

The PRODUCTION of smoke in a vase or other container, a very old effect, is still used by many performers. There are various HANDLINGs for the ROUTINE, but all require the fumes of hydrochloric acid and ammonia to combine to create a smoke-like vapor.

(*Please note*: though this vapor has the appearance of tobacco smoke it is *considerably* more harmful; under no circumstances should the performer inhale the vapor.)

The effect was performed by CHUNG LING SOO with a glass vase, the lid of which was prepared with a valve which allowed him to let the chemicals combine at any time (this vase was described in the *New Pentagram* magazine). Another popular version of the effect was done with two clay pipes and later by BILLY MCCOMB with a single pipe; McComb's routine is described in his *McComb's Magic*. Lee Noble performed a routine with corncob pipes which can be found in BRUCE ELLIOTT's *Classic Secrets Of Magic*.

Many modern performers have done the effect with a brandy glass which is covered with a beer mat; FRED KAPS featured this version.

See SMOKING THUMB.

SMOKING THUMB

An effect in which the performer closes his fingers and extends his thumb to simulate a pipe, and then puffs on his thumb and blows clouds of smoke. It has been featured by ADE DUVAL, FRED KAPS, PETER PIT, BILLY MCCOMB and many others; McComb's version was inspired by his viewing of a Laurel and Hardy film in which the EFFECT was simulated.

SNADER, CRAIGE (b. ?)

Writer on magical subjects for many years resident in Mexico; editor/publisher of *Magic Sounds*, a periodical devoted to audio recordings relevant to magic. Also noted for his interest in MENTAL MAGIC (which he performs as Alex Redans), he is the author of *Mind Square*, a treatise on the MAGIC SQUARE.

SNAKE BASKET

A comedy card effect using an obvious imitation snake which is placed in a wicker basket; a card is selected and returned to the deck which is likewise placed in the basket. With considerable byplay the snake slowly rises from the basket, the selected card in its mouth.

The effect is mechanical, and few spectators would perceive it as anything else; its value lies in the basis it creates for comedy situations. This one effect comprised almost a complete act for comedy magician RUSSELL SWANN.

SNOWSTORM IN CHINA

See WINTERTIME IN CHINA.

SOFT SOAP

A SUCKER EFFECT in which "soiled" handkerchieves are put into a detergent box; clean handkerchieves are withdrawn but the spectators are led to believe that the dirty handkerchieves remain in the box. Eventually it is torn apart and shown to be completely empty.

SOLDIER'S PRAYER BOOK AND ALMANAC

A narration in which the performer shows how various aspects of a deck of cards are used to recall stories from the Bible, and also how the cards may be used as a calendar (fifty-two cards = fifty-two weeks, four suits = four seasons, etc.).

The ROUTINE is said to be over two centuries old; it is described in HUGARD and BRAUE's *Encyclopedia Of Card Tricks*.

SOO, CHUNG LING

See CHUNG LING SOO.

SORCAR, P.C. (1913-1971)

Indian performer (born Pratul Chandra Sorcar in East Pakistan) who toured an elaborate ILLUSION show through his own country and (with a smaller show) many others, including France, Russia, Britain, and the United States. He was noted not only for the magnificence of his show and wardrobe but also for the huge amounts of publicity he created and generated.

Sorcar received a great deal of publicity from a television appearance in Britain in 1952; he performed his version of the BUZZSAW illusion, and the program went off the air before the assistant could be shown "restored." The television station's switchboard was immediately jammed by alarmed viewers wondering about the assistant's fate. Several newspapers headlined the story the next day.

He often billed himself as "The World's Greatest Magician," and it was not unusual to see him referred to in magic magazines by the acronym TWGM.

On his death his show was taken over by his son, Prodip Chandra Sorcar (born 1946), who has toured throughout Asia, Europe, Britain and the U.S. with considerable success.

An interesting potpourri of magic, history and reminiscences is his *Sorcar On Magic*.

SORT-EDGE DECK

A type of MARKED DECK using cards of the BEE back design. Since in printing these decks there will be some variance in how the pattern appears on the backs, it is possible to sort various printing runs by whether the cards have full or half-diamond patterns at the long and short edges. While such a deck cannot indicate all values, and thus is not often used for magical purposes, it can indicate high/low or court/spot, and thus is useful for such games as Blackjack (Twenty-One).

SOUND CHECK

A testing of the audio equipment at a venue (tape decks, speakers, microphones, etc.) to insure proper sound reproduction, and/or to balance and calibrate equipment to the acoustics of the venue.

Sound checks are important when the performer provides the sound equipment, and essential when using that provided by the venue.

SOUTHALL, GUS (1902-1971)

British magician highly regarded as a CLOSE-UP MAGIC performer, particularly with cards. A few of his effects will be found in PENTAGRAM Magazine.

SPECTATOR CUTS THE ACES

A PLOT devised by Bob Veeser in which a spectator divides the deck into four piles, and an Ace is found at the top of each pile. Considerable work has been done on this effect by ED MARLO and many others.

SPELLING BEE

A type of card SPELLING TRICK in which the cards of a suit or of the entire deck are spelled out in sequence (by dealing a card for each letter in the name of the card). Such demonstrations are more in the nature of mathematical curiosities than magical effects.

A somewhat more entertaining variant of the above is to have the spectator attempt to spell various cards without success, the performer then spelling the card correctly; this routine is the invention of HERBERT MILTON. A routine for this effect will be found in JOHN SCARNE's *Scarne On Card Tricks*.

A version of this latter routine, using cards with titled pictures of various objects, is VAL EVANS' An Invitation to Lunch—*With Beer*, which can be found in THE JINX Magazine.

SPELLING TRICK

A card EFFECT, believed to have been invented by DR. JAMES WILLIAM ELLIOT, in which a chosen card is found by spelling its name, dealing one card from the deck for each letter; the chosen card turns up on the last letter. Variations include spelling several cards in sequence, spelling thought-of cards, or spelling the spectator's name.

See LIE SPELLER; SPELLING BEE.

SPHINX

A famous ILLUSION invented by Professor Thomas W. Tobin and first presented by COLONEL STODARE in 1865. A small box was placed on a bare, three-legged table; when the box was opened, it revealed a living human head which would converse with the spectators.

The illusion was accomplished by a specific use of the MIRROR PRINCIPLE; here, mirrors were mounted between the front leg and the two side legs, each set at an angle of 45 degrees to the audience. Thus it appeared to the spectators that they were looking under the table to the back curtain, while actually they were seeing reflections of the side curtains. (This general arrangement of the mirrors is sometimes given the name **Sphinx Principle**.)

A discussion of this and related principles will be found in SAM H. SHARPE's *Conjurers' Optical Secrets*.

SPHINX (Magazine)

Founded in 1902 by WILLIAM J. HILLIAR; after struggling under various owners for a few years it was given to DR. A. M. WILSON, who was editor and publisher until his death in 1930.

At that time it was taken over by JOHN MULHOLLAND, who continued as editor until the magazine ceased publication in 1953.

For much of its life the SPHINX Magazine was the most influential of magic journals; with the colorful Dr. Wilson and later the scholarly John Mulholland, it managed to be both staid and controversial and packed a great deal of magical history and invention into its pages.

SPIDER

A coin GIMMICK consisting of two thin flesh-colored rods clipped to the first and fourth fingers, with a coin suspended between them by a wire or rod; its purpose was to allow less-than-dexterous performers to BACK-PALM a coin without fear of dropping it. Though spiders of various kinds are described in T. NELSON DOWNS' *Modern Coin Manipulation* and *The Art Of Magic*, it is doubtful that such gimmicks were ever extensively used by professional performers.

More recently the term has been applied to a GIMMICK invented by Philippe Socrate of France, which stores over thirty feet of thread on a REEL arrangement which will slip into the pocket, greatly simplifying the preparation for effects involving thread as an operating principle.

The Spider was also the name given by STANLEY COLLINS to his effect in which pips vanished one at a time from a playing card and were found on a sheet of tissue which had previously been shown blank.

A magic-themed play by FULTON OURSLER was also titled *The Spider*.

SPIDER'S WEB

Invented by J.F. Orrin, this is a large web of gold cord mounted on a circular black velvet background with wood backing, on which an imitation spider sits; when the web is spun on its central pivot, a chosen card appears on the web under the spider's legs.

SPIDORA

A sideshow and carnival ILLUSION in which a very large (stuffed) spider resting on its web appears to have the head of a living woman. Similar in general design to the HEAD ON SWORD, this illusion relies on an application of the MIRROR PRINCIPLE; and is generally credited to HENRY ROLTAIR.

SPIKE CABINET

An ILLUSION invented by P.T. SELBIT in which a woman is placed in a cabinet standing in front of a wall

Mark Wilson performs the lighted-bulb version of the *Spike Cabinet*, assisted by Nani Darnell (*photo courtesy GENII Magazine*).

of large spikes; a curtain is drawn closed and a wheel is turned, forcing the spikes out through holes in the cabinet wall and apparently through the woman. When the spikes are withdrawn the woman steps un-harmed from the cabinet. (In some models the curtain is replaced by a door, and/or the wheel by a lever.) Selbit called this illusion **human pincushion**; it is better known now as the **spike cabinet**, a name given to it by CHARLES CARTER.

There have been many later versions of this illusion, including one where the spikes are replaced by long lighted bulbs; this version (invented by LEON) is climaxed by having the outer wall removed to show the bulbs apparently visibly penetrating the ASSISTANT.

SPIKER

An ILLUSION which uses two posts approximately four feet tall, each with a l-inch hole drilled from side to side near the top. A person stands between the two posts, and a metal rod is apparently passed through the holes in both posts and the person's body.

Also known as the *Pillars Of Fear* and by various other names.

SPIKE TABLE

See TABLE OF DEATH.

SPINNING COINS

Coins which, when spun on a hard surface, will always come to rest with the same face upwards. The coins are FAKED by grinding the edge at a slight angle, so that the edge slants fractionally and thus one side of the coin has a somewhat smaller diameter than the other. Such coins are usually sold in sets of two, one of which will always land heads, the other tails.

A somewhat more sophisticated application of this principle is to prepare the coin in a half-and-half manner so that, viewed from a particular point, it is a slanted parallelogram in cross-section; with such a coin, either side may be made to come up at the con-clusion of the spin depending on which area of the coin rests on the table at the beginning of the spinning action.

SPIRIT BELL

A pseudo-spiritualistic effect in which a bell on a tripod, usually covered with a glass dome or wicker basket, rings in answer to questions.

In actuality the covered bell does not ring at all; the sound comes from a device worn by the performer or otherwise concealed. There are a number of other methods of accomplishing the effect, ranging from threads to mechanical devices.

A precursor to this effect, involving a bowl-like crys-tal bell with an external clapper, was featured by ROBERT-HOUDIN; this bell would ring when suspended either from a hook or the performer's wand. Mechanisms in the hook and wand raised a thin rod which actuated a lever within the bell's supporting ring which was attached to the clapper. A later variant of this version of the spirit bell effect is described in PROFESSOR LOUIS HOFFMANN's *Modern Magic*.

Unquestionably the most bizarre method was created by ALEXANDER HEIMBURGER (see BIRD MAGIC).

SPIRIT BONDS

The term *Spirit*, when applied to a restraint such as a metal *collar* or *cuff*, indicates a device from which the performer can escape without needing to remove the lock. This may be accomplished by removing the pin from a hinge, by separating a magnetic hinge, or by other mechanical means.

Such devices are sometimes used in conjunction with an ILLUSION to apparently restrain a person in a particular position.

SPIRIT CABINET

A classic stage ROUTINE, inspired by the DAVENPORT BROTHERS, in which a MEDIUM is secured to a post or chair and placed in a curtained cabinet; various physical manifestations take place—the tooting of horns, the flinging from the cabinet of various objects, etc.—but when the medium is examined he or she is still tightly secured.

One of the most effective feats in this routine uses the borrowed coat of a spectator; placed into the cabinet, it is revealed being worn by the medium, who is still bound—an apparent demonstration of MATTER THROUGH MATTER. This effect was featured by JOHN NEVIL MASKELYNE in his cabinet routine, and has been used by many performers since.

This demonstration was a feature with many who demonstrated it as a genuine spiritualistic phenomenon, or implied as much; the most famous of these was *Anna Eva Fay*, and the effect is still sometimes referred to as the Fay Cotton Bandage Test. (Miss Fay was secured with strips of cotton bandage, a method still used.)

Among the magical performers who have featured a version of the Spirit Cabinet are KARL GERMAIN, FREDERICK EUGENE POWELL, HOWARD THURSTON, GUS RAPP, HARRY WILLARD, LES LEVANTE, VIRGIL and Julie, MILBOURNE CHRISTOPHER, ANDRE KOLE and many others. Its most accomplished exponent at present is FRANCES WILLARD.

SPIRIT COUNT

A COUNT procedure for a PACKET of four cards which apparently displays the face of each of the four cards, in actuality showing only two faces (the two cards shown must, however, be identical, for example, two Jokers or two blank cards).

Invented by Gene Castillon, it is described in JERRY MENTZER's *Counts, Cuts, Moves And Subtleties*.

SPIRIT GUM

A rubber-cement-like adhesive used to adhere false hair, rubber prosthetics and/or other components of a stage make-up to the face or body. It may be dissolved with ACETONE.

SPIRIT LOCK

This term is applied to two different kinds of faked padlocks:

1. A lock which can be opened without the use of the key, either by pressure at a particular point or by insertion of a rod into a cavity. Such locks are sometimes used in ESCAPES.

2. A lock which, fastened to a rod or other object, opens itself and falls to the floor. Descriptions of differing designs for such locks may be found in CRAMER's *Germain The Wizard* and HOPKINS' *Twentieth Century Magic*. An excellent model of this lock was for a time manufactured by JON MARTIN.

SPIRIT NUT

See BRASS NUT.

SPIRIT PAINTINGS

Originally performed as a genuine "spirit manifestation" by two professional mediums known as the Bangs Sisters, this ROUTINE involves the creation of finished oil paintings on examined blank canvases—the canvases having been illuminated from the rear to demonstrate their blank state.

The methodology of the Bangs Sisters was analyzed by DAVID P. ABBOTT, who greatly improved it; in correspondence he described it to a Dr. Wilmar (W. S. Marriott) who promptly sold it to SELBIT and KELLAR. It was some time before the truth of the matter was known; later, when HOWARD THURSTON presented the effect, he billed it as *Abbott's Riddle Of The Century*.

For many years the **spirit paintings** were featured in the performances of VIRGIL, but in recent years the effect has been rarely seen. The most thorough discussion of it is still that of Abbott and will be found in *David P. Abbott's Book Of Mysteries*.

SPIRIT RAPS

Knocking sounds produced on tables, floors, etc., apparently by the agency of spirits. Questions could be addressed to the spirits and would be answered with three raps for yes (Y-E-S), two for no (N-O). Such raps, produced by the young Fox sisters in 1848 in Hydesville, New York, are generally conceded to be the beginning of modern Spiritualism as a religion. (One of the sisters, Kate Fox, confessed in later life that it had all been fraud; by that time, however, she was an alcoholic, and her statements were of little value to people on either side of the question.)

Magicians were quick to simulate the phenomenon, and a number of methods were developed to accomplish it; these included a metal "clicker" set into the belt and operated by pressure of the stomach, and an elaborate piston-operated arrangement strapped to the performer's leg. Some of the methods employed may be found in Hereward Carrington's *Physical Phenomena Of Spiritualism.*

Such demonstrations lacked visual appeal, however, so magicians tended to discard them in favor of more interesting demonstrations along the same lines, such as the SPIRIT BELL and the RAPPING HAND.

SPIRIT SLATES

School slates, usually employed in pairs, on which a message appears after the slates have been cleaned and examined. A number of methods for creating this effect exist, ranging from those requiring ingeniously prepared mechanical slates to routines which can be done with unprepared slates.

The primary source for effects of this kind is PETER WARLOCK's *The Best Tricks With Slates.* Much useful information will also be found in *Master Slate Secrets* (four volumes) by Al Mann.

SPLIT DECK

A deck of cards which has been cut in half diagonally; spectators choose half-cards from the two halves of the deck—and of course these are revealed to be the two halves of the same card. This MECHANICAL DECK, the invention of ROBERT HASKELL, is simply a ROUGH-AND-SMOOTH FORCE deck which has been cut in two (*see* ROUGH-AND-SMOOTH PRINCIPLE).

Variations include a JUMBO DECK on the same principle, and a comedy routine in which the two halves do *not* match—but the prediction card is seen to be composed of the two chosen halves.

SPLIT FAN

A type of CARD FAN PRODUCTION technique (see BACK PALM), in which the fan is secretly divided into two portions—one portion being backpalmed as the other portion is allowed to fall into a receptacle. The ILLUSION is, of course, that all the cards have been dropped.

The concealed cards may now be produced and the procedure repeated as long as there are enough cards to make the technique visually convincing.

This technique, according to DAI VERNON, was invented by a sideshow performer billed as "Ardo, The Frog Man."

SPONGE BALLS

Balls, generally about 2 inches in diameter, made of a highly compressible sponge rubber or similar foamed substance. Because of this compressibility, it is impossible for a spectator to ascertain how many he or she may be holding—and this fact, along with SLEIGHT OF HAND, makes sponge ball magic very effective in close-up situations. Other things being equal, magic which appears to take place in the spectator's hand always has a stronger appeal, which accounts for the unfailing popularity of this effect. The use of **sponge balls** within magic is credited to Jesse L. Lybarger. The most popular **sponge balls** available at present are those marketed by ALBERT GOSHMAN.

Many ROUTINEs for this effect may be found in works by AUDLEY WALSH, FRANK GARCIA, and FRANCES MARSHALL.

A variant of this routine, using small sponge rabbits, is the MULTIPLYING RABBITS.

SPOOK SHOW

Also known as a **Ghost Show**, this is a specialized kind of theatrical magical performance, usually taking place at midnight. The magic is of the grotesque or bizarre kind—e.g., the GUILLOTINE illusion, the SPIRIT CABINET, etc.—and the traditional climax for such shows is the BLACKOUT, in which glowing ghosts, skeletons, and assorted apparitions float and fly over the heads of the spectators.

Many MENTALISTs and magicians have used this as an adjunct to their regular shows; the greatest success, however, has been made by those who specialized in this area, including George Marquis and Jack Baker (Dr. Silkini). Undoubtedly the best show of this kind was the *Madhouse Of Mystery* presented by WILLIAM NEFF.

SPOT

A particular position in the running order of a show which uses a number of acts; for example, **closing spot.**

Also, a complete ACT or ROUTINE used to replace or supplement the regular act, as for the second or third performance of the evening for the same audience.

Also, abbreviation for SPOTLIGHT.

SPOT CARD

An Ace, Two, Three, Four, Five, Six, Seven, Eight, Nine, or Ten of any of the four suits; also called *number card.*

SPOTLIGHT

A light, created by an incandescent bulb or carbon-arc, and using a lens and mechanical iris, used to illuminate a particular area of the stage. Some spotlights are fixed in position, while others (such as the **follow spot**) can be moved to follow the performer; these are most often operated from a light booth at the rear of the theater, usually in the upper balcony.

The **pin spot** is usually fixed in position on the stage itself, illuminating a very small and specific area; however, a BABY SPOT with a small iris opening is sometimes used.

SPREAD

See RIBBON SPREAD.

Also, as a noun, the deck or a portion thereof lying in a ribbon-spread condition on the table; as a verb, to perform the ribbon-spread action or, to push the cards from one hand to the other while maintaining their sequence.

SPREER, EDMUND (1902-1983)

Born in Germany, he combined his interests in engineering and magic to become show mechanic for MAURICE F. RAYMOND on a tour of Latin America. For a time he left magic, working as a master mechanic in Buenos Aires, Argentina. Around 1928 he joined forces with DAVID BAMBERG, building and reworking ILLUSIONs, and toured with him for over a decade.

Later, living in Mexico City, he worked for Mexican television as a master mechanic for twenty-five years, taking a brief hiatus during this time to build illusions for the last of Bamberg's elaborate shows.

In 1979 he was the recipient of a Creative Fellowship from the ACADEMY OF MAGICAL ARTS. He is the subject of a book by Robert Olson titled *Illusion Builder To Fu Manchu*.

SPRING FLOWERS

Paper flowers made to fold flat, with a flat metal spring which causes them to open fully; a packet of such flowers small enough to conceal in the hand makes a very large bouquet. They are used in various ways, often with PRODUCTION devices.

Since they do not really resemble any real flowers, they should not be left for any extended scrutiny by the audience. The most convincing display is made from a large number of green flowers in which are placed a smaller number of red ones (an idea credited

Edmund Spreer (*photo courtesy GENII Magazine*)

to DAVID DEVANT); this gives the appearance, at a casual glance, of a bouquet of roses.

Spring Flowers are the invention of BUATIER DE KOLTA, who kept the secret of their construction to himself for a time. Then, at one performance, a breeze from a door opened backstage blew some of the flowers into the audience, where they were quickly snatched up by magicians present.

SPRINGING THE CARDS

A FLOURISH in which the deck is held in one hand and squeezed at the two short edges between thumb and fingers so that it develops a downward bend. The cards are then allowed to escape from thumb or fingers one-by-one in rapid succession, the release of tension causing them to spring through the air in a continuous ribbon to the other hand.

This Flourish is described in GIBSON's *Complete Illustrated Guide To Card Magic* and many other publications. An interesting variant of the usual technique is described in HUGARD and BRAUE's *Expert Card Technique*.

SPRING OBJECTS

Objects which are apparently solid, but which are actually made of a cloth covering over an inner spring. A large number of such objects may be compressed and placed into a PRODUCTION device. Among the many items so prepared are rabbits, large dice, and strings of sausages.

See also SPRING FLOWERS.

SQUARE CIRCLE

A popular PRODUCTION device invented by LOUIS S. HISTED, it consists of a small platform on which is a square wooden chimney with a slotted or grillwork front, through which a brightly colored metal tube can be seen. In performance, the chimney is removed and shown empty and replaced; the tube is then extracted and also shown empty, while the slots or grill in the chimney allow spectators to see its interior. The tube having been replaced, a large production of various items can be made.

Many models of the **square circle** are available, from a tiny one which will produce a small SILK to one large enough to produce a full-grown person. Versions of intermediate size will produce doves, flowers, fishbowls, and the like.

The **square circle** operates on the principle of a BLACK ART load chamber. Sometimes the tube is constructed as a PHANTOM TUBE, to allow for an additional production without using the chimney.

A similar effect was marketed in Britain as *Wunda Villa*.

SQUARE PIG

A commercially marketed EFFECT invented by U. F. GRANT in which a slate is shown bearing a picture of what the performer claims is a pig; since the picture consists entirely of straight lines, it is difficult to tell.

The performer is asked to make the pig "look round," and eventually it does—the triangular head of the pig visibly turning to look in the opposite direction.

SQUARE THE DECK

To even the cards so that the sides of the deck are perfectly smooth; often done to establish that the performer is not keeping track of a particular card.

SQUASH

An effect invented by PERCY ABBOTT in which a partially filled shot glass held in the performer's hands is caused to vanish.

This is accomplished by an ingenious PULL, consisting of a small rubber ball on an elastic cord; the ball is wedged into the glass, effectively sealing it, and the pull is released.

SQUEEZAWAY BLOCK

An APPARATUS effect invented by EDWARD M. MASSEY in which a yellow block placed between two black blocks in an open-sided box is seen to get progressively thinner as the two outer blocks are pushed together. Finally the yellow block vanishes altogether and is found elsewhere.

The apparatus operates on an ingenious variation of the SHELL principle.

SQUEEZERS

Nickname given to the first decks of cards to use identifying INDEXES in diagonally opposite corners; from the squeezing action used to spread the cards slightly to learn their identities.

Prior to this, it was necessary to view the whole FACE of a card to ascertain its value.

It is now used to denote Bulldog Squeezers, a brand of poker-size playing cards sold by the U. S. Playing Card Company.

SQUIRCLE

Commercially manufactured effect invented by Ken Bowell in which a square is torn from a folded newspaper. When the paper is opened, however, a circle has been torn out of it! A later addition to the ROUTINE is to open the torn piece—which is seen to be the circle.

STABBED DECK

See CARD STAB.

STACK

A particular arrangement of a deck of cards; or, to so arrange a deck.

While gamblers used prearranged or "cold" decks to deal a specific hand to themselves or their partner, a stacked deck in magical use is most often employed to ascertain the identity of a chosen card. In the most elementary application of this, the magician cuts the deck at the point where the selected card is removed and completes the cut; noting the new bottom card, it is an easy matter to calculate the next card in the arrangement—the chosen card.

There are two basic kinds of Stack employed by

magicians—the **cyclical stack** and the **memorized stack**.

A **cyclical stack** is an endless chain arrangement; of these the most popular is the SI STEBBINS Stack. Here the suits rotate in a specific order of Clubs, Hearts, Spades, Diamonds—remembered by use of the mnemonic word CHaSeD—and each card is of a value three higher than the preceding card. Thus if the Ace of Hearts is the top card, the second card will be the Four of Spades; then the Seven of Diamonds, Ten of Clubs, King of Hearts, Three of Spades, and so on for the remainder of the cards. So popular is this stack that such items as **Deland's card locator** and the **Deland dollar deck** (both invented by THEODORE H. DE LAND) have been marketed for use with it.

One of the drawbacks of the Stebbins stack noted by magicians is its mathematical nature which, with its 3-6-9 sequences, may be noted by a spectator. To eliminate this, mnemonic couplets have been devised to indicate the sequence of values.

The most popular of these is called the Eight Kings Stack; the rhyme used here is *"Eight Kings Threatened To Save/Ninety-Five Queens For One Sick Knave"*—which symbolizes the values Eight, King, Three, Ten, Two, Seven, Nine, Five, Queen, Four, Ace, Six, Jack.

Another such arrangement, created by JOHN MULHOLLAND, is called the **jackass stack**: *"Jackass Ate Live Tree, King Intends To Fix Several For Benign Queen,"* suggesting Jack, Ace, Eight, Five, Three, King, Ten, Two, Six, Seven, Four, Nine, Queen.

The repeated sequence of suits is also a problem, and while at various times formulas have been devised to determine the suit of one card by the value of the one preceding, these are rarely used. Two systems of this type have been developed by GEORGE SANDERSON (in his *Concealed Art of Magic*) and GEORGE BLAKE (in his *Set-Reset*).

A non-cyclical stack in which succeeding cards are determined by a mathematical formula is Richard Osterlind's Breakthrough Card System.

A completely memorized stack, using card MNEMONIC systems, is also rarely used. Of these the most famous and popular is LOUIS NIKOLA's *Nikola Card System*, published as a small book and later as a chapter in the *Encyclopedia Of Card Tricks*. The Nikola Stack may be used not only for locations but also for GAMBLING DEMONSTRATIONs, SPELLING effects, and other feats.

Later mnemonic arrangements have included the Ireland Stack (created by L. L. IRELAND), the **Walsh stack** (created by AUDLEY V. WALSH), and many others; a notable recent addition to this literature is Simon Aronson's *A Stack To Remember*.

One other type of stack which should be mentioned is the **specific-purpose**, or **dedicated stack**; this is an arrangement of the cards used for only one effect; for example, the arrangement used in NAME-O-CARD; and the *Gambler's Rehearsal*, a GAMBLING DEMONSTRATION routine in the TARBELL COURSE IN MAGIC (Volume 6). **Dedicated stacks** are by their nature used far less than **cyclical** or **memorized stacks**.

The most convincing use of a **stacked deck** depends on the performer's ability to do a convincing FALSE SHUFFLE or DECK SWITCH—preferably both.

STACK OF QUARTERS

A close-up EFFECT with coins in which a stack of five or six quarters is placed on the back of a spectator's hand and covered with a paper or leather cone. The cone is tapped, and the coins drop from beneath the spectator's hand, having apparently passed right through it; the cone is empty. This effect is the modern version of the **cap and pence**.

The loose coins are switched for a stack which is held together with a rivet (which allows the stack to be spread slightly), and it is this stack which is covered with the cone; after the loose coins are dropped from beneath the spectator's hand, the cone is squeezed and the stack carried away beneath it to be PALMed and/or secretly disposed of.

There are many variations of the basic effect: in some versions the riveted stack is hollow, so that a miniature die (or other small object) may be placed within. In the routine, a duplicate die is placed on *top* of the stack before it is covered with the cone, and the presence of (apparently) the same die when the cone is lifted is subtle reinforcement that the coins have vanished from beneath it.

Several ROUTINEs for this effect are described in J.B. BOBO's *Modern Coin Magic*.

STACK OF TIRES

An ILLUSION invented by HARRY BLACKSTONE SR. in which a woman was placed into a stack of automobile tires; the stack was then quickly disassembled (the tires being rolled offstage one by one) and the woman had vanished.

STAGE ILLUSION

See ILLUSION.

STAGE LEFT/STAGE RIGHT

The left and right sides of the stage from the point of view of the performer facing the audience; the reverse of left and right as seen by the audience.

See also DOWNSTAGE; UPSTAGE; PROMPT SIDE; OPPOSITE PROMPT.

STAGE MONEY

Imitation currency, often switched for a borrowed bill prior to burning or some other form of destruction.

Spring bills are folded stage money equipped with springs much like SPRING FLOWERS; they are often used as a climax to the MISER'S DREAM.

See also FLASH BILL.

STAMP ALBUM

A stamp album is shown to have blank pages. Stamps are shaken from a bowl or clear envelope into a cone, from which they vanish; when the album is shown again, the stamps are affixed in place within it. This effect is the invention of John Brearly.

The stamps vanish from the cone by means of a secret pocket into which they are poured. The album consists of pages alternating long and short; each alternate page is blank. Depending on which direction in which the album is riffled, it may be shown to consist of blank or filled pages—much as with the handling of the SVENGALI DECK. (It should be noted that the basic principle used in the construction of the stamp album is over three centuries old.)

A variant construction has alternate pages cut with a bevel; thus the change can be shown by riffling in the same direction, but at the upper or lower end of the pages' outer edge.

STANLEY, HARRY (b. ?)

British magic dealer and publisher; former band singer and drummer. He was the operator of the UNIQUE MAGIC STUDIO in London (initially, in partnership with ARTHUR DOWLER and JACK HUGHES), for many years one of the leading magic shops in the world. Editor and publisher of THE GEN Magazine, he also published a number of important books written by LEWIS GANSON and featuring the magic of VERNON, SLYDINI, and many others.

Stanley was also instrumental in developing the careers of new performers, notably JOHNNY HART. Retired since 1970, he continues to be active in the magical community, writing articles and reminiscences.

STANYON, ELLIS (1871-1951)

Born in Britain; noted magic dealer and writer. In addition to his Serials (several books, each dealing with a specific EFFECT), he was also the editor of *Magic*, a magazine which had a two-decade run beginning at the turn of the century.

He is the author of *Conjuring for Amateurs* and *Conjuring with Cards.*

STAR TRAP

A circular opening which is closed with a number of pie-slice shaped doors hinged around its circumference; these doors are held closed by spring tension, but an object may be pushed through them into a waiting container below.

While the **star trap** has an advantage in that in action it uses a smaller opening, its drawbacks—mechanical complexity, the tendency of objects to "hang up" on the points of the doors, etc.—have caused it to fall into disuse. While versions of the **star trap** are still found in smaller APPARATUS, it is almost never used as a device set into a stage, since its design renders it somewhat dangerous to a person passing through it.

STAY-STACK

A card-shuffling principle (discovered by RUSDUCK) derived from the use of the REFLECTED STACK in combination with the FARO SHUFFLE; it states that, while the positions of actual cards may be moved, the relationship between pairs of cards in the upper and lower half of the deck will remain in the reflected stack.

A related point is that, if a deck in reflected stack is evenly divided and given a genuine RIFFLE SHUFFLE, each of the two halves will contain one card of each value and color.

See also GILBREATH PRINCIPLE.

STEAL

To secretly remove an object under the direct or indirect observation of the spectator. An example of the former would be to steal a pea from under a shell during a performance of the SHELL GAME; of the latter, to steal a cigarette from a CIGARETTE DROPPER.

STEAMBOAT BACK

An early card back design consisting of crosshatched diagonal lines, usually against a beige background.

STEBBINS, SI (1867-1950)

Born William H. Coffrin, he worked for many years as an acrobat and rube clown in circuses, billed as *Vino*; under the Vino name he published a book of card tricks. A later book, describing his card stacking system, was published under the Stebbins name.

He was the inventor of the STACK which bears his name, in which the suits follow a repeating sequence and each card is three higher in value than the one before (A-4-7-10-K-3-6-9-Q-2-5-8-J).

It should be noted that the above stack was *not* the one he employed in performance; for his own use Stebbins preferred a sequence in which each card was *four* higher than the preceding one (A-5-9-K-4-8-Q-3-7-J-2-6-10). Stebbins revealed this in a pamphlet published quite some time after the earlier books.

STEELE, RUFUS (1879-1955)

Born William F. Steele; a professional gambler early in life, he became well known as a card expert, and compiled several books of card effects, including *Card Tricks That Are Easy To Learn, 50 Card Tricks You Can Do,* and *The Last Word On Cards.*

STEINMEYER, JIM (b. 1958)

Born near Chicago, Jim Steinmeyer has acquired a considerable reputation as an CONSULTANT to many top illusionists, including DOUG HENNING (with whom he has been associated since 1981). He created illusions for several Henning television specials and for the Broadway show MERLIN which featured Henning.

Steinmeyer conceived the spectacular vanish of the Statue Of Liberty which was featured by DAVID COPPERFIELD on a television special. He served as TECHNICAL ADVISOR for the recent *Blacke's Magic* television series, and has also created effects for Doug Henning's Chrysler television commercials. He has devised magic for various theatrical productions, from *A Christmas Carol* to the Las Vegas production of the *Folies Bergere.*

He is the author/editor of the excellent revised edition of *Jarrett Magic and Stagecraft Technical* by GUY JARRETT, published by MAGIC, INC.; Steinmeyer has added clarifying annotations, illustrations, and further information to the Jarrett book, including considerable biographical material. It is essential reading for performers interested in ILLUSION magic.

He has also written *The Mystery Of Psycho*, a book on the famous PSYCHO automaton.

STEP

A point at which the two halves of the deck are out of alignment, made by not replacing the upper half precisely; as the deck is picked up the performer can locate the step by touch and get a BREAK at this point.

This technique is often used as part of the procedure for RESTORING THE CUT.

STERANKO, JAMES (b. 1938)

Editor and illustrator by profession. He is noted within magic for two sizable supplements he contributed to GENII Magazine; one dealt with card magic, the other concerned ESCAPES, and both were marked by considerable originality. Indeed, twenty-five years later the escape concepts Steranko originated are *still* ahead of their time.

He is also the author of *Steranko On Cards*, which expands on concepts in the *Genii* supplement, along with considerable additional material.

Steranko is the editor and publisher of *Prevue*, a popular magazine covering all aspects of the visual media.

STERLING EGG

An egg-skin, either real or of thin rubber, which can be collapsed but which, when inflated, has the appearance of a real egg.

See EGG ON FAN.

STERLING, MAX (1870-1941)

Born in Britain; he claimed to have invented the EGG ON FAN effect, but it is more probable that he devised a specific presentation for the already existing effect.

He is the author of *Problems In Mystery.*

STERN, DEANE (b. 1944)

A specialist in CLOSE-UP MAGIC, he has worked almost exclusively in the TRADE SHOW field, appearing at corporate exhibitions as well as in hospitality suites and at sales meetings. His clients include Lear-Siegler, Litton Industries, Piper Air, Humana, Hyatt Medical and others.

Stern was a featured performer at the first aerospace trade show held in the People's Republic of China. He has appeared for his clients in many countries, from Uganda to Katmandu to France.

Not well known within magic circles, Stern is highly regarded by his corporate clients, many of whom have hired no other magical performers.

STERN, DUKE (1913-1973)

Born Maxwell Stern; performer with long professional career, specializing in comedy magic. For many years he was associated with Abbott'S Magic Co. in various capacities.

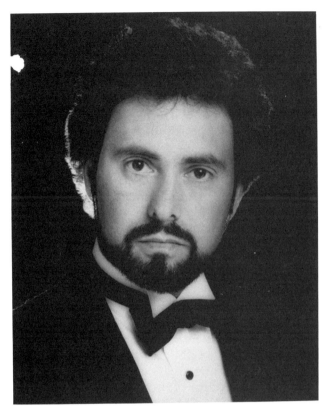

Deane Stern

He is remembered for his tireless efforts on behalf of magic and magicians, and also for the hilarious skits he performed, most often with KARRELL FOX, at the yearly Abbott's convention in Colon, Michigan.

STEVENS, JOE (b. 1935)

For many years associated with the Fuller Brush Company, in 1975 he opened Stevens Magic Emporium in Wichita, Kansas. The store was immediately successful, becoming noted for its many quality items including several from Britain's KEN BROOKE. Stevens has also created the Greater Magic Video Library, which has produced instructional videotapes from many top performers.

He is also noted for producing the Desert Magic Seminar, a magic convention begun in 1977 and held annually in Las Vegas, which features competitions and instructional lectures as well as several shows.

STICKLAND, WILLIAM G. (1904-1984)

Born in Britain; for many years he specialized in private parties for society functions, and also worked as a children's entertainer. During World War II he entertained the troops in Britain and Europe as an ENSA performer. He later developed several different acts, including a fast-paced cabaret show; he was, however, most noted for his several routines using dice of all kinds.

He was very active in the British Ring of the I.B.M., as Honorary Secretary for many years and also as Ring President; he was subsequently elected to the international vice-presidency and then to the presidency.

He originated a number of effects, many of which will be found in his *Wessex Wizardry, Interesting Tricks,* and *Introducing Bill's Magic.*

STILLWELL BALL

Term sometimes used to denote HANDKERCHIEF BALL; from its use by George Stilwell in his SILK act, described in PROFESSOR HOFFMANN's *Later Magic.*

STOCK

A particular group of cards within a deck (i.e. top stock, bottom stock); such a group may be in a particular STACK required for the effect at hand.

STOCK ESCAPE

A set of hinged wooden stocks (two pieces of wood, each with two semicircular cutouts) is used to secure the performer, who may then instantly make his escape.

Stocks can be prepared in various ways, from the simple (a pin which can be drawn from the hinge opposite the lock) to the complex (spring-loaded inner sections operated by a secret release mechanism).

While escape stocks have an imposing visual appearance, they suffer from the fact of being virtually unknown in contemporary western society; the only place most people have ever seen such a device is in the escape artist's performance, and thus there is the danger that the stocks will seem to be "magic apparatus."

STODARE, COLONEL (1831-1866)

Born in Britain; his birthname is variously recorded as John or Jack English, Jack or Alfred Inglis (Stodare had a brother—also possibly a performer—and thus there is some confusion in the historical record). He performed often at the EGYPTIAN HALL, where he introduced the SPHINX illusion. He was also noted for his bloodcurdling presentation of the BASKET illusion, worked by an original method.

He wrote two books: *The Art Of Magic* (not to be confused with the book of the same title by DOWNS), and *Fly Notes.*

He is also credited with the invention of the STODARE EGG.

STODARE EGG

Term (now rarely used) to describe the hollow egg with a small hole in one side, employed in the SUCKER EFFECT of the SILK TO EGG and also in KLING KLANG.

Stodare Egg Expose is the term used in Britain for the SUCKER EFFECT version of the SILK TO EGG.

STONE, PAUL (b. ?)

Born in Britain; partner with KEN BROOKE in the latter's shop for many years. On Brooke's retirement he took over the shop, which is now called The Ace Place; it is the only authorized British source for many of the ROUTINEs formerly marketed by Brooke. (In the U.S., the authorized dealer for the Brooke/Stone line is Stevens Magic Emporium, operated by JOE STEVENS.)

STOOGE

See CONFEDERATE.

STOP TRICK

A card effect in which the performer deals through the deck, stopping whenever specified by the spectator—the card stopped at being one previously selected by the spectator.

There are many variations on the basic effect, which is quite old; it is believed to be the invention of HOFZINSER (*see* Association Of Thoughts in *Hofzinser's Card Conjuring*).

Depending on the specific presentation, the performer may transfer cards from one hat or box to another, move the cards from one holder to another (see ATTABOY), or have the spectator himself do the dealing.

A variety of methods are available, ranging from psychological influence through SLEIGHT-OF-HAND and MECHANICAL DECKS to special APPARATUS.

STORY EFFECT

Routine in which the effect or illusion is used to illustrate a story; a classic example is the FOUR BURGLARS.

Properly presented, story effects can be quite entertaining and effective; this is, however, not easy to accomplish, and the performer must possess considerable charm as a storyteller in addition to magical competence in order to create worthwhile presentations.

Story effects are quite popular with performers specializing in CHILDREN'S MAGIC.

STRAITJACKET ESCAPE

Made popular by HOUDINI, the escape from a straitjacket is still featured by escape artists; most often it is performed as an outdoor BALLY stunt, the performer suspended upside-down from a cable while making the escape.

Most straitjackets are unprepared; it is, however, possible to GAFF them in two basic ways. The first way enables the performer to hold back a few inches of the arm strap from inside the jacket; in the course of the escape this is released, giving extra slack which simplifies the escape.

A much more subtle preparation is to enlarge the armholes at the shoulder of the jacket; escape from a jacket thus prepared is still difficult but is made marginally easier by this preparation.

For the most part, however, straitjacket escapes are done by ability, technique, sheer strength and endurance.

The best book on the subject is John Novak's *Escapes From A Strait Jacket*, Volume IV of his eight-volume *Art Of Escape* series (essential reading for anyone contemplating escape work).

STRANGER CARD

A card from another deck of differing back design, introduced into the deck in play; this may be done openly (as, for example, in the REMOTE CONTROL effect) or secretly, in which case the **stranger card** acts as a duplicate card. In this latter case, the performer must exercise care that the different back is not seen.

Also, a card from a matching deck which replaces the identical card in the working deck; such a card, taken from a new deck and put into a deck which has been broken in, will have a noticeably different feel and can thus be used as a KEY CARD. When this technique is used, the performer should make certain that the unsoiled edge of the **stranger card** does not stand out too prominently against the edges of the other cards.

STREET MAGIC

Performances in the open air, on city streets and in urban parks; many performers have worked in this demanding and sometimes dangerous situation, notably HARRY ANDERSON.

An excellent book on the subject is *Street Magic*, by Edward Claflin with JEFF SHERIDAN.

STRETCHING A ROPE

The performer takes a short length of rope and stretches it to several times its original length. The effect was invented by MILBOURNE CHRISTOPHER, and is described in his *Stretching A Rope* booklet; it can also be found in HILLIARD's *Greater Magic* and in *Encyclopedia Of Rope Tricks* edited by STEWART JAMES.

STRETCHING A WOMAN

See ELASTIC LADY.

STRIKE

In theatrical terminology, to remove an item (PROP, furniture, or scenery) from the performance area.

STRIKE MOVE

Term used to denote a move or SLEIGHT which does not require any preliminary get-ready movement or preparation.

STRIPPER DECK

A MECHANICAL DECK in which the cards are narrower at one end than the other; thus a card reversed end-for-end can easily be located by the projecting edges.

In actual practice, it is the deck which is reversed while the spectator looks at his card. The usual procedure is to fan the cards for selection and then, after the chosen card has been removed from the deck, to close the fan in a motion that turns it end-for-end.

Most decks are stripped, or "beveled" along the long edges; decks stripped along the short edges are called END STRIPPERS.

An excellent book on this subject is *The Stripper Deck* by JEAN HUGARD and FRED BRAUE.

STROBEIKA

An ESCAPE illusion in which a male ASSISTANT is manacled to a large horizontal board which is suspended from chains within a curtained cabinet; the curtains are briefly closed, and when they are re-opened, a young woman is found chained to the board. The missing assistant makes his reappearance from the audience.

A full description of the working of the illusion may be found in CHARLES HOPKINS's *Magic*.

See also ASSISTANT'S REVENGE; MANACLE BOARD VANISH.

STRUNG DECK

See ELECTRIC DECK.

STUART, J. MARBERGER (b. ?)

Performer of long experience, most noted for his New York production of *Make Me Disappear*, written by himself in collaboration with Marjorie Stuart. The off-Broadway production debuted in 1969, and received favorable reviews.

Stuart is also noted as the creator of *You Don't Have To Slay A Dragon*, a book used in feats of MENTAL MAGIC.

STULL, ROBERT (1893-1981)

Inventor by profession; noted in magic for his invention of the STULL WATCH, a unique version of the CLOCK DIAL, and many other effects, which were marketed through his Stull Magic Company. Many of his items, including his extensive handcuff collection, are on display at the MAGIC CASTLE.

He was the recipient of a Creative Fellowship from the ACADEMY OF MAGICAL ARTS.

STULL WATCH

A pocket watch designed by ROBERT STULL for a feat of MENTAL MAGIC; with the **Stull watch**'s case closed, a spectator turned the stem to reset it, and the performer was able to reveal or predict the new setting.

The watch, while precision made, had the drawback that it was not a functioning timepiece; also, in recent years, few people carry pocket watches, and this has rendered it somewhat suspicious and unusual. The basic effect of the **Stull watch** can now be duplicated with functioning analog watches.

STUNG!

A SUCKER EFFECT using three jumbo playing cards; after showing the faces of the cards they are placed under a handkerchief. Two cards are removed; when the third is uncovered, however, it now bears only the word *Stung*. After some byplay in which spectators are led to think that the card face is on the other side, it is eventually turned around to show the words *stung again*.

The basic effect has been marketed in a number of different versions.

STUTHARD, JOE (b. ?)

Born in Britain; performer who worked in variety, music-halls, and other venues. He is noted as the inventor of the TRILBY deck and also for his excellent book on the use of CONFEDERATRES titled *Stooging Around*.

SUB TRUNK

Illusionist's nickname for the METAMORPHOSIS effect.

SUCKER EFFECTS

There are two basic kinds of such ROUTINEs; (a) those in which the performer seems to inadvertently reveal the working method, and (b) those in which the performer apparently shows how the effect is accomplished, only to mystify the audience again at the conclusion.

Sucker effects are popular with magicians, primarily because such routines often take up considerable time. Unless, however, the performer has an exceptionally pleasing personality, these routines run the risk of alienating at least a portion of the audience. It should be noted that sucker effects are very popular with some performers specializing in CHILDREN'S MAGIC, where the accent is on noisy audience participation rather than mystification.

In Great Britain sucker effects are sometimes known as UP-THE-GARDEN-PATH (UTGP) routines, after a popular routine invented by Cecil Tebbett.

SUGAR CUBE TRICK

A close-up EFFECT based on **the potsherd trick**, a very old effect which is possibly of Middle Eastern origin. A spectator writes his initials or draws a design on a sugar cube, which the performer drops into a glass of water, instructing the spectator to hold his hand over it. When the cube has dissolved, the spectator turns over his hand at the performer's behest, and finds the initials or design written on the palm.

The initials are written on the cube with a pencil containing a very soft grade of lead; the performer has secretly moistened his thumb, and in dropping the cube into the glass gets an impression of the design on the ball of his thumb. In the action of moving the spectator's hand over the glass, the performer grasps the hand with his fingers above and his thumb in the spectator's palm, thus transferring the impression.

A variant of this effect can be done with certain varieties of ball-point pen, writing on a slip of paper which is then burnt; this is, however, not as effective as the original version.

SUN AND MOON

A borrowed white handkerchief has a large hole cut in its center; the performer does likewise with his own colored handkerchief and then attempts to restore them. This happens—except that the white handkerchief has the colored center and vice versa. After various other misadventures the two handkerchieves are restored to their original condition.

This rarely seen example of PERVERSE MAGIC is at least a century old; it is described in C. LANG NEIL's *The Modern Conjurer* and other sources.

The **sun and moon** title has also been applied to a coin trick with a similar plot, of comparatively recent vintage.

SUNKEN KEY

A KEY CARD which is at a particular position within the deck; if, therefore, a selected card is placed on top of the deck which is then repeatedly cut, the selection always remains a given distance from the **key card**.

If the **key card** is also a SHORT CARD or other type of LOCATOR CARD, it may be cut to the top; this will bring the chosen card to a previously determined position, depending on the key card's original location.

SUNSHADE TRICK

See MUTILATED PARASOL.

SUNSHINE, MARTIN L. (1897-1978)

Performer who traveled the world as Kismet, performing both as magician and MENTALIST. When not traveling, he was the featured performer at the Northernaire Showboat in Wisconsin for over thirty-five years. He was also, at various times, a magic dealer; he is noted as the inventor of **color vision**, a pocket DIVINATION effect, and is also believed to have originated the CENTER-TEAR technique.

SUPER-ROUGHING

To apply ROUGHING FLUID to the upper half of a playing card on one side, and to the lower half on the other side. If, for example, ten cards are prepared this way, alternating red and black suits, the PACKET can be spread at one end and will show only five red cards; with a card shifted from top to bottom, and spread at the other end, the packet will show only five black cards.

The principle is believed to be the invention of Dr. Lazlo Rothbart, and was used by him in his **Coloroto** effect which appeared in THE JINX Magazine.

See HALF-ROUGHING.

SUPER-X

Name of a popular form of SUSPENSION. A spectator lies on a board resting between two supports; the performer wraps a cloth around the spectator and then removes the supports, the board bearing the spectator remaining suspended in the air.

The effect is manufactured by ABBOTT'S MAGIC NOVELTY CO.; the basic device is commonly used by performers to create interesting poses with celebrities for publicity photographs.

SUPREME MAGIC COMPANY

Manufacturing company and dealership which has, from its out-of-the-way location in Bideford, Devon (in Britain), become one of the three largest magic companies in the world (TANNEN'S and ABBOTT'S being the other two).

It was founded in the early 1950s by Edwin Hooper, now retired (a performer who specialized in CHILDREN'S MAGIC and PUNCH AND JUDY); since that time, specializing in mail-order sales, it has served thousands of customers. In addition to the manufacture of magical effects, Supreme also publishes an extensive line of books, pamphlets and manuscripts as well as two magazines—MAGIGRAM and *The New Pentagram*, a continuation of the original PENTAGRAM Magazine. In addition to original works, they have obtained the rights to and reprinted several of the UNIQUE MAGIC STUDIO books and other publications. Much of the publishing end of the business is overseen by IAN ADAIR; several of Supreme's books and instructions have been written by KEN DE COURCY.

SURE SHOT DICE BOX

A small round box of wood or plastic. It is unfaked, but is designed so that a pair of dice placed within will make one quarter-turn with each up and down movement of the shaking; four such movements bring the dice back to their original position.

SUSPENSION

An ILLUSION in which a person rests in the air, either only partially and insufficiently supported, or completely unsupported. An example of the first type would be the **broomstick illusion**, in which a person lies horizontally with her arm resting on the brush of a broom which stands vertically on the stage or a small platform; of the second type, the SUPER-X.

A suspension differs from a LEVITATION in that it is stationary, the supports being partially or completely removed to demonstrate the suspended condition. (It should be noted that in some early versions of the suspension, the illusion began with the person standing vertically next to the supporting cane or rod, then slowly rising in a pivoting fashion to a horizontal position; this was accomplished by a rotating rod within the support engaging a cog mechanism in the harness worn by the person.)

There have been many variations of the basic suspension, the supporting rod being a cane, a crutch, a neon tube, a spiral of newsprint, or other similar item. (A version featured by THE PENDRAGONS uses a large broadsword in combination with sophisticated illusion mechanics and physical control to produce a very strong effect.)

In some cases the support is taken away, turning the illusion into one of the second type.

There have been several versions of the "unsupported" suspension as well; in addition to the Super-X, notable versions have been invented by JACK GWYNNE (**The Flying Carpet**), ROBERT HARBIN and WALTER BLANEY (**The Blaney Suspension**). A recent suspension of this type is known as the **Yogano Suspension** after its inventor.

The basic effect is thought to be of Indian origin, but this is far from certain; while it was seen in India in the early part of the 19th century, it may well be several hundred years old.

This illusion is thoroughly discussed in the *Encyclopedia Of Suspensions And Levitations* by Bruce Armstrong.

See LEVITATION.

SVENGALI DECK

A MECHANICAL DECK which uses twenty-six ordinary cards, and twenty-six identical cards which are trimmed slightly shorter than regular length. The ordinary and duplicate cards are arranged alternately.

When the cards are riffled by thumb or finger, the trimming of the duplicates causes the cards to fall in pairs, the duplicates remaining hidden behind the different cards. However, a spectator taking a card from the top of the lower group during a RIFFLE or CUT will always get a force card.

The SVENGALI DECK is generally believed to be the invention of BURLING HULL; it may, however, have been invented by W. D. Leroy.

A variation of this deck uses the ROUGH-AND-SMOOTH PRINCIPLE on the pairs of cards so the deck may not only be riffled but also fanned before the spectator; in such decks the duplicates are sometimes not trimmed, and selection is made as the deck is spread.

As with other mechanical decks, Svengali decks are rarely used by professional performers, not only because of the widespread knowledge of such decks gained through watching television pitchmen, but also because there are very few effects possible with such decks which can't be done with ordinary cards.

SWAMI GIMMICK

Term often used to denote the NAIL WRITER.

SWANN, RUSSELL (1905-1980)

Performer who specialized in comedy magic and was highly successful; he appeared in every major nightclub in the U.S. in the 1930s and 1940s, also performing in Britain and Canada.

Swann also made several appearances on television and film.

He is a recipient of the Performing Fellowship of the ACADEMY OF MAGICAL ARTS.

Russell Swann experimenting with the hat of an alarmed Eddie Cantor (*The Mulholland Library of Conjuring & the Allied Arts, Los Angeles, California*)

SWINFORD, PAUL (b. ?)

Noted inventor, particularly of effects dependent on mathematical principles. In addition to contributions to PALLBEARER'S REVIEW, EPILOGUE, ARCANE, and other periodicals, he was also for a time the editor of the LINKING RING Magazine Parade section.

His books include *Faro Fantasies* and *More Faro Fantasies*.

SWITCH

To secretly exchange one article for another; or, the exchange thus accomplished. Not to be confused with a TRANSPOSITION in which two items are made to exchange positions in an apparent magical fashion, in which a switch may be the method employed.

SWITCH WALLET

A wallet which will secretly exchange an item placed in it for another. The most popular kind of **switch wallet** is the FLIPOVER WALLET; other varieties include the Miracle Wallet, equipped with a pocket the performer may easily STEAL, and the Dalal Wallet, so designed that anything placed in its "window" section is indetectably switched.

SWORD BOX

A stage ILLUSION in which a person is put in a small box, through which are then thrust a number of sharp swords; on removal of the swords the person emerges unharmed.

In many versions of the effect the box is opened at the front after the swords are in place, and is seen to be empty except for the crisscrossing blades (see CANE CABINET; DOLL HOUSE; SPHINX).

An incredible version of this illusion is performed by HANS MORETTI; here, after he is placed an apparently ordinary cardboard box bound in chains and handcuffs, *spectators* put the swords in place in seeming random fashion—and after the swords have been removed Moretti emerges not only free of the manacles but in full clown costume and makeup, and carrying two large birds!

SWORD SWALLOWING

It is ironic that, while many circus and sideshow acts which employ various GAFFs (strong man, "torture" act, sharpshooter) are thought to be genuine demonstrations of skill, the genuine feats of sword swallowers are thought to be accomplished by faked swords that "fold up."

Collapsible swords have, however, been used by magicians to simulate sword swallowing, usually for comedy effect; these swords are available from time to time on the magical market.

SWORD THROUGH NECK

A wooden stock-like frame is placed around a spectator's neck; a sword is then inserted at one side and pushed through, apparently passing through the neck.

The "sword" is flexible (often being made from two lengths of steel rule bound together with convex sides outward); it thus will bend around the neck, guided by a secret channel in the stocks.

Most models of the APPARATUS are singularly unconvincing, thus the effect is usually presented for its possible comedy aspects rather than as a mystery.

SYMPATHETIC CLUBS

A stage card effect invented by HERBERT MILTON using two sets of the thirteen club cards. One set is shown to be arranged in numerical order and then is placed on an easel or in a clear glass. The other set is mixed, apparently at random, and an indicated card is turned face down in the group.

When the other packet is again examined, it is seen to have changed its order to exactly match that of the mixed packet—including the face-down card.

The effect was a favorite of NATE LEIPZIG, whose handling of it is described in HILLIARD's *Greater Magic*.

SYMPATHETIC COINS

The name formerly used for a SYMPATHETIC ROUTINE using coins; these are now usually called MATRIX effects, after AL SCHNEIDER's influential routine of that name.

SYMPATHETIC ROUTINE

Effect in which a number of objects (usually cards or coins), placed under separate covers, congregate one-by-one under a single cover. One popular version uses the four Aces from a deck of cards, which are placed at the four corners of a sheet of newspaper and covered with mats or folded sheets of paper; they assemble under one cover. Routines for this have been devised by DAI VERNON, Clyde Cairy, and DR. JACOB DALEY, among many others.

Such EFFECTs when performed with cards are now sometimes called BIRDS OF A FEATHER (this phrase is also used as a title for a chapter on FOUR-ACE effects in HUGARD and BRAUE's *Expert Card Technique*). When performed with coins, these are most often called MATRIX routines.

See MATRIX; CHINK-A-CHINK.

Also (rarely) a routine in which actions performed on one object are magically duplicated on a similar object.

SYMPATHETIC SILKS

Three silks are tied together in a chain and set to one side; three others are shown to be separate. The knots pass from one group of silks to the other—the tied silks now being separate and vice versa.

At one time this was a very popular effect, but with changing styles it has all but disappeared from the professional repertoire. It is believed to be the invention of EDWARD VICTOR; several versions are described in RICE's *Encyclopedia Of Silk Magic*.

TABARIN

Born Jean Salomon in France; a sixteenth-century clown entertainer credited by some with the invention of CHAPEAUGRAPHY.

TAB CARD

A card which has been made into a KEY CARD by the addition of a small tab of metal, plastic, or cloth or metal tape. Such cards are described in HILLIARD's *Greater Magic*.

TABLE

Used by the performer to hold APPARATUS and sometimes as a working surface. Most commercially-available tables intended for magicians are of questionable design, doubtful utility and tasteless appearance. Unless the table is a prime focal point of the audience's attention (which is almost certainly inadvisable), or must fit in with a particular decorative theme, it should be as utilitarian and unobtrusive as possible.

Two books on the subject are available from MAGIC INC.; they are titled (not surprisingly) *Table Book I* and *Table Book II* (the latter by GENE GLOYE).

See BLACK ART TABLE; CANE TO TABLE; NIGHTCLUB TABLE.

TABLE-HOPPING

Term used to denote close-up performance at patrons' tables in a restaurant.

This term has fallen into some disrepute among performers in this field, as it does not imply any importance or seriousness to the performer's role.

Regardless of a performer's feeling about the phrase, it should not be used to laypersons (specifically including employers at restaurants); they will not know what it means, and are unlikely to formulate a definition favorable to the performer.

TABLE LIFTING

Originally performed by MEDIUMs in a SEANCE setting, this effect has often been featured by magical performers; among those currently presenting it are HARRY ANDERSON and DAVID BERGLAS.

Within magic, there are two basic versions:

The first version uses a small four-legged table on which the performer places his hand, and which then seems to cling to or push against the hand—the table rising well above the floor, sometimes over the performer's head. It is accomplished by means of a slotted finger ring, worn by the performer, which engages a stud which can be made to rise from the center of the tabletop. This version has been credited to CHEFALO.

The second version uses an unprepared table on which members of the audience place their hands; it lifts from the floor and moves about, the spectators following. Two of the spectators (on opposite sides of the table) are CONFEDERATEs, and have rods strapped to their arms which can extend out under their hands. These rods go beneath the table-edge and provide the lift. Variants of this method use special harnesses with hooks or linking straps to lift heavier tables.

An effect related to this is **table-tilting**, in which a table surrounded by spectators who place their hands on it will rock back and forth and move around the room. This routine, not often used by performers, relies on psychomotor response—involuntary muscle movement on the part of the assisting spectators. A book describing this approach is EDDIE JOSEPH's *Come, Good Spirits*.

TABLE OF DEATH

An ESCAPE ILLUSION invented by ANDRE KOLE (based on WALTER CERRETTA JEANS' *The Death Of Cora*) in which the performer is chained to a table above which is suspended a board with downward-pointing spikes. A curtain is drawn in front of the imprisoned performer, and shortly thereafter the board of spikes descends with a crash, the spikes penetrating the table and visible beneath it. When the curtain is pulled aside, the performer is lying comfortably on *top* of the board.

This very popular illusion has been featured by inventor Kole, by DAVID COPPERFIELD and many others; it has also been used in a number of television dramas in which magic plays a part.

TABLE RAPPING

See SPIRIT RAPS.

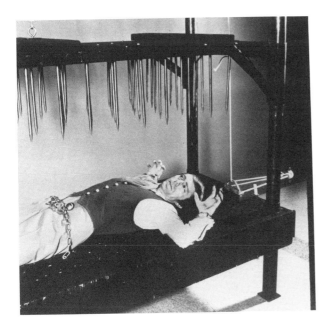

Andre Kole facing an array of steel spikes on his *Table Of Death* (*photo courtesy GENII Magazine*).

TABLE SPREAD

See RIBBON SPREAD.

TABS

Another name for the FRONT CURTAIN; more specifically, the edges of the two curtains where they meet.

TAILS

Full formal evening wear, including a tailcoat, as distinct from a dinner jacket or tuxedo; also, specifically, the actual "tails" of the tailcoat.

Though such formal wear is thought to be the "uniform" of the magician in popular image, comparatively few modern performers attire themselves in this way. This may be for the best, since tails look attractive only on a performer of a particular physical type (lean and graceful) and personal manner (commanding and confident), and notably inappropriate on anyone else.

TAKAGI, SHIGEO (b. ?)

Born in Japan; Librarian of Japanese Library Of Congress by profession. Considered to be one of the most important figures in contemporary Japanese magic, and largely responsible for the present popularity of CLOSE-UP MAGIC in Japan.

He has written over a hundred books, dozens of them concerning magic and its allied arts. He is noted for his invention of the **Takagi turnover count** (a sleightless procedure for counting cards in a seemingly fair manner while concealing several surfaces) and for his **Card Monte**, which was published in HARRY LORAYNE's *Apocalypse* (an adaptation of this routine titled **Miracle Monte** by Takagi and Busby is marketed by JEFF BUSBY).

TALK

In magician's parlance, an accidental noise made by an object which may give a clue to the methodology, e.g., two palmed objects clicking together, or the sound of the two halves of the deck brushing against each other as a SHIFT is made. Also, a sound from an apparently empty container which betrays the presence of an object within.

TALKING BUDDHA

Also known as the **Whispering Buddha**, this was a wood or papier-mache statue which could be heard to speak—this being accomplished by means of an induction coil arrangement similar to that used in the TALKING TEAKETTLE.

The Talking Buddha was used occasionally by magicians and mentalists, but more often by fraudulent mediums. It is described in C. A. ALEXANDER's *Life And Mysteries Of The Celebrated Dr. Q.*

TALKING SKULL

A misnomer in that the skull does not actually speak, but rather answers questions by raps or clicks made by the movement of its jaw. Methods to accomplish this have ranged from simple thread hookups, to hidden electromagnets, to concealed clockwork mechanisms. Of these perhaps the most famous within magical lore is the **Skull of Balsamo** created by JOSEFFY—but it is by no means the first; Lewis Spence, in his *Encyclopedia of Occultism*, describes the use by one Alexander the Paphlogonian of such a device in the middle of the Second Century A.D.

TALKING TEAKETTLE

A papier-mache teakettle which could be examined by a spectator, who would then drop into it a folded slip on which he had written a question. When the spectator held the spout of the kettle to his ear, a "spirit" voice would speak to him, giving an answer to the written question.

The kettle was invented by DAVID P. ABBOTT, and is fully described in *David P. Abbott's Book Of Mysteries*. It operated by means of electrical induction—*not* radio, as was speculated by HOUDINI and others.

TALKING VASE

A large vase, usually of light wood or papier-mache, from which a "spirit" voice would issue; its operation was similar to that of the TALKING TEAKETTLE.

An excellent description of the vase, and a routine in which it may be employed, will be found in THOMAS H. CHISLETT's *The Spirits In The House* and in *David P. Abbott's Book Of Mysteries*.

TALK-THROUGH REHEARSAL

A kind of limited REHEARSAL in which the performer goes over the general BLOCKING and CUES for the act with the stage manager and orchestra, describing what happens at various points rather than actually performing the effects.

Although not as thorough and useful as a full rehearsal, the talk-through is often the only sort of rehearsal permitted by the exigencies of the business.

Talma, a souvenir postcard

TALMA, MERCEDES (1861-1944)

Born Mary Ann Ford in Britain, she married SERVAIS LEROY and joined his show. Becoming extremely skilled at COIN MAGIC, and taking the stage name of *Talma*, she soon became a major feature of the act, manipulating coins and BILLIARD BALLS.

She was noted not only for exceptional accomplishments in pure SLEIGHT OF HAND, but also for her quite remarkable beauty. As part of the Leroy, Talma and Bosco act she performed for over three decades.

TALON

The cards remaining in the hand after a portion of the deck has been removed.

TAMARIZ, JUAN (b. ?)

Born in Spain; noted not only as a major theorist of magic, but also for his skills at card and COIN MAGIC—and for his very funny close-up presentations. He has created a system called *Methodo*

Symbolico for discussing magic across language barriers; is one of the founders of a school of magic in Spain; and is an important figure in the ESCORIAL convention.

Tamariz has contributed to a number of periodicals; he is also the author of *The Five Points In Magic*, an excellent work on MISDIRECTION and presentation.

TAMBOURINE

A device for PRODUCTION routines consisting of two metal rings which nest together (like embroidery hoops). A piece of tissue paper is sandwiched between the rings; a hole is poked in the center of this improvised tambourine, and a large production of paper ribbon is made. From the ribbon a further production of items may often be done.

Some tambourines use a LOAD CHAMBER which may be hidden behind the piece of paper as it is picked up, or secretly added later; these chambers can contain a variety of production items.

Also known as **tambo rings**.

See COIL.

TAMPA (1888-1939)

Born Raymond Sugden; performer who worked in vaudeville with an ORIENTAL STYLE act, and later did a FULL EVENING SHOW under the management/ sponsorship of HOWARD THURSTON.

TAN HOCK CHUAN (b. 1910)

Born in Malaya; schoolmaster and mathematics instructor by profession. He is noted for his many original EFFECTs.

His work is described in his *The Magic Of Tan Hock Chuan*.

TANNEN, LOUIS (1909-1982)

Founder of Louis Tannen Inc., one of the three largest magic dealerships in the world (the other two being Abbott's Magic Co. and SUPREME MAGIC CO.). In addition to running the company, Tannen also found time to create a number of EFFECTs, including Salt-Go, a popular version of the HAUNTED DECK, and many more.

TANNER, DON (1924-1981)

Telephone company technician by profession; he was for many years the director of the Magi-Fest, an annual magic convention in Columbus, Ohio. He was the editor of The New PHOENIX for several years; he also

Tan Hock Chuan (*The Mulholland Library of Conjuring & the Allied Arts, Los Angeles, California*)

founded and edited a periodical devoted to MENTAL MAGIC called *The Mentalist*, as well as contributing to the LINKING RING Magazine and numerous other periodicals.

Tanner's books include *Coffee Break Magic, How To Do Cigarette Tricks, How To Do Headline Predictions, Manual Of Magic*, and many others.

TAP DICE

A variety of LOADED DICE which may be set to favor any number; the dice have a dense, honeycomb-like interior structure containing mercury or any heavy, viscous liquid.

By positioning the dice with the desired faces upward, and tapping them, the load within is made to shift to the bottom; thus that side becomes weighted and alters the percentages accordingly.

See also LOADED DICE.

TAPPING EFFECTS

A variety of MATHEMATICAL MAGIC in which a spectator secretly counts as the performer taps each of a group of items in apparent random fashion; at a previously specified point the spectator calls stop, at which point the performer is tapping the item thought of by the spectator.

The principles and general structure of such effects may sometimes be similar to those used in SPELLING effects. Thus, variations include having the spectator mentally spell out the name of a thought-of item chosen from a list; the spectator advances one letter with each of the performer's taps, and as before the final tap is seen to be on the selected item. Many variations of this effect are described in MARTIN GARDNER's *Mathematics, Magic and Mystery.*

See MATHEMATICAL MAGIC.

TARBELL, HARLAN (1890-1960)

Performer, illustrator, and author; creator of the monumental TARBELL COURSE IN MAGIC. Tarbell performed throughout the U.S., Canada and Mexico, most often being booked through lecture bureaus rather than theatrical agencies.

He also wrote and illustrated numerous instructional sheets for various magic dealers, and illustrated a number of books, including 1150 technical illustrations for HILLIARD's *Greater Magic.*

Tarbell's *Course,* and his many lectures to magic

Dr. Harlan Tarbell (*photo courtesy GENII Magazine*)

groups, influenced a whole generation of magicians, and he had a profound effect on the direction of the art. He was undoubtedly the most influential writer on magic since PROFESSOR LOUIS HOFFMAN, and was not only respected but admired and held in strong affection by thousands of his contemporaries.

TARBELL CONE

See CONE.

TARBELL COURSE IN MAGIC

A complete course in the basics of magic, originally a mail order course published in photo-offset lessons; later published, with considerable additional material, in book form by Louis Tannen Inc. (*see* LOUIS TANNEN). The first six volumes were written and illustrated by HARLAN TARBELL; the seventh and final volume, produced after Tarbell's death, was written by HARRY LORAYNE. Volumes 1 through 5 were edited by Ralph W. Read, Volume 6 by BRUCE ELLIOTT.

TARBELL GIMMICK

A device invented by HARLAN TARBELL, it consists of two small rods which can be inset into the ends of ropes. By means of the single-turn male screw in one rod and the receiving female socket in the other, they can be quickly joined together to make the rope appear as one continuous length.

Variant versions of these GIMMICKs were designed as tubes which fit over the end of the rope; though finished to resemble rope, these could only be deceptively used at stage distance.

Tarbell himself called the device a ''Caesar Gimmick'' (after its manufacturer, Chicago magic dealer Frank Caesar) but the name never caught on. Ropes prepared with **Tarbell gimmicks** are often used in CUT AND RESTORED ROPE effects and—less often—in ESCAPES.

TAROT CARDS

Forerunner of the modern deck of playing cards, the Tarot deck consists of twenty-two titled cards, called the **greater arcana**; and fifty-six cards of four suits—Wands, Swords, Cups and Pentacles—with values from Ace to Ten and with court cards of Page, Knight, Queen, and King. These suit cards were known as the **lesser arcana**.

The origin of the designs used in the Tarot— particularly the Greater Arcana—are the subject of much speculation; within occultism they are believed to be the symbolic representation of a secret philosophical tradition. They are used by occultists today within ritual and visualization practices; by fortunetellers as a divinatory device; and by performers as an interesting PROP to incorporate into effects, most often in the category of MENTAL MAGIC.

TAUNT, SERL (1902-1961)

British performer who worked in ORIENTAL STYLE as "Chan D'Or, the Eurasian Illusionist," later in a Turkish-style COSTUME. He was noted for his work in a number of magical societies, and also for his LINKING RINGS routine.

TAYLOR, HAROLD (b. ?)

British performer of wide experience who is known not only for his magic but also for his skills as a MASTER OF CEREMONIES; his approach to his work is discussed in his *The Angle Of A Pro.*

TAYLOR, MERV (1904-1974)

Noted manufacturer of high-quality APPARATUS; he was the first to use acrylic plastic (plexiglas) in magic manufacturing, and was also known for his many items made in stainless steel. In addition to magic apparatus, he often designed and constructed special PROPS for films, and also made a number of items on an exclusive basis for many performers.

In the mid-1950s his company became a part of Owen Magic Supreme.

TEAR-APART VANISH

A box into which a small animal or bird is placed, which may then be taken apart piece by piece to show the vanish of the creature; all sides of the box are simple frames covered with newspaper, and as each piece is removed the performer pushes his or her hand through the paper to show the frame empty.

A similar version of this EFFECT, but using solid wood pieces rather than paper-covered frames, is termed a **Take-Apart Vanish.**

TEARING A DECK

A card is selected and returned to the deck, which the performer then tears in half; dealing down through each half in turn, the performer stops where indicated by a spectator. The half-cards thus arrived at prove to be the two halves of the selected card.

The EFFECT was a favorite of JOHN

MULHOLLAND, who elaborated it by tearing one of the halves into two parts.

The effect is described in HILLIARD's *Greater Magic,* and also in THE JINX Magazine, among many other sources.

As with TEARING A PHONE BOOK, this can be done with an unprepared deck but is much easier with one baked to brittleness; this preparation will not, however, work with plastic or plastic-coated cards (which should not be used for this effect in any case).

TEARING A PHONE BOOK

The feat of tearing a telephone directory in half as a strong-man stunt has at times been used by magicians in comedy presentations. It can be done legitimately without great difficulty if a technique of beveling the pages is employed; however, it can also be accomplished with much less effort by previously baking the book in an oven until it becomes brittle. The book will then tear easily.

TECHNICAL ADVISOR

One who supplies technical expertise on magic to stage, motion picture and television productions. Most often this will consist of teaching an actor how to accomplish magical EFFECTs in a convincing way, but it may also involve suggesting specific magical material as indicated by the requirements of the production.

It is not unusual for a technical advisor to actually perform some of the magic, particularly in close shots where the face of the actor will not be seen.

Technical advisors include JIM STEINMEYER, RICKY JAY, MARK WILSON, MAX MAVEN, and T.A. Waters.

This term should not be confused with CONSULTANT.

TELEPATHY

A term coined by 19th-century psychic researcher F.W.H. Myers to indicate mind-to-mind communication, or the perception by one person's mind of a thought or feeling in that of another person. Often used as a premise in MENTALISM and MENTAL MAGIC.

TELEPHONE TRICK

An EFFECT invented by JOHN NORTHERN HILLIARD in which a spectator makes a telephone call to a friend of the performer; the friend is able to tell the spectator the identity of a previously chosen card.

Many versions of the effect have seen print, and there have even been two books—*Tele-Trickery* by Corinda and *Handbook of Telephone Telepathy* by Al Forman—devoted to this feat alone.

The term may also refer to an effect which can be done by the performer over a phone line; most such effects are with cards, and many of these rely on mathematical principles.

TELEVISION CARD FRAME

See CARD FRAME.

TELL

An indication of the presence or condition of an object; in gambling parlance, the body language and other actions of a player which indicate the value of the hand he or she holds.

Also, a mechanical or physical device or preparation for indicating the presence or condition of an object; as (again in gambling parlance) the **tells** used in Faro-dealing boxes or dealing shoes to reveal the value of the card beneath the top card. (Note: usually such **tells** will only discriminate between, say, high and low values, or a similarly limited range of differences.)

See also TELL-TALE.

TELL-TALE

An indicating mark or thing which reveals the identity or condition of an object. A playing card, for example, may be marked with a NAIL NICK which can be felt or seen; a coin may have a thin horsehair attached to it which will project from beneath a covering cup and reveal its presence; a box may have a pin which projects or retracts to indicate the presence or absence of a particular object within.

TEMPLE SCREEN

A PRODUCTION device invented by U.F. GRANT, this consists of a three-fold screen which is shown on both sides and then folded into a triangular tube; from it a large production can then be made.

TEMPLETON, MAX (1883-1964)

Born George Alfred McQuire in Britain, he had a long professional career which included several command performances; he was also honored by many British magical organizations, and was a founding member of the London Society Of Magicians.

In addition to magic, Templeton performed SHADOWGRAPHY expertly and may have been the first person to do so on television (1933).

TEN CARD DEAL

A GAMBLING DEMONSTRATION effect using only ten cards; though these are repeatedly shuffled by the spectator, the performer always gets the higher poker hand.

The ten cards consist of three sets of three cards of the same value—the Fours, Sevens and Tens, for example—and one other card of any other value; the performer has only to see that the spectator gets this odd card, for whoever holds this card has the losing hand.

This odd card is sometimes referred to as the *Jonah Card*.

Many ROUTINEs and presentations for this EFFECT are found in magic literature; a relatively recent and influential version is **cider**, described by PAUL CURRY in *Paul Curry Presents*. A multiphase routine based on this principle is **Psych-Out**, created by Bruce Bernstein.

TEN ICHI

Three people are known to have performed under this name; the first was a Japanese whose real name was *Shokyoku Hattori* (1852-1912), whom some consider to be the patriarch of modern Japanese magic; he was noted not only as a performer but as a teacher. One of Hattori's students, named Tenji, took over the name after his *sensei*'s death.

The third Ten Ichi was Jules De Nijs (1893-1967), a Dutch citizen who performed in ORIENTAL STYLE and who is thought to have taken over the original Ten Ichi troupe when it toured Europe. De Nijs claimed that his grandfather had originated the Ten Ichi stage name (a phonetic arrangement of the family name); also that his father (performing under the same name) had originated the THUMB TIE. All were noted for their performance of the WATER FOUNTAIN effect.

TENKAI (1889-1972)

Born Tenkai Ishida in Japan; he began his career as a helper to a magician, and later worked as a musician. He then joined the troupe of a performer named Tenmatsu (later Tenyo), where he performed as a comedy magician.

With his wife (Iwa Kato, later called Okinu) he performed in various theaters for a time, and then joined the company of a noted female magician, Madame Tenkatsu, where he stayed for a decade; during this time the company made a tour of the U.S., and

Tenkai (*The Mulholland Library of Conjuring & the Allied Arts, Los Angeles, California*)

Tenkai decided to remain in the U.S. in order to learn the western approach to magic. He stayed, in fact, for thirty years, returning to Japan in 1958.

He is noted for many originations, of which the best-known is the TENKAI PALM technique. His work is described in his *Tenkai's Manipulative Card Routine* and *Six Tricks By Tenkai*, and also in *The Magic Of Tenkai* by GERALD KOSKY and ARNOLD FURST.

TENKAI PALM

Term commonly used to denote a technique invented by TENKAI; a misnomer in that the card is not actually palmed, but rather gripped near its front narrow edge between the first joint of the thumb and the palm. The card is supported only where its two front corners touch the palm and thumb, and lies in a horizontal position with the back of the hand toward the audience.

This technique first attracted attention when it was described in the *Dai Vernon Book Of Magic* by LEWIS GANSON. An excellent book on the uses of the Tenkai palm is *Practical Impossibilities* by RICK JOHNSSON.

TENT VANISH

With the deck held face-down in dealing position in the left hand, a face-up card is levered upward by the thumb at its inner long edge, so that it slants downward toward the fingers at about a forty-five degree angle. The right hand approaches with a card hidden face outward in a PALM. In the act of apparently taking the face-up card, both cards are allowed to drop flat on the deck as the right hand moves away; the concealment of the face-up card by the card above it creates the illusion.

Invented by ARTHUR FINDLEY, this move is described by DAI VERNON in his SLOW-MOTION ACES routine in the *Stars Of Magic*.

TENYO

Major Japanese magic manufacturing company, begun in 1931 by performer Tenyo Shokyokusai; in 1950 Tenyo's son Akira Yamada took over the management of the business. The Tenyo Company's

Tenyo in the 1930's (*photo courtesy GENII Magazine*)

creative staff includes Hiroshi Kondo, Shigeru Sugawara, Hideo Kato and Takuya Yoshizawa.

The company has sponsored many lectures by performers from all over the world, and each year holds a convention where new products are introduced. Among their many highly popular products, marketed throughout the world, are **Squeeze Play**, **Sidetrack**, and **Zig-Zag Cigarette**.

TEST CONDITIONS

A style of presenting EFFECTs (usually of the MENTAL MAGIC or MENTALISM type) in which the procedures are so closely observed and controlled by members of the audience that the possibility of trickery or fraud is apparently eliminated.

THAUMATURGIST

A Greek term meaning "wonder-worker"; now sometimes applied ironically or satirically to the present-day magical performer.

THAYER, FLOYD G. (1877-1959)

Magical manufacturer and publisher; noted for the exceptionally high quality of his handcrafted APPARATUS (primarily of wood), from the smallest set of BILLIARD BALLS to the largest of ILLUSIONs.

Many of the effects marketed by Thayer are described in *Thayer Quality Magic*, a four-volume collection of instruction sheets and manuscripts edited by GLENN GRAVATT.

THICK CARD

A kind of KEY CARD made by glueing two cards together to create a card of double thickness; it can be easily located by touch.

Some thick cards are made with a razor blade or other strip of thin metal between the two layers so they can also be used as SHIM cards.

THIEVES AND SHEEP

See ROBBERS AND SHEEP.

THIMBLE HOLDER

A device which holds four thimbles in concealment under the coat, in position for the fingers to obtain all four simultaneously. Holders vary in design, using elastic cord or straps or metal clips to hold the thimbles in position.

THIMBLE MAGIC

A specialized area of SLEIGHT-OF-HAND magic and MANIPULATION, in which thimbles appear, disappear, change color and multiply. The usual ROUTINE commences with the appearance of a thimble which vanishes and reappears and then passes from one forefinger to the other; there is then an interlude of such effects as a change of color or size; and the routine concludes with the PRODUCTION of eight thimbles, one on each finger of each hand.

One problem with such routines was suggested by a cartoon (by JAY MARSHALL) which appeared many years ago in GENII MAGAZINE: it showed two men in balcony seats, one of whom was viewing the stage with binoculars and announcing to his companion, "He just produced another thimble." Like coins, thimbles are not very visible at any distance; unlike coins, they do not have a characteristic sound to point up the productions.

There have been various attempts to solve this problem, including glitter-plastic, jeweled and sequinned thimbles; such props have been less than successful since they no longer look like thimbles and the audience is not sure just what the performer is

Michael Skinner performing *Thimble Magic* (*photo courtesy GENII Magazine*).

doing. Nickel or chrome plating of the thimbles, in concert with careful selection of lighting and background (including the performer's clothes), may help to increase the visibility of the thimbles.

By far the best solution is that of Danish performer VIGGO JAHN, who performs in black gloves and—using classic thimble sleights—manipulates the *white knob* taken fron the head of his formal walking stick.

In spite of the limited appeal of thimble magic to audiences, there has been a good deal of work published concerning techniques and sleights. Major sources are JEAN HUGARD's *Thimble Magic*, *Loyd's Master Manipulation Of Thimbles* by E. LOYD Enochs and CAMILLE GAULTIER's *Magic Without Apparatus*.

Notice should also be made of the several routines, complete with props, marketed by SAMUEL BERLAND.

THIMBLE RICE BOWLS

A marketed novelty version of the RICE BOWLS, in which two small thimbles substitute for the bowls in a CLOSE-UP routine.

THIMBLE-RIGGING

A variant of the THREE-SHELL GAME, using three thimbles and a small pea; this gambling game is a distant cousin of the CUPS AND BALLS.

THINK INK

A clear liquid (presumably water) poured from a pitcher into a glass remains clear for several moments; then, apparently at the performer's mental command, it changes instantly and completely into ink.

The effect is created through a timed chemical reaction; the presentation, and method for allowing the two necessary chemicals to secretly combine, was devised and marketed by ORVILLE MEYER and Wilber Kattner. A full description of the routine later appeared in Meyer's book *Magic In The Modern Manner*.

THINK OF A CARD

A category of MENTAL MAGIC with cards in which the spectator does not make any sort of physical selection of a card but rather simply thinks of one (usually from a displayed fan of cards).

Location of a thought-of card can employ a wide variety of techniques, from the purely mental to combinations of psychological subtleties with SLEIGHT-OF-HAND. Experts at the purely mental technique in-clude MAX MAVEN in the U.S., DAVID BERGLAS and CHAN CANASTA in Great Britain.

Many of the techniques now used are heavily influenced by the work of DAI VERNON. The best general discussion of this type of effect was a series of articles by FRED BRAUE which appeared in *Hugard's Magic Monthly*.

THINK STOP

A presentational variation of the STOP TRICK with cards; here the spectator, having selected a card, watches for his card as the performer deals the cards into a face-up pile from the shuffled deck. On seeing the selected card the spectator is to simply *think* "stop"; the performer seems to pick up this mental message, stopping on the selected card.

Since all that is required to create the effect is knowing the identity of the selected card, there are dozens of ways of accomplishing the necessary technique.

THIRTY CARD TRICK

See CARDS ACROSS.

THIRTY-ONE, THE GAME OF

See NIM.

THOMPSON, FRANK (?-1976)

Gambler by profession; he was noted for his absolute mastery of many card and coin SLEIGHTs and for his card routine using a special STACK.

He is the author of *The Cold Deck*.

THOMPSON, JAMES KATER (1889-1972)

Performer with long professional career in various phases of show business; he worked in vaudeville in a unicycle act, later as a magician, performing in all the major vaudeville circuits and in CHAUTAUQUA. Still later he became a theatrical booking agent.

He was noted for his expertise with cards and CLOSE-UP MAGIC; with GEORGE DELAWRENCE he wrote *Modern Card Tricks And How To Do Them*.

THOMPSON, J.G. JR. (1910-1975)

A banker by profession, he created a number of EFFECTs and ROUTINEs and wrote extensively on magic and MENTAL MAGIC. Among the effects he invented are **Mentalism by Design, Jet Thought, Telastrophy**, and **Moonlight Madness**.

In addition to columns in M.U.M. and LINKING

J. G. Thompson Jr. presenting his Telastrophy routine (*photo courtesy GENII Magazine*).

RING Magazine (for the latter of which he was associate editor), he contributed effects to numerous magazines. He also wrote a number of books, including *My Best, Magic To Delight, The Living End, Centermental, Top Secrets Of Magic, Miracle Makers*, and (with Ned Rutledge) *Card Party* and *Between Two Minds*.

THOMPSON, JOHN (b. 1934)

Performer who began his performing career as a harmonica player, touring and recording with Jerry Murad's Harmonicats for seven years. Influenced by a performance of CANTU, he created an act of DOVE MAGIC, but continued with music; he formed the Harmonica Jazz Quartet, which toured for five years. He later became part of a comedy team, and reworked the dove act as a parody of serious performers. Unlike most parody acts, however, in Thompson's the magic worked, and worked well. Of Polish ancestry, he began using the billing of "Poland's Finest Magician," and later "The Great Tomsoni, The Wizard Of Warsaw."

In 1972 he began performing in Reno; two years later

he went into the *Vive Paris Vive* show at the Aladdin in Las Vegas, where he performed every night for three years. He continued with the show when it moved to the Flamingo. In 1976 wife and partner Pam joined the act; the billing became "The Great Tomsoni And Company"—Pam being . . . *And Company*, and playing the bored and dizzy ASSISTANT to the hilt.

In the years since then they have become known as one of the top revue acts in the business, appearances include the Nugget in Reno, the *Folies Bergere* show at the Tropicana, the *Lido de Paris* show at the Stardust, and Trump's Castle in Atlantic City. They have performed on *The Tonight Show* and many other television shows in the U.S. and elsewhere. Thompson also created a revue called *Les Sorcery* which played for several months in Reno.

In addition to his stage work, Thompson is a noted close-up performer, and is highly respected in the TRADE SHOW field. While many performers become accomplished in one of these areas, Thompson is considered a virtuoso at all of them. He is also an experienced actor in theater and television.

He is the author of *Polished Polish Prestidigitation* and *Coin In Bottle—Plus*.

Thompson is a recipient of the Best Stage Magician Award from the ACADEMY OF MAGICAL ARTS,

The Great Tomsoni & Co. (John and Pam Thompson)

which has also awarded a Performing Fellowship to The Great Tomsoni And Company.

THOMPSON COIN

A FAKE coin of the DOUBLE-FACED variety, showing a half-dollar on one side and a smooth brass surface on the other; it also has a magnet embedded within it.

The coin was designed by J.G. THOMPSON JR., for use with a brass OKITO BOX which may have a magnet or a SHIM built into it; thus the coin, with its half-dollar side showing, may be dropped into the box so the brass side is up. The box may immediately be shown apparently empty (the brass surface of the Thompson Coin appearing as the interior bottom of the box), and may even be turned upside-down—the magnet holding the faked coin within.

THORNTON REEL

A type of REEL which had an an exceptionally long thread; it was used in versions of the CARD FOUNTAIN, the RISING CARDS, and many other EFFECTs Invented by John Thornton, it has not been manufactured for many years.

THOUGHT-READING

See TELEPATHY; also sometimes used specifically to denote CONTACT MIND READING.

THREAD

The medium through which motive power is applied in a number of effects, including versions of the RISING CARDS, FLOATING BALL, and DANCING HANDKERCHIEF, to name only a few.

Thread is also sometimes used as a generic term to indicate any sort of line used in a magical EFFECT—even when it is, for example, **monofilament** used in such close-up effects as FRED KAPS' **floating cork** and FINN JON's **Silver Stick**, or thin gut employed where high tensile strength is required.

Ordinary sewing thread is often used; it is most often black, and usually silk thread. Gut line is available from hardware and sporting goods stores. Monofilament line can be purchased from magic dealers, or extracted from panty hose.

In using thread a great deal of attention must be paid to background and lighting. A common mistake is to use a solid black or dark background, against which a thread will stand out clearly; the background should be heavily patterned, to break up the line created by the thread. (Another approach to this is to dye black short sections of a dark brown thread [easily done with

a marking pen]; as with the patterned background, this classic camouflage technique breaks up the line.)

Sometimes the thread must be treated with a matte spray to prevent it from reflecting light. Adjustment of lighting angles and intensity can also affect this, but it is somewhat futile to bring the light level down so low that the effect could be as easily accomplished by BLACK ART.

FINN JON is well-known for his many effects employing thread of various kinds; several ingenious applications of thread have also been developed by GAETAN BLOOM. It is also extensively discussed in *Floating Routines For Table And Stage* by Ralf Wichmann-Braco.

THREE-CARD MONTE

A classic but still very popular gambling game, doubtless a descendant of the THREE SHELL GAME, in which the victim tries to keep track of one of three cards. Usually the game is played with a Queen and two identical spot cards, and the victim is urged to ". . . find the lady."

Magicians have long used the game as a premise for entertainment, and a great number of routines have been published; some of these use pure SLEIGHT OF HAND, some use specially-printed or otherwise prepared cards, and some use a combination of techniques. An excellent book on the subject is *Why You Can't Win: A Treatise On The Sucker Effects Of Three Card Monte* by JOHN SCARNE, as told to AUDLEY WALSH. Another excellent book, aimed specifically at the needs of magicians, is *Three-Card Monte As Entertainment*, by LEWIS GANSON.

Please note: Acquiring a knowledge of these techniques will not help you at all in encounters with street "monte mobs," for in no sense of the word are these operations games. At best you will be shut out of the game; at worst, you may not survive it.

THREE GRACES

A presentation created by SERVAIS LEROY in which a cabinet is shown empty and the performer holds a sheet before it; a form appears under the sheet and moves forward. This is repeated twice, after which the performer steps into the cabinet.

When the figures are uncovered, two are revealed to be assistants, and the third is the performer; the cabinet is then shown empty.

(It should be noted that LeRoy's original presentation of this title was the straightforward production from a cabinet of three women dressed as the Three Graces [Euphrosyne, Aglaia, and Thalia, daughters of Zeus]. In a later presentation, both LeRoy and his wife and partner TALMA entered the cabinet, vanished, and reappeared under the cloths, the third figure being revealed as an ASSISTANT in devil costume.)

Any production cabinet or device of sufficient size may be used for this presentation, including the MODERN CABINET, the CABINET OF PROTEUS, and the MILLION DOLLAR MYSTERY. Many variations of the basic ROUTINE are possible; in the version currently being presented by DOUG HENNING (titled **Things That Go Bump In The Night**), a large jungle cat is produced from the cabinet to conclude the illusion.

THREE SHELL GAME

See SHELL GAME.

THREE-TO-ONE ROPES

An EFFECT in which three separate lengths of rope, knotted together, instantaneously become one piece. It was invented by CARLYLE (Lyle Laughlin) and later commercially marketed by TOM OSBORNE. Several variations on the EFFECT have been created and published.

THROUGH THE EYE OF A NEEDLE

A stage ILLUSION invented by P. T. SELBIT which employed two large barrels resting in separate metal racks. After an assistant was placed in one barrel, its mouth was barred with four long steel rods; the other was sealed with a large metal plate having only a small opening in the center. When the two barrels were placed "mouth to mouth," however, the assistant was able to pass from one barrel to the other, apparently penetrating the rods and metal plate. In various forms the illusion has survived to the present day.

Typically, in versions of **Through the Eye of a Needle** presented in the U.S., the barrels (or similar containers) are positioned horizontally on twin racks; in Europe, one barrel is placed on top of the other in a vertical configuration. Given identical methodology, there does not seem to be any ready explanation for this presentational dichotomy.

THROUGH-THE-HANDS FLOURISH

Apparently *only* a FLOURISH, this move can also be used to indetectably turn over a PACKET of cards; this application is credited to DAI VERNON.

The packet rests on the fingertips; the hand is turned over and closed simultaneously, the cards remaining in the same position relative to the floor. The thumb now pushes the packet through the hands, where it is taken by the other hand. Done this way, the flourish does not reverse the packet; if, however, the packet is resting on the *palm*, the turning over of the hand and resultant push-through act to turn the packet over. Both versions of the flourish, however, appear identical.

Done with a pocket-knife, this flourish can also be useful in COLOR-CHANGING KNIFE routines.

THROW

In an overhand FALSE SHUFFLE, to bring a specific group of cards from the bottom to the top of the deck in a tossing motion.

THROWAWAY

An incidental magical EFFECT to which the performer draws no attention; an example would be the PRODUCTION of a lit match from the pocket in order to light a candle for a subsequent effect.

Careful selection of throwaways can enhance an act considerably, giving the impression that everything the performer does is magical; the presentation, therefore, can be blandly matter-of-fact, as though (to continue the above example) the performer is so used to taking lighted matches from the pockets that he or she doesn't even seem to realize that this may be a bit unusual.

THROW CHANGE

Generally, any type of SLEIGHT in which one object is switched for another in the act of tossing it from hand to hand or to a table or other working surface.

Specifically, a card change in which two cards are held as one, the face card being displayed; in the act of tossing the card to the table, the face card is drawn off by the thumb and palmed, the rear card being allowed to fall to the table. Usually the other hand holds the deck, and the hand with the palmed card goes back to the deck and deposits its card while attention is on the card on the table.

THROW-OUT CARDS

Printed advertising cards, usually with the performer's picture, of the same size and shape as playing cards. Often distributed by the performer in the course of a demonstration of CARD THROWING.

THRUST STAGE

A type of stage which has a performing area which projects out beyond the PROSCENIUM, and which usually has spectators seated at the sides as well as in front. In such venues it is necessary to select effects which are or can be made ANGLE-PROOF, and to BLOCK the presentation in such a way that all the spectators—and not merely those in front—can appreciate the performance.

THUMB COUNT

With the deck held in dealing position, the left thumb moves to the upper left corner of the deck and bears down, allowing one card at a time to move past it; in this way a certain number of cards can be counted off. In most cases the right hand may act as cover for the counting, and for the transfer of the BREAK thus created to the inner right corner of the deck.

In a variant version, it is the *right* thumb, at the rear of the deck, which does the counting; this can be either from the bottom (face) of the deck or the top. The action is screened by the back of the right hand.

Both counts are employed most often in connection with the DOUBLE LIFT or other multiple lifts, but they have many other uses.

THUMB CUFFS

Restraints made to fit on the thumbs, carried by security officers when regular handcuffs would be too bulky; often sold by magic shops for use in ESCAPE routines. It should be noted that thumb cuffs used in such routines are ungimmicked, the release depending on a handling technique known to the performer.

THUMB GRIP

A more accurately descriptive synonym for THUMB PALM; most often used, however, to refer to cigarettes concealed in this manner.

THUMB OFF

To deal cards using the left hand only, the action being accomplished with a push of the thumb.

Not to be confused with the THUMB COUNT.

THUMB PALM

To grip a coin or other small object by its edge between the inner side of the thumb and the side of the hand. If the object projects toward the back of the hand (so that the palm can be shown), the position is known as a **reverse thumb palm**.

Tenyo performing the *Thumb Tie* (*photo courtesy GENII Magazine*).

THUMB TIE

The performer's thumbs are securely fastened together, yet hoops and various other objects apparently penetrate and end up on one arm or the other. Though there is speculation that the **thumb tie** originated in the Orient, there is also evidence to suggest that it was independently created elsewhere; it was, for example, featured in the European performances of CHEVALIER GUISEPPE PINETTI in the latter half of the eighteenth century.

The first performer to achieve a major reputation with this EFFECT was the Japanese magician TEN ICHI; it has been featured by several performers of past and present, among them DE BIERE, CARL ROSINI, JEAN HUGARD and HARRY WILLARD. (The consensus of those who saw him perform is that Harry Willard's was the most impressive presentation of the **thumb tie** they had ever seen.)

Methods of securing the thumbs have ranged from paper-covered twine to cords, straps, wires, pipe cleaners and adhesive tape. A good introduction to the subject is *Sixteen Thumb Tie Gems* by MAX ANDREWS; among specific ROUTINEs marketed are **The Jaspernese thumb tie** by JAY MARSHALL and the **Red Tape Tie** by IRV WEINER.

THUMB TIP

A shell which fits over the thumb, which it is shaped and colored to resemble. The **thumb tip** may be made of metal, rubber or plastic, and is a utility device with countless uses. (A smaller version, made to fit on the finger, is, not surprisingly, known as a **finger tip**.) One performer suggested as a possible inventor of the **thumb tip** is JOSEPH HARTZ; this is, however, only speculation.

In many applications the **thumb tip** is held in one hand, and a small item (silk handkerchief, cigarette) placed into the hand—and secretly into the **thumb tip**. Often the performer will then poke his thumb into the hand on some pretext of pushing the item in further; the thumb comes out wearing the tip with the item concealed within. As has been pointed out by EUGENE BURGER, this action is awkward and peculiar, the thumb being used in this manner only by very small children or those with motor impairment. A preferable method is to angle the tip backward through the fingers, so that it can be taken by the thumb as the first finger does the poking action.

Several books are available on the use of the **thumb tip**, including MILBOURNE CHRISTOPHER's *Fifty Tricks With A Thumb Tip*, PATRICK PAGE's *Book Of Thumb Tips*, STUART ROBSON's *Tips On Thumbs*, John Kenyon's *Thumbs Up!*, Bob Chesbro's *The Tipnician*, and GARY DARWIN's *Thumb Tip Secrets*, *Thumb Tip Miracles*, and *Thumb Tip Thinking*.

THUMB WRITER

Most often used as a synonym for NAIL WRITER.

Also, specifically, a THUMB TIP adapted for secret writing by the addition of a small holder for pencil lead or crayon.

THUMM, MANFRED (b. ?)

Born in Germany; for many years he performed semi-professionally (while working for Philips Electronics) with his BLACK LIGHT act called The Magic Hands Black Light Show.

In 1973 he left Philips and founded his own magic company which he named after his trophy-winning act: The MAGIC HANDS.

Through his company, Thumm has sponsored a yearly convention—The Magic Hands Fachkongresse—since 1978.

THURSTON, HOWARD (1869-1936)

He began his career with a vaudeville act which featured BACKPALMING of cards; he also featured the QUEEN OF THE AIR version of the RISING CARDS. (After a performance of this EFFECT for LEON HERRMANN, Thurston used the billing of "The Man Who Mystified Herrmann.") He toured the

Howard Thurston (*The Mulholland Library of Conjuring & the Allied Arts, Los Angeles, California*)

U.S., Britain and Europe with this act, and was quite successful.

Thurston later created one of the most elaborate ILLUSION shows in the history of the theater (as the designated successor to HARRY KELLAR), and was the most famous magician in the U.S. for over three decades. He also toured to many other countries with equal success.

TIHANY (b. 1916)

Born Franz Zzeisler in Hungary, in his teens he worked as an ASSISTANT to a performer named Blackaman, then began performing his own show, taking the name *Tihany* from his birthplace.

With a large FULL-EVENING SHOW he toured throughout Hungary and other European countries; emigrating to Brazil, he bought a circus and combined it with his magic show, touring many South American countries as well as Mexico.

Tihany retired briefly, and then built an even larger show which is presented in a spacious 4000-seat tent; it does not use a circus ring, but rather a fully equipped modern stage.

Tihany (*photo courtesy GENII Magazine*)

He is the recipient of both a Performing Fellowship and a Masters Fellowship from the ACADEMY OF MAGICAL ARTS.

TILT

The title given by ED MARLO to a card subtlety developed by DAI VERNON, with additional work by EDWARD VICTOR, KEN KRENZEL and Marlo. In the action of this technique (also known as the **Depth Illusion** or **Illusion Of Depth**), a playing card is apparently placed in the approximate center of the deck; in reality it is only one or two cards down from the top.

The move and its applications are fully described in Marlo's book *Tilt*.

TIONG, PHOA YAN (b. ?)

Holland-based performer of Chinese ancestry; he is noted for his colorful and poetic act, with which he has appeared throughout Britain and Europe.

He has contributed a number of items to the GEN Magazine and other publications; he has also written a

manuscript on his **Cut and Restored Silk** which has attracted considerable attention, particularly since being featured by DOUG HENNING. He is the author of a book called *The Seasons*, which is a very thorough treatment of the WINTERTIME IN CHINA effect.

TIPOVER BOX

Also known as the INEXHAUSTIBLE BOX and erroneously as the JAPANESE BOX, this utility item is most often used for the PRODUCTION of various items.

The box is tipped forward (hence the name) and the lid is lifted to show the box empty; after a reversal of these moves the lid is again lifted and a large production is made.

The actual bottom of the box, and an inner front wall, never move; when the box is tilted forward and opened, the front of this extra wall is assumed by the spectators to be the bottom of the box. After the box is closed and returned to an upright position, a production may be made of any objects previously placed on the true bottom of the box.

This principle is also used in stage ILLUSIONs, and was probably first employed by COLONEL STODARE in his unique version of the Indian BASKET TRICK.

TIP-TILT VANISH

A SLEIGHT for the vanish of an unlighted cigarette. With the fingers of (say) the left hand pointing upward, the cigarette is held at the right-hand fingertips and pushed downward into the left hand; when this action is almost completed the right fingers push slightly forward, pivoting the cigarette against the left-hand fingertips so it is levered up into the right hand, where it may be finger-palmed.

The sleight is described in HILLIARD's *Greater Magic*, and in many other books.

TONGUING

Concealing a lighted cigarette in the mouth by using the tongue to lever the inner end downward and then allowing the cigarette to flip backward so that it lies on the tongue with the lighted end toward the rear of the mouth.

This movement is generally executed under cover of the hand, which is apparently taking the cigarette from the mouth and throwing it on the floor. Care and practice are required to execute this movement without burning the lips or tongue.

Descriptions of the technique of tonguing may be found in KEITH CLARK's *Encyclopedia Of Cigarette Tricks* and in HILLIARD's *Greater Magic*.

TOP CARD

The card at the back of the deck; the topmost card of a face-down deck. It should be noted that, in most technical descriptions of card EFFECTs (unless otherwise noted) the card at this position is still called the top card even when the deck is face-up and thus the *actual* top card is the FACE CARD of the deck.

TOP CHANGE

A card SLEIGHT in which a card held in the right hand is switched for the top card of the deck; it is described in HUGARD and BRAUE's *Expert Card Technique*, GIBSON's *Complete Illustrated Book Of Card Magic*, and many other places.

The mechanics of the sleight are quite simple; the timing to use it effectively and deceptively, however, are much more difficult to acquire, and usually come only with considerable experience.
See BOTTOM CHANGE.

TOPIT

Invented by British magician Harold Comden, this is a large bag affixed inside the performer's jacket. Objects can be secretly tossed into it or, less commonly, secretly acquired. Though **topit** bags which can be pinned into position are commercially available, they have serious limitations, thus most professional performers using this device have it tailored into their performing wear, these tailored **topits** are sometimes designed so that the performer may openly regain an object by reaching into (and through) the outside jacket pocket. This type of "magical tailoring" requires a rare knowledge of both disciplines; one person specializing in this exacting field is LYNN HEALY.

Topits are used quite often in various kinds of manipulative acts, and are also used extensively in PICKPOCKET ACTs (to dispose of the "dipped" objects). Books on the use of **topits** include PATRICK PAGE's *The Topit Handbook*, MICHAEL AMMAR's *The Topit Book*, and Bob Fitch's *Topit Again And Again*.

TOP OF POCKET

A subtlety by which a front trouser pocket may be shown empty while actually containing a small object.

Most such pockets are cut square at the top; if an object is wedged in the inner top corner, the pocket can be pulled out and shown without the object being seen. This should not be done with tight-fitting trousers and can only be used with pockets having a vertical rather than horizontal opening.

TOP PALM

With cards, to palm a card or cards from the top of the deck; this action may either be done with both hands—in which case the card is usually palmed in the hand not holding the deck—or with one hand—which palms the card in the action of putting the deck on the table or placing it into the other hand. (The one-handed top palm is believed to be the invention of British magician John Elrick.)

The techniques are described in HUGARD and BRAUE's *Expert Card Technique*.

TOPS AND BOTTOMS

Dice which are mis-spotted, usually with duplicate numbers on opposite sides of the die; they operate on the fact that only three sides of a die can be seen at once.

Rarely used by crooked gamblers, but sometimes employed by magicians in the execution of a RANGING FORCE.

TOPS (Magazine)

The house organ of Abbott's Magic Company, it was founded in 1936, and had a continuous run until 1957, at which time it ceased publication.

In 1961 it was revived as *The New Tops*, under which name it continues its run. *The New Tops* is noted for its many columns of news, reviews and information by SID LORRAINE, FRANCES MARSHALL, GEORGE JOHNSTONE, and others.

TOPSY-TURVY

There are two basic premises for this class of EFFECT:

1. An object or person mysteriously turns upside-down, usually in a confined space which makes such a maneuver impossible.

2. An object or person, turned upside-down by the performer and in the same confined situation, mysteriously returns to a right-side-up state.

An example of the first type would be DAVID DEVANT's **the new page** ILLUSION; of the second, ROBERT HARBIN's **topsy-turvy**.

A smaller version of the effect, which can be presented either way, is the **topsy-turvy bottles**; here a bottle placed in a tube can be shown right-side up or inverted, as the performer wishes. The effect usually involves a spectator who, provided with a similar bottle and tube, is unable to match the performer's movements.

An interesting routine was created and is currently being presented by PETER PIT, in which a wooden chair placed inside a snug square chimney-like tube apparently turns upside-down and vice-versa within its narrow confines.

TORN AND RESTORED

A highly popular class of EFFECTs; the objects torn range from cigarette papers to signed playing cards and dollar bills to napkins to newspapers. There are literally hundreds of ROUTINEs for such effects.

Many of these routines incorporate a SUCKER aspect—i.e., in the napkin routine the performer will "expose" the method by showing how he switches the torn pieces for an undamaged napkin; at the conclusion of the routine, the supposed torn pieces are also magically restored.

A subtlety often used is that of the TORN CORNER; one of the pieces is handed to a spectator to hold, and when the item is restored, the spectator's piece fits into a remaining gap. In such routines the corner given to the spectator does not come from the bundle of torn pieces, but from the paper later to be shown as restored.

Well performed, these routines have a strong audience appeal; AL KORAN featured the **torn and restored cigarette paper** in his nightclub performances, and one of DOUG HENNING's favorite feats is the tearing and restoring of a newspaper.

TORN CORNER

The marking of a particular item (playing card, bill) by the removal of a corner section which is handed to a spectator, so that it may be checked against the item at a later point. *See* TORN AND RESTORED.

TORN DECK

See TEARING A DECK.

TORRINI

See DE GRISY, EDMOND.

TOUCH

A commercially marketed MENTAL MAGIC effect with cards created by PAUL CURRY, in which predictions written on two cards match two other cards which later are freely selected by spectators.

The Curry effect, which uses a specially prepared deck and the DOUBLE BACK and DOUBLE FACE principles, has been widely imitated, plagiarized, and simply ripped off; indeed, one such "variation" won its "creator" an originality prize at a magic convention!

This is not to say that some of the variations have been without value; a number of interesting versions have been developed. It is more than likely, however, that none would exist without Curry's brilliant creation to show the way.

TOURNIQUET

A basic SLEIGHT in which a small object is held between thumb and first finger of one hand; the other hand apparently takes it from this position, but the object is allowed to fall to the base of the fingers. From this position it is PALMed.

Also known as the **French drop**, the sleight is described in virtually every book on basic sleight-of-hand.

TOWNER, ROBERT (b. ?)

Performer who has appeared in varied venues, primarily on the west coast; he is noted for his original and dramatic presentations of ILLUSION effects. Also known as *Torchy Towner* (he has performed FIRE EATING), he has performed under the names of *Rinaldi* and *Harlan*.

He was for many years on the staff of MARK WILSON's *Magic Land Of Allakazam* television show.

TRADE SHOW

A business exhibition of various companies which is sometimes open to the public and sometimes restricted to those involved in relevant industries and businesses. Many companies hire magicians to attract attention and/or act as spokespersons for their exhibits. Noted performers in this field include EDDIE TULLOCH, JOHN THOMPSON, PAUL GERTNER, BUD DIETRICH, DEANE STERN, MARSHALL BRODIEN, MIKE CALDWELL, and many others.

Books on this subject include *The Trade Show Handbook* by BUD DIETRICH and Dick Jarrow and *Trade Shows—An Inside Insight* by FRANCES MARSHALL.

Not to be confused with INDUSTRIAL SHOW.

TRANSFER

Another term for CHANGEOVER PASS.

TRANSPARENT CARD

A card with a secret inner layer bearing extra pips or a court card face; if such a card is held before a light source, its back to the audience, it will show a different identity than that visible on its FACE, and thus the effect of a magical change may be created. The card may be designed so that extra PIPs will be visible, those on the inner layer blending in with those on the exterior face; a court card design on the inner layer will obscure any pips on the outer face.

A routine in which the **transparent card** plays a part is described in HOFZINSER's *Card Conjuring*; Hofzinser is generally credited with the invention of this card.

TRANSPOSITION

In general usage, movement to a different position; in magical terminology, the switching of position of two objects or persons by apparent magical means. Examples would be the COPPER AND SILVER coin effect, FOLLOW THE LEADER, and METAMORPHOSIS.

TRAP

Trapdoor, usually in the floor of the stage but sometimes in the backing scene. Trapdoors were used for many illusions in the early part of this century, but changes in performance conditions and the development of new ILLUSION techniques have rendered them (for the most part) unnecessary. They can still be effectively employed when a show will be in a fixed location for a long run (and thus the stage can be altered as required) or when "one-shot" sets are constructed (as for a television presentation).

While magicians rarely use traps at present, audiences are not aware of this, and will often hypothesize their use to explain an illusion; the performer, accordingly, must so present the illusion as to eliminate this possibility.

See ARTHUR.

TRAP PASS

A BILLIARD BALL SLEIGHT in which a ball is placed on top of the fist, so that it rests in the circle formed by the first finger and edge of the thumb. As the other hand closes around the ball, the fist is opened slightly to allow the ball to descend into the hand.

As the other hand moves away, apparently taking the ball, it is allowed to slip into a PALM position.

The SLEIGHT is described in HENRY HAY's *Amateur Magician's Handbook* and RALPH W. HULL's *Expert Billiard Ball Manipulation*.

TRAVELER

Sliding metal holder from which the stage curtain is suspended at its leading vertical edge; the travelers of the two halves of the curtain, operating on separate parallel tracks, are designed to overlap.

If a performer onstage is uncertain of which way this overlap is set, a glance up to the travelers will reveal the situation. The performer may then push back on the UPSTAGE curtain and exit with a minimum of fumbling.

TRAVELLERS

A card EFFECT invented by DAI VERNON in which four cards, placed into the deck, travel to four different pockets in the performer's clothing. Many versions of the effect are in print.

TRAVERS, ROLAND (1891-1970)

Professional magician who began his career in 1901, performing in ORIENTAL STYLE an impression of CHING LING FOO. He toured with ADELAIDE HERMANN, and later performed in vaudeville as "The Illusionist Extraordinary." For this act he originated a famous illusion in which a girl vanished from the top of a ladder. Travers also developed some original techniques for the use of the BLACK ART principle.

In later years he created special equipment for a number of magicians, notably DELL O'DELL, with whom he was associated for many years.

TRAVERSE CURTAIN

A curtain running parallel to the FRONT CURTAIN and located at any point between it and the rear of the stage; it is almost always rigged to divide in the center.

TRAY GIRL

Slang term for female ASSISTANT who carries smaller properties on and off stage, or holds items of APPARATUS (often on a tray) while the performer executes the ROUTINE.

TREGETOUR

One of the very earliest words in the English language (ca. 1300 A.D.) to denote a trickster, magician, or SLEIGHT-OF-HAND performer.

TREWEY, FELICIEN (1848-1920)

Born in France; a versatile performer who was skilled not only in magic but also juggling, gymnastics, singing, poetry and painting. He is best remembered, however, for his skills in SHADOWGRAPHY and

CHAPEAUGRAPHY; his act featuring the latter was called "Twenty-Five Heads Under One Hat."

TREY

With cards or dice, a value of three.

TRIANGLE

A presentation of the CARDS ACROSS; this version was created by DAVID DEVANT, and is described in *Our Magic* by Devant and NEVIL MASKELYNE.

TRICK

Term used by laypersons to indicate a magical feat; the word is rarely employed in this sense by magicians, who prefer the term EFFECT.

"Trick" as a popular term is unfortunate in its suggestion of cheating, swindling and harmful deception—and also in its stress on the puzzle/challenge aspect of magical feats, to the detriment of true mystery entertainment.

TRICKSTER

One who executes the procedure of a magical effect without any attempt to perform, or who conceives of and presents magic as a type of puzzle exhibition or battle of wits with the onlooker.

TRILBY

An ILLUSION of the SUSPENSION type, invented by ALEXANDER HERRMANN, in which a plank was placed across the backs of two chairs and a woman reclined on it. The chairs were then removed, the board and woman remaining suspended in midair. At a gesture from the performer the board and woman turned to a slight angle, and then returned to the horizontal. The chairs were replaced and the woman got up from the plank.

Also, **Trilby deck**, a MECHANICAL DECK invented by JOE STUTHARD; it is similar in operation to the SVENGALI DECK, but uses the STRIPPER DECK principle instead of short cards. The twenty-six FORCE cards can thus easily be removed and, in the course of a routine, replaced with the twenty-six indifferent cards which will complete the deck. Thus the performer is able to routine a number of effects using the Svengali and STRIPPER DECK concepts.

TRIPLE ALLIANCE

Title billing of an act which featured SERVAIS LEROY, IMRO FOX, and FREDERICK EUGENE POWELL.

TRIPLE DIVINATION

A centuries-old feat of MENTAL MAGIC in which three people take three objects; they are then given one, two and three counters respectively. From a pile of eighteen more counters they take the same amount, twice as many, or four times as many according to which of the three objects they chose. After the objects and counters are hidden, the performer divines the holder of each object; he is able to do this by noting how many counters remain.

Many versions of the EFFECT have been devised; the best general overview is in MARTIN GARDNER's *Mathematics, Magic And Mystery*. An excellent presentation for this type of ROUTINE, created by M. S. MAHENDRA, will be found in HILLIARD's *Greater Magic* (an expanded version of this presentation was marketed in manuscript form by Mahendra as *He Can't Read My Mind*).

TRIPLE TRUNKS
See CANNON ILLUSION.

TRIUMPH

A card ROUTINE invented by DAI VERNON in which half of the deck is turned face-up and riffled into the face-down half; all the cards turn face-down with the exception of a previously selected card.

The basic Vernon routine is described in *Stars Of Magic*; there have been many later variations.

TRIUMPH SHUFFLE

A FALSE SHUFFLE devised by DAI VERNON for his TRIUMPH card effect. In this SHUFFLE, after the cards are interlaced the performer appears to SQUARE THE DECK; this is, however, only an illusion, and the two interlaced halves may be separated in an apparent cutting action.

The technique is thoroughly described in the relevant section of the book *Stars Of Magic*.

TROST, NICK (b. ?)

Prolific writer on all phases of magic; his books include *Ace Tricks, Cardman's Secrets* (two volumes), *Challenge Poker Deal, Close-up Card Tricks, ESP Card Magic, ESP Session With Nick Trost, Gambling Tricks With Cards* (two parts), *Subtle Card Magic* (two parts), *Routine With The Cups And Balls*, and many others.

TROUBLEWIT

A novelty ROUTINE, similar in form to CHAPEAU-GRAPHY, in which the performer manipulates an accordion-pleated piece of heavy paper into various shapes, with accompanying PATTER.

It is at least three hundred years old, was featured nearly a century ago by FELICIEN TREWEY, and is in the programs of many present-day performers, notably JAY MARSHALL and TOM OGDEN. Troublewit is thoroughly described in C. LANG NEIL's *The Modern Conjurer*; more recent works on the subject are *Troublewit Routines* by KEN DE COURCY and *Troublewit Simplified* by Herb Morrisey.

TROUPER

A touring performer, usually a member of a company of players or performers.

Also, a powerful type of SPOTLIGHT; the most powerful such light is appropriately known as a **super trouper**.

TRUNK ESCAPE

A variant of the BOX ESCAPE, in which the performer is secured inside a large steamer trunk and mysteriously makes his escape. The most famous early escape of this kind was invented by JOHN NEVIL MASKELYNE.

A later trunk, designed by HERBERT BROOKS, is still known as the **Brooks trunk**; it could be carefully examined and yet the performer, locked inside, could escape from it with rapidity.

Trunk escapes as such are rarely seen today; a much more popular ILLUSION using this PROP is METAMORPHOSIS.

See BOX ESCAPES.

TUCKER, TOMMY (b. ca. 1915)

Performer with long professional career, at first featuring comedy magic; he is best-known, however, for the TWO PERSON MENTAL ACT performed with wife Liz. The Tuckers are now considered by many to be the best performers of this act; they have appeared in varied venues throughout the U.S., Britain and Europe, and have also worked in numerous TRADE SHOWS for corporate clients.

The Tuckers also operate a company called Magitronix, which supplies various kinds of electronic devices to performers.

Within magic Tucker is noted as the inventor of the SIX-CARD REPEAT.

TULLOCK, EDDIE (b. ?)

Specialist in TRADE SHOW work, at which he is considered to be one of the most successful performers in the business. In addition to trade shows, he also appears in corporate hospitality suites, sales meetings, and related venues. Tullock performs card magic exclusively, adapting his effects to his client company.

He is a recipient of a Performing Fellowship from the ACADEMY OF MAGICAL ARTS.

TUNED DECK

An elaborate sequence of card locations routined by RALPH W. HULL; it is the subject of an entire chapter of HILLIARD's *Greater Magic*.

TURNOVER BOX

Another name for the FLIPOVER BOX. Not to be confused with the TIPOVER BOX, the two having entirely different working principles.

TURNOVER CHANGE

See CURRY TURNOVER CHANGE.

TURNOVER PASS

With playing cards, a type of SHIFT executed in the act of turning the face-down deck face-up (or vice versa). Also known as the HERRMANN PASS (from its possible inventor), it is in some situations preferable to the standard shift in that it can be deceptively performed while the deck is under close observation by the audience.

It is described in HILLIARD's *Greater Magic* and HUGARD and BRAUE's *Expert Card Technique*, and many other standard works.

TURNOVER SPREAD

After a deck is in RIBBON SPREAD on the table, to cause the entire deck to turn over in wave-fashion by lifting the exposed edge of the bottom card and turning it over—causing the other cards to move in similar fashion.

Also known as a **wave turnover; spread turnover**.

A flourish often incorporated into this procedure is known as **Walking The Dog**: here the turnover is controlled to stop in the center (the cards at one end face-up, at the other end face-down). One card is then removed from one end and its edge is used to move the crest of the wave back and forth. It is possible to break the single wave into two smaller waves and perform the **Walking The Dog** procedure with both hands.

TURN UP

To deal cards face-up; alternatively, to turn the top card of the (face-down) deck face upward.

TWENTIETH CENTURY SILKS

Two silk handkerchieves are tied together and rolled into a ball; a third (usually of contrasting color and design) is vanished, and when the two silks are unrolled the vanished silk has reappeared knotted between them. This effect is believed to be the invention of FRANK DUCROT.

There are many methods for this effect, ranging from SLEIGHT OF HAND or APPARATUS switches to specially-prepared silks; the effect is well-covered in HAROLD R. RICE's *Encyclopedia Of Silk Magic*.

TWENTY-FIVE CARD TRICK

A venerable feat of MENTAL MAGIC with cards, in which five spectators each think of a card from a hand of five dealt to each of them; gathering the cards, the performer deals them into five new hands and asks each spectator in turn if he sees the thought-of card in these new hands as they are shown one-by-one. The action of redealing the cards has redistributed the cards in a mathematical sequence; thus if the third spectator sees his card in a given hand it will be the third card in that hand. Thus, the performer is able to locate the cards.

This principle is variously known as the FIVE-BY-FIVE, INTERSECTING SETS or CROSS-REFERENCE principle; a bald performance of it as described above will deceive few spectators. Over the years, however, magicians have developed ways of disguising the principle, among them S. LEO HOROWITZ (see *Greater Magic*); STEWART JUDAH (*The Magic Of Stewart Judah*); LOUIS S. HISTED (*The Magic Of Louis S. Histed*); and SIMON ARONSON (*The Card Magic Of Simon Aronson*).

A recent book by Peter Tappan titled *The Impostress Princess* is devoted entirely to this effect.

There have also been marketed GIMMICKs employed in this effect, including AL BAKER's **Vocalepathy** and PAUL FOX's **Miracle Gimmick**.

In recent years there has been a tendency to confuse the above effect and principle with the PRINCESS TRICK; the two effects are quite different both in method and presentation.

TWENTY-ONE GIRLS FROM A CABINET

The title explains the EFFECT of this GUY JARRETT illusion; twenty-one women are produced from a cabinet that is of a size that apparently could hold no more than six at most. Like many of Jarrett's illusions, it involves his use of the HONESTY PRINCIPLE; Jarrett knew no one would believe that all the women were in the cabinet at the outset.

Incredible in effect though it is, the ILLUSION is rarely seen, since it involves maintaining a troupe of twenty-one people well-trained in the necessary techniques. It was presented on a recent DOUG HENNING television special for what was probably the first time in several decades.

TWENTY-ONE CENT TRICK

A commercially available EFFECT using two nickels, a dime, and a penny; it is so designed, using the SHELL principle, that the four coins may be made to appear as a single nickel.

A number of different effects are thus made possible; an excellent ROUTINE for this coin set will be found in J.B. BOBO's *Modern Coin Magic*.

TWENTY-SIXTH DOWN LOCATION

A type of location using a SUNKEN KEY which is twenty-six cards down from the top of the deck; if a selected card is replaced on top and the deck is cut, the selection will always be half the deck distant from the key. This property can be utilized with the FARO SHUFFLE and other techniques.

TWIRL

In the MULTIPLYING BILLIARD BALL effect, any move which causes the SHELL to remain with its convex side to the audience as the hand is turned. A **twirl** may be accomplished by the holding hand only or with assistance from the other hand.

TWISTING EFFECTS

Card EFFECTs using a small PACKET of cards, in which different cards turn face-up, face-down, or change their identies in mysterious fashion, the effects usually being revealed as the face-down packet is counted from hand to hand. Most of these effects rely on such SLEIGHTs as the ELMSLEY COUNT, JORDAN COUNT, SIVA COUNT, etc., often in combination with other sleights and subtleties (and, in some cases, specially printed cards).

The term comes from DAI VERNON's **twisting the**

aces effect in his *Inner Secrets Of Card Magic,* in which a "twisting" motion of rotating the packet end for end is the supposed "secret move" by which the effect is accomplished. Vernon devised the motion to give a reason for the grip between thumb and fingers at each side of the deck required for many of the above-mentioned counting procedures.

TWO-CARD MONTE

An effect invented by THEODORE H. DE LAND in which two cards are shown and one of these is placed behind the performer's back; the cards appear to instantly change places.

Specially-printed cards, in concert with a very simple MOVE, accomplish the effect.

TWO-EIGHTY-FIVE TRICK

A set of coins consisting of two silver dollars, a half-dollar, a quarter and a dime. The coins are placed in the hand and a single silver dollar removed; when the hand is opened, it is seen that the other coins have vanished.

This set of FAKE coins operates on an extension of the SHELL principle.

See also DOLLAR-THIRTY-FIVE TRICK; TWENTY-ONE-CENT TRICK.

TWO-HANDED PASS

See SHIFT.

TWO INTO ONE WILL GO

A SLEIGHT-OF-HAND effect invented by E. BRIAN MACARTHY in which two candles are placed one at a time into a metal tube which will hold only one. It is described in PENTAGRAM Magazine.

A similar effect using small colored pencils was developed by Cecil Keech.

TWO-PERSON MENTAL ACT

A classic ROUTINE in MENTAL MAGIC in which a blindfolded performer on stage describes objects handed to a partner in the audience. In a variation of this, spectators may whisper questions to the audience performer; these are immediately answered by the "medium" onstage.

Most such acts employ complex verbal and silent codes; contrary to audience speculation, electronic gimmickry is rarely used. Though acts of this type such as those of the Zancigs, Mr. and Mrs. Tree, The Zomahs, Lucille and Eddie Roberts, and the Piddingtons were once quite popular, few are seen today—undoubtedly because it is an extremely difficult act to do well. One of the best such acts today—by a considerable margin—is that of Tom and Liz Tucker (*see* TOMMY TUCKER), whose work is much in demand both for stage and trade show work.

ULTRA-MENTAL DECK

A variant of the BRAINWAVE DECK, with which any card freely named may be shown as the only face-down card in a face-up deck; it was invented by JOE BERG.

Like the Brainwave Deck, it operates on the ROUGH-AND-SMOOTH PRINCIPLE.

ULTRA-VIOLET LIGHT

See BLACK LIGHT.

UNCANNY HANKS

A ROUTINE created by GEORGE BLAKE in which four handkerchieves tied to a length of tape visibly untie themselves in any order indicated by spectators. The routine is marketed, and also thoroughly described in Volume VI of the TARBELL COURSE IN MAGIC.

UNDERCUT

To CUT the deck in the reverse of the usual manner (i.e., to draw off the bottom half and place it on top). This can be done from the normal dealing position, but is more usually executed with the deck being held at the sides from below by thumb and fingers.

UNDER-DOWN DEAL

See AUSTRALIAN DEAL.

UNEQUAL ROPES

A commercially marketed ROUTINE, also known as the **Professor's Nightmare**, in which three lengths of rope—short, medium and long—become the same length, only to finally revert to their original state. The ropes are ordinary; the illusion is created by the handling. Many variations of the original routine have been published.

A related EFFECT, sometimes given the same name, is that in which a spectator tries to trim one rope to match another in length, with amusing lack of success. This latter effect is credited to Harold Sterling.

UNIQUE MAGIC STUDIO

British magic shop which operated in London for over two decades after World War II, under the proprietorship of HARRY STANLEY; it was noted for the generally high quality of its books and EFFECTs, and also for its chief "demonstrator"—KEN BROOKE.

UNTYING SILK

A silk handkerchief is held by diagonal corners and an overhand knot is tied in it; one corner is released and the silk allowed to hang from the other hand. Slowly the lower end of the silk crawls up and through the knot, untying it.

The basic methodology employs a thread, either hanging freely or attached to a REEL; handlings are described in RICE's *Encyclopedia Of Silk Magic*. The EFFECT is also known as the *Serpent Silk*.

UP AND DOWN

A mathematically-based card trick invented by DAI VERNON in which the performer predicts the positions at which two thought-of cards will be found. The effect is fully described in GARDNER's *Mathematics, Magic And Mystery*.

UPSTAGE

The part of the stage furthest from the audience; so called because at one time most stages were RAKEd, being higher at the rear than at the front. (In Britain and Europe, many such stages still exist.)

As a *verb*, to divert attention from another performer; in technical use, by moving to an upstage position so that the other performer has to turn away from the audience to interact with the performer in the upstage position. More generally, the term is used to denote any technique used by someone to divert the audience's attention from another performer.

Magicians rarely have this problem with assistants or partners, but it can occur when a stagewise spectator is brought up to assist and is not carefully kept within the framework of necessary action.

See DOWNSTAGE; STAGE LEFT/STAGE RIGHT; PROMPT SIDE; OPPOSITE PROMPT.

UP THE GARDEN PATH

A phrase sometimes used in Britain to denote SUCKER EFFECTs; it comes from a routine of that title devised by Cecil Tebbett.

U.S.O.

United Services Organization, a group which provides free entertainment and other services to members of the military; many magicians have performed on U.S.O. shows.

See ENSA.

UTILITY ITEM

Any item of magical APPARATUS which can be used in a number of different ROUTINEs; usually such an item can cause objects to appear, vanish or change. Examples of utility include the CHANGING BAG, MIRROR GLASS and THUMB TIP.

UTILITY MOVE

Term sometimes used to denote a SLEIGHT-OF-HAND technique used to show both hands empty except for a certain number of items. As an example, after three coins are shown in the left hand they are tossed into the right hand; however, one coin is palmed in the left hand and the other two join a coin already there. Credited to STANLEY COLLINS.

There are many variations of this general technique.

UTILITY SLEIGHT

Any SLEIGHT used secretly to accomplish a magical effect, as opposed to a FLOURISH.

VALADON, PAUL (1869-1913)

Born Adolph Waber in Germany, he emigrated to Britain where, with his wife, he presented a TWO-PERSON MENTAL ACT as well as a number of ILLUSIONs, appearing at EGYPTIAN HALL; he was particularly noted for his invention of an illusion called *"Well, I'm . . .,"* in which a woman vanished from the top of a table, and also a precursor to the DRUM ILLUSION.

Valadon emigrated to the U.S. and appeared for a few seasons with HARRY KELLAR; it was planned that Valadon would be Kellar's successor, but a conflict of personalities prevented this. Valadon then went into vaudeville for the remainder of his career.

VAMP

Within current theatrical usage, to improvise with words or actions, usually to cover a delay.

Within magic, this may occur when the operation of an EFFECT or ILLUSION through malfunction takes longer than planned; also, when the elimination of a nonfunctioning effect puts the performer ahead of a musical accompaniment and it is necessary to stall slightly in order to resynchronize the music with the act.

VAMPIRE

Another name for the CREO illusion, from the Rudyard Kipling poem of the same title, and the apposite line therein: "A rag, a bone, a hank of hair . . ."

VAN BERN, CHRIS (1871-1950)

British performer who had an exceptionally long career in music halls and many other venues; his act featured, in addition to magic, vocal and instrumental music and QUICK-CHANGE effects.

With DE VEGA he wrote *Whirlwind Of Wizardry.*

VANEK, JOSEPH (1818-1889)

Born in Hungary, he spent the early years of his life working for the government as a scientist; at about the age of thirty he began his professional career and was immediately successful, traveling throughout Europe and the Middle East.

Vanek made a well-received tour of the U.S. in 1873, then returning to Europe for the next few years until his retirement from the stage.

His featured EFFECT—an apparent decapitation of a hapless assistant—was so realistic as to cause many spectators to faint.

VAN HOVEN, FRANK (1886-1929)

British performer who scored a major success in U.S. vaudeville after switching from serious to comedy presentation. His act was known for rapid-fire comedy lines and slapstick humor, and his most famous ROUTINE involved a hapless "volunteer" from the audience who was made to hold a large block of ice. He often used the billing of "The Man Who Made Ice Famous."

In the early part of his career Van Hoven worked briefly as ASSISTANT to ROLAND TRAVERS.

At his retirement Van Hoven sold his act to DELL O'DELL.

VANISH

The disappearance of an object, person, etc.; it is most often used between magicians to denote an *action* rather than a *state of being*, e.g., "I will vanish the card," rather than "The card will vanish." The word *vanish* should not be used in this manner when speaking to laypersons.

VANISHING BIRD CAGE

Invented by BUATIER DE KOLTA, originally cylindrical in shape; in its modern form a small cubical cage (usually about four or five inches on a side) which is held between the performer's hands, containing within it a small bird. Without covering of any kind the cage visibly vanishes.

It is constructed of a frame of square steel rods into which the wire bars are fitted so they can swivel freely; thus the cage can collapse into a long, lozenge-like mode no more than an inch in diameter. The cage is fastened to a cord attached to a strap on one arm; the cord goes up the sleeve, across the back, and down the other sleeve to the cage. In its collapsed state, the cage is rapidly pulled up the sleeve by extending the arms. Variant hookups allow slack in the cord which is taken up by a REEL before the vanish procedure is executed. *See* PULL.

The bird is almost always a FAKE made of thin rubber, held in position within the cage by threads. At one time live birds were used and, while an inner bar kept the cage from collapsing too tightly around its occupant, this provision often failed to work; the bird might be crippled or (in the phrase of HARRY LEAT, a writer/magician who detested this practice) ". . . be jerked into eternity."

Indeed, CARL HERTZ, who featured the EFFECT using a live bird, was called into court on this account, where he "proved" that the bird survived its journey. There is speculation that the bird eventually shown by Hertz was not the one originally seen in the cage. Over the years bad publicity would crop up again and again for performers using live birds for this effect, and the practice is now almost unknown.

The **vanishing bird cage** was a reputation-maker for magicians from the days of DE KOLTA and Hertz; later performers to feature it were JOHN BOOTH, FRED KEATING, BERT ALLERTON (as a close-up effect!), and most notably HARRY BLACKSTONE SR. and his son, HARRY BLACKSTONE JR., in whose hands it became a masterpiece of stage presentation.

The Elusive Canary, by MYSTIC CRAIG, is devoted to this effect.

VANISHING CANE

A coil of metal or plastic which can be drawn out and secured in its extended position by placing a cane knob at its wide end. When the knob is removed, the coil instantly contracts to its former shape. The cane may be wrapped in a sheet of paper to conceal this action, or a silk may be placed within the cane—the EFFECT then being a transformation of cane to silk; in like manner a FEATHER FLOWER bouquet may be used.

Invented by RUSS WALSH.

VANISHING CLOTH

Not, as may be imagined, a cloth which vanishes; the term instead refers to a cloth square, usually of a fairly heavy material, which contains a wire frame representing the upper edge of an article apparently held underneath the cloth, but in actuality no longer present. The article may be anything from a bowl of water to a large dove cage.

Often these frames are loosely jointed, so that when the cloth is shown empty and allowed to hang from one corner there is no telltale bulk.

Some interesting **vanishing cloths** are described in OKITO's *Quality Magic*.

VANISHING ELEPHANT

An EFFECT most often performed for the publicity angle rather than as a mystery. Indeed, a classic backstage joke of WALTER GIBSON's origination makes this clear: "Four men push a cabinet on stage. Houdini puts the elephant in the cabinet. Houdini shows the cabinet empty. Twenty men push the cabinet off stage. Where did the elephant go?"

If the presentation used by HOUDINI was not quite that bad, it was still far from an impressive mystery—but it did lend itself to exploitation, accomplishing that purpose to Houdini's complete satisfaction.

The elephant vanish was featured in a television special by DOUG HENNING, who used no cabinet as such and a far more deceptive method. It is also featured by HARRY BLACKSTONE JR. (in whose presentation the elephant visibly vanishes) and SIEGFRIED AND ROY.

VANISHING LADY

An ILLUSION invented by BUATIER DE KOLTA a century ago, in which newspapers were spread on the floor of the stage (to preclude trapdoors) and a chair placed on them; a woman sat in the chair and was covered by a thin silk drape.

Suddenly the drape was whisked away and the woman had vanished, seemingly in that same instant. (Some performers, including DeKolta himself, would cause the drape to vanish as it was whipped away from the chair; others thought this addition confused the effect).

The directness and simplicity of this illusion have appealed to many performers over the years; it was a major effect in the show of ALDO RICHIARDI, and is currently featured by JOHN THOMPSON, DOUG HENNING, DAVID COPPERFIELD, SIEGFRIED AND ROY, and many others.

In magical parlance this effect is usually referred to as the **DeKolta chair**.

An excellent description of the **vanishing lady** will be found in WILL DEXTER's *This Is Magic*.

VANISHING WAND

A magic WAND is wrapped in a sheet of paper, which is then torn to bits, the wand apparently having vanished; it is reproduced from the pocket or elsewhere.

The effect is accomplished by an application of the SHELL principle; only the white tips of the wand are solid, the black central section is made of heavy paper. When the paper-wrapped wand has been torn up, the pieces are crushed together and discarded. In doing this care must be taken that the solid tips do not reveal their presence by a clunking sound.

The Vanishing Wand is the invention of THEO BAMBERG.

VANITY FAIR

An ILLUSION in which a large (about four feet by nine feet) mirror is mounted in a wheeled wooden frame, with the bottom of the mirror well above the stage, so that spectators can see beneath it. At the front of the mirror is a small platform on which a woman stands; she is then concealed with a folding screen, but the mirror is visible all around the platform and screen. When the screen is removed, however, the woman has vanished.

There have been many later variations of this illusion. In some versions the person is changed into an entirely different individual; in a variant of the basic EFFECT but using the same general technique, a person is caused to pass through the solid mirror. For this latter effect the mirror is sometimes replaced by clear plate glass or heavy lucite.

Vanity fair and its later variants work on the principle that movement of a smooth transparent or reflecting surface within an enclosing frame is extremely difficult for the eye to detect.

The illusion is explained in Albert A. Hopkins' book *MAGIC*.

VAUDEVILLE

A stage show consisting of a number of individual performers doing separate acts. The equivalent British term is *music-hall* or *variety*.

VEESER CONCEPT

With the cards held in a BIDDLE GRIP, the side-JOG of certain cards to facilitate various counting and/or switching sequences; this action has many applications, thus the term has been applied to a number of sleight sequences in which it is used. It is the invention of Bob Veeser.

There are many variations of the basic **Veeser Concept** move; an interesting analysis of these variants, together with their application to the CARD PUZZLE, will be found in JUSTIN BRANCH's *Multiple Assemblies*.

VEESER COUNT

A counting technique for a small packet of cards which accomplishes the same thing as the ELMSLEY COUNT; however, the cards are held from above in a BIDDLE GRIP position and the technique is slightly different, employing an application of the VEESER CONCEPT.

The move, created by Bob Veeser, is thoroughly explained in JERRY MENTZER's *Counts, Cuts, Moves and Subtleties*.

VERMEYDEN, HENK (b. ?)

Dutch magic dealer, producer, and publisher; founder of FISM, and tutor/advisor to many of the prize-winning entrants in its competitions. His Triks Magic Studio for many years published a house organ (also called *Triks*).

VERNON, DAI (b. 1894)

Born David Frederick Wingfield Verner in Canada, he became interested in magic at the age of six; in the years since then he has come to be the single most influential figure in modern magic, and is known throughout the world as The Professor. He is considered by most magicians to be the greatest card expert who has ever lived, and also has an unrivaled reputation as a close-up performer.

During the early part of his career he performed a stage act; its most elaborate version was the COSTUME ACT known as the Harlequin Act, performed in New York City at Radio City Music Hall and at the Rainbow Room. The act was a critical success, but so costly to produce that it was not financially viable.

At this same time Vernon had begun to perform at private parties for society clients, at which he was very successful; he also, at various times, worked as a silhouette cutter (an art at which he is also expert), on Atlantic City's Boardwalk and elsewhere.

Vernon's first writing was the anonymously published *Secrets*; later came the legendary *Twenty Dollar Manuscript*. In the 1940s he contributed several sections to the *Stars Of Magic* book. After a lecture tour of Britain he worked with LEWIS GANSON to produce *The Dai Vernon Book Of Magic* and the Card Secret Series—*Inner Secrets Of Card Magic, More Inner Secrets, Further Inner Secrets* and *Ultimate Secrets*; in addition, Ganson produced two booklets describing Vernon's routines for the CUPS AND BALLS and the LINKING RINGS.

He has made a number of lecture tours of the U.S., Britain, Europe and many other countries. For many years he has written a column called *The Vernon Touch* for GENII Magazine.

VESTING

Secretly disposing of a palmed object by pushing it up under the vest or waistcoat; less commonly, obtaining an object therefrom. The vest is sometimes prepared for this by having an elastic ribbon sewn into it at the lower edge, but for many applications of the technique this is unnecessary.

Vesting was regularly employed in the EFFECTs of turn-of-the-century performers but has gradually fallen into disuse; properly applied, however, the technique is still quite worthwhile and deceptive. Some current performers use this general technique with a cummerbund, sometimes fitted with elastic along its lower border.

VEST TURNING

A cord is tied between the performer's wrists; without disturbing this bond, he is able to cause his vest to turn inside out—either in a cabinet or under cover of darkness. The EFFECT is often performed as part of a SEANCE or SPIRIT CABINET routine. Depending on the restraint, the performer may either turn the vest inside out without removing his bonds (through topological manipulation) or—using a KELLAR TIE or similar restraint—remove his bonds while accomplishing the reversal of the vest.

The effect was originally used by fraudulent spirit mediums as evidence of spirit power; it is described in Hereward Carrington's *The Physical Phenomena Of Spiritualism*.

VICTOR, EDWARD (1887-1964)

Born Edward Neuschwander in Britain, he had a long and highly successful professional career. He began as an entertainer at private parties, then turned to stage work and a long run at EGYPTIAN HALL. His act consisted almost entirely of manipulative magic and SHADOWGRAPHY, two skills in which he excelled.

In the course of his career he performed in all sorts of situations and venues, from variety and music-hall to theatrical revues; for many years he played ABANAZAR in the traditional Christmas pantomime.

Victor's excellent books on SLEIGHT OF HAND include *Magic Of The Hands, More Magic Of The Hands*, and *Further Magic Of The Hands*; he also wrote a pamphlet (My Rope Trick) on his version of the CUT-AND-RESTORED ROPE, and several sections of WILLANE's *Methods for Miracles* series.

Edward Victor in makeup and costume as Abanazar (*The Mulholland Library of Conjuring & the Allied Arts, Los Angeles, California*)

VICTOR COUNT

See E.Y.E. COUNT.

VICTORY CARTON ILLUSION

Specifically, an ILLUSION created by U.F. GRANT in which two large cardboard cartons (without top or bottom) are shown empty, and from which a person is immediately produced.

More generally, any of a number of illusions created by Grant which use similar cartons; these are described in his *Victory Carton Illusions*. The basic illusion is also described in MARK WILSON's *Course in Magic*.

VINTUS, LEN (b. ?)

Born Melvin J.G. McMullen; holder of membership card #1 in the I.B.M., which he founded with GENE GORDON and W.W. DURBIN.

VIRGIL (b. 1900)

Born Virgil Mulkey, he began his career with an act featuring silk magic which he performed in vaudeville

Virgil (*The Mulholland Library of Conjuring & the Allied Arts, Los Angeles, California*)

for many years. He later created a FULL EVENING SHOW and toured throughout the U.S., the British Isles, India, and the Far East.

Returning to the U.S, he continued to tour with wife and partner Julie, primarily in the western part of the country. They were particularly noted for the many new effects presented on each tour, and for their presentation of the SPIRIT CABINET.

In recent years Virgil and Julie have continued to perform, with a smaller version of their stage show presented in combination with feats of MENTAL MAGIC.

VISIBLE COINS IN GLASS

The JACK HUGHES marketed version of the APPARATUS coin effect COPENETRO. This should not be confused with a JOHN KENNEDY effect titled **visible coins to glass**, which is completely different in presentation, routine, and method.

VOLLMER, RICHARD (b. ?)

Magical translator located in France; responsible for (among many other works) French editions of popular English-language magic books, published by Jean-Pierre Hornecker's *Editions du Spectacle*.

VOLTAIRE, BOBBY (1910-1986)

Born Robert Arrendorff in Britain, he moved to Canada as a child and there began his career as assistant to a medicine-show performer; later, in Britain, he performed in many different types of venues with varying results until he developed an act featuring electricity and lightbulbs, with which he very quickly became successful.

On his retirement he sold the rights to a number of his electrical effects to MARVYN ROY.

VOLUNTEER

A member of the audience brought into the performing area to assist in an effect (*see* AUDIENCE PARTICIPATION).

Use of the term in a technical description implies that the spectator is innocent and uncoached; in other words, not a CONFEDERATE.

VON ARX (1873-1959)

Born Charles Nicol; elder brother of NICOLA. Performing at first in his brother's show, Von Arx later created an elaborate illusion show with which he toured the world. In later years, after various reverses, he performed a pared-down version of the show, and also occasionally presented a SPOOK SHOW.

VOODOO

The Haitian occult religion has lent its name to a number of magical and mental magic effects:

1. An effect by Arthur Monroe which appeared in THE JINX, in which the performer seemingly has the ability to astrally project himself to a distant spot, bring back an object from that location, and then return it!

2. A marketed effect with several claimants, in which the performer predicts which area of a voodoo doll will not be pierced by needles handled by spectators.

3. A marketed effect by Albert Spackman in which a manikin figure printed on a card suffers an alteration to match that shown on a card chosen by a spectator.

There have been any number of other effects using the word Voodoo as part of their name (e.g., **voodoo glass**, **voodoo rings**), but in most of these the relationship between the prop/effect and the powers of voodoo is tenuous at best.

V-SHUFFLE

A type of FALSE SHUFFLE invented by HUGH JOHNSTON in which the two halves of the deck are interlaced with a riffling action in the form of an acute V. In the action of apparently closing the V and Squaring the deck, the cupped hands lift one half above the other at the outer end; this half becomes the upper half of the deck as the cards are freed of the interlacing at the inner end.

The shuffle is described in MAHENDRA's *Amazing Card Miracles*. It may be based on a procedure described in the ''Blind Shuffle'' section of ERDNASE's *Expert At The Card Table*.

WAKELING, ALAN (b. 1926)

Performer who began his career as a demonstrator in a magic shop, later working for FLOYD THAYER. After military service in World War II, he worked as an assistant to PETER GODFREY, and was also employed by DANTE. He also assisted MERV TAYLOR in the creation and manufacture of magic props.

He was simultaneously developing an act which he played in various venues; in 1951 he married singer Helen Whalen, who became his partner in the act. For the next decade they performed in theaters and nightclubs along the West Coast.

Retiring from performing, Wakeling became a CONSULTANT to a number of performers, including direction of the Peter Reveen show; he also created effects for Disney shows.

In 1966 he joined MARK WILSON's organization as Creative Director, a position he has held since that time. He is generally considered to be one of the most knowledgeable persons in this field.

He is the author (with EARL NELSON) of *The Chop Cup Book*.

Wakeling is a recipient of the Creative Fellowship from the ACADEMY OF MAGICAL ARTS.

WALKING AWAY FROM A SHADOW

A stage ILLUSION in which the performer steps behind a roller blind shade which is then brightly illuminated from the rear; the performer's shadow appears in strong relief on the shade. After a few moments the performer walks out from behind the shade—but the shadow remains. This illusion has been said to be the invention of BURLING HULL and U.F. GRANT.

Alan and Helen Wakeling, 1951

The original version used a shade prepared with luminous paint, in conjunction with special lighting; it was featured by LEVANTE, SORCAR and BLACKSTONE SR. Some modern versions use far more complex optical techniques.

WALKING THROUGH A BRICK WALL

An ILLUSION in which the performer, under cover of three-fold screens set up on each side of a brick wall, apparently walks right through it.

HOUDINI made a feature of this illusion, which he purchased from SIDNEY JOSOLYNE; there is some evidence, however, that the first version of this feat was created by C. A. ALEXANDER, who walked through an ice-block wall in Alaska well before Houdini's performance of the brick-wall illusion.

Because of the expense in having such a wall constructed, and the jurisdictional problems of the various unions involved, the illusion has almost never been seen since Houdini's time. DOUG HENNING performed a new presentation of the effect on a television special (based on a DEVANT principle); for the *Today* show, RANDI walked through the still-standing wall of a partially-demolished building; and DAVID COPPERFIELD has also presented the feat on a television special—the wall in question being *The Great Wall Of China!*

WALKING THROUGH A RIBBON

A long length of ribbon is held by two spectators; the magician (or a third spectator) apparently passes right through it.

A variety of methods have been devised for this EFFECT; some are scaled-up versions of the BLOCK AND FRAME effect, others use specially prepared ribbons, and still others require complex mechanical devices. The simplest versions make use of the principle employed in CORDS OF PHANTASIA or its predecessor GRANDMOTHER'S NECKLACE.

WALLER, CHARLES (1884-1960)

Australian inventor and author of many books, including *Happy Magic, Magic From Below, For Magicians Only*, and *Waller's Wonders*.

He also contributed items to many magazines. A posthumously published work is his *Magical Nights At The Theatre*, a fascinating account of magicians of many countries who appeared in Australian variety.

He is noted as the creator of the concept of PERVERSE MAGIC.

WALSH, AUDLEY (1894-1957)

Policeman by profession, he was an expert on gambling fraud, often lecturing on the subject and presenting a GAMBLING DEMONSTRATION. A number of his magic and gambling EFFECTs and ROUTINEs will be found in the PHOENIX; among his books are *Dice Dexterity* and *Why You Can't Win* (a treatise on THREE-CARD MONTE, written with JOHN SCARNE).

WALSH, RUSS (?-1972)

Born William Walsh; best known as the creator of the Walsh VANISHING CANE and APPEARING CANE, he also manufactured and marketed a number of other items, including a rubber top hat and appearing table.

WALSH CANE

See APPEARING CANE; VANISHING CANE.

WALTON, ROY (b. ?)

Born in Scotland; operator of L. Davenport & Co.'s shop in that country. Walton is noted for his card and close-up magic, and is perhaps best known for CARD WARP (his adaptation of a JEFF BUSBY routine).

His books include *Card Script, Cardboard Charades, The Devil's Playthings, Tale Twisters, Trigger, That Certain Something*, and others.

WAND

The traditional symbol of the magician's power, and one of the major implements in occult magic; also a symbolic representation of the generative power.

Within stage magic the Wand has largely fallen into disuse, except as an object to be used for an effect—as, for example, the VANISHING WAND. The wand is sometimes used in CLOSE-UP MAGIC, primarily in performances of the CUPS AND BALLS; its employment, however, is hardly ever consistent and continuous through a presentation, and most performers treat it primarily as a decorated pointer rather than as the focusing agent for their powers.

An exception to this casual usage is in BIZARRE MAGICK, where the wand is presented as an instrument of real magic; this may perhaps be its only theatrically valid use in present-day performance magic.

WANDAS, SUZY (ca. 1900-1986)

Born Suzy Van Dyk in Belgium; her parents, Charles and Elizabeth, were both magicians using the stage name of Wandas, and Suzy became part of the act while still a child.

Specializing in manipulative magic, Wandas performed an act consisting almost entirely of sleight of hand; she was considered to be one of the half-dozen best manipulators in the history of magic.

After the death of her father, she and her mother performed for many years as the Wandas Sisters; when her mother retired, Wandas continued perform-

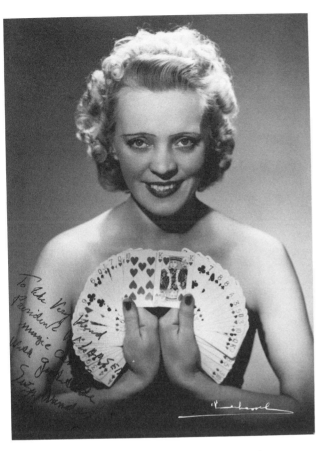

Suzy Wandas (*photo courtesy GENII Magazine*)

ing throughout Europe and Britain. She later toured the U.S., appearing at the Abbott Magic Co. Get-Together in Michigan. In 1959 she retired, marrying DR. ZINA BENNETT and making her home in the U.S.

She was a recipient of the Performing Fellowship from the ACADEMY OF MAGICAL ARTS.

WARLOCK

Term often (and erroneously) used to denote a male witch.

In fact a witch may be of either sex, and the word *Warlock* is a tropism of the Old English *waer-loga*, which meant traitor, enemy, or devil—the witch being considered such in relationship to the predominant Christian faith of the time and locale. A male witch obviously does not consider himself in these terms, and thus the term is not used within witchcraft tradition or practice.

This term is sometimes used (in its erroneous sense) to denote a male stage performer of impressive or mysterious bearing, or in an intended ironic or satirical sense.

WARLOCK, ELIZABETH (b. 1932)

Born Mary Bell in Britain; daughter of PETER WARLOCK, with whom she shares the distinction of winning the BRITISH RING Shield for excellence in performance.

For many years a resident of Canada, she wrote a column titled Toronto Tricks for LINKING RING Magazine; now returned to Britain, she writes the *Our Side Of The Pond* column begun by her father for the same magazine.

WARLOCK, PETER (b. 1904)

Born Alec Bell in Britain; a banker by trade, he is one of the most important and influential figures in British magic. For many years Editor of the PENTAGRAM, he continues with its successor, *The New Pentagram*. In addition, he has written several books, including *Designs For Magic, Plans For Deception, Warlock's Way* and *Peter Warlock's Book Of Magic*.

He also writes on matters magical for the British show-business paper *The Stage*, and for many years wrote a column called *Our Side Of The Pond* for LINKING RING Magazine. (The column is now written by his daughter ELIZABETH WARLOCK.)

Though best known for his interests in and performances of MENTALISM and MENTAL MAGIC, he is also accomplished at "straight" magic and with it has won the BRITISH RING Shield, a trophy given for excellence in performance. (This trophy was, incidentally, won the next year by daughter Elizabeth.)

WARNING CUE

A type of CUE used shortly prior to a specific cue for action, to alert the listener to be ready to act on the action cue.

WATCH BAG

There are two basic types of watch bag, both of which accomplish the same purpose: the apparent destruction of a borrowed watch.

The first variety has a small inner pocket near the top, and it is into this pocket that the borrowed watch is placed. At the bottom of the bag are various pieces of an old watch, and these the performer pounds on with some enthusiasm before spilling them out onto a tray—the spectator's watch remaining hidden in the small pocket.

The second type is actually two bags sewn together so their mouths are at opposite ends; into one bag is placed a duplicate watch, and the performer then grips this through the fabric as he holds the bag with the other mouth upward.

A spectator drops his watch into the bag; at the same time the performer releases the gripped watch, and the illusion is that the spectator's watch has fallen right through a hole in the bottom of the bag.

In both cases the borrowed watch remains in the bag, which can be taken offstage so that the watch may be loaded into some other device for reproduction.

WATCH BENDING

This somewhat Daliesque effect, in which a pocket watch appears to bend in the performer's hands, is actually an optical illusion. The watch is held between the fingers and thumbs of both hands, and the hands are moved slightly in and out, bending at the wrists. The varying amount of visible area of the watch between the fingers, coupled with the movement of the hands which are apparently gripping the watch securely, produces a very strong illusion of bending.

The move can also be effectively performed with a coin of half-dollar or silver dollar size.

WATCH BOX

A small wooden box, often equipped with a lock, into which a borrowed pocket watch may be placed; pressure at a certain spot on the box causes a side to flip up so that the watch can be secretly extracted.

Some **watch boxes** had a watch movement concealed within one wall; thus a spectator could hold the box to his or her ear and hear the ticking of what the spectator presumed was the watch still safe within.

Pocket watches having largely been replaced by wristwatches—which, because of the strap, cannot be cleanly removed from the **watch box**—use of this apparatus is now extremely rare.

WATCH MAGIC

EFFECTs with borrowed watches were in the past far more popular than at present; PROFESSOR LOUIS HOFFMANN, in his *Modern Magic* and *Later Magic*, devotes a chapter to such feats—in the latter book a lengthy section of nearly fifty pages. It should be noted that in Hoffmann's time the pocket-watch was used almost exclusively, and its shape—similar to that of a coin—lent itself to various kinds of SLEIGHT OF HAND techniques.

Few stage effects with watches are now popular; of these the most often seen is the vanish of a borrowed watch (in some cases first being damaged or destroyed with a WATCH BAG or similar device), only to be reproduced from a NEST OF BOXES.

One other effect which has created interest in recent years is the altering of the setting of the watch hands,

apparently by mind power alone—an effect featured by URI GELLER. With the increasing popularity of digital watches, this interesting feat is not likely to be often seen.

A few effects with digital watches have appeared in the magical marketplace; there is, however, the possibility that a spectator may be somewhat suspicious of electronic devices for—since the spectator doesn't understand their *ordinary* workings—he may be inclined to believe the device can be made to do anything, even when this may not be the case.

One performer who featured magic with watches and clocks exclusively was GUS FOWLER.

WATCH TARGET

A borrowed watch is smashed and "loaded" into a pistol which is fired at a target; the undamaged watch appears visibly in the bull's-eye.

The borrowed watch, having been secretly switched, is hung on a hook at the rear of the center section of the target; this section is on a pivot and spring-loaded, so that when a catch is released it spins around rapidly to the front, causing the visible appearance of the watch.

It is not uncommon for the watch to fly off the target and crash to the floor when the center section spins around, which may explain why this effect is rarely seen.

WATERFALL

A card FLOURISH in which the cards cascade from one hand to the other in a continuous ribbon; it is accomplished by squeezing the deck in a gradual fashion to space the cards evenly before release.

WATER FOUNTAINS

An EFFECT in which a jet of water appears, springing up from a bowl or item of furniture. The water-jet is transferred to a wand, and in rapid succession to a fan, the performer's hand, various items of furniture, etc.—finally multiplying into a large number of water-jets appearing all over the stage.

A traditional Japanese effect, it was introduced to western audiences by the TEN ICHI troupe. It was later featured by JEAN HUGARD, DANTE and other performers; however, because of the elaborate preparations required it is now not often seen.

WATER JARS

Invented by KARL GERMAIN, this LIQUID EFFECT uses six opaque jars which are shown empty—both by visual inspection and by nesting them to show the absence of double walls. Nevertheless, water or other liquid appears in several of the jars.

While ingenious in method and convincing in effect, the water jars suffer from the leisurely procedure of showing them empty made necessary by the method; as a consequence this baffling mystery is now rarely seen. It was, however, featured by KALANAG.

WATER RATS, GRAND ORDER OF

British performers' group organized for charitable purposes; some British magicians—BILLY MCCOMB, HAROLD TAYLOR, PAUL DANIELS, DAVID NIXON, and DAVID BERGLAS—are members, and the latter two have served terms as King Rat.

WATER TORTURE CELL

Spectacular ESCAPE ILLUSION devised by HOUDINI and first performed by him in 1911; its first public presentation was at the Circus Busch in Germany in 1912.

A heavy metal tank with a glass front was filled with water; Houdini's feet were locked into stocks and he was then lowered upside-down into the tank, the stocks being secured to the top with padlocks. The cell was concealed by a screen or curtain and Houdini then made his escape, seemingly in the nick of time.

In a later variation, Houdini was first locked upside-down in a metal cage with inward-pointing spikes; this cage was then lowered into the water-filled cell and locked in place.

It should be noted that Houdini performed this escape successfully many, many times—contrary to the depiction in a theatrical film of his death while attempting it.

The escape has been presented by a few other performers since Houdini's death, including Britain's Timothy Dill-Russell and Howard Peters; a version in which the escape was combined with a VANISH was a feature of the first network television special of DOUG HENNING.

WATSON, MONK (1894-1981)

Born Donald Watson, he began his career with the Buffalo Bill Circus; later he toured with the Elsie Janis Show as bandleader and dancer, and then formed his own vaudeville band.

Watson's approach to comedy and performing is described in his book *The Professional Touch*; this was also the title of his long-running column in TOPS Magazine.

WAVE CRIMP

See MEXICAN JOE CRIMP.

WAYNE, DON (b. ?)

Best known as a CONSULTANT to DAVID COPPERFIELD, for whom he has created a number of EFFECTs, Wayne is also noted as a manufacturer of original effects, including his **Pranky Hank, The Don Wayne Floating Ball,** and many others.

WEAVE SHUFFLE

See FARO SHUFFLE.

WEBER, MICHAEL (b. 1962)

Highly regarded as a performer of CLOSE-UP MAGIC, and for his many original EFFECTs which routinely baffle other magicians, Weber is a very successful private-party worker, appearing at many Beverly Hills functions. He has won prizes in several Desert Seminar competitions, and has lectured on magic throughout the U.S. and in several other countries.

He is a recipient of an Achievement Award from the ACADEMY OF MAGICAL ARTS.

Michael Weber

WEDGE BASE

A low table-like platform on which the main structure of an ILLUSION is set; the front of the platform is thin, but widens from front to back; the rear area is of sufficient size to partially or completely conceal a person. It operates on an optical principle similar to that used in the PHANTOM TUBE, and is most efficiently employed in conjunction with other illusion principles.

Unlike a BEVEL BASE, a **wedge base** is not completely ANGLE-PROOF, and is best only used in performance venues where the audience is seated only in front of the stage (as for example a standard proscenium-arch theater).

WEDGE SHUFFLE

See FARO SHUFFLE.

WEINER, IRV (b. ?)

Performer who appears primarily at colleges and universities, billed as "Mr. Fingers"; he is considered to be one of the most popular and successful performers in these venues.

Briefly a dealer who operated a shop in Boston, he continues to market his EFFECTs and manuscripts. Of his many effects, perhaps the best known are his **soft dice** (a SPONGE BALLS routine with sponge dice) and **red tape tie** (a variant of the THUMB TIE in which the performer is secured with red adhesive tape).

His manuscripts, which he markets under the name *Manu-Secrets*, include *Cut Control*, *Dabbling With Daub*, *Impromptu Impression*, *Miracle Move*, *Out Of My Notebook*, *Patriotic Cups And Balls*.

WELL

See BLACK ART TABLE.

WELLES, ORSON (1915-1985)

Born George Orson Welles; one of the best known stage and film actors in the world, he had a long association with magic, and often incorporated it into his dramatic productions. In 1942 he created the *Mercury Wonder Show*—a magic show in a large tent presented for servicemen. Assisting in this show were Rita Hayworth, Marlene Dietrich, Agnes Moorehead and Joseph Cotten.

(In this show Welles featured an EFFECT in which he linked a dozen borrowed finger rings into a chain; while done by a different method, this is a clear precursor to the now popular LINKING FINGER RINGS routine.)

He also performed magic in Las Vegas, on numerous television shows and in films, and in three appearances for the British Royal Family. Welles was also a contributor to PHOENIX Magazine.

He is the recipient of a Special Fellowship from the ACADEMY OF MAGICAL ARTS.

WEST, FIELDING

Performer who began his career as magical host of a children's television show. He later did an act with wife and partner Pam which featured a hilarious burlesque of the METAMORPHOSIS ILLUSION.

He has appeared in many Las Vegas venues including the Tropicana, Sahara, and Mint; he has also performed in Reno, Tahoe, Atlantic City, and many other venues.

WESTCAR PAPYRUS

Egyptian manuscript giving the earliest recorded description of a magical performance.
See DEDI.

WETHERED, ERNEST H.C. (1879-1975)

British jurist and highly regarded amateur; he created many sophisticated and well thought out ROUTINEs which he contributed to PENTAGRAM Magazine and other publications.

He is perhaps best known for his ingenious BLACK ART TABLE, which is described in Trevor Hall's *Reading Is Believing* and also in TARBELL COURSE IN MAGIC (Volume 6).

WHERE DO THE DUCKS GO?

Title used by W. J. NIXON for his DUCK VANISH.

WHISPERING CARD

A presentation for a card discovery in which a particular card (usually a Queen or the Joker) "whispers" to the performer the identity of a selected card.

WHIST DEAL

See BRIDGE DEAL.

WHITE, BRUNEL (?-1944)

Born in Britain; highly-regarded inventor of many EFFECTs and devices, including the GLOVES TO

DOVE, a version of the CHANGING TRAY, and others.

His books include *Original Mysteries For Magicians* and *Modern Master Mysteries*.

WHITE, FRANCIS (b. ?)

Long associated with the MAGIC CIRCLE, he was its secretary for many years and has served as President since 1958. As a performer he is noted for his presentation of the BILL IN LEMON.

WHITE, JOSEPH M. (b. 1925)

Performer who began his career in a carnival under the billing of "Prince Tiny"; he later worked in the Ringling Brothers Circus, and also was a children's entertainer. He has been billed as The Midget Magician, The Wee Wizard, and Micro, The Miniature Mentalist; he states that he is the world's smallest adult magician.

He has also appeared in films (*Under The Rainbow*) and in many other venues.

White has contributed effects to GENII, LINKING RING, TOPS, and several other magazines. His books include *Big Magic For Little Kids*, *Micro Mental Miracles*, *Micro Mental Programs*, *Scotch Brand of Magic*, and *Select Mental Effects*.

WHITE BORDER CARDS

Decks in which the back pattern does not extend to the edges; BICYCLE and TALLY-HO are examples of white-border cards, while BEE decks are not.

This aspect of the card's back design is important in those effects in which a card is turned face-up in a face-down deck; if the deck back does not have white borders, the reversed card will be immediately evident even when the deck is squared and will render a number of card EFFECTs unworkable.

WHO-HAS-WHICH

A category of EFFECTs in MENTAL MAGIC in which spectators choose from among a small group of objects—five colored balls, ESP symbols, a few coins—and the performer is able to reveal who among the spectators has which object.

Methods for this type of effect are many, and range from the mathematical (*see* TRIPLE DIVINATION) through the purely psychological to the use of CONFEDERATES or complex mechanical devices.

WICKS, CHARLES (1900-1967)

Australian magician, very active in the I.B.M (of which he was an International Vice President). He is also noted as the originator of the ROUTINE in which the performer goes through a number of actions—rearranging a numbered stack of blocks, breaking a match, etc.—and then "turns time backwards" to show the various items are now as they were at the beginning of the routine.

WIDE CARD

A card fractionally wider than the rest of the deck; used as a KEY CARD.

As with the LONG CARD, the **wide card** is created by trimming the edges of the rest of the deck (here the long edges are trimmed). It can also be constructed by glueing two cards together, stepped slightly out of alignment; such a card also acts as a THICK CARD.

WILD CARD

Title given by FRANK GARCIA to an excellent PACKET TRICK invented by PETER KANE and widely copied, in which eight cards change their faces to match that of a ninth. Its original title was **Watch The Ace**.

A variation, also invented by Kane, uses seven Tarot-style cards and is marketed as GYPSY CURSE.

WILLANE (?-1955)

Born William H. Lane in Britain; a wholesale food dealer for most of his life, in the latter part of his life he decided to become a successful stage performer, and did so. In addition to an intriguing act combining magic and music, he also created (with the assistance of CLAUDE CHANDLER) a DRUNK ACT titled The Immaculate Inebriate which he performed in music halls and at magic conventions. He also presented, at various times, performances of ventriloquism and hypnotism.

In addition to this, he founded the publishing house of ARCAS (Academy of Recorded Crafts, Arts and Sciences); among the magic books it brought out were works by TREVOR HALL, PETER WARLOCK, and others. ARCAS also published the *Methods For Miracles* series of booklets; these have recently been republished, with additional material, as a single volume.

WILLARD, FRANCES (b. 1940)

She was for many years an ASSISTANT in the ILLUSION show of her father, HARRY WILLARD. In a

Frances Willard being secured at the beginning of the *Spirit Cabinet* routine, assisted by Glenn Falkenstein (*photo courtesy GENII Magazine*).

featured ROUTINE of that show, she acted as a MEDIUM in the classic SPIRIT CABINET presentation; with her husband, Glenn Falkenstein, she continues to present the traditional "cabinet act," and is generally considered to be the best performer of this feat in the world.

WILLARD, HARRY (1896-1970)

A tent-show magician who toured an elaborate FULL-EVENING SHOW under canvas throughout the American southwest for many years; he was the last of a family of magicians, all billed as "Willard the Wizard," who began performing in Ireland in the 1860s and moved to the U.S. twenty years later.

Willard, like CHUNG LING SOO, was one of that rare breed who are genuinely obsessed with their profession; it is said that his performance of a number of feats (the THUMB TIE, for example) has never been equaled.

WILLIAMS, ERIC (1911-1981)

British amateur performer who specialized in comedy magic, creating such weird and hilarious characters as The Great Pong, The Schoolgirl, and The Nit-Wit. In addition to creating a number of marketed EFFECTs, he contributed to several magazines; a long-running column was his Nit-Wittian Natterings which appeared in ABRA Magazine. He was a member of the Inner MAGIC CIRCLE with Gold Star.

WILLIAMS, OSWALD (1880-1937)

Born in Britain; performer who was highly successful while still in his twenties, appearing at varied venues throughout the British Isles (including several seasons at ST. GEORGE'S HALL, where he was the successor to DAVID DEVANT).

Williams invented a number of EFFECTs and ILLUSIONs, of which the best-known is the still-popular DIZZY LIMIT.

WILLMAN, CARL (?-?)

Late 19th-early 20th century German magic dealer; he founded a German magazine called *Die Zauberwelt* (The Magic World). He was noted for the manufacture of precision mechanical GIMMICKS (such as REELS) and stage APPARATUS.

WILLMARTH, PHILIP (b. ?)

Marketing consultant by profession; he has for many years been the Parade editor for the LINKING RING Magazine. He is particularly noted for his effects in which metal rings pass on and off ropes, and is the author of *The Ring And Rope Book*.

His other books include *Fun With A Handkerchief, The Magic Of Matt Schulien*, and *Jim Ryan Close-up* (three volumes).

WILL, THE WITCH, AND THE WATCHMAN

Title of an elaborate ILLUSION playlet created by NEVIL MASKELYNE; its central focus was a large cabinet which contained an interior cell (possibly inspired by the CABINET OF PROTEUS, but using a different application of the general principle).

In the course of the playlet there were several EFFECTs; a person locked in a trunk instantly escapes, various characters seem to change places with astonishing rapidity, and there are various subsidiary effects.

A later version of the playlet was know as **The Witch, The Sailor And The Enchanted Monkey.**

A thorough description of this illusion playlet, an article by JOHN BRAUN and the dialogue script, will be found in S.H. SHARPE's *The Magic Play.*

WILSON, A. M., DR. (1854-1930)

After a brief and unsuccessful career as a professional performer, he became a doctor; still interested in magic, he took over the editorship (and ownership) of the SPHINX Magazine in 1904. He continued as editor until his death, and during his tenure with the

Dr. A. M. Wilson (*The Mulholland Library of Conjuring & the Allied Arts, Los Angeles, California*)

magazine was involved in a number of feuds and controversies.

His oft-quoted slogan was "Magic is an art that sometimes instructs, often amuses, and always entertains." Many later writers, notably DARIEL FITZKEE in *Showmanship For Magicians*, have taken issue with what was perhaps the stating of an ideal rather than an intended statement of fact.

WILSON, MARK (b. 1929)

Born James Mark Wilson, he began his career with a local television show in Dallas. The show, marketed to other cities, proved successful, and in 1960 Wilson created *The Magic Land Of Allakazam*; this was the first show featuring a magician to run as a weekly network series, running for two years on CBS-TV and three more on ABC-TV. It made Wilson one of the best-known magicians in the U.S., and featured wife and partner Nani Darnell. The show also employed the talents and skills of ROBERT TOWNER, BEV BERGERON, JOHN GAUGHAN and several others.

Wilson also produced several one-hour *Magic Circus* specials which were syndicated nationally by the *Pillsbury* company. In 1964 he created the *Hall Of Magic*

Mark Wilson

Ron Wilson

pavilion at the New York World's Fair; since that time he has created countless exhibits and shows for a long list of corporate sponsor and clients such as Allis-Chalmers, Burger King, Honeywell, ITT, Motorola and several more. He has also been a TECHNICAL ADVISOR for numerous film and television dramas including *The Magician, Circus Of the Stars* and *The Six Million Dollar Man*.

Wilson is one of the best-known performers in the world, having made countless television appearances over the years, including shows hosted by Johnny Carson, Mike Douglas, Merv Griffin, Cher and many others. He has also appeared in Las Vegas and throughout the U.S., and was the first western magician to perform in the People's Republic Of China.

He is the creator of the *Mark Wilson Course In Magic*, noted for the exceptional clarity of its instruction. He has also published *The Chop Cup Book* by ALAN WAKELING and EARL NELSON.

He has for many years served on the board of directors of the ACADEMY OF MAGICAL ARTS, and has twice received the Academy's *Magician Of The Year* award; he has also received numerous other awards, including the *Star Of Magic* from the INTERNATIONAL BROTHERHOOD OF MAGICIANS and the Magician Of The Decade award from the Show Business Shrine Club.

WILSON, RON (b. 1926)

Born in Scotland, he emigrated first to Canada, and later to the U.S.. He is adept at many kinds of magic (he once performed a DOVE ACT), but prefers to specialize in close-up work. Billed as The Uncanny Scot, he performs at private parties for clients in Beverly Hills and elsewhere, and is noted for the considerable charm of his performances as much as for the immaculately-executed magic. His work is described in *The Uncanny Scot: RON WILSON* by RICHARD KAUFMAN.

He has served on the board of directors of the ACADEMY OF MAGICAL ARTS for many years; he is a recipient of the Academy's awards for Best Close-Up Magician and Magician Of The Year.

WINDSOR, TOMMY (1906-1978)

As a boy he became a cartoonist, later becoming involved with magic and working as an ASSISTANT in the show of MACDONALD BIRCH; still later he worked as an actor on a showboat.

Returning to magic, he played school assembly shows for many years, at which he was highly successful; he also had his own (local) television series in Parkersburg, West Virginia—but ended it when he felt it was interfering with his "live" shows.

Among his books are *The Real Svengali Pitch, The*

Balloon Pitch, *The Street Faker Act*, and *Sixty-Four Ways To Make Magic Pay*; marketed EFFECTs include his **Golden Egg Bag** and the very popular **Popcorn** DYE BOX.

WINE AND WATER

A popular EFFECT of the past in which clear liquids poured from a pitcher go through various color changes, with the presentation of water changing into wine. The effect was accomplished by means of CHEMICAL MAGIC.

WINEGLASS PRODUCTION

The appearance from beneath a handkerchief of a wineglass filled with liquid, which the performer drinks to prove its genuineness.

There are many techniques for accomplishing this production, some requiring special holders, etc.; one of the best methods, needing no clips or holders but requiring superior technique, is that invented by JARDINE ELLIS and described in BRUCE ELLIOTT's *Classic Secrets Of Magic*.

WINGS

The area at either side of the stage behind the PROSCENIUM, out of the audience's line of sight; also, the vertical FLATs which mask this area from the audience's view.

WINTERTIME IN CHINA

A classic EFFECT (which despite its title is most probably of Japanese origin) in which a napkin or strip of paper is torn into small pieces which are then dipped in water; as the performer squeezes the sodden mass and "dries" it with an opened fan, the water drips from it and suddenly tiny dry pieces of paper erupt from the performer's hand in a cloud, creating the "snowstorm" of the title.

There are many versions of the effect in print; an entire book on the feat titled *The Seasons* was written by PHOA YAN TIONG.

Also known as **Chinese snowstorm** and **snowstorm in China**.

WISHBONE RING

An item of jewelry much favored by magicians, it is in appearance two curved *V*'s (or wishbones) joined together at the ends to make a ring which shows a V at front or back of the hand.

In addition to its aesthetic appeal, it can be used as a device to aid in certain moves; if worn so that the point of a V is toward the palm, a card or coin may be secreted under this point and held by pressure of the palm against the object. Similarly, a STEAL in the act of pushing a card into the deck may be performed by clipping the card beneath the hand as it is apparently shoved flush.

An interesting account of the wishbone ring will be found in JOHN BOOTH's *Wonders Of Magic*.

WITCH

A person of either sex who practices the arts and traditions of witchcraft (in this connection see WARLOCK).

In general usage the term is erroneously confined to females only, and is often applied in a pejorative sense to any female who practices any form of occult art. Within occult tradition, the term is more limited, referring to a person who follows a specific body of beliefs and practices, and who may worship a specific deity such as the Celtic Cernunnos or the Egyptian ISIS, or something as general as a Nature principle.

The term may sometimes be used in ironic or laudatory fashion to denote a female magical performer.

WITKOWSKI, DAN (b. 1956)

Founder of MagicCom, an organization which creates magical presentations and shows for corporate

Dan Witkowski

sponsors. Witkowski's clients include Bell Telephone, Kraft, A.T.&T., General Mills, Polaroid, Honeywell and many others.

Witkowski also works as a motivational speaker, using magic to accent his points, and has done seminars for many communications and advertising companies. He has also mounted stage shows such as the *Easter Spectacular* at New York's Radio City Music Hall, where one of his ILLUSIONs involved the production of all thirty-six Rockettes. Other venues have included Las Vegas appearances, Disney World, Disneyland, and President Reagan's inaugural gala.

WIZARD DECK

A name under which the STRIPPER DECK is sometimes sold.

WIZTAX

Brand name for a type of double-sided adhesive material formerly sold as a magical aid, similar to double-stick cellophane tape currently available.

A book on its uses—*Tricks With Wiztax*—was written by SAM BERLAND. Also, a number of EFFECTs employing double-stick tape have been contributed to magic literature by JOSEPH M. WHITE.

WONDER, TOMMY (b. ?)

Born Josef Bemelman in Holland (and performing for a time as Jos Bema), he is well-known for his excellent general magic and close-up work, and is particularly noted for his excellent use of MISDIRECTION.

His work is described in his *Wonder Material* and *Tommy Wonder Entertains*.

WOODWARD, MILTON (1901-1964)

British performer who worked throughout Britain and Ireland for over three decades; he had a number of different acts, but was best known for his BAR ACT which he billed as *Wonder Bar*.

WOOFLE DUST

An imaginary powder with supposed magical properties, the obtaining of which gives the less-than-skillful performer an excuse to reach into a pocket—in order to secretly(?) obtain or dispose of an object. It should be noted that this is a very transparent ploy to all but the most obtuse observers.

WORK

Originally a gambling term referring to secret preparation of the gaming objects, either prior to play (e.g., SHADE WORK) or during the course of the game (to CRIMP a card is to "put the work in").

More recently, within magical parlance, it has come to mean information regarding the ideal procedure or technique for a given effect; the "real work" is the (often little-known) best way to bring about a desired magical result.

WORLD'S FASTEST CARD TRICK

A comedy routine by JOE KARSON adapted from a Stephen Leacock humor piece; in it, the performer's attempts to do a simple card trick are foiled by the assisting spectator (who is subtly and unknowingly guided by the performer into doing the "wrong" thing). The title is ironic in that the routine will sometimes run ten minutes or more.

WRESTLING CHEESE

A stage ILLUSION invented by P. T. SELBIT which used a large circular object decorated to look like a giant piece of cheese. Volunteers from the audience were unable to tip it over or move it in ways it didn't "want" to be moved. As a climax, ropes threaded through pulleys were attached to the cheese and the spectators hauled it up into the air; at a command from Selbit ("Cheese, do your stuff!"), the cheese immediately sank to the floor again, pulling the spectators off their feet.

Though electromagnets were sometimes suggested as a method, the cheese's powers depended in part on a flywheel inside it which produced gyroscopic effects, and also on ingeniously constructed pulleys.

WRIST CHOPPER

See CHOPPER; DISECTO.

WRIST TIE

See ROPE TIE; KELLAR TIE.

WYMAN, JOHN (1816-1881)

Noted in magic history as the first U.S. performer to present a FULL-EVENING SHOW; also noted as one of the first performers to do the GIFT SHOW. He performed primarily in the eastern U.S. and Canada. He was also one of the first U.S. performers to feature the BULLET CATCH, having obtained it (according to HOUDINI) from JOHN HENRY ANDERSON.

X-ING THE DECK

See CROSSING THE CUT.

X-RAY EYES

A phrase often used in billing and publicity matter by performers specializing in BLINDFOLD work.

YETTMAH, CYRIL (?-?)

Born in Britain; inventor of a number of popular EFFECTs and ILLUSIONs, including the PIGEON CATCHING, IASIA, and others.

YOGI

A male practitioner of the spiritual and physical disciplines of *Yoga*. (A female practitioner of Yoga is called a *Yogini*.)

Within show business, the term has often been applied to a performer of FIRE-EATING or the FIREWALK, or other apparent demonstrations of imperviousness to pain such as sticking pins and needles into the body or lying on a bed of nails.

The term has also been used (particularly in the early part of the 20th century) by performers of MENTALISM or MENTAL MAGIC.

YOST, THOMAS (1832-1917)

Magic dealer who, after a brief performing career, founded Thomas Yost & Co. in Philadelphia, Pennsylvania.

YOU DO AS I DO

A class of EFFECTs most often done with two decks of cards; a spectator matches the performer's movements in selecting a card at random and then replacing it in his deck; at the conclusion it is shown that both have selected the same card. These effects are sometimes done with only one deck, performer and spectator each taking a half and choosing cards of same color and value.

YOU DO AS I DON'T

A category of EFFECTs in which the spectator apparently matches the performer's actions exactly but concludes with a different result. Examples of such effects are the TOPSY-TURVY bottles, the HUNTER KNOT, and certain kinds of SPELLING TRICKS.

ZARROW SHUFFLE

See FALSE SHUFFLE.

ZIG-ZAG GIRL

A striking ILLUSION created by ROBERT HARBIN in which a woman, standing in a narrow cabinet with face, hands, and one foot visible, is apparently trisected by two large blades thrust in at the front of the cabinet. The central section of the cabinet is then slid completely out of alignments with the upper and lower sections, so that an empty space exists where the woman's midsection should be.

The illusion is very popular with magicians not only for the strength of its effect but also because it is ANGLE-PROOF, can be performed under almost any conditions by just the magician and his assistant, and is designed to be easily disassembled for transport.

Indeed, this illusion is so popular that it has the questionable distinction of being the most widely pirated illusion of the present era (*see* PIRACY; COPYISTS).

ZIMMERMAN, DIANA (b. ?)

Performer who created a number of themed ACTs as a teenager; these included the **hula act** and the **French maid** act. Later, with partner and husband DICK ZIMMERMAN, she performed their noted **magic circles** act, as well as the **record act**—a solo presentation featuring EFFECTs with phonographs and records.

She now devotes much of her time to the Junior Magicians program at the MAGIC CASTLE, which she has shepherded since 1975.

ZIMMERMAN, DICK (b. ?)

Best known as a creator of magical ROUTINEs (such as **Dancing Ring, Linking Hula Hoops, Sticky Fingers** and **Computer Vision**), he has also worked as a CONSULTANT for MARK WILSON, DAVID COPPERFIELD, DOUG HENNING, HARRY BLACKSTONE JR. and ANDRE KOLE among others. He has worked as a TECHNICAL ADVISOR for many entertainment companies, including Universal Studios and Walt Disney Productions.

With his wife and partner DIANA ZIMMERMAN, he created their **magic circles** act, consisting entirely of EFFECTs with hoops, rings, and similar items; the act has been seen on stage and television in the U.S. and many other countries.

He has received several awards, including the Lecturer Of The Year award from the ACADEMY OF MAGICAL ARTS.

ZOMBIE

See FLOATING EFFECTS.

A rare photograph, taken in the 1940's, of several of magic's greats: standing, left to right: Cardini, Dr. Jacob Daley; seated, left to right: Arthur Finley, S. Leo Horowitz, Al Baker, Charles Miller, Dai Vernon.